THE POLITICS OF THE IMAGINATION

SANDRA DJWA

*The Politics of the Imagination:*
# A Life of F.R. Scott

Canadian Cataloguing in Publication Data

Djwa, Sandra, 1939–
The politics of the imagination

Includes bibliographical references and index.
ISBN 0-7710-2825-3

1. Scott, F.R. (Francis Reginald), 1899–1985
2. Poets, Canadian (English) – 20th century – Biography.*
3. Lawyers – Canada – Biography.
4. Socialists – Canada – Biography. 1. Title.

PS8537.C62Z59 1987    C811'.54    C87-093985-8
PR9199.3.S362Z59 1987

DESIGNED BY RICHARD MILLER
Printed and bound in Canada

McClelland and Stewart
*The Canadian Publishers*
481 University Avenue
Toronto, Ontario
M5G 2E9

# Contents

❦

# F.R. Scott: A Brief Chronology

❦

1899:  born August 1, in Quebec City, the sixth of seven children of the Rev. Frederick George Scott and Amy Brooks Scott.

1914:  father serves overseas as army chaplain during the Great War.

1916:  loss of eye in accident; enrols at Bishop's College, Lennoxville; brother Harry killed in Battle of the Somme.

1918:  tries, unsuccessfully, on five occasions to enlist.

1919:  graduates with B.A. from Bishop's.

1920:  enrols at Oxford University on Rhodes Scholarship, where he will publish poetry in student magazine, *Isis*.

1922:  earns third class on B.A. exams, Oxford.

1923:  B.Litt., Oxford; accepts teaching post, Lower Canada College, Montreal.

1924:  enters McGill Law School; indentured to law firm where brother William is a rising lawyer.

1925-27:  founds and edits *The McGill Fortnightly Review* with A.J.M. Smith, Leon Edel, and others.

1927:  joins law firm where he had apprenticed; meets J.S. Woodsworth.

1928:  accepts teaching position, McGill Faculty of Law; marries Marian Dale, an artist.

1929:  only child, Peter, born.

1932:  founder of League for Social Reconstruction, with Frank Underhill and others; travels to England rather than attending founding meeting of Co-operative Commonwealth Federation (CCF); "An Up-to-Date Anthology of Canadian Poetry" in *The Canadian Forum*.

1933:  *Labour Conditions in the Men's Clothing Industry*, with Harry Cassidy; helps to write Regina Manifesto for CCF convention.

1935:  major contributor to *Social Planning for Canada*; journeys to Soviet Union.

1936: *New Provinces*, poetry anthology edited with A.J.M. Smith; American Institute of Pacific Relations conference, Yosemite, California.

1938: travels to Australia for Sydney Conference of the Institute of International Affairs; edits *Canada Today*.

1930s: publishes numerous essays on Canadian neutrality, Quebec politics, democracy, constitutional law, civil liberties.

1940-41: Guggenheim Fellowship for a year at Harvard to research and write book on BNA Act; impact of war precludes completion of project: instead, writes "The Democratic Manifesto."

1942: elected national chairman, CCF; founds and edits *Preview*, with Patrick Anderson, Margaret Day, P.K. Page, and others.

1943: death of mother; *Make This YOUR Canada*, with David Lewis.

1944: death of father; Guarantors Prize, *Poetry* (Chicago).

1945: first book of poetry, *Overture*.

1946: "Laurentian Shield" in *Northern Review*, an outgrowth of *Preview* (now disbanded).

1949-50: passed over as Dean of Law at McGill because of political activities and affiliation.

1950: resigns as CCF national chairman; helps to found Association of Law Teachers.

1952: United Nations technical assistance resident representative in Burma, contracts amoebic dysentery.

1953: Keewaydin Poetry Conference.

1954: *Events and Signals* (poetry).

1956: Kingston Writers' Conference; trip down Mackenzie River with Pierre Trudeau; argues Padlock case before Supreme Court of Canada.

1957: *The Eye of the Needle* (satiric verse); wins Padlock case in Supreme Court decision of March 7; *The Blasted Pine* (anthology of satiric verse), with A.J.M. Smith.

1959: Roncarelli case won in Supreme Court of Canada.

1961: around-the-world trip on Canada Council grant to study the making of constitutions in parliamentary democracies; appointed Dean of Law at McGill.

1962: successfully argues *Lady Chatterley* case before Supreme Court; *St-Denys Garneau & Anne Hébert: Translations/Traductions*.

1963: appointed to Royal Commission on Bilingualism and Biculturalism.

1964: leaves deanship after difficult three years; *Signature* (poetry); *Quebec States Her Case*, with Michael Oliver.

1966: *Selected Poems*.

1967: *Trouvailles: Poems from Prose*.

1970: *Dialogue sur la traduction*, avec Anne Hébert.

1973: *The Dance Is One* (poetry).

1977: *Poems of French Canada* (trans.).

1978: Governor General's Award for non-fiction for *Essays on the Constitution: Aspects of Canadian Law and Politics*.

1981: F.R. Scott Conference at Simon Fraser University; *The Collected Poems of F.R. Scott*.

1982: Governor General's Award for poetry (*Collected Poems*).

1985: died January 31, with wife Marian at his side.

This book is dedicated
to Ann Herstein above all,
and to Frances Hord, Marilyn Flitton,
and Perry Millar.

For man's political life is more intimately an expression of the general quality of his imaginative life than we are in the habit of noticing: and those who are concerned with man's imaginative life are therefore concerned with the area in which his political concepts are shaped – are *shaped* – they do not shape themselves, but are shaped in his imagination, not only by man's mortal destiny and metaphysical questions to which it gives rise, but also by particular contexts of nation, doctrine, class, and race. By these forces, all of them together, the imagination and the politics of a man are both shaped and made to interact, and the study of one cannot be fully separated from the study of the other.

CONOR CRUISE O'BRIEN, 1976

# MOUNT ROYAL

No things sit, set, hold. All swim,
Whether through space or cycle, rock or sea.
This mountain of Mount Royal marks the hours
On earth's sprung clock. Look how where
This once was island, lapped by salty waves,
And now seems fixed with sloping roads and homes.
Where flowers march, I dig these tiny shells
Once deep-down fishes safe, it seemed, on sand.
What! Sand, mud, silt, where now commuters go
About their civic clatter! Boulevards
Where crept the shiny mollusc! Time is big
With aeon seconds now, its pendulum
Swung back to ice-pressed pole cap, that drove down
This chest of earth until the melting came
And left a hollow cavity for seas
To make into a water waiting-room.
But sea-bed floated slowly, surely up
As weight released brought in-breath back to earth
And ground uprising drove the water back
In one more tick of clock. Pay taxes now,
Elect your boys, lay out your pleasant parks,
Your gill-lunged, quarrelsome ephemera!
The tension tightens yearly, underneath,
A folding continent shifts silently
And oceans wait their turn for ice or streets.

F.R. SCOTT, 1962

# ONE

# The Scotts

❦

On a clear Sunday afternoon in November, 1979, F.R. Scott pointed out the old John Ross mansion, now the Faculty of Law at McGill University in Montreal, as we drove up Peel Street to Pine Avenue. Turning west, we travelled up Côte-des-Neiges Road across Mount Royal, the mountain that gives the city its name. On one side of the road lies exposed the skeleton of the mountain: ribbed layers of sedimentary rock, once under the sea and now raised into light and air.

As the road ascends, these layers of rock give way to square-cut greystone blocks, the retaining walls of substantial old houses built at the turn of the century by Montreal tycoons. The city, moving inward and upward from the St. Lawrence, rises more than halfway up the mountain. Very near the top is a roadway that winds down into the Mount Royal Cemetery, where for more than a hundred years the Protestants of Montreal have buried their dead. On a gentle incline toward the south side of the cemetery, facing north, is the burial ground of the Scott family.

Here are the tombstones of four generations of Scotts. Oldest is the grey stone of John Scott who, with his wife, Caroline Neate, came to Montreal from England in 1831. Next in line is the black marble of their son, Dr. William Edward Scott, and his wife, Elizabeth Sproston. Behind their gravestone stands an old English oak. Time has dimmed the lettering on the stone, but the oak rises high, its trunk deeply etched and ribbed, its spare branches, still glowing with the last few autumn leaves, arching far up into the sky.

Dominating the scene is a large white stone cross that marks the grave of John Scott's grandson, the Reverend Archdeacon Frederick George Scott and his wife, Amy Brooks – the parents of F.R. Scott; two of their children, Mary and Charles, lie buried near the cross. Frank Scott pointed out the spot beside them where he thought his own ashes should lie. Knowing that his time was limited, he was searching out his own place in what he called "the dance" of creation.

ON TUESDAY, AUGUST 1, 1899, the Reverend F.G. Scott wrote in his diary: "Little Boy born at 5.50. Slept in afternoon. Dinner to Dobell's."[1] What with the house in an uproar over his wife's confinement and five other children to be fed and put to bed, supper with one of the wealthier families in his Quebec City parish must have been a happy escape. Francis Reginald, as the new baby was christened, sixth in a family of seven, was both to resent and enjoy his position as the "little boy" of the family.

As one of the two youngest boys, "the dregs" as their father jocularly called them, Frank was always far down the line of command. Not only did he feel the pressure of the immediate family but, as he grew older, he felt a great pressure to live up to the Scott name. His father, Canon – and later Archdeacon – Scott, was a formidable churchman and a brave chaplain whose watchwords were duty, honour, courage, virtue, and purity. These values he imprinted on each of his children. "To be a good Scott one must live without spot," the young Frank was to write just before his seventeenth birthday.[2] This legacy, and burden, of high performance was handed on by Frank Scott to the next generation of Scotts. In the thirties his son, Peter, carved into his desk at the old Westmount High School in Montreal: "100% not good enough for a Scott."[3] The family was a dominant one, motivated by high idealism. Ever since the arrival of the Scotts in Canada these ideals had helped shape not only the immediate family but also their professions and an emerging Canadian society.

JOHN SCOTT, F.R. Scott's great-grandfather, came to Canada with his wife and family in 1831. Born in England on October 8, 1791, he was a lieutenant in the 4th Regiment of the local militia in Surrey.[4] He married Caroline Neate on January 15, 1818, and produced a large family – six surviving children and three who appear to have died in infancy in England; the last child, a girl, was born in Quebec in 1834.

The family's introduction to Canada was clouded by death and the threat of civil war. The same year they arrived, 52,000 immigrants disembarked in Quebec City and Montreal, bringing the cholera germs that produced the epidemics of 1832 and 1834. In 1832 British troops fired into a boisterous Montreal election crowd, killing three young Frenchmen and helping to precipitate the 1837 rebellion in Lower Canada. By 1835 John Scott was dead, possibly of cholera, and his wife was left to raise six young children. The eldest boy, John, was then fourteen, his younger brother, William Edward, thirteen.

W.E. Scott, Frank Scott's grandfather, became first an apothecary and then a physician. Medical care in Montreal during the mid-nineteenth century was no better, and perhaps worse, than elsewhere in North America. The city had no proper sewage system and the water supply was regularly contaminated, leading to outbreaks of typhoid. Immigrants brought with them new outbreaks of cholera and influenza, and many thousands died. Like the victims of the plague in Europe a century earlier, they were then buried without ceremony in mass graves. Dedicated physicians like Scott faced insurmountable odds in battling the disease. A fellow Montrealer, J.W. Shaw, recalled visiting him at his apothecary shop at the time of the great typhoid epidemic in 1847. He found Dr. Scott dispensing medications by day and tending patients at night. Depressed and overworked, he beckoned Shaw into the back room of his apothecary shop and urged him to talk of "school days and books," adding, "though my time is worth a guinea an hour I am sick of business, and unless I get a respite soon I shall fall victim myself."[5] His great courage and dedication in attending the victims of successive epidemics, patients shunned by many of his contemporaries, were applauded in Montreal newspapers of the day.

He was powerless, however, to prevent the deaths of five of his own nine children. Dr. Scott did not believe in the "germ theory." Ironically, an ailing Mrs. Scott may have been the unwitting carrier of the "galloping consumption" that killed her children, for the younger boys who survived were all tended by an orphaned Englishwoman, Matilda Preddy, brought into the household in 1857. It was her responsibility to look after F.R. Scott's father, Frederick George, born in 1861, and his younger brothers, Frank and Charles. Partly as a consequence of the loss of so many of his children, Dr. Scott was openly loving with those who remained. In letters he addressed his son as "My Darling Fred," using terms of affectionate endearment that Frederick George was later to apply to his own children.

Dr. Scott was appointed lecturer in forensic medicine at McGill and, in 1852, was given one of the major chairs, professor of anatomy, a post he held until his death in 1883. Between 1871 and 1874 he served as president of the College of Physicians and Surgeons of the Province of Quebec, one indication of the high regard of his professional colleagues. He numbered among his students William Osler, Ernest Shepherd, and Sir Thomas Roddick, forerunners of the new science of medicine, who developed the Faculty of Medicine at McGill into one of the greatest in North America.

When he died in 1883, his colleagues in the McGill medical faculty observed that as he had been "a pupil of some of the founders of the school and having subsequently served as one of its active members for a period of 38 years, [he] formed the only remaining link connecting the present staff with the various names of those who laid the broad foundations of the existing college." He was, they noted, "high-minded, honourable and courageous, but withal firm in his own convictions and eminently conservative ... a colleague of whom his university has long been proud ...."[6]

Life changed drastically for the Scott family after Dr. Scott's death. Several months later, on Dominion Day, his widow, Elizabeth, lamented in her diary: "What a sad change has come over our lives since this time last year. My darling husband is in heaven, and Oh, how sad and lonely I feel. Everything is changed and I feel as if I should never know happiness again." She added, "there is nothing to look forward to now but dear Fred's return home. Poor fellow, what a change for him."[7] The daughter, Emily, remained at home with her mother, but the surviving boys were now responsible for making their own living. Frank found a job in the treasurer's office at the Grand Trunk Railway, a company of which he later became vice-president; the youngest brother, Charles, emigrated to the United States, where he died in Duluth in 1894; the eldest, Fred, was studying theology at King's College, London.

FREDERICK GEORGE SCOTT, to judge from his mother's letters, had a kindly, impulsive nature. "I do not like you to go so much among the poor miserable wretched people of London. I think it dangerous," she wrote to him on March 11, 1883, "I like your taking the little, miserable, hungry children into bakers' shops and feeding them with buns, but take care, my darling, you may be waylaid and robbed."[8]

F.G. Scott received his early religious training at St. George's in Montreal, the church of his father and grandfather. St. George's was respectably Low Church – the Anglo-Catholic Oxford Movement was alien to most Canadian members of the Church of England – and young Fred was cautioned by his parents never to enter the doors of the Church of St. John the Evangelist in Montreal, where the service was so High Church as to be considered "popish." In a memoir about Scott, Canon Sydenham Lindsay wrote that Fred, "like many another small boy ... was curious to do what was forbidden, and so he went, but when he saw surpliced choir boys, proceded by a processional cross, and followed by Father Wood [the parish priest] in vestments, he was terrified and ran out of the church."[9] Despite his fears, or perhaps because of them, this scene permanently imprinted itself on F.G. Scott's religious imagination: the cross became the dominant symbol of his religious life, Father Edmund Wood his spiritual mentor, and Anglo-Catholicism his faith.

Up to the age of nineteen, Fred Scott was a typical young romantic who wrote love lyrics with such classical tags as "To Celia." After "ploughing out" (flunking) at McGill, he was sent to Bishop's College, Lennoxville, in Quebec's Eastern Townships, where he did well in his examinations and graduated with a B.A. in 1881. The following year, the emotional tone of his life abruptly changed. By 1882 he had courted, and then lost to death, a young girl whose memory never left him. In December, 1882, he travelled to England to study theology at King's College, London, and while there received news of his father's death. His mother died later that year and his older sister Emily died in January, 1884. His father's illness, the history of death in the Scott family, the loss of a sweetheart – all combined to generate a feeling of depression tinged with both fear and guilt.

In March, 1882, Scott wrote of his intense fear of death. Since earliest childhood a "demon" had haunted him with "death and dreams of death":

> And, when I gaze in rapture on the face
> Of whom I love, he casts a hideous light,
> That lets me see, behind the sweet, warm flesh,
> The lightless skull ...[10]

The young Scott was a sorrowful romantic figure, dressed in black, writing poems on death, and recognized as the archetypal "young Werther" by the admiring young women in his circle.

Behind this dramatic persona was a sensitive, anxious young man who, when told of his father's impending death, found refuge and consolation in the Church of England. The highlight of his 1883 stay in England was a pilgrimage to Birmingham to visit Cardinal Newman, the celebrated Anglo-Catholic who had been converted to Roman Catholicism. His eyes, Fred reminisced on his return to Canada, looked far beyond him to some "wide plain ... where the shining battlements of the New Jerusalem, the City of God, were growing hourly clearer through the mist."[11] Newman was the physical embodiment of devotion to a living faith.

The grieving young poet-priest found spiritual comfort in Anglo-Catholic ritual, especially in the mystery of the mass with its doctrine of incarnation and its promise of spiritual resurrection. High Church practices kindled Scott's emotions, as did the demand for complete dedication of self to the Church, which offered a sense of vocation he had not found in the Anglicanism in which he was raised. Fred's theological convictions put him on the wrong side of a pre-existing schism in the diocese of Montreal. Members of the Church of England in Canada, even more so than those in the mother country, were strongly opposed to Anglo-Catholicism. That Dr. Scott fully understood the depth and radicalism (by Montreal standards) of his son's religious commitment is apparent in a few lines dictated just before his death: "If it is the will of the Almighty" he would like to have a talk with his dear boy before his ordination. "I would like him to be moderate in his views and church ritual and not do anything to displease the Bishop who will get him a position in this diocese."[12] Dr. Scott's worst fears were justified. Fred did well in theology at King's College, but when he returned to Canada and applied for ordination in September, 1883, he was refused. The Bishop found his theology "crude and contradictory."[13] In one of his answers to a question on his examination for ordination he had moved dangerously close to the Anglo-Catholic doctrine of the real presence of Christ in the elements.[14]

As a result Scott spent 1883-84 back at Bishop's College, marking time and writing verses on nature, death, and ecumenicalism. The following year he appears to have taught at St. John's School with Father Wood. This year proved one of the most important in his life, for he seriously considered entering a monastic order. He made application to the Anglo-Catholic parish of Coggeshall in Essex, England, for ordination. Then, quite suddenly, just before leaving Canada, he proposed to a young Montrealer not long out from England.

In 1878, Amy Brooks had come to Canada to live with her mother's childhood friend, a Mrs. Hutton, after the sudden death of her father, church organist George Brooks of Barnet, England. A spirited young woman with a good upper-middle-class education, she read widely, spoke passable French, and was an accomplished needlewoman. Above all, she was a fine pianist who frequently took her turn at the church organ. A contemporary portrait shows a young woman with a gentle face and softly curling hair; her arms reach out to a small white terrier. Despite her gentle expression, however, Amy Brooks was not the sort of young woman to be swept off her feet by a grand passion, even by so dashing a figure as Fred Scott.

She considered their engagement precipitous. In a letter written to Scott after he had gone to England for ordination, she explained that she knew that he wanted to marry her, but that "I think it was because you felt impressed with the idea that you would be happier married and I was about the only girl you knew intimately enough to propose such a thing to."[15] It was a shrewd comment. When Fred left Canada again he had already suffered the series of bereavements that included the deaths of his parents. He was undoubtedly looking for stability in his emotional life, and Amy was an ideal candidate. She and Scott were the same age and they met frequently in a circle of young people at St. George's Anglican Church.

Amy continued to be very careful about committing herself; she wanted to be persuaded. Her first letter, written on New Year's Eve, 1885, just after Fred's departure for England, spoke of the great changes that had taken place in their lives since the start of the year: "It positively makes me quake to look forward to the end of '86 or allow myself to contemplate all the changes that may have taken place before then. Don't *you* shrink a little from the thought dear Fred and look back longingly to the superior joys of life in a brotherhood?" Then, recollecting herself, she put forward a strong case against the monastic life: "There always appears to me a kind of moral cowardice in entering an institution of that sort as it takes away so much of the feeling of individual responsibility attached to this life ...."[16] By midsummer 1886, Amy could write frankly that there was now such a marked change in his letters that she doubted if he could have loved her at all before. But now she was fully persuaded – at least to the extent that she considered it decorous to admit: "I might almost say I am as ready as you are."[17]

While Amy's love for her future husband was deepening – and while she was very subtly courting him – events also took a sudden turn for the better in his professional career. There was a position open for a rector in Drummondville, a good rural parish in the diocese of Quebec in the Eastern Townships. The Bishop of Quebec was willing to have Fred Scott in his charge: "I am very fond of Scott, he is a great friend of my son's, and if he would like Drummondville, he can have it, if he writes to me,"[18] Bishop Williams told his old nurse, Matilda Preddy. She was pleased: "You cannot think dear boy what a pleasure this news was for us *all* ... *this* is the way opened out for you in answer to our prayers."[19]

Fred applied to the bishop and his application was ratified at Drummondville. The resolution of his spiritual turmoil came two months later in a poem entitled "The Soul's Quest," dated Coggeshall, November 12, 1886. Should one, as did Newman at Littlemore, retreat from the world to serve God in an Anglo-Catholic brotherhood? Or should one, as did Arnold of Rugby, find his spiritual vocation in a life of active service? For Scott the cloistered life, highly attractive aesthetically, did not bring peace to the troubled soul. It was the active life that brought communion with God – a life spent on the human highway and filled with service. But this choice did not preclude the occasional visit inside the sanctuary, where:

> The altar-lights are shining fair,
> And Jesus' cross is standing there;
> The darkness brightens everywhere.[20]

In these stanzas Scott put forward his own resolution to pursue a life as an active churchman on the broad highway of the Anglican middle way, with his aesthetic sensibility nourished by occasional forays into High Church rituals.

In practical terms this meant that he would try to raise the practices in his Canadian parishes from Low to High Church. His Canadian congregations stoutly resisted such elevation. The Reverend Fred Scott arrived in Drummondville in late January, 1887; on March 27 he preached a controversial sermon that took an Anglo-Catholic position on the role of the elements in holy communion. His church wardens promptly complained to the bishop, and two weeks later he was in grave danger of losing his parish.

Bishop Williams considered the matter judiciously, hearing a second delegation supportive of Scott. He then issued a firm but tactful reprimand.[21] Nearly ten years later, his successor, Bishop Andrew Hunter Dunn, wrote to Scott in sweetly reasonable accents, pointing out that "the Wafer Bread – the Walking out in Cassock – the Erecting a Crucifix ... the Eucharistic Vestments – the use of a sign of a [Patée cross] – Genuflexions, prostrations, etc." could not, after all, "be said to be Essential." As they were not practised in any other church in the diocese, the Reverend F.G. Scott, should he care to move up to a larger parish, for "peace's sake" would have to "give them up." Why not attempt to do so now?[22]

Such requests were as impossible for Scott to follow in 1895 as in 1887. The heart of his faith rested in the Anglo-Catholic conception of holy communion, or "mass," as he liked to call it. The symbol of his religion was the crucifix, which he insisted on placing on the altar. What matter if an irate parishioner should throw his silver candlesticks into the river? He defended his own position with the assertion that "Mine is a higher law than some Privy Council Decisions."[23]

Scott and Amy were married on April 27, 1887, three months after his arrival in Drummondville. That she entered marriage with no illusions about his character is apparent from her remarks on the Drummondville controversy: "I shall always regret that it ever occurred ... the tone of your two last letters was so excessively jubilant that I might almost fancy you *enjoyed* the situation (providing always that you came out ahead)." She also recognized that her own nature differed strongly from his: "I could never thrive under opposition as you appear to be doing." Although she had come to feel that peace was the most desirable quality life offered, she gave him a strong warning: "I don't want to delude you with the idea that you will find me as clay in the hands of the potter."[24] But, most important, Amy had reached a turning point in her life. She had come to see their marriage as the will of "Divine Providence": "Although my future were not to turn out all I hope it to be, I should still feel satisfied that I was walking in the appointed way."[25] The young couple were married in Montreal, but only after Amy requested a postponement to allow her to attend a performance of the visiting Boston Symphony Orchestra.

Five children were born in Drummondville: William Bridges in 1888, Henry Hutton in 1890, Mary in 1892, Elton in 1893, and Charles Lennox in 1895. Scott revelled in the role of *paterfamilias*. To each of his male children, all of whom inherited his large beaked nose – "the Scott nose" – he gave a reward of ten dollars. He claimed a chivalric stag's head as "the crest of the Scott family," and he had it engraved on a commanding black stone ring that he wore on his little finger.[26] As each son came of age, he was presented with his own "Scott family ring." Each wore it proudly throughout his life. Undoubtedly, Scott wished to link the family to an aristocratic English past, a concern that became all the more pressing after he discovered that there were "brewers" in the family line. The father's myth proved potent, for several of his sons felt the pressure to strive to be worthy of the Scott family, a pressure intensified by their father's heroic life.

Because Elton weighed only four pounds at birth, his father felt it would be a shame to waste a Scott family name on a baby who might not live.[27] He named the child after the hero of a novel he had just written, *Elton Hazelwood*, a tale of a young man destined for the priesthood that emphasizes the ideals he was to pass on to his children. When Elton falls from chastity he explains: "You remember how we used to talk about knighthood and Sir Percival and the vision of the Holy Grail. We used to say that we would strive to live like Christian knights, but, Harry, old man ... I have been out in the world a good deal since then, and, in short, I've fallen from my ideal."[28] The novel, linking chivalry with the code of the English gentleman, dramatizes the Victorian crisis of faith. With its thinly disguised autobiographical elements, the book suggests that F.G. Scott was weighing the two vocations of priest and artist. The novel vindicates the priesthood, through which the fictional narrator finds assurance of life beyond death.

The question of vocation was all the more pressing because he had been keeping his hand in at poetry, privately printing *Justin and Other Poems* in 1885 and *The Soul's Quest* in 1886. In 1888 this early verse was republished by Kegan Paul, Trench of London and two lines from "In Memoriam," a poem for the young English Canadians killed in the Northwest Rebellion of 1885, became an epitaph to W.D. Lighthall's *Songs of the Great Dominion*, the major anthology of nineteenth-century Canadian poetry. His later verse, especially *My Lattice and Other Poems* of 1894 and *The Unnamed Lake and Other Poems* of 1897, described his strong attachment to the solitary northern landscape:

> Among the cloud-capt solitudes,
>   No sound the silence broke,
> Save when, in whispers down the woods,
>   The guardian mountains spoke.[29]

In 1892 Scott received a letter from his old friend the Reverend Lennox Williams, son of the Bishop of Quebec, saying he had a vacancy for a curate to assist him at St. Matthew's parish in Quebec City; perhaps Scott would know of someone? F.G. wrote back promptly: "Look no further. I am your man."[30]

By the turn of the century, in Canada as in the larger Empire, the Reverend F.G. Scott, now rector of St. Matthew's Anglican Church, was becoming well-known. Chaplain to the Quebec Citadel, he preached to the Canadian troops just before they left Canada for the Boer War. In 1901, after the death of Queen Victoria, he gave a moving eulogy reported in full in the Quebec papers. He commended the doughty Queen, a "mother," for having "drawn together by a subtle bond the young brood of fledgling nations that make up the imperial family" and castigated those who "foment racial antipathies, and tribal exclusiveness, in the pursuit of some ideal less than the national one."[31] Scott was alluding specifically to the Boer War and French-Canadian objections to it, but his remarks applied to the larger relationship between French and English in Quebec.[32]

To be sure, Scott's extremely personal cordiality leapt over many prevailing cultural tensions in the province. As an Anglo-Catholic, he preached and practised ecumenicalism; consequently he saw the whole community – whether Anglican or Roman Catholic or Greek Orthodox – as his parish. Quebecers of all religious persuasions tended to call upon him for help. He looked, and to some degree acted, like a Roman Catholic priest; he was fond of wearing a long, black ecclesiastical cape; he displayed the crucifix. He had a habit of dropping into Roman Catholic churches, as he explained to his children, "to smell the incense." He loved the ritual of the mass, the gilt of the statues, the holy water.

Then there was his charm. A tall, somewhat whimsical figure, he was "exuberant with good nature. [His] face was wreathed in smiles, and his whole body & spirit buoyant with pleasure."[33] Invariably trailed by his mongrel dog Jack, he would stop acquaintances in the street, proffering little cards with copies of his latest poem. These attributes were well known in Quebec City, as was his poetry about the Laurentians. French Quebecers felt that it had affinities with the poetry of *le terroir*.

Above all, there was the legend of his bravery. It was well known that he had received a Royal Humane Society Award for saving the life of a Quebecer who, after celebrating too much, had fallen beneath the Point Lévis ferry on a cold, dark night. Scott, a strong swimmer, had dived into the black, near-freezing water and pulled him out. "And to think that you did it for a French Canadian," marvelled one of the reigning Anglican ecclesiastics. "My Lord," replied Scott, "I did it for a fellow Canadian."[34]

For many French Canadians, there were irreconcilable differences between English and French in Quebec, not the least of which was the English assumption of social and political superiority. But Scott's genuine social concern, his winning personality, his northern poetry, and later, at the time of the Great War, his incredible courage in ministering to his English and French "boys" at the Front did much to ameliorate these differences. Yet Scott's Canadianism was closely allied with his imperialism. His "Hymn of Empire," set to music, was sung by Canadian schoolchildren throughout the Dominion. He published a controversial article near the start of the century supporting Chamberlain's policy of free trade within the Empire, to which Henri Bourassa, then editor of *Le Devoir* and one of the most prominent Quebec spokesmen, responded that while he did not share Scott's views, he concurred "most heartily in your warm appeal to a broad and deep sentiment of Canadianism .... I equally agree with you that our differences of race, creed and language should not be an obstacle to our being united by a common sentiment of strong attachment to our common land."[35]

It was in this hothouse atmosphere of Canadianism, Anglo-Catholicism, and imperialism that Frank Scott spent his formative years. The boy was fully aware of his father's doctrinal links with the French-Catholic community.[36] Rev. Scott would bring the young Frank, whom he intended for the Anglican priesthood, surreptitiously to the Roman Catholic high mass, saying, "one day soon the two churches will be reconciled."[37] To the small boy he passed on his perception of a worldwide Christian brotherhood and his belief in the mass as an assertion of eternal life triumphing over the omnipresence of death. Often, alluding to the series of tragic bereavements in his own early life, he would say "you can't imagine what it's like to lose both your parents in the same year – within a year."[38] And by his actions he demonstrated both the depth of his faith and the solace that it brought.

## TWO

# A Quebec Childhood

❦

WHEN FRANK SCOTT WAS BORN, Quebec City was a small self-contained town divided by geography, history, and language. Lower Town, the area closest to the St. Lawrence, was the site of Old Quebec, which was established by Samuel de Champlain in 1608 under the Norman seigneurial system. Largely French-speaking and Roman Catholic, Lower Town had successfully absorbed thousands of Irish immigrants by the late nineteenth century. Upper Town, the area above the escarpment near the top of the promontory, sprang up after the English conquest of Quebec in 1758 and was originally an outgrowth of the English military garrison at the Citadel.

By 1890, the English population had begun to decline, but a substantial enclave still existed in Quebec City, mercantile in its social composition, imperialist in its politics, and Church of England in its religious practices. The two major Anglican churches in the city were the cathedral, presided over by the Bishop of Quebec and serving the whole diocese, and St. Matthew's Church, a grey stone edifice built in 1876 by the local congregation. It had a fine steeple, good stained glass, a great stone altar extending down to the foundations, and a marble baptismal font. There Frank Scott and his younger brother Arthur were baptized.

The rectory of St. Matthew's Church at 5 Simard Street, where the Scott family resided, was poised on the escarpment that overlooked Lower Town. Located about a mile outside the original walls of the old city, it was a brisk twelve-minute walk from the church. The house was a large brick building; set in a large, treed garden, it had the air of a rambling country home. The northern windows of the rectory looked out upon the St. Charles River and the Laurentian Mountains beyond. To the east stood the rock of Cape Diamond, flying the Union Jack; to the south and west stretched the Plains of Abraham, a constant reminder of the last decisive struggle between the French and English in Canada.

This house was home to Frank Scott from birth till adulthood. He experienced the rectory as a world unto itself, with its own emotional climate and beloved geography. The house was large but reassuringly familiar. Inside the front door the study was immediately to the left, the sitting room to the right. In the study F.G. kept his books, a couch for napping, and a red leather armchair that the children called "Day Dreams Castle." (Elsewhere in the house was another large armchair called "The Death Chair" because Uncle Walter Scott had died in it.) From time to time Father would come rushing out of the study calling to the family, "I have written a new poem! Amy! Amy! Children! Come and hear." Everyone would gather around while he exuberantly recited his latest poem. The cup of his emotional life, always full, often overflowed at these times. Frank would stand there listening, not knowing quite what to do or how to express his feelings. He learned not to say anything at all, to shy away from demands on his emotional responses, or to deflect them by turning the highly serious into the humorous or satiric.[1]

In the sitting room a fire often burned in the grate. Frank liked to gather twigs for the fire from the garden. In one corner of the room was Mrs. Scott's piano, a Steinway grand, a great square instrument of dark wood on which she taught Frank to pick out the notes. From the main floor a stairway led up to the master bedroom, two smaller bedrooms, and an adjoining nursery with French windows looking out upon the Laurentians. From the time they were four or five, Frank and Arthur slept together in a large double bed in the nursery. Frank would drift off to sleep with the sound of his mother's piano coming softly from below; she would sometimes play Beethoven sonatas, sometimes church hymns. He remembered he felt content there under the warm heavy quilts, secure in the knowledge that he would soon be fast asleep. Once or twice he awoke from sleep, suddenly afraid, and called "Mother, Mother, come here," and she came quickly up the stairs.

Frank's fears in the night were the usual fears of childhood, but death also intruded. "The brother next above me called Charlie died of pneumonia or some lung ailment when he was seven, I think, and I was five .... And I can just remember kneeling down by the bed; Father was having sort of a little family memorial service."[2] Canon Scott was obviously deeply affected by the death of Charlie, who had become seriously ill while his father was away from home, allegedly visiting the pope. About this time the Canon instituted a custom of lining up his children in a row to kiss them good-bye affectionately, just in case one should expire while he was away. "Come children, come gather for the last embrace," he would demand.[3]

The world of the rectory was a strongly Victorian one where Father was a demanding patriarch, death was a large part of life, and Mother seemed quietly happy to be mother. Amy Scott provided the stability in the family, her husband being a perennial Puck to the end of his life. His ruling dictum, "God will provide," carried the corollary that the Reverend Mr. Scott did not have to do so. The burden of the organization of the family fell on Mrs. Scott, the eldest son, and the rest of the children in succession.

The youngest children grew up in a lively world of picnics and pets and outdoor games. In a family photograph taken during a summer vacation in 1903 at Cap à l'Aigle, a hundred miles from Quebec City, F.G. Scott and five of his six children are ranged in descending order in front of a log fence.[4] At the end of the line is Frank, about four, wearing a sailor suit. The boy looks abashed; he stares down at the grass in front of him. At the top of the line is the father, at ease; then William, the eldest boy, somewhat truculent in expression: William gave the orders. Harry, open-faced, cap in hand, is the pivot of the picture. Everyone liked Harry. Elton, the middle son, turns towards the younger children, Charlie, Frank, and Arthur. When Charlie died a year later, Elton moved closer to Frank and Arthur. Absent from the photograph is the only girl, Mary, vivacious and full of fun, who was born after Harry, and Mrs. Scott, whom her sons remember as trim in a navy skirt and white shirtwaist.

As the second youngest in this large family, Frank experienced all the benefits of a protected childhood, but also a sense of powerlessness. Decisions came from above, primarily from Mother and Father, but also from the eldest brother, William, or "Willum," as he was nicknamed. Frank and Arthur, as the babies of the family, were raised in the relative affluence of St. Matthew's (compared to the austerity of Drummondville) and enjoyed a privileged childhood. They were, as Frank later quipped, "trained to irresponsibility." Their father soon dubbed them "the two little Sirs" because of their habit of calling to each other: "Si-i-i-r, let's go and play."[5]

Play most often took place in the garden behind the rectory. Canon Scott found nature a retreat – a comfort that his children also came to appreciate – so he determined to keep the garden in a state of nature; nothing was to be trimmed, uprooted, or cut. His only concession to art was his rustic bench, where he communed with nature, wrote poems, and received guests, some of them Canadian poets such as Archibald Lampman and Wilfred Campbell. One day Arthur, then eight or nine, came rushing into the house: "Frank, do you know who is out on the Poet's Seat with father? Charles G.D. Roberts!"⁶ The boys were greatly excited because Frank had been reciting to Arthur selections from Roberts's animal tales.

Mrs. Scott liked a garden where things grew in an orderly fashion, but her attempts to bring order to it were doomed to failure. She also augmented the family's inadequate income with her vegetable plot, a hazelnut tree, red currant bushes, and white raspberries. One year there was corn; Frank pulled away the husks and ate the succulent ears raw. And in the fall he enjoyed raking the leaves to make a huge bonfire where potatoes could be roasted.⁷

At the bottom of the large garden was a stream, a stable, and tall trees – oak, maple, birch, and willow – all of which Elton, Frank, and Arthur climbed to the top. Whenever he caught them clinging to dangerous limbs, their father would impose a ban, but it was soon forgotten. Even after Elton had broken his arm three times by falling out of trees, the boys persisted. The stream cut across the large field behind the rectory. When spring came and snow still covered the field, the children hardly knew where the stream was until their feet disappeared suddenly into a watery mess. Later, during runoff, the boys built dams and scooted one of Elton's marvellous home-made toy motorboats around their artificial pond. Just before the stream dropped over the edge of a small cliff, it went through a thicket of almost impenetrable hawthorn bushes where the boys cut a path to make a secret fort.⁸

The stable in the garden was empty because Canon Scott could not afford the luxury of a horse. He walked to church, where the celebration of early-morning Anglo-Catholic mass was to him his chief religious duty and consolation, even though few parishioners attended. "The sexton was there and the church was filled with angels," he told his chaffing family.⁹ A small boy, watching his father set out on foot without breakfast at 7:15 a.m. in all weather, learned to understand that "duty," or Christian service, must always come before personal comfort.

LIFE IN THE SCOTT HOUSEHOLD revolved around the festivals of the Anglican Church, especially Christmas, Easter, and the Harvest Festival, which coincided with the seasons. It provided a rhythmical life, replete with what the children sensed were eternal verities. On Sundays the whole family went to church three, sometimes four times a day.¹⁰ As a young boy, Frank sang in the choir. There were many buttons on the choir cassock and during the long time it took to get them fastened his eyes focused on "Duty," one of F.G. Scott's poems, hanging on the vestry wall just in front of them:

Duty from thy golden wings
God on man his glory flings
And all the harps of God are strung
With the songs that Thou hast sung.[11]

By the time Frank was twelve, Canon Scott had introduced a processional cross behind which the choir entered singing "Holy, Holy, Holy, Lord God Almighty." The choir, together with his mother's music, laid the foundation for Frank's strong aesthetic sense. He internalized the measures of the old church hymns and the image of the cross. Concepts often considered opposite – like duty and poetry, or religion and art – were fused for him.

The focus of the religious year for young Frank was the birth of Christ. A hundred and fifty candles blazed on the altar. Balsam boughs filled the church with the scent of resin. At home there was never a Christmas tree, considered by Canon Scott a "pagan symbol," but there were Christmas pillowcases strung on a rope stretched across the nursery.[12] Canon Scott wrote a nativity play, *The Key of Life*, and in 1913 it was staged at the church hall with Frank as First Angel. Before "the starry canopy of space [that] stretches far away into the infinite distance," he announced the Nativity:

Dear Brother, canst thou see,
Far down the gulfs of night,
That world to which so joyfully
Great Gabriel speeds his flight?[13]

The tableau gave Frank a poetic sense of the starry heavens and their great distance from earth. He, the younger child, the smallest angel, was absorbing a tangible sense of a relation between the religious infinite and human beings. On clear winter nights the snow spread like a carpet beneath Frank's bedroom window; the Laurentians were silhouetted in the distance, the stars hung in the sky with absolute clarity. For the child, the heavens shone forth with the Glory of God and he lay in bed thinking about eternity: "When I get to heaven, it's not going to end, no, it's *never*." This thought was so overwhelming that "you'd almost faint."[14] In later years, eternity became highly vulnerable when contrasted with the infinity of Eddington and Einstein, but Frank Scott never lost his sense of man as a microcosm silhouetted against the greater movements of the universe.

His first memory of nature was beneficent. Around the age of four, playing on an old wooden dock at Lake St. Joseph near Quebec City, he suddenly tumbled into the water:

What surprised me was that I floated.... The water was over my depth and I didn't know how to swim. But I remember lying on my back on the surface of the water, looking up at the sky and saying to myself and feeling, "I'm floating." It surprised me.... Instead of being a frightening accident, the event sort of encouraged me in some kind of way.[15]

His father used to tell him, "You've a guardian angel looking after you," and Frank associated the idea with a beneficent universe.[16] To the small boy saying his prayers, his guardian angel was a real presence. This notion was transformed in adolescence by thoughts of a Divine Providence that helped shape one's life and, in later years, a mature Scott joked about "little hands." Underlying this concept was the belief, at first literal and then metaphoric, in a power for good that guided and supported, especially when one was engaged in a just cause.

The young Frank was rebellious, clashing with his father at an early age. Years later, Elton told Frank that the younger boy, when two or three years old, had refused to leave the toilet. The father repeatedly dragged him away, but the boy just as persistently returned. His father shouted angrily, "you have to show who's master at the start," and spanked him so hard Elton was alarmed.[17] Apparently, Frank did learn. In several photographs of him, from ages four to twelve, he looks abashed, eyes directed down toward the ground.

Spankings took place quite frequently in the Scott household, sanctioned by the Victorian adage, "Spare the rod and spoil the child." On another occasion, Frank and Arthur made a pile of hay in the middle stall of the stable in the garden and set a match to it. A column of smoke arose and the child became terrified. "I got frightened and I crouched in the back of one of the stalls. Father came charging in and eventually found me and dragged me out. This resulted in a very severe spanking. I can remember hiding under the bed in the nursery after the spanking, trying to recover. Instead of being pleased that I wasn't burned to death, he was furious that I had been so stupid."[18]

Later, when the boys were adolescents, Canon Scott caught Elton, Frank, and Arthur masturbating, a practice they had just learned from a schoolmate. It was Elton who took the brunt of the punishment, a lecture Arthur remembered as "the most God awful going over that a man could ever have from his father." The Anglo-Catholic practice of confession, which the father had always insisted on, began to take on overtones of an inquisition. Frank recalled "for the few years in which certainly I went to confession, something called impurity was about the worst sin you could commit."[19] Canon Scott's extreme reaction, and his rigid distinction between the purity of the spirit and the impurity of the body, engendered a sharp body-spirit polarity in his sons' minds. They remained painfully inhibited about expressing emotions, especially of a sexual nature. None of the Scott men, Arthur once remarked, could ever kiss their wives in public.[20]

Another of Canon Scott's maxims was "be ye angry and sin not." The family understood this to mean that unexpressed righteous indignation was itself a sin. Yet, the children also feared their father's power while absorbing his aggression. As a result of his father's behaviour, Frank brought into adult life the conviction that one had a right to be angry – in fact, one must be angry about wrongdoing and injustice. But he also learned to dislike and to fight against unbridled power of any kind.

Yet, Frank Scott's memories of his father were largely positive. He continued to imbue the children with his appreciation of the natural world and young Frank was receptive to these experiences. The Canon used to take the child outside at night to look at the street lights reflecting on the snow crystals, and to look at the constellations. "Frank, see the sparklers! Look Frank, there's the Great Dipper," he enthused. Soon Frank began to visit the library, where he studied astronomy books. And during picnics in the Laurentians, the children were taught geology. Frank recalled his father telling them at Montmorency Falls, one of the family's favourite spots, that the limestone was once under the sea, that the Laurentians were "the oldest mountains in the world." They learned that the soil covering the rock underfoot was so shallow that in places, if you stamped on it, the ground sounded hollow underneath. They were impressed with a sense of the newness of the Laurentian forest, in terms of geologic time. Above all, their father emphasized the great open spaces of the Canadian North: "Frank, stand on this stone and look north. There's nothing between you and the North Pole."[21] Father, as an older Frank was later to joke, "never thought of the Indians."

Frank also began to absorb a sense of the relationship between the French and English in Quebec and, beyond that, of Canada's place in the empire. In 1909, Quebec celebrated the three-hundredth anniversary of the city's founding. A replica of one of Jacques Cartier's ships rode at anchor in the harbour, and platforms and bell tents were erected near the Citadel to accommodate the festive crowds. The French workmen's voices rang out in the distance as they sang such old French songs and ballads as "J'en va à guerre."

On the day of the tercentenary, the townspeople re-enacted the historic battle. Throngs of redcoats moved across the Plains of Abraham to meet the bluecoats pouring out of the Citadel. There, in the centre of a wooden stage, representatives of the two nations met and shook hands. Frank Scott, son of an English-Canadian clergyman, in a blue uniform representing the French, greeted Jack Price, son of an English-Canadian lumber baron, in a red coat representing the British.[22] With this handshake, or so it seemed, all differences between English and French were obliterated.

The old Quebec High School, a tall building with huge Gothic windows, was built high on the promontory near the old Citadel. On their way to school Frank and Arthur passed by one of the mass graves dug some sixty years earlier for the countless immigrants, many Irish, who died in the epidemics tended by their grandfather, Dr. Scott. Some of the skulls had become disinterred and the boys occasionally used one as a football, kicking it along and shouting ferociously, "There you go, McGinty."[23] Inside the Quebec High School, in one of the classrooms, was a large mercator map of the world showing all of the British possessions in a bright red. "The empire is my country, Canada is my home," read the motto. On the playing field as in the classroom, Frank was absorbing a sense of the Canadian past. He was also emerging as a leader, as both he and Arthur began to take the high school awards for proficiency.

THE HIGHLIGHT of each summer was camping out on the shores of the St. Lawrence. About the middle of June the Scott family packed up, boarded a train or a paddlewheel boat in the harbour at Quebec City, and travelled down the St. Lawrence to camp at Beaupré, or Cap à l'Aigle, or Cacouna, fashionable resorts of the period where their father's family had summered. Canon Scott had acquired a large bell tent left over from the tercentenary and he and the boys customarily set up four other smaller tents on the beach at Beaupré. Mother and Mary at first slept in a nearby farmhouse; later a special tent with a wooden floor was rigged out for their use. There was an outdoor fireplace made of stone and a table under an awning where the family ate breakfast and supper. For breakfast one of the bigger boys, Harry or Elton, would make porridge in a large billycan. At mid-day the whole family would troop to a nearby boarding house owned by a family named Tremblay for the main meal of the day.[24]

The tenting life at Beaupré was a continuation of the joys of the rectory garden. At night the boys fell asleep in their blankets, lulled by the "constant conversation" of running water. Water was always their favourite element and there were many fish in the St. Anne River. Harry, an accomplished fisherman, instructed the younger children. He was a great favourite with Frank and Arthur. As the second oldest, he had none of William's pressing sense of responsibility; he was gentle, with a spontaneous sense of humour.

During his summer holidays, Canon Scott would come to camp usually on a Saturday, but by Monday mornings he began to feel anxious about his duties at St. Matthew's. He also missed the bustle and excitement of Quebec City. "I have got to get back to my parish," he would announce and then disappear. However, in spite of his absences, he continued at Beaupré many of the religious rituals of rectory life. Halfway up the cliff, he found a niche with a great pine tree and a fine view. There he would say his prayers, evensong or matins. Family prayers were said as usual after breakfast. A special family communion service was always conducted on Sundays, among the trees near the tents, on a little altar made of a box covered with a cloth, on which the Reverend Scott placed the cross.[25]

From 1912 to 1914 the family moved away from the beach, further downstream and closer to Beaupré, to a log cabin belonging to the manager of the local pulp mill, Ferdinand Van Bruysel. The family also retained a tent for visitors. By 1914, Harry had become engaged to an attractive, dark-haired young woman, Constance Hall. The younger boys were very curious about this engagement, especially about the mechanics of the proposal. One evening while Harry, Frank, and Arthur washed the dishes, Arthur began to probe. "When was it," he demanded, "a handkerchief was placed upon the ground and a lowly knee was bent?"[26]

The exaggerated chivalric language of Arthur's question reflected the parodying style of Stephen Leacock's *Nonsense Novels*, which F.G. had been in the habit of reading aloud. They heard much Leacock – *Literary Lapses*, and *Sunshine Sketches of a Little Town* – as well as Dickens's *Pickwick Papers*. Arthur and Frank would roll on the grass laughing loudly at Leacock's account of young Lord Ronald who, when disappointed in love, said nothing but "flung himself from the room, flung himself upon his horse, and rode madly off in all directions." They also enjoyed his parody of the knight errant in "Guido the Gimlet of Ghent: A Romance of Chivalry," particularly the opening paragraph, which they were fond of declaiming: "It was in the flood-tide of chivalry. Knighthood was in the pod."[27]

# THREE

# *Knighthood*

W ITHIN TWO DAYS of the announcement of war on August 4, 1914, Canon Scott notified his astonished church wardens that he would be going to the Front. He was fifty-three years old and, as Chaplain of the Eighth Royal Rifles, he had told a friend, "I must volunteer."[1] He liked to boast, when stationed at training camp at Valcartier, that he had beaten to the punch by twenty-four hours his eldest son William, who enlisted as a private. The declaration of war came three days after Frank's fifteenth birthday.

After enlisting, F.G. rejoined the family on holidays at Beaupré. There he wrote a poem, "Blood Guilt," describing the coming struggle as a Holy War against a bloodthirsty despot:

> The brand of Cain is on your brow,
>     Emperor!
> A crown of gold may hide it now,
>     Emperor!
> But when the day of reckoning comes ...
> A people's wrath will rend the skies
> And topple down your dynasties,
>     Emperor![2]

Shortly after, Frank was appalled when Ferdinand Van Bruysel, manager of the local mill, egged on his dog who attacked a woodchuck and tore the animal to pieces before their eyes. Frank wrote an indignant verse:

> The brand of Cain is on thy brow
>     Ferdinand!
> Although you may not know it now
>     Ferdinand!

If you a great big house would build
I'm sure that you could have it filled
With all the woodchucks you have killed,
Ferdinand![3]

He discovered one of the joys of authorship when his cousin Bertha confided how much she admired this poem. Frank had begun to sense the power of words on January 1, 1912, when his sister gave him a pocket diary as a Christmas present. In it he made brief daily entries about school, outings, friends, and books. Occasional glimpses of the young boy emerge from the large scrawl: "1. My rat died / 2. Got a canary / 3. Lost the canary / 4. Got two more canaries / 5. Buster ate one canary." There is no mention of the Great War in the innocent summary of the "chief events of 1914" contained on the flyleaf of his diary of that year.[4]

By September, 1914, the war had begun in earnest for the Scotts as the Canon and William, now at training camp at Valcartier, prepared for service overseas. Assigned to Salisbury Plain, Scott disregarded orders and travelled surreptitiously to France. There he attached himself to the nearest Canadian detachment, the 15th Battalion of the First Division.[5] Taking no pains for his own safety (and believing "the Lord will provide"), from then on he was often found at the front lines administering the last sacrament. His belief in the miracle of the mass now brought comfort to young men dying at the Front.

During the war years Frank greatly missed the male companionship of his family. Harry and Elton, following the example of their father and William, each joined up when they turned eighteen. Poor health, too, often added to Frank's low spirits. His childhood had been an alternating cycle of activity and rest: robust boyish activities were followed by periods of sickness, with weeks at a time spent in bed. He ran the gamut of illnesses: appendicitis, pneumonia, whooping cough, bronchitis, influenza, recurrent grippe, and, now in 1915, tonsillitis.

While in bed Frank read voraciously, cosseted by Mother and Mary. He made an annual list in his diaries of the books he had read that year. In 1912 he read children's classics such as *The Jungle Book*, *Tom Brown's School Days*, and *Chums*; in 1914 he read *The Story of the Heavens* and in 1915 *Lorna Doone*, *Rob Roy*, *Stalky and Co.*, and Foxe's *Book of Martyrs*, which impressed him more than any other he had read. It had illustrations of martyrs tied to the stake and writhing in the flames, their faces contorted with suffering and ecstasy. These images of martyrdom and suffering were later to appear in his poetry and to condition his view of religion. His initial response to the book was admiration for the sacrifice, encouraged by his father and by the popular view of World War I as a crusade in which the heroic young soldiers were new martyrs.

During this year Willum was sent home from the Front, a war casualty. A German sniper had shot a bullet through his field glasses as he surveyed the battlefield, splintering his face and causing the loss of an eye. A year later, in June, 1916, when Elton reached the age of eighteen it was his turn to go to the Front. To celebrate the departure, Frank decided to organize a fireworks display. He set up a rudimentary firebomb, perhaps unconsciously exposing himself to the same dangers faced by his brothers in battle. He arranged a large pile of gunpowder, lit the fuse, and waited, shielded by the corner of the rectory. When it failed to go off, he came back to investigate. At that moment the gunpowder exploded in his face, sending fragments of metal into both eyes.

As Frank stood there, blood dripping down his face, it seemed to Mrs. Scott he would lose the sight of both eyes. A message for help was sent to Willum, now practising law in Montreal. He contacted Uncle Frank, at that time a vice-president of the Grand Trunk Railway. A special train was chartered to rush the boy from Quebec City to the Jeffery Hale Hospital in Montreal. As Frank lay in bed, his eyes covered with bandages, he, too, was convinced that he would never see again. Stoically, he tried to comfort himself. Even if he was blind he could still fish for perch off the wharf at Cap à l'Aigle. In his mind's eye he began to follow the rough, timbered contours of the wharf and tried to determine how he would set out his fishing line.[6] Mrs. Scott stayed constantly by her son's bedside. She now made the daily entries in his diary, and she wrote to her husband at the Front, telling him that Frank had "the spirit of a true soldier in him."[7] Canon Scott, surrounded by maimed and broken bodies, was not disposed to sympathy. "Do not allow the boys to go in for explosions. We have enough of them, too much of them here. It is a mercy he did not blow out both eyes."[8]

Frank endured a week of anxiety before he was told the surgeons had been able to save his left eye. He would have to wear a black patch over the right eye for a year or so until it healed and later, a glass eye. In future years, he would turn his left profile to the world. The accident also caused him to miss his formal graduation from high school. When the results came out, however, Frank learned he had won two silver medals: one for proficiency in French and another for writing the best literary composition in the school.[9] He had written on kindness to animals. Narrowly missing coming first in his class, he ranked just one mark behind his best friend, Sydney Williams, the son of Lennox Williams, his father's old friend.

That summer of 1916 at Cap à l'Aigle, Frank and Arthur contributed to the war effort by catching smelt and peddling them from house to house to raise money for the Red Cross. They rolled bandages and they staged concerts.[10] Frank, now seventeen, was tall and gangly, with a shock of fair hair falling over his forehead. He played Prince Charming – dashing with a black patch over his one eye – to the Princess of Margaret Cundhill, a young neighbour.[11]

He was beginning to be known as one of the adventurous Scott brothers, who were considered "different." On a train journey, Frank and Elton had been known to ride on the top of one of the carriages, clinging with bare hands, hair flying in the wind. Instead of staying at the conventional boarding houses in the country, they camped on the beach and bathed naked. They went on long hikes, climbed the local mountains, and paddled out to islands in the St. Lawrence.[12]

In September he left home for the first time to attend Bishop's College, in Lennoxville, Quebec. Frank liked Bishop's. The professors were pleasant, the work was congenial, and his friend Syd Williams was a classmate. There was a happy social life of outings, concerts, and pageants, usually for the war effort. Frank discovered he had a gift for comedy when he starred in a play called "The Hoodoo."[13] Syd and Frank spent many happy afternoons paddling on the river just outside the college gates. The only shadow, a gradually deepening one, was the war. In his room, just above his desk, Frank arranged photographs of his father and three older brothers – all resplendent in uniform.[14]

By the fall of 1916, William's part in the war over, Elton was on leave in England awaiting active service. But Harry, who had enlisted in 1915, was a lieutenant leading a company in a battery about to enter the front lines at the Somme, where his father served. Canon Scott worried about his son, but like many of his background and sensibility, he saw the Great War in chivalric terms and expressed this in an epitaph called "Knighthood," written for a dying soldier:

> In honour, chivalrous;
> In duty, valorous;
> In all things, noble;
> To the heart's core, clean.[15]

Nevertheless, the father's anxieties for Harry, who he knew must face the enemy fire, grew. Few returned from such engagements.

In a letter home he told of a communion service in murky weather on a hillside with Harry's 87th Battalion, which was to go into battle the next day. He had preached, "I beseech you, walk worthy of the vocation wherewith you are called," and he had been overjoyed Harry could be among the communicants. After the service, father and son had an opportunity to speak of the old days at Beaupré and of the last communion held by the Canon under the trees by the river. He continued the letter with the promise, "When I get home, one of the first excursions will be to the riverside camp and the cross on the big boulder."[16]

A week later Frank received a telephone call at Bishop's College from his sister Mary. Harry was missing in action. Frank left immediately for Quebec City and the rectory. There, all the members of the family, including Harry's wife Constance, gathered to await further news. Confirmation of the tragic news came on October 30, 1916, in a cable from Canon Scott: "Harry died nobly leading his Company in attack. He did not suffer. Hope to get his body later. May God give you courage and strength. We must keep on unflinchingly to the end."[17] Frank never forgot Constance, who collapsed "as if she had been hit a blow on the head."[18]

Frank took the news with fortitude and returned to Bishop's and his university work there. Two weeks later, in early December, he received a large packet of the letters written home by his father with the request they be preserved in "the Scott family archives." In one eleven-page letter scribbled on legal-size paper, the Canon described his journey into hell – the search for Harry's body. Also included with this description was a further page, apparently written for Elton: "I am so proud of my boys. Fancy being the father of two boys who have shed their blood for the Empire and of another who is coming to the front. You are all so noble."[19]

Harry, the Canon wrote, had been killed by a sniper's bullet while waiting to lead his battery in attack. His body had been buried hastily in no man's land. Anxious to conduct a proper burial service, the Canon described, for his family, the frantic horror of his twenty-four-hour search in the Regina Trench for the grave. He found it in an area described by the soldiers as a "drear, weird" hollow called "Death Valley." In the shell-ploughed landscape, in mud both slippery and sticky, and lit by the flash from nearby shelling, Canon Scott finally came across "a little lonely white cross." He and a soldier assisting him dug but did not find the body. Just before a new bombardment, they dug near this cross and another unpainted one nearby. Eventually, "after [the soldier] had taken off a few shovelfuls of earth something white was laid bare and there was darling Harry's left hand with the signet ring on his little finger. It was like a miracle – to think that I had found him on that waste on which I could see many bodies still unburied."[20] With the sound of shells whistling overhead, Canon Scott recited the burial service.

A few days later Frank replied he was glad to read the letters about Harry's death. He had learned his father's lessons well: the letters "made me feel proud to belong to a family like ours, and made me want to live up to our standard. 'To be a good Scott one must live without spot,' I think ought to be our motto."[21]

This task laid a great burden of duty on the young man, for it demanded far more than ordinary virtuous conduct. It required, quite literally, that he emulate the knight, an idea common to Canadians of the war generation.[22] While at Bishop's, Frank purchased the Canadian edition of Edward Marsh's *Memoir* of the young soldier-poet Rupert Brooke. He read it and Brooke's poems over an extended period of several years, musing on each occasion on the nature of greatness and his desire to emulate Brooke. This emotional climate – the chivalric temper of the age, the influence of his father, the death of his older brother – brought out that potential knight errantry, the desire to serve and be of some use in the world, that is so often a part of an idealistic youth's character. In Frank Scott this idealism was at first thwarted – and then intensified – when he found himself unable to serve at the Front.

By the spring of 1918 Frank's diary had begun to reflect some of the pervasive anxiety of the war years: "Everybody is anxious about the big battle on the Western Front. All sorts of rumours are afloat."[23] When he returned to the rectory for the Easter weekend on March 30, 1918, Quebec City was in the grip of the conscription riots: "On Thursday and Friday nights there were riots, and more trouble was expected tonight. Squads of soldiers were patrolling the streets and protecting important buildings. The trouble is over the enforcement of the Military Service Act. These French-Canadians are not British."[24] For the first time, Frank was beginning to perceive that the easy pageantry of the Quebec tercentenary did not hold true.

The following day, Easter Sunday, public meetings were postponed and women and children were not allowed out after dark, but brief church services were permitted. As the Scott family knelt in prayer at St. Matthew's, the roar of the crowd coming up from Lower Town sounded ever louder. The closer the mob came, Frank later quipped, the more earnestly the congregation prayed. After the service ended, Frank and Arthur walked down from the church toward Lower Town. There, on Palace Hill, they were met by a policeman who pointed a gun into Arthur's back and said, "Get up there ... now go on, go on or I'll shoot."[25]

On the following night, Easter Monday, the Scott family sat on their little balcony at the rear of the rectory, overlooking Lower Town. The electric lights had been cut off by the rioters; the whole of Lower Town was in fog and darkness. They heard shouts. Now and then they would hear a group singing "O Canada," and then more shouts. Suddenly they heard the terrifying sound of machine-gun fire. In fact, the army had turned their guns on the brick walls. When the night was over, the bodies of five French Quebecers lay in the morgue. Frank never forgot the roar of the mob. It gave him a sense of the extreme vulnerability of the *entente cordiale* between French and English in Quebec. He became determined to work toward its preservation.

When Frank turned nineteen on August 1, 1918, he tried to enlist. "Went up & saw Major Peppel at the St. Louis camp re enlisting. He told me I wd. be in category B.2, wh. wd. mean service in Canada only, so I didn't join up." Category B.2 ruled out service at the Front. Two days later he tried again by ringing up some military officials. But despite five attempts, by November 3 he was forced to give up hope; he concluded that "one-eyed men" were not in demand. "I wonder what course my life would have taken had I enlisted!" he wrote. "A small thing may change one's future." Eight days later, on November 11, 1918, the Great War was over. In spite of the chivalric war rhetoric and his own attempts to enlist, he was conscious of false sentimentality. He wrote in his diary on Armistice Day: "As I write this the whistles of all the factories around here are shrieking to the world at large the news of the signing of the armistice. Imagine how lightheartedly the mothers of the Empire will go about their work today! (Bosh)."

ON SUNDAY, MAY 4, 1919, the Scotts received news Canon Scott would be arriving that morning on a troop ship. The Chaplain was arriving as a war hero: all the family, and much of Quebec City, were there to greet him. There was to be a special ceremony in which he would be presented with a Nash motorcar as a token of the city's gratitude. The family stood on the dock as the *Empress of Britain* steamed into the harbour. They saw, all along the decks of the great vessel, crowded against the railings, long lines of khaki as 2,700 men waited to disembark. Frank watched his father inspect a guard of honour. Canon Scott held up his hand and a hush descended over the great crowd. "I told them what they had done for Canada and what Canada owed them, and how proud I was to have been with them. I asked them to continue to play the game out here as they had played it in France ... I pronounced the Benediction, said, 'Good-bye, boys,' and turned homewards."[26] Frank was deeply moved at the time and never able to recall the scene in later years without tears stinging his eyes.[27]

The following month Frank graduated from Bishop's College with a bachelor's degree in arts. His four years there had been happy and productive. He had discovered an aptitude for history and literature and his favourite teacher, Professor Boothroyd, a Cambridge graduate who taught both subjects, encouraged these interests. "Boots," as he was familiarly called, had done more to awaken a love of poetry in Frank than anyone else. His father had never read poetry aloud – none, that is, other than his own. But Frank found Canon Scott's habit of importuning acquaintances with his latest poems embarrassing. Poetry as read by Boots – the colloquial verve of Browning and the rhythmical sweep of Tennyson – was quite different. And Boothroyd made it clear a poem ought to make sense. To Frank, nurtured as he was on his father's poems, the spontaneous overflow of natural feeling, this emphasis was quite new.[28]

Boothroyd also gave Frank a sense of European history. One essay topic suggested by him was "Socialism." When Frank said he knew nothing about it, Boots said, "Look it up in *The Encyclopedia Britannica*." He did and found an article by G.B. Shaw, which stated: "In Socialism, private property is anathema and equal distribution of income the first consideration."[29] Frank was also encouraged to consider the newly emerging League of Nations, an interest reflected in his earnest valedictory address on "The Brotherhood of Man":

> The Armistice placed the College at the parting of the ways, but it does far more than this.... Bishop's has always aroused in her students a patriotic love for their nation and Empire. But now there is a higher duty for her to discharge: she must instill into those who study within her walls that love of humanity as a whole, that feeling of the brotherhood of man – that universal spirit which alone can make the League of Nations possible.[30]

In the summer of 1919 the Scott family journeyed to Cap à l'Aigle, where Frank, for the first time, felt the pangs of calf love when smitten by Kan Dennis, a pretty dark-haired girl from Nova Scotia, whose charming profile showed to advantage under the wide leghorn hats of the period. They sat around bonfires together and discussed poetry. His emotions were galvanized when his foot accidentally met hers.[31] In September, at summer's end, Kan wrote an adieu directly into Frank's diary: "goodbye-ee Franco! Don't forget we are *good friends* and not merely 'ships that pass in the night'." After she had gone, he moped. No one had engaged his emotions and his intellect as Kan had when they discussed poetry. Pulling himself together, he diagnosed his condition as "Kanlessness,"[32] and cheered himself by writing verse.

By October, 1919, Frank had acquired a temporary position as the form master for the preparatory class at the Quebec High School, the class formerly taught by the teacher he had most admired, Adam Elliot.[33] He was once more living at the rectory, where returned soldiers frequently visited to pay their respects to Canon Scott. After one such evening, in October, Frank summarized his response: "Father brought some men in evening. They talked war all the time. I wd give 10 years of my life to have been able to get to the front."[34]

The fact that he had missed the war still rankled. What made it worse was that the Canadian post-war climate was saturated with the war. When he went down to Bishop's to visit Arthur, he found a lecture on war poetry in progress. Each night as he sat down to summarize the day's activities, he found at the start of every page in his new 1920 diary the motto "Lest we forget." By early spring 1920, he was helping his father with a book Canon Scott had begun to write. Published in 1922, *The Great War as I Saw It* described the war as "the great adventure of [my] life among the most glorious men that the world has ever produced."[35]

It had been decided Frank would go to Oxford, in January, 1920, to join Elton, now studying theology on a Rhodes Scholarship, and the family would endeavour to support him. But as the year turned, he came down with another of his recurrent bouts of tonsillitis. Physically and emotionally depressed, he read George Eliot and responded deeply to what he recognized as the tragic happiness of Maggie Tulliver's death in *The Mill on the Floss*. Like Maggie he realized he, too, had come to a turning point in his life. "I suppose it marks the change from boyhood to manhood, from the stage of parental support to that of self support."[36] He wondered if he could ever make good and was concerned that he had not proven himself.

> So far I have done nothing to justify my existence. My life has resembled that of a family pet – a dog or a canary – which is fed and housed by the master of the house.... Now the time has come to prove that that expenditure of love and money has not been in vain.... Last night in answer to my anxiety, I opened the Bible by chance at Matthew VI 25-34. May God give me strength to make that my creed and my practice.[37]

The message of the gospel, simply put, is that "God will provide," an echo of F.G. Scott's prevailing creed.

As the year ended Frank's tonsillitis became steadily worse. Early in January, 1920, Canon Scott announced the Oxford plans must be postponed. Frank could not possibly endure the damp English climate in his present health. For the next three months the younger Scott was at loose ends. He spent much of his time, while recovering, chauffeuring his father around Quebec City on pastoral calls. While waiting in the car, he read; at night he helped correct his father's war book. Canon Scott thought Frank ought to find more lucrative employment, so he consulted an old friend who owned a leather factory, who offered Frank a job carrying bales of leather at a decent salary.[38]

One day, just before Frank was to begin work, he and his father were walking up a street in Quebec City when they encountered the Anglican Bishop of Quebec. "Frank, what are you doing?" "Well, I think I'm working down in [a] Tannery." "Why don't you apply for a Rhodes Scholarship?" asked the Bishop. "I think you've got the qualifications. You might get it."[39] Frank did apply. He travelled to Montreal, where he was interviewed by the Rhodes Committee and its chairman, Mr. Edward Beatty, president of the Canadian Pacific Railway. Frank was required to "show his points" but he was not accustomed to performing on demand: "Felt like a poodle at a dog show," he wrote in his diary. "Went to Loew's Vaudeville to take away the taste."[40] A few weeks later, Frank Scott received the astounding news that he had been awarded a Rhodes Scholarship to Oxford. "God had provided," as He did for the young Fred Scott some twenty-five years earlier, and again through the agency of Lennox Williams, now Bishop of Quebec.

# FOUR

# Oxford: "My Great Adventure"

☙

THE WORLD THAT Frank Scott entered when he and his brother, Elton, went past the porter's lodge at Magdalen College, Oxford, under the great stone arch with its effigy of Mary Magdalen, had changed little since medieval times. As the Scotts walked around the vaulted quadrangle of the old Cloisters, a Gothic window to their left opened on a square of green; to the right were steps leading up to Hall, while just around the corner was the Junior Common Room, where undergraduates met, talked, smoked their pipes, and read the papers. Still further down the corridor, a door led out through a painted iron gate and over a bridge on to the Water Walks.

Beyond the gate, Addison's Walk followed the bank of the river, bordered by large hawthorns, oaks, and willows, through the Deer Park and widening meadows, winding back in a circle until one could see the crenellated towers of Oxford in the distance, with Magdalen Bridge on the right. Under the bridge were the brightly coloured punts, oblong with square ends. This walk became Scott's favourite at Oxford; lost in the trees, listening to the sound of running water, he might well be back in Quebec.

On September 24, 1920, when Frank and Elton Scott left Quebec City for Montreal on the first lap of the journey to England, Frank had taken from his pocket a small cloth-covered book and begun to write: "Packed our grips for Oxford.... My great adventure has started." That adventure, at first, lay not in his academic program at Oxford so much as in the College itself, especially the antiquity of its buildings and the traditions they embodied, and in the lovely undulating green of the English countryside: "just the same sort of peaceful prettiness that I expected."[1] His first great discovery in England was the romance of the past.

AFTER HIS INITIAL delighted exploration of Magdalen and Oxford, Scott settled down to undergraduate life, in a routine that included study in the morning and occasional lectures; afternoon sports; tea and talk with friends at 4:15, followed by dinner in Hall; then attendance at clubs or study until eleven or twelve, in the rooms he shared that year with his brother.

Each night Scott recorded the day's events in his diary. A typical entry, for February 26, 1921, gives an account of lectures attended, library work, a rehearsal for a tableau, a hockey match, tea with friends, a lecture on modern poetry, a meeting to form a dramatic society, evening reading (that day it was Pollard's *Evolution of Parliament*), terminating with a report on the weather: "Nice cool day." Near the end of this entry is the terse remark: "Beginning to perceive more and more how miserably formed is my character."

Two voices report on Scott's years at Oxford, the first, and most clearly defined, is the public voice of the diaries, offering a calendar of events. The second and smaller voice is a private one: it enters, usually at the end of the day's activities, often undertaking a spiritual inventory. As a High Anglican, Scott was accustomed to make confession; now at Oxford he begins to confide these matters to his diary, reporting on the difficulties of his new life.

First among those difficulties was meeting the academic demands of the honours school of modern history. That history, under the Oxford syllabus, included the Dark and Middle Ages and encompassed the history of England from the landing of Julius Caesar to the latter half of the nineteenth century. Because history and law were once under a single faculty, the study of history at Oxford has as its backbone the study of constitutional law. Some of the great Oxford historians – Stubbs, Bryce, Anson, and Dicey – worked notably in the field of constitutional history and law. Of equal importance, social and economic history were studied in the context of the general history of the country and the development of arts and letters – a perspective that profoundly influenced Scott's later vision of the social function of law.

The candidate for an Oxford degree in "Mods" was required to write a paper illustrating the development of the nature of English law and government, the first option being from the earliest time to 1307, including Stubbs's *Charters*. Also required was a theoretical paper on political science based on a textual study of Aristotle's *Poetics*, Hobbes's *Leviathan*, and Rousseau's *Du contrat social*. On December 10, 1920, Scott notes that he is reading Stubbs on constitutional history and working on Aristotle's *Poetics*.

A Canadian compatriot, Stephen Leacock, who much to Scott's pleasure visited Oxford early in 1921 and chatted with the undergraduates in their rooms, later reported on the difference between Oxford and North American universities. At Oxford, he explains, lectures don't matter; the key figure is the tutor, yet it is hard to understand how he works. " 'We go over to his rooms,' said one student, 'and he just lights a pipe and talks to us.' 'We sit round with him,' said another, 'and he simply smokes and goes over our exercises with us'." "From this and other evidence," Leacock concluded, "what an Oxford tutor does is to get a little group of students together and smoke at them. Men who have been systematically smoked at for four years turn into ripe scholars.... A well-smoked man speaks and writes English with a grace that can be acquired in no other way."[2]

Scott's education had begun in earnest on October 9, 1920, when he picked up a list of suggested readings and recommended lectures from his tutor, and went to his first lecture, on October 12, at Trinity [and Brasenose] College. During his first term he attended thirteen lectures a week. Attempting to keep up with the recommended reading, he would often read till after midnight. Once a week he reported to his tutor on work done, frequently presenting a paper; he usually saw him in the company of two or three other men. Scott found the English system arduous. The graduate of Bishop's was ill prepared to shine at Oxford; yet he expected, and was expected, to excel. The Oxford system demanded continuous reading, thinking, and writing – a cycle that did not come easily. And he did not write fluently. Every sentence was an agony: "wrote out more rot in evening,"[3] he noted early in 1921 of his latest essay. His tutor, Lewis Namier (later Sir Lewis, the well-known historian of European politics), sometimes agreed.

One of the first papers Scott wrote for Namier, on British policy at the Congress of Vienna, was pronounced "bunkum." Scott was taught not to rely on any one authority, to view each opinion with a question and to attempt to test it. Namier, who had been present at the peace talks at Versailles and observed how practical politics shape history, had no patience with high-minded cant, even if well intentioned. Under his influence, Scott became aware of post-war ideas in Europe, and politics, especially labour politics, began to interest him. He observed the fall of Lloyd George and began to read books on the state of politics in England.

In 1921 he was reading the pseudonymous *Mirrors of Downing Street*, which set out to show the decline in virtue among the great men of England, and castigated Asquith, for example, as a man who had fallen from the moral strenuousness of his youth. "There are some men, and those the strongest sons of nature, for whom the kindest commandment is, 'Uphill all the way'."⁴ Scott liked the book and he liked the motto. He wrote in his diary that he would like to live so that it could never be said of him (as was said of Asquith) that "the force of his youth was ambition, and the goal of his energy was success."⁵ (Years later, when rereading these diaries, Scott remarked: "What a young prig I was!"⁶)

Scott's Oxford years were dominated by the theme of vocation. Youth, for him, was a capitalized imperative: "The great thing," he reflected after reading the *Memoir* and poems of Rupert Brooke, "is to realise the presence of opportunities before they disappear.... And in youth more than any other time this is important. Youth is the apprenticeship for life; the training before the race; the choice of a mould to receive the clay."⁷

In January, 1922, he is again making resolutions for "Youth" and attempting to strengthen his character through injunction: "It is absolutely no use living if the end of a day finds you merely 24 hours nearer the grave. Service, not happiness, is the only thing that can possibly justify existence. We don't live to be happy; we live in order to help others to be happy, which is a very different thing." In 1919, early in 1920, and again in 1921, he was reading and re-reading Tennyson's *Idylls of the King*, particularly "Elaine" and "Guinevere" – he already knew "Sir Lancelot" by heart – and in 1921, when visiting his cousins, the Blakes, at Castle Cary in Somerset, he sought out "many-towered Camelot" and the glorious panorama of the surrounding countryside. "This," he recollected, "is Arthur's country – just what I had imagined it would be like – only more beautiful."⁸ Again in 1923 when visiting the Blakes, he hears: "Wild wind howling through the trees outside as I write – even as it did in the days when Arthur and his knights lived in this country." But, he goes on, "were they really more bold and chivalrous than we today? Once a man dies, he passes into the hands of the historian."⁹ Scott's tutorials with Namier had taught him that "History is too often read in the light of after events."¹⁰ Had the historians mythologized Arthur?

The concept of knighthood was still a resonant one. In 1923 he hung a reproduction of Raphael's "Vision of a Knight" (sometimes entitled "The Dream of a Knight") in his rooms at Magdalen.¹¹ The picture may be seen as the artist's vision of a knight, as the knight's vision, or as both. Looking at a reproduction of the painting many years later and observing the knight lying at rest in the foreground, his eyes closed and his sword at hand, guarded by the two Graces, Scott remarked, "It's a Galahadish position." Raphael's painting reminded him of "a knight who had been killed in noble battle and who is being appreciated." He added: "It's a vision of knighthood and all its duties. He knows that he is supported by the true spirits around him."[12] Even for the elderly Scott, the young knight was associated with high ideals, service, and battle.

Not that the young Scott consciously cast himself as a Christian knight. For him, as for many of his generation, the imagery of knight-errantry pervaded much of his thought because the language of chivalry had been so strongly associated with the Great War. The imagery also emerged in less guarded moments, as when, for example, he received news that Margaret Cundhill, his princess of Cap à l'Aigle, had become engaged to another man. "V[ide] Tennyson's 'Guinevere'," he wrote in his diary in April, 1923, noting the passage beginning "Ah my God, what might I not have made...."[13] Scott casts himself as Arthur; in rejecting him, Guinevere has chosen the lesser man.

Some of this high seriousness was soon to be lost. As he matured, Scott recognized that there were aspects of Sir Lancelot as well as Sir Galahad in his character, and gradually he moved toward a greater urbanity. He was helped in this by the friends he made at Oxford. There were a good many Canadians there during this period, often Rhodes Scholars, many sons of the rectory or manse, among them King Gordon, Jack Farthing, Arnold Heeney, Terry MacDermot, Roland Michener, Graham Spry, Lester Pearson, and Norman H. Rogers. For Scott, Gordon, Farthing, and Spry, as earlier for Frank Underhill, a political pattern was to assert itself in a conversion to Fabian socialism at Oxford followed by the determination to work for a less colonial Canada. For others at Oxford in the 1920s, the English undergraduates especially, the pattern was strongly aesthetic: a life of privilege, wit, and pranks. Evelyn Waugh, whose time at Oxford overlapped with Scott's, evokes such a life in *Brideshead Revisited*, as does the Canadian diplomat, Charles Ritchie, in his Oxford diaries published as *An Appetite for Life*. Both currents of thought – a highly serious Fabian socialism on one hand and a more apparently frivolous aestheticism on the other – were available to Scott. Unlike most of his contemporaries, he responded to both. He joined the Bach Choir, the Oxford Student Christian Union (OSCU), and undertook regular military drill with the Officers Training Corps. He also frequented the Musical Society's Tuesday evenings, where he was first introduced to chamber music. On Sundays the Scott brothers attended early service at Magdalen Chapel and, often, morning and evening services at local churches.

Scott's closest friends at Oxford were three Englishmen, John Darlington, John Madden, and Peter Girdlestone, and a Canadian, Raleigh Parkin. Darlington and Girdlestone were both sons of Anglican canons; Madden was preparing for the Egyptian civil service. Parkin, who had been at Winchester, was a gentle, cultivated man, a veteran of the Great War and the son of Sir George Parkin, the organizing representative of the Rhodes Scholarship Trust. Scott and Parkin were to remain close friends for life. Darlington was reading theology; also a veteran, he felt isolated from what he called the "mayfly" life of the College, but when he entered the rooms shared by Frank and Elton Scott, he knew he had "fallen among FRIENDS."[14] With Darlington, Scott went to Labour meetings, with Girdlestone he rowed, and with Parkin he visited family friends and listened delighted as Raleigh, "the maestro," swayed dramatically over the keyboard of a pianola, producing waves of classical music. In his second year, Scott frequently climbed the staircase in Magdalen Cloisters to play the piano of another Canadian, Terry Sheard of Toronto.

The Frank Scott of this time was an active figure, tall and slim, his light brown hair falling over a high forehead. His long bony face with its aquiline nose was highly mobile; when animated it lit up. And he laughed easily. Yet his manner was reserved; in photographs from the twenties his expression is dreamy, his gaze focused inward. He was not given to pushing himself forward.

During his second year at Oxford he began to move more easily within a widening circle of acquaintances. In his year were Alfred Denning, Gerald Gardiner, and Gerald Thesiger, all to become prominent English barristers and jurists. Denning became the controversial Master of the Rolls of the Court of Appeal. Much later, in 1959, Gardiner was to defend D.H. Lawrence's *Lady Chatterley's Lover* against charges of obscenity in England while Scott did the same in Canada. Others in his year included Adrian Stokes, a painter, soon to become an art critic; Eric Berthoud, who entered the British foreign service, becoming ambassador to Poland; Howard Florey, an Australian, who became Professor of Pathology in Oxford and a Nobel Prize winner. A rowing mate of Scott's, A.K. Warren, became Archbishop of New Zealand.

With his closest friends, Scott shared his developing love of poetry and art. Parkin, he reported, nearly gave him a poetry "repression" when Scott read some of his own first verse to him. Darlington appreciated Frank for "the way in which he opened my eyes to the treasures of art and beauty. Good pictures intensely interested him. His interest in them was contagious."[15] Scott loved beauty, whether it was found in the English countryside, the Bach Choir, or the art of Botticelli. He also enjoyed physical activity. In his first year at Magdalen, he played hockey and joined the shooting team. He rowed during his second and third years. In the "long vac," he and Elton and several of their new friends visited the Continent: he climbed the Wetterhorn, sailed in the Mediterranean, saw a bullfight in Spain, and flew across France in an old German war plane.

Visits to country houses, Wadham House in Somerset, Sorrento at Torquay, and Stonely at Curry Rivel in Somerset, were emotional highlights of these years. At Drokes in the New Forest, the home of Colonel Dudley Mills, whose wife was a de Lotbinière of Quebec, there were two attractive daughters, Ottalie and Verity. The house overflowed with groups of young people intent on enjoying themselves. The two Scotts happily joined the hayrides, the dancing, and the moonlight picnics by the oyster beds. One evening they slept out under the stars as they had done so often in Quebec: "Made a small fire, wriggled into a small hollow full of dead leaves, wrapped ourselves up and had a fine sleep. Not a bit cold."[16]

At Christmas at Drokes the young people played games like "Bob," "Suffragettes," and "Old Maid." Scott, who occasionally rebuked himself for calf-love ("looked at girls in a silly way"), thanked Heaven for the purity of Tennyson's *Elaine*. He thanked Heaven again, after a visit to Paris and the Folies Bergères, that such "displays" would never be allowed in England.[17] On a second visit, when his friend John Madden left in mid-chorus, Scott agreed that the show should be stopped: "I shall never go again. My money [shall not] go to pay women to expose themselves."[18] His indignation masked, even from himself, the strength of a normal sexual response. A few months later, smitten by Cecily Carter, an elegant young visitor at Drokes, his feelings found expression in the lament: "I was dull, oh! incredibly dull."[19]

In February, 1921, he had shown himself dull in another way. Members of the Oxford Cadet Corps at Magdalen were to provide a guard of honour for a visit from the Prince of Wales, who had been up at Magdalen before the war. Scott, the tallest man in the Corps, was placed at the extreme right of the front row, as the sergeant-major gave his instructions: "When I say 'fix bayonets' file number one [Scott] will smartly step forward three paces and pull his bayonet out and do this." The drill was taking place in one of the loveliest quadrangles at Oxford; over in the corner was the Grammar School dating back to the fifteenth century. Suddenly, the command rang out, "Fix bayonets!" But Scott, drinking in the beauty of the scene, remained motionless. The whole Corps was immobilized. Scott was demoted. A short fellow on the other side of him, who had won a Military Cross in the Great War, was given his position.[20] That night "Scott chucked his essay" and went for a moonlight walk with Elton. "Exhibited my inefficiency before the company," he reported. "No use forgetting we are alive, in our efforts to be of considerable importance."[21]

As Scott strove to reconcile the conflicting strands of his evolving personality, he arrived at one clear realization: the social order was unjust, and a Christian was obliged to improve it. He came to this while attending Oxford Student Christian Union study groups. In the fall of 1920 and throughout 1921, the OSCU was reading and discussing the fifth report published by the Committee of the Anglican Archbishops of England entitled *Christianity and Industrial Problems*, and based on mission work in the slums of east London (which both J.S. Woodsworth and later F.G. Scott had visited). The Committee included Albert Mansbridge, well known for his work in adult education, and socialists such as R.H. Tawney and George Landsbridge. The bibliography lists writings by Beatrice and Sidney Webb, G.D.H. Cole, John Ruskin, and Karl Marx. By early December, 1920, Scott had begun to discuss Cole, Follett, syndicalism, and guild socialism with Elton. Soon he reported that he was reading *Fabian Essays*. By early February, 1921, he and Jack Darlington were attending socialist meetings: they heard Malcolm Sparkes of the London Builders Guild at the Oxford Union, Graham Duncan and Margaret Bondfield on the "pool for wages" at the Oxford Town Hall, and G.D.H. Cole on "Systems of Wage Payments" in Lincoln Hall. After the first lecture they went to the rooms of a fellow undergraduate, Cecil Campbell, at Hertford College. "Sparks [*sic*] was there. Went further into Guild Socialism. I am convinced," Scott noted in his diary, "that something like that is very much needed. Industrial democracy is no mere catchword."[22]

Scott learned a good deal in this 1921 study group about conditions among village and farm labourers in England as a result of the Industrial Revolution. He was later to echo the question set in *Christianity and Industrial Problems*, asking how "men who were really religious ... sincerely patriotic and personally benevolent ... men even of common sense [could] defend as a quite natural state of things [that] ... children of six [were] kept at work in factories from 5 a.m. to 9 p.m., girls under eight crawl[ed] through coal seams eighteen inches high, boys of four [were] sent up flues seven inches square, in 'a country renowned for its humanity'?" The faults of the industrial system were an expression of "deficiencies deeply rooted in the nature of that order itself,"[23] in the co-existence of poverty and riches.

In 1922, the OSCU group read Tawney's *The Acquisitive Society*, and Tawney himself, a pleasant man with the endearing habit of stuffing his lighted pipe in his jacket pocket, came to Elton and Frank's rooms in the Cloisters to answer the group's questions on the book. Tawney took the long view of English history. Where society was once ordered by function, by a man's role in society, it now operated by privilege, by the mere acquisition of material goods. He attacked acquisitiveness or greed as the main cause of the breakdown in English post-war society. It was wrong, he argued, that an absentee landlord should take the greatest profits from an industry when he, in fact, did nothing more than supply the capital. The results of industry should be divided among all who contributed labour as well as capital.[24]

Tawney's recognition of the need for social reconstruction, his belief in the necessity for social planning, and his perception that such planning must be based on moral principles – all of this found fertile ground in Scott's thinking. He read *The Acquisitive Society* carefully, underlining phrases that struck home, itemizing points of the argument in the margins. The book, he concluded, "is certainly fine." On the flyleaf at the end of the book, preserved in his library, he noted salient passages: "p 32, Definition of Acquisitive Society; p 117, How to remove Capitalists."

Another important text for these years was *The Imitation of Christ*, written by the Roman Catholic monk Thomas à Kempis in the early part of the fifteenth century.[25] Scott's copy, which he came across early in 1922, opens by long usage to a section on the love of Christ. He read through the book a number of times during his last two years abroad; many chapters have multiple dates indicating that he read them at least three times; occasionally when his reading happened to coincide with his visit to some European city he noted this fact on the flyleaf. Scott found the book "a revelation." The author's distrust of intellect, his castigation of intellectual vanity, corresponded with Scott's own view: "Intellect doesn't really count for much in God's sight. Character is what the world wants – men are quite clever enough now."[26] The book encouraged a continuing dialogue with conscience, a dialogue Scott appreciated, especially with so acute an interlocutor. Responding to the emphasis on the spiritual life and the sacrifice it demands, he found a bulwark against materialism.

Scott had first read Rupert Brooke's *Memoir* at Bishop's; shortly after, he wrote in his diary how much he regretted not going to the war, on the way to which the English poet had died. In 1921, at Oxford, as he began to re-read this *Memoir* and Brooke's poems, he wrote introspectively: "I know very little, and can do very little for my age. Of course character and not knowledge is the really important thing. I am afraid I hanker too much after an outstanding position."[27] When, on July 30, 1921, Scott finished reading the *Memoir*, he concluded that "Greatness can only be got by learning to put our very best into little things of everyday life." Scott committed to memory Brooke's sonnet:

If I should die, think only this of me:
That there's some corner of a foreign field
That is forever England.[28]

Brooke, who in dying young had sacrificed life and art for his country, was a catalyst for Scott's feelings that he must accomplish "something great."

Scott also turned to H.G. Wells, the critic of the social order, in the early 1920s. Between 1920 and 1923 he read several of Wells's many books: *Kipps*; *The Research Magnificent*; *The Outline of History*; *The Undying Fire*; *Men Like Gods*; *God, the Invisible King*; and *The New Machiavelli*. In the summer of 1922 Canon and Mrs. Scott visited Oxford and Frank and Elton accompanied them on a tour of France, visiting the battlefields and the war graves. Frank brought with him Wells's novel of contemporary life, *The Undying Fire*. The idea of the undying fire – the spirit of God in man impelling him to struggle up and onward – he considered "a fine idea. I believe Wells is trying to help things on."[29] The book, though hardly typical of Wells's best-known work, was an oddly appropriate one to bring to the battlefields of France. The main character, Job Huss, is a latter-day Job whose faith is sorely tried, above all, by the loss of an only son, missing in battle. Scott was reading *The Undying Fire* on July 19, 1922: "[Wells] makes you think – something gained," he remarked.[30]

The next day the Scott family left for Albert and the Tara Hill Cemetery. They laid a wreath and planted geraniums on Harry's grave and prayed. The three men then continued on to Adanac Cemetery, where they found the first cross that had stood over Harry's grave. They walked together over "untouched ground, still full of shell holes: heaps of debris, shells, rifles" – everywhere. Every scene brought back a new memory to the father. Here and there such and such happened, he would recall.

When Frank sat down that night to recapitulate the day's activities he tried to come to terms with his mixed feelings. "Felt that the best thing I could offer Harry was the resolution to spend life fighting those things which make war possible." Again drawing on his reading of Wells, he observed, "Must know what we fight for, as well as what we fight against." He then added, "Love demands sacrifice: therefore it involves some pain. 'There is no living in Love without some sorrow': à Kempis (*De Im. X [Imitation of Christ]*)."

That Scott found comfort in Thomas à Kempis is apparent in the form and content of his entry. As he was writing the last few sentences regarding

---

human and divine love his pen ran dry. He refilled it with new darker ink. When he had finished the entry he went back to the faint mid-section of the diary entry which described the desolation and rubble surrounding Harry's cross in Adanac Cemetery: "There found the first cross that had been on Harry's original grave. Looked towards Pys, and saw the approximate spot where he was killed. Drove back through Courcellette and Contalmaison. Desolate looking country still – specially the trees. Albert is 75% ruins. Road through Courcellette is composed of Brick rubble. To Amiens again for dinner." He then added, in dark blue ink, a final sentence. "Larks singing everywhere."[31] The larks were, in effect, spiritual emissaries.

His earlier romantic notions of war had altered partly through reading Wells's graphic descriptions of battle and largely through seeing Harry's grave – the cross, the rubble, the desolation. But the implications of all this could not be faced at the time. Comforted by à Kempis, Scott's imagination added divinity to the battleground. Strangely, his diary does not mention his father at all, but many years later he retained in his mind's eye an image of Canon Scott, transfigured by his recollections of war, wearing out his tall, strapping sons, who, by the end of the day, were limping tiredly behind him.[32]

THAT SUMMER OF 1922 was a crucial one in Scott's Oxford career. A few weeks earlier, in May, 1922, in a dark suit and gown with a white tie, he had presented himself at "Schools," the final examination for the B.A. degree. Before that, reviewing the list of books required for "Mods" and assessing his own performance, he had perused copies of past examinations in his field. "Can't hope for more than a second," he decided, "... [but] better to assimilate a second's worth than to gain a first by cramming."[33] By the Easter break of 1922, on a reading party at Dalmaly, Scotland, he remarked in his diary that he was getting fed up with work. "Too many professors are living on other professors' mistakes. A lot of the stuff we have to get up doesn't really matter a scrap."[34]

The written examinations over, on July 17 he was summoned back for his *viva voce*, the oral exam. He went to the Schools Building at 9:30 but was told to return again at 2:45, which meant that his *viva* would not be perfunctory. A prolonged *viva* implied that the candidate was on the borderline between classes. While waiting to be called, Scott alleviated his nervousness by scribbling some doggerel.

I am waiting my turn to be asked to relate
What I know of Hobbes, Hooker and Mill;

> And I ask myself now 'Is it awful, my fate
> Is it horribly bitter, my pill'?[35]

His tutor had told him that he showed signs of first class ability; he would undoubtedly get a second, "even if a brick falls on your head."[36] Nonetheless, he performed badly at the oral. The questions were so easy, there must surely be a catch somewhere. What did they *really* want? While he pondered the catch he failed to give the obvious answer. Much annoyed, he left his examiners: " 'So you think the Sept. massacres were in the Reign of Terror, do you?' Cheap!"[37]

On his birthday, August 1, back from the visit to France with his parents, he saw posted the results of the Oxford Schools. A third! That night he poured out his feelings to his diary. "For what does it all mean? Ever since I was a small boy people have told me I was clever; I took prizes at school and prizes at college, and a first in history at Bishop's and now, now, after two years' quite steady reading I only get a third! A third – the easy course at Oxford!" The past year had given him hope and he believed that the results might confirm it. "Then said I, having once proved my ability – having once known *for certain*, – the rest will be plain sailing." But – a third! "That pretty well tears to pieces your old ideas about yourself, doesn't it, Frank? God, what an awful thing – to doubt one's ability, to have one's confidence in oneself shaken! Not to have faith!"

As he continued to write, his emotions, objectified on the page, became less overpowering. He began to reason with himself. "After all, a 3rd in history only means that I don't know history or that I can't express my knowledge on paper. Not so awful, is it?" Two weeks later, again abroad, touring in Germany, he returns to the subject. Shouldn't he take a job and give up his idea of a third year at Oxford and the B.Litt. his mother had agreed to finance? At least that would be "helping instead of just absorbing [money] .... Shall I give up worrying and just take things as they come – be an ordinary person?" The answer from his diary alter ego came back loud and clear. "No! Try big things, so that at least the idea of them will be left to you."[38]

By October, 1922, the Michaelmas term having begun, he advanced one step further in conquering his chagrin. In a sonnet, "Lament, after Reading the Results of Schools," published in the Oxford *Isis* under a pseudonym, he both expresses his discomfiture and controls it – through a parody that concludes: "I am a man who, by ambition stirred, / Aimed at a first, and only got a third."[39]

Scott still held high aims ("great men ... like myself") but unlike his English contemporaries who, understanding the system, quickly narrowed their studies to a specialty and "swotted," his interests were far broader. He also had much more to absorb – in large, Europe itself. Near the end of his university career he talked about this to Alfred Denning. "Discussed professions and other things – and the two kinds of life possible at Oxford: the one devoting itself with singleness of heart to one particular line of work, the other aiming instead at general knowledge and experience rather than special ability. Denning followed one, and got two firsts; I the other, and got a third – but spent vacations travelling."[40]

Scott did not spend his vacations reading prescribed texts; instead, he travelled to the great European centres of art, "soaking up culture." At Oxford he spent much of his free time on music, poetry, and books of art. Rowing practice and serious training filled his afternoons and extended into his evenings. Frank Scott, like Evelyn Waugh who came up to Oxford in January, 1922, got a third. And for much the same reason. Scott was marching to his own drum.

MAGDALEN IN THE EARLY 1920s was pre-eminently the college of gentlemen and the "Pres," Sir Herbert Warren, was a snob,[41] notorious for removing the college's brewery (and with it the undergraduates' cheap beer) in order to install a private bath to entice the Prince of Wales to become a resident. Frank and Elton Scott, certainly not aristocrats, were accepted as Rhodes Scholars at Magdalen because of their father's distinguished career. After the publication of *The Great War as I Saw It* Scott wrote to his father, "What a noble example for your sons to follow! The President stopped me in the quad, too, and told me he had read the book through and thought it was very beautiful."[42] Many of Scott's classmates were titled and one, Sir John Hanran, was a baronet. At the monthly ritual of "Wine and After" when the members of College stood to toast "England's Senior Bart," Sir John remained seated. Scott, who scrambled to his feet with the rest, was at first uncomfortable as he reached for his glass, for he was a teetotaler. Before leaving Quebec he had given his father a pledge of abstinence.

The question of what is "good form" for a gentleman member of College had preoccupied Scott during his first terms at Oxford. He recalled the story of the American jurist A.L. Goodheart, who was said to have gone to his tutor at Cambridge asking to be told the rules so he could be sure to follow them. His tutor replied, "Goodheart, there are no rules in this College, but if you break any of them you'll be sent down."[43] Scott found himself in the same quandary. Some things simply were not done. But what were they? It was good form, for example, to wear light flannels with a dark blue jacket but never a light blue jacket with dark trousers.

As a North American he had no inkling of the complex web of social prohibitions that most of his English contemporaries had absorbed at public school. He was often uncertain how he should behave and conscious of his responsibility to perform well: "As a Canadian in the mother country I must always try to be a type, not an individual – for any individuality will be sure to be mistaken for Canadian manners, and I can't afford to damn Canada."[44]

His father often remarked that a gentleman is known for the things he will not do. This dictum fused with some aspects of the code of behaviour Scott encountered at Magdalen. The smaller prohibitions regarding conduct, manners, and dress were assimilated relatively easily. He soon wrote home asking to be released from his pledge of abstinence; thereafter he drank cider, beer, and wine. He began to talk, and eventually to write, more easily and fluently. The essence of being a gentleman, he reflected at one point, is "to be always at ease."[45] Gentlemanliness involved a code of behaviour in which integrity, virtue, loyalty, courage, and concern for the weak, many of the characteristics he had earlier associated with the knight, were important components.

Scott looked and, to a degree, sounded like his contemporaries at Oxford: at six foot three he did not tower above all of his class as he had once done at Bishop's. Back at the rectory, his father had drilled each of his children in turn so that they might escape the flat, plebeian vowels of Canadian speech: "Now Frank, say after me, '*bath, calf, half*'."[46] He acquired a tweed jacket and grey flannels and a long wool scarf and gloves; overcoats were disdained. After 1921 he could wear the Magdalen rowing blazer on special occasions and by 1923 when he sported the wide, shorter flannels – "Oxford bags" – he looked like a typical English undergraduate.

But it was another matter to think and act with the same assumptions as the English upper classes. Certain aspects of English life, above all the class system, Scott found alien. English countryhouse life, as he observed during his first experience of it, was "the last word in comfortable living. Its justification is that it raises intelligent and cultured citizens, I think – though it does not tend to make for class sympathy, perhaps."[47] A year later, following his absorption of Tawney, he visited the same estate, reflecting: "East House grounds were open to Pinner villagers today – they stood and watched us playing tennis. Not a word said to any of them by us. At dinner we talked of the 'funny people'."[48]

At Magdalen, class and privilege were sanctioned by tradition and reflected even in the physical arrangements and social life of the College. In his second year, Scott acquired his own sitting room and bedroom at the College. Served by a scout who laid the fire and saw to breakfast and tea (the latter usually taken in front of the fire, talking with a group of friends), Scott felt he was "architecturally a gentleman." He took part in numerous social functions and mastered the minor rituals of dinner in Hall (where the penalty for saying more than three Latin words in succession was to quaff, without pause, a very large tankard of beer, and where there was bread-throwing when the dons were impossibly late). At regular gatherings like the "Wine and After" ceremony in the Junior Common Room, following the wine there was an "after" of Scotch, and they sang the Old English drinking songs, such as a variation on "The Owl and the Pussy Cat" begun by scouts who were chosen for their good bass voices and who afterwards helped put thoroughly sodden older members of the College to bed.[49]

At Magdalen in the 1920s, there was less emphasis than in other colleges on results obtained in Schools, on participation in debates, or in the Oxford Student Union, and greater emphasis on social life.[50] The Oxford emphasis on training an intellectual elite co-existed here with a more general, gentlemanly "philistinism," as Scott termed it. The "heavy" or important man, if not a peer, was often one who was outstanding in sports, particularly rowing. The studious man, one who got a double first as Denning did, also had his place, but in general too much grind was not appreciated: such a man lacked the requisite college spirit.

It was far easier for a gentleman to be a philistine than to be an aesthete. Aesthetes, sometimes objects of derision, retaliated by affecting even greater preciosity. Scott's classmate John Strachey (later the author of *The Coming Struggle for Power*) timed his visits to the baths to coincide with the exit of the rowing team from Hall where they had been breakfasting. To the hearties, Strachey was unspeakably decadent in his toga-like purple dressing gown, a shock of black hair falling over his hawk-like nose, and his sponge bag spilling unguents as he tottered across the Quad. The two Canadians, Terry Sheard and Scott, savoured the confrontation from the sidelines, and sometime after this Scott observed in his diary "the incompatibility of the gentleman and the artist – the ideal of the one being reticence and of the other personal expression (hence Shelley an outcast)."[51]

Frank had already begun to realize that he was in an equivocal position at Magdalen. As a rower he exulted in those vigorous afternoons on the river and he liked the comradeship of the rowing fraternity. But he was never happier than when wrapped in his own dressing gown, sitting in front of his fire, writing and reading verse. Yet the very opposition of his interests – the division between what he saw as the "aesthete" and the "philistine" in his own character – made him feel guilty.

He had begun to row in his second year abroad. His brother Willum, who had come over on business later in 1920, had been horrified to find Frank playing hockey at the College. "You'll lose the other eye. Don't be foolish!" Rowing, he thought, would be more appropriate.[52] In the fall of 1921 Scott dutifully presented himself at the river to be "tubbed." As he showed some promise in the two-man tubs, he was moved up into a coxswainless four. Then the hard work began. He wrote home: "We are all in strict training now; have to walk round Addison's Walk before breakfast at 8:15; bed by 10:30 every night; light teas and enormous breakfasts and dinners."[53] By 1922 he had advanced to a "Togger," a chunky eight-man boat with fixed seats.

The rowing at Oxford was entirely different from that which Frank had done in Quebec. There was one man per oar; more importantly, the impetus for the stroke came not from the arms but from the legs, by what is called "the drive from the stretchers": all the oars had to move in unison if the boat was to go forward smoothly and rapidly. More than once, Scott came back tired and discouraged from an afternoon's rowing, reporting, "[I] know that I am [the] cause of the boat going not quite as well as it should."[54] None the less, he stuck with it. He liked the companionship of the rowing team. He loved those rare afternoons on the river when the English sun showed itself. And he was feeling extraordinarily fit.

He was soon rowing with the First Togger, and in the Torpids or Toggers race, which took place in the last week of February that year of 1923, his crew went "Head of the River" the first day. The object of each boat is to eliminate the distance between it and the boat ahead by bumping it. When the races ended on March 1, Magdalen's First Togger was still Head of the River. At the Bump Dinner, in celebration, Scott sat at High Table. The evening became very merry as the night proceeded. Streamers were thrown about the room; signatures were scribbled upon white shirt fronts. Scott's name was mentioned in a toast. "Small sip of the cup of fame!" The men went on to one of the crew's rooms for more toasts, then to another's. Finally they "ran about outside – rode bicycles around cloisters, shut people in the history library. Bed tired."[55]

Eights Week, the apex of the Oxford year, began on May 24, a lovely spring morning. Scott went down High Street to purchase the lilies traditionally carried by the cox of the Magdalen boat. When he returned he found huge crowds on the tow-paths, sporting their college colours. The Magdalen barge was filled with well-wishers: young women in bright frocks and sashes, young men in white flannels, wearing "blues." Scott's boat, the Magdalen Second Eight, did not fare so well this time. By

May 30 they were out of the contest. "We started frightfully hard, but were rowed by Pembroke by the Ferry. Couldn't do anything about it – were outclassed." The Magdalen First Eight stayed Head of the River, however: "It was a splendid effort on their part – sheer pluck did it."

By great good luck, when there was a change in the crew of the Magdalen First Eight, Scott was invited to row at the Henley Regatta. The day "dawned cloudy but rainless." The crew changed and went down to the starting place at mid-morning. They moored there and lay on the grass, Scott reading George Moore's *Confessions*, until it was time to go out. F.I. Pitman, the Rowing Society president, started them. "I shall say, are you ready, once, and if I receive no answer, I shall say, go. Are you ready? – Go." And they did. The boat soon drew away and settled at a hard paddle. That afternoon, however, they lost to the First Eight of Jesus College. "Exit Magdalen Eight – and me from the rowing world."[56]

When Scott brought Moore's *Confessions* to the Henley Regatta he was carrying the very bible of aestheticism into the camp of the philistines. Here, as when he had earlier brought Wells's *The Undying Fire* to Harry's grave, he may have been attempting to right a balance. With considerable self-awareness he set out these opposing strains in his character in a poem entitled "The Problem," which he signed satirically "De Profundis" when it appeared in *Isis* on November 8, 1922.

> No problem can be worse than mine,
> My state is quite pathetic;
> One half my soul's a Philistine,
> The other half's aesthetic.

The division Scott set up in the poem's thirty lines is far-ranging. Which should it be: the philistine life of sports, prose, strong beer, and chorus girls or the aesthetic life of art, religion, and fine old wine?

The question, posed facetiously, makes the same distinction between the active and the contemplative life as Scott's father had faced in the 1880s. In January, 1922, thinking of Canada and the future, Scott had written in his diary, "Would one be justified in devoting one's life to poetry when it is not certain whether one can write? Would life have been a failure, if, after years of trial, one turned out [to be] a 3rd rate poet?"[57] After he had returned to Canada, he read one of his compositions aloud to his father. "Father quite impressed: with his usual paternal enthusiasm he told me I must be the greatest Canadian writer before I die."[58]

Scott's own "aesthetic" had sprung into life during the Easter vacation of 1921. Up to this point he had been recording each day's activities in brief notations, a mere calendar of events. Suddenly, in April, 1921, the diary entries change dramatically. His world had expanded, as he later recalled, "like one of those dried Chinese blossoms that are dropped in water to suddenly flower."[59] The forces that impelled this flowering were diverse, but fundamentally they sprang from European culture, augmented by modernism. The sceptical turn of mind fostered by his readings in history was supplemented by the new science: Bergson, Eddington, and Einstein. He followed the arguments of the Fabian socialists and had acquired a smattering of psychology, notably Hadfield and his new post-war psychology of "complexes." Most importantly, there was the impact of England and the continent of Europe upon a young and impressionable sensibility.

Scott responded intensely to the beauty of Europe: he was dazzled by Chartres and the Louvre, by the Sistine Chapel and the paintings in the Uffizi. The architecture and especially the art of Europe released his emotions. At the Uffizi, he was particularly impressed by Botticelli's *Madonna del Magnificato* and *Calumny*, Andrea del Sarto's *Maddona delle Arpie*, Albertinelli's *Virgine and S. Elizabeth*, Perugino's *Assumption* and *Descent from the Cross*, Correggio's *Adoration of the Child*, Sassoferrato's *Madonna*, and Raphael's *St. John*. "Saw the Medici gems, and a marvellous inlaid mosaic table. Went to San Marco in afternoon. Saw the loveliest Fra Angelico's – specially like his *Last Judgement*. Looked at the frescoes in many of the cells, and went into Savonarola's old rooms. Bartolommeo's picture of him is wonderful. One could almost feel his spirit hovering about the place."[60] As Scott's pen tried to keep pace with his eyes and his heart, the writing in his diaries grew smaller and more crabbed, while the entries blackened the pages and filled the margins.

He returned to Oxford inspired, seeking out books on art and art criticism. He read Walter Pater's *Studies in the History of the Renaissance* with a Medici society print of Botticelli's *Birth of Venus* on his knee; Croce and Tolstoy on art; Bernard Berenson's *Florentine Painters of the Renaissance*. Whole evenings were spent with friends admiring and sorting re-productions from the great museums. He studied Carl Thurston's *The Art of Looking at Pictures*. The world of beauty, of the imagination, became opposed to the world of "fact," of his studies in history.

There was a strong component of romantic idealism in the young poet's sensibility. One night he reflected, "if only everybody before retiring at night would try to think one thought really worth thinking, the world would soon be a better place." And that, he concluded, would have to be his thought for the day. Lying face down on his bed, with two candles standing on a book of poems for light, he was too sleepy to write any further.[61]

Not surprisingly, Scott's early poetry is religious and chivalric. His first attempt at a long poem in 1922, "Domine, Quo Vadis," was on the subject of martyrdom. The poem turns on the psychological process by which St. Peter, "the doubting saint," questions martyrdom: "Still knowing in his heart that he was swayed / By that same fear of death which made him seek / In three denials, safety from the Jews."[62]

His reading of Tennyson was giving way now to Arnold and the Georgians, particularly Brooke, but also to Alfred Noyes and James Elroy Flecker. In his last year at Oxford, Frank bought Matthew Arnold's *Collected Poems*. Every now and then he escaped the deadening grind of writing the B.Litt. thesis to walk and cycle about the Oxford countryside, himself a scholar-gypsy: "Crossed Marston ferry, turned sharp left on reaching the road and discovered the most delightful grass lane. English fields around, English trees rustling overhead, and in the distance English hills made lovely by the blue haze of an August day. The sight gave me a spiritual bath. Wood-Eaton, Islip, Ellesfield, Oxford."[63]

Wonder in response to the vast panorama of nature become integral to Scott's poetry. Not coincidentally, his first two satires were parodies of a well-known Romantic sonnet, Keats's "Much Have I Travelled in the Realms of Gold" with its superb expression of awe and wonder. The first parody came out of an encounter with an ancient book in the Bodleian, its pages still uncut: "Much Have I Rummaged in the Realms of Mould." The second was the sonnet, "Lament after Reading the Results from Schools," comparing the disappointed scholar to "stout Cortez." This early verse, topical and self-directed, asserts Scott's modernism, for the satiric temper, endemic in the post-war years, develops as an attempt to gain balance. Wit, and its extreme manifestation, parody, is essentially a levelling device and only one who feels very deeply the romance of history, "the dead past come to life"[64] (as Scott remarked of his first delighted encounter with genuine historical documents), needs to counterbalance it with satire.

In his last year at Oxford, through Pater and later through George Moore, he became particularly interested in aestheticism and the concept of "Art for Art's sake." His first response to Moore's *Confessions* was that the book revealed "depths of insight in its criticisms but leaves one angry at a life ill-spent – purposeless. Makes one cry for order and design." He concluded: "They are aesthetic in a way that at once attracts and repels me – attracts by its appreciation of true art, repels by its conscious assumption of superiority; by its selfishness. This is why aesthetes at Oxford are looked at rather askance by undergraduates; and rightly so."[65]

The problem with aestheticism was that it was not compatible with Scott's primary aim. He wanted to be "great," but to achieve greatness through the Christian way of service to others. He sometimes felt guilty when reading the aesthetes and later some of the Georgians. One night he stayed in front of his fire reading Flecker's *Hassan* rather than talk with a rowing mate, Podge (R.P.) Slade. "Was it right?" Scott wonders. He answers himself with a string of quotations from *Hassan*: " 'Allah gave man dreams by night that he might dream by day.' 'I corrupted my soul that I might set ten words in a row like gems,' says the Poet! 'My girdle is the chain of love, which breaks at the touch of my lover'."[66] The problem with erotic verse was that it was not compatible with Scott's views on purity. As he later recognized, he was encased in "armour," an armour so strong it was not to be penetrated until the late 1920s when he read D.H. Lawrence seriously.[67]

Little by little, he reached toward a synthesis that enabled him to be faithful to the opposing aspects of his character. In the spring of 1923 he went with John Madden to Bagley Wood to hear the nightingales. They gave him a feeling that he had had too little "a sense of things unseen." The steady grind of his history thesis had been killing his imagination. "Facts," he recognizes, "are dull food." Yet there was a still larger vision, an essential Arnoldian view, which he accepted: "If one can keep that gift of being able to view things as a whole, to see the world with larger eyes, a part of our imagination will grow."[68]

The Henley Regatta in June, 1923, signalled the end of term. Now the question of vocation reasserted itself. Scott's first hope had been to get into university teaching. This would provide work he had been trained for as well as free time in the vacations for his own writing. "Educational work, especially in a young country like Canada, is worth the best we can do for it – worth all we have got in us."[69] He was also interested in foreign affairs. In March, 1923, he had written home saying, "the Dept. of External Affairs at Ottawa – wh. I shd. very much like to join – tell me they are full."[70] Canon Scott did not think much of the civil service. "You are perhaps right," Frank replied late in April, 1923, "... but I believe this Department has got a future before it.... If one got into the work in its infancy there should be a good opportunity of rising as it grows.... I am much attracted by anything in the nature of international relations – probably as a result of four years in history."[71] He added that he would be seeing G.M. Wrong, of the University of Toronto history department, later in the term about university work.

In July, Scott was interviewed in London by Professor Wrong. The next day he had appointments with C.S. Fosbery of Lower Canada College,

Montreal, and the Reverend G. Woodcombe of Ashbury College, Ottawa. Wrong "was not encouraging," he reported, "can see that my third has queered me with him." Wrong advised Scott to "get into print" so that he could "disprove the slur" of his third-class degree by publication. He also said to "avoid getting into a school" if he intended university teaching. "Get branded as a school-master and you won't get out of it easily, he says."[72] Scott, however, had no choice. The next day, he accepted C.S. Fosbery's offer of a job at Lower Canada College with the understanding that Scott would not begin until early November. His B.Litt. would not be completed until the end of the summer term and he would have to wait at Magdalen to take his *viva* in October. Happily, he would be at Oxford long enough to row in one more race!

The work on the B.Litt. thesis, on "The Annexation of Savoy and Nice by Napoleon III, 1860," now became more intense. Scott was particularly interested in the struggle between Italy and France for the territory in question, and in the use of a plebiscite to settle the issue. Working with documents held in repositories in Paris, he analysed the reasons for intervention by the countries concerned, by the Catholic clergy, by Garibaldi and also Cavour, who wanted to unite the area. For the first time a territory was given permission to vote on its future: Savoy and Nice voted in a public referendum in 1860, the vote favouring France. (Years later, in the 1970s, Scott discussed the novel mode of a referendum with a leading cabinet minister in the Parti Québécois.[73] Shortly after, it was announced that a referendum would be held in Quebec on the question of sovereignty-association. Scott believed that his suggestion had fallen on fertile ground.) When he was writing his thesis, however, he was convinced of the total inadequacy of such a referendum, describing it as the "misshapen product of a disconnected intellect."[74] His tutor pronounced it one of the best B.Litt. theses he had read.

As the time of his departure for London drew nearer, Scott became more and more morose at the thought of "going down" from Oxford and leaving his good friends. "Oh Oxford! Oxford!" he wrote, in language reminiscent of Pater and Keats. "How sweet and yet how very cruel thou art! for thou heapest blessings upon thy sons, and fillest them with all manner of riches, so that they come to love thee more than they can say; and then, when they are bound to thee by ties that can never be loosened, thou dost cast them from thee into a world with little sympathy."[75]

Two days later he rowed with the Magdalen First Eight. They won the morning race but lost in the afternoon. "We couldn't have done more," he concluded. "Defeat but not disgrace." At dinner he found at his place a present, a book on art, from his rowing mate, Peter Girdlestone. Later another crewmate, E.C. ("Goat") Garton, sang a special song, "old man Sco," which he had written in honour of Scott's departure. Frank Scott found that he was beginning to feel "tearful inside" both then and later when the whole group sang "Auld Lang Syne."[76]

The next day, November 3, he was scheduled to leave for Canada. He finished his packing and sat at the end of the usual table for rowing men in Hall. As soon as Goat saw him he got up from where he was sitting and came to sit beside him. After the meal Scott went to the Junior Common Room and said good-bye to the man in charge. He then went back to his digs and piled his bags in a taxi, tying the great oar (trophy of his rowing success) on the outside of the taxi and cycling back to College with the taxi following. There he found a crowd of rowing men, and said good-bye all around. As he jumped in the taxi and drove away, a small cheer rose from the group. This was a scene that Scott was not to forget. It gave him something to take away from Oxford which he valued more than the B.Litt. or any academic distinction. "Good men, and true, these were: in whom was no conceit, nor any pretense: men who did not talk about virtues, or art, or high sounding things, yet men who possessed that supreme virtue, and who practiced that highest art – that of being English gentlemen."[77]

# FIVE

# *A New Soil*

❦

O N NOVEMBER 4, 1923, Scott left England for Montreal on the s.s. *Canada*. "New era starts," he wrote in his diary, "– Life, in fact. Period of Assimilation is over: period of Expression, in every way that is good, must commence."[1] But after three years abroad, Canada was a great disappointment. He found his fellow train travellers from Quebec City to Montreal "commercial looking" and the "country ill-kempt and dull, as though it had been all drawn out and got thin in the process."[2]

After his European feast, Canadian culture seemed oppressively thin and new. Montreal, with its muddy back streets, its foot-high curbs, and its burgeoning industry, bore no relationship to the great cities of his travels. As he later recalled,

> A kind of shock treatment now began to take the scales from my eyes. My sensibilities were offended by much that I saw around me. Montreal seemed ugly and shoddy, full of false values and outworn attitudes. One day walking on the mountain I came to the Cross erected where Jacques Cartier had once stood: it was made of crude steel girders, and on the bottom was a sign reading: "Electricity supplied by courtesy of the Montreal Light, Heat and Power Co. Ltd." These and many other things shook me into self-consciousness, forcing me to redefine my own standards.[3]

Much of his first year back in Canada was taken up by "the shock of recognition" – by the inevitable contrasts between the old world and the new, between Oxford and Lower Canada College, between London and Montreal, between the polish of British statesmanship and the Canadian political muddle. He greatly missed the intellectual companionship and the civilized beauty of England and Europe. It was depressing, too, to leave the good life of Oxford for the old familiar scene and an uncertain future. Scott felt provincial horizons closing around him. It was not until he escaped to the bush of northern Quebec with Arthur and Elton that he began to find in the geologically ancient Laurentian Shield a sense of an authentic past which he craved. "Child of the North," he was to write,

> Here is a new soil and a sharp sun.

> Turn from the past,
> Walk with me among these indigent firs,
> Climb these rough crags.   (*C.P.*, p. 37)

In this Laurentian landscape Scott found the basis of an indigenous beauty and a Canadian identity.

He had returned from England an anglophile, and something of an aesthete, far different from the unpolished young Victorian who had started out on his great adventure. Tentative in manner, he was still in the process of forming his opinions. Yet, by Montreal standards, he was an accomplished young man with a recognizable patina. He was sought out by society matrons for dinners and teas, and by young ladies for dances, skiing, and excursions. The patina was not deceptive. Scott had acquired standards of "good form" that applied to society and to art just as they did to social behaviour. As a trained historian, he soon grasped the dimensions of the Canadian situation. Within two months of his return, he wrote, "we are faced with problems in the country which, if not solved or at least attacked now, will prove impossible to handle at all."[4]

Montreal was then Canada's major city. St. James Street, despite the challenge of Toronto's Bay Street, was still the centre of the Canadian financial empire; McGill University, despite the growing prestige of the University of Toronto, was the Canadian university best known in Europe and the United States. Along the busy thoroughfare of St. James Street stood many of Canada's greatest financial institutions: the imposing buildings of the Bank of Montreal, the Canada Life Insurance Company, and the offices of *The Star*, which advertised itself as "Canada's finest newspaper." The offices of the Canadian Pacific Railway, which saw no need to advertise itself as Canada's wealthiest company, were in the monumental Windsor Station.

Yet, as Scott's depression began to lift, he discovered post-war Montreal retained pre-war attitudes: it was still a tight, mean little world dominated by business. Sir Frederick Williams-Taylor, as general manager, controlled the Bank of Montreal and Sir Arthur Currie, as principal, ruled McGill University. But the sway of the financial tycoon, Edward Beatty (later Sir

Edward), head of the Canadian Pacific Railway, was all-embracing. It extended from the CPR to "kindred institutions like the Bank of Montreal and McGill." Scott considered these "interlocking directorates" (as they were later called) abuses of personal power. Such abuses made him angry; ultimately they depressed him.

> So many things about me in our civic and national life here simply make me angry – McGill, American influence blindly copied, rotten press ... dirty civic official life and very questionable politics in Ottawa, CPR officials being directors of McGill and generally considered to be worthy of authority in education because they have made money in other lines, the whole acceptance of business as an end in itself – all these things weigh upon me, as though they were my own wrongs (as in a sense they are) and I find it hard to be cheerful at heart.[5]

It was a society dominated by wealth, a plutocracy just as extreme as that satirized by Leacock a decade earlier in *Arcadian Adventures with the Idle Rich*: there, practical education is respected because it generates a profit, but pure learning is considered worthless. In Leacock's satire the earnest attempts of good old Dr. McTeague, the Presbyterian divine of St. Osaph's, to reconcile Christianity with the practices of his congregation are met with derision. The businessmen of Plutoria Avenue know better.

Scott soon began to make similar Leacockian discoveries. Carleton Stanley, a McGill professor of Greek, told him a revealing story about a Swiss emigrant named Beck who had come out to Canada to see about settling emigrants throughout the country: "he interviewed Sir Frederick Williams-Taylor, who seemed pleased with the scheme, but when asked to sign his name as a person favourable to the idea replied 'I must first see Mr. Beatty of the CPR.' Beck then went to [Principal] Currie at McGill and was also well received, but given the identical answer to his request – 'I must first see Mr. Beatty of the CPR'."[6]

The rights of labour, generally respected by the British press, were given short shrift in the Montreal newspapers. On May 21, 1924, the *Montreal Gazette* objected to the proposal to establish an eight-hour day in Canada: "The International Labour Conference costs Canada much as it is; it is not well to sacrifice any business interests at its behest. *Time and economic conditions will settle wages and hours of labour*, and generally in favour of workers, *without legislative action*" [Scott's italics]. "Ye Gods!" he protested. "Are we living in Malthusian days?"[7]

Scott was not the first to make such observations. A decade earlier Harold Laski, then a young instructor of economics at McGill, had publicly praised the British labour leader Kier Hardie. Laski was castigated in a Montreal newspaper, whose editor was on the McGill Board of Governors. Laski's appointment was not renewed. In later years Scott was to find himself under similar pressures.

Compared with England, there was little in the way of good concerts, lectures, or plays. Social activities seemed to consist almost entirely of dances and teas. The dances took up an inordinate amount of time and the teas rarely had good conversation to recommend them. "I do miss what I call a good talk," Scott lamented. The Montreal debutante, "the unnatural product of an unnatural social atmosphere,"[8] spoke only of "dances, movies and cars." The one woman he could admire was the charming and attractive wife of a McGill University professor. "Why can't I discover girls of that sort in the making here?"[9] In the spring of 1923, he had given some thought to the kind of marriage he hoped for:

> The question is, should one venture on the married life with no stronger feelings about one's partner than friendship and high esteem? Is it wise to be content with that – or is it greater to hold on in the hope of something nearer one's early beliefs. With friendship and respect a happy and useful life is possible; many unfortunates have less than that to carry them through. Of such matings good citizens are made. But for one's own soul, for that personality which we strive daily to perfect and make whole – for that we require more than mutual goodwill in marriage, if we would touch the heights and taste the glory of completion. Better never to have loved at all than to walk rationally and deliberately into that state which cannot be of much value to either party without love. Some one to look after you ...! Heaven preserve me from that.[10]

In England, Scott had considered many of the "possible girls" attractive and easy to talk to but not as engaging as Canadian girls. They lacked a "healthy upbringing." Once back in Canada, he found these illusions swiftly dispelled. "Ye Gods!" he exclaimed, "save me from the Montreal flapper!"[11] He had returned during a new era of jazz and gin and short skirts and silliness. He disliked jazz – "civilisation will have to answer for Jazz at the day of judgement"[12] – and disliked, even more, the sense of being helplessly propelled by the same "primitive forces" that moved the crowds of dancers at the Mount Royal Hotel. Among the young women of his set there was a craze for breaking plates at popular restaurants like Childs. "At the word 'go,' slowly counted out, Mary and Meg each smashed a plate, to the horror or amusement of all around us." Writing in his diary late that night,

Scott ruminated, "No good, really, that sort of thing"[13] – overlooking the fact there is little difference between plate smashing in Montreal and bun throwing at Oxford.

Within a year of his return he had begun to choose his friends by whether or not they could distinguish "the little leaven of decent people from the great lump of money-seeking, pleasure-satiate babbits."[14] His closest friends were also ex-Oxford: Terry MacDermot, a Master at Lower Canada College, and Raleigh Parkin, who had taken a position with the Sun Life Assurance Company. With both, Scott often attended evening services at Knox Presbyterian Church, followed by visits to the Savage household. He was soon taking "Annie" Savage, an artist and "a very live person," to an occasional dance.

Scott's circle of acquaintances was widening gradually to include McGill academics. Besides Carleton Stanley, he also met George Glazebrook and Basil Williams. In the spring of 1924, Scott, Parkin, and MacDermot walked up Mount Royal to join Raleigh's mother, Lady Parkin, for tea with the Stanleys. They all listened while Carleton Stanley, in a "quiet, measured voice," gave his views on Canada. "He was pessimistic," Scott reflected, "as all good Canadians I believe must be. Money has become the sole god that owns the unimpeded allegiance of the country. As yet there seems to be no willingness to shoulder the sacrifices involved in the maintenance of a distinct nationality, and consequently we are daily growing more and more like our southern neighbours."[15]

The commercial spirit did indeed reign supreme in Montreal and Canada was rapidly becoming more Americanized. Yet Stanley's condemnation of Canadian nationalism, religion, and education, as outlined by him in *The Hibbert Journal* a year earlier, had been considered extreme.[16] It drew a chorus of protests in Montreal and two long letters of rebuttal to the journal. Canada, his detractors pointed out, was still a young country, preoccupied with establishing the material base on which a future culture might be built. Moreover, materialism was not confined to Canada but characterized most countries during the post-war period. Education in Canada was not as bad as Stanley had asserted. As for Canadian literature, what about Roberts and Carman?

The problem, as Scott summarized it half a year later, was the extreme difficulty of developing a Canadian nation when there was so little to build on – in Canadian history, in Canadian politics, in Canadian letters. Echoing Henry James's earlier remark about America, Scott noted in his diary "one had to be ten times a genius in order to be – a genius." "Really, I get very depressed about the condition of things out here. How the devil can we make a good nation out of ourselves?"[17] As his sense of being "out here" reveals, Scott, like many young men of his generation, also thought of himself as an Englishman in exile. This ethos, the product of childhood training and his education at Oxford, reflected the prevailing English-Canadian cultural climate up to the early twenties.

During his first years back in Canada, he tended to look to England for standards, especially in education. He was angered by the absence of a critical spirit and objected to the commercial spirit, "the almighty dollar," which had replaced what ought to have been national vision. "All I value most highly in a race I see lacking here: disinterestedness, public spirit, political integrity, a consciousness of the international duties of nations, a love of the beautiful, family life, dignity. It won't come in my lifetime."[18] In particular, he objected to the discrepancy between Canada's assertions of nationhood and her failure to act in matters of national defence: "When shall we realize what T.H. Green has expressed for all time, that 'rights' are inseparable from 'duties'."[19] His real hopes for Canada centred on something Scott called "soul," an all-embracing concept that included the spiritual, the aesthetic, and the cultural. This concept had begun to form at Oxford a few years earlier when he wrote, "... I am determined to work at something that I feel is for the good of Canada's *soul*; so long as my profession satisfies me on that point, it doesn't much matter what it is."[20]

FOR THE LAST THREE MONTHS of 1923 and the first half of 1924, Scott found himself immured in Lower Canada College in Montreal, a preparatory school for boys that had grown out of the old grammar school where his father had taught forty years earlier. The headmaster, C.S. Fosbery, a short and bustling Englishman, had been brought to Canada by Father Edmund Wood in 1900 to teach at the school of St. John the Evangelist Church. In 1909, he had taken over the school at a new site where it was renamed Lower Canada College. A figure of great energy, "universally known as 'the Boss'," Fosbery demanded regurgitation of fact, honesty in speech, good manners, and proper dress. There his conception of education ended. Herded in classrooms like so many sheep, the boys frolicked whenever opportunity provided.

Frank was soon describing LCC, with metaphors drawn from Milton's Hell, as "chaos" and "pandemonium": "In the dormitory I rang a bell, and each boy prayed; a brief space later I rang it again and pandemonium resumed its sway."[21] Mrs. Scott, visiting her son at the school, looked about her and observed succinctly, "It might easily have been – but it is not quite ..."[22] The classes were ill-ordered, the texts ill-chosen, and the walls of the schools so thin that the headmaster's voice boomed through the corridors, drowning out the other masters' voices just as his forceful personality ignored their suggestions for change. Scott was soon composing a satiric sonnet: "There was a booming in the corridor."[23]

During his first week of teaching, Scott found two allies: fellow master Terry MacDermot and Raleigh Parkin. One afternoon Parkin came to visit Scott and MacDermot at LCC, bringing a copy of Henri Bergson's *Creative Evolution*. The three men, after a cold supper in the dining hall, settled down to a discussion of Bergson. Scott was fascinated by Bergson's conception of "flux," and by his vision of all matter, whether human or natural, animated by a common *élan vital*. He enjoyed the friendliness, the intellectual talk, and the frequent bright remarks that brought with them the ambience of the Oxford life the three young men had left behind. After Parkin's departure, he and MacDermot "groused" about their common objections to Fosbery's methods and concluded: "Got down to the root principles of teaching boys: out-calling instead of in-pushing."[24]

Scott had not been at LCC two weeks when he recognized, "If I continue as I am at present, I shall never be anything more than a school assistant in this life. I am not working at bigger things than occur in my daily round of teaching – not reaching out to new worlds. Unless I strive, things will not come my way."[25] At the end of the school term he came down with one of his recurrent bouts of tonsillitis. Distressed and ill, he pondered the question of a vocation. Now, urged by Canon Scott and his brother William to consider law, he decided to leave the school. Although he enjoyed teaching, he most often felt "divided in spirit," that he lacked unity and driving purpose in his life. What he really wanted to do was write poetry. But how could this be reconciled with the practical business of earning a living?

In the pages of his diary he began to balance the possibilities for a future career that might include his need for expression in poetic forms. Schoolteaching, with its long summer holidays, could provide the leisure required for art, but without a specific educational goal he risked the danger of becoming a mere dilettante. Although law held, as Nathaniel Hawthorne had said, the danger of making one's living by other men's quarrels, it nonetheless provided a professional life and the possibility for public service. This would be a sound foundation for a possible future career in politics. And it was the political aspect of public service that especially attracted him. "Service to the nation provides me with a philosophy of work."[26] With this resolution, he determined to take up the profession of law and enrolled in the Faculty of Law at McGill University for the fall term of 1924. On June 11, 1924, he recorded his thoughts on his "last day of school-teaching at LCC – perhaps forever."

> The last thought rather than the former causes me sorrow. I can imagine no more pleasant – and, if honestly done – profitable life than working in a well-run school. Had I private means, so that I could supplement my school salary so as to make marriage and an educated family possible, I might continue at the work, though probably not at this detached portion of chaos. But I want to send a son to Magdalen....

Nostalgic for Oxford, Scott and MacDermot evolved a "Grand Scheme" to get back to England during the summer holidays. They organized a tour to introduce boys from LCC to the glories of England and Europe; as guides they would have their passage paid and receive a small allowance. On June 27, 1924, the trip to England began. When the two masters and their four charges docked at Southampton, they were met at the dock by one of the boy's relatives, who promptly whisked the children off for a weekend on the estate of the Prime Minister of England. The two masters were not invited. Neither could have cared less. Terry MacDermot was courting Anne Savage's sister, Elizabeth (or "Queenie"), who had been teaching in England; Scott was blissfully happy to be returning to his beloved Oxford.

Back at Oxford he met Leonard Hodgson, chaplain at Magdalen, and they discussed the ideas from Hodgson's recent book, *Birth-Control and Christian Ethics*. A few years earlier Scott had written in his diary that he believed in marriage because any relaxation of the divorce law would weaken the social bond. Moreover, after discussions with the OSCU, he had come to agree with Hodgson that "birth-control must be self-control." At the time he had repeated this maxim to John Strachey, who promptly retorted, "You just get in bed with a woman and try that."[27] Hodgson now was most interested in Scott's impressions of Canada, especially in his idea that the country would evolve a better system of education once it had acquired an educated elite. Scott also sought out his old rowing friends at the Henley Regatta with great anticipation. But he found things had changed and that the rowing talk at dinner was "the most shoppy kind of shop."[28]

After a short stay at Oxford, Scott, MacDermot, and the boys travelled through England and Europe. The British portion of the trip was largely devoted to visiting the cathedrals; in Europe, their chief interest was touring the art museums. Scott was especially moved by the great cathe-

drals, in particular Salisbury, where the service included the 23rd Psalm
and the comforting words, " '... Thou being our ruler and helper, we may
*so pass through things temporal* that we lose not the things eternal'." Taking
this thought to heart, Scott resolved, "I can face the legal world with
that."[29]

Having given his allegiance to the spiritual, he was now free to enjoy
the natural world. The poet was uppermost in his sensibility as the group
travelled through Devon. The eye that appreciated the Devonshire countryside and the small seaport of Clovelly – the trim whitewashed houses,
the flowerpots, the quaint winding alleys – was the sensuous eye of a lyric
poet.

> And when the moon came full over the darkening coast line, I felt
> I must get naked, and bathe. The others had retired to their rooms,
> so I slipt away unperceived, with a face-towel crammed in my pocket.
> Along the slippery wet pebbles I stepped, till a large rock offered
> shelter from Clovellian eyes. There I stripped. As I crawled to the
> water a wave larger than usual foamed up to greet me, and in the
> rough manner of the sea flung its cold and clinging arms about me.
> And then I was swimming, with all the spiritual lightness that attends
> an almost complete suspension of the force of gravity. I could see the
> last liquid glows of twilight in the west, and the clear freshness in the
> rising moon reflected above the cliffs that towered over me. It was
> magnificent, for I was naked, and all nature was about me.
> That is our secret, Clovelly and I. None other shall know.[30]

For a few glorious uninhibited moments the pressures of the daylight
world had been lifted.

"IN SEPTEMBER 1924, still starry-eyed from the timbered halls of Oxford,"
Scott entered the McGill law faculty, housed on the upper floors of what
was then the east wing of the Administration Building.[31] The administration offices were renovated former pantries, kitchens, and cellars. Above
them, Leacock remarked, "[was] housed the Law Faculty, crookeder still."[32]
A different kind of crookedness in the law faculty first struck Scott – a
lack of aesthetic harmony: the incongruity of an institution of higher
learning equipped with fixed desks and spittoons.

The law students sat at what appeared to be school desks, each carved
with the names of former students.

One desk showed a detailed map of the Western Front in World War
I, drawn, it was rumoured, by Erskine Buchanan, who had known it

well. Most of the lecturers were practising lawyers or judges who talked about their latest cases or read from ancient notes. All lectures were compulsory, and the roll was called at the beginning of each. There was virtually no library.[33]

Law students were expected to copy verbatim the notes dictated by their professors, and these notes, Scott indignantly reported, were not always accurate. "Consider the state of education in a country where a lecturer in the law faculty can solemnly inform his class that the Edict of Nantes was revoked in *1620*, and that that date marked the extermination of the Protestant party in France!"[34]

In retrospect, he was to see that there had been valuable influences at work in the law faculty. McGill had three full-time law professors – Percy Corbett, H.A. Smith, and Stuart LeMesurier – all keen reformers who strongly supported the idea of a true university law school with full-time professors and full-time students, rather than part-time professors drawn from the legal community. In Scott's day the teaching of law at McGill was in a transitional stage: full-time lectures were supplemented by part-time work in legal offices. For this aspect of his training he was indentured to the Montreal law firm of Lafleur, MacDougall, Macfarlane and Barclay, where his brother William was a rising lawyer. Scott was stimulated by the teaching of several professors, particularly Smith, whose lectures convinced him the current decisions of the British Privy Council on Canadian constitutional matters were opposed to the wishes of the Fathers of Confederation.[35] At the time, however, and throughout 1925 and 1926, he was most conscious of being engaged in "automatic writing" at McGill and in "office boy erranding" at the law firm.[36] He also began to recognize the inherent difficulties in his own position: "What will happen when a person with a mind philosophically inclined and a soul poetically inclined finds himself treading the straitened pathway of the lawyer?"[37]

Despite his reservations about fraternities, while a student at McGill he joined Alpha Delta Phi, where Harry and William had been successive presidents. But he loathed the conformity encouraged by the members and his diaries are subsequently punctuated by "seven blasts of all resounding trumpets" against secret societies.[38] It was also during this time that he began to attend family dinners, most often at the home of William and his wife Esther.

He found relief from university, law firm, and the strictures of society and family with a small group of friends: MacDermot, Parkin, Jack Farthing, Ronnie McCall, Brooke Claxton, Arthur Terroux, and V.C. Wansborough. Except for McCall, all were lawyers, and except for Claxton and

Terroux, all had been to Oxford; all, with the exception of Scott, had been to war. Scott rented "digs" jointly with Raleigh Parkin and Dr. Ernest MacDermot, Terry's brother, at 90 St. Matthew's Street. One evening Scott, Parkin, and Jack Farthing, who had come to dinner, "discussed [the] question of young men's groups for [the] purpose of studying and endeavouring to better Canadian social and political life. Agreed [that] much might be done if we went at it carefully and yet with determination." Farthing spoke optimistically of the rise of many such groups with similar aims throughout Canada. The idea was a captivating one; they "talked till 12 on that subject and art."[39] Thus the Group was born.

The Group was one of many manifestations of the prevailing nationalism of the twenties. This post-war spirit accelerated a desire for a truly Canadian art and literature that would, as the argument ran, confirm the existence of a Canadian political nationality. This new nationalism was reflected in the revival of interest in Canadian Clubs, in the founding of *The Canadian Bookman* in 1919, *The Canadian Forum* in 1920, and the Canadian Authors' Association in 1921. It was also displayed in the first official exhibition of the Group of Seven in 1921. The editorial that launched *The Canadian Forum* expressed the spirit of the times when it declared its aim was "to trace and value those developments of art and letters which are distinctively Canadian."[40] It also pointed to a problem the artists and poets of the period, particularly the younger ones, would have to come to terms with. What was a distinctively Canadian art?

The Group eventually embraced politics, art, and current literature. For Scott, it helped consolidate his Canadianism – in art as in politics. He remained concerned about the question of a new nationality, summarizing late in 1924, "I have no real faith in Canada yet, no instinctive faith," a statement he then promptly qualified: "Perhaps that statement is too strong – I mean that I am not sure developments in Canada are all in the right direction."[41] During 1923-24 he had begun to read Canadian history, in particular W.L. Grant's *History of Canada*, just one step ahead of the boys he was teaching. His initial view of the Canadian past was not encouraging. "Not much 'give' in it: mostly 'gain',"[42] he concluded after reading of the successive exploitations of fur, fish, and timber.

During the Group's first-year meetings, the topics for discussion were mainly political: the development of Canadian autonomy up to Lord Elgin's time, the possibility of an independent foreign policy for Canada, Canadian immigration, the problems of the Jews in Montreal, Canada's position in the Empire. On colonization in Canada there was "no lack of opinions aired."[43] In March, 1925, each of the Group read short papers on Canada's position in the Empire. "Fairly advanced attitude adopted: agree on necessity of being allowed some control of our own for[eign] affairs." All the members, with the exception of Scott (ironically, considering his later convictions), agreed on the possibility "of one part of the Empire going to war without involving others."[44]

Croce, his synthesis of philosophy, science, and art, the Group of Seven, D.H. Lawrence, psychology, alternate ways of looking at history, and the current conditions in Russia[45] were topics that were also examined and discussed. Labour socialism was occasionally mentioned, but it is clear the Group's interests were primarily nationalist and aesthetic.

By June, 1925, several members of the Group, including F.R.S., as he was beginning to designate himself, were making arrangements to open a print shop in a section of Burton's, a Montreal bookstore, to distribute fine art reproductions, particularly those masterpieces of European art produced by the Medici Society. While still at Oxford, Scott had expressed a desire to bring European art to Canadians. The purpose of the Leonardo Society, as the "print directorate" of the Group called themselves, is apparent in Scott's response to their first sales, Andrea del Sarto's *Head of St. Phillip* and Leonardo's *Head of Christ.* "Nice to think," he jotted, "of two such civilizing influences being let loose in Montreal through our efforts."[46]

Although he was often pessimistic about the direction of Canadian political life, Scott had a strong foundation for his Canadianism – the land itself. In December, 1924, he began to prepare a paper for the Group to determine the extent to which Canadian nature and climate need be detrimental to art. On Christmas Eve at the rectory in Quebec City, he mused in his diary.

> Mild snowy day. It is a most beautiful Christmas eve. The clouds have cleared away, the air is fresh, and impulsive gusts of wind disturb the rim of snow that lines every bough of the trees and make silvery cascades to descend from time to time. The flickering arc-lights cast sharp outlines of shadows over the glossy whiteness of the undisturbed surfaces of snow, and the atmosphere seems to take on as it were the very spirit of whiteness. There is the stuff of art here if we have wits to see and tell.

The arc lights flickering on the snow brought back his childhood sense of the intense beauty of Canadian nature, first glimpsed in the rectory garden. A year later, while in the company of Jack Farthing at the Gruppe Platz at Lake Manitou (a summer cottage owned by Ronnie McCall and a weekend meeting place for the Group), Scott spoke of his belief in "the necessity of getting back to nature" for a Canadian art, the culmination of his own experience of camping in the Laurentians and his growing appreciation of the art of the Group of Seven.

The link between art and national identity, always strong in Canadian life, was never stronger in Canada than in the mid-twenties. By the fall of 1924 the Group of Seven had come into national prominence; its enormous success at the Wembley Exhibition of that year had convinced British, and subsequently Canadian, audiences of the existence of a distinctive Canadian art. Not surprisingly, members of Scott's Group had close affiliations with Canadian artists and with patrons of the arts. McCall was an early enthusiast and owned a collection of Group of Seven paintings.[47] Terry MacDermot and Brooke Claxton, both members of the Group, married sisters of the painter Annie Savage. In her home, and later at the MacDermots and Claxtons, exhibitions of the Group of Seven were held. And Scott was soon inviting to local dinners, for walks, climbs up Mount Royal, or ferry rides to Ste. Helen a young Montreal artist, Marian Dale, whose early work shows the influence of the Group of Seven.

On January 10, 1925, Scott attended a skating party and dance given by a Mr. and Mrs. Miller at "Surrey Gardens" near the top of Mount Royal. There he had met Marian Dale, the daughter of Robert John Dale, a Montreal executive. Her light brown hair, gathered in a soft knot at the nape of her neck, was secured by a looped ribbon. She spoke with intelligence on art and literature, and her opinions were expressed in a most distinctive voice. It was low, resonant, well bred. She had just returned from a Cook's Tour of Europe where she had visited England, France, and Italy. Miss Dale and Mr. Scott exchanged opinions on the European galleries they had visited. She, like Scott, favoured Florence. He asked her to dance and, when the party was over, walked her home; both recalled there was a light snow, softly falling, as they talked and walked the long distance down Mount Royal to the Dale home at 451 Pine Avenue.[48]

Marian Dale was intrigued by Frank Scott. On her tour of Europe she had been chaperoned by a Montreal matron, a Mrs. Wigmore, who as a girl had encountered the dashing young Fred Scott. Marian had been fascinated by her chaperone's recollections of the grieving poet-priest, dressed in black, writing poems on death. Then, too, just a year before, at Murray Bay, she had heard Canon Scott preach. He was a visible presence – tall and rosy-cheeked, radiating energy. Then, at the party,

Marian had seen Frank – tall, ruddy from playing hockey, talking attractively – just across from her in the Millers' drawing room. Someone said, "That's Archdeacon Scott's son."[49]

The Dales, like the Scotts, were well established in Montreal. Marian's father was born and raised in England, had attended Merton College, Oxford, and then volunteered for service in the Boer War. After the war he had felt unsettled in England and welcomed the opportunity to go out to Canada to establish a branch of the family business, Dale Marine Insurance. There he fell in love with the Canadian countryside, and with a Montreal girl, Marian Barclay, the daughter of the Reverend James Barclay of St. Andrew's Presbyterian Church.[50] Dr. Barclay was the original of Leacock's good and upright Dr. McTeague of St. Osaph's. His daughter was an attractive and intelligent woman with literary interests whom Leacock is reported as describing as "the most charming woman I have ever met."[51] While her children were young, Mrs. Dale's considerable creative energy was expended in bringing them up; later in life she wrote a novel, under the pseudonym V.V. Vinton, which, published in England by Jonathan Cape, was well received.

There were three Dale children: Cluny, a son, and two daughters, Marian and Anna. Marian's generation was the first that was heir to women's emancipation; in her character, traditional values were to unite with the revolutionary impulse. She had been taught by a French governess, Mlle. Boucher. One day, as Marian turned the globe in the nursery and remarked that the sun never set on the British Empire, her governess, a descendant of Charlotte Corday, the French revolutionary, gave her to understand that such sentiments were not so admirable as Marian believed. Aided by Mlle. Boucher, Marian escaped the imperialism of many English Quebecers. She had sympathized with the French-Canadian farmers who, during World War I, had hidden in the woods in the winter to evade conscription while their wives brought them food and water. They were so poor, the soil of their farms thin and exhausted, how could they possibly make a living? When Marian was twelve and Anna ten, their portraits had been painted; Anna as a blue girl, Marian, in pink. She had not wanted to sit for her portrait but had been induced to do so by the promise that if she sat quietly for twenty minutes, she would be allowed to paint her doll, Christabel, in oils. The doll's name, a wry joke of her mother's, was that of the oldest daughter of the famous Pankhurst family of suffragettes.[52]

She began as a romantic. As a young girl vacationing in England with her family, she would go out on the downs near the Folkestone Cliffs in the mornings to read Thomas à Kempis. She was attracted by his emphasis on the spiritual life, but she recalled thinking at the time that she could never agree with the notion of a retreat from the world. The world was so incredibly beautiful, even the mists on the downs and the large slugs so frequently underfoot that one had to be careful not to step on them. One couldn't possibly give it all up![53] Although she shared many of the values of her mother's generation, which had been bounded by home and family, women of Marian's generation also sought, as Dora Russell remarked, "to prove our capabilities as individuals, not merely as wives, mothers and daughters."[54] Marian was determined to pursue an independent career. Early art classes with governesses had been followed by courses at the School of Art of the Art Association or, as it was known in those days, The Montreal Art Gallery, where she won a scholarship. Later she worked under the Montreal artist, William Brymner, and won another scholarship. At seventeen, she toured Italy and France, viewing the European masters, and then returned to Montreal to complete her two-year course at L'Ecole des Beaux-Arts.

When she met Scott in the spring of 1925, Marian had been home for a half year, struggling against the conventional – the conventional life of the Montreal debutante and the conventional teaching techniques put forward at the Beaux-Arts. Once her mother had urged her to paint the picturesque lighthouse at Métis, but Marian had refused and put her paints aside for a time. She knew her real subjects were elsewhere. Outside her bedroom on Pine Avenue, an arc light sparkled through the leaves. She was fascinated by this glimmering light making shifting designs on the bedroom wall. "That's what I'd love to paint," she remembered.[55]

In due course, Mr. Scott called upon Miss Dale, and, as time went on, Scott shared his album of European art reproductions with her and "got the right reaction." Was this the girl he had hoped to meet? Scott was cautious about committing himself. He wanted to be persuaded. "M.D.," he confided to his diary, "(almost) a discovery of great value."[56] Although he was no longer expressing himself in biblical terms, whenever emotionally moved he reverted to origins: his phrase, "a discovery of great value," is rhetorically parallel to "a pearl of great price." As time went on, he discovered he and Marian Dale shared an ideal of the creative life. Determined to paint, she understood his desire to write poetry.

A year after the young couple had met at the Millers' skating party, Marian wrote in her own diary of how greatly her life had changed. That afternoon Frank had reminded her that this was the anniversary of their first meeting.

How funny. I can remember seeing him so well for the first time, tall and rather red from the exertion of hockey, talking to a group of older people. I watched him with a certain interest though with an instinctive dislike. Specially when I heard from all around how clever he was supposed to be. Then later, upstairs, we were introduced.... And while we were dancing I said some foolish thing and he looked down at me and smiled his smile. And I knew that I would like him. And I began saying more foolish things just to get that smile again. We walked home together and we both found we had a longing for travel. And we talked about a great many places we had dreamed of and wished to go to. But I did most of the talking. And when, at last, I was alone in my room I began to feel sorry I had talked so much and so impulsively because I was sure he must have thought I was a great gabbler.

How long a time ago it seems, how distinctly I remember it all and yet how changed I am. Strange to look back; a debutante tired of the life but always trying to play up to the part. Discontented but not exactly knowing what I was or wanted to be. Had I not grown since then? I know better what I am and what I want to be and I have certain objects ahead. And instead of just drifting then I try as much as possible to be what I am.

Frank, she thought, would never know how much her friendship with him had brought about this great change in her life. "From the very beginning I felt that I need only be myself with him and that I could talk about the things that interested me instead of pretending that dances and movies were the only things of interest. He had made me ambitious, given me a longing to grow in all."[57]

# SIX

# The Orthodox was Wrong

> So here I am, twenty-six years old, and not even started upon my life work: not even certain where it lies. Were I Napoleon, I would be one year only away from the Italian Command; were I the younger Pitt, I should be two years prime minister of England or Delane, and three years editor of the Times. But I am Frank Scott instead, and so one of the countless millions that give material expression to the "élan vital" for a brief space. But I believe my opportunity will come.

S O WROTE FRANK SCOTT on his twenty-sixth birthday. Overwhelmingly conscious that he had not yet found his life's work, he was once again setting up impossible standards of comparison and indulging fears that he might, after all, be ordinary.

Yet his life had begun to change in significant ways. One of the catalysts was the Group. By October, 1925, it had been meeting for a year. Already the members had absorbed the art of the Group of Seven and had run the gamut of the more pressing political issues of the day. They were now ready for culture in a broader sense. They decided to reconstitute themselves as a loosely organized literary society devoted to "expression." Earlier, Scott had published a story and an Oxford sonnet in the *Literary Supplement* of *The McGill Daily*. In the fall of 1925, he wrote a letter of protest to the *Daily* opposing the establishment, at McGill, of an American hospitality society. The next day he was approached by two students, A.J.M. Smith and Allan Latham, the past and present editors of the *Supplement*, asking him to join its editorial board. An "invitation," he wrote in his diary, "I was only too glad to accept."[1]

Just a few weeks later, Smith published a verse by Aldous Huxley on a then unspeakable subject – "spermatozoa." At the instigation of the paid secretary of the Student Union, the *Supplement*'s publication funds were withdrawn. The editors were now in a quandary. Should they attempt to go it alone, raise their own funds, and start their own rag? "It is high time," Scott decided, "someone stood definitely on something in the great mass tides at McGill."² On November 21, *The McGill Fortnightly Review* appeared. It was an independent literary magazine controlled and funded by its editorial board. The board was made up of Smith, Scott, Latham, and A.P.R. Coulborn, with Leon Edel as managing editor. Edel, the youngest, was a third-year student in English. Smith and Latham were seniors, Smith studying chemistry and Latham, economics. Scott and Coulborn, an Englishman studying history, were the oldest members.

Like *The Canadian Forum*, which had begun in 1920 with an avowal to "secure a freer and more informed discussion of public questions,"³ the *Fortnightly* announced itself as a journal of "independent opinion." The first editorial declared the existence, among the students, of "a new and more lively spirit of criticism."⁴ This new spirit was soon manifested in editorials critical of current practices at McGill and in a series of articles and reviews defending literary experimentalists such as Yeats, Joyce, and T.S. Eliot, the iconoclasm of H.L. Mencken, and the new drama of Eugene O'Neill. One trait in the twenties was "debunking," and Mencken's wit, or "smartness," as it was popularly termed, set the dominant critical tone for Canadian radicals. It characterized the pronouncements of F.H. Underhill in his "O Canada" column in *The Canadian Forum*, as well as those of Douglas Bush in his literary articles. Smith and Scott in the *Fortnightly* and Leo Kennedy and S.I. Hayakawa in its successor, *The Canadian Mercury*, all absorbed it in varying degrees.

The first issue of *The McGill Fortnightly Review* appeared in mid-November, with faculty members Eugene Forsey and Stephen Leacock contributing articles. Smith contributed an anonymous editorial congratulating McGill for inviting "so distinguished a poet as Bliss Carman" to the campus.⁵ Leacock sent the *Fortnightly* his reflections on the role of little magazines and the more tangible support of "one Canadian dollar," a year's subscription. Forsey contributed "After the Ball Was Over," a whimsical summary of Mackenzie King's dilemma following the disastrous 1925 election. In another article, a budding young nationalist, under the pseudonym "Nordic," concluded Canadian nationalism was a myth. What Canada had was a national "inferiority complex." Because students considered the American Scarlet Key Society a good idea, they had adopted it instead of evolving a Canadian equivalent. They were becoming denationalized, looking south instead of east and west. "As I see it," Nordic taunted, "the students of McGill were told that opposition to American ideas was useless because we were already organised on American lines. And yet we still talk about the Scotch tradition, and vote our Lord Rectorship. Ye Gods!" Needless to say, "Nordic" was F.R. Scott.[6]

It may have been the slighting reference to the possibility of a Lord Rector for McGill in the first issue of the *Fortnightly*, or the disparaging view of education offered in the second, or simply the suspicion of more to come. In any event, two weeks after the magazine began publication, Scott and Smith were summoned to the office of the McGill principal, Sir Arthur Currie, where they were asked to provide good reason why the name of the university should be attached to their review. What if the editors should go too far, he demanded, by injuring McGill's "esprit de corps" through "dangerous doctrines"? Even worse, what if they turned "Bolsheviki"? Surely they needed a board of advisers to help them? No, countered Scott, the spokesman for the group, this would show that Currie distrusted his students. Currie was outflanked. He agreed to "risk it" and Frank returned home jubilantly to versify his first battle for freedom of speech.[7]

Currie's appraisal of the first two issues of the *Fortnightly* was shrewd. Once students began to criticize university institutions, there was good reason to suspect they would move beyond the university to the society whose values it embodies. The editors of the *Fortnightly* also understood this principle very well. In a February, 1927, editorial they cited H.L. Mencken: " 'All over the country,' said Mencken in his recent *Prejudices: Fifth Series*, '... in scores of far-flung colleges the students have begun to challenge their professors, often very harshly. After a while they may begin to challenge the masters of their professors. Not all of them will do it, and not most of them. But it doesn't take a majority to make a rebellion; it takes only a few determined leaders and a sound cause'."

The *Fortnightly* had the leaders and they soon found a number of suitably sound causes. Literary essays by Smith on Yeats ("Symbolism in Poetry"), and on Eliot ("Hamlet in Modern Dress"), and on "Contemporary Poetry" were implicit criticisms of the nineteenth-century emphasis of the English department, which was divided between authoritarian conservatives, led by the dogmatic department head, Cyrus MacMillan, and a few liberals. All, however, interpreted a tradition extending from Beowulf down to, but not too far into, the twentieth century.[8] The *Fortnightly* staffers, advocates of modern literature and independent opinion, were soon thumbing their noses at an anonymous professor, recognizably MacMillan:

Professor Windbag, Ph.D.,
Astounds his Freshman class
With 1880 heresy
That shocks each lad and lass
Into a most profound respect
For his courageous intellect.[9]

When MacMillan combined with the Dean of Arts to refuse use of the Little Theatre in Moyse Hall to a newly constituted Student Players Club, Smith and Scott published the letters of refusal and rebutted each argument in turn. The next issue of the *Fortnightly*, which set the campus abuzz, announced that the Players Club had been granted the right to Moyse Hall.[10]

Scott wrote several prose satires, including a pre-Orwellian description of a machine card university world controlled by a military big brother.[11] On the larger issues that affected society in general, the editors condemned the importation of the Ku Klux Klan to "Kanada"; J.A. Taylor tackled Bertrand Russell's *What I Believe*; Allan Latham surveyed trade unions in Canada; and J.S. Woodsworth, MP, contributed a brief but moving survey of "The Labour Party in Canada." The most pointed criticism of McGill's relationship to its Montreal masters was "College $pirit," by "Vincent Starr," Smith's pseudonym. His verse directly reflected the interview of the *Fortnightly* editors with Sir Arthur Currie: "Suffer the little children / To come unto me. / Said the Big Business Man / As he endowed a University...."

*Esprit de corps*
Won the war,
Did it not?...
And our students shall grow God-fearing,
That is, respectful of money,
And learn to distrust Scott Nearing,
And think Poets funny....[12]

In a later unsigned editorial, Scott remarked sharply, "Already students whose opinions have not in the past been other than orthodox are wondering whether the authorities do not wish them to hear Scott Nearing [the American socialist] because it is feared that the speaker's unquestionable honesty and humanity will win converts to a system of ideas not altogether in accord with those of our rulers."[13]

Raleigh Parkin and Scott were now living in shared quarters near the university. Parkin, considered a younger member of the establishment, had been invited, one evening, to dine with Sir Frederick Williams-Taylor when Sir Arthur Currie was present. There the principal had declared: "The S.C. [Student Christian] Movement needs watching." And, in the course of the evening, Currie revealed that whenever speakers were scheduled to come to McGill, he wrote to the Intelligence Bureau at Ottawa asking for their records. When "wild men," like Scott Nearing, came to the campus, the students needed to be told they were wild. Parkin and Scott were equally appalled: "That is no university head," Scott concluded that night. "The forces of the enemy are thickly massed and firmly entrenched. As Raleigh said, it is useless thinking of a Labour party over here when we haven't even got Liberalism."[14] Scott knew independent opinion and freedom of expression went hand in hand with a repudiation of orthodox opinion. In the past his criticisms had been stifled, confined to his diary and to a small group of intimates, but now, with growing self-confidence and surrounded by literary friends, he was encouraged to speak out publicly.

The young editors sparked each other's creativity. During their first winter they would gather at Coulborn's basement apartment at 989 Atwater Avenue. Smith and Scott would differ amiably about the poems to be included. Scott, however, "tall, endlessly energetic," and radiating self-assurance in his tweed jacket and Oxford "bags," deferred to Smith's superior taste in poetry. When agreement was reached on the verse to be included in the *Fortnightly*, Smith would pile the heap of rejected manuscripts to one side and place the one or two accepted poems neatly beside it.[15]

There were few good poems and articles by undergraduates. "Those students whose opinions most nearly coincide with those of the orthodox majority," Scott pontificated, "seem unable to garb their thoughts in printable clothing."[16] The editors filled this vacuum by soliciting articles from their professors and by signing only their best pieces; the rest they published under pseudonyms. Scott was Nordic, Bernard March, Brian Tuke, T.T., and XXX; Smith was Vincent Starr, Michael Gard, and Simeon Lamb; Coulborn was Vespassiano; Edel was Leonard Noble. With new opportunity to write – and to be read – Scott began to question his decision to practise law. "Literature is and always has been, had I only known it, the only love with whom I can contract a compatible marriage: would it not be saner and more righteous to abandon all striving other than that which gets me bread and butter, and give myself to her?"[17] Like his father before him, Scott was often to experience this conflicting pull between his poetry and his profession.

Of the group who worked on the *Fortnightly*, A.J.M. Smith most influenced Scott's developing poetic aesthetic, although ultimately they were to diverge in their general outlooks. Smith saw the modern movement divided by the war into two periods, the first characterized by the attempt of older poets like Masefield and Yeats to throw off the effete diction of an outworn romanticism, the second by younger poets such as Edith Sitwell, T.S. Eliot, and Wallace Stevens, who looked back to the seventeenth century and the sophistications of the metaphysical technique. Because Smith was convinced that the image extended into symbol (actually the Yeatsian symbol) distinguished the striking new poetry from the old, he accompanied his essay on "Symbolism in Poetry" with two of his own poems constructed from a pastiche of symbols and concepts, borrowed from Eliot and Yeats.[18] On the whole, Smith's determined search for the modern and his recognition that the modern movement was both anti-romantic and anti-nationalist led him to reject Canadian subjects.

For Scott, the path was somewhat different. From the very first issue of the *Fortnightly*, where Smith tackled the question, "What makes modern poetry modern?" Scott worried another: "Can we have a Canadian art?" His question reflects contemporary nationalist debate in *The Canadian Forum* in its assumption that Canada lacked a national spirit. In the second issue of the *Fortnightly*, in a discussion of an exhibition by the Royal Canadian Academy, he wondered why, of all the arts, only painting should have taken a firm root in Canada's soil? Scott found the most distinctive part of the exhibition was a group of winter landscapes: "All the loneliness and brooding silence of the northern hills are here."[19] In the third issue, again writing under the pseudonym "Nordic," he is wondering whether Canada's northern climate can provide a suitable environment for literature. Scott had been pondering this question for some time now. He had decisively answered the question a year earlier in his Christmas Eve diary entry when he contemplated the snow: "There is the stuff of art here if we have wits to see and tell."[20]

In January, 1926, Smith provided direction with the publication of "The Lonely Land" in the *Fortnightly*. In context, the poem was a pastiche of the pictorial images of the windswept landscapes of the Group of Seven, with echoes of the American poet H.D.'s (Hilda Doolittle) "Oread." It took its title from two of J.E.H. MacDonald's paintings, "The Solemn Land" (1921) and "The Lonely North" (1913).

> Blown spume and windrift
> And thin, bitter spray
> Snap
> At the whirling sky;
> And the pine trees
> Lean one way.[21]

For Scott the images were resonant. He recognized this poetic landscape and soon wrote his own Canadian poem. His subject – the northern landscape and the threat of winter – reflects his own experience, the landscapes of the Group of Seven, and a Canadianized version of Sir James Frazer's fertility myth, all by way of Eliot and Lawrence. In these granite mountains, by ice-rounded valleys and rocky shores, Scott writes, "When the first ominous cold / Stills the sweet laughter of northern lakes, / ... I cannot bring myself to your embrace."

> For love is an impudent defiance
> Flung into the teeth of time,
> A brazen denial
> Of the omnipotence of death,
> And here death whispers in the silences,
> And a deep reverence is due to time.[22]

Even while affirming man's ephemerality within nature, Scott suggests that the force which animates man as well as nature – Bergson's *élan vital* – is the same. This image of the evolutionary northern landscape was to provide the basis of the new Canadian poetry. Very shortly he wrote two additional poems on Canadian themes: "Below Quebec," a love poem for Marian Dale, and "New Names," a manifesto for a new Canadian poetry.

> Who would read old myths
> By this lake
> Where the wild duck paddle forth
> At daybreak?   (*C.P.*, p. 40)

Smith had shown Scott how to transpose the Canadian image to a modern context; Scott had the emotional attachment to the images to continue to make poetry from them.

Smith and Scott had entered the modern world by way of the questioning, experimenting twenties. Everything was challenged. Smith wrote verse that scoffed at religion; Scott satirized politics. As Scott explained in a paper on "Modern Poetry" and later reiterated in a 1931 article, a new world demanded a new way of thinking. There was no going back. Poetry no longer meant Tennyson and the Georgians of *Poems of Today* (1924); rather it was the Munroe and Henderson anthology, *The New Poetry* (1924), with Lawrence, H.D., Wilfred Owen, e.e. cummings, and T.S. Eliot. The Imagists had a strong influence on his own poetry; he loved the spare verbal pictures that passed so cleanly before the mind's eye. Under Smith's tutelage Scott began to write free and imagist verse. One of his first attempts was the e.e. cummings-like "Fantasy," where the flight of an arrow is described typographically with an arching "up": "... whish! / UP ... Up ... up ... up...." (*C.P.*, p. 28).

But it was Lawrence who most shaped the sensibility of the young poet. He had been reading Lawrence's early novels, *The Rainbow* and *Women in Love*, and the poems of *Amores, New Poems, Birds, Beasts and Flowers*. His light verse began to reflect a new whimsical humanity and, more importantly, a new emotional freedom: "Is a tree kinder / Than a doormat / With frayed edges? ..."

> Trees have only birds, and insects, and crawly things.
> There is no vulgarity in these,
> Only poetry, and evolution, and innumerable legs.
> But in doormats there is much
> Vulgarity
> Humanity
> Futility
> Dust, bootmarks, and sunlight.[23]

Scott also read *Pansies* (1929) where, in a late poem, Lawrence epitomized some of the themes that were to characterize his own early verse:

> And man and woman are like the earth, that brings forth flowers
> in summer, and love, but underneath is rock.
> Older than flowers, older than ferns, older than foraminiferae
> older than plasm altogether is the soul of a man underneath.[24]

The sense of the ephemerality of human life and vegetation, silhouetted against the great aeons of geological time and rock, is similar to that which Scott developed in his own verse.

If Lawrence most influenced Scott's artistic sensibility, it was Eliot who had the greatest effect on his developing thought. What Scott absorbed from *The Waste Land* (1922) was the profound belief that the old ideals no longer held, for he recognized in this poem the pattern of a modern new world: non-linear, disjunctive, disillusioned. His first perception of the modern, gleaned from Eliot, was that all was chaos:

> Civilization was crumbling and pretty rotten at the core.... There was no core or center from which everything worked its way forward. It was in a state of confusion. People were lost.... It was all part of the reaction to the early enthusiasm of World War I in the sense of collapse, spiritual collapse first taking place.... Idols were not very important.... They didn't have much to say that related to the world that you were living in at the moment.... [And then you] had to start with the realization that so much of it had to be remade and replaced.

"It looked," he recalled in the seventies, "[as though] *The Waste Land* had given it all to you – made you aware."[25]

Scott and Smith were willing to take their poetic nourishment wherever it could be found; in the twenties, this meant primarily in England but also in the United States. A Canadian literature, barely emerging, was considered a pitiful thing. Scott purchased a contemporary book on Canadian poetry as a wedding gift for a friend, took a quick look, and registered his scorn: "Laughed over Garvin's ridiculous book on 'Canadian Poets'."[26] In the last quarter of the *Fortnightly*'s existence, Scott and Smith contributed an unsigned editorial:

> Canadian literature – if there be such a thing – is overburdened with dead traditions and outworn forms. We are a pitiful extension of the Victorians. If a living, native literature is to arise we must discover our own souls, and before that can happen a mass of débris has to be removed. No better helpers in this task can be found than amongst our contemporaries in England and America.[27]

Both men were appalled by the Victorianism of past and contemporary Canadian poetry. By the mid-1920s, the Canadian Authors' Association was in the midst of its "Made in Canada" program to promote the buying of Canadian books: preferably books made in Canada by Canadian authors on Canadian subjects. Sir Charles G.D. Roberts and Bliss Carman, who had spent most of the years between 1890 and 1920 abroad, were brought home on lecture tours and enthusiastically promoted as "our younger Canadian poets." This was galling for the coming generation, especially

for Scott, who had met Carman when he visited McGill in 1924 and had
had lunch "in digs" with him and Parkin. Scott was not at all impressed.
Carman's table talk was not aesthetic but concerned with material things;
worse, he affected an eccentric stetson-like hat and long embroidered
chaps. Stuart LeMesurier, later Dean of Law at McGill, was at the University Club when Carman visited and saw that instead of a handkerchief
in his breast pocket Carman had "a little leather thing with some sort of
medal on the end." Someone said to LeMesurier, "What's that Carman
has got in his pocket?" LeMesurier replied with great good humour, "It's
his poetic license."[28]

Not surprisingly, Scott was soon to categorize Carman's verse as "me-
diocre." The judgement was unfair because it was based only on the late
verse. Like most Canadians, Scott and Smith read English poetry and they
knew very little of their Canadian predecessors. Scott had read his father's
verse, Smith the later Carman, they both knew Roberts for his animal
stories, and had read little of Archibald Lampman and Duncan Campbell
Scott. Like young poets everywhere, they tended to denounce the older
poets in order to carve out a niche for their own poetry.

Early in 1927, Smith and Scott attended a meeting of the Canadian
Authors' Association at the new and elegant Ritz Carlton Hotel on Sherbrooke Street. Smith recalled he went up to the podium to claim first and
second prizes for two sonnets (one mischievously submitted under the
pseudonym "Max" to test the CAA for possible anti-Semitic leanings), while
Scott sat at the back of the hall scribbling his impressions of the Canadian
literary establishment: "The Canadian Authors Meet."[29]

> Expansive puppets percolate self-unction
> Beneath a portrait of the Prince of Wales.
> Miss Crotchet's muse has somehow failed to function,
> Yet she's a poetess. Beaming, she sails
>
> From group to chattering group, with such a dear
> Victorian saintliness, as is her fashion,
> Greeting the other unknowns with a cheer –
> Virgins of sixty who still write of passion.
>
> The air is heavy with Canadian topics,
> And Carman, Lampman, Roberts, Campbell, Scott,
> Are measured for their faith and philanthropics,
> Their zeal for God and King, their earnest thought.

> The cakes are sweet, but sweeter is the feeling
> That one is mixing with the *literati*;
> It warms the old, and melts the most congealing.
> Really, it is a most delightful party.  (*C.P.*, p. 248)

Here, as elsewhere, the young modernist poet rejected the Victorian back-wash of an exhausted romanticism. In Canada of the twenties, the old poetry (like the old politics) still had an imperial flavour: poetesses burbled verse as mechanically as that handy new gadget, the coffee percolator, under the prevailing English conventions symbolized by the portrait of the Prince of Wales. The parade of Confederation heavies – "Carman, Lampman, Roberts, Campbell, Scott" (presumably D.C. Scott, but not excluding F.G., Frank's father) – is given short shrift. Dismissed also are the non-poetic standards by which poetry in Canada was habitually judged. "Faith and philanthropics," "zeal for God," "earnest thought" – these phrases describe Victorian social and religious attitudes.

Smith and Scott were serious about their art: they believed it was of value in itself and did not have to be justified by reference to external political or moral standards. They objected to the dilettantism of the CAA, the notion that poetry was just another pleasant activity in the social round, to be taken before or after tea as one pleased. They were hotly opposed to the prevailing belief that if verse displayed the maple leaf it was Canadian and thereby worthy of support.

> Shall we go round the mulberry bush, or shall
> We gather at the river, or shall we
> Appoint a Poet Laureate this fall,
> Or shall we have another cup of tea?
>
> O Canada, O Canada, Oh can
> A day go by without new authors springing
> To paint the native maple, and to plan
> More ways to set the selfsame welkin ringing?  (*C.P.*, p. 248)

By employing poeticisms and inverted syntax, and by parodying the first line of "O Canada," Scott pinpointed the technical weaknesses and the sentimental nationalism that vitiated much contemporary Canadian poetry.

The poem also demonstrates the critical double bind in which Scott and Smith, by the accident of time and place, were inevitably caught. Both condemned the old romanticism, yet both, like most modern poets, were essentially romantic in sensibility. Both agreed with the current view that modernism was international and anti-romantic. Yet such theories, which had emerged from the United States and Great Britain – where national literatures had been established and where periods of romantic nationalism had already been experienced – had little relevance to the Canadian situation. Indeed, for an emerging nation like Canada in the twenties, where romantic nationalism and modernism coincided, such theories were inevitably restrictive. Smith, who rejected Canadian and romantic subjects in favour of the cosmopolitan, effectively cut himself off from much of his natural audience. Scott, whose conception of the modern did not exclude a somewhat romanticized Canadian landscape, continued, together with E.J. Pratt, to write the northern (and romantic) poem, which consistently found an appreciative public.

In the spring of 1927, *The McGill Fortnightly Review* came to an end. A.J.M. Smith, Scott recalled, was the catalyst that had changed the direction of his poetry – and his life – from the Victorian to the modern. Years later, when both were in their seventies, on the eve of an American symposium honouring Smith's achievements, Scott wrote to Leon Edel, by then the internationally recognized biographer of Henry James:

> I think you and I ... both looked upon Arthur as the man who most surely understood the new movements stirring in the literary world around us.... Certainly I find it hard to exaggerate to myself the value of what I may call the whole Fortnightly experience. It helped me escape from the shell of my Victorianism, which Oxford may have cracked somewhat but within which I was still neatly folded. This release was of course brought about not only by our own influences on each other, but by the whole range of modern literature to which I was for the first time introduced.[30]

As a journal of independent opinion, the *Fortnightly* was a new phenomenon for McGill and for Montreal. Reaction to it had been mixed: some were delighted; others were appalled. The editors took a lofty view, remarking that some minds could not understand the nature of criticism: "We are looked upon as dangerous beings possessed of radicalism, socialism, Bolshevism."[31] Nevertheless, official retribution, whenever it could be applied, was sharply and swiftly administered. Cyrus MacMillan, who controlled the fate of Latham's father, a professor in the English department, and that of Edel's teaching fellowship, had to be considered. In the interests of survival both officially resigned from the *Fortnightly* editorial board halfway through the second year, but unofficially they continued their editorial duties.[32] MacMillan, and possibly Currie also, ensured that Smith, although a fine scholar and poet, would never be hired at McGill. This determined Smith's academic future; he was forced to choose between high school teaching in Montreal and university lecturing at Michigan State University.[33] Scott, whose outspoken reasonableness was admired by Dean Percy Corbett of the law faculty, escaped this penalty. Nonetheless, one F.R. Scott went down in Sir Arthur Currie's mental files as a man to be watched. And by 1932 Currie's aide-de-camp, Colonel Bovey, was corresponding with the authorities at Ottawa on the subject of Scott's "file."[34]

IN 1925, AN EXHIBITION of Russian paintings took place at Morgan's department store. It was a beautiful exhibition, one of the best Scott had ever seen in Montreal. But "when Raleigh and I heard from McBride himself, the organizer, that Dr. Shepperd had refused to allow the pictures to be hung in the Art Gallery because they were painted by Russians (i.e. Bolsheviks!), we became first speechless, then incoherent, and then filled with expletive wrath. 'O God, O Montreal!' As [Prof.] Waugh said, Montreal is now as it was 20 years ago when Butler knew it."[35]

Years before, Samuel Butler had coined this phrase in his satiric "Lament for Montreal":

> Stowed away in a Montreal lumber room
> The Discobolus standeth and turneth his face to the wall;
> Dusty, cobweb-covered, maimed, and set at naught,
> Beauty crieth, in an attic and no man regardeth –
>                   O God! O Montreal![36]

The chorus provided Scott with a convenient shorthand for expressing his dismay as when, for example, the promoters of Palm Olive soap, using an advertisement featuring the Venus de Milo, were forced by the Quebec censors to stick a plaster over her breasts. Even charitable organizations in Montreal could not be trusted. Marian's younger sister Anna, who had been collecting for the Federated Charities, informed Scott that when requesting contributions she had been instructed by the organizers to put her thumb over the amount contributed by individuals the previous year. When they were tempted to state a larger figure than had actually been given, she was to remove her thumb and embarrass the individual into giving a larger donation.

On the larger scale, Scott's sense of social justice was violated by three closely related civic scandals. The Westmount Water Company bought up a municipal utility at a fair market price and, after amalgamation with the city, sold its interest for an exorbitant price to Montreal. In January, 1927, over seventy-five children suffocated in a fire at a city theatre when they were trapped behind exit doors that were designed to open inward. Although the city had been negligent in the enforcement of safety measures, it responded to the tragedy not by regulating that doors in public buildings should open outward but by forbidding children under the age of sixteen to go to theatres. In March and April, a typhoid fever epidemic raged in Montreal, the source of which was traced to a contaminated milk supply; the city council had passed a by-law regarding the pasteurization of milk, but had not enforced it. What was worse, the vaccine, patented by a large drug company, was to be sold in the city at the prohibitive cost of fifteen dollars per inoculation – practically a month's wages for a domestic servant.[37]

These larger examples of what an R.H. Tawney would have described as the greed of an acquisitive society, reaping where it had not sown, were reinforced by Scott's personal experience:

> I was in a palatial mansion this evening. All that wealth could purchase of beauty in pictures, hangings, carpets, furniture, china – all that was there. Not a chair, but would sell for enough to feed a slum family for a month: not a picture but would provide a home for every beggar in Montreal.
>
> In the house was a little, tired woman, with a magnificent gown and necklace of large pearls.
>
> She had a cross as a pendant. And down in the Railway Shops men toiled half-naked round roaring fires, and beside clanging machinery, for hours a day at ... cents an hour. And whenever he wanted to do so, the husband of the tired woman with the pendant cross would tell these men there was no more work.[38]

Scott was beginning to recognize mere criticism was not enough. Direct action would have to be taken, the genuinely Christian action of the cross militant, if society was to be improved.

On July 1, 1927, the sixtieth anniversary of Confederation, attention was directed to the wider sphere of Canadian unity. Montrealers gathered on Fletcher's Field to hear the Governor General speak from Ottawa by the still novel medium of radio, relayed by means of loudspeakers set up in the park. Scott "listened in" on the wireless to the broadcast: "They didn't say anything not obvious," he concluded glumly, "but then though we have existed 60 years we haven't learnt how to produce statesmen. Will that come? Or shall another 60 yrs. find us merely a 'two billion dollar dominion' instead of a 'billion' dollar one? Science at any rate has made a country the shape of Canada possible as a political unit."[39]

It was to H.G. Wells that Scott turned again for reform of the social order. Wells, as he later remarked, "taught us vividly that science could be turned to great purpose, how squalor and misery and ignorance could be replaced by bold imagination and large-scale planning."[40] In a paper probably presented to an audience in Burton's book shop in 1925, Scott concluded that all of Wells's teaching might be reduced to the same important message: to "indicate to man the things he should avoid, and the way he should go."[41]

Wells's vision of socialism, as Scott recognized, was a twenties form of Christianity. He visualized, in *The Research Magnificent*, the earth "hus-banded and harvested. As Christians have dreamt of the New Jerusalem so does Socialism, growing ever more temperate, patient, forgiving and resolute, set its face to the World City of Mankind" (HGW, p. 20). Scott was attracted to the cadre of intellectuals portrayed in the book, especially to the primary figure Benham, who asserted, "We have to choose each one for himself and each one for the race, whether we will accept the muddle of the common life, whether we will ourselves be muddled .... Whether we make that choice or whether we succeed in realising ourselves is a small matter to the world, but it is a great matter to ourselves...." (HGW, pp. 25-26) Scott considered *The Research Magnificent* "a call to individual service" (HGW, p. 26). He recognized Wells's dogmatism but still believed "for all [Wells's] egotism we should be grateful to him, for he is not afraid to ask us to think while we read. And we need rebels occasionally ... for they compel us to take stock of ourselves" (HGW, p. 29).

Frederick George Scott,
ca. 1884.
(*Scott family*)

F.G. Scott and his sons:
William, Harry, Elton,
Charlie, Frank, and
Arthur. Cap à l'Aigle,
1903. (*Scott family*)

ABOVE St. Matthew's rectory in winter.   (*Scott family*)

LEFT Amy Brooks, ca. 1887. (*Scott family*)

BELOW Arthur and Frank, ca. 1910. (*Scott family*)

Harry's grave.
Killed at the Battle
of the Somme, October, 1916.
(*Scott family*)

Frank at Montmorency, 1916.
(*Rosemary Cartwright*)

LEFT A young aesthete, 1923. (*Scott family*)

BELOW Graduation from Bishop's: Frank Scott on left, others unknown, 1919. (*Scott family*)

OPPOSITE, ABOVE Touring the continent: John Darlington and Frank Scott, 1921. (*Scott family*)

OPPOSITE, BELOW May morning, Oxford, 1923. (*Scott family*)

TOP Elton and Frank preparing their gear.   (*Scott family*)

ABOVE The Murray River.  Ca. 1925.   (*Scott family*)

Discovering the Canadian wilderness: Frank, Elton,
and Arthur Scott. (*Scott family*)

Marion Scott    THE THIRTIES    Frank Scott

BELOW Archdeacon Scott's funeral, 1944.    (*Public Archives of Canada*)

LEFT The *Preview* Group, c. 1942. Back row: Kit Shaw, Neufville Shaw, Bruce Ruddick, F.R. Scott; front: Peggy Anderson, Patricia Kathleen Page, Patrick Anderson (on floor). (*Public Archives of Canada*)

BELOW Campaigning in Winnipeg, 1948. (*National Film Board*)

Frank Scott.

The Poets' Group celebrating publication of Gael Turnbull's *The Knot in the Wood*, 1955.   (*All photos, Public Archives of Canada*)

Irving Layton.                    Eli Mandel.

Louis Dudek.

LEFT F.R. Scott and Prime Minister Louis St. Laurent with his daughter, Mrs. O'Driscoll, at the Governor General's garden party, June, 1957. (*Capital News Service*)

BELOW F.R. Scott in Burma, 1952. (*Public Archives of Canada*)

BOTTOM The Kingston Conference, 1955. From left: unknown, John Marshall, F.R. Scott; background: Phyllis Webb. (*Public Archives of Canada*)

ABOVE North Hatley, c. 1969: Frank Scott, Marion Scott, Raleigh Parkin, Louise Parkin. (*Lois Lord*)

BELOW LEFT "Iconics" by Marion Scott. Private collection, Montreal. (*Brian Merrett*)

BELOW RIGHT Frank and Marion at North Hatley, 1952. (*Scott family*)

Frank and Marion: discovering democracy at the Acropolis, 1961.

TOP Recollecting *The McGill Fortnightly Review* in 1963: Leon Edel, F.R. Scott, A.J.M. Smith.

ABOVE AT the Scott Conference, 1981, David Lewis and F.R. Scott. (*Sarah H. Tobe*)

TOP Pierre Trudeau and F.R. Scott.   (*Sarah H. Tobe*)

ABOVE Marion and Frank Scott.   (*Sarah H. Tobe*)

SEVEN

# A Search for Form

ON AUGUST 12, 1927, Scott began his professional career with Lafleur, MacDougall, Macfarlane and Barclay, the law firm where he had apprenticed. His eldest brother, William, was still with the firm and Marian Dale's uncle, Gregor Barclay, was a senior partner. Earlier William had brought Harry into the firm; now Frank was assigned the role of potential junior partner. On his first day at work, he found the practice of law involved sitting in his office until 5:30 p.m. attempting to solve other people's "material problems": once a solution was found, he sent a large bill. This life he found silly and unreal. "I should prefer to be solving my own problems: how to understand, how to create beautifully. And for this I now have but sleepy evenings and hurried week-ends." He consoled himself by quoting a sentence from Baudelaire's *Journaux intimes*: " 'To be a great man and a saint for one's self, that is the sole important thing'."[1]

He was quickly disillusioned in his belief that the private practice of law could change society or lead toward any ideal system of justice: "It is the old business of trial by battle in another form – less chivalrous. Each side hits its hardest strokes: the weaker loses."[2] This opinion was consolidated when, in the name of his firm, he wrote a letter to a man who had moved to Montreal while still owing $12,000 in Vancouver, requesting that he pay or face "consequences." To everyone's astonishment, the man paid. Scott's superiors charged a fee of $1,000 since, they reasoned, their client had not expected a return.[3] The cynicism of this equation, $1,000 for ten minutes work, distressed Scott. More and more frequently he found himself writing of the need to protect the world of the spirit, the "fair garden" of his poetry, safe from "all the batteries of industry."[4]

A.J.M. Smith, who had received a fellowship to study with Sir Herbert Grierson in Edinburgh for a Ph.D. on the subject of seventeenth-century poets, wrote home in early December: "What epics have you written?

97

What barbs of irony have you hurled? Now that the *Fortnightly* is no more, into what new channels have you directed your energy?"[5] The question was an appropriate one. Only that summer Scott had been wondering if his "whole being will ever find one channel in which to flow."[6] Taking stock of his education over the decade, he concluded that it had been "fundamentally a failure."

> To be successful, an education should teach a man what he wants to do in life, and how to do it. Mine has not done that for me. Bishop's advanced me along that line not one whit: it gave me a smattering of general knowledge, a little maturity, but nothing more. Oxford stirred me to the depths, revealed to me the longing for artistic expression that had lain till then dormant in me, gave me the first taste of the intense exhilaration that comes from literary creation, but taught me no technique, and left me still a writer in embryo, a literary youngster. McGill taught me how to earn a living in a profession which does not attract me. Voilà tout! And twenty-eight good years gone, not to mention the expense.[7]

Scott's search was for form in life as in art. Still divided between the conflicting pulls of "aesthete" and "philistine," it irked him to have reached the age of twenty-eight and not be settled in his profession. This search was radiating out, not only to forms of the new art and poetry, but also toward the kind of new society that must replace the old. But in all three – in his own life, in poetry, and in social vision – his starting point was Canada, the land itself.

AFTER SCOTT'S RETURN from England, he and Arthur, occasionally joined by Elton, had begun an annual pattern of wilderness camping trips. Each fall, just before the start of the university term, they would head out for a week in the bush, the first year to Baie St. Paul and St. Urbain, the second year, and often thereafter, up the Murray River.

Their usual wilderness gear was a khaki shirt, heavy pants, puttees to protect the legs from underbrush, and boots. A knapsack was suspended, Indian style, from a tump-line – a broad leather band across the forehead. They carried flour, bacon, tea, and oatmeal, expecting to round out each meal with trout. On a typical trip in 1925 they set out by car, finding, about eight miles beyond Grand Lac, an ideal camping site by the side of the old road to Ha Ha Bay. It was fine hiking weather, warm yet slightly overcast.[8] Even at camp, Scott kept his diary, remarking as he settled at night that the boughs on which they were sleeping filled the tent with the "wonderful smell of gum, familiar to every Eastern Canadian. With Herodotus to chatter to me before I go to sleep, I have all that a civilised resident in this country could desire."[9]

The following three days the Scotts climbed, scaling 3,500 feet on Indian Head Mountain. They posed in turn on a huge boulder precariously balanced over sheer cliffs that dropped 2,000 feet. Then they rolled the boulder over the height. The next day they trekked on but were disappointed in not finding any peaks over 3,400 feet; Arthur had an aneroid barometer and their goal was to climb one of 4,000 feet.[10] They had a ticklish time that night canoeing down the river in the dark, almost sinking on a large rock as they fought their way down the rapids. The numerous portages added to their difficulties. After seven hours in wet clothes and without food, they discovered a ranger's cabin with wood, a stove, and a large barrel of pork. On the stove they dried their clothes and from the barrel Frank extracted a huge hunk of pork, "of uncertain age and very definite distastefulness." This they fried up with bannock and ate hungrily.

Later that day they reached Camp des Erables and telephoned for a "voiture" – "four wheels held together by two axles and three planks" – which brought them out to Grand Lac. There they joined a French-Canadian family, the Maltaises, with twelve children at their evening meal. The meal was unpleasant because of the presence of a consumptive invalid, who groaned and coughed over the food. The visit, Scott recorded, "showed us French-Canadian life in its most typical form; a plain wooden house, obviously built by the father himself; a few excruciating prints of a religio-superstitious nature; a large and cheerful family, quite ready to joke with us, and interested in our experiences in the bush; plain food, no table manners (one child used the plate and spoon of another, quite happily) and no conversation outside of a few comments on the day's work in the fields." Later, resting in the comforts of civilization at the home of a friend, he balanced this judgement by reflecting: "What a material contrast between Maltais' home and this – yet the former builds a nation, while this leaves things as it found them."[11]

For Frank Scott the wilderness was to leave its imprint on him and on his poetry. On their first day in the bush, the Scott brothers had paddled up the river on an expedition to Les Eaux Mortes, the dead or still waters, to a low-lying lake where there was almost no current. Suddenly they found themselves in "quite the most beautiful scenery I have ever met in the Laurentians. [We] were in a deep valley with sheer, and almost sheer granite cliffs on either side. Fresh vistas opened as we rounded the corners. Altogether lovely. Rich foliage at the valley bottom and early slopes."[12]

Images of this experience and his childhood memories of the sounds of the river near Ste. Anne de Beaupré fused in the poem "Old Song," published in *The Canadian Mercury* in 1927.

> far voices
> and fretting leaves
> this music the
> hillside gives
>
> but in the deep
> Laurentian river
> an elemental song
> for ever
>
> a quiet calling
> of no mind
> out of long aeons
> when dust was blind
> and ice hid sound
>
> only a moving
> with no note
> granite lips
> a stone throat   (*C.P.*, p. 38)

The ephemerality of human life and vegetation contrasts with the eternal resonance of the river. This is an evolutionary vision in which the land is associated with a timeless process. Man is evanescent, a brief interval. The chief attraction of the poem is the suggestion of a force that lies beneath physical reality, a Bergsonian *élan vital* personified in the powerful last image of "granite lips / a stone throat." In effect, Scott vivifies nature: but, faithful to the scene, he emphasizes a sense of inanimate strangeness in the comparison. This was a new romanticism, post-Darwinian: nature was no longer like man; rather, man was seen in nature's terms.

To Scott, Canada at first had nothing in the way of an historical past to match that of Europe – nothing, that is, except the immense stretches of the Precambrian Shield. "But the Laurentian country was wonderful, open, empty, vast, and speaking a kind of eternal language in its mountains, rivers and lakes. I knew that these were the oldest mountains in the world .... Geologic time made ancient civilization seem but yesterday's picnic."[13] For him, the enormous age of the land seemed to have been transmuted into a substitution for an historical past. But at the same time, because of its subsequent associations with the new nationalism and because it was open, unexplored, unpeopled, the land presented itself as an open page or clean canvas for the artist's impression.[14] He soon articulated his belief that it was in this ancient land that a new Canadian poetry must take root. Smith, the Group of Seven, and the Imagists had guided Scott toward an external form for his poetry. The nationalism of the Group and his own deep love of the land gave it heart.

DURING THE SUMMER OF 1926 the Scotts summered at Cacouna, a resort on the north shore of the St. Lawrence where the large square homes of the summer residents, among them the Dales, were set in wide lawns spaced along the banks of the river. Here Scott resumed the pleasures of his childhood: picnicking, boating, and fishing. One night after a bonfire and a long talk with Marian, as they walked leisurely home, he noted a pleasant discovery: "An intelligent woman is a most companionable person."[15]

Marian, sharing Frank's progressive and aesthetic interests, was reading Freud, Roger Fry, and Clive Bell on the role of the artist. She was distressed to find Freud considered art a sublimation. The creative spirit, she felt, had far higher importance than this. To Bell's concept of "significant form," the organic unity of a work of art, she gave wholehearted assent. She and Scott compared opinions on Thomas à Kempis, who had profoundly influenced them both, although in different ways. For Frank, à Kempis meant spiritual retreat from the world; for Marian there was more of a sense of an internal retreat within the self, while still remaining in the world.[16]

Scott subscribed to *Dial*, and together they read through its pages discovering the latest in art and poetry. Scott was also rereading H.G. Wells's *God, the Invisible King*, which, in its sense of God as a spirit permeating all, recapitulated ideas he had first encountered in Bergson's *Creative Evolution*. In poetry he was engaged by the Decadents. To Marian he read aloud from Swinburne's "Faustine" and Ernest Dowson's "Non Sum Qualis Eram Bonae Sub Regno Cynarae."

> I have forgot much, Cynara! gone with the wind,
> Flung roses, roses riotously with the throng,
> Dancing, to put thy pale, lost lilies out of mind;
> But I was desolate and sick of an old passion,
>      Yea, all the time, because the dance was long....[17]

By the end of the summer of 1926, when she left Montreal for a year's study at the Slade School of Art in London, they had reached an unofficial "understanding" that they would become engaged on her return. Marian felt honour-bound to tell her mother and, somehow or other, the Scott family soon knew as well. William was annoyed; it was quite wrong for Frank to make a commitment of this sort when he had not yet established himself in the world.[18]

That fall Scott began to savour the later novels of D.H. Lawrence with their emphasis on the integrity of the self. The Lawrence of *Look! We Have Come Through!* and *Studies in Classic American Literature* expressed many feelings that, for him, hitherto had been vague.

> The only sin is to be untrue to one's integrity: the unforgivable sin is that against our own Holy Ghost. Love is a distinction of individuality and an achievement of unity at the same time: there is never complete merging with the one loved though in love alone does individuality find completion and wholeness.[19]

No longer did he read Thomas à Kempis daily, write religious sonnets, and attend church three times on Sunday. Now he wrote verses descriptive of the religious "dimness" of churches and a neo-Lawrentian sonnet on frisking, like Pan, naked down the streets of Montreal.

> Why not bare arms and legs that gleam in the sun,
> A fillet of leaves in my hair, flowers in masses
> Of startling hues on my body, grass on my feet?
> By all the old gods of Christendom
> I think this would be good for the upper classes
> Whom one meets on Sunday morning on Sherbrooke Street.[20]

For Christmas, 1925, Scott had sent Marian a reproduction of one of Botticelli's madonnas with a blue transparent veil – an expression both of his affection for her and their joint love of Italian religious art.[21] At Christmas, 1926, the modern asserted itself when he introduced Marian, then in England, to D.H. Lawrence's poetic cycle of his life with Frieda, when he sent her *Look! We Have Come Through!* "The whole," Lawrence writes in his foreword, "revealing the intrinsic experience of a man during the crisis of manhood, when he marries and comes into himself."[22] In this book Scott marked a series of poems on roses and Lawrence's "Manifesto." There is a degree of ambivalence in the "Manifesto," as there is in the larger cycle of poems, the ambivalence of the free spirit who is both attracted and repelled by the intimacy demanded by giving oneself to another.

When Marian Dale returned to Canada in April, 1927, she, too, had qualms about marriage; she feared especially that it would mean the end of her career. "There goes Mainey's art," her father had sighed when Scott asked to marry her.[23] But when she disembarked at Halifax and started the long train ride to Montreal, some of these fears were allayed as she began to read Havelock Ellis's *The Dance of Life* (1923). On her return to Montreal she brought the book to Scott. Together they read and reread it, underlining vital passages. What Ellis offered was a call to creative living that reconciled life and art: the two were not distinct but one. He also proposed a new morality: a happy combination of the traditional and the modern. "Our only valid rule," Ellis pointed out, "is a creative impulse that is one with the illuminative power of intelligence."[24] For Scott, the book laid the basis for a vision of life in which the "creative" impulse, the "dance," can be seen as informing all spheres of human activity: art, philosophy, religion — even law, politics, and behaviour. The old Victorian structures of rigid morality were beginning to loosen.

The "dance" was a highly appropriate metaphor for the twenties, as the forms of ballet, hitherto rigid, were becoming more flexible under the pressure of the modernist spirit. Years later, celebrating a shared life together, Scott wrote "Dancing," a poem for Marian, included in a book of late poems.

> ... Now I dance
> seeing her dance
> away from me
>                     she
> looks at me
> dancing
>           we
> are closer
> held in the movement of the dance
>
> I no longer dance
> with myself
>
> we are two
> not one
>
> the dance
> is one   (*C.P.*, p. 166)

That summer Marian visited the Scotts at St. Matthew's rectory. She endeared herself to Archdeacon Scott by rushing out in the early morning, still in her nightgown, to rescue a bird from a marauding cat. Willum, however, was not pleased by the timing of her visit. How could Frank study for his final bar examination while distracted by a young lady? Scott managed. He read Byles on "Bills" while paddling a canoe with Marian and placed a respectable second in his class in the province.[25] Marian's family, in turn, were weighing Scott. He was pale and frequently ill, a result of long years of tonsillitis. Was it wise for Marian to marry such a sickly young man? Then there was the problem of the dominant father; poor Mrs. Scott had become something of a doormat, it was thought. Shouldn't Marian be warned? A visitor to the Dale household, a prominent Montreal bluestocking, passed severe judgement after meeting Frank Scott. She concluded that he was an "intelligent but very conventional young man."[26]

The last verdict, at least, Scott could legitimately deny. He and Marian Dale were rapidly rejecting the conventional as they began a fascinated exploration of the worlds of Havelock Ellis and Bertrand and Dora Russell. Ellis's *The New Spirit* (1890) outlined the possible dimensions of the modern age – the new scientific discoveries, the emergence of women into a larger public role in society, a possible socialist reconstruction of democracy. Scott had begun to read Russell's iconoclastic *Free Man's Worship* (1903) and both were intrigued by the new Mrs. Russell's manifesto, *The Right to Be Happy* (1927). Dora Russell deplored society's refusal to see that sexuality and parenthood were separate issues. "What hinders us from establishing a social system in which young men and women who are out in the world earning may enter into open temporary sex partnerships without harm to the work and legitimate ambitions of either? ... We must have freedom and courage to learn if we are to be worth anything as human beings."[27]

Marian and Scott, like the Russells, began to discuss "free love." Perhaps they could just live together? This notion received a cool reception at the Dale household. Mrs. Dale ceased to speak to Mr. Scott for a week until the young couple presented a white azalea as a peace offering.[28] After this incident, there was no more talk of unconventional arrangements. As Scott already recognized, there was a great difference between decrying convention and actually bucking it. When Marian had first returned from London, he had regretted that they could not spend a night together. "We are about as free from convention as an ant from instinct – all we who talk of emancipation."[29]

On February 28, 1928, Frank Scott and Marian Dale were married in a High Anglican ceremony at St. John the Evangelist Church, the church where the elder Scott had first glimpsed the processional cross that was to condition his Anglo-Catholicism. Three clergymen officiated: Archdeacon Scott, the Reverend Elton Scott, and Dr. Davidson, the Dean. The young couple had proposed the 29th, Leap Year's Day, as a wedding date but Mrs. Dale objected to the notion of celebrating the anniversary only every four years. Still, Frank and Marian managed to express a degree of individualism: in their wedding ceremony the bride was not given away. And the organist played Bach rather than hymns. But as might have been expected, Archdeacon Scott managed to dominate the occasion. With time to spare before the ceremony, he decided to explore the crypt below the church and became lost. The wedding had to be delayed while a search party was organized.[30]

A month before the wedding Scott had received a letter from McGill University. He sensed, before opening it, that it contained an offer to join the McGill law faculty. He knew, if he accepted, there would be strong objections from both the Scotts and the Dales. William was incensed. How could he be so foolish?[31] Yet the offer was an excellent one: it would provide a salary of $5,000 per year, more than twice the $1,800 he was getting in the law firm. The Dales were unhappy, but polite: Marian was urged to use her influence to dissuade Scott from exchanging an assured profession with an established firm for the dubious status of teaching law at the university. Marian did not. She urged him to follow a life that would be "creative" in the largest sense.[32]

William, however, continued to exert pressure and the two brothers quarrelled. Early in February, Scott wrote to "Dear Willum" explaining that he could not abandon freedom of choice in determining his livelihood:

> my choice was dictated ... because I believe a greater part of me can work for McGill than could ever work for the office. I happen to be made that way. A still greater part of me – the whole, in fact – would be employed if I could devote my time entirely to writing. That is a disturbing fact that I only realized at McGill, and if you don't believe that you will never understand me. Beside it nothing really matters.[33]

Despite these brave assertions Scott found himself divided on the question. He wanted to get back to university life, but what if it didn't work out? Law did not attract him in practice. And what about his poetry? His final decision was not made until over a month later when he spelled out the pros and cons in his diary.

> It seems to be a choice between "stimulaggers" and "stagnaggers," artistically speaking.

Later

To accept, not to accept: to be a lawyer, to be a professor: to do this or to do that – it all seems rather trivial.

I have no ambition to be a lawyer.

I have no ambition to be a professor.

I want to write a word and a word, curiously.

I have an unposted letter accepting McGill's offer in my pocket. It will drop into the letter box, without being pushed....

It tumbled in, and lay silent. McGann vs. Auger applied, I suppose.[34]

Scott is consciously Hamletesque in pose: the burning question was still to be – or not to be – an artist. He lacked a strong vocation for law or teaching and wanted to be a poet, "to write a word and a word, curiously." Yet this desire was not unqualified: his choice was between "stimulaggers" and "stagnaggers." The art that excited him did not carry its own stimulus for the artistic life; yet law, which he feared would lead to artistic stagnation, nagged him into action. Given the strong emphasis on duty that had moulded his character, and considering that few Canadians in the twenties could conceive of a life of poetry without some other means of support, the choice of a university post offered synthesis – a middle way between the opposites of poet and lawyer. With the leisure provided by university life, he would have some free time for composition; and, as he later rationalized, as a professor rather than a practitioner of law, he would be challenged by the theory behind law and could discover those principles of design that are the basis of good government and social order.

The problem was resolved, providentially perhaps, when his letter of acceptance, poised on the lip of the mailbox, fell in. There was some degree of irony in his perception: "It tumbled in, and lay silent. McGann vs. Auger applied, I suppose." Scott was referring to a legal precedent holding that once a letter had been posted, it no longer belonged to the sender but to the addressee. Even if he wished to retrieve the letter – there was a sense in which he did – he could no longer entertain this possibility because he was bound by his first decision. By addressing his letter to McGill and bringing it to the post box, he had committed himself to his future. With this entry Scott ceased to keep a daily record of his activities. He no longer needed his diary as a confidante, as he had found one in Marian. And the question of vocation had at last settled itself. Henceforth he would express himself through his poetry, his correspondence, and his legal and political writings. Only occasionally, when travelling, would he keep a diary as an *aide memoire*.

Following their marriage the Scotts lived briefly on Hutchison Street. Less than a year later, their only child, Peter, was born. They had not planned on a child quite so soon, but family planning, despite the pioneer work of Marie Stopes among English intellectuals, was still a taboo in Canada. The birth of their son brought joy –

> Little cell-colony
> Puffed with vitality
> You predominate.
>
> Cry, and we tremble,
> Laugh, we are hysterical,
> Run a fever –
> Rooms grow tomb.
>                 (Little Body of Baby)[35]

– and change. Marian's art had to wait. Their joint travels had to wait. And Frank, who had just acquired a wife, his longed-for companion, complained in the accents of a D.H. Lawrence that he had lost her to motherhood.

> I married a woman.
> She could do the things I did
> And go with me.
>
> We climbed high rocks together
> And in dark pools
> Bathed
> Swimming out into strong currents.
>
> But suddenly she turned into a mother.
> Life used our love as a tool
> For its own selfish ends.
> Life overreached us.
>
> Now I have to take care of her.
> She is not the woman I married.
>
> I don't like this thing.
>                 (Metamorphoses)[36]

To accommodate the new baby the young couple moved to Highland Avenue in Westmount, near the top of Côte des Neiges Boulevard, where they rented the upper floor of an old brick house. From their living-room window they had an unbroken view of Montreal and the valley of the St. Lawrence. And, when their landlady was away, they were sufficiently isolated to experiment with the "sun-exposure" for infants that Dora and Bertrand Russell had recommended. The Scotts, once launched into parenthood, were resolved to be progressive parents. Their new son thrived under such treatment. And Marian, pushing the pram with a sketching board propped up against the handle, seized whatever spare moments she could for her art. Ultimately, however, she bowed to the inevitable and, for several years, put aside her paints and easel to raise Peter.

IN THE LAST YEARS of the decade as Scott acquired the wife he had always wanted, his social idealism was also finding an outlet. Since his return to Canada, he had been aware of his father's efforts for Christian social justice. Some years earlier, at a family dinner between Christmas and New Year's, 1924, he recognized he shared his father's beliefs and completely opposed the more conventional views held by his older brother William.

> Willum and Esther in to dinner. Had an immense argument about religion, Willum putting forward the age-old doctrine of the pagan gentleman – that conduct was the essential thing, and that belief mattered little. Father presented the Christian position strongly, I interpreted his religious attitude as well as possible in lay expression in order to make it appeal more to Willum, and Arthur kept the company sane by witticisms. We might have been at it still if the manager of the Chateau had not rung up to complain of Father's remarks about the sin of drunken revels on New Year's Eve.
>
> Then Father told me a lot more about his visit to the Besco works in N.S. with Elton – about the miserable conditions of living, the utter lack of feeling amongst the directors, and so forth. This, combined with the fact that I had to argue a case for Christianity with my own brother, made me feel intensely that unless my life was devoted to something bigger than the attainment of a position of ease for myself, I shall be of all men the most utterly damned. May God grant me the opportunity of service and the strength to serve.[37]

His father's influence, however, was soon supplemented by that of J.S. Woodsworth. In 1927 Woodsworth had contributed an article to *The McGill Fortnightly Review* on the Labour Party in Canada. The idea of independent political representation by labour, Woodsworth reported, was slowly gain-ing ground. The "most difficult task," he wrote, "has been to attempt to convert labour to the necessity of sending its own representatives to the House, and, hardly less important, to establish that sense of common interest which will lead to a larger spirit of unity and to efficient organization." In England, he continued, "the Labour Party has been reinforced by a number of so-called 'intellectuals.' Why not in Canada?"[38]

Why not in Canada, indeed? Woodsworth, who had suffered for his socialism, knew very well why not. In 1919 when he had taken over the strikers' paper at the time of the Winnipeg Strike, he was charged with seditious libel. To be sure, Woodsworth was never prosecuted on these charges, yet he knew only too well the strength of Canadian conservatism. He had experienced resistance to change at every level of society. There did not exist anywhere in Canada those basic freedoms of speech, assembly, and individual liberty that were taken for granted in Great Britain.

Woodsworth's election to Parliament as the member for Winnipeg North in 1921, his outspokenness in the House of Commons on the folly of attempting to extract reparations from Germany, and his arguments for the repeal of Bill 98 soon consolidated his reputation as a man of principle.[39] Yet he was a "socialist": as such he was persona non grata with the Canadian establishment, especially in Montreal, its heartland. Throughout the twenties he slipped in and out of the city, always inconspicuously, and sometimes meeting with Canon Scott. The younger Scott was aware of his presence, but did not perceive the full force of the man until some time in 1927 when he attended a small meeting of the McGill Labour Club addressed by Woodsworth. He recalled his appearance: "a rather aesthetic yet noble face, very trim and quiet, reserved, soft-spoken." As a speaker Woodsworth was "never an impassioned orator," but in his frequent use of charts, sometimes painted on bed sheets and illustrated with statistics, he taught clear, simple lessons.[40] On this occasion he spoke of the accumulation of wealth by capitalists in Canada and the corresponding absence of trade unions – facts that illustrated the injustices of Canadian society.

Shortly after this meeting, Scott invited Woodsworth to the Dale home on Pine Avenue near the top of Mount Royal. There Woodsworth met and talked with Marian Dale. As the two stood before the large living-room window looking out onto the panorama of the city of Montreal and the St. Lawrence River below them, Marian remarked she had attempted to paint the city in various lights, once or twice at dawn. Woodsworth mentioned he had once wanted to be a writer. He spoke of his own feelings, when standing on the Mount of Olives, looking down on Jerusalem. Before he left, he gave the young couple a copy of a pamphlet, *Following the*

*Gleam* (1926), which described this experience. His title, drawn from Tennyson's poem "Merlin and the Gleam," carries overtones both of godhead and of the creative spirit – to follow the gleam was to follow the divine impulse. Marian was most attracted to the creative spirit she sensed in this slight man with the sharp face and the little foxy beard,[41] Scott to his social vision: the new "forms" of society. Many years later, Scott spoke of the "underlying spirit of [Woodsworth], the indomitable courage, both moral and physical, and the largeness of vision, which are so truly the essence of his character and of which his work for humanity and for socialism is but the natural outward expression."[42]

Woodsworth personified those ideals Canon Scott held, but they were embodied in a new and more modern form. Nevertheless the social activism of the two men was strikingly similar. Canadian-born, both clergymen had studied in England, both were influenced by the new theology of the 1880s and 1890s, and each found himself in opposition to the orthodox views held by his respective church. As a result, each turned increasingly to a social gospel, speaking out against injustice whenever occasion demanded. Their careers frequently converged. In 1919 they shared the platform and addressed the Winnipeg strikers.[43] In 1923 they both took up the cause of miners striking the British Empire Steel Corporation in Nova Scotia.[44] Later, when Woodsworth argued in the House of Commons against selling Canadian nickel (obviously destined for use in armaments) to Manchuria, F.G. Scott publicly criticized the federal government's attitude.[45] And so did his son. A few years later, with Harry's death still in mind, Frank Scott wrote in "Lest We Forget":

> The British troops at the Dardanelles
> Were blown to bits by British shells
>   Sold to the Turks by Vickers.
> And many a brave Canadian youth
> Will shed his blood on foreign shores,
> And die for Democracy, Freedom, Truth,
> With his body full of Canadian ores,
> Canadian nickel, lead, and scrap,
> Sold to the German, sold to the Jap,
>   With Capital watching the tickers.   (*C.P.*, p. 95)

J.S. Woodsworth and F.G. Scott were also alike in their work for the Kingdom of God on earth, in their belief in the brotherhood of man, and in their insistence on the primary importance of spiritual values. The differences between the two men were the result of age and temperament. Woodsworth, fourteen years younger than Scott, escaped both a Victorian imperialism and a Victorian faith. Highly suspicious of the British connection, especially Canada's participation in England's wars, he was sensitive to the emerging demands for Canadian autonomy: thus his social vision took a distinctively modern and progressive turn. A true child of the early twentieth century, he had left the organized church when it could not be reconciled with his social activism. The Archdeacon, on the other hand, accommodated his social mission within the strongly imperialist fold of the Church of England in Canada.

A tall, assured man, Archdeacon Scott was a resonant and powerful speaker; it was difficult to be in his presence without feeling a compelling, charismatic power. Woodsworth was slighter in figure, more hesitant in approach, with a thinner staccato voice projected by his keen intellect and profound faith. In general conversation, Woodsworth would quietly and firmly rely on the Socratic technique: "Do you think?" "Is it possible?" "Why not some sort of Labour code for Canada?" "Why not also investigate the dealings of our financial promoters and manipulators?"[46] As Frank Scott later mused, the word he would least associate with Woodsworth was "power."[47] But, in fact, Woodsworth did have power, enormous power, but one would not call it that: it was a shared force. It was the vision of the socialist commonwealth ("power is brought to pooling/ And outcasts share in ruling") that emerged strongly in Scott's thirties poem "Dedication." (*C.P.*, p. 88)

In short, both Archdeacon Scott and J.S. Woodsworth were charismatic leaders who attracted a large and devoted following; but one was a Victorian and the other was a modern; one reached his zenith in war and the other in peace; one was Frank's father and the other was not. After a young manhood spent in vigorous emulation of his father ("As Father says ..." was a twenties catch phrase somewhat dismaying to Marian Dale), the pendulum began to swing. It had started on Scott's return from Oxford when he found himself amused to see his father, like some Ancient Mariner, buttonholing guests at a wedding with his verses. Family loyalty blocked off rejection of his father, or his father's ideas or verse. But Frank, at twenty-eight, was embracing the modern with an enthusiasm that repudiated the Victorian. In this *bouleversement*, his father, for a time, was pushed to one side as the young man took centre stage. Yet he brought with him into maturity his father's – and Woodsworth's – pressing sense of duty and the conviction one must always speak up when injustice is found.

The younger Scott had already delivered judgement on the Confederation poets. Now his readings in the new science were leading to a re-evaluation of religion. Eddington, Einstein, and Bergson had convinced him of the primacy of matter and of a universe of flux. He became engrossed in Eddington's new book, *The Nature of the Physical World* (1928), especially his anthropomorphized discussion of energy in the universe: "the mind-stuff of the world," as Eddington termed it, "is, of course, something more general than our individual conscious minds; but we may think of its nature as not altogether foreign to the feelings in our consciousness."[48] Scott registered his disagreement with this argument on a little piece of yellow paper and tucked it into the book: "Science cannot tell us about absolute reality," he concluded. "Granted, but what can? The search for absolutes is silly: none but priests and a few priestly-minded scientists have attempted it." His old vision of eternity, the heaven that would never end, was fast metamorphosing into infinity: vast stretches of infinite space. Against this macrocosm, man was but an insignificant speck and, as Bergson asserted, "the essence of things escapes us ... the absolute is not in our province; we are brought to stand before the unknowable."[49]

Scott was also drastically revising his view of war. H.G. Wells's *The New Machiavelli* had helped. He had read the book in London in 1923 and reread it in 1925 when preparing his paper on Wells. Scott wrote:

> I start with two conflicting ideas: one a firm belief in the value of Nationalism, Pride in race, Patriotism. The other, a conviction of the internationalism of Christianity. We are all one in Christ. One sees the Union Jack flying over the House of Parliament in Whitehall – one thinks of it flying over the House of Parliament in Ottawa, Capetown, Melbourne, and one feels a stirring of the heart that is too great to be pride, too fundamental to be un-Christian. And yet one sees the same flag flying over armies in conflict, over fortresses and battleships, standing as the symbol of the great barrier of race. One sees the nation's communal welfare put before the most natural dictates of morality. One sees the crime of the individual becoming the duty of the citizen and one cannot fail to realize the utter divergence between Christianity and this form of Nationalism.[50]

On Armistice Day, 1926, he recognized he was "changed in many ways now. Don't write this diary regularly as I used to. Beliefs all topsy-turvy too: Christianity? Morality? Yet indignation at certain things still comes, thank God."

As the whistles blew at 11:00 in memory of the Armistice I read Grenfell's "Into Battle" and then Nichols['s "Fulfillment"]: the one singing the glory, the other the utter brutality of war. I prophesy that every succeeding war will produce more Nichols and less Grenfells.[51]

Scott had good reason to be thinking about the brutality of war. Not only did Nichol's poem graphically present the nightmare of dying at the Front – the gasping, the choking, the cold and decaying bodies – but this horror had new resonance. He was beginning to learn more about the circumstances surrounding Harry's death. Returned soldiers told Frank that on the eve of the Battle of the Somme at which Harry was killed, he had been suffering from a bad case of nerves and nearly had a breakdown. Harry had told their father he expected to be killed the following morning.[52] Frank Scott, by this time, seemed to have suppressed his early desire to enlist and forgotten his father's letter from the Front and his own response. But he now knew, if only subconsciously (for he did not voice this insight), that his father when preaching that last communion service for Harry the night before battle – "I beseech you walk worthy of the vocation where with you are called" – was asking his son to be brave unto death.

None of these apprehensions found voice in an emotional confrontation with his father. Scott had learned to avoid emotional scenes. And he understood perfectly well that his father's strong Christian faith lessened the horror and sanctioned the nobility of Harry's sacrifice. Instead, Frank now devoted all of his energies to an understanding of the causes and conduct of war. During these years, like many of his generation, he became profoundly anti-war. He began to express his disagreement with the militarism sanctioned by Christianity and his belief in the kind of pacifism J.S. Woodsworth advocated. In the following decade Scott saw less and less of his father as he turned increasingly to Woodsworth as moral exemplar.

By 1929, the publication of Robert Graves's *Good-Bye to All That*, Erich Remarque's *All Quiet on the Western Front*, and Henri Barbusse's *Le Feu* consolidated one generation's changed view of war. Scott, who was avidly reading Graves and Remarque, soon began to recite with great relish a current anti-war ditty,

> Gott mit uns, the Germans sing,
> The British chant, God save the King,
> God this, God that, the nations cry,
> Good God, says God, whose God am I?[53]

Not surprisingly, at this time he also repudiated his former hero, Rupert Brooke. In a paper prepared for the Group, he called into question the language and sentiments of Brooke's sonnets, which so easily coupled God and Flanders. Brooke, he said, "typified the willing self-sacrifice of youth on the altar of patriotism."

> And yet how is a generation which demands war to be treated as in "All Quiet on the Western Front" ever going to take Brooke's war sonnets seriously? ... The world has at least learnt one lesson from the war, and that is that patriotism, like all forms of love, is blind. Such poets as lived to the end saw the truth; compare with Brooke's galahadism Siegfried Sassoon's lines
>
> > O martyred youth and manhood overthrown
> > The burden of your wrongs is on my head.
>
> and Wilfrid Owens'
>
> > What passing-bells for those who die as cattle?
> > Only the monstrous anger of the guns.[54]

In the decade between 1919 and 1929, Scott had completely reversed direction from the youth who had five times attempted to enlist. He had also repudiated his own early galahadism. Now strongly opposed to war, he later affirmed he had always held this opinion.

In these opinions J.S. Woodsworth concurred but he had reached them earlier. Ever since his visit to England during the Boer War, he had been convinced of the "horror and futility and wickedness of war." When, in 1918, he tendered his final resignation to the Manitoba Conference of the Methodist Church, it was because of such principles. If he no longer accepted Methodist theory regarding the Lord's Supper, how could he practise the forms? "Forms should be more than forms, or they become a mere mockery."[55]

Scott had read Woodsworth's *Following the Gleam* carefully, underlining those sections that most impressed him. One was Woodsworth's observation that religion is new with each generation: "Many to-day are experiencing a social re-birth that is as distinct and far-reaching in its effects as was the 'conversion' of an earlier day."[56] And the very heart of the teaching of Jesus was to set up the Kingdom of God on earth. For an increasing number of individuals who have attempted the task of "Christianising the Social Order," Woodsworth declared, individuals whose study of history and economics had led them to the socialist position, the Ideal

Kingdom of Jesus was easily associated with the co-operative common-wealth of socialism.

J.S. Woodsworth had much to offer Frank Scott: a faith reshaped by the modern age; a modern view of war; and a blueprint for a new order of society. Significantly, this new order rested on the Christian social ideals Scott had absorbed from his father and from R.H. Tawney and the Fabians. And Woodsworth was a strong Canadian. He believed a Canadian socialism must be shaped by Canadian conditions and grow from Canadian soil. Woodsworth, in the late twenties, helped Scott to find a new faith, socialism, adjusted to the new forms of the contemporary world.

At the end of the decade Scott summarized his modernist odyssey. Every line of investigation, Scott remarked, led to the discovery that "the orthodox was wrong."

> The old order of politics needed no consideration; the fact of the war was proof enough of its obsolescence. The old order of Deity was shown by anthropologists to be built not upon rock, but upon the sands of primitive social custom. Socialism and Communism cast overwhelming doubt upon the value of the old economic order. Psychologists unearthed buried portions of the temple of the mind.... The universe itself, after Einstein's manipulations, ceased to be an easy movement of heavenly bodies through infinite space, and became a closed continuum as warped as the mind of man.... Morality disappeared in mere behaviour. Amid the crash of systems, was Romantic Poetry to survive?[57]

The whole gamut of human society – religion, politics, the Great War, socialism, Marxism, science, morality, poetry – all were to be questioned. In politics the old imperialism had led 60,000 young Canadians to their deaths on the battlefields of France, deaths sanctioned by Christian teachings. And had not Sir James Frazer's *The Golden Bough* demonstrated that the myths of the Old Testament Jehovah were built on earlier fertility customs? The Fabians and Karl Marx had proven the capitalist system was devised for the benefit of a privileged few at the expense of the many. Freud, the Russells, and Havelock Ellis all argued that the buried areas of the mind were of primary importance, and often concerned with sexual matters. And how did one view the universe, now that Einstein had demonstrated and Eddington had confirmed that $E = mc^2$? Morality, as Ellis and the Russells were pointing out, could be as simple as mere preference. With the whole world topsy-turvy, surely poetry must reflect the change? In all these matters the decade had led Scott to the conclusion that the outmoded conventions of an earlier world were no longer applicable. "The modernist poet, like the socialist, has thought through present forms to a new and more suitable order. He is not concerned with destroying, but with creating, and being a creator he strikes terror into the hearts of the old and decrepit who cannot adjust themselves to that which is to be."[58]

# EIGHT

# Politics – The Only Road to Heaven Now

(Day of news of attempt on Roosevelt's life)
I write this today in order to leave a record of my present feelings. I am living in a country abounding in natural resources. It possesses at the moment some 1,200,000 persons on direct relief. Not one of these people is being properly nourished. Children are having their constitutions undermined by malnutrition, and their characters permanently affected by poverty and insecurity. Yet great numbers of other Canadians still possess far more than they need for their daily welfare. There is great wealth in the form of money and credit locked up in the estates of the upper ten percent of the population. The government refuses to remedy this flagrant injustice. It is allowing property rights to stand in the way of human welfare. Children must starve in order that dividends and interest may go on being paid to wealthy people.

In such a situation, I predict a growth of assassination. I predict that desperate men will be goaded beyond endurance, and will throw away their lives in a gesture of defiance and complaint. If anti-social acts deserve punishment, do not our present leaders, who are permitting this injustice to continue, deserve punishment? This will be the argument of the assassins, and there will be primitive justice behind it. Only in one way can such a development be prevented, and that is by a supreme act of sympathy and justice toward the whole working class by those in power – a release of our natural wealth for the needs of the starving, a placing of human welfare above property rights, and an insistence that the burden of the depression shall be distributed equitably over *all classes* in the community.

WITH THESE WORDS the writer scrawled a large "Frank Scott" over the last third of the letter and addressed it "To my future self."[1]

In 1933, the pivotal year of the depression, the world had been collapsing all around Scott for three long years. Now, with the attempted assassination of President Roosevelt, the one leader who stood for social justice, Scott's emotions erupted. At the start of the decade, he and many of his friends had hoped society could be reformed by practical Christianity working through the established churches, but now this no longer seemed possible. On the other hand, President Roosevelt's New Deal in the United States seemed to prove the state could provide social justice.

A number of events led up to this crucial date in February: the 1929 crash of the stock market; widespread bankruptcies; snowballing unemployment; and drought on the Prairies. All were spoken of by Prime Ministers Mackenzie King and R.B. Bennett as phenomena that would disappear if "the market was allowed to right itself." The old ideas of free competition and freedom of trade persisted. Bennett trumpeted that he would blast Canada's way into foreign markets while the bright young men of Scott's set, beginning to grasp what was to become the new Keynesian economics, objected to a tight money policy during a recession.

Not only was there no "New Deal" for Canada, but the economic insecurity of the depression brought with it a drastic curtailment of civil rights. Demonstrations by the unemployed had been severely suppressed in Montreal, Toronto, and Vancouver on the grounds these meetings were communistic or seditious. The authorities were empowered to put down such demonstrations by amendments to the Criminal Code, passed at the time of the Winnipeg Strike, when "bolshevik" revolutionary violence was a perceived threat. Just a few weeks after Scott's letter to his future self – a letter acknowledging the primitive justice of the revolutionary – an unemployed labourer, Nick Zynchuck, was shot in the back by a Montreal policeman before a large crowd of fellow labourers and sympathizers.

Several days later, when Zynchuck's funeral cortege wound slowly along Sherbrooke Street, a crowd of men, many unemployed, walked behind the hearse. As the procession approached Royal Victoria College, a whistle blew and plainclothes policemen leapt from behind the snow banks, knocking members of the procession into the snow and kicking them about. Incidents like this were common; Scott himself saw a plump little man in a bowler suddenly step up to a labourer, who had been standing by the edge of the road, and knock him to the ground with a ferocious punch to the jaw. Scott was shocked when he discovered the man in the bowler was a policeman. With Warwick Chipman, a respected older colleague in the McGill law faculty, and Arnold Heeney, a former student and practising lawyer, Scott quickly formed a committee that met with the mayor to insist that policemen be uniformed when on duty. Other tactics, he decided, merely induced a contempt for the law.[2]

Like all Western nations, Canada was thrown into economic chaos by the depression. In a democracy without relevant social legislation – no minimum wage, no unemployment insurance, no health insurance – charity was a luxury, not a right. The depression generated at least five new political parties in Canada: the Co-operative Commonwealth Federation (1932), the Reconstruction Party (1935), Social Credit (1935), Union nationale (1936), and the National Social Christian Party. The Communist Party, started in the twenties, was active but still largely underground. All these groups offered radical, if not revolutionary, solutions to the economic ills of the depression. Some of these solutions were eventually to be accepted by the major parties, albeit in a piecemeal manner.

Internationally, Canada began to chafe against its status as a colonial nation within the Commonwealth. The Balfour Declaration of 1926 had asserted that Canada was a member of "autonomous communities within the British Empire, equal in status, in no way subordinate one to another in any aspect of their domestic or external affairs."[3] The Statute of Westminster, which appeared to declare an end to imperial sovereignty, was passed in 1931. However, as Scott was quick to point out in *The Canadian Forum*, what had been gained was little more than a "gentlemen's agreement" regarding Canadian autonomy – in point of law the British Crown was still the final authority for the Canadian Parliament.[4]

The road to full nationhood for Canada was strewn with impediments. The federal and provincial governments had not been able to agree on how to amend the BNA Act; indeed, it became a matter of serious dispute in the 1930s as the social measures required to meet the miseries of the depression demanded clarification of the division of power between the federal government and the provinces. Though provinces were responsible for social welfare under the constitution, they had no money; the federal government, which did have access to funds through its wide taxing powers, lacked jurisdiction. And, not surprisingly, all levels of government tended to evade responsibility. Scott's passion for social justice, his love of country, and his training in constitutional law coincided with the primary concerns of the decade, especially with the "obsession," as H. Blair Neatby has termed it, of national identity.[5] Thus far, national identity had been defined by the provisions of the British North America Act. Now, for many individuals of all parties, the reshaping of the BNA Act to bring it more into line with Canada's pressing internal social needs and with her growing external responsibilities became the single most important political issue of the decade.

If the young Scott of the twenties had been preoccupied with the search for a vocation, for a Canadian art and nationality, in the thirties he became caught up in the larger issue, the reshaping of Canadian society through politics and law. The constitution, he believed, in the widest sense, defined the form of an independent, just, and socially responsible Canada. As Scott later quipped, "politics is the art of making constitutions."[6] While he paid careful attention to the letter of the law of the constitution, which led him to a critical analysis of leading judicial decisions on it, he also kept before him a vision of its spirit, "the kind of Canada that I believed the BNA Act was intended to create, which I thought and still think was infinitely worth creating."[7] In law, politics, and poetry his rational and academic self walked hand in hand with his moral and creative self.

That Scott's social and constitutional concerns were expressed within the context of a stalwart Canadian nationalism is apparent from the structure of a group of verses published in *The Canadian Forum* in February, 1932, a collection called "An Anthology of Up-to-Date Canadian Poetry." A catalogue of contemporary injustice, his "Anthology" was framed by an excerpt from the national anthem: "We see thee rise, O Canada, / The true North, strong and free ..."

This mini-anthology concluded with an early "found" poem, "My Creed," based on a statement written in December, 1931, and distributed to Canadian manufacturers by H.H. Stevens, then Conservative Minister of Trade and Commerce:

> I believe in Canada.
> I love her as my home.
> I honour her institutions.
> I rejoice in the abundance of her resources....
>
> To her products I pledge my patronage,
> And to the cause of her producers
> I pledge my devotion.

Scott's satiric poems replying to this attitude are fuelled by the discrepancy between the vision of Canada put forth by the Fathers of Confederation – a nation "strong" and "free" – and the weak, fettered Canada of this manufacturer's "creed." For the Conservatives in power, advocating the support of Canadian manufacturers (who had raised their own dividends while firing workers), he had nothing but contempt. In another poem, "Natural Resources," he writes of a Canada without national planning:

> Come and see the vast natural wealth of this mine.
> In the short space of ten years
> It has produced six American millionaires
> And two thousand pauperized Canadian families.(*C.P.*, p. 65)

"British Traditions" describes a Canada without social justice, where Sections 86 and 98 of the Criminal Code can be used to deprive men of their rights to freedom of speech and assembly.

> Crack this man's head open with a police baton,
> And send him to gaol for sedition.
> He said the present economic system was rotten,
> And actually told the workers they wouldn't get a square deal
> Unless they organised and fought for their rights.

Religion is also controlled by the profit motive ("Treasure in Heaven"), and judges are too often ignorant both of the law and of social conditions ("Justice"). Indeed, prominent politicians are associated with graft. Another of Scott's verses referred directly to the main figures of the Beauharnois scandal, Senators Andrew Haydon and W.L. McDougald, whose names are parodied in Leacock's manner.

> Meet Senator Haymond D. Belgan McLocourt
> Whom the Canadian people have chosen as lawmaker.
> He was unsparing of his private means (or his shareholders')
> In helping his party – sheer public spirit
> Justly rewarded by the lease of a power site.

Verses such as these in *The Canadian Forum* brought a flurry of attention. Many of Scott's colleagues in political science, history, and law were delighted someone dared to speak out. Others, especially older members of the Montreal establishment, began to feel Frank Scott was a dangerous young radical.

One of those who admired Scott's courage was J.S. Woodsworth. As he wrote to Scott, "I think you will agree with me that the man who loots the public to the tune of millions, or who corrupts governments, is a great deal more dangerous than the poor boy who may attempt to hold up somebody on the highway."[8] Prominent Liberal senators and businessmen went apparently unscathed, although they were shown to have profited by the Beauharnois Waterways Project. And no one spoke of legal proceedings when it was whispered that members of the McGill Board of Governors had invested university money in their own companies, losing, it was rumoured, over a million dollars in the process. Indeed, so far only one man in Quebec had protested against this sort of financial chicanery: a Quebec small businessman (the owner of the printing press that had earlier published *The McGill Fortnightly*) alleged that the federal cabinet had advised the Sun Life Assurance Company to put forward its equity shares at a greater than market value to avoid bankruptcy. As Scott ironically summarized the case: "one lone Galahad – Harpell – assaulted the financial fortress...."[9] Subsequently Harpell was sued for libel by Sun Life and sentenced to jail for a year. Liberal senators and large corporations, it seemed, were immune from prosecution; lone Galahads were not.

For Scott, the thirties were the decade in which he consolidated his revolt against "the orthodox" – especially orthodox solutions to the economic and social catastrophe of the depression. Families were going hungry yet unemployed men were being clubbed in the streets of Montreal simply because they dared to protest against injustice. A product of his father's teaching that the Christian must oppose injustice, and a man who was attempting to integrate the warring opposites of his personality through law, Scott could not stand idly by as each new day brought yet another example of social injustice. The year 1933 proved to be a watershed for Scott. It turned the academic, poet, and embryonic political activist into a stalwart fighter for social justice – Sir Galahad in socialist armour.

Scott's social verses were prophetic since they anticipated his work during the following decade – his attempts through newly founded socialist organizations (the League for Social Reconstruction and the Co-operative Commonwealth Federation) to establish national social planning; his work as a committed citizen and a constitutional lawyer in insisting that all Canadians have a right to the elementary justice of freedom of speech and assembly; his activities in helping to establish a Canadian Penal Association. Beyond these specific concerns, Scott the satiric poet flailed away at those who considered themselves above the law.

Scott found this verse – "pregnant doggerel," as he called it – extraordinarily easy to write. Verse after verse tripped forth just as they had when he and Smith prepared issues of *The McGill Fortnightly Review*. But his own reaction was now quite different. As he began to read what he had written, he found himself a little shocked by poems like "The Hero":[10]

> Having stuck several Germans with a bayonet
> For Canada, the Empire, and Civilization,

> This unemployed ex-service man
> Surveys the fruits of his endeavour.

The blunt statements, this rude loud voice, these accusations – all seemed almost a betrayal of class, of friends, and even of family. Where had this voice come from? Others were no less horrified. (Galahadding was a dangerous profession.) Scott began to experience the force of social rebuke, first at the university, later among prominent Montreal acquaintances. One evening at a party at Brooke Claxton's, a society matron pulled aside his Oxford classmate, Terry Sheard: "Do you see that man," she hissed, pointing at Scott, "he's a Communist."[11]

In Montreal, dominated as it was by the big money of Canada on the Anglophone side and by the Roman Catholic Church on the Francophone side, little distinction was made between socialist, bolshevik, "red," and Communist. Writing for *The Canadian Forum* in May, 1931, Scott objected to the view, which he attributed to the upper classes, that a socialist is "a man whose sole aims are bombs, blood, and burglary, or possible riot, rebellion, and rape." The truth, Scott concluded with a rhetorical flourish, is that "the modernist poet, like the socialist, has thought through present forms to a new and more suitable order." A year later, writing about the trial of some Toronto Communists, he was less sanguine when he concluded: "*Malheur à qui fait des revolutions: heureux qui en hérite.*"[12]


DESPITE SCOTT'S BRAVE ASSERTIONS in the pages of *The Canadian Forum* that "the orthodox was wrong," he and many of his contemporaries turned, at first, to orthodox solutions to the problems of the depression. In particular, they looked to the church as a leavening agent in society. The message that Scott had absorbed at Oxford, from the writings of Tawney and the English Fabians, had much in common with a social gospel and even the Victorian Christianity in which he had been raised.

Many of the bright young men of the early thirties, including Graham Spry, King Gordon, Frank Underhill, and Eugene Forsey, were ex-Oxford and Fabian socialists. For King Gordon, an Oxford conversion to socialism had been augmented by the Christian socialism of Union Theological Seminary in the United States. Gordon had been strongly influenced by Reinhold Niebuhr and Harry Ward, who were preaching and teaching the practical application of Christian ethics on society. Niebuhr's *Moral Man in an Immoral Society* (1932) was a particularly important book. During the first few years of the depression, an attempt was made to put the social gospel into practice: it was no longer just preached from the pulpit but was taken out to the breadlines. Jack Farthing, for example, organized soup kitchens for the Protestant unemployed at the Anglican cathedral. Gordon and Forsey began to produce a report describing the social conditions of the unemployed and how they might be met by the church.

During the thirties, the Scotts were seeing three groups of friends. The groups visited separately but sometimes overlapped. There were old friends from the *Fortnightly* and the Group. There were new friends, nourished on Fabian socialism, who were looking for outlets for political action, many of whom were beginning to attend meetings of the Young People's Socialist League at McGill. And there were Marian's friends from her student days at the Beaux-Arts, artists like Pegi Nicol and Edwin Holgate, augmented by others, Francophone or European, who clustered around the Montreal artist John Lyman, just back from Paris in 1931 because he sensed that a new conflagration was about to overrun Europe.

In 1932 the Scotts moved to a house on Oxenden Avenue, northwest of McGill. From there they could take skis on their shoulders, walk across Pine Avenue and up Fletcher's Field, and be skiing on the slopes of Mount Royal in five minutes. Here, in contrast to the situation at their previous flat, they gradually became part of a full and happy community life. Lyman had taken a house half a block down their street. Nearby were more artists – Holgate and André Bieler and the Jean Palardys were one block down. Gordon lived nearby, as did John Bird, a South African journalist now living in Canada, and his American-born wife, Florence.

From the *Fortnightly* days came A.J.M. Smith and Leon Edel, back from obtaining their doctorates in Europe, and Leo Kennedy, wanting to start a new literary magazine. Ultimately all were unable to find positions in Canada because of the depression and emigrated to the United States. Smith considered himself lucky to find a permanent position at Michigan State University in 1936. Edel took newspaper assignments until 1936, when he received a Guggenheim to work in Paris on the plays of Henry James. A year later he went to New York to work with the American Wire Service. Kennedy eventually found a job with an American advertising agency. The members of the Group, all a few years older and better connected, were securely established before the depression started. Claxton went to a Montreal law firm, MacDermot taught history at McGill.

The Group was still a loosely knit collection of friends, meeting fairly regularly to discuss literature, art, and politics. At gatherings at Oxenden Avenue, poetry took its place with socialism and legal discussions. No one had much money, but that did not seem to impede having a good time. Parties were frequent and informal; beer was cheap and plentiful. On other occasions, less often, they would mix up a good punch with a gallon of *alcool* from the Quebec Liquor Board. The large living room on Oxenden Avenue was lined with low bookshelves, painted blue. There were paintings hanging on the walls. A gramophone would play the new orthophonic records; the large punch bowl or beer was set out and chairs pushed back for an evening of talk and dance – both going on at the same time. There was a great craze for dancing to the popular music of the day, "Smoke Gets in Your Eyes," or "Night and Day."[13]

All who came to the Scotts were young and full of energy, with high aims for Canada's future. The Reverend J. King Gordon intended to change the social order through the United Church; Graham Spry and Alan Plaunt wanted to establish a Canadian equivalent of the British Broadcasting Corporation; Brooke Claxton was looking forward to a career in Liberal politics; Florence Bird was an aspiring novelist; her husband, John, wanted to be one of the important newspaper editors in Canada; Hazen Sise aimed to be a great Canadian architect; Dr. Norman Bethune spoke of a new society to help his tubercular patients and drew up blueprints for a model town. And Frank Scott, as Florence Bird recalls, "was going to change the world through the LSR,"[14] the new social organization that was just in the process of coming into being.

During these parties Scott was most likely to be found in a corner, arguing or joking – or both. One night he and John Bird tilted over the question of relief to the unemployed. Bird, who had recently concluded writing a series of articles on the plight of the unemployed, considered the work of a new research group Scott was initiating in Montreal far too theoretical. Bird preferred King Gordon's missionary work with the church, which involved establishing breadlines and supplying clothing for the poor. Scott retorted that the ideas and research generated by the new group would set out the principles essential for the remaking of society. The two men debated with vigour and at length. That night, as the Birds walked home, an acquaintance who accompanied them asked, "Why do you go on seeing Frank Scott, when you hate him so?" "Hate Frank Scott?" responded Bird indignantly. "He's my closest friend!"[15]

Not everyone shared the same ideas yet they found each other's company stimulating. New ideas were in the air, the old orthodoxies were being discarded: "the sacred cows were out of their pasture and cluttering the highways."[16] The experts had not foreseen the depression; nor could they now find any solution for it. It was a field day for the amateur. In such discussions, all shades of political opinion were represented, from the far left to the extreme right. J.M. Macdonnell, who had married Raleigh

Parkin's sister, was a staunch Conservative; Claxton and McCall were active in Liberal circles; Dorothy Livesay and Bethune gravitated toward the Communist Party. Bethune, short and rather stocky, his large head of grizzled hair balding slightly, was a man of great vitality. His abundant sense of life and his attractive voice, with its trace of Scottish brogue, were magnetic. But in Scott's memory the artist Pegi Nicol became, through an elegiac poem, the epitome of the spirit of all these people. She was, he recalled, "a Canadian of these difficult days / When greatness is in our thoughts / And our hands are numb.... / Her alive is alive." (*C.P.*, p. 163)

At gatherings at the Scotts, as King Gordon later quipped, "Moral man in an immoral society sat down with Lady Chatterley." Ethical concerns were paramount but they took their place within a larger context that included art and literature. Members of the Group were still quite interested in Lawrence. Scott and McCall were collecting first editions of his works. His poems, Scott felt, were so fluid that his images evoked the plasma of a quivering leaf; in fact, "even if he wrote of a tree you could feel not only the outside of the tree but also what it felt like inside."[17] They read Middleton Murry's *Son of Woman* as soon as it appeared and liked the later *Letters of D.H. Lawrence* with Aldous Huxley's sympathetic introduction. Hemingway, too, made a great impression. Both Frank and Marian Scott continued to be intrigued by Bertrand Russell. They read *The Conquest of Happiness* (1930) and liked Russell's suggestion that a sense of unhappiness too often stems from an irrational sense of sexual sin. Scott, who had been conditioned by his father's spankings to equate sexuality with guilt, found Russell emancipating.[18] There was a great deal of talk about a "new morality" and the freedom to live spontaneous and creative lives.

Scott was still reading poetry, especially *Dial* and *Poetry* (Chicago), and receiving the occasional copy of *transition*. There he was delighted to find the Stein-like dictum: "The poet does not communicate; he expresses." Like that of his favourite poets in *transition*, Scott's own style began to change; he started "hot-hoofing it over the fence rail."[19] He was also keeping up with British poetry. Stephen Spender, Cecil Day-Lewis, and the Auden of the 1930 *Poems* with his convoluted syntax and psychological insight were favourites. Auden, above all, conveyed a sense of a new decade dawning.

The Group also continued to read the iconoclastic H.L. Mencken and began to absorb the social criticism implicit in the novels of Aldous Huxley and Wyndham Lewis. And, as the depression deepened, they discovered the new American novelists of social realism: Dos Passos, Thomas Wolfe, and Steinbeck's *The Grapes of Wrath*. Scott soon subscribed to the new Left Book Club, which brought him, almost every month, the latest in socialist writings. He was particularly interested in the comments of the Russells and the Webbs, who wrote approvingly of new developments in Russia, especially social planning.

Scott was now rapidly becoming a political activist. In 1929 he had begun to meet with a second group of people who were actively committed to Fabian socialism in the context of Canadian nationalism. These were the ex-Oxford Fabians, friends like Underhill, Forsey, Spry, and Alan Plaunt, a wealthy young Ottawa businessman of French descent. Scott and Plaunt held one another in high regard, and whenever they met would greet each other exuberantly with the "Y" salute – two arms outstretched – to indicate the united Canada of the French and English races.[20] Plaunt's nationalism, in collaboration with that of Spry and Brooke Claxton, was manifested in various forms: in the establishment of the Canadian Radio League; in his support of the soon to be developed Co-operative Commonwealth Federation; in his attempt, in 1939, to bring together Canadians of all political persuasions to establish Canada's right to neutrality.

Forsey, after a Rhodes Scholarship at Oxford in 1926, returned to McGill where, near the end of the decade, he had begun to attend meetings of the McGill Labour Club, much to the disgust of his mentor, Stephen Leacock. There Scott had met a young engineer named Jacques Bieler, the son of a Swiss professor of theology at United Theological College and brother of artist André Bieler. In 1929, at the home of Leo Kennedy, Scott had also met David Lewis, an earnest young undergraduate, who later described himself as "the only Philistine" present in the poetry meeting.[21] He was the son of Jewish immigrants, and, although not a Marxist himself, was already well versed in European Marxist socialism. Lewis was also attending Scott's lectures in law at McGill.

By the early thirties, the severity of the depression had given strength to the arguments of those who thought R.B. Bennett's protectionism and laissez-faire economics were no answer to the problems faced by Canadian agriculture and industry. New acceptance of socialist, and more specifically Marxist, interpretations of society was in the air. Many in Scott's circle found such solutions to the current economic crisis appealing. They shared the Fabian belief in "a society based on equality of opportunity and equality of rights, in which the economic process is subordinated to the principle of production for use rather than for profit."[22] They believed in the gradual reform of existing institutions through the democratic processes of discussion, public education, and the ballot box. For several, there were personal reasons for a commitment to socialism. Scott, Gordon, and Bieler were the sons of clergymen, and David Lewis had absorbed an ethical, even Old Testament, sense of justice from his father, a Jewish radical. All these young men shared a "common concern for the human condition, the human tragedy, itself the result of outworn orthodoxies enforced by power."[23]

Early in 1931 Scott addressed a meeting of the Young People's Socialist League on the future of socialism. Although he was not a member of any political party, he said, his sympathies were with those who wanted to create a co-operative in place of a competitive society in Canada. "I believe there is no other road toward a civilized state of society than the long & hard road of study, organization and political action .... You cannot grow a socialist tree in unprepared soil." Scott foresaw the gradual propagation of reformist ideals as young men carried new ideas into the legislature. Because of "their growing numbers and the superior justice of their ideas [they would] gradually and surely attain control of the organs of state and use them for the benefit of the masses." That it was a *young* people's league particularly appealed to Scott. "We are governed by old men in Canada, and that is disastrous because you cannot produce solutions for modern problems out of antique minds."[24]

In his speech, Scott referred warmly to "my friend" David Lewis, then chairman and leader of the Young People's Socialist League, and whom Scott was encouraging to apply for a Rhodes Scholarship. Subsequently, in 1932, Lewis left for Oxford where he, too, became a Fabian socialist, and the first "colonial" elected president of the Oxford Union. In this position Lewis forged links with members of the British Labour Party, notably Sir Stafford Cripps and Malcolm MacDonald, the son of Prime Minister Ramsay MacDonald. He kept himself abreast of socialist happenings in Canada through a frequent exchange of letters with Scott. Lewis, one senses, wanted Scott as a confidant: he reported his successes at Oxford with the Labour Party and wrote amusingly of mutual friends. But it was hard, he explained, to make really close friends at Oxford, and he was not sure if he cared to.

Scott replied amiably. He undertook errands for Lewis and made arrangements to have him registered at the Quebec bar, but he appeared not to see the personal overtures.[25] "I loved the man," Lewis was later to reminisce, "he gave me a sense of the worth of the human mind and human spirit. Very few people have the inner elements that enable them to give you that sense. I loved him always because he exuded life and verve and a sense of humour and a sense of the absurd and because it was a joy working with him."[26] Yet, from the first Lewis felt he had never penetrated to the deeper core of the man: "I cannot say that I got to know his private person. In this respect, he was a typically reticent WASP."[27] After Lewis's return to Canada in 1935, he took up work for the socialist cause, and the two men began what was to be fifty years of a close working friendship.

Among the third group of acquaintances the Scotts saw regularly were members of Montreal's artistic circles. The Lymans held a salon every Saturday night that brought together the English and French avant-garde, including the painters Alfred Pellan, Jean Palardy, and Jeannette and André Bieler. Lyman, fresh from Paris, soon established new standards for art in Montreal. He considered the Group of Seven derivative of the Impressionists and resented their imitative followers. "The popular notion is that the subject all but makes the picture," he complained. "There is nothing so conventional in Canada today as the 'New North' ... henceforth, the public will have to look deeper for the Canadian character." In 1931 he was instrumental in starting an art school, The Atelier, through McGill's Department of Extension. Marian occasionally attended. In his personal contacts with other artists and through his teaching, Lyman was instrumental in encouraging Montreal artists, the Scotts among them, to move from a nationalist to an international art.

As the depression deepened, its effects on the three groups with which Scott associated were intensified. For the Group, it resulted in an attempt to write a book outlining Canada's problems and suggesting solutions; for the socialists, the worsening depression began to demand direct political action; for the poets and artists, the depression required a new art of social realism.

The repression of civil liberties that accompanied the depression forced socialists to recognize the need for political alternatives. This lesson was learned independently and within the same month by Frank Underhill, a professor of history at the University of Toronto, and by Frank Scott at McGill. The Fellowship of Reconciliation, a newly founded pacifist organization, announced an Open Forum to be held in January, 1931, in a Toronto movie house. A nervous theatre owner, fearful of a possible $5,000 fine for which he was liable under the provisions of Section 98 of the Criminal Code, cancelled the lease. On January 15 a letter criticizing this infringement of civil rights appeared in Toronto newspapers. Drafted by Underhill, it said "the right of free speech and assembly is in danger of suppression in this city" and was signed by sixty-eight persons, many of whom taught at the University of Toronto.[28] The letter sparked an immediate public controversy. Professors, it was thought, should not pass opinions on political matters; indeed, the expression of such opinions was clear evidence that the universities were becoming dangerous seedbeds of communism.

A week later in Montreal, two speakers at a meeting of the Canadian Labour Defence League, a Communist-run organization, were arrested and charged with sedition. On February 3 *The Gazette* published a letter from Scott protesting that the Montreal police had broken up meetings of the unemployed by force. It made no difference, Scott wrote, whether the meetings were attended by Communists or unemployed labourers. Furthermore, sedition had not been defined with any exactness by the courts. "To order a crowd assembled in a hall to disperse when all that it has done is to listen to what may be seditious words, is high-handed and probably illegal. To begin tearing down bunting and destroying pictures, even of Lenin, is clearly illegal, and obviously likely to cause a riot." The methods of the Montreal police amounted to judging the case before any evidence of a crime existed, thus violating rights – and they were rights – to freedom of speech and assembly. Why interfere at all? The British method was simply to let radicals blow off steam for repression merely encourages dissent. Only 250 people had attended the first meeting but at the last there were over 1,500: "It would be interesting to know how many converts to communism had been made by this procedure."

Scott, who had signed himself "Associate Professor of Constitutional and Federal Law," soon found himself in public debate with the Montreal chief of police, Director Langevin, who responded indignantly to *The Gazette* on February 5. "According to Professor Scott, the British method is to let the radicals blow off steam, but against this I have my orders. At every meeting over three-quarters of the crowd consists of Communists. I cannot allow this sort of thing to take place in Montreal."

A statement as authoritative as this, observed Eugene Forsey ironically, summarizing the events for the readers of *The Canadian Forum*, ought to satisfy even the academic mind. But not Scott. Once again he spoke out, saying that the police chief was acting illegally, for even Communists had a perfect right to attend any meetings they wished until the Criminal Code was amended by Parliament, unless, of course, they preached sedition or caused a riot. Indeed, Langevin's statement that "he intends to forbid one class of British subjects from exercising their undoubted rights itself seems to satisfy one recognized definition of sedition, 'the utterance of an intention to promote feelings of ill-will and hostility between different classes of His Majesty's subjects'."[29] Scott soon found himself on the carpet before Principal Currie; he had no right, he was told, to indicate his association with McGill University when writing to the newspaper. The real issue, of course, was that Currie feared Montrealers would associate Communist predilections with a McGill professor.

Scott found a new outlet for his social concerns in August, 1931, when Dean Percy Corbett invited him to accompany him as his secretary to the annual Round Table Conference held at Williams College in Williams-town, Massachusetts. There he met Frank Underhill, recently censured for speaking out on Section 98, and whose acerbic "O Canada" column he had long enjoyed in *The Canadian Forum*. A committed North American, Underhill recognized that sooner or later Canadians would demand "a more direct and a more responsible activity by our government in internal questions. Then we shall run up against the restrictions of the British North America Act."[30]

Frank Scott and Frank Underhill found they had much in common. On a free day at the conference Underhill said, "Let's have a picnic." The three Canadians, Scott, Underhill, and Percy Corbett, drove to the foot of Mount Greylock in the Berkshires. As the men started to walk, Underhill, much to Scott's surprise, began to speak on what became known as the "uses" of history. He was convinced the present depression would have the same effect as the depression that followed the Great War: it would generate a new progressive party. But without clearly enunciated principles to guide it, any new party was sure to fall into the clutches of Mackenzie King and the Liberals – as had the Progressives of the mid-twenties. A research group was needed, along the lines of the British Fabian Society, to provide a theoretical socialist framework. By the end of their jaunt, Underhill and Scott were determined to start a research group with branches in Toronto and Montreal. Underhill, later summarizing for the *Forum* in April, 1932, wrote that they wanted to attract those "unattached critical spirits who find no haven in either of the two national political parties, and whose circumstances do not make it possible for them to join Labour or Farmer political movements."

Although Scott and Underhill were primarily concerned with Fabian socialism, there was also keen interest in Soviet Russia, the Mecca of the planned economy. Woodsworth visited in 1931, Gordon and Forsey in 1932, and Scott would go in 1935. In Lincoln Steffen's phrase, Gordon and Forsey "had seen the future and it worked." Both returned eager to talk about Russia and made several public speeches reporting on their trip. On one occasion Forsey, lecturing to the St. James Literary Society, was reported as saying, "I prefer the hard-headed, practical proposals of Socialism."[31] Unless Forsey was misquoted, this suggests that, at the start of the decade, socialists themselves were not precise when distinguishing socialism in general from the Russian version. Forsey also opined that capitalism – "Blessed are the greedy for they shall inherit the earth" – could never survive. A storm of protest from Montreal manufacturers soon demonstrated the strength of capitalism. Among those who demanded that Principal Sir Arthur Currie "muzzle" his young "idiots" was Arthur Purvis, the president and managing director of Canadian Industries Ltd. Even Premier Taschereau made a formal complaint.[32]

Scott, in the meantime, had been adding fuel to the fire by continuing to defend Communists in his public writings. He took up the cudgels for free speech in the August, 1932, issue of *Queen's Quarterly*, in an article on the trial and imprisonment of eight Toronto Communists. The treatment of the accused had caused many Canadians to wonder "just what our British traditions of freedom of speech and association really mean, if anything." Moreover, he argued, the Communist Party was considered legal in all democracies but Canada, and the ordinary laws of sedition, treason, and unlawful assembly had always been considered adequate protection for public security in any situation short of impending rebellion.

> Yet Canada in 1919 proceeded to graft on to her criminal code a special section – the now notorious section 98 – which for permanent restriction of the rights of association, freedom of discussion, printing and distribution of literature, and for severity of punishment, is unequalled in the history of Canada and probably of any British country for centuries past.

As Scott observed, the Communist Party had been operating publicly since 1924, and although its program was well known to the authorities, no action had been taken against the party until 1931, when the economic crisis intensified.

> Nothing will convince Canadian radicals that the trial is not simply an example of the class war, a temporarily successful attempt on the part of the privileged classes in Canada to defend their position against proletarian attack. Nothing will convince conservatives in Canada that the trial was not a perfectly reasonable enforcement of the criminal law against a lot of foreign "reds" who had clearly broken it. So the matter must rest. Which view will prevail will depend upon which class prevails.[33]

To the very conservatives that Scott described, his writings had an ominous ring. Surely those who spoke so easily of the class war must be in favour of it? Letters from prominent Montreal businessmen, many of them members of McGill's Board of Governors, began to reach the office of Principal Currie. And Scott himself began to suspect he had come under RCMP surveillance. B.K. Sandwell, on receipt of a letter from Scott, noticed a disquieting tear in the envelope. "Have you any reason to suppose your mail is being opened?" he asked Scott.[34]

In fact, the RCMP had launched an inquiry into the presence of "Communists" at McGill. Chancellor Beatty told Principal Currie that the superintendent of the RCMP, Major General J.H. MacBrien, wished to have the university suppress them. Gordon, Forsey, and Scott were all suspect. Currie, however, was not easily coerced. On October 26, 1933, he prepared an internal memo affirming McGill's right to academic freedom.

> We may be called upon to fight a battle, not for socialism, so-called, in universities, but for the existence and development of universities themselves. An institution which tries to stimulate a respect for truth and sincerity, for honesty and honour, for justice and fair play, may not be one that selfish interests like.[35]

In earlier letters of December 12 and 17 sent through Colonel Bovey, his unofficial aide-de-camp, to the RCMP superintendent, Currie had described the three young professors as not Communists, but "parlour socialists." Gordon and Scott, he explained, were "Ramsay MacDonald socialists," disapproving of the existing economic arrangements but desiring change by parliamentary action. Forsey, whom he completely underestimated, he categorized as having "no knowledge of the world, and could have no possible influence over anyone who knew him, least of all over the students." What Bovey, however, had feared was that active and clever members of the Communist Party could use these parlour socialists for their own ends.[36]

While the political activists of Scott's circle were demanding greater freedom of speech and assembly, for the artists the depression generated new questions about the nature and function of art. One of the key questions debated during the thirties at the Scotts', at the Lymans', at the Samovar Restaurant on Peel Street, was "Should art be art or should art be put to a social purpose?" Even if one did agree that the social content was important, and many did, there was a further debate between the dictates of socialist realism and independent theories of art. This debate affected both Scotts; neither believed that art could be subordinated entirely to a party line, yet Scott felt that art could no longer be enjoyed for itself alone.[37]

A strong "art for art's sake" aesthetic had lingered on in Canada – a delayed inheritance from the Decadents of the 1890s. Some of the poems written by Scott and Smith for the *Fortnightly* (mostly under pseudonyms) were characterized by a languid "beauty" and by euphony. But during the early thirties both poets began to write a new kind of poetry informed by social comment, poems like Smith's bitter summation of the depression decade in "Son and Heir: 1930," Scott's 1932 "Anthology of Up-to-date Poetry" and his 1935 "Social Notes," both published in *The Canadian Forum*. Marian, whose early work reflected the Group of Seven, now came under the influence of Cubists. By 1935 she was teaching east-end children with Fritz Bradner at classes for the underprivileged started by Bethune. She was now developing a series of escalator paintings. Groups of individuals, fluidly expressed, are grouped en masse on staircases, on escalators, on city streets – all with blank expressionless faces.[38] She was particularly fascinated by the new "moving staircases" that she felt epitomized society in the thirties – the individual was not giving direction but rather was directed.[39]

The larger currents of society were also affecting Scott's poetry. In 1936 he and Smith edited the first anthology of modern Canadian poetry, *New Provinces: Poems of Several Authors*. When Smith's initial preface condemning the old order of Canadian poetry was predictably rejected by one of the older poets in the group, E.J. Pratt, Scott developed a new preface with distinctly socialist overtones. He pointed out the book had been assembled in recognition of "the need to restore order out of social chaos, [and that] the economic depression has released human energies by giving them a positive direction." Of the six poets whose work was collected in *New Provinces*, the poems of A.M. Klein, Pratt, and Scott most often show clear evidence of social consciousness. Robert Finch, Leo Kennedy, and Smith were less concerned with social issues and more preoccupied with art for art's sake. Scott's verses, especially "Summer Camp" and "Efficiency," have a clear, didactic social message.

> The efficiency of the capitalist system
> Is rightly admired by important people.
> Our huge steel mills
> Operating at 25 per cent of capacity
> Are the last word in organization.
> The new grain elevators
> Stored with superfluous wheat
> Can unload a grain-boat in two hours.

Marvellous card-sorting machines
Make it easy to keep track of the unemployed.
There isn't one unnecessary employee
In these textile plants
That require 75 per cent tariff protection.
And when our closed shoe factories re-open
They will produce more footwear than we can possibly buy.
So don't let's start experimenting with socialism
Which everyone knows means inefficiency and waste.   (*C.P.*, p. 71)

At the same time he was preparing an article for *Queen's Quarterly*, "The Efficiency of Socialism," which attempted to contradict prevailing myths of its inefficiency.[40]

The early thirties had been an extremely busy time for Scott. Constitutional change had been initiated; a new political movement was under way; and he had worked hard for reform, propagandizing even through his verse. But there were moments of respite. On winter weekends the Scotts and their friends often took the ski train to the Laurentians, to St. Sauveur, where there was a pension run by a Madame David. Or, occasionally, they would stay at Jacques Bieler's ski cottage. His brother André, who had learned the art of fresco in Italy, had painted one side of the house with a huge fresco of St. Christopher, the patron saint of travellers. Marian Scott had a sense, as the skiers went out in the morning, that all were "blessed" as they passed. They would ski all day and come back at night to the family table of villagers; always in the middle of the table was a huge bowl of pickled beets – a splash of vivid colour.[41]

Life in the Laurentians was effortless and filled with natural beauty. Yet once Scott was back within the city limits, the call to act could not be denied. Men walked the streets in shabby overcoats, too often herded by policemen with truncheons; long lines of unemployed workers gathered before the church soup kitchens that Jack Farthing and King Gordon had helped to organize. Gordon's university career had already been terminated because of his socialism; he was informed by the Board of Directors at United Theological College that his services were no longer required. A professor of Christian Ethics, as *Saturday Night* ironically commented, seemed to be the very last thing needed at a theological college.[42] One evening, after a day's skiing at Westmount Park, Scott and Gordon bantered as they walked home together. Scott quipped, "If someone were to ask you, say for a *Who's Who*, what your recreations are, tell him: 'skiing and changing the social order'."[43]

# NINE

# Missionaries of a Political Character

❦

Perhaps it is because I am a Canadian of several generations, and have inherited the individualism common to all born on the American continent; yet with political and social ideals profoundly influenced by British traditions and so-called Christian idealism ... I am convinced that we may develop in Canada a distinctive type of Socialism. I refuse to follow slavishly the British model or the Russian model. We in Canada will solve our problems along our own lines.

J.S. WOODSWORTH, 1933

J.S. WOODSWORTH, as David Lewis later reminisced, was "preacher, teacher, and missionary" to many of the CCF leaders who, like Scott, came to socialism through the social gospel.[1] In all these roles, the integrity of the man was paramount: Woodsworth was truly "the conscience of the nation." From the inception of Section 98, Woodsworth spoke against the bill, and after his election to Parliament in 1921 he began calling for its repeal and protesting the violation of civil liberties. He also urged the Western nations not to insist on reparations from Germany, as he foresaw that their continuance could only lead to another war. Woodsworth also persistently advocated amendments to the BNA Act that would allow the federal government to protect civil liberties, institute basic social benefits to workers, and relieve "urgent economic problems."[2] He spoke, again and again, in Parliament and out, about the necessity of building a new society in Canada, a co-operative commonwealth. In the mid-twenties it was not difficult to dismiss these ideas: a contemporary cartoon captioned "Bzzzzz" shows Woodsworth as a mosquito attacking a gigantic pillar labelled "the Foundation Stone" – the BNA Act.[3] But with the financial crash in 1929 and the social disruption of the depression, his concerns suddenly took on new relevance.

It was to Woodsworth that Underhill and Scott first turned in the early thirties. Would he accept the office of honorary president of their new research group? The excitement generated at Williamstown had spilled over into meetings held in Toronto and Montreal. To Oxenden Avenue and occasionally, on Thursday afternoons, to the cheery downstairs bar with its red-checked tablecloths at the Ritz-Carlton, came Forsey, Gordon, Bieler, Lewis, and a new member, Leonard Marsh, a professor of economics at McGill. They began drafting a manifesto setting out the principles to guide the new organization.

Both the Montreal and Toronto branches of the new group were to be modelled on the lines of the Fabian Society, the early tutor of the British Labour Party, and some aspects of American League for Industrial Democracy. The influence of both societies was reflected in an initial debate over the name of the fledgling organization. Underhill preferred the League for Social Reconstruction. Scott wrote to Underhill that he favoured the League for Economic Democracy: "For one thing, it would tend to exclude Communists by suggesting only democratic action. Again, it confines our activities to the economic sphere: the name LSR might suggest that we [are] also going to reconstruct odd things like the Roman Catholic Church."[4] Underhill and the Torontonians prevailed – through the simple expedient of holding a public meeting and thus ratifying the name before the Montreal group did.

In the meantime, Scott and the Montreal members drafted a socialist manifesto and sent it to the Toronto group where, with some modification, it was accepted. The association was described as "working for the establishment in Canada of a social order in which the basic principle regulating production, distribution and service will be the common good rather than private profit." The manifesto expressed dissatisfaction with "the present capitalist system [which] has shown itself unjust and inhuman, economically wasteful, and a standing threat to peace and democratic government." The LSR would "support any political party in so far as its programme furthers the [social] principles" outlined by the manifesto. However, research interest dominated; the group wanted to build up a body of information on such questions as public ownership, planning, and the social services.[5]

The first public meeting of the League for Social Reconstruction was held at Wymilwood Hall, Victoria College, Toronto, on February 23, 1932. Most of the seventy-five men and women attending took out memberships at two dollars per year, and they approved the manifesto and constitution drawn up by the founding group. A provisional national committee consisting of Gordon, Havelock, Parkinson, and Scott was appointed. Underhill was elected president and Isobel Thomas, a Toronto teacher, secretary-treasurer. J.S. Woodsworth accepted the office of honorary president. A Montreal meeting followed on March 11, 1932. Again, approximately seventy-five people attended,[6] including a Montreal alderman, Joseph Schubert. King Gordon was elected president of the Montreal chapter while Scott, Forsey, Lewis, and J.K. Mergler, a Montreal lawyer, formed the working committee. B. Fernihoff, a McGill student who later became a member of the Communist Party, offered her services as secretary.[7]

The primary task, as Woodsworth believed, and Scott and Underhill agreed, was to educate the public about socialist principles and goals through lectures and pamphlets. Woodsworth was convinced, perhaps naively, that if individuals could be shown the truth, as he saw it, they would undoubtedly agree and follow socialism. Subsequently, the LSR commenced a vigorous program of public speaking undertaken by members of the executive as well as by more illustrious speakers. On May 1, 1932, Agnes Macphail, MP, was invited to speak on the possibility of a farmer-labour party. Visitors came from the American League for Industrial Democracy, including Norman Thomas, head of the Socialist Party in the United States, who spoke in May. In 1933, at King Gordon's request, Reinhold Niebuhr spoke in Montreal to the League on the topic "The Challenge of Reconstruction." He reminded his listeners of the necessity to take a public stand on moral principles despite the inevitable public opprobrium. Niebuhr was aware that there is always some egotism within a desire to pursue a cause: "Man's devotion to his community always means the expression of transferred egotism as well as of altruism."[8]

Scott spoke on twenty occasions during 1933 on a wide variety of topics – "Section 98 and Its Consequences," "The Place of Government in Modern Society," "The Need for Social and Economic Reconstruction," "Some Modern Theories of Prison Treatment," "The CCF and the Constitution," "Canada's International Position" – to groups as diverse as the Ottawa University Women's Club, the Verdun Unemployed Organization, the Montreal LSR, and the Toronto CCF.[9] And in 1934 he gave a lecture in a second series of radio lectures begun by the LSR. At the same time, in Toronto, Underhill was giving a series of public lectures, sponsored by the LSR, on "Canada and the World Crisis."[10]

In the winter of 1933-34, John Strachey, Scott's classmate at Magdalen, now author of *The Coming Struggle for Power*, visited the LSR in Montreal and stayed with the Scotts. He dismayed members of the Montreal Men's Canadian Club (who had been expecting the Strachey of *Eminent Victo-*

*rians*), when he alluded to a known Communist by remarking brightly at the beginning of his address: "I understand you put my colleague, Tim Buck, in one of your penitentiaries."[11] In April, 1934, Sir Stafford Cripps, KC, MP, a cabinet member in Ramsay MacDonald's National (coalition) government in England, made an extended visit to Montreal under the sponsorship of the LSR.

The publicity resulting from such widespread lecturing had the desired effect. By January, 1933, seventeen branches were scattered across Canada, most quite small except for those in Toronto and Montreal, which had about 150 members each.[12] In reply to a Mr. Allen of Oxbow, Saskatchewan, who was working to set up an LSR branch, Scott wrote that when selecting members it was important to have people who understood the manifesto: "We want to build a new type of society in Canada, not merely to brush up the old. And the basis of the new order must be economic equality, and the elimination of a privileged, profit-sharing class through the spread of public ownership to all the sources of wealth. Our natural resources must become national resources." The danger was the LSR could become filled with well-meaning individuals "who think we can achieve social justice merely by passing stricter company laws and more severe regulations for the control of privately owned industrial enterprises." Scott ended on a very firm note: "We have no faith in these half measures."[13]

Woodsworth did not believe in half measures either. By spring 1932 he was actively engaged in plans for a new political party. On the afternoon of May 26, 1932, in the office of William Irvine, an MP and a member of the "ginger group" in Parliament that included Woodsworth, a number of people met who were convinced the time had come to form a national political party based on socialist principles. A committee of two, Woodsworth and Robert Gardiner, the head of the United Farmers of Alberta, was formed to "consider ways and means of carrying out the wishes of the group as expressed during the discussion – that is, drafting a tentative plan of organization for future action thereon."[14] That future action was to be the founding conference of the new party in Calgary in July, 1932.

On June 14, Scott received a letter from M.J. McPhail of Montreal asking for an interview to discuss the founding of a new socialist party. Scott excused himself as he was just about to leave for England. In any event, he was not sure this was the time to start a new socialist party in Canada: "better to work through the existing Labour Party, however ineffectual, than to attempt to create an entirely new party."[15]

As it happened, none of the members of the LSR executive, all of whom were invited, were present at the founding convention of the new party.

"Following a meeting that packed the Legion Hall [in Calgary] with 1,300 people on the night of July 31, 1932, the representatives of the leading Farmer and Labour Organizations in the four western provinces met in the Labour Temple on August 1 and decided to launch the Co-operative Commonwealth Federation."[16]

The new organization, a federation of farm, labour, and socialist organizations, was to have a National Council made up of representatives from the various organizations with a national president and secretary to be elected by the annual convention. Woodsworth was elected as president and Norman Priestley of the United Farmers of Alberta as secretary.[17] The Calgary conference accepted a provisional program with the understanding that the definitive party program was to be decided at a conference in Regina to be held in one year's time. The August issue of the U.F.A., official organ of the United Farmers of Alberta, caught the excitement created by the conference. It quoted Woodsworth as saying, "The launching of the new movement [is] of far greater consequence to the future of Canada than the Imperial Economic Conference now in session in Ottawa; for while the Ottawa Conference is seeking to restore prosperity by adding a few patches to the disintegrating system of capitalism, the object of the Federation is fundamental social reconstruction."[18]

After Scott returned to Canada from England he wrote to Underhill on September 7, 1932, remarking that the new party, the Co-operative Commonwealth Federation, seemed like "the long looked-for article," the progressive party he and Underhill had anticipated. He agreed the LSR should help the CCF but added, "I am doubtful whether any sort of official connection should be established however. At the present I rather favour keeping the LSR at its educational job alone."[19]

After an October visit by Woodsworth to Montreal, Scott again wrote to Underhill. Woodsworth had approached the Montreal group regarding the drafting of a manifesto for the new party. "Woodsworth practically invited us to write out a proper programme for the party, and this is the sort of work which we could certainly do without involving the League as a whole."[20] It is likely Woodsworth first approached Scott and the Montreal branch rather than Underhill, as is often assumed, because it was the Montreal group that had drafted the highly satisfactory LSR manifesto.

Two months later, on December 1, 1932, Underhill wrote to Scott announcing the first public meeting of the CCF:

Last night the CCF was launched with a bang in Toronto. There was a public meeting in Hygeia Hall (an ex-church) which was so packed that the police had to send in asking that the aisles be cleared, and an overflow [was put] in another hall, and still people were turned away. Woodsworth, Irvine, Gardiner, Miss Macphail and Dr. Salem Bland spoke at both places.... [Those] who heard the broadcast of the last hour of the proceedings (all that could be got from the radio companies) said it sounded like a football match, there was so much applause.

He added that Woodsworth wanted a draft of a CCF manifesto ready by the end of the year to be submitted to the National Council in January: "I propose to try a draft of my own unless I hear that you have made progress with one of yours. I could submit it to you for revision and to our inner group here."[21] This would seem to suggest the Montreal group had been dilatory and that Underhill, for reasons of his own, had determined to undertake the drafting of the manifesto. He had access to both the CCF resolutions passed at the Calgary conference and the LSR Manifesto, but the latter was most prominently reflected in his own draft. Underhill later told Michiel Horn that he, Harry Cassidy, and Escott Reid, a political scientist active in the Canadian Institute of International Affairs, and possibly Joe Parkinson, had gone over the draft. Parkinson brought Underhill's draft to a YMCA conference on politics held at Lake of the Woods and there he, King Gordon, and Eugene Forsey, all conference participants, revised the document.[22]

A month later the first annual convention of the CCF was held in Regina. Delegates came on foot and by bus; they rode the rails; they hitched up horses to their gasless automobiles and drove these "Bennett buggies" into town. Scott drove across the country in his prized air-cooled Franklin. He, Forsey, Gordon, and Parkinson came three days early, on July 16, to meet with the National Council of the CCF to undertake the final drafting of the proposed manifesto for presentation to the convention. All came to Regina, as T.C. Douglas later recalled, "with little of this world's goods but with a vision of the future."[23]

The vision was that of a "co-operative commonwealth," a term borrowed from Laurence Gronlund's utopian and Marxist blueprint for a new society.[24] But it was infused by Woodsworth with Canadian and Christian content. Concerning this vision Scott was to write to King Gordon four years later:

Old J.S.'s power in Canada has come from his vision and there is no political cunning or tactic which is a substitute. The objective of a good society, which is all that socialism is, must be clarified and stated simply to this baffled generation.... It seems to me we have to express through the CCF the idea that our people came to North America to build a fair city, so to speak, and that we have obviously fallen down lamentably on the job. This sense of purpose, I am sure, is a more cohesive force than any detailed program. It is latent in the Regina Manifesto but buried under blueprints.[25]

Woodsworth's vision of the fair city, the new Jerusalem on earth, was based on the biblical concept of the brotherhood of man, the socialist commonwealth. A sketch prepared for the Regina convention shows a husband and wife with their three children walking through a dark landscape toward a rising sun, captioned "the CCF." The spreading rays of the sun are emblazoned with promise – "Prosperity, Justice, Democracy, Unity, Equality, Freedom, Security."[26]

As the delegates gathered in the old City Hall it seemed apparent a new day was dawning. The old capitalist order was collapsing around them. On the second day of the conference, Thursday, July 20, *The Leader-Post* of Regina carried the headline: "Wheat Slumps 17¢ in Two Days." The following day the Moose Jaw *Evening Times* reported near panic at the close of the stock market on Thursday in Chicago and Kansas City. Prime Minister Bennett declared: "If President Roosevelt wants to save the world he will close the New York Stock Exchange." The bottom had fallen out of the commodities market on the American Stock Exchange, the market on which the whole prairie region, and for that matter the prosperity of Canada as a whole, depended.

The CCF National Council made plans for a public meeting on Thursday at which Woodsworth would give the primary address; Scott was also to speak. The delegates then settled down to the business of laying out the blueprint for a new society. During the first day of the convention, Norman Priestley, the secretary, presided and read the manifesto down to the twelfth clause. Years later Scott wrote: "I shall not forget Priestley standing on the platform reading to us in a great booming voice, paragraph after paragraph of denunciation of capitalist evils and promise of socialist benefits, nor the way in which when he finished the whole Convention rose as one man to its feet to express its enthusiastic approval."[27] Five of the fourteen clauses drawn up by LSR members were accepted by the convention, although the National Council who reviewed it before the convention had made changes to other clauses, particularly the one on agriculture.[28] In response to questions from the floor and further objections to specifics in the manifesto, the academics and the executive worked over the document clause by clause.

The most acute point of controversy in the ensuing debate was over the question of compensation for nationalized industries. Some of the older diehard British Columbia socialists "were insistent that the owners should get nothing when society took back what rightfully belonged to it. To the farmer delegates from the UFA and the UFO this was far too radical a position. To resolve the conflict a committee was struck off during a lunch hour to find a formula that would reconcile both sides." Scott recalled that he, King Gordon, and Eugene Forsey were three of its four members; they sat in a small booth in a Regina restaurant drafting a paragraph dealing with compensation, which was scribbled on a cigarette box. "Later when the Manifesto had to be rethought in the light of post-World War II conditions, and old-timers in the CCF thought this was sacrilege, that not a word should be touched, I could not help remembering how casually some of the words had been thrown together. But this is true of all Bibles."[29]

At the end of the third day the manifesto consisted of a preamble with fourteen points. The plan was national in scope, a blueprint for the day when a CCF government might be elected in Ottawa. At the heart of the manifesto was the belief that the capitalist system was inhumane and led to gross injustice. The purpose of the CCF was the "establishment in Canada of a Co-operative Commonwealth in which the principle regulating production, distribution and exchange will be the supplying of human needs and not the making of profits."

The preamble emphasized that the program of the CCF could be accomplished through a democratic election and support by a majority of people. Change through violence was not advocated, yet there can be no question about the radical, even revolutionary, tone of the manifesto. The inequalities of capitalism could be remedied only through a planned economy "in which our natural resources and the principal means of production and distribution are owned, controlled and operated by the people." What was wanted was "a proper collective organization of our economic resources such as will make possible a much greater degree of leisure and a much richer individual life for every citizen."[30]

Just as the manifesto began with a clear indication of belief in its program, so it ended with an equally clear and succinct statement: "No CCF Government will rest content until it has eradicated capitalism and put into operation the full programme of socialized planning which will lead to the establishment in Canada of the Co-operative Commonwealth."[31] This final paragraph, as Coldwell later remarked,[32] was to prove a "millstone" about the neck of the new party, reflecting as it did ideological conflict between the eastern intellectuals and the western socialists. Many of the British Columbia socialists in particular had their roots in the Clydeside struggles; they were tough and they were militant. The pressure of this more radical faith led to the assertion that the CCF was not just a reformist movement, but rather a revolutionary one determined to abolish capitalism.

On the second day, July 20, a public meeting to discuss the principles of the newly formed Federation was held, again in the auditorium of the old City Hall. Robert Gardiner, MP, presided, and F.R. Scott, M.J. Coldwell, and J.S. Woodsworth spoke. The main floor of the auditorium was packed with eager listeners, as was the long U-shaped gallery that looked down into the hall. Of the three speakers, Scott stood out in the estimation of one observer in the gallery, George Curtis, a young city lawyer.[33] Slim, earnest, and articulate, Scott allayed the fears of those who believed it impossible to create the Co-operative Commonwealth by peaceful means. He believed the constitutional aspects of the CCF program could be accommodated within the British North America Act and stated that the CCF would not interfere with minority rights guaranteed in the constitution. However, the CCF would encourage the learning of French and, Scott added, "There is no reason why we might not come out with a bilingual currency."[34] Scott's comments on French language rights, not surprisingly, were immediately applauded by an editorial writer in Le Canada as a source of great satisfaction to French-speaking Canadians because obviously exempt from electioneering tactics. The writer was convinced of this because Scott's audience at Regina was composed of Anglophones.[35]

As Michiel Horn points out, the role of the LSR academics in formulating the policy of the new party had proven to be of great importance. Articulate, knowledgeable, and efficient, they had established the theoretical principles to guide the CCF and had shepherded the Regina Manifesto through the convention. Scott, in particular, had played a large part in clarifying the legality of the proposed program. George V. Ferguson in the *Winnipeg Free Press* on July 19 quickly identified a "brain trust" among the young professors, much on the lines of the expert advisers on whom Roosevelt had relied for his New Deal. Scott knew the academics had scored a great hit, a judgement confirmed by others. Cassidy wrote to the economist, Kenneth Taylor, "Frank Scott called me this morning on his way back from the CCF convention.... He said that the LSR had scored a brilliant success at the convention, since the members of our group who were on hand had succeeded in having their views accepted pretty generally with respect to the programme." And Graham Spry, who had also attended the conference, wrote to Cassidy: "The opinions of Scott, Parkinson, Forsey and Gordon were almost always deferred to."[36]

The night the Regina Manifesto was adopted, Mackenzie King, then Leader of the Opposition, was beginning a speaking tour in the West. Rather than denounce CCFers, he announced equitably that "a large part of their program would gain the support of anyone." However, he could not agree with the socialization of industries. "Confiscation of property would mean revolution," he reminded the Liberal faithful at a picnic.[37] Prime Minister Bennett soon promoted a similar but more vicious attack on the new party. In a speech in November, 1932, at the annual convention of the Ontario Conservative Party in the Royal York Hotel, he roundly denounced socialism and communism and advised "counter-destruction" against such pronouncements. "We should use the iron heel of destruction against propaganda of that kind," Bennett declared.[38] *The Ottawa Journal* reported this talk under banner headlines: "BENNETT URGES RUTHLESS WAR ON SOCIALISM; Premier says Communists Sowing Their Seeds Everywhere ... Being Led by Cooperative Commonwealth Movement."[39]

Three days later, Scott picked up the gauntlet at the People's Forum in Ottawa. "If the Prime Minister [does] not know the difference between socialism and communism," Scott declared, "he might learn it from 'any university graduate.' ... Things are coming to a pretty pass," he went on, "when the Prime Minister of this country incites the people to ruthlessness."[40] At the beginning of the brouhaha that followed his speech in Ottawa, when the young professor returned to his lectures in constitutional law at McGill, his first class of the morning stood up in a body and applauded.[41] Scott had practised what he taught: freedom of speech and expression. It was a heady experience. It also provided a pattern that would characterize his actions for the next three decades.

This speech provoked an outraged response from *The Ottawa Journal* on November 15. "Mr. Bennett did nothing of the sort," the lead editorial asserted; "the iron heel" of ruthlessness was to be applied to foreign propaganda aimed at the destruction of Canadian institutions. "Would even McGill's professor of constitutional law say Mr. Bennett went too far?" McGill's professor of constitutional law would. He promptly replied to *The Ottawa Journal*, stating he had been correct in his assertion that Bennett had confused socialism and communism:

> May I refer you to your own report of Mr. Bennett's speech in your issue of November 10th? The headline is "BENNETT URGES RUTHLESS WAR ON SOCIALISM" and the subtitle is "PREMIER SAYS COMMUNISTS

SOWING THEIR SEEDS EVERYWHERE." Clearly your reporter was confused even if Mr. Bennett was not, and your paper was guilty of the
same "loose thinking" of which you accuse me. All the other press
reports I have seen treated Socialism and Communism together in
the same way.

In any case, he pointed out, there was nothing illegal about foreigners
seeking to alter or even abolish Canadian institutions as long as legal means
were employed. The Prime Minister, Scott argued, had no greater freedom
than anyone else. If a professional agitator were to call upon an audience
of unemployed men for ruthless treatment of the capitalist class he would
be promptly jailed for sedition; "And I think it is permissible to hold the
Prime Minister, who speaks with greater authority and is himself a lawyer,
to a stricter accuracy and to a nicer appreciation of British traditions than
a professional agitator."[42]

While Scott jousted with the Prime Minister, he and other members of
the LSR decided to produce publications to educate the Canadian public.
A research committee was formed under the chairmanship of Harry Cassidy, who told the LSR national convention in January, 1933, that the
committee proposed "to prepare a book, comparable in scope to the British
Liberal 'Yellow Book,' containing a detailed statement of the LSR programme." He added they hoped the book would be "an amplification of
the [LSR] manifesto, [would] be accepted by the CCF as a semi-official
statement of policy, and that it [would] be ready for circulation during
the coming summer."[43]

Work was begun on *Social Planning for Canada* in 1933 with Cassidy as
the editor-in-chief and Graham Spry as associate editor. Eugene Forsey,
Irene Biss, a young economist from the University of Toronto, and Joseph
Parkinson were to work on the chapter on economics, Underhill was
responsible for politics, Scott for the chapter concerning the constitution,
and Escott Reid for external affairs.[44] A number of others were brought
in to supplement the work in these areas or to enhance areas in which
they had special expertise. Ultimately the project became much larger than
first envisioned; it was not until September, 1935, that it was published.
The original run of 1,500 copies sold well and by 1936 a second printing
of 1,500 came out.[45]

J.S. Woodsworth contributed the foreword to the book. The preface,
signed by Scott, Marsh, Spry, Gordon, Forsey, Parkinson, and Underhill,
stated the aims of the group. Through its analysis of Canadian resources
the book was intended to educate the public on the inadequacies of the

present system. The proposals sprang from socialist ideals, "the endeavour to put governments *by the people* and *for the people* into modern terms." The writers also called for reason to counteract the emotionally based charges of communism levelled against socialists.[46]

*Social Planning for Canada* sparked great controversy during the election campaign of 1935 as it was attacked indiscriminately by both the right and the left. Tim Buck, the Communist leader, considered the book "interesting, but inadequate and naive." However, it was the criticism from the right that really hurt. A public relations officer with the CPR, P.C. Armstrong, wrote and distributed anonymously a forty-page booklet entitled: *Criticism of the Book*.[47] "As though *Social Planning* was a bible," Scott was later to remark.[48] Armstrong dismissed the book as "a Marxist-inspired document in which misinformation and faulty logic were put to the service of a sermon preaching class hatred."[49] Underhill was infuriated by this kind of criticism. But Scott asserted, "I am delighted that the incident has occurred. The vicious style of the document, its use of contempt for argument, its complete failure to answer the main thesis of our book, are admissions of great weakness.... On the whole, our prestige – and our sales – should go up considerably."[50] Scott was grossly overestimating the acumen of the average Canadian voter; it was precisely this kind of criticism that was to vitiate Canadian socialism. Strachey, writing in England in 1933, was both more cynical and more astute: socialists need not expect capitalists to stand meekly by while their privileges were threatened.[51]

Even as the first printing of *Social Planning for Canada* was coming off the press, the publisher recognized the need for an abridged version. Forsey, Marsh, and Scott promptly began work on the project and in February, 1938, the shorter *Democracy Needs Socialism* was published. It was not, strictly speaking, an abridgement. It contained an expanded chapter considering women's rights and clarified the questions of economic recovery, the challenge of fascism to democracy and parliamentary institutions, and the drift to a major war.[52] But of all the documents produced by the LSR, it was *Social Planning for Canada* that was "judged by reviewers in Canada and abroad to be a significant socialist statement, an assessment that the passage of time has modified but little."[53]

Throughout 1933, Trade and Commerce Minister Harry H. Stevens from Vancouver had been busy speaking on behalf of the Bennett government. Bennett was frequently away that year and, while standing in for the Prime Minister, Stevens became acquainted with reports on growing economic hardship. He also began to receive reports of the questionable conduct of a number of industries, among them several first-hand accounts of poor conditions in the clothing industry and unethical practices by buyers for chain and department stores. These practices were forcing small manufacturers into bankruptcy. Frank Scott and Harry Cassidy played an important role in bringing to light many of the practices exposed by Stevens's subsequent charges.

In 1932 Scott had been approached by the Montreal alderman and LSR member, Joseph Schubert, to do a study of wage rates in the men's clothing industry in Quebec and Ontario. Although the request came from Schubert, the report was jointly commissioned by the Canadian Garment Manufacturers' Association and the Amalgamated Clothing Workers' Union of America. The survey was conducted independently of the LSR, but Scott had invited Cassidy to undertake the study jointly. He felt he lacked sufficient experience in designing and conducting a survey whereas Cassidy, an economist at the University of Toronto and research secretary for the LSR, was experienced in such work.[54] In their report, *Labour Conditions in the Men's Clothing Industry*, completed in December, 1933, Scott and Cassidy had described an industry in chaos:

> Both the manufacturers and the workers have suffered greatly in recent years, the former from cut-throat competition, disorganized marketing and general industrial instability, and the latter from unemployment, under-employment and the revival of the sweatshop in its most obnoxious forms.[55]

Concluding that existing labour laws were not effective enough, they recommended that their proposals – fair wages, shorter workday, restriction of unfair business practices, improved management, concern for consumers – be implemented by an extension and enforcement of the current labour laws and that a board of control, composed of employers, labour, and consumers, be established as a self-governing body within the industry.

The editor of *Saturday Night*, in a column entitled "People Who Do Things," spoke highly of the two young reformers, lauding their zeal and sincerity:

> Because Frank Scott is an energetic, sincere and earnest young man, deeply moved by human problems, he is devoting his time to many other problems of paramount importance. Penal Reform is one, and as a member of the executive of the new Canadian Penal Association we are bound to hear from him. Furthermore, he and H.M. Cassidy did a piece of work for the Institute of Pacific Relations [the report's publisher] exposing sweatshop conditions ... in the Clothing Industry

in Quebec and Ontario, which was so thorough that it was submitted subsequently as evidence before the Stevens Committee.[56]

The Scott and Cassidy report was absorbed into Stevens's charges of monopolistic practices in business and industry. In early 1934 the Select Committee on Price Spreads and Mass Buying was formed under Stevens's chairmanship. It met for four months and, due to the prorogation of Parliament, was scheduled to reconvene as a Royal Commission in October, 1934. Among the witnesses appearing before this committee was Harry Cassidy, who presented the report on wages and conditions in the men's clothing industry. This information, together with that received from other witnesses, was incorporated in a speech Stevens delivered to the Conservative Study Club in June, 1934. In the speech Stevens accused the Canada Packers Company and the Robert Simpson Company of unethical business practices. When the text of the speech found its way into the press, Simpson threatened to sue and pressure was put on Stevens to apologize. He received no support in the cabinet meeting that followed the Simpson threat, and in the aftermath of the incident, when it was rumoured he had agreed to apologize, the furious Stevens resigned.[57]

The Stevens controversy and the publication of *Social Planning for Canada* and of *Labour Conditions in the Men's Clothing Industry* were strong evidence of the hardship created by the malfunctioning of the economic system. Another problem, as Scott saw it, was that Canada needed the approval of the British Parliament to alter the BNA Act in ways that would allow moderate social changes. In 1934 he addressed this problem in "Social Reconstruction and the BNA Act," one of four pamphlets published by the LSR. A clause in the BNA Act, the Dominion residuary clause, attempted to designate areas in which the federal government could enact legislation. This clause could be used in a time of emergency and, in Scott's opinion, the wider effects of the depression qualified as an emergency. A second use of the residuary clause related to laws "giving effect to Canadian treaties and conventions." Scott argued that the judgements of the Privy Council in the Radio Broadcasting and the Aeronautics cases had given the Canadian government an important precedent, leaving "the way open for Dominion control of any aspect of the internal life of Canada, so long as the matter is covered by an international agreement to which Canada is a party." He believed "a progressive government at Ottawa might feel reasonably sure of constitutional support in any attempt to bring the industrial and economic life of Canada into line with a general world programme agreed upon at an international conference." He asked why legislation on wheat production or hours of work, for example, could not come under the same authority as radio. Social questions could, he believed, be considered under conventions drawn up by the International Labour Office.[58] Bennett, who borrowed Scott's pamphlet from the library in External Affairs, did not return it, and Scott's arguments soon appeared in Bennett's text of his New Deal.[59]

These events and ideas, and above all an impending general election, encouraged Bennett to put forward his own version of a New Deal for Canadians. In January, 1935, in a series of six radio broadcasts, he advocated reform based on a wide variety of economic measures that made use of Scott's arguments. He referred to unemployment insurance, minimum wages, and a scaling down of mortgages. By 1935 these were no longer new ideas but, if instituted, would constitute reform. What was new was the promise by the government to do something. His intent appears to have been to use Parliament as an instrument of social justice. However, as members of the LSR concluded, his proposals would serve only to preserve and even revitalize a capitalist system responsible for the present injustice. As Bennett said: "When capitalism is freed at last from its harmful imperfections, when government exercises the intended measure of regulation over capitalist groups, capitalism will be in fact your servant and not your master."[60]

The LSR was not enthusiastic about Bennett's "half-measures" – reforms, as Underhill sourly remarked, that would merely satisfy a capitalist. The marketing legislation provided security to producers and processors, but at the expense of the consumer. The editors of *The Canadian Forum* (probably Underhill) felt Bennett was turning back the clock on behalf of "a group of small manufacturers and retailers who are out to get Eaton's and Simpson's and the chain stores."[61] Scott's reaction was guardedly optimistic: he was not convinced the Prime Minister's "death-bed" conversion to socialist principles was real. Moreover, he did not consider the measures sufficiently far-reaching. Yet this was the first attempt by a federal government to assert Canadian direction in her internal constitutional affairs. If these measures went into effect, it would signal the beginning of Canadian initiative in planning its society. This hope was to be disappointed.

Midway through the summer of 1935, Bennett had a heart attack and shortly thereafter called an election for October. It was an active election campaign. Besides the two traditional parties, there were five other parties campaigning for the protest vote, including the CCF and the Reconstruction Party, founded by Harry Stevens after his break with the Bennett government. With so many new parties competing for office, the protest vote was split. Mackenzie King, cannily sizing up the situation, sailed to victory on a slogan of "King or chaos." The newly formed CCF did badly: only seven candidates were elected.

After the defeat of the Conservatives in 1935 and a deadlock in the Supreme Court as to the constitutionality of Bennett's measures, the new Prime Minister, Mackenzie King, submitted them to the Judicial Committee of the Privy Council in London. In January, 1937, the Judicial Committee decided that much of the legislation submitted, including the Weekly Day of Rest Act, the Minimum Wage Act, the Limitation of Hours Act, the Natural Products Marketing Act, and the Employment and Social Insurance Act, was *ultra vires*. The labour acts that had been justified under the International Labour Organization Conventions[62] were rejected by the Privy Council because such conventions were not empire treaties and infringed on provincial powers. The government argument that the legislation fell under federal jurisdiction over trade and commerce, or came under the federal government's residual power for "peace, order and good government," was also ruled *ultra vires* because it, too, conflicted with provincial jurisdiction over "property and civil rights."

In a sense King had ensured this decision by submitting the cases in their weakest state – as reference cases and not as enacted legislation. Indeed, in Scott's view, he need not have submitted the cases at all. Scott recounted years later that he "felt something collapse within" him when he read of the Privy Council's decisions in the morning paper.[63] A wider interpretation of federalism was instantly dissipated. He launched a blistering attack on the Privy Council in *The Canadian Bar Review*, charging Canada had been destroyed as a federal and international entity, that she had virtually ceased to be "a single nation in the conduct of her international relations" since treaties, other than strictly empire treaties, could not be implemented by the federal government if they interfered with "property and civil rights." Most offensively, the Privy Council's decisions seemed to negate the national status that Canada had so recently acquired with the Statute of Westminster.

He concluded that the "Privy Council is and always will be a thoroughly unsatisfactory court of appeal for Canada in constitutional matters; its members are too remote, too little trained in our law, too casually selected, and have too short a tenure."[64] Scott's views on the Privy Council reflected the prevailing opinion of the thirties: the miseries caused by the depression demanded a strong federal state rather than provincial balkanization, a view strengthened by Scott's belief in socialist planning. Later analysis of the Privy Council's role takes an opposite view but Scott's interpretation was characteristic of the thirties and forties.[65]

In addition to his legal writings and his continuing work with the LSR and the CCF, Scott also became actively involved in penal reform. He had been asked by Dean Corbett, early in the decade, to become a member of the Prisoner's Aid and Welfare Association, a charitable organization in Montreal. For Scott this was the beginning of his recognition of the complex problems involved in the administration of justice and penal reform. On June 13-14, 1935, the Prisoner's Aid and Welfare Society became the Canadian Penal Association. Scott was the guest speaker at the founding conference. In his address, he noted the depression had made it possible to see connections between social problems: "child welfare," for example, "related to slum clearance, juvenile delinquency related to unemployment, medical and dental care related to education, and the whole problem of social security [is] inescapably bound up with the working of the economic machine." Scott clearly stated his attitude to his profession: "Law," he said, "is 'social engineering,' and it seems to me that the most fruitful development of law in the years ahead will come from the treatment of law as an experimental social science rather than an inherited set of untouchable and mysterious dogmas."[66]

The speech reflected both Scott's participation in the LSR and the CCF and his concern about his role as an educator of future lawyers and judges. Certainly its tone evidenced his socialist idealism: some of the recommendations can be found in the Regina Manifesto. Moreover, with his awakening interest in penal reform, he began to recognize the issues he could raise in the minds of the future lawmakers he had the responsibility of teaching: "Modern penology is a science, one of the new social sciences. It is not philanthropy.... Being a science, it should be as completely divorced from politics as it is humanly possible to make it in a democracy." As J.A. Edmison said later, not only did Scott's comments portend a shift in Canadian thinking toward the rehabilitation of the offender, but they also raised the critical issue of the role of political considerations in the judicial process.[67]

In 1937, when a commission was established under Judge Archambault to look into the penal system, Scott gave testimony. He recalled that when he appeared before the commission, Judge Archambault said to him: "You know, Mr. Scott, before I went on this job I didn't know what penology was."[68] For Scott it must have seemed as if life imitated art. Early in 1932 he had written a satiric verse entitled "Justice":

> This judge is busy sentencing criminals
> Of whose upbringing and environment he is totally ignorant.
> His qualifications, however, are the highest ....

Who should know better than he
Just how many years in prison
Are needed to reform a slum-product ... ?    (*C.P.*, p. 66)

In addition to his work on penal reform, Scott also prepared a report for the Rowell-Sirois Commission. The emphasis of the Commission was not on an analysis of the role of government but on a reallocation of existing revenues and expenditures by provincial and federal governments. However, in a retrospective examination of the Rowell-Sirois Report, Donald Smiley has argued that "in its analysis of federal-provincial relations [Rowell-Sirois] has had surprisingly little influence on the directions that the theory and practice of Canadian federalism have taken since 1945."[69] Scott, however, suspected the Royal Commission was another of Mackenzie King's delaying tactics, and he did not feel that its scope was sufficiently broad. Writing in 1938, he outlined crucial problems in federal-provincial relations that were beyond the purview of the Rowell-Sirois Commission. He was concerned that the national budget remained unbalanced, that the national debt continued to grow, that monopolistic economic power was expanding, and that the Canadian economy was still subject to the debilitating cycle of boom and bust. What was more, he wrote, "in certain parts of the country the principle of democracy itself is openly challenged and violation of civil liberties condoned by high authorities in church and state."[70]

In spite of his personal reservations, the LSR presented a brief to the Commission entitled *Canada – One or Nine? The Purpose of Confederation*, largely written by Scott and presented to the Commission by him and Leonard Marsh. Because the Privy Council forced Canadian federalism to conform to a looser, inefficient English model, the brief argued, it encouraged sectionalism and had allowed a "parallel government" of monopoly capitalism to emerge, thus vitiating the quality of Canadian democracy. That sectionalism or regional interests might have encouraged the Privy Council to make its decisions seems not to have occurred to Scott. He advised the Commission that the original aims of the Fathers of Confederation were still essential for Canada and that efforts should be made to bring the constitution into conformity with the broad principles of Confederation in order that new national purpose could be implemented. Most important, there should be federal responsibility for a basic social security for every citizen, not only because the Dominion government alone had the necessary funds but because social security was a matter of national concern. As a second broad objective, the federal authorities should undertake long-range planning to help maintain stability in the economy and provide for the proper development of natural resources.

The brief also recommended that the BNA Act should be amended to give the Dominion the necessary power to pass social legislation and that treaty-making power should be placed with Ottawa. More specifically, Scott recommended the creation of a National Welfare Code and a Department of National Welfare. Taxes should be based on wealth, not consumption, and revenues should be used more creatively as an instrument of economic and social policy. It was suggested that the national debt be reduced by a profits tax, a debt redemption levy, and the nationalization of profitable industries.[71]

When the Commission presented its report in 1940, the LSR gave the document its "qualified approval." But at the Lake Couchiching Conference in the summer of 1940, Scott repeated his earlier view that the Rowell-Sirois Commission "failed to do the job it might have done by a consideration of the whole economic structure of the nation with a view to proposing basic changes leading to a better economic and political order."[72]

EARLIER IN THE DECADE, Scott had had an opportunity to see the socialist state in action and what he saw was not entirely encouraging. In August, 1935, Scott travelled to Russia. Earlier that year he had made arrangements with a Montreal travel agent to shepherd a party of tourists through Russia in exchange for a reduced fare. Throughout the late twenties and early thirties, the Russian experiment was particularly attractive to socialist intellectuals elsewhere in the world. Socialized planning, as the reports of the Five Year Plan seemed to suggest, was working. Prominent English socialists – the Russells, the Webbs, and poets W.H. Auden, Cecil Day-Lewis, and Stephen Spender – were all keenly interested in Russia and there was a great deal of curiosity to have a first-hand look at conditions there. Scott and others kept in touch with these visitors' impressions through their travel reports in *The New Statesman and Nation* and through the Left Book Club.

Woodsworth, Gordon, and Forsey had all visited Russia before Scott. His reaction to Russia was not as enthusiastic as that of Forsey and Gordon, but neither was it as tempered as that of Woodsworth or of Edmund Wilson, the American literary and social critic whose visit to Russia overlapped with Scott's. In truth, Scott was divided in his reaction. The poet in him loved the "vision" of Russia while the intellectual balked at the reality of Russian totalitarianism. On his return, Scott reported this ambivalence in *The Canadian Forum*: "The USSR is a bible with a text for everyone. Conservatives ... find the expected backwardness and hardship, the communist enthusiast enters a thrilling world. Where lies the truth? Truth lies, I think, in the significance of things."[73]

It was this task of determining the significance of the Russian revolution that Scott, the tourist, set himself that August when he left Canada with two other Canadians, Mrs. W.B. Somerset and Miss Aileen Ross, the daughter of one of McGill's Board of Governors, and an American couple who were Seventh Day Adventists. The five members of the tour met in London, where they embarked on the Russian ship *Co-operation*, then travelled through the Baltic and disembarked at Helsinki. There they took the train to Moscow and continued on to Kharkov, Kiev, and Yalta. On the first lap of their journey to Moscow they met M. Charpentier, the first secretary of the French Embassy. Charpentier spoke Russian, and he had an ample supply of rubles, then difficult to obtain. A charming man, he soon became a part of the group.

Scott found Russia – and the Russians – highly enigmatic. "These atheists," he confided to his diary, "practising Christianity, humanely brutal, and creating freedom through their ruthless dictatorship, are certainly a challenging paradox."[74] He was satisfied that the planned economic system was working, but clearly not to the extent the West had been led to believe. It was clear, too, that the dictatorship of Russian state power cost millions of lives and involved tactics that "positively hinder" the attainment of socialism. Nonetheless, he believed Russian communism would achieve its general purpose. In particular, he found the confidence of the younger people infectious. "Just as people perish when there is no vision, so they live when there is vision. The Soviet Union has its vision. It sees a brave new world where there is no war, poverty or insecurity, and in which free and equal men and women live active and cultured lives."[75]

Scott's *Canadian Forum* report gives the substance of his intellectual impressions of Russia, but not their aesthetic import. These he reserved for the pages of his travel diary. He first glimpsed the vision of the new Russia embodied in the difference between a shabby, stooped sculptor and his art. The sculptor led Scott's group through the mean streets of Leningrad to a dark basement room that served as his studio.

In the middle of the studio, on a table, stood one of the most beautiful statues I have ever seen. Perhaps it was the unexpectedness, or the contrast between artist and creation, which accentuated the sense of beauty, but I have never been more instantly aware of that sudden exaltation which art alone can give. The figure was a life-size clay figure of a girl standing with a ski against her shoulder. She had the well-proportioned solidity of the peasant woman, standing with firm ease on the ground, but her face had that slightly upward look of fearless confidence that the revolutionary art has evolved to symbolise its new womanhood. I looked round at the sculptor again, and then I felt I understood Communism. He was the actuality of today, a creative soul embodied in an ugly frame; the clay figure was the new social order that will certainly come into being.

In the room was a sickly, tired girl. Who was she? The sculptor's wife, his model. "Of course, he explained, he had had to change her somewhat to make his clay figure; she was not very strong."[76] The reality of life in Soviet Russia was other than its vision. Scott found this apparent, too, in the obvious fear felt by the Russians he met. " 'I would not talk like that, if I were you'," warned one Russian lawyer to a carelessly chattering American tourist. Later another lawyer remarked: " 'It is all very well for you to talk about a revolution. You have not lived through one'."[77] For Scott, the negative aspects of the revolution were epitomized by the attempt to eliminate the kulaks, or prosperous peasants. Scott had talked with many Communists before, but he had never heard such cold-blooded planning. "The inhumanity of the blueprint," as he called it, must have cost Russia millions of lives. "Scratch the Communist," he aphorized, "and you find a Tartar."[78]

The group decided to take a side trip to Yalta, on the Black Sea. Charpentier hired a car and took Scott and Aileen Ross three or four thousand feet up a cliff above Yalta, to a place called Bakchiserai. There Scott looked northwest and realized one could travel for about six or seven thousand miles through Soviet Russia, right up to Siberia – a huge expanse. Then he looked northwest toward Moscow fourteen or fifteen hundred miles away and realized there were about twenty-five men sitting there who had the power to say, "We are going to make the whole of this country fit our concept of the state and of man in the state."[79]

Scott found a metaphor for this dichotomy of Communist Russia when the group went to see the Fountain of Bakchiserai. Built in the fifteenth century by a local khan after the death of a favourite princess, it consisted of a stone wall into which were built tiers of cups, almost like little breasts. From the top, half-moon shapes were cut into the stone, and water dripped in stages into cups below. Here, at Bakchiserai, was the fountain weeping perpetually; there, in the far distance, was Moscow. How could Russians bother about the individual when they were looking after one hundred and fifty million people at a time?[80] For Scott the fountain symbolized the importance of the individual – and of human love – as opposed to the tyranny of the collective. It was characteristic of him, even as a political thinker, that he needed an image – the poet's way to truth – to crystallize his thoughts.

After leaving Russia, Scott went directly to Sweden, landing in Stockholm with a letter of introduction to a prominent government official. When he discovered the man was away, he went to the office of the primary socialist newspaper, the *Social Demokraten*. Going up to the first desk, he said: "I am a social democrat from Canada." To his astonishment Scott was received as a virtual ambassador. That afternoon he was talking to a cabinet minister in the Swedish government. Later, he was taken on tours of socialized industries and co-operative housing. He returned to Canada highly enthusiastic about the co-operative movement. More importantly, he had received first-hand assurance that socialism, as implemented in Sweden, could provide the basis of a just and prosperous economy.[81]

# TEN

# *Canada*

FRANK SCOTT'S CAREER as a teacher and interpreter of law was profoundly influenced by the fact that his appointment at McGill coincided
with the onset of the depression. Following Stephen Leacock, who was
said to have quipped that he joined the Department of Economics at
McGill at the end of the century and the next year the good old Queen
died, Scott echoed that in 1928 he joined the Faculty of Law at McGill
University and in 1929 the whole economic system collapsed about him.[1]

Scott's outspoken conviction that capitalism was responsible for the
crash brought him into direct confrontation with McGill's Board of Governors. Moreover, all of those issues on which Scott held distinctly nationalist and socialist views – the necessity for economic planning on a
national scale, the repression of civil rights, and the larger constitutional
questions of Canada's internal relations between the provinces and the
federal government, and external ones with Great Britain, the Commonwealth, and the League of Nations – were to bring him into further conflict
with the Montreal Anglophone establishment.

Since the early twenties, Scott's nationalism co-existed with his internationalism. At Oxford he had written that his line of work must be
"(1) Canada, (2) the Empire, (3) the English speaking peoples and (4) the
League of Nations."[2] On his return to Canada his nationalism was strengthened by the teaching of H.A. Smith and by the Group. The Group was
not an isolated Montreal phenomenon (as Scott tended to think), but
rather part of a larger movement generated by the Canadian nationalism
of the twenties. The Group, looking at the historical ties with Britain with
a new perspective, had decided Canada should be a self-governing nation
within the world community. Once this decision had been reached, a new
view of French-Canadian nationalism began to emerge and Group members became more fully aware that in French-Canadian eyes, Canada's

continuing involvement in European wars was due to the British connection.[3] These young men, despite their service overseas (Claxton and Farthing had served in the McGill Battalion), and because of the prevailing attitudes toward Great Britain in the Anglophone community, were still not fully aware of the intransigence of French Quebecers with respect to the British connection. And this was even more true of Scott. His father's insistence on the existence of an ecumenical Catholic community – of which Anglo-Catholicism was a part – and his father's privileged and accepted position within the little world of Quebec City had tended, in the past, to insulate him. It was not until the late thirties, after repeated condemnations of the CCF by Quebec clergy and after the emergence of Adrian Arcand's fascist party, that a recognition of the implications of French-Canadian nationalism was to dawn.

Claxton and Scott, in reassessing Canada's internal affairs, were also part of a movement to reshape her external affairs. Issues dealt with in the Balfour Declaration in 1926, which had proclaimed Canada an "autonomous" member of the Commonwealth, were reflected in 1928 in Canada by the formation of the Canadian Institute of International Affairs. This Institute, started by Sir Robert Borden, soon established branches in the principal cities across Canada and, without any formal arrangement, absorbed most of the members of the older Canada League. Not surprisingly, several members of the Montreal Group, including Claxton and Scott, joined the CIIA. Scott was taken to a meeting at the house of Sir Arthur Currie, McGill's principal, by Dean Percy Corbett. It was the beginning of an involvement with the CIIA that continued for many years. For the first few years, discussions at the Institute centred primarily on the gold standard and Canada's relationships with Great Britain and the United States.[4]

In 1929, several members of the Group, including Scott, Claxton, and MacDermot, along with some Toronto-based individuals who had been members of the Canada League, had planned to collaborate on a book dealing with the political, economic, and social problems of Canada. The book was inspired by a strong nationalism. It proposed "to fill the widespread need of a general description of the distinctive Canadian character" and to put forward a consistent political theory that would be national – "neither anti-British nor anti-American." A projected chapter on the constitution, discussing the aspirations of the Fathers of Confederation and the frustration of such aims by the British Privy Council, prefigured Scott's legal scholarship in the thirties. The book also proposed an extension of Canada's responsibility in obtaining constituent powers to implement treaties, to control and develop resources and commerce, and to pass social legislation. The abolition of all appeals to the Privy Council was recommended, as well as the cutting of all purely legal ties with Britain, except the throne.[5]

Although the editors contacted a number of people, including John Bird, Percy Corbett, J.W. Dafoe, George Ferguson, Hugh Keenleyside, J.M. Macdonnell, Chester Martin, Norman Rogers, Graham Spry, and E.J. Tarr, about the possibility of collaborating in the writing of particular chapters, the book was never completed. Probably because, as Terry MacDermot speculated in a letter to Frank Underhill on September 10, 1931, the concerns to be dealt with became specific issues addressed by the League for Social Reconstruction in its series of pamphlets.[6]

At the Williamstown Conference in 1931, Scott's knowledge of international affairs had broadened when he had acted as a secretary to Percy Corbett, a specialist on American-Canadian relations, in the Round Table discussions. In preparation for his duties, Scott wrote Lester Pearson at the Department of External Affairs asking for information on "the machinery of co-operation" among members of the British Empire.[7] "The situation itself is far from clear," Pearson replied. "The fact is that the obscurity of inter-Imperial relations tends to express itself in the indefiniteness of our methods of communication."[8] Ever the punctilious civil servant, Pearson instanced such occasions and his remarks were promptly incorporated into Scott's report at Williamstown, "The Determinants of Canadian Foreign Policy." Afterward he expanded the Williamstown address into an article, "The Permanent Bases of Canadian Foreign Policy," and innocently submitted it to the prestigious American journal *Foreign Affairs*, not knowing that such articles were always solicited. The essay, however, was accepted and published in July, 1932.

In it Scott expressed pessimism about the chances of trade reciprocity with Britain, a matter scheduled for discussion at the Imperial Economic Conference to be held in July in Ottawa. Reviewing Canada's foreign policy in terms of her geographical position in North America, her membership in the League of Nations as well as in the British Commonwealth, and her economic dependence on American trade, Scott concluded, "the association of Canada with the other members of the British Commonwealth is but one aspect of her international relations, and by no means the one that is necessarily uppermost in the mind of the Canadian who faces the problems of his country and of the world."[9]

With the windfall of $118 received for his article, Scott travelled to England on the *Empress of Britain* in 1932. His primary purpose was to attend meetings of the Royal Institute of International Affairs. He also attempted, unsuccessfully, to have some of his early poetry published with Mrs. Dale's publisher, Jonathan Cape. At one of the meetings of the Royal Institute at Chatham House in London, Scott stood alone when he expressed a distinctly nationalist view on the question of tariff preferences and imperial defence. The question of currency, he observed, involved not only "the whole problem of inter-Imperial debt payments," but also the question of preferences. "It was difficult to see on what basis preference could be established until there was some form of agreed stabilisation of currency." Scott's speech continued: "Canadians looked at it from the point of view that, if they were to become an independent nation tomorrow, Great Britain would not spend any less on armaments, and they consequently did not feel it necessary to contribute any more."[10] Scott was distinctly rebuked for his stand by the chairman, Sir John Power, who hoped the other colonials would not share Scott's opinion.[11] Shortly after, however, at an Imperial Trade Conference in Canada, Prime Minister R.B. Bennett remained intransigent on the question of imperial preference.

After the enactment of the Statute of Westminster in 1931, some Canadian members of the CIIA began to feel it would be desirable to call together individuals from the various Commonwealth countries to discuss developments resulting from it and the Balfour Declaration. This conference, organized by the Royal Institute of International Affairs, was held at Hart House, Toronto, September 11-21, 1933. Forty-six delegates were at the meetings, among them the Honourable N.W. Rowell, KC, chairman; John W. Dafoe, vice-chairman; Brooke Claxton, Dean P.W. Corbett, the Honourable Vincent Massey, E.J. Tarr, and J.S. Woodsworth, MP. Scott attended as one of the thirty-five secretaries, for the most part college professors. The British delegation included the chairman, Viscount Cecil of Chelwood; a Labour representative, Philip J. Noel-Baker; and two distinguished scholars, Professor Arnold J. Toynbee and H.V. Hodson, then assistant editor of *The Round Table*. The Australian delegation was under the chairmanship of Archibald Hamilton Charteris, Professor of International Law at Sydney, and the New Zealanders under the chairmanship of the Honourable W. Dowine-Stewart.

Opinion on the Balfour Declaration, the Statute of Westminster, and the nature and role of the Commonwealth was divided. On the one hand were those, like Charteris, who held that the Commonwealth was an entity involving legal and moral obligations on the part of all constituent bodies. On the other hand were those who felt that "since every nation in the Commonwealth was not 'master of its destiny,' co-operation between

Commonwealth members was ... voluntary." The difference was not academic. The first view meant that if one Commonwealth country was at war all the others were also at war. Claxton's pragmatic summation of the conference deliberations was probably shared by most Canadian delegates: "While we had prized our loyalty to the Crown, or a common regard for British institutions and traditions ... these were unlikely to be the decisive factors in determining questions of war and peace. The policy of the Dominions, as of the United Kingdom, would ultimately be determined by the individual interests of each country."[12]

At this conference J.W. Dafoe discerned a distinctly Canadian view emerging, a view that Canada was a North American nation, that is, a country with a history of democratic institutions, situated on the North American continent, which held a unique role in the British Commonwealth of Nations. This view of Canada as an independent country was in distinct opposition to the view of Canada as a colony held by many British delegates. Dafoe, who was invited to give three lectures at Columbia University during the academic year 1933-34, published these lectures the following year as *Canada: An American Nation*. There he reiterated his arguments that Canada and the United States share a geographical isolation from Europe and a similar tradition of evolving democratic institutions.

Scott seems to have absorbed and extended Dafoe's views expressed both at the Commonwealth Conference and through the CIIA. He participated actively in debating Canadian foreign policy through the CIIA and through an associated American body, the American Institute of Pacific Relations, founded by the Council on Foreign Relations, the body that produced the journal *Foreign Affairs*. Canadians did not begin to participate in the IPR until 1929, after the formation of the CIIA, but by 1935 Scott had become a member of the CIIA national executive. He and Raleigh Parkin were among the delegates appointed to attend the 1936 Yosemite Conference sponsored by the IPR.

The Scotts and the Parkins had continued their friendship. They now shared a summer home at Lachute, Quebec, a large, rather primitive establishment built on the sand. There was a hand pump in the kitchen and it delighted Scott that great blocks of ice for the ice chest, cut from the river in winter, were stored in an old wooden shed and covered with sawdust. To get ice, from blocks weighing as much as 400 pounds, they would have to crawl into the low-roofed shed and dig down into the sawdust, heave up a block, and saw off a chunk.[13] Reporting on Lachute life to King Gordon, Scott remarked:

Lachute life continues as usual. Marian spends most of her time up in her bedroom painting the interiors of street cars. To some it might seem an odd use for a farmhouse but you know Marian. Occasionally she will break away to paint a flower, but only if it has some ungodly shape. Everyone is well, and the standard of living is constantly rising. There are now two open cess-pools instead of only one. The children's house is almost completed, and is so airtight that it is like an oven most of the day. Peter and Elizabeth [Parkins' daughter] are planning a vast marriage ceremony, in which Raleigh is to be Archbishop and I am to be best man and organist, playing the wedding march on the sweet potato. Marian is to be flower-girl "because she knows so much about flowers." It will be a positive orgy of sacrilege, as far as I can make out.[14]

After several weeks of this rustic life in midsummer 1936, the two men left their wives to contend with nature and set off for the IPR conference.

Scott and Parkin travelled to Yosemite by train and stopped to see the Grand Canyon, which Scott thought wonderful.

The biggest hole in the world, fantastic. As you walk up on the horizon you see the hills around you and then an absolute cliff just plummets. It takes strong nerves just to look down. It goes down over a mile. There are mountains down below you that are 3500 feet high that don't come up to the rim. A little tiny thread of the Colorado River running through. All the strata laid down geologically, little stone s's marked away in this great iibrary .... [The colours were] spectacular, every kind of colour, the yellows of sulphur, the reds ....[15]

Yosemite was also a beautiful valley of rounded, contoured rock quite different from the Laurentians. For two weeks the delegates had the valley practically to themselves; they slept in tents and were provided with good food at a large central eating place. Scott was aware, as the delegates discussed Pacific relations, of being "surrounded by great rounds of granite bluffs smoothed by ice," and "beautiful greenish water running down smooth stones."[16]

There were 150 delegates from eleven countries, of whom eighteen were Canadians, under the leadership of the Honourable Newton W. Rowell, recently appointed Chief Justice of Ontario. Among the other delegates were Dr. R.C. Wallace, principal of Queen's University, and Dafoe of the *Winnipeg Free Press*. Also attending for the first time was a delegate from the Soviet Union; from Britain came Lord Snell, Labour leader in the

House of Lords, and Sir Kenneth Wigram, former chief of the Indian General Staff; from France, M. Albert Sarraut, Premier of France before the Blum cabinet was formed; Dr. Hu Shih, the prominent Chinese philosopher and intellectual leader; Mr. Yoshizawa, former Japanese minister in China and later ambassador to France; and Mr. Newton D. Baker, Secretary of War under President Wilson.

The inevitable onset of the war was not formally recognized. The topics discussed included trade, defence, national policy, and areas of conflict. The general subject of the conference was the changing balance of power in the Pacific and the possibilities of peaceful adjustment. The delegates began by studying the internal, economic, and social structure of the four chief countries of the Pacific – the United States, Japan, China, and the Soviet Union – pursuing such topics as the effects of the American National Recovery Act, the reconstruction movement in China, economic developments in the Soviet Union, particularly in the Far East, and population pressure and trade expansion in Japan. This, Scott believed, proved to be the correct approach, for it showed that foreign policy was largely the result of domestic policy. In a later radio broadcast describing the conference he remarked: "It is not a mere coincidence that the three countries which are so much alike in their aggressive foreign policies – Japan, Germany and Italy – are also alike in their internal opposition to democratic ideas, whether in politics or economics."

Japan had invaded China in 1933, but the League of Nations had proved ineffective. Moreover, it also seemed apparent that the Soviet Union and Japan were bound to come into conflict, yet the majority of delegates at Yosemite agreed that the Soviet Union was pursuing a peaceful policy. "Her one great aim today is to raise her internal standard of living."[17] Japan was considered the trouble spot because of its internal needs and aggressiveness. Yet Scott greatly underestimated the extent of its militarism perhaps because, in contrast to other nations, Japan was then apparently quiescent. Mussolini had invaded Ethiopia in October, 1935, the Spanish Civil War was now raging fiercely, and Hitler, supporting Generalissimo Franco, was a frightening presence on the world stage.

In 1937 Escott Reid, secretary of the CIIA, wrote to Percy Corbett saying a "prominent member" of the Institute had suggested that the most pressing need in research at present was a book on Canada's right to neutrality in the event of a war in which Great Britain was involved. He suggested also that after Corbett had finished reading the letter he pass it along to Frank Scott for discussion. This proposal resulted in *Canada Today*, the CIIA position paper for the Sydney Conference of the Institute of International Affairs. Scott was invited to write the volume, which was to be based on reports from experts in local branches of the Institute throughout the country. In the preface he states that his aim has been to show "the various schools of opinion within the country, and particularly to show the relation between internal forces and external policy."[18]

Scott's view of Canada as a North American nation draws considerably from Dafoe's conception. The argument in *Canada Today* is directed toward the conclusion that Canada had a right to neutrality for a number of reasons: because of her geographic isolation from European areas of conflict, because of the existing rift between French and English over participation in a possible European war, because of her tradition of democratic institutions, and because of her status as an autonomous member of the British Commonwealth of Nations. *Canada Today* is an important statement about the country near the end of the decade. It acknowledges the danger of a major division in political thinking at the time and the threat of French-Canadian nationalism and expresses an opinion on Canada's autonomy. On the settlement of this division would rest Canada's future.

*Canada Today* was published in August, 1938. The following month, Scott and the other Canadian delegates of the CIIA left Vancouver to attend the Sydney Conference. The delegates left on an old tub, a World War I steamer called *Mauganui*. The trip took them to Honolulu, Fiji, New Zealand, and finally Sydney. E.J. Tarr was the chairman of the delegation and he asked Frederick Soward, the secretary, to try to arrange the shipboard tables so that members could meet each other informally. The British, not keen about this arrangement, did not always comply. Still, the delegates got to know one another fairly well through various social occasions. On the trip out, there was a fancy dress party. The five tallest Canadians, all about six feet, went as the Dionne quintuplets: each wore a diaper, a ribbon, and a quint's name written on his back with lipstick. Scott was Emilie – "the most loathsome sight I've ever seen," he later recalled.[19] But to his fellow delegate, Soward, Scott seemed free and light-hearted during these years, "quite the dashing intellectual."[20]

At Lapstone, the resort hotel at which the conference was held, the main topic was the Czech crisis. When the delegation from each country was called on to answer questions from the others the Canadians were given a tough examination, chiefly on the question of their alleged isolationism and pro-Americanism. When the British delegates' turn arrived they had added a Newfoundlander to their group who had little grasp of international politics. Clearly they hoped the other delegations would ask questions about Newfoundland so the British would not have to discuss their role in the coming world crisis. Edgar Tarr, at one point, turned to the Canadian delegation and said, "For goodness sake, somebody ask a question and break this thing up or we'll never get anything out of them." Obligingly, Percy Corbett, who had a very penetrating voice, said "Mr. Chairman, I wonder how long the British government will continue its present policy of compounding a felony?" His question blew the lid off the proceedings and the best discussion of the conference ensued. Half the British delegation were unhappy about the British position and about leaders such as Bevin and Sir Alfred Zimmern. In fact, the conference helped change the view of Philip Kerr, the Marquess of Lothian, who had favoured appeasement.[21] The New Zealanders and many of the Australians felt much as the Canadians did, that the British were deceiving themselves by thinking they would get peace. And, as Scott recalled, they all despised Chamberlain.

Not all members of the Canadian delegation shared this view. The Canadian senator in the party, William A. Griesbach, described by one of the party as "a die-hard old Tory," asked on one occasion that each of his countrymen give his view of Canada's relation to Britain. They all felt the same: the British tie must inevitably recede; Canada must establish her own position. Griesbach was horrified. Here was a nest of vipers, supposedly representing Canada. On his return to Canada he broke the in-camera tradition of the CIIA by telling *The Montreal Star* the Canadian delegates conveyed the idea that Canada would secede from Britain in the event of war. In his opinion Canada could not be neutral even if she wanted to be. *The Star* commented that such sentiments by "our 'pink professors' are nothing new": these doomsayers were like Hyde Park orators letting off "professorial pink steam." The editors tacitly supported Griesbach's view that the conference was not worth a "hill of beans."[22]

Tarr instantly responded to Griesbach's comments.[23] Several days later both Scott and Corbett also denied Griesbach's charges. But the damage had been done. One British visitor, Sir Maurice Hankey, sent memos back to the United Kingdom raising "the brutal question of whether Canada would come to our assistance in another war," a question that he resolved to his own satisfaction by discounting the influence of the " 'highbrows,' isolationists, French Canadians, Irish disloyalists ... and 'intellectuals'."[24] This incident also convinced a number of influential Montrealers that Frank Scott was a man who denigrated the British connection, a man of no credit to the Scott name. In part this was true. Scott did want to cut the ties with the British imperialism that his father had so energetically proclaimed. He did not, however, want to endanger his personal relationship with his father, his older brother William, and those Montrealers he had known for many years. Coming events were to make these links harder and harder to maintain.

THROUGHOUT THE THIRTIES when Scott was fighting for a new Canadian nationality based on political parity with Great Britain, a parallel nationalism was developing in French-speaking Quebec. It, too, was precipitated by the depression and was similarly based on a desire for equality of political status – but with English Canada. However, some Quebecers went further and were beginning to demand national sovereignty: "the creation of an independent French and Catholic republic on the banks of the St. Lawrence."[25] This patriotic movement was primarily engendered by the racial and historical theories of Abbé Lionel Groulx. It had gained impetus during World War I, particularly among those who had been conscripted to fight the "English war," but with the prosperity of the twenties it had lapsed until now.

The depression reactivated Quebec nationalism. The effects of it were severe in Quebec, partly because of the extent of industrialization in the province. And there was a feeling among the French that the blame for the depression in Quebec lay with the English industrialists. The new nationalism of the thirties sprang into prominence with a new political reform party, l'Action libérale nationale. But there were other nationalistic groups, such as Les Jeunesses patriotes, whose official organ, *L'Indépendance*, expressed the character of the movement most clearly. In March, 1936, that journal called for independence in ringing tones: "the French-Canadian people will not exist as a nation until it has freed itself from the foreign yoke."

Scott had taken measure of the province fairly early in the decade: "The Liberal government in Quebec is liberal in the sense that the National-Socialist government in Germany is socialist – that is to say, in the non-sense." So began "The Fascist Province," an article that appeared in *The Canadian Forum* under the name of J.E. Keith in April, 1934. Keith was a *nom de guerre* for Scott, who had been ordered by the McGill administration to cease bringing the name of the university into contentious issues. He wrote bitterly of the harmonious relations between the three persons of what he called "the provincial trinity": the Liberal Party, the industrialists and bankers of St. James Street, and the Roman Catholic Church. None was willing to take progressive action during the depression.

Premier Taschereau, Scott wrote, stood for private ownership of the oil industry and public utilities; he refused to bring the province under the Dominion old-age pension scheme; inadequate labour legislation on the Quebec statute books was not even properly enforced, as evidence to the Stevens committee had made clear, and the government's policies played into the hands of the Quebec industrialists whose power had been consolidated during the depression. The Montreal Light, Heat and Power Company had absorbed some twenty municipal systems; and the Beauharnois project, after the supposed 1930 investigation, had passed quietly into the hands of the Holt interests. Not one of Quebec's major financial scandals had been exposed. If the stewardship of St. James Street was ever to be called to account, Scott went on, the call would have to come from outside (and presumably from above) Quebec: "not a person here who knows the facts dare open his mouth." The outlook for remedy was dark, Scott thought, yet he recognized that "there are currents moving, bodies of criticism forming, but they have not reached the surface."

At the same time he was concerned that some of these bodies, especially Quebec nationalist youth groups, seemed to be guided by the Catholic Church, which saw the depression as a punishment from God upon greedy individuals. The youth groups, despite apparent similarities with the CCF, were potentially, if not actually, fascist. If discontent grew among the French-speaking masses, Scott expected a concerted move by those in power to deflect it into fascist channels in order to provide Quebecers with scapegoats. There was evidence of this: in the emerging fascist party of Adrien Arcand, in anti-Semitism, and in the tendency to associate financial manipulation with the English "race."

Other bodies of criticism, such as the CCF and other radical groups, were denounced more strongly by the Catholic Church than were the social injustices that produced them. But there were no French socialist leaders, Scott wrote, to

> show how public ownership is the easiest method by which the French-Canadian may regain control of the natural resources which English and American capitalists have stolen from him.... the masses are being taught that all will be well if only English capitalists are replaced or controlled by French ones, and all chain and department stores replaced by small, independent retail merchants, and all unemployed persons set to work on the abandoned farms.[26]

Scott's response embodies the double bind of the liberal in the Quebec of the thirties. He is critical of the domination and extreme views of the Roman Catholic Church, which infringe on the rights of others, yet there is no doubt he believed in freedom of religion. Moreover, if Scott was harsh in his criticism of the church, his judgement of capitalism was equally harsh. Nothing short of a dismantling of the present system would suffice. What must be kept in mind is that Scott stood outside both the predominant power structures in Quebec: the English-speaking Protestants who formed the business class and employed the predominantly French-speaking working class, and the Roman Catholic government and hierarchy with whom French-Canadian workers were aligned. What he could not perceive was that solutions to Quebec's problems proffered by English-Canadian socialists were automatically suspect. In time, Scott was seen as a threat to both Quebec groups. To some English he seemed to deny his own class and racial roots; to some Roman Catholics he was a leader of a socialist movement that took direction from Russia and the ideals of post-revolutionary France.

The Quebec leader that Scott expected was soon to emerge – but from a nationalist source. Paul Gouin had formed L'Action libérale nationale as an alliance of reformist liberals with a group of Quebec City nationalists. But in 1935, eighteen days before a provincial election, the ALN merged with the provincial Conservative Party under Maurice Duplessis to form the Union nationale. In the ensuing election Taschereau's majority was reduced to six seats. Duplessis then used the Public Accounts Committee of the legislature for a brilliant and relentless exposure of government corruption. Taschereau resigned in June, 1936; his successor, Adélard Godbout, called an election immediately, and the Union nationale won with a large majority: 76 out of 90 seats. The new party was made up of the most conservative forces in Quebec, largely Catholic, predominantly French, and supported by industrialists and by the rural vote. The new leader of Quebec was Maurice Duplessis.

Since the Dominion Parliament had repealed Section 98 of the Criminal Code in 1936, there was no longer an all-inclusive statute under which the Montreal civic authorities could ban "communistic meetings." Thus in March, 1937, the Quebec legislature adopted the Act Respecting Communist Progaganda, popularly known as the "Padlock Act," which gave the Attorney-General of Quebec the power to place a padlock on any building suspected of being used to "propagate communism or bolshevism." Neither term was defined. The owners of padlocked property had to come before the court and prove their innocence before the padlock would be removed; there was no appeal from the verdict of a single judge.

The "attack on civil liberties" was showing itself in other ways as well. A Baptist mission was forbidden to distribute Bibles and "members of the sect known as the Witnesses of Jehovah were frequently persecuted on charges of 'sedition'." What attracted the most attention, however, was the banning of public meetings by supposed "reds."[27] Efforts to test the validity of the Padlock Act failed on the ground that the Act fell within provincial legislative jurisdiction over property and civil rights.

Writing under the initial "S" in *Foreign Affairs* in April, 1938, on "Embryo Fascism in Quebec," Scott pointed out that, even though fascist political groups were most strongly supported by French-Canadian youths, and even though the National Social Christian Party, under the leadership of Adrien Arcand, was an almost complete copy of European fascism, with its swastika emblem, blue shirts, and policy of violent anti-Semitism, the term "fascist" must be applied with reservations, because Arcand's party had no great influence in the province as a whole: the legislature was composed of devout Catholics and did not contain one fascist, and the large industrial complexes were not supporting fascism. Because big business in Quebec was largely English-Canadian and American, it was frequently attacked by young French Canadians. Scott shrewdly diagnosed this kind of nationalism as, in large part, a response to the rapid urbanization of Quebec. He also posed an important question. If, as he argued, there was only a small Communist movement in Quebec against which a frightened government needed to pass undemocratic laws, and no frightened industrialists financing a local fuehrer, why then was there a marked tendency toward fascism in Quebec at that time? The answer, he suggested, was related to symptoms of wider unrest in French Canada. The coming into power of the Union nationale under Duplessis, combined with a revival of French-Canadian nationalism, suggested that a new liberal spirit in the province threatened the "totalitarian" control of the Catholic clergy. The church was sensitive to the threats and determined to yield as little as possible. In Scott's opinion it was "the effort on the part of the church to prevent the spread of anti-clericalism and anti-Catholic doctrine which accounts for many of the manifestations in Quebec that are called Fascism."[28]

Scott had just been theorizing about the power of the Catholic Church in *Foreign Affairs*, but six months later, with the visit of a delegation from Republican Spain, he saw some implications of his theory in action. The delegation, consisting of Marcelino Domingo, then Minister of Education in the Spanish government, Isabella de Palencia, the former Spanish delegate to the League of Nations and later ambassador to Sweden, and Father Luis y Sarasola, a Franciscan priest, visited Toronto, Hamilton, Ottawa, and Montreal to present the case for democracy in Spain and to raise money for the beleaguered republic. The group's visit to Canada was variously sponsored by a number of left-wing organizations – in Montreal, it was the Committee for Medical Aid to Spain, chaired by F.R. Scott.

Headlines in Montreal English-language newspapers stated that the delegates had denied belonging to either the Popular Front or the Communist Party. Yet a photograph published in the New York *Daily News* showed a party of five Spaniards – two women, smiling and elegant in their tilted hats; a young girl in a beret; and two gentlemen in dignified dark coats and homburgs – four of whom were shown with their arms upraised in the clenched-fist salute of the Communist Party. Only one, Father Sarasola, abstained.

On October 23, the delegation arrived in Montreal, where feeling ran especially high against the Spanish Republicans. The coalition that formed the government in Spain was perceived as a revolutionary, anti-clerical mob, guilty of murdering priests, disrupting the Spanish church, and seizing private property. There was a profound admiration for Generalissimo Franco, who was seen as attempting to restore law and order against atheistic communism. To be sure, a small group of liberals, socialists, and Communists in Quebec, largely English-speaking, viewed the Spanish Civil War as a struggle between democracy and fascism. Scott was one of this group. He was convinced that the war represented a struggle between a democratically elected government and the powers of privilege and repression.

For Quebec Catholics, however, the visit of the Spanish delegates was highly threatening. Not only were the Spanish Loyalists regarded as Communists, but this delegation included a Franciscan priest, which seemed to contradict the church's teaching that the Catholics of Spain stood against the Loyalist government. Archbishop Gauthier of Montreal promptly issued a warning to Montreal Catholics implying that Sarasola was an unfrocked priest. And the municipal authority quickly reinforced this ecclesiastical stand. The visit of the Spanish delegates coincided with a giant Catholic rally against communism planned for the same weekend, Sunday, October 25, celebrating the Feast of Christ the King. There was great uneasiness among civic authorities when they discovered that the Mount Royal Arena meeting of the Spanish delegates had been declared a "Communist" meeting by local fascists, French-Canadian university students, and members of patriotic organizations, all of whom planned to "wreck the affair." If put into action, these plans would undoubtedly engender reprisals from Popular Front adherents at the Catholic rally on the following Sunday.

A chief organizer of the Catholic rally was Alderman J.M. Savignac, also chairman of the City Council Executive Committee. This body was advised by its legal counsel that it had no legal basis on which to ban the meeting at the Mount Royal Arena. Indeed, Police Director Fernand Dufresne, who had been given carte blanche, stated in a newspaper interview that as two of the four delegates were accredited representatives of the Spanish government, "the Montreal police will see to it that they have full protection."[29] Scott, however, sensing trouble, phoned the chief of police on the 22nd to express his concern. To his consternation Director Dufresne replied with animosity that Montreal was a Catholic city: did Scott really know what he was doing, holding a meeting such as this?[30]

The following morning, the day the Spaniards were scheduled to speak, an unruly mob of about three hundred University of Montreal students invaded City Hall. They occupied the corridors and offices demanding that the meeting be stopped. Alderman Savignac, supported by the acting mayor, announced that Dufresne had been ordered to cancel the meeting. In making the announcement Savignac said, "We will not allow communism to take roots here."[31] Upon hearing this news Scott attempted to book the evening meeting at Victoria Hall, Westmount.

On the afternoon of the 23rd, Scott took two of the Spanish delegates (Father Sarasola had withdrawn from the group rather than cause further embarrassment) to the auditorium of the old Student Union Building at McGill on Sherbrooke Street. It was a large hall, holding about four or five hundred, with a raised stage at the front. There Scott witnessed the most moving tableau he had ever seen. Señor Domingo and Señora de Palencia stood alone on the bare stage. Domingo would speak a sentence or two quietly. Then de Palencia would translate, putting even greater emphasis on the words. Domingo spoke poetically: "It is yesterday in a struggle with tomorrow. It is the past trying to prevent the future from living. They are assassinating the soul of a people."[32] In the great hall there was absolute silence as McGill students and professors listened. Scott recalls the essence of their speech: "There was no ranting or anything – just an incredible story of the destruction of a legitimately elected government by force of arms, the invasion by Franco, followed by Nazi planes and things."[33] It was a simple story of the demolishing of a legitimately elected government by the force of arms, and by the failure of the democratic Western nations of England and France to step in. "Spain," said Señora de Palencia, "is not only fighting for her own democracy but for that of the world."[34] Her words were prophetic. The Spanish Civil War provided a testing ground for Hitler's Luftwaffe, a flexing of muscles in preparation for a yet greater world conflict.

The address at the McGill Union was all that the Montreal municipal authorities allowed. Scott's committee was informed that the alternative location, Victoria Hall, had been rented, and he was obliged to cancel the large general meeting planned for the evening of the 23rd. At the last minute, about 150 people – largely professional men with a few academics and the organizing committee – met informally at a salon in the Mount Royal Hotel. At this meeting, Dr. Norman Bethune, about to leave for Spain, said the lives of at least a thousand innocent women and children had been sacrificed by the Montreal city authorities. "This meeting was to raise money to send into Madrid vaccines and serums for use against preventable diseases ... I would never have believed that a meeting of this sort could have been stopped in Montreal.... The right of free speech had been denied us – in a free country."[35] It is hard to believe that Bethune, or Scott, did not know what might be expected in Montreal: what does seem likely is that the degree of control exercised by municipal and provincial authorities was greater than either had experienced before.

As Bethune was speaking, a large group of students was demonstrating before the Mount Royal Arena, where the original meeting had been scheduled to take place. Sent on their way by a squad of Montreal police, they paraded through the main streets of the city chanting "à bas, à bas, à bas les Communistes!" "A bas les juifs!" Hearing the rumour that the meeting was to be held in Victoria Hall, they invaded Westmount, among them a high school student named Pierre Elliott Trudeau who had been attracted by the roar of the crowd. At 9:15, after Señora de Palencia had been speaking for just a few minutes, the Mount Royal Hotel management came to say that the approaching mob made it necessary to stop the meeting. Despite indignant protests the lights were then turned off and the assembly dispersed, grumbling but quietly at the request of the chairman.

The following day Scott issued a statement on behalf of the committee, protesting that responsible citizens of Montreal had sponsored a meeting for representatives of the Spanish government, travelling on diplomatic passport, in order that the Loyalist side of the story might be told. Such meetings had already been held in Toronto, Ottawa, and Hamilton.

> They did not come as exponents of any political theory, but simply as democrats to state the case for their democratically-elected government. If it is true that such a meeting could not have been held in Montreal without rioting, then the Montreal police were justified in banning it. Canadian democracy is in a precarious condition if a sane and considered statement for a lawful government is prevented

from being given in a British country by threats of violence from irresponsible elements.[36]

There was a degree of ambivalence in Scott's response. He was indignant at this curtailment of civil liberties. Yet, also the lawyer, he acknowledged that if indeed a riot was about to take place, the municipal government had a right to invervene.

On the following day a rally of 100,000 Catholics was held in Montreal: in a newspaper photograph a sea of faces extends as far as the eye can see. Archbishop Gauthier spoke first, and then, first among the lay speakers listed, Alderman Savignac. Communism was condemned and Catholics were called to join in a crusade for its extermination. Also denounced was Canadian support of the Spanish Loyalists: "a group comprised of new barbarians who have covered the lands of Spain with desolation and blood."[37] In Quebec City Cardinal Villeneuve and Premier Duplessis addressed a crowd of twenty thousand on the same subject. After insisting that there could be no compromise "between us and Communism," the Premier stated: "The grand theories of liberty, of equality, of fraternity are of no account [ne valent rien]. Those which do count are the three theological virtues: faith, which illumines the intelligence, charity, which enriches the heart, hope, which brings comfort."[38] Duplessis was once again expressing the old objections of the Quebec clergy to the principles of the French Revolution that had vitiated the church in France. (Thus, post-revolutionary France was described in Quebec as "France athée." From this perspective, the brotherhood of man advocated by Canadian socialists could also be seen as a preliminary to atheism.)

The Spanish Civil War became a litmus test, sharply distinguishing conservatives from radicals on both sides of the Atlantic. For many younger progressives it represented a loss of innocence greater even than World War II, as it seemed to prove that a good cause – democracy in Spain – could be defeated. W.H. Auden, Stephen Spender, Robert Graves, and Beatrice and Sidney Webb all travelled to Spain. For some, especially Auden, Spender, and Graves, the Spanish reality was discovered to be much more complicated than the theoretical concept of democracy against fascism. There was merciless blood-letting on both sides. The Loyalist atrocities were directed particularly at the clergy, and thus there was basis for the charges of anti-clericalism levelled by the Quebec clergy. Yet the number of people killed by Franco and his allies was far greater. Foreign observers reacted with horror to this carnage. As Auden later remarked, " 'Just seeing what Civil War was like was a shock. Nothing good could come of it.... One asked oneself, did one want to win'?"[39]

This Scott did not know. His main sources of information about the Spanish war came from Bethune, by now an avowed Communist, and from a little booklet on the Spanish Civil War issued by the Left Book Club under the pen name "Vigilantes." He was also reading generally positive accounts of the war by the Webbs and Auden in *The New Statesman and Nation*.[40] Auden, who did not want Franco to win, did not feel free to make his severe reservations public. He had gone to Spain with the understanding he could be useful as a stretcher-bearer, but once there discovered he had been brought for propaganda purposes. Consequently he had returned to England with deeply mixed emotions that his report in *The New Statesman* attempted to censor. Shortly after, however, Auden's pessimism escaped in "Spain 1937" (1937) with its telescoping of history and its recognition that the Spanish Civil War was not so much the struggle of socialism against fascism as the struggle of humanity against itself – its own fear and greed. Auden also perceived that the war had become a juggernaut. If the struggle failed, there was little that history could do to help, for "History is only the sum of men's actions."[41]

To this view Scott took great exception. Early in the forties he wrote his own "Spain 1937," a rebuttal to Auden, which asserted his own faith that the ideals of the Spanish Loyalists continued to endure.

> For these we too are bleeding: the homes burning,
> The schools broken and ended, the vision thwarted,
> The youths, their backs to the wall, awaiting the volley,
> The child staring at a huddled form.
>
> And Guernica, more real than our daily bread....
>
> Behind the gilded cross, the swastika,
> Behind neutrality, the will to kill.   (*C.P.*, p. 96)

Behind the cross is its perversion – the swastika: the amalgamation of the Spanish clergy with Franco, all supported by the might of the Nazi bombers. Behind the facade of neutrality, the Non-Intervention Pact signed by England, Spain, Italy, and Germany, lay the will to destroy the democrats of Spain. The tragedy of the Spanish Civil War for Western liberals was that the democratic side was also the Communist side. The spectre of communism made it virtually impossible for many moderate liberals to recognize that democracy was also at stake. But for Scott, the poet Lorca, martyr for the Loyalist cause, becomes the symbol of hope and freedom.

> And Lorca, rising godlike from fascist guns.
>
> In the spring of ideas they were, the rare spring

That breaks historic winters. Street and field
Stirring with hope and green with new endeavour,
The cracking husks copious with sprouting seed.
Here was destruction before flowering,
Here freedom was cut in its first tendrils.

This issue is not ended with defeat.   (C.P., p. 96)

The visit of the Spanish Loyalists caused repercussions in Montreal. The high-handedness of the municipal authorities and the threat of mob violence in the Montreal incident led some English-speaking Quebecers to recognize that the time had come to form a civil liberties association to organize against future incidents of this kind. In Scott's mind the threat of mob violence to the Spanish delegates recalled the violence of the conscription riots in 1917. This new example of the volatile nature of French Quebec later conditioned his attitude to World War II. And the failure of the Western powers to intervene on behalf of Spain, a democratic nation, infuriated and sickened Scott. This aspect of the Spanish Civil War finally hardened his attitude to England and set him against Canada's participation in any future imperialist war.

The visit of the Spanish government representatives to McGill was a factor in the dismissal of Eustace Morgan, the new principal of McGill. While Premier Duplessis had been stating in Quebec City that liberty, equality, and fraternity were of no importance, Morgan issued a statement to a Montreal newspaper affirming the university's right to freedom of speech. "As long as I am Principal of McGill University, I shall help them [students] to the utmost of my ability to maintain that right to the search for truth."[42] Six months after the event, on May 5, the *Montreal Witness* expressed shock and dismay at the sudden end of Morgan's career in Canada. The editor offered two reasons for his resignation. The principal did not move to "padlock" radical utterances of the younger faculty and he, unlike his predecessor, Currie, had taken seriously the ideals of a university by attempting to improve standards and cut away dead wood. Both actions, speculated the editor, gave mortal offence to the businessmen who dominated McGill.

Morgan was succeeded briefly by Lewis W. Douglas, who accepted a post in the United States soon after his installation. McGill's next principal, Cyril James, was a dapper, dark-haired Englishman. Sharp-witted and conservative, James kept the university faculty under tight control by the simple expedient of making himself the bottleneck through which all university business passed. He never made a public statement without first consulting the Chancellor and Board of Governors and quickly came to enjoy the full confidence of the Montreal business establishment.[43] Not surprisingly, Scott soon began to feel that the degree of political freedom enjoyed at McGill was becoming increasingly limited.

THE PERIOD OF EUROPEAN CRISIS that began with the Spanish Civil War culminated in 1938 with the Munich Agreement: "the last victory," as the British historian H.R. Trevor-Roper remarked, "of those who, through fear of war, believed in unconditional 'appeasement'."[44] For Scott the choice now was between "old-style imperialism and new-style Canadianism."[45] Since the early thirties he had been crusading vigorously against war. In 1934 he had told a Couchiching Conference that Canada must not be dragged into yet another European war just because of her political connections, a comment that led to a stern editorial rebuke from *The Montreal Gazette*: disarmament talks had failed, Empire defences were weak; was this the time for people like Professor Scott to be telling Canadians that they should not honour their British connections?[46]

But with the Spanish Civil War Scott became convinced that the European situation was primarily the result of imperial politics. Britain, he thought, was no longer concerned with preserving democracy in Europe. What was more, he believed that the majority of Canadians agreed with him. Discussing the question "Will Canada take part in the next war?" at a supper club meeting of the Montreal Junior Board of Trade, Scott said: "If you took a straight vote in Canada as to whether we should participate in a war just because Great Britain was involved, I believe the great majority of the people would say no."[47] This view was shared by O.D. Skelton, Undersecretary of State for External Affairs. He wrote to Prime Minister King a few years later: "it is very doubtful if a majority of the people of Canada would in a free plebiscite have voted for war." Skelton's shrewd analysis of the situation was that the anti-war feeling "has not found greater expression [because] it has not found leadership, [because] the organs of opinion are in control of the old and conservative, and not least [because of] the masterly strategy of the Prime Minister."[48]

Chief among the shapers of public anti-war opinion was the CCF. And the most prominent of those committed to Canada's right to neutrality were Woodsworth, Scott, and Underhill. On March 3, 1937, Scott spoke at Strathcona Hall on "Our Position When Britain Enters War" and elaborated his position. Had the Statute of Westminster given Canada the right to neutrality? No, he concluded. The Statute conferred upon the dominions additional power to make laws on any matter they liked, but until each made use of this extra autonomy its position remained the same. If Great Britain went to war, Canada was immediately involved. Scott remarked that Mr. King and Mr. Lapointe had recently said in the House of Commons that "parliament will decide," but had neglected to say *what* it was that Canada could decide. Neutrality, he reminded the crowd, was not secession from the Commonwealth.[49] Scott felt strongly about the issue. He had written to Woodsworth that he considered the attitude of the Prime Minister, who was also acting as Defence Minister, little short of "criminal" in that he deliberately left in doubt so fundamental a question,[50] one that Scott described elsewhere as the primary constitutional question of his generation.

King's answer, although certainly deceptive, was not criminal. As the Prime Minister had remarked in 1923, even if Canada was constitutionally committed to war when any other member of the Commonwealth was at war, she would not be recognized as an active belligerent until Parliament had voted.[51] Scott knew this. What infuriated him was King's deliberate deception. The Prime Minister meant to mislead Canadians into believing war was not at hand while, in fact, the cabinet and Canadian industry were gearing up for it.

There are two issues here. The first was whether Canada should remain isolated from the European conflict or engage in defence spending in preparation for the inevitable war. The second was Canada's right, in terms of constitutional law, to decide whether or not to go to war. It is clear that the Prime Minister had decided it was now too late to sort out the constitutional question. Complete non-preparedness would alienate many English Canadians just as overt preparedness would antagonize Quebec. Then, too, as England's experience was soon to show, lack of preparation might well precipitate a future disaster. In such a case, there would be no choice but isolation. But isolation, or even neutrality, could not be squared with the moral problems raised by a Hitler dominant in Europe. Up to this period, many Liberals, including Lester Pearson, Jack Pickersgill, Hugh Keenleyside, and especially O.D. Skelton, would have shared many of Scott's assumptions about the desirability of Canada remaining neutral. But after Munich they could no longer entertain such views. And Scott, who saw very well that Mackenzie King was determined to remain in power, did not credit him with the desire to preserve a united Canada. In the poem "W.L.M.K.," written after King's death in 1950, he wrote:

We had no shape
Because he never took sides,

And no sides
Because he never allowed them to take shape.

He skilfully avoided what was wrong
Without saying what was right,
And never let his on the one hand
Know what his on the other hand was doing.

The height of his ambition
Was to pile a Parliamentary Committee on a Royal Commission,
To have "conscription if necessary
But not necessarily conscription,"
To let Parliament decide –
Later.

Postpone, postpone, abstain.   (*C.P.*, p. 78)

As a Quebecer, a constitutional lawyer, a socialist, and a nationalist, Scott was staunchly opposed to Mackenzie King's manoeuvrings. It was apparent that there would be a war and that a colonial Canada, again subordinate, would be treated as cannon fodder. The heart of the matter was the injustice of the coming war. But then, could war ever be seen as just? Like Woodsworth, Scott now had a strong strain of pacifism in his character, in direct contrast to his early militarism. This anti-war feeling, fuelled by the revisionist accounts of war he had absorbed in the twenties, also may have contained subconscious anger: anger that he had been fooled in 1916, that the "noble cause" for which Harry had given his life was the foolishly mistaken charge of the Somme. He was also angered by the reports of war profiteering, especially the selling of Canadian nickel, indispensable in the manufacture of armaments, to belligerents like Japan in the late twenties and early thirties, and to Japan and Germany even up to 1939. This anger generated "Lest We Forget," where Scott had satirically foreseen that many "a brave Canadian youth" would die with his body full of Canadian ores sold to Germany and Japan. In the late twenties, in the early thirties, and even at so late a date as the spring session of Parliament in 1939, only J.S. Woodsworth spoke for the conscience of the nation. " 'Is this to go on'?" he demanded. " 'Are profits to continue being made from shipments to possible future enemies? Why not stop the shipments now? For the life of me I cannot see why any private manufacturer should be allowed to make any profit out of war munitions'."[52]

As a Quebecer, Scott had strong memories of the conscription riots of 1917, of the violence present then and bursting out again at the visit of the Spanish government delegates. With another war might come another conscription crisis that would surely split the country along ethnic lines. And what for? Britain had failed to support the League of Nations and sold out democracy in Spain and Czechoslovakia. Why should Canada, from her position of relative isolation in North America, imperil her own emerging national unity for the sake of a European war that would not directly affect her and, indeed, need not have occurred? Finally, as a constitutional lawyer, Scott resented the fact that Canada was being led into a war that she had not agreed to and might have avoided altogether by a policy of neutrality.

Actually, King and Scott shared the same priority – staving off involvement in the war to preserve a united Canada. Where they differed was in how to achieve this objective. King endorsed Chamberlain's appeasement to stay out of war; Scott endorsed Canada's right to neutrality for the same reason. King's policy to "never let his on the one hand / Know what his on the other hand was doing," a policy so accurately diagnosed by Scott, was, in large part, as Frank Underhill later recognized, his strategy to keep the English and French in Canada marching together without the rift of open disagreement. Such a policy Scott could not accept.

At issue was a question of style – perhaps ultimately the difference between theoretical and applied politics in a Canadian context. King's route was the middle way; his tools were obfuscation, persiflage, and behind-the-scenes negotiations that traded concession for limited agreement. Scott was committed to the open forum, the frank discussion of issues and recognition of differences that led to the discovery of shared truth and joint action. That Mackenzie King's middle way accommodated both extremes without excessively agitating either; that his own idea of an open forum required a relatively sophisticated electorate; that recognized differences might prove volatile capital in the hands of one's political opponents – these ideas would not have occurred to Scott. King, however, had taken to heart the failures of Laurier. His political strategy combined expediency with the preserving of a united Canada.

Fiercely responding to what appeared to be King's policy – equivocation indicating no policy – Scott was soon engaged in a public debate on defence spending before a largely imperialist audience at the Young Men's Canadian Club in Montreal. His opponent, R.L. Calder, KC, a prominent Montreal lawyer and CCFer, but an exponent of Empire solidarity, saw defence spending as a buffer; he feared isolation would put Canada in the hands of the United States. Scott opposed defence spending and argued for isolation. He pointed out that there was little danger of invasion from the Pacific or from Europe. Besides, the Monroe Doctrine guaranteed that the power of the United States would protect Canada.[53]

The debate on Canada's right to neutrality raged throughout 1937. In June, Scott reiterated his arguments in an article entitled "Canada and the Outbreak of War" in *The Canadian Forum*. At a dinner at the Ritz-Carlton in Montreal on October 10, celebrating the achievements of the CIIA over the last ten years, Governor General Lord Tweedsmuir entered the fray by agreeing to make a real speech, something that was more than the usual "Governor-Generalities," as he called them. Public response was instant and indignant when he had the temerity to remark that Canada was a sovereign nation and should not docilely take her attitude to the world from Britain or the United States: "A Canadian's first loyalty is not to the British Commonwealth of Nations, but to Canada and to Canada's King, and those who deny this are doing, to my mind, a great disservice to the Commonwealth."[54]

The difficulties of reaching a common policy acceptable to both French and English in Canada were becoming increasingly apparent. While Senator Griesbach had been reminding English Canadians of their duties and loyalties to Great Britain in the event of war, Maurice Duplessis had been reminding French Canadians of their Quebec heritage and the necessity of keeping out of future imperialist wars. While Scott was in Australia attempting to determine Chamberlain's intentions from the British delegates at the Commonwealth Conference, Chamberlain was negotiating the Munich settlement. After Munich, on September 30, Prime Minister King wrote to Chamberlain, the "great conciliator," thanking him for bringing peace: "on the very brink of chaos, with passions flaming and armies marching, the voice of reason has found a way out of the conflict which no people in their heart desired but none seemed able to avert."[55]

Scott, however, held quite different opinions about Chamberlain's conciliation. "Where Do We Go from Here?" he demanded in an article for *The Winnipeg Tribune*. Before Munich it was possible to argue that the Chamberlain government was ultimately working for collective security and the support of democracy in Europe. Now, neither of these arguments held. "Sacrificing European democracy is a price Mr. Chamberlain will pay for peace," Scott declared. Therefore, all Canadians who wished to fight for other than racial reasons must decide whether they now wanted to support England for imperialist reasons. If not, they must turn isolationist. "Canadian foreign policy becomes much simpler since Munich. Now it is a straight choice between old-style imperialism and new-style Canadianism based on Canada's interest as an American nation." Although the Prime Minister's verbal policy had been one of "no commitments," his real policy was the opposite, one of old-style imperialism. He had not obtained for Canada the right of neutrality; he left the naval bases of Halifax and Esquimalt to the British Admiralty and he continued to make preparations for war. Why should an unthinking patriotism to Britain be considered more loyal than loyalty to Canada? A new and genuine sense of Canadian nationality was growing throughout the country, especially in the West. "After Munich, English Canada is going to become more Canadian. Then perhaps it will understand French Canada and we shall have a real country."[56]

In January, 1939, in an article entitled "A Policy of Neutrality for Canada" published in *Foreign Affairs*, Scott reviewed the diplomatic revolution of the 1930s that had led Canadians increasingly to turn away from participation in European wars. Canadians with "more loyalty to Britain than to democracy," he argued, "helped to subjugate the Boers in 1899; hence they accepted the automatic belligerency imposed upon them in 1914 without a murmur. Even the growth of 'Dominion Status' in the 1920s did not make them reconsider their European commitments, for then the League of Nations was in existence." When, however, the League proved unwilling or unable to prevent the old power methods of settling disputes, little remained but racial sentiment or self-interest. Canada, which at least had a voice in the old League, now had no voice in British policy. As a result, the contemporary imperialist in Canada found that his policy met opposition from two sources: "from all those who want a permanent withdrawal from European commitments, and from the self-respecting Canadian nationalists who want Canada first of all to have complete control over the major issues of peace and war, whatever path she may choose to follow in the future."[57]

The feeling of dissociation from Great Britain, Scott claimed, was fuelled not only by a Canadian patriotism but also by the fact that at least half of the Canadian population had no racial ties to Great Britain, giving Canada serious concern about the problems of maintaining national unity:

> If an idea is to be found great enough to evoke a common loyalty amongst all races in Canada and to overcome their differences sufficiently to make stable political union possible, it can only be found in *the idea of Canada, the nation. The building of an orderly and just society within this vast territory*, the elimination of poverty and insecurity through a wise utilization of natural resources, the development of arts and sciences, of political liberty and spiritual freedom

– all of this while maintaining a fair balance between the claims of racial and religious minorities – that is a task ... that can hardly be achieved, however, except at the expense of the old imperialist foreign policy.[58]

Since the spring of 1939 Scott had been considering the idea of a "just society" and meeting with a group of French-Canadian nationalists and left-wingers to discuss Canadian foreign policy. All were opposed to the coming war. The group consisted of François-Albert Angers, a professor at the Ecole des hautes études commerciales and head of the St. Jean Baptiste Society; André Laurendeau, editor of *L'Action nationale*; Gérard Filion of the Union des cultivateurs catholiques; Dr. Georges E. Cartier, who became a stalwart of Bloc populaire; Madeleine Parent, a student at McGill and a former LSR secretary who soon became a Marxist trade union militant; Neil Morrison and Alec Grant from the Student Christian Movement; and George Laxton from the Fellowship for a Christian Order. In all, this group met six times to try to find a common ground. They worked on a document entitled "Toward a Canadian Foreign Policy in the Event of War / Pour une politique canadienne en cas de guerre prochaine," which was to be submitted to the federal government as "the only one acceptable to all those who have the peace and prosperity of the country at heart."[59] The French version was completed on June 2, 1939, and Scott was to translate it. As Michael Oliver later remarked, a preamble that recognized Canada as one country made up of two official groups was an achievement in itself.[60] It concluded with a statement against conscription and against the raising of contingents to fight outside Canada, but it agreed that those, who might wish to, be allowed to leave Canada to enlist with Britain. It also suggested an embargo on exports to nations attacking Britain but stated that there should be no financial support of Britain by Canada.[61] However, the document was never sent to the government or published. The group issued a statement in the fall of 1939, but was overtaken by events on the world stage.

Scott, like many other Canadians, felt a sense of impending chaos during that pre-war summer of 1939. Chamberlain's attempts at appeasement continued into the spring of that year, but in March, when Hitler invaded Czechoslovakia, neither Britain nor France could any longer delude themselves that Nazism could be contained. During the next few months, Britain began to rearm and Canada agreed to provide assistance. Britain also guaranteed to support Poland, Rumania, and Greece in the event of German aggression. During the summer, while the Western powers were bargaining with Russia for support, Stalin entered into secret negotiations with Hitler and in August, 1939, Russia and Germany signed a non-aggression pact. This was a great blow to those left-wingers everywhere who idealized the Russian experiment. It was a grim summer, the end of a long decade of greed, broken agreements, and double-dealing. On September 1, 1939, Poland was invaded by Germany. World War II had begun.

On the weekend of September 2, 1939, a meeting, which included members from the French Canadian Group, was hastily called by Alan Plaunt and Scott to discuss war policy. Held at Scott's home on Summit Circle, the meeting included George Ferguson, David Lewis, Arthur Lower, R.O. MacFarlane, Georges Pelletier (the assistant editor of Le Devoir), Alan Plaunt, Ken Taylor, and Frank Underhill. As Lower recalled, the group was sitting in Scott's living room on the Sunday morning, wondering if there was anything immediately useful they could do about the emergency – listening anxiously, as Lower wrote, with one ear to the radio and another to the discussion. Scott dropped a remark on modern art: " 'A picture of a dead donkey on top of a piano, or some such combination,' he said, 'there you have the confusion, the anarchy, the lack of reason in our modern life.' Just about that moment the radio brought in the voice of a popular preacher who pictured Christ marching down the street in uniform along with the enlisting men. Someone turned [the radio] off in disgust." During the ensuing discussion several expressed the fear that this new war would split Canada along French and English lines. In the middle of the conference a call from Ottawa came for Taylor, asking him to become Deputy Minister of Finance.[62] He came back and told the assembled group about the request, but expressed uncertainty about what to do. They urged him to accept. If war was inevitable, it had "better have some good people" in key positions in it.[63] (Ironically, the war accomplished what Scott and his fellow socialists had long desired – greater control by the federal government of the economy. The Wartime Prices and Trade Board administered by the Department of Finance was to become one of the biggest planning instruments ever established by the government.)

During the following week Scott went to Ottawa for meetings called by the CCF National Council to hammer out an official party policy on the war to be presented in the special session of Parliament called by the Prime Minister for September 8. Scott went to the meetings a convinced pacifist and isolationist. The initial meeting was held on September 6 in the cafeteria on the fifth floor of the Centre Block of Parliament. M.J. Coldwell, the national chairman, presided. Woodsworth sat on his right and David Lewis, the national secretary, on the left. In all there were twenty-eight people in attendance, including Underhill, Forsey, and Angus MacInnis. There were also MPs and party members from across Canada, including provincial presidents such as George Williams from Saskatch-ewan and visitors such as Mrs. Woodsworth, Agnes Macphail, and Geof-frey Andrew, then a teacher at Upper Canada College.

The first day was spent in debate on the nature of the war. Was this a war to save democracy or an imperialist war? What were Canada's best interests in relation to its own political situation and what was the proper official attitude of the CCF? Woodsworth began the discussion by pointing out that he had opposed the last war and conscription, and that he opposed this war. As a socialist he felt that the war was the inevitable outcome of capitalism; as a Christian he felt that war must be opposed. It was essential that Canadians build up their own culture in Canada. He added that he felt so strongly on the matter that if his opinions were not those of the CCF he would have to cease to be a spokesman for the party in the House of Commons.

At mid-morning Scott presented his views. In many respects they were similar to Woodsworth's. Speaking from the heart, and using no notes, he expressed his belief that this was an imperialist war. He also spoke as a Quebecer, forcefully arguing that the war threatened Canadian unity and the position of the CCF in Quebec. Scott's speech seems to have been pivotal, as some speakers who followed, including Underhill, Andrew, and J.C. Arrowsmith, began by agreeing with his position. However, the majority urged full or partial participation in the war. Williams argued, and Abraham Heaps supported him, that the failure of the Allies and the victory of Germany and Italy, backed by Russia, would destroy democratic government in Canada. Others, such as Andrew and MacInnis, who had experienced Nazism at first hand, pointed out the dangers of Hitler's racial policies. This was indeed a war for democracy. As the debate proceeded, it was clear that schism threatened to divide the party.

Angus MacInnis most clearly articulated the dilemma facing the CCF. Party considerations would have to be overruled by the larger issue of world democracy. There were three possibilities open to the party. One would be total opposition to the war, but this would mean that the CCF would not be able to raise its head after the war. A second possibility would be full co-operation, but MacInnis also opposed this action. How-ever, there was a third option. Because of Canada's automatic engagement in the war, the CCF should attempt to develop a position between extremes. Before sitting down, MacInnis remarked: "Scott's position is false: he wants the Allies to win and yet he will not help them." This statement was copied in a careful hand by Scott himself. He had recorded the opinions of all the delegates and he did not eliminate MacInnis's severe judgement of his own position.[64]

Yet, after the meetings were over, Angus MacInnis said to Scott: "Frank, you held the party together. You avoided a split,"[65] an opinion confirmed by David Lewis.[66] What MacInnis seems to have meant was that Scott, a member of the committee elected to draft an official CCF policy, had accepted some of the arguments put forward by the supporters of the war and swung his influence in their direction. He had taken a new tack during the discussion. Accepting the fact that Canada would have to go to war, he decided against a position of isolationism. The committee appointed also included MacInnis, Lewis, Williams, Bert Gargrave, and Ingi Borgford, the last two the British Columbia and Nova Scotia provincial secretaries respectively. The compromise statement they worked out contained an analysis of the events that led to the war and a "condemnation of the fact that Canada had been 'committed to a war policy' before Parliament ... met." It acknowledged that the war was a "struggle which may involve the survival of democratic institutions," and expressed the belief that "Canada's policy should be based first on the fundamental national interests of the Canadian people, as well as on their interest in the outcome of war." In essence, it stated that "Canada should be prepared to defend [its] own shores, but [that] assistance overseas should be limited to economic aid and must not include conscription of manpower or the sending of any expeditionary force." The statement was presented to the meeting and adopted in a vote of fifteen to seven.[67]

After the vote was taken, Kenneth McNaught reports that Woodsworth rose and said, "You all know, as I know, what this must mean ..." and placed his resignation from the office and the party before the meeting.[68] As none of the delegates could accept his resignation, he was persuaded to let the question wait until the next morning. Scott had championed Woodsworth's right to make an individual statement – "wasn't the party big enough to have a true pacifist inside of it because everything else about it he [Woodsworth] liked" – an argument that also helped move the party to a more humane compromise.[69] It was agreed that Woodsworth would be the first speaker from the CCF in Parliament and would present his position; Coldwell would follow and present the party's official policy. For Woodsworth these few days marked the end of his career as leader of the party he had brought into being.

Scott continued to be one of the most vocal critics of the war and the way in which it was fought. On January 5, 1940, after the dispatch of the

First Canadian Expeditionary Force to England, he wrote a personal letter to the Prime Minister, one which, as J.L. Granatstein observes, must have caused some "uncomfortable squirming" in Ottawa.[70] In it he pointed out that the practice of the Liberal government so far in this war was quite at variance with King's previously declared policy. King had stated in 1937 that only Parliament would decide on the extent to which Canada would participate in the war. Yet, King's cabinet had taken so many steps to place Canada in a state of active belligerency before Parliament met on September 7, 1939, that he had greatly limited parliamentary freedom of action to decide what course to follow. Scott wrote:

> Your government has already established two most dangerous precedents in this war, which go far to undo the theory of Dominion autonomy which has been built up over the past twenty years. The first is that, so soon as Great Britain declares war, Canada must be placed on a belligerent footing before Parliament meets. The second is that the Canadian Cabinet is competent to decide, without Parliamentary discussion, whether Canadian soldiers shall be sent to die in Europe. Both these precedents suggest that Canada still occupies a completely colonial position....
>
> The second point I wish to urge upon you is this: Canada's participation in this war must be strictly limited if we are to emerge as a nation. The two conditions of our survival are that we should not become so involved militarily as to make conscription necessary to maintain the overseas forces, and that we should not sink so far into debt as to endanger our self-government through national insolvency. We cannot be destroyed by military defeat in this war, for no enemy will be able to cross the Atlantic to attack us; but we can be destroyed by internal stresses and strains. Our greatest enemy is therefore not Hitlerism, evil though that system is, but participation "to the last man and the last dollar."[71]

A reply carefully justifying the Prime Minister was prepared by J.W. Pickersgill, but the letter was never sent. King doubted the wisdom of attempting any correspondence "on a matter which has been raised for purposes of controversy, and is certain to lead to such." He could not imagine Mr. Chamberlain replying in detail to letters critical of his government's policy. Perhaps Mr. Pickersgill would show the letter to Dr. Skelton for his opinion?[72] Skelton agreed with King. He found, however, that Mr. Scott's points "are not easy to answer."[73]

# ELEVEN

# Who Hears a Shot?

IN FEBRUARY AND EARLY MARCH, 1940, Scott had taken a respite from active politics to help adjudicate a dispute between the Dominion Coal Company of Nova Scotia and employees who were members of District 26, the United Mine Workers of America. Scott's name, now well known within CCF and labour circles, had been put forward by the miners. Other members of the commission were R.R. Stewart, H.J. Kelley, vice-president of Dosco and mine manager, Mr. Justice C.F. McTague, P. Belle, Arthur Cross, D.W. Morrison, A. McKay, and Silby Barrett. He remembered that his father, who had gone to Nova Scotia to help the miners at the time of the Besco strike in the mid-twenties, had said that Dominion #2 was the worst of all the mines. When Scott informed the other commissioners of this they all asked to go down Dominion #2.

The mine was at least a mile underground. To get there the commissioners were equipped with helmets and taken underground by elevator. There they were told to lie prone on a flat car that trundled through about three miles of tunnels. They felt they were near to the centre of the earth. There the temperature was eighty-five degrees and the air full of flies clustering around the ponies used for hauling carts. Water splashed across the runways for the carts. Scott, stooping as he walked through the tunnels, recalled that every now and then a miner, black-faced and sweating, would come forward to wave them on saying, "Step this way, Professor!"[1]

The commission was able to recommend some relief for the mine workers but the experience had greater relevance to Scott's poetry than to his politics. He found the experience of visiting the mine profoundly moving. The idea of the "cutting edge" particularly intrigued him. He learned that "rock under great pressure bends; it doesn't just break and fall down – it just slowly bends." As the miners cut into another seam they continually had to support the walls of the mine with pit props. Scott recalled they worked in a kind of v-shaped wedge to remove the coal. Eventually, the pit props, too, were crushed into the earth after the seam of coal was pulled out.

For Scott the technique of cutting into the new seam of coal became a metaphor for the role of the avant-garde in life as in art. "You've got to keep cutting into the new," he was later to say, "otherwise you get crushed down and become stone – fossilized!"[2] It was an appropriate image for the forties. Throughout this decade Scott was forced again and again to bend under pressure. Each time he learned to cut into the new, trusting in that impulse that guides man, often without his full recognition, toward the "cutting edge." Much later he summarized this turbulent decade in a poem of homage, "A l'Ange Avant-Gardien" – to the spirit or angel of the avant-garde.

> We must leave the hand rails and the Ariadne-threads,
> The psychiatrists and all the apron strings
> And take a whole new country for our own.
>
> Of course we are neurotic; we are everything.
> Guilt is the backstage of our innocent play.
> To us normal and abnormal are two sides of a road.
>
> We shall not fare too well on this journey.
> Our food and shelter are not easy to find
> In the *salons des refusés*, the little mags of our friends.
>
> But it is you, rebellious angel, you we trust.
> Astride the cultures, feet planted in heaven and hell,
> You guard the making, never what's made and paid.   (*C.P.*, p. 132)

IN APRIL, 1940, the "phoney war" suddenly turned into a real war. Germany invaded Norway in the early spring; by summer the whole of Europe was threatened. Scott, who had been planning to leave Canada for Harvard under a Guggenheim Fellowship, now hesitated when, in the first week of July, Hitler began to bomb Britain. On July 15 he wrote to Dr. O.D. Skelton, Undersecretary of State for External Affairs, explaining that he would be happy to remain in Canada if there was any work in External he could do. He received no reply. J.W. Pickersgill, then in External Affairs, later speculated that King had been overwhelmed with volunteers at the time and that Scott's offer might have been overlooked.[3] Judging from the reception of Scott's earlier letter to External Affairs about the way the war was being fought, however, it is quite probable that Mackenzie King had decided to ignore the request. As Scott whimsically recalled, "answer came there none ... for he'd eaten every one."[4] Like the walrus and the carpenter in Lewis Carroll's doggerel, the Prime Minister had already gobbled up most of the opposition. Why bring to Ottawa yet another troublesome academic who would then be in a position to create more difficulty?

In late August, as the Scotts prepared to leave Montreal for Harvard, Scott felt reluctant to go. He remembered the opprobrium Mackenzie King had suffered by leaving the country during World War I to work for the Rockefellers. He considered his own situation respecting the Guggenheim not too different except that his proposed research, a book on the BNA Act, was highly relevant to the Canadian situation. Despite these reservations, however, by early September the family was settling in at Cambridge, determined to make the best use of their time in the United States. Scott intended to synthesize a collection of materials on the constitution he had gathered while preparing various articles during the thirties; Marian looked forward to visiting the art galleries of Boston and environs; and Peter, now eleven, was enrolled in a progressive private school.

Scott was greeted by his American colleagues with considerable kindness. He was provided with a room in the law library where he could keep his work and his books; and he was elected a member of the Senior Common Room at Eliot House. As a result, he had quite a different status from that of an ordinary visitor and moved freely among the faculty. Harvard was a strong centre for Wendell Wilkie, then running against Roosevelt for the U.S. presidency. But Scott noted among his colleagues "a quiet certainty" that Roosevelt would win. He was pleased to see much more "outspoken partisanship" among the Harvard professors than at McGill or Toronto.[5] Although a majority of the Harvard faculty approved the nation's official policy of isolationism, there was also a strong interventionist lobby. Prominent among the lobbying group was William Yandell Elliott, a professor of government and the unofficial adviser to the Militant Aid to Britain Committee formed by law students. Elliott and Scott had literary interests in common. Elliott had been a member of the southern "Fugitives" group of poets and, as a Rhodes Scholar at Oxford, he had been part of a circle that included Edmund Blunden, Robert Graves, and Richard Hughes. But as a political scientist and government adviser, he had strong opinions regarding the necessity of American intervention.

At dinner one evening at Elliott's house, Scott enraged his host by telling him bluntly that he thought the United States should remain isolationist.[6]

Despite this belligerent defence of American isolationism Scott seriously doubted North Americans could stay out of the war. The conflict in Europe had drastically accelerated over the summer; with the fall of the Maginot Line a bulwark of Western defence had crumbled; and now, in September, the bombing of Britain was accelerating daily.

At first, with the flurry of meeting new people and getting established at Harvard, Scott had little time to think about the war. On September 20, 1940, he began his work on the BNA Act by jotting a few paragraphs in his notebook:

> Critical dates in Canadian history are 1663, 1763, 1774, 1791, 1840, 1867, 1931. At each of these periods a change was made in the governmental structure, to give effect to some new purpose or plan for the Canadian people. Legal changes were, as always, a means to an end.
>
> What were the underlying purposes producing each constitutional form? Who defined these purposes – who selected them and rejected others?
>
> To spread Catholicism and French culture, to spread Anglo-Saxon power and trade, were two non-Canadian concepts. Has the Canadian amalgam a purpose for itself? Above all, has it a democratic purpose?[7]

Any consideration of Canada's constitution, or so it seemed, also involved the question of democratic purpose. It became clear that he would have to define more exactly what democracy meant.

Attending a faculty tea party at Harvard in the fall of 1940, Scott's mind revolved on the differences in the forms of democratic government that distinguished the former American colonies, the Boston of the famous tea party of 1774, from the Cambridge of 1940. As his satiric eye roamed about the room he observed "the Harvard pundit's tea" served amid the comfort of "ample female forms":

> While D.A.R.'s and Ph.D.'s
> And "How-d'ye-do's" and "Is-that-so's"
> Are wafted on a scented breeze
> That piles the orchid on the rose.
>
> The English butler scarce is heard
> Purveying the historic drink.

His servile mien, without a word,
Provides the true historic link

With colony and ruling class,
Commons by royalty dissolved,
Declared dependence of the mass
And revolution unrevolved.

O serve me, Butler, mild and meek,
Your gentle tea so piping hot.
No rebel here shall dare to speak,
And round this world, who hears a shot?     (*C.P.*, p. 98)

The last line of Scott's "Boston Tea Party 1940" echoes Emerson's "Concord Hymn" with its reference to the American Revolution and "the embattled farmers" who "fired the shot heard round the world."[8] But Scott's poem is satirically ambiguous. He relishes the historic reversal of status that has led the British butler to serve the new American aristocracy. The United States, unlike Canada, has achieved its revolution. No longer a colony dependent on the whims of the mother country, it is by now the dominating power. The key words in the poem are *dependence* and *revolution unrevolved*. The reader expects the two opposites of each term yet Scott is asserting that the wheel did not revolve fully for the American "masses" (nor, one suspects, did it revolve any more fully in Canada; Harvard faculty teas were duplicated at McGill). Indeed, he sees the United States suffering from that same hardening of the revolutionary arteries that had once affected Britain. "No rebel here shall dare to speak, / And round this world, who hears a shot?"

Scott may have been attempting to deceive himself about the power of the individual. Certainly, in the fall of 1940 shots were echoing around the world. Each day the newspapers, radio, and newsreels brought new accounts of the bombing of Britain by the Luftwaffe. On September 7 the first bombing of London completely immobilized the city: the dock area on either side of the Thames was gutted and a conflagration followed. The words of Air Marshal Goering addressing the German nation reverberated throughout the Western world. "This is the historic hour when for the first time our air force delivered its thrust right into the enemy's heart."[9] With the start of the Battle of London, the so-called phoney war began to look like a war for survival. And it was not only a battle for England's survival but for Western democracy.

The bombing of London persisted night after night until November 3. As each new day brought worse news, Scott became more and more agitated. The external conflict generated an internal one, reflected in the poem "Conflict":

> When I see the falling bombs
> Then I see defended homes.
> Men above and men below
> Die to save the good they know.
>
> Through the wrong the bullets prove
> Shows the bravery of love.
> Pro and con have single stem
> Half a truth dividing them.   (*C.P.*, p. 97)

The metre, parallelling the traditional hymn stanza, suggests Scott's early training. The moral question that had followed World War 1 – "to the Christian how can war ever be just?" – was resurfacing with all the old anguish. All that war could ever prove, or so his experience told him, was "the bravery of love" and the sacrifice of young men like his brother Harry.

With those feelings against war came a resurgence of his emotional attachment to Great Britain. After the fire-bomb attacks began Scott worried that England would fall. The murderous Nazi bombers had blitzed Spain and destroyed democracy there. Could England hope to stand? He began to have nightmares and recurrent "strange seizures" during the day "in which a dream of the previous night comes suddenly to life along with an intense sensation."[10] Outwardly he gave little sign of this turbulence. To the young Douglas Le Pan, also ex-Oxford and at that time an instructor at Harvard, Scott was witty and articulate, a stimulating companion in discussions of poetry and the fine arts.[11] Socially and in the university context, he appeared actively engaged in his studies of the constitution; inwardly, however, Scott began to fear that he was on the verge of a nervous breakdown.[12]

The head was in conflict with the heart. Intellectually he had been fighting British imperialism throughout the thirties. Britain had, he felt, let the world down. She had become almost an ally of the fascists in Spain. She had killed the League of Nations. She had made pacts with Hitler; one of the pacts had given away democratic Czechoslovakia. Yet despite all Scott's objections to Britain's international policies there persisted his strong love of the country forged in the twenties. It was precisely because he idealized British traditions and statesmanship that he found Chamber-lain's appeasement cowardly. Scott habitually thought in terms of abso-lutes, of blacks and whites. He had reached his decision on Canada's right to neutrality – and thus her right to stay out of the war – on an intellectual basis that had ignored this emotional component. But now Hitler's bombs were destroying the England he loved. They were falling on St. Paul's Cathedral, they were threatening Westminster Abbey. This was *his* Eng-land, that green and pleasant land – "just the way I imagined it" – of his Oxford idyll.

What was worse, he recognized that he had been guilty of intellectual arrogance: "My nearly total isolation was based on a false assumption that this was another war like the Kaiser's war."[13] He had considered the war a squabble among a number of European nations. But he now realized it involved a much broader issue, threatening democracy and the breakup of the civilized world itself. If England fell, the whole world might become the vassal of a totalitarian state. The collapse of the Maginot Line and the inexorable spread of Hitler's panzers across the whole of Europe threatened a new "Armageddon":

> Suddenly the last boundary broke
> And every land was used by somebody else.
> The closed world swarmed with a throng of roads
> Where caterpillars span a thread of our blood
> And sewed our flags into the history-quilt.    (*C.P.*, p. 102)

Scott had gone to Harvard to write a book on the British North America Act but when the bombing started, he recalled, "I said to myself, there won't be a BNA Act when we are through with this! What am I doing, pottering around here?"[14]

His anxiety began to lift on November 3, the eve of the American national election, and also, perhaps not coincidentally, the first night since September 7 that London was not bombed. On this day he achieved a degree of emotional peace. On the grand piano in the house they rented he played a Mozart sonata better, he thought, than he had ever played in his life. He read Rilke's *Duino Elegies* (1930, 1939) in the translation by J.B. Leishman and Stephen Spender. The preface describes Rilke's anguish during the terrible war years of 1914-18 and his discovery of grace through poetry: "Who, if I cried, would hear me among the angelic orders?"[15] Rilke's dark angels owe little to Christianity, yet they speak of the inner voice for which Scott had been waiting. And they may well have resonated with childhood memories. "Frank, you've a guardian angel looking after you,"[16] his father used to say, sometimes jokingly, as the family passed the small village of L'Ange Guardien on their way to summer camp at Cap à l'Aigle.

That night Scott listened to a spectacular radio program in support of President Roosevelt. On the basis of his advocacy of democracy and human rights, many top stars of American stage and screen spoke eloquently in favour of Roosevelt's candidacy. Scott felt inspired. The democratic ideal, always integral to his thinking, became numinous. It was, he recognized, "something you could give your life to."[17] He began to work on a manuscript that would define his vision of democracy.

Two nights after the Roosevelt program the bombing of Britain recommenced. But Scott was now more able to deal with his feelings. The process of recovery had begun. In *The New Statesman and Nation,* in early November, he read an article by John Strachey entitled "Digging for Mrs. Miller," about the search for survivors after one of the London blitzes. Strachey described an air raid rescue group that dug into the ruins and found two human shapes – a woman and a man – crushed and pressed into the debris of several houses, "locked in reluctant intercourse."[18] On the woman's wrist was a metal disc identifying her as Mrs. Miller.

Scott used Strachey's account as a vehicle to embody his own collapse and restoration. In a poem called "Recovery" he transformed the search for survivors in war-torn London into a symbol of the intellectual's predicament during World War II. More specifically, Scott was writing of his own predicament when confronted with the bombing of Britain.

> Now thought seeks shelter, lest the heart melt
> In the iron rain, the brain bend
> Under the bombs of news.
> Fearfully the mind's hands dig
> In the débris of thought, for the lovely body of faith.
> Is she alive after this shock, does she yet breathe?
>
> O say that she lives, she is ours, imperishable,
> Say that the crypt stood.   (*C.P.,* p. 105)

The body of Strachey's Mrs. Miller becomes "the lovely body of faith" and the poem is a recapitulation of the political events of the thirties. His generation, the narrator says, "had played in the hanging gardens." The betrayal of democracy in Spain, in Czechoslovakia, and at Munich are all hinted at in symbols of a pleasure-loving generation that had loved the "facade" more than the "foundation." Now that the whole building has collapsed into ruins, what can man build on? In Scott's poem, as in Strachey's article, the search is successful. But to the poet the search is for a new foundation of belief. With the discovery of "the lovely body of faith," expressed in hyperbole – "O clutch her to you, bring her triumphant forth. / Stand by her side now, scatter the panzer doubts." – he can go forward. "More roads are opened than are closed by bombs / And truth stands naked under the flashing charge" (*C.P.*, p. 105).

One suspects the description of the search for the body of Mrs. Miller had great emotional resonance for Scott; and like Canon Scott's search for Harry's body in the Regina Trench, it was a quest with transfiguring overtones. Through the metaphors of his poetry (just as earlier for his father through the symbols of the mass) death is transformed into life. The religious element is still present but less overt. The abstraction of Mrs. Miller into "faith," the explicit reference to "hope," and the implicit reference to "love" all suggest the trilogy of faith, hope, and charity found in 1 Corinthians 13. It is charity or love that "beareth all things, believeth all things, hopeth all things, endureth all things." In the early forties Scott felt he had lost his faith and his sense of truth. Now he affirmed a "rock," which he was increasingly to identify with the democratic ideal. Poetry was always important to Scott as a means of finding his way toward truth – a symbolic truth expressed through metaphor.

In January, 1941, the English poet George Barker gave a reading at Harvard. His visit, and a projected issue of *Poetry* (Chicago) edited by E.K. Brown and devoted entirely to Canadian poetry, stimulated Scott to new writing. He and Barker enjoyed each other's company. They talked poetry, drank beer, and speculated whether England could hold out against the Nazis. Scott was both horrified and delighted when Barker exclaimed that "If England should fall, think of the wonderful elegies the poets could write!"[19] Barker's remark somehow put a new perspective on the blitz of London and eased Scott's crisis by helping him achieve a measure of aesthetic detachment. After a full night of good spirits, the two poets wove their way up the stairs toward bed. They met the Scotts' French-Canadian maid on the stairs. She was carrying a tray with a glass of orange juice meant for her employer's breakfast and Barker reached out, took the glass, and drained it in one long shuddering mouthful. For the young woman, French-speaking and alone in this unfamiliar Anglophone world of Cambridge, Massachusetts, Barker's gesture was the last straw. She was later found in an almost catatonic state, her arms stretched out in the form of a cross. It was she who had the nervous breakdown Scott had anticipated for himself.

DURING HIS YEAR AT HARVARD, his teaching in the following summer session there, and then in the fall of 1941 at McGill, Scott began to search out and write down definitions of democracy, clarifying his views as he wrote. He entitled his study "The Democratic Manifesto." It indicates that his concept of democracy, like his earlier consideration of socialism, was determined by a basically religious value system. Scott explored the democrat's relationship to the state and to international tyranny, in the context of war, and also devoted a long section to the relations between the internal and external policy of states. He appears to have been attempting to determine the circumstances under which a Christian and a democrat might support war.

Democracy, he wrote, is characterized by "faith" and "vision." It is more than an inner life; it is a faith expressing itself in social action. Scott had come to certain conclusions about the individual democrat's "rights" and in some extremes his "duty" to civil disobedience. But democracy exists "as much by its restraints as by its toleration." It cannot countenance the freedom of a majority to persecute a minority, the freedom of capital to exploit labour, or the freedom of individuals to destroy public property, to slander races, or to engage in private vengeance. All these freedoms are denied by democracy to ensure a more widespread liberty.[20]

The democratic attitude toward conflict "is found in the Christian doctrine of loving your enemies and doing good to those who hate you." For these reasons, many democrats doubt whether violence is ever justifiable as a means to reach a democratic end. On the other hand, most democrats, while recognizing that violence is evil,

> distinguish coercion with a democratic purpose from coercion with an undemocratic purpose. Instead of refusing all personal participation in violence, they seek to canalise and direct its use.... Force is used within the state to put down individual violence, and so it will be in the world society. War as an instrument of national aggrandisement is wrong, but war as a final means of international defence against the law-breakers is justified. Such a war is preferable to a victory for undemocratic forces which would destroy all immediate hope of a democratic internationalism.[21]

Hitler's tyranny had forced Scott to reconsider democracy and led him to question his former anti-war position. He concluded that war against tyranny was justified.

Scott believed that democracy finds its finest expression in the socialist state. Moreover, his vision of democracy places the national within the context of a world vision: "This democracy opposes all selfish patriotism which blinds men to the world vision. It recognises a loyalty due to the state, but places it below the other and higher loyalty due to the concept of world-wide democracy." Scott concluded, "Only a supra-natural authority can satisfy men's political aspirations, provide men with security, and free their creative energies for spectacular achievements."[22]

Throughout the thirties Scott's aestheticism was largely overshadowed by the struggle for the social good. But now, again, he began to rethink the old categories of the good, the true, and the beautiful within the perspective of a humanist and internationalist framework. In rethinking the concept of democracy he perceived its relation to beauty. For Scott there was an important place for the artist among the leaders of democracy. Democracy "will hunger for the beauty it knows awaits creation. The mainsprings of democracy are truth, beauty, order, design, mastery, making; these too are the springs of art. Man making life, man living life, man understanding life – these blend the two endeavors."[23]

On November 24, 1941, Scott wrote several sentences in his notebook suggestive of Thomas Paine's remark: "My country is the world, and my religion is to do good."[24] Scott wrote, "Democracy is my government; the world is my country. The spirit of man is my god; the future of man is my heaven."[25] His reformulation shows that a revived belief in democracy, the spirit of man, had led him away from what he now saw as a narrow nationalism into a wider internationalism. That nationalism had led him to take such an intransigent position on World War II. Henceforth he was to be severe in his judgements of this concept; as a result he came to undervalue the depth and significance of his own nationalist motives as they existed in the thirties and forties. Just as in the late twenties he had revised his views about World War I and forgotten the young man's anxiety to serve king and country, so now, embracing a strong internationalism, he came to think he had always had these values. This new belief was later codified in the fifties in the poem "Creed":

> The world is my country
> The human race is my race

The spirit of man is my God
The future of man is my heaven   (*C.P.*, p. 89)

Scott is substituting the modernist "spirit of man" for the older "spirit of God," but it is clear that he considers the two analagous. This connection has a long history in Scott's thought. In 1921 he had read Robert Bridges's *The Spirit of Man*, an anthology of inspiring poetry and prose first published in 1915 and designed to cheer an England at war. The preface suggests that the proper work of man's mind is "to conquer the natural aspects of the world so as to bring them in subjection to the spirit" – thus the human spirit echoes the divine. This view, supplemented by H.G. Wells's description of the immanence of the divine in *God the Invisible King*, seems to have provided Scott, then an orthodox and idealistic young Anglican, with an important transitional metaphor in which the human spirit – political, artistic, or scientific – can be seen as infused by the divine.

While gathering his material on democracy, Scott often implicitly compared it with what he saw as the opposite form of government – communism. When he entitled it "The Democratic Manifesto," he suggested a parallel with *The Communist Manifesto*. He submitted the manuscript to a New York publisher who rejected it. Several months later another book on democracy by the American writer Emery Reves appeared; it was entitled *A Democratic Manifesto*.

AFTER THE EARLY YEARS of laying the groundwork for the new socialist party in the thirties, the early forties brought an increase in CCF popularity and greater success at the polls, both provincial and federal. Although its war policies were somewhat at variance with the public mood, in the federal election of 1940 the party held its own. Then, after the war had been in progress for about a year, it became clear to many in the CCF that Britain must have help if Western democracy were to be saved. Accordingly, party policy began to moderate. At the 1942 national convention the party supported a plebiscite on conscription even though it elected as national chairman one of the chief opponents of conscription – F.R. Scott.

After Scott's election, E.B. Jolliffe, the Ontario CCF leader, said to him: "Frank, you are everything that a national chairman ought *not* to be. You are lean instead of fat. You are aloof instead of approachable...." And Scott cut in, "Yes, and I'm unpopular instead of popular."[26] The question of Canada's role in the war and support for Great Britain was a controversial one for CCFers. During 1940-41 Frank Underhill had nearly been fired from the Department of History at the University of Toronto for making critical comments at a Lake Couchiching Conference on the British connection: behind this incident, however, were more than ten years of annoyance to some members of the University of Toronto board. Scott, who had been quite active while at Harvard in gathering the support of American academics for what he liked to call "l'affaire Underhill," now also found himself in hot water.

In the fall of 1942 Bartlett Brebner, the Canadian historian at Columbia who had helped Scott rally the support of American professors for the outspoken Underhill, wrote to Scott reporting that Underhill, for whom a Guggenheim had been secured, was now busily at work at Columbia. He added, "you seem to have inherited his mantle as whipping boy for various discontents."[27] And, indeed, "l'affaire Scott" was mushrooming. *Saturday Night* had called him a Nazi sympathizer; the McGill governors were up in arms over his stand on conscription; and his brother William, a pillar of the Montreal establishment, was not speaking to him.

The trouble had started with an article on conscription, "What Did No Mean?," that appeared in *The Canadian Forum* in June, 1942, in which he seemed to condone, as well as explain, French-Canadian attitudes to the war. Under the National Resources Mobilization Act of 1940 the government had sweeping powers to mobilize for war. Throughout the debate on this act in Parliament the CCF had urged conscription of wealth before conscription of manpower for military service, arguing that any conscription of manpower should merely be for home defence. Yet after the national plebiscite of April, 1942, which released the government from pledges made in the 1940 election not to introduce conscription for overseas service, the government introduced Bill 80, which stated that overseas service could be imposed on conscripted men by order-in-council without further reference to Parliament. At the same time the Prime Minister had declared, "not necessarily conscription, but conscription if necessary."[28] The CCF had supported a national plebiscite on believing a "yes" vote would indicate support for conscription of national resources. But it opposed Bill 80 giving what was, as Coldwell said, in effect a "blank cheque" to the government for rule by order-in-council rather than by Parliament.[29]

Scott was particularly disturbed when all the provinces voted "yes" in the referendum, with majorities of 69 per cent to 82 per cent, except Quebec, where 73 per cent voted "non."[30] The referendum, he felt, was largely misunderstood by English Canadians, who did not perceive the significance of the overwhelming "no" vote by French-speaking Quebecers. He was in touch with Quebec opinion and, just before writing the conscription article, had met with a mixed group of French and English at the home of Thérèse Casgrain, a prominent French-Canadian advocate of women's rights, to discuss the issue. Among those present were André Laurendeau, then a nationalist writing for *L'Action nationale*, Edmund Turcotte, editor of *Le Canada*, and Leslie Roberts, a Montreal journalist. Scott reported to M.J. Coldwell that all of the group were agreed upon three points: first, a large factor in the "no" vote was a protest against the "continuing colonialism of Canada's relationship to Great Britain;" second "the extent ... of the 'no' vote has astonished even French Canadians themselves and made them feel strong and united;" third, "conscription now would be followed by far greater opposition in Quebec than during the last war."[31]

In his article Scott pointed out the "yes" vote was ambiguous, and the "no" vote (largely that of French Quebec) was misunderstood by English Canadians. The small "no" vote in all provinces but Quebec was interpreted as majority support of Mackenzie King's war policy whereas in fact, for Quebecers, it was a protest against imperialism. No political issue in Canada had so many imperialist associations for Quebecers as conscription for overseas service. The Boer War had produced Henri Bourassa, founder of *Le Devoir*, and, together with the compulsory conscription of the Great War, had influenced contemporary feeling in Quebec.

Scott was condoning as well as explaining. The new factors in the war situation, he thought, particularly the bombing of Pearl Harbor by the Japanese, the subsequent United States entry into the war, the initial sweeping Japanese victories, and even the fall of France, did not alter Quebec's belief that it was an imperialist war. "Along both shores of the St. Lawrence it still looked like conscription imposed by imperialists...."[32] Quebec voted not on the question of whether the government should be free to introduce conscription but on the question of whether Canadians should be forced to defend the British Empire. Canada, which had failed even to provide symbols of nationhood (its war posters and publicity were filled with suggestions that it was just a little lion fighting alongside a big lion), should make up its mind whether it was fighting the war as a British colony or as one of the United Nations. The French Canadians, he concluded, will do everything necessary for the defence of Canada, but the "no" vote says that Quebec "does not wish her children to die for any country other than her own."[33]

Scott's personal logic was open to question. At Harvard he had experienced a crisis of faith and decided that the war was just and "for the preservation of democracy." In 1941-42 France was overrun and England seemed to be losing to Hitler. In this context Scott's arguments regarding imperialism verge on quibbling, for Pearl Harbor went far beyond the imperialism that had led up to the war. Even in terms of Scott's earlier conception of Canada as a North American nation, the fact that the war had now spread to Hawaii suggested it had already become a matter of survival – for French Canada as well as English. Also, his suggestion that French Quebecers would fight only for "French-Canadian soil" implied they would not fight for "freedom" or "democracy." The answer, perhaps, was that Scott had reached a pragmatic position based on his understanding of the views held by a number of Quebec intellectuals. As an Anglophone Quebecer his views were directed toward the preservation of peace in Quebec – a peace on which he felt the future of Canada depended. To some degree, this was a position to which Scott clung all the more fiercely when challenged, because he was unaware of the degree to which he was rationalizing.

His summary of the Quebec position was overwhelmingly appreciated by Francophone Quebecers, who were delighted to find there were some Anglo-Canadians who understood. Gérard Pelletier of Le Devoir immediately responded by reprinting Scott's article in its entirety and thanking him in a personal letter for his sympathetic analysis "in the present circumstances."[34] Louis Morisset, a Quebecer who had felt obliged to vote "yes," wrote to thank Scott: "It is my humble opinion that you have exposed the problem in the clearest possible way and permit me to tell you that your attitude forces my admiration."[35] Emile Vaillancourt, one of the most important liaisons between French and English in Montreal, was so delighted with the article that he acquired funds from the Quebec government for publication of several thousand copies to be distributed to influential individuals and embassies throughout the world.[36] And there were also English Quebecers who approved of Scott's article. Louis Dudek, a young Montreal poet, wrote to thank Scott. "In this world of today," he philosophized, "where everything is bought and sold for money, it is hard for truth to walk in the market-place."[37]

But the article was greatly resented by many prominent English Canadians, especially by two of the most significant moulders of public opinion, J.W. Dafoe of the Winnipeg Free Press and B.K. Sandwell of Saturday Night. Both editors saw Scott as a traitor to the cause, as did J.M. Macdonnell, general manager of National Trust, a leading Toronto Conservative. Macdonnell was appalled. He complained that Scott, under the guise of explaining the Quebec vote, had actually written a "philippic virtually justifying French-Canadians up to the hilt."[38] Perhaps, he suggested, in writing an article supporting the extreme French element, Scott was seeking to extend the CCF following among the French?

The *Winnipeg Free Press* of July 2, 1942, ran an editorial under a banner headline, "Those Who Render Disservice," claiming that the unity of Canada was "threatened with disruption" and that, among those responsible for this, Frank R. Scott, professor of civil law at McGill University, was guilty of mischief. "Ostensibly the article was designed to explain objectively and in sympathetic terms the reasons for the attitude taken by the 'No' voters in Quebec; but actually it is advocacy, subtle and skillful, of the case for a limited contribution to the war." In the meantime, fellow socialist Eugene Forsey, a Newfoundlander and thus a staunch imperialist by birthright, attacked Scott's position in *The Canadian Forum*.[39]

*Saturday Night* began to run a series of articles critical both of the CCF stand on the conscription issue and of Scott in particular. Echoing the objections of the *Winnipeg Free Press*, an editorial complained that Scott's attempt to explain Quebec's revolt against British tyranny did not seem either useful or historically correct.[40] A month later, in the same journal, Scott's name was linked with Theodore Dreiser, the American novelist turned Communist who had a Toronto lecture cancelled after he mentioned to reporters his admiration for Russia and his hope that the Nazis would overrun England. "The advantage of a man like Mr. Dreiser," said the editor of *Saturday Night*, "is that he blurts out frankly what is in his mind, while people like Professor Frank Scott say the same things in subtle and polished phrases which do far more damage and which cannot be dealt with by the Toronto police commissioners or the Minister of Justice."[41] In the next issue Sandwell extended a partial retraction: "It was far from our desire to suggest that Professor Scott has been guilty either of adulation of Russia or of hot-gospelling for a Second Front." What infuriated the editor was Scott's apparent refusal to recognize the "life-and-death struggle between democracy and tyranny" and his failure to recognize that England "for almost two years stood alone between us and the preponderant might of Germany." To Sandwell such an attitude of mind was incomprehensible. As such, it invited comparison with Dreiser's pro-Nazism.[42]

Scott's reply, published October 17, 1942, was prompt and incisive. The Dreiser comparison was unjust and libelous. Moreover, he was not expressing a personal opinion but representing Quebec's attitude. Also, in his opinion, the war for democracy had begun long before September 3, 1939 – by inference, it had not for Sandwell. Scott's nationalism rose to the fore in his final point. "It may be difficult for you, as an Englishman resident in Canada, to understand how some Canadians can advocate for Canada a policy based on an independent estimate of what is needed to save humanity." Scott's objection was to colonialism, to the habitually deferential attitude that dominated Canadian foreign policy. "I want to eliminate, as the best elements in England want to eliminate, the last relics of economic exploitation and Anglo-Saxon domination from the British Empire."

Sandwell was to have the editor's prerogative – the last word. He had come to Canada at the age of twelve. M.J. Coldwell, the CCF leader, had come at a much later age and had not lived in the country nearly so long. What Scott was really objecting to was not Englishmen *per se* but Englishmen of particular political persuasions. Only the "best elements," as Scott defined them, had a right to speak. If he, Sandwell, could not speak on Canadian policy how then could Scott speak out on the way that England was treating India, representing the United Kingdom "as tyrannical, exploiting and obstructive to a potential true democracy."[43] Indeed, if Scott considered Sandwell an Englishman then it was just as well to talk about Sir John A. Macdonald as a Scotsman resident in Canada.

Emotions ran high on either side. Scott was not without his defenders. Arthur Lower promptly responded to Dafoe's "unfair attacks."[44] Harold Innis, the University of Toronto political economist who in the thirties had severely criticized Scott for taking a stand on political issues, now changed his mind. He didn't like to see the establishment ganging up on Scott. "*Stick to your guns and give them some more,*" he advised.[45] Brooke Claxton approved: "It is one of the best pieces of writing done about Canadian affairs. It made your brother Willum mad as hell."[46]

As the son of Canon Scott and the brother of William Scott, a pillar of the Quebec Anglophone establishment, Scott was in a highly visible position. *Saturday Night* tweaked his nose none too gently when it printed one of Canon Scott's poems next to the editorial condemning his son. And when his brother William walked into the University Club to find prominently displayed this anti-war essay in *The Canadian Forum* bearing the Scott name, he was humiliated and enraged.[47] An angry salvo of letters ensued, each brother attempting the impossible task of persuading the other of the logic of his position. Failing, each lapsed into denunciation of the other's position. William and Frank Scott ceased to speak to each other for almost two decades.

Even Elton, the middle brother, was drawn into the controversy. Writing from Bishop's College, where he was now a member of the theological faculty, he told Frank it was a fallacy to think only imperialists believed that war was necessary. Elton could not remember when he had last met a Canadian of the type most French believed the English to be. English

Canadians who were for an all-out war policy, including conscription, were not motivated by imperialism; they simply saw clearly that Canadians must go all out and anywhere, to win. The chief danger that he foresaw for Canadian unity in the future was "the virtually totalitarian nationalist machine in this province; Religion, language, education, youth societies, the press and radio of the province are all directed by one closely integrated body of people, of one race. The rest of Canada has no such unity or such machinery. It is always going to be very hard to get the non-French to even see the French point of view, and the French to care for what the rest of Canada thinks."[48]

Scott's stand on the conscription issue, including his minority position within the CCF Executive Council, had been preceded by yet another unpopular cause. A number of Montreal matrons, members of the Municipal Chapter of the Imperial Order of the Daughters of the Empire, wrote a letter to *The Gazette* in which they expressed "profound disapproval of the sentiments which [Thérèse Casgrain] set forth some days ago in connection with Canada's participation in this present war."[49] Madame Casgrain, wife of Pierre Casgrain, Liberal MP, running as an Independent Liberal candidate in Charlevoix-Saguenay, had spoken out on the electoral platform against conscription, although she had also urged people in the riding to enlist voluntarily. In a letter to *The Gazette*, Scott came to her defence:

> All this fuss and bother over Mrs. Casgrain's position is surely very tiresome and petty. Her record of public service is well-known. What dreadful thing has she done to merit this burst of Anglo-Saxon indignation. She is opposed to overseas conscription, it is true. But so are some four million Canadians, not to mention the Canadian government, Australia and South Africa.... People may disagree with this view, but look a little silly when they pose as moral superiors because they do not hold it.... Mrs. Casgrain is entitled to the view she holds, and her irate friends might spend a little time thinking the matter over.[50]

Thérèse Casgrain was extremely grateful. At a time when many English Canadians were censuring her and few French Canadians spoke on her behalf, Frank Scott, "a great Canadian," came to her rescue.[51]

Shortly after the conscription fuss, Archdeacon Scott was to complain, half-humorously, to his son, "There you are, Frank, you and Thérèse Casgrain, each of you with a hand on either side of the pail, drifting up to heaven."[52] Neither, he implied, had a strong enough sense of reality to keep his or her feet on the ground. It was not that the Archdeacon did not admire his son. One night in the mid-thirties, coming home with Jacques Bieler from an LSR meeting, he had spontaneously poured forth his love and admiration. Frank was his kind of person.[53] And it was not that he did not approve of his son's socialist principles. Indeed, he felt he shared them. After the Winnipeg General Strike, he had announced that henceforth he would "dedicate the rest of my life to fighting labour's battles."[54] But the Archdeacon's socialism, a social manifestation of his religious faith, was inextricably tied to his "boys," as he called them, the war veterans who had led the Winnipeg and Besco strikes. It did not interfere with his imperialism or his social life, which revolved around the activities of the Canadian Legion. On September 1, 1939, when Germany was invading Poland, the "beloved Padre" officiated at ceremonies to open yet another Canadian war memorial.

Frank's socialism was undeniably different. His strident denunciations of capitalism, his anti-imperialism, his frequent speeches on the necessity of freedom of speech for Communists, and even his verse were alienating. "Frank, is this poetry?" asked the father, struggling through "Teleological," a thirties version of the argument from design, first published in *New Provinces* (1936):

> Note, please, the embryo.
>                    Unseeing
> It swims into being.
> *Elan vital*,
> Thyroid, gonads *et al*…. (*C.P.*, p. 250)

He might just as well have asked, "Frank, is this theology?" because his son's poem, offering a scientific explanation of creation, implicitly rejected his father's belief in Genesis. So many of Frank Scott's beliefs and activities were now in opposition to those held by his father and old friends in uppercrust Montreal. The Archdeacon, a military hero, was frequently invited to dine out and preside at official gatherings. When Prime Minister Churchill conferred with President Roosevelt and Prime Minister King at Quebec City on August 23, 1943, Mackenzie King informally presented the Archdeacon to the party on August 24th.[55] He was astonished when his son mentioned he was rarely invited to such galas. "Oh, that's too bad," he would say.[56]

The Archdeacon liked a joke and he was not above twitting his son about his own greater popularity and importance. In the late thirties, when Scott was still in the thick of his most strident anti-imperialist phase, he wrote to his father explaining that should the Archdeacon die and have a military funeral, his son could not in good conscience attend. "That's all right, Frank," his father replied. "As long as I'm there, it will be a success."[57] Later, when the Archdeacon was setting out on one of his periodic jaunts across the country to visit branches of the Canadian Legion, his son brought him down to Windsor Station in Montreal. There, as they passed three railway cars, each of the three porters greeted the senior Scott affectionately by name and paid absolutely no attention to his son. "You see, Frank," he said, "you may work for *them*, but they know *me*."[58] Scott said nothing but he later recalled the incident as "one of father's great 'put-downs'."

With the outbreak of war Archdeacon Scott had rushed immediately to Ottawa. There, in a corridor of the Parliament Buildings, he met Brooke Claxton, one of the "boys." Claxton understood instantly that the Archdeacon had come to help with the war effort. And when Claxton, then in External Affairs, told him that his son Frank was also in Ottawa but taking part in an anti-war conference held by the CCF, the old trooper sighed. "Oh," he said.[59]

In 1939 and 1940 the elder Scott seemed indestructible. Tall, erect, and witty, "a gallant Christian gentleman,"[60] he still managed to galvanize audiences by his devotion to duty, his humour, and his poetry. And he still ruled his household with a rod of iron although it now consisted only of himself and Amy in an apartment building, the Château Louis, on the Grande Allée. When the notion to compose verse overtook him in the small hours of the morning, "Amy!" he would thunder, "Amy! Come here." And he still persisted in bringing home strangers. When Mrs. Scott yet again protested about feeding unexpected guests, the irrepressible old man went out and lugged home several cases of tinned beans and soup. "There," he said. "Don't tell me that you don't have enough food now."[61]

In June, 1943, Mrs. Scott became ill and suddenly died. It was then that F.G. came to recognize, as did the rest of the family, that the mother had been the heart of all, holding the family together. In "Bedside," Scott's elegy on his mother's death, the central image is of a tree uprooted: with the main root gone, all the smaller roots are gasping in shallower soil. With her death, as a line from his poem said, "... five no longer integral departed" (*C.P.*, p. 170). No longer held by the old bond, William, Elton, Mary, Frank, and Arthur scattered.

The Archdeacon felt the loss most keenly. Less than a year after the death of his "beloved Amy," in January, 1944, he became seriously ill and was brought to the Royal Victoria Hospital suffering from pneumonia.

Frank found his father in an oxygen tent. He peered through the mica window cut into the tent. The old man seemed dead, a pallor on his face, his eyes closed. Suddenly he opened his eyes. In a fraction of a second, life and consciousness came flooding in. "Frank," he said, "is this the revolution?"[62] Jesting, even on his deathbed, the father wittily fused his son's faith in the socialist millennium with his own belief in the afterlife.

For Frank, his father's imminent death called up the old thirties conflict between science and religion. One of his finest poems, "Last Rites," came from the experience of sitting at the bedside of his dying father.

> Within his tent of pain and oxygen
> This man is dying; grave, he utters prayers,
> Stares at the bedside altar through the screens,
> Lies still for invocation and for hands.
> Priest takes his symbols from a leather bag.
> Surplice and stole, the pyx and marks of faith,
> And makes a chancel in the ether air.
> Nurse too is minister....
> But nurse will stare
> This evil in the face, will not accept,
> Will come with stranger and more cunning tools
> To other bedsides, adding skill to skill,
> Till death is driven slowly farther back.
> How far? She does not ask.
>                                        Priest does not fight.
> He lives through death and death is proof of him.
> In the perpetual, unanswerable why
> Are born the symbol and the sacrifice....
> And I who watch this rightness and these rites,
> I see my father in the dying man,
> I am his son who dwells upon the earth,
> There is a holy spirit in this room,
> And straight toward me from both sides of time
> Endless the known and unknown roadways run.   (*C.P.*, pp. 168-69)

In the poem science and religion are accepted as equally valid truths. In the line "I am his son who dwells upon the earth," Scott recognizes the kinship in the two faiths, but he has chosen "science," making "the heaven on earth" and rolling back the area owned by "death." Scott, who later remarked that "a holy spirit" was a real presence in the dying man's room, was reaffirming not only the trinity of High Anglicanism but also the endless continuity of the human spirit. In effect, the poem expresses man's endless search for truth. In reaching the conclusion that there are two kinds of truth – rational as well as intuitive – the younger Scott was also reconciling his own belief in science with his father's faith. He later wrote, in September, 1944, "One can live as fully by faith as by emotion."[63]

Shortly after he joked with his son, Archdeacon Scott slipped into a coma. He died several days later, on January 19, 1944. The expected military services for the "beloved Padre" were held on January 21 in Quebec City and on January 22 in Montreal. The funeral in Montreal was a great civic affair with dignitaries of both church and state attending. William and Frank, Elton and Arthur, in top hats and morning coats, walked in procession through the main streets of Montreal followed by "the Canon's boys," the veterans from the Canadian Legion. They were there in the thousands – his old comrades from Valcartier Camp, Salisbury Plain, 2nd Ypres, Kitchener's Wood, Festubert, Givenchy, Pozier's Ridge, Regina Trench, Courcellette, Vimy Ridge, Arleux, Fresnoy, Hill 70, Passchendaele, Canal du Nord. The procession travelled up the tiered slopes from the city of Montreal to the Protestant cemetery near the top of Mount Royal.[64]

The funeral service at Christ Church Cathedral in Montreal was simple and dignified. It included the 23rd Psalm and on the cover of the "Order of Service" was printed F.G.'s poem "Knighthood":

> In honour, chivalrous;
> In duty, valorous;
> In all things, noble;
> To the heart's core, clean.[65]

At the top of Mount Royal, the clear call of the Last Post was followed by the crash of guns of the firing party's salute. Frederick George Scott was laid to rest.[66]

## TWELVE

# *Preview*

❧

A FEW DAYS AFTER his father's funeral, Scott received a letter from Leon Edel, then in the United States Army, expressing his regrets. Scott wrote back promptly, thanking him and urging him to return to Montreal – to live: "a) because Canada is moving rapidly ahead, ideologically, while the U.S. isn't (to put it mildly) b) because we have a group of poets writing here better than anything since the Great Days of the 14tly [*Fortnightly*] [and] c) because we'd like to have you back."[1] The group of poets was the *Preview* group, which had come into being shortly after Scott's return from Harvard.

The mimeographed *Preview* was, as its name implies, not meant to offer a finished poetry but rather to provide an opportunity for practising poets to preview their own verse. The group was a lively one, leftish and international in its sympathies, intrigued by the new discoveries of psychoanalysis, avidly reading such major new poets as George Barker, Dylan Thomas, and Karl Shapiro. Politically, *Preview* represented a movement from individual isolation to a communal war effort. In the first editorial the editors remarked they had all "lived long enough in Montreal to realise the frustrating and inhibiting effects of isolation. All anti-fascists, we feel that the existence of a war between democratic culture and the paralysing forces of dictatorship only intensifies the writer's obligation to work."[2]

In the spring of 1942 Scott had met a young Englishman, Patrick Anderson, at a tea given by Montreal poet Margaret Day, later the wife of artist Philip Surrey. Anderson was ex-Oxford, fair-haired, and intensely vocal: a stimulating conversationalist, he always enjoyed (as did Scott) a verbal joust. He had been active in the Oxford Student Union and in 1938 was awarded a two-year Commonwealth Fellowship, a kind of reverse Rhodes Scholarship, to Columbia University in New York. His fellowship in the United States over, Anderson, who feared war, decided to avoid the draft in England by emigrating to Canada with his American-born artist wife, Peggy.³ Following the example of his mentor W.H. Auden, he preferred to contribute to the war in a literary manner. At Columbia he and his wife had edited a mimeographed poetry magazine called *The Andersons* that he had shown to Scott in Montreal. Shortly after, when Scott, Anderson, and Margaret Day were again talking together, Scott said, "I've got an idea. Let's start a poetry magazine."⁴

The "little mag" was *Preview*, the refuge and stimulus Scott spoke of in "A l'Ange Avant-Gardien." For some time Scott had been conscious he had not been faithful to poetry. "I used to wake up in the mornings and a voice was saying, 'You've got to write, you've got to write,' and I knew I had to write. And all my frenetic activity in *not* writing – or in writing, but not poetry – was to excuse me for not writing poetry to which I would come when I had finished all my other duties ... and I kept working to clear away something that seemed to be keeping me from it."⁵ Now, under the stimulus of Anderson's presence he was back to poetry again.

When the first issue came out in March, 1942, the editors included Scott, Anderson, Day, Neufville Shaw, and Bruce Ruddick. P.K. Page was to join the editors with the next issue, and, several months later, A.M. Klein. Anderson, politically committed and a poet, was the acknowledged catalyst of the group. "Weedy and extremely thin, he looked like one of those Englishmen who'd grown up under a rock. No colour in his cheeks ... just very pallid.... He looked as if he drank nothing but tea."⁶ Indeed, many *Preview* meetings were held in his kitchen around a big coal stove with kettle bubbling and Anderson exclaiming, "Peggy, make the tea!"

To the Montrealers Anderson looked and sounded the way a poet ought to look and sound. He knew of the new poets; he spoke eloquently of their concerns and techniques. And he wrote enviably well. He also thought that the other members of *Preview* should look and behave like poets. They should wear capes and grow their hair. They should read *The Communist Manifesto* and speak out for a second front for "Holy Mother Russia." All this advice was dispensed with the utmost kindness. To P.K. Page he seemed a kind of giant cuckoo, force-feeding his fledglings with poetry and communism.⁷

Although much of this advice fell on deaf ears, his messianic sense of the poet's role was contagious. It affected the whole group. But there was no question about the political commitment of the *Preview* poets. Anderson, his wife Peggy, and Margaret Day were Marxists; Scott and Klein were staunch CCFers and Klein, in addition, was a fervid Zionist. Page and Ruddick also leaned to the left. *Preview* poems and reviews were largely devoted to the war controversy: there were articles on the role of factories, offices, and universities in the war and stirring injunctions to members of the armed forces. Anderson even managed to dedicate one issue to the Red Army "whose recent heroic successes have done so much for the cause of human freedom and culture everywhere."[8]

Several months after *Preview* began, a second Montreal poetry magazine called *First Statement* came into being. Years later, editor John Sutherland was to write a story about a young man who was rejected by one poetry group and promptly set up a rival publication with its own printing press. The story was largely autobiographical.[9] *First Statement* began in antithesis. The group soon consisted of Sutherland, Louis Dudek, Irving Layton, and Audrey Aikman. As Dudek recalled, there was a sense of rivalry built into their position as the younger generation of poets.

> Layton and I, the first night that we met, we went over to his house and we looked at ... *New Provinces* [the thirties anthology of new Canadian poetry]. We thought it was very lukewarm stuff as far as modernism was concerned. We laughed at some of the experimental gimmicks in there, words running down the page – superficial and silly forms of modernistic poetry. We would want something much more energetic, more visceral than that. From that moment, and probably before, there was a considerable rivalry between ourselves built into the whole situation of ourselves as the younger generation.[10]

For Dudek this sense of rivalry was modified by an opposing fact – Scott was a socialist. In 1941 Dudek had gone to the Montreal Museum of Fine Arts to hear Scott talk about Roosevelt's WPA Recovery Project for artists in the United States. Long before the creation of the Canada Council, Scott the socialist was giving a picture of what could be done when government takes an interest in the arts and stimulates them. Dudek later recalled his feelings at the time. "Here was a man talking straight and intelligent and he was saying the right things. Nobody else was saying these things at the time.... we're all dependent upon the whole social structure, and it's not working, when there's no work for people. Something is terribly wrong. We've got the machines, we've got the land, we've got the productive capacity. Let's organize things better."[11]

For *First Statement* members incipient admiration of *Preview* co-existed with rivalry – not the least because several members of the executive had been rejected as members of the *Preview* group. They were reading and, in many cases, emulating the magazine they editorially attacked. *First Statement* members dismissed *Preview* as elitist, internationalist, and not realistically political, while describing their own practices as proletarian, nationalist, and politically engaged. Although this account has been accepted by literary history many of the distinctions were mythic.

The *Preview* group did read and emulate the British poets, notably Auden, Day-Lewis, Spender, and Dylan Thomas. But *First Statement* writers were reading the American poets, Pound and W.C. Williams. From the *First Statement* point of view, to read the American poets was to be North American and hence not British or "colonial."[12] To be American (that is North American) was less imperative for *Preview* members. They felt a residual anger against America for not entering the war until after Pearl Harbor and a corresponding desire to support Britain. Anderson was English and Scott had worked through the strongest phase of his anti-colonial feelings about England in the political sphere. The rest of the group were willing to take poetic nourishment wherever it could be found.

Although generational and class differences, especially as felt by the Montreal east-enders of *First Statement*, undoubtedly played an important part, differences in aesthetic theory also were important. The younger poets were convinced that Scott, Smith, and the first wave of Canadian modernists had not gone far enough. As Dudek recalled:

There's no question that Layton and I always felt, and probably still do, that the other poets were too refined.... In fact, I do think that any kind of civilization or refinement involves leaving out aspects of existence, that's what refinement means – take the rock from the ore – leave only the fine metal. Same thing happens in civilization, a man refines himself and says "Don't belch; don't fart." He leaves out things, so that gradually what is left is a very fine thing but a very thin business.[13]

Yet, the primary difference between the two leftish poetry groups was political. The *First Statement* Marxists were largely Stalinists and believed in a national communism. The *Preview* Marxists inclined toward Leninism; they advocated an international communism. One evening when the *Preview* members hired a hall at the Ritz-Carlton Hotel to discuss with *First Statement* members "nationalism versus internationalism," this political distinction emerged as most significant.[14] In later years the Marxist political origins of the antithesis between the "national" and the "international" positions were long forgotten and the literary differences emphasized.

In fact, there was a strong interest in the Canadian poem in *Preview*. The major nationalist poems of the forties – Anderson's "Poem on Canada," Scott's "Laurentian Shield" and "Lakeshore," and Klein's "Montreal"

– all emerged from the *Preview* context. Scott had long been interested in the "Canadian" poem and Anderson gave this interest new dimension. As an Englishman, he continually questioned the national identity. His "Poem on Canada" saw the country with new eyes as "a cold country, 'America's attic,' an empty room."[15] *Preview* members were soon discussing the question of Canadian content and about developing a Canadian voice. One evening they held a long discussion attempting to isolate the essentials of the Canadian poem. It "was not Canadian because it talked about moose, or about ice, or about snow, or a mountain," they concluded, but nonetheless "a poet writes out of a geographic milieu and a social milieu, and this is Canada, and therefore something will come out that speaks of the place [the poet] is in."[16] That is, it was not the number of references to moose, ice, snow, or mountains that made a poem Canadian, but rather the evocation of some essential national quality – what they called the "moosey-ness of the moose."

Through *Preview* Scott was directed again to the poetry of the Canadian landscape. He also began to read the "new" poetry. As a result, his own poetry was significantly altered. The somewhat dry and satirical social verse of the thirties gave way to a poetry deepened by a psychological awareness, by a new emotional openness and an exuberance of language. Anderson's influence was partly responsible, as well as the new psychology introduced to Scott by Dr. Prados, a refugee from the Spanish Civil War. Scott's poetry also reflected the British poets of the forties, especially George Barker and Dylan Thomas, whom he was now reading. A.J.M. Smith, visiting in Montreal, joined the *Preview* poets for a party. Standing in his hotel room one night, a little drunk, he swayed back and forth, reading from *Deaths and Entrances*. This was Scott's introduction to Dylan Thomas.[17]

For Scott, *Preview* was not quite the emotional experience of *The McGill Fortnightly* – it was not the opening of a whole new world. But he was now forty, not twenty, and certainly the group provided emotional companionship as well as literary direction. *Preview* reminded him he was still a poet. Five poems written during the *Preview* days (including "Resurrection" and "Villanelle for Our Time") were accepted by *Poetry* (Chicago), the most prestigious journal of the period. They were published in March, 1944, and awarded the Guarantors Prize, which had gone to Stephen Spender in 1939 and Kenneth Fearing in 1940. During the same year another member of the group, P.K. Page, won the Oscar Blumenthal Prize for Poetry.[18] Scott's prize, and the fact that some poems were anthologized in Ralph Gustafson's *Penguin Book of Canadian Verse* (1941) and A.J.M. Smith's *Book of Canadian Poetry* (1943), encouraged him to put together his first book of poetry, which he called *Overture*.

In "Overture," the title poem written early in the thirties, the speaker listens to a Mozart sonata in a darkened room "... under a cone of light," and hears "The bright / Clear notes fly like sparks through the air / And trace a flickering pattern of music there."

> But how shall I hear old music? This is an hour
> Of new beginnings, concepts warring for power,
> Decay of systems – the tissue of art is torn
> With overtures of an era being born.   (*C.P.*, p. 87)

Indeed, the Spanish Civil War gave way to the greater tragedy of World War II. The thirties had proved to be a decade of "concepts warring for power."

The book begins with "Dedication," a call for world brotherhood, and ends with "Villanelle for Our Time." "Conflict" reflects an Audenesque awareness of the duality of human motives – "Persecution's cruel mouth / Shows a twisted love of truth" (*C.P.*, p. 97). A new recognition of the individual as well as the collective self is conveyed in "Armageddon": "This foe we fight is half of our own self" (*C.P.*, p. 103). The poems in the book, written in the forties, burst forth with a sudden profusion of metaphors:

> Suddenly the last boundary broke
> And every land was used by somebody else.
> The closed world swarmed with a throng of roads
> Where caterpillars span a thread of our blood
> And sewed our flags into the history-quilt.   (*C.P.*, p. 102)

Although it can be argued he is simply reporting the actual political and military events of 1940, the opening metaphor of "Armageddon," which invokes the unknown yet ominously familiar landscape, as well as the subsequent map imagery and the witty personification, does suggest Auden. The opening stanza of "Flux" is neat, epigrammatic, and knowing, suggesting both Eliot and Auden in its distinction between present catastrophe and former "trim routine": "Trained to the tram-line and the office walk, / The weekend outing and the game of bridge, / Little avails us now the trim routine" (*C.P.*, p. 99). But other lines in "Flux" indicate that Scott was beginning to find his own direction by rejecting one solution to the cataclysm of World War II, that of becoming "refugees of the mind": "On the piled ox-cart of tradition; make for the rear. / This self-imprisonment obstructs the roads / And only the mobile heart allows escape" (*C.P.*, p. 99). Scott's values are those of human feelings and brotherhood; and his program for political action ("Strip for this venture forth, my pretty man. / Props and property are caving in") rests with conscience expressed as insight: "... the thunder of the still small voice.... the ultimate I, the inner mind" (*C.P.*, p. 99). The new direction of the poem reflects widespread new concerns of the forties, but the implicitly religious substratum is his own.

By 1945, *Preview* had run out of steam, whereas *First Statement*, which had acquired a printing press, seemed to be full of life. Under Scott's impetus, the two rival publications decided to merge into a new magazine, *Northern Review*. Sutherland was appointed editor. This merger was short-lived. Trouble began almost at once when the *First Statement* group, at a preliminary get-together at Scott's, began to feel they were kept below the salt because their host, wanting to provide them with food and drink, had ushered them into the kitchen, while *Preview* members commanded the living room. At this party Earle Birney, a teetotaller for six months because of an allergic reaction to alcohol, took his first sip of Scotch. He became violently ill. Irving Layton then charged that Birney (who, one suspects, had committed the unforgivable sin of twice winning the Governor General's Award for poetry) was a drunkard.[19] It was an inauspicious beginning and worse followed. Sutherland was soon packing the editorial board with friends and students to ensure control. In 1946, he launched a cruel attack on the poems of Robert Finch, which had just been given a Governor General's Award. The *Preview* editors withdrew from the magazine in dismay, and Scott went back to politics and law with a deepened poetic sensibility.

The political concerns of the forties, the new poetry, and, above all, a new psychological awareness had humanized Scott's poetry. He had come to realize the socialist planners had not included in their neat blueprints the irrational drives and urges of human nature. The issue was no longer confined to the classic struggle between monopoly capitalism and socialism. It concerned "the kind of new order which shall arise on the ruins of the old." In reviewing Arthur Koestler's *The Yogi and the Commissar* in the first issue of *Northern Review* (December / January, 1947), Scott stated the problem: "Can democracy and humanism not only survive the revolution but be in fact its active cause and pre-eminent spirit?" Koestler, rejecting the extremes of the saintly yogi on the one hand and those of the Communist commissar on the other, is commended for his synthesis, for what Scott calls "revolutionary humanism."

In the same issue of *Northern Review* Scott published "Laurentian Shield," a poem about politics and poetry generated by his work in the CCF. This poem provided Scott's answer to some of the problems posed by Koestler, in particular a consideration of the nature of the new order in Canadian

terms. But unlike the early thirties verse, where poetry is largely subordinated to politics, with "Laurentian Shield" Scott lets the imagery and
rhythm of the poem embody his thought and feeling. *Preview* had released
the poet from some of the political activist's constraints.

# THIRTEEN

# Make This Your Canada

B Y 1942, CCF SUPPORT was rapidly increasing across Canada – except in Quebec. There the Liberals, the traditional choice of Quebecers, enjoyed the firm support of business and the press. In contrast, the CCF was popularly regarded as both Communist and atheist, was consistently attacked by church and nationalist movements, and had little financial support. As national chairman and the party's primary Quebec lieutenant, Scott worked hard to develop a social welfare policy to appeal to a broad spectrum of Canadians, especially those in Quebec and Ontario. Drawing heavily on the United Kingdom's Beveridge Report, he helped formulate a CCF policy demanding that welfare be provided by the federal government, free of private interest, in tangible forms such as health benefits, education, and good housing.[1]

In a climate of ill will, however, it was extremely difficult to persuade Quebecers and a majority of Canadians that socialism offered a means of bettering their personal situations, especially when the Liberals appropriated the CCF's health and welfare policies. In the early 1940s, Scott, David Lewis, and a recently elected CCF organizer for Quebec, Jacques Casgrain, a Catholic lawyer, struggled to articulate CCF policy in Quebec. Scott, as the son of Canon Scott and as a distinguished constitutional lawyer and bilingual speaker, lent some national credibility to the CCF. And despite an initially lukewarm response, he worked indefatigably. Although sometimes irritated with the day-to-day work, Scott was an effective organizer. David Lewis recalled he demanded from other executive members the same discipline he imposed on himself. "He was a relatively strict presiding officer: he demanded order, discipline and tidiness in thought and action, but he did so in orderly, disciplined and tidy phrases, without offensive shrillness.... Although Scott did not have direct experience with the electorate – he was never a candidate for public office – he showed realistic political sense which took into account relevant electoral considerations." In particular, Lewis asserted, Scott knew very well that the CCF had been established by the Regina Manifesto as "a political party seeking to win power by the parliamentary electoral route."[2]

Gradually, Scott's influence and hard work began to pay off. His stand on the conscription issue, especially, began to attract a group of young Francophone intellectuals. During 1942-43, as the issue of conscription came to a head, a number of young Quebecers, including author Roger Lemelin, began to attend CCF meetings. Lemelin, in response to the Regina Manifesto, wrote to Lewis that he was interested in helping found the Quebec City section of the CCF. He recalled that he "was soon joined by Jean-Marie Bédard, a Trotskyist of Quebec City who became a major officer in labour unions, and Jean Phillipe Vaillancourt, who did the same." Jacques Casgrain, who later became a CCF organizer in the West, also joined about the same time.[3]

Although the CCF received some initial support in Quebec from the Bloc populaire canadien, a more constant source of membership in Quebec over a longer period was the trade unions. Scott had met a number of Francophone organizers when he was investigating conditions in the Montreal garment industry; in the forties, his work with trade unions made him relatively well known. Individuals such as Omer Chartrand, Roger Bédard, Roger Prévost, and Claude Jodoin of the Ladies Garment Workers, A.L. Hepworth of the Canadian Brotherhood of Railway Employees, and Paul Marquette of the Montreal Tram Workers, all of whom had been struggling against Duplessisism, found support in the CCF's socialist policies. After Jacques Casgrain had become active and Thérèse Casgrain and Guy Desaulniers had successively become provincial organizers, CCFers began to feel that they were at last making headway in Quebec.[4] But Jacques Casgrain proved unreliable and Thérèse Casgrain, although representative of the Quebec establishment, was, as she sadly recalled, "a woman" – and thus not a credible politician in 1940s Quebec.[5] Quebec women, after all, did not get the vote until April 25, 1940.

Nationally, as the forties progressed, the CCF began preparations for the inevitable election that would follow the end of the war. Consequently, in the summer of 1943 Scott and David Lewis collaborated on a review of CCF history and policy entitled *Make This YOUR Canada*. It was designed to present the CCF as attractively as possible, but it was the spirit and inspiration of J.S. Woodsworth, who had died on March 21, 1942, that dominated the book. In the foreword M.J. Coldwell recommended the book to readers in Woodsworth's own words: "Every socialist should have a reason for the faith that is in him." The book also included, as a frontispiece, a Karsh photograph capturing Woodsworth's "other-worldly" aspect. This photo, a favourite of Scott's, hung in his office thereafter. Speaking of Woodsworth's death in *Make This YOUR Canada*, Scott and Lewis stressed his devotion to the people of Canada, his "great moral courage and faith in the future of his country, [that] had won for him a permanent place in the front rank of the builders of Canada."[6]

In the book Scott and Lewis ask "Who owns Canada?"[7] It had been forced, they insisted, to conform to capitalism; Canadians must reverse the process to make the economy conform, instead, to the democratic ideal. In a chapter entitled "The CCF Comes to Power," a blueprint for the new Canada is given. M.J. Coldwell, visualized as the Prime Minister giving his inaugural address, warns: "Any attempt by vested interests to sabotage the people's programme will be promptly and energetically stopped by proper legal action in accordance with the democratic principles of Canadian justice."[8] The book concludes with an expression of faith and vision. What is needed is "a social faith which we can express in our personal conduct and in our national policies. We realize that without vision we perish."[9]

"Vested interests" were not slow to react. The *London Post* of December 30, 1943, ran an article with a cartoon entitled "How to Make This *Their* Canada." A tall simpleton, clearly Scott, is depicted standing in front of an office door labelled "Patents." He carries a little contraption tagged "How to Run the World" with another tag saying "Perpetual Motion." It was not surprising that the gains made by the CCF and publication of the book generated such responses. Industrialists recognized that the CCF represented a genuine threat. And there was more to come.

Even Scott and Lewis's vision, strongly social democratic, was not sufficient for other members of the CCF, such as Harold Winch, who leaned further to the left. Nationally, the party suffered a setback on November, 1943, when Winch, a British Columbia MLA, was goaded into saying that under a CCF government "the power of the police and military would be used to force those opposed [to the party's program] to obey the law." Elaborating later, he added: "Those who defied the government's will would be treated as criminals.... If capitalism says no, then we know the answer – so did Russia." He added that "a CCF government would scrap the BNA Act and give Canada a Canadian constitution."[10] Some of Winch's remarks were taken out of context and distorted. Yet the general import was accurate. The implications of totalitarianism and the notion of tampering with the British North America Act, a particularly touchy subject for Quebec, caused the whole country's censure of the CCF. "A-Winching we will go" was A.M. Klein's ironic summary.[11]

An earlier setback had been suffered by the CCF in August, 1943, with David Lewis's defeat in a by-election in the Cartier riding in Montreal, a working-class district with a large Jewish population. Lewis, who had grown up in Cartier, was a natural choice as the CCF candidate, but he had refused to run earlier because the riding was notoriously corrupt. Encouraged by gains the CCF had made in other parts of Canada, he agreed in 1943 to stand for office. The other candidates were Lazarus Phillips, a Liberal, Paul Massé of the Bloc populaire, and Fred Rose, who represented the Labour Progressive Party, the Communists.

Lewis had difficulties from the outset. He lost significant support at the nominating meeting because he would not endorse a statement by a group of labour Zionists. He insisted he represented all the riding's working people. When the first voters' lists came out, the CCF discovered they were extensively falsified. They protested, achieved a re-enumeration, but the improvement was slight.[12] Rose won the election by appealing to immigrant population sympathies for the Russian war effort against Germany. Massé, representing the anti-war, anti-conscription feelings of the French populace, was only 150 votes behind. Lewis came last. The CCF had run a scrupulously clean campaign but had had little to offer the riding's special interests and could not compete with its rivals' powerful election machinery.

In contrast to failure in Quebec, the CCF achieved a great victory in Saskatchewan when, in June, 1944, a CCF provincial government was elected. T.C. Douglas, the new premier, immediately asked Scott to come to Regina as a constitutional adviser to the government. When he arrived and walked into the legislative buildings with Douglas, Scott was struck by the apprehension of the civil servants present. Clearly they all expected to be fired by the CCF revolutionaries.[13] The popular press did not help matters. *Saturday Night*, for example, warned that the totalitarian revolution had begun.[14] In Saskatchewan, Scott attempted to allay these fears.[15]

By midsummer 1944, all parties were girding up for a federal election. After the CCF's Saskatchewan success it was evidently a serious contender. The Liberals in particular were fighting back with a virulent anti-CCF newspaper campaign, especially in the *Winnipeg Free Press*. George Ferguson, who had written such editorials for the *Free Press*, was moved to *The Montreal Star*, where he continued the attack on the CCF. He then published an editorial alleging the CCF had not replied to an earlier one. Scott wrote the paper, pointing out that the CCF had responded but the newspaper had not published the letter. Not surprisingly, *The Star* did not publish the second letter either. A stormy confrontation between Scott and *The Star*'s publisher, J.W. McConnell, brought no satisfaction. McConnell simply insisted that CCF principles promoted foolish notions and lies and refused to listen to arguments to the contrary, even from the eloquent Scott.[16]

Immediately following the argument, Scott wrote a rebuttal of *The Star* editorials, had it privately printed, and sent it to many prominent Montrealers, personally addressing a copy to each member of the McGill Board of Governors. "That was a good letter you wrote, Frank," Principal Cyril James was heard to observe. McConnell began to be twitted by several other members of the Board of Governors.[17] Socialism might be beyond the pale, but they considered yellow journalism even more so. The all-powerful McConnell was not accustomed to being thwarted. He retaliated by barring the use of Scott's name in *The Star*'s columns.

The other major English-language paper in Montreal, *The Gazette*, was equally conservative. This fact was confirmed later in the decade by the novelist Brian Moore, then a young newspaper reporter. His report of an excellent speech given by Scott was blue pencilled out of existence by editors who "weren't interested in anything [Scott] had to say politically."[18] Reporting the incident to Scott, Moore remarked, "You won't get your name in the *Gazette* unless you rape a girl on the corner of Peel and St. Catherines."[19]

Dealing with virulent anti-socialism in the Canadian context was occasionally balanced by the successes of socialism elsewhere. Shortly after the war began, David Lewis and M.J. Coldwell had corresponded with labour parties in the Commonwealth urging an international meeting of socialists to exchange ideas about common objectives. The New Zealand Labour Party had formed the government since 1935, and the Australian Labour Party since 1941. In Britain, Labour was a partner in the Churchill government. On behalf of the CCF National Executive, Lewis urged the British Labour Party to hold a conference, for two reasons: "[to] arrive at some common policy regarding the peace negotiations and international order which will follow the defeat of the Nazis in Europe," and to establish a precedent for other such conferences.[20] The British party accepted the idea, and the conference was convened in London in September, 1944.

Five delegates went from Canada: Scott, Coldwell, Lewis, Claire Gillis, a labour representative, and Percy Wright, a Saskatchewan farmer and MP. The participation of the Canadian delegation was important because it helped establish the CCF as part of the Commonwealth's social democratic community. One item on the Canadians' agenda was to insist that India be given its freedom after the war. But their major task was to describe the CCF's history and future. Other conference delegates were surprised at the extent and importance of farmers in the party. Scott's own presentation dealt with the "world assembly" to be established after the war. He suggested a structure and purpose in some detail. "The Commonwealth of the future is a Commonwealth of absolutely independent nations, whose association is not based on a constitutional tie, but a voluntary and free association which is the standard definition of our relationship."[21]

Scott found many British Labour leaders depressing. Apart from Morrison, they seemed old and empty. He appreciated Harold Laski's comment in reaction to James Walker, a Labour MP who fulminated like a Tory. Laski whispered to Scott: "You see what I have to work with. I wish I had died in 1913 and not lived to witness the disintegration of this great movement."[22]

While in London, the group was also taken on a tour of the war-ravaged city. It was a disheartening experience for all. On September 12, Scott woke at 6:15 a.m. when "an enormous bang woke me to the sickening realisation that this was a live bomb." Later he "saw a dead man on a street corner, creating an enormous vacancy." After several days in London, and again in response to the bombs, he began to have seizures like those experienced in 1941 at Harvard.[23]

But there were lighter moments. After a visit to Canada House to call on Vincent Massey, then High Commissioner in London, Scott noted in his diary: "We must abolish the uniformed flunky there when we take over."[24] Meeting a Canadian officer with a glass eye who had recently fought with Tito in Yugoslavia, he reflected, "I might have seen combatant service after all." And at a lunch given by Massey, he sat next to Sir Benjamin Jowett, "who discussed nice points of constitutional law like (1) Edward VIII's rights to Sandringham, Balmoral and the furniture in Buckingham Palace after he renounced the throne; (2) the lack of precedence for the Dominion High Commissioners; (3) what would happen if a son were born to the Queen seven months after the King had died and after the Princess had ascended the throne."[25]

When Scott returned to Canada preparations for a federal election were in high gear. In the spring of 1944 the CCF had appointed Coldwell, Lewis, and Scott to establish a program to be presented to the CCF national conference to be held in Montreal in November, 1945, where delegates were to hammer out a CCF platform. Before leaving for London, they had met in the Maritimes to prepare a draft to go before the National Council. On their return Lewis and Scott clarified this draft and sent copies to provincial secretaries. Despite this attempt at internal democracy in the CCF, when the meeting convened in Montreal a small but determined group of the 203 delegates strenuously opposed the program.

One of the main debates concerned the proposed nationalization of the banks. Lewis and Scott argued for a less militant policy. This was, after all, just the first round of a proposed program; there would be plenty of time to introduce more rigorous tactics later. Harold Winch and Colin Campbell, two of the outspoken radicals from British Columbia, were adamant. The old tension between the purists and those who wanted a more pragmatic vote-getting policy again flared up.[26] Ultimately Lewis and Scott won, but there were sore feelings within the party and the more militant speakers, especially Winch, played into the hands of the party's opponents.

Despite increasing pressure to call an election, Prime Minister King delayed until June, 1945. He had hoped that if he waited long enough the war would end and he could avoid facing the voters on the conscription issue alone. At the beginning of 1945, CCF members were optimistic. They could count among their achievements formation of the official opposition in the Ontario legislature in 1943, formation of the government in Saskatchewan in 1944, winning three federal by-elections since 1942, doubling the CCF vote in Alberta, an increase in membership in the Maritimes, and the election of a member to the Quebec legislature. The party held 109 seats in provincial legislatures. Scott, visiting Regina in July, 1944, for the CCF provincial convention, told a capacity crowd of delegates: " 'The CCF is going to win the next Federal election. We can win it – and we will win it'."[27] In January, 1945, however, the CCF came in a poor third in a crucial by-election in Ontario.

After the January by-election, King continued to postpone announcing an election date, while trying to consolidate the Liberal Party in Quebec, where an independent Liberal movement was being formed. Eventually, in April, he called the election for June 12, and in Ontario where a provincial election was to be held June 4, the campaign was intertwined. The Liberal Party was in better shape than he expected: the war in Europe had ended on May 8 and the subversive Liberal movement in Quebec had died. The party based its campaign on King's record and experience, concentrated on post-war reconstruction, and was aided in its campaign by ongoing registration for family allowance, which kept the Liberals' CCF-inspired social programs prominent. The Conservatives, misjudging the conscription issue, continued to call for conscription. Initially they also attacked family allowance as a "political bribe," but then retracted.

Despite the 1944 Gallup polls, which had shown that the CCF was in an exceptionally strong position relative to the other parties, by 1945 King had again turned the tables, convincing the electorate that liberalism was the only safe middle course, untainted by the rigidity of the Conservatives or the radicalism of the CCF. Moreover, the Liberals had the great advantage of having co-opted a number of the CCF's welfare programs. With the end of the war and a return to normality, much of the electorate returned to traditional political loyalties. Moreover, recent anti-CCF campaigns were taking their toll. All these factors contributed to the disastrous results, both federally and provincially, for the CCF. It was no longer the official opposition in Ontario and federally it lost all its Ontario support. The twenty-eight seats it did win were all from the West, with the exception of one seat from the Maritimes.[28]

Despite the bitter disappointment of the 1945 election, the election of a CCF government in Saskatchewan still seemed a harbinger of a new social order. T.C. Douglas, following the precepts on social planning put forth in *Make This YOUR Canada*, set in motion new social measures designed to restore Saskatchewan to its citizens, engaging experts to advise the new government, among them an English specialist, George Cadbury, appointed as the director of an Economic Advisory and Planning Board.

As legal adviser to the new CCF government, Scott frequently travelled by train to Saskatchewan. On one such trip in the summer of 1946, he read an article by Stephen Spender in *The Partisan Review* on "The Making of a Poem." Its setting is another train journey, one across the "Black Country" of England. Surveying the wounded landscape of gaping pits and pitheads, of slag heaps and jagged cuts in the ground, Spender had felt as devastated as the land. Then a poetic line had flashed into his head, "a language of flesh and roses." Analysing the associations that gave rise to these words, Spender decided that the world man creates is a symbolic language for his inner thoughts and wishes; the Black Country, the industrial landscape, enslaving both employers and employees, is an expression of human will. But what language does man really aspire to? The answer was "a language of flesh and roses," that is, an ethically and aesthetically beautiful language embodying a humane and harmonious social world.[29]

As Scott read Spender's essay, his own train sped through northern Ontario and across the huge spaces of the Laurentian Shield. An image of the land began to form in his mind, shaping the poem. It was one that found Koestler's middle ground, the synthesis Scott had admired in *The*

*Yogi and the Commissar*. He began to move toward a language that merged with social ideas and the landscape.

> Hidden in wonder and snow, or sudden with summer,
> This land stares at the sun in a huge silence
> Endlessly repeating something we cannot hear.
> Inarticulate, arctic,
> Not written on by history, empty as paper,
> It leans away from the world with songs in its lakes
> Older than love, and lost in the miles.   (C.P., p. 58)

Scott the punster enjoys the play between "arctic" and "inarticulate" – the voice of the land that cannot now be heard. Because "arctic" or uncultivated, the land is without a history or language; to man it seems a *tabula rasa*. Yet, in the depths of its lakes, it has "songs" of its own. These songs, like the geographically ancient Shield, were produced in the aeons before humanity emerged. They are "older than love," than the first man or woman, and far away, "lost in the miles" of time and geography. Canada, a new place that "leans away from the world," must also develop its own ways.

   Articulation of the land's old songs, like the characteristics of its physical development, is dependent on human "technic."

> This waiting is wanting.
> It will choose its language
> When it has chosen its technic,
> A tongue to shape the vowels of its productivity.
>
> *A language of flesh and roses.*   (C.P., p. 58)

Now, travelling to Saskatchewan, contemplating the new socialist experiment and his role as a contributor to it, Scott considered the wedding of technocrats and politics it represented. His pun on "technic" fuses the concepts of technological development and artistic technique. Technique, as Arthur Lismer had said in a 1933 radio talk, is a "double-barrelled word. It implies *how* a thing is done-style-mannerisms-directions-process. Or, it means the actual material employed – a technique for oil painting, a different one concerning water colour."[30] This concept of "technic" leads into Spender's "a language of flesh and roses." What is desired is a technology conditioned by aesthetic and material considerations: one that will lead to fruitful cultivation of the land, a language of love and poetry. Like Spender, Scott uses the phrase to imply culture in its highest sense.

Scott also begins to consider Spender's vision of man's relation with the land in terms of the Canadian experience. Several years earlier, in 1943, he had written about this northern land when the Shipshaw Power Development threatened to exploit Canada's North. This is, in the words of the poem, "The long sentence of its exploitation . / ... the bold command of monopolies, big with machines, / Carving their kingdoms out of the public wealth" (*C.P.*, p. 58). The proposed development had "very serious implications," Scott had said at the time, "not only for the future of democracy in North America, but for Canadian-American relations.... On what terms is this development to occur?"[31] Scott demanded. Now, the Saskatchewan experience, that brand-new socialist utopia, offered the possibility of bringing together the best in man's technical and political knowledge.

The poem sketches the history of Canadian development, determined by geography and characterized by differing forms of exploitation. The land has music ("songs") to which man brings words, "... pre-words, / Cabin syllables, / Nouns of settlement," but ominously, the language is moving through "steel syntax" toward "The long sentence of its exploitation," with its implicit legal and linguistic pun. The danger is that a technology of exploitation, of rape, is replacing the ideal of love and nurture. Thus development of the land is expressed through an evolutionary language. But it is not until the land acquires a "history" – interpolating with the human – that the "sentences" can be connected.

The land's "first cry" was that of the hunter and gold-digger; then came the "bold command of monopolies, big with machines, / Carving their kingdoms out of the public wealth." Now "... the drone of the plane ... links our future over the vanished pole" (*C.P.*, p. 58). The plane, unlike the railroad, is seen as a friendly force, it shrinks the northern waste and "Fills all the emptiness with neighbourhood," creating the global village.

All these aspects of the poem are implicitly linked to the Saskatchewan experiment, where northern social and economic development was an important aspect of the CCF program. George Cadbury later remarked, "Saskatchewan Government Airways visited every lake and settlement monthly and the communications centre at Lac la Ronge maintained radio contact. These activities led to head-on competition with the Hudson's Bay Company who had previously maintained a monopoly after their agreement with the Nor'Westers."[32]

The conclusion of "Laurentian Shield" affirms that it is in such "neighbourhood," in human closeness and social co-operation, that future hope is to be found.

But a deeper note is sounding, heard in the mines,
The scattered camps and the mills, a language of life,
And what will be written in the full culture of occupation
Will come, presently, tomorrow,
From millions whose hands can turn this rock
　　　　　into children.　(*C.P.*, p. 58)

Scott's poem affirms the Canadian North's potential, one to be nurtured into being by social co-operation. For many socialists in the 1940s, the new CCF government in Saskatchewan represented the vision Scott expresses in the poem. The poem itself embodied the politics of his own imaginative process.

"Laurentian Shield" marked the beginning of a new stage in Scott's life. He seemed, at this time, to have been balancing the rival claims of poetry and politics. Gradually he began to move away from politics and into the period of his best poems. Just as Koestler had shown him the weakness of a socialist blueprint that did not consider man's irrational side, so Spender provided a rationale for the argument that poetry (rather than politics) provided the higher vocation. Like Scott, Spender had experienced a political disillusionment in the thirties and was now turning with renewed energy to poetry. Four years later, in 1950, Scott was to resign as national chairman of the CCF.

At the August, 1946, national conference, the CCF delegates assessed their 1945 election defeats and the subsequent decline in popularity of the party. At the root of many important debates was the party's dualistic nature: it was a socialist movement dedicated to the tenets of the Regina Manifesto, but in the interests of attempting to win elections, principally the 1945 federal election, some party members had moved the CCF to a more moderate stance. They now argued that a more pragmatic approach was necessary to win votes. At the 1946 convention Scott noted: "It is as though we had lost faith in ourselves; zeal is lacking, because inside each CCF member there is an element of doubt about his function and role at the present moment."[33] At its core, however, he believed the party was correct in its analysis of society. It would have to rethink its position, but this did not reduce the importance or necessity of the CCF program for Canada. Coldwell, too, dropped his electioneering rhetoric and reiterated some of the party's basic premises. By the mid-forties there was a moderation in the CCF program, particularly with respect to the role of business in a social democratic Canada.

While the CCF by 1946 was not experiencing the popularity it had in the early forties, it was holding its own across the nation. It increased its efforts to improve ties with and support from the unions and ran an extensive education campaign resulting in a number of publications. But the situation in Quebec had not changed. Scott wrote sadly in 1947: "Had lunch with our French group today – all 5 of them.... [They] say we cannot operate in Quebec outside Montreal – we have been too effectively labelled as communist, centralist, Anglo-Saxon and imperialist."[34]

In 1949, a small organization called L'Equipe des Recherches Sociales received financial support from the Canadian Congress of Labour in the hope that it might stimulate political action. Scott, Forsey, Gérard Pelletier of *Le Devoir*, Jean Marchand, secretary of the Canadian and Catholic Confederation of Labour, and Pierre Elliott Trudeau, a Montreal lawyer close to the CCF, attended a meeting of the group. Lewis recalled that little was accomplished and Trudeau, "who [had undertaken] a number of projects, went to work in the Privy Council Office." However, none of these associations substantially advanced the CCF cause.[35]

# FOURTEEN

# The Law Teacher

❦

I N 1945 AND 1946 Scott the teacher found himself facing, in his first-year constitutional law classes, a new type of student: veterans. In his lectures he talked about the nature of Canada and what it meant to be a Canadian – topics of considerable interest to a serious and hardworking group of men whose war experiences had led them to think seriously about the shape of the post-war world.[1] The law faculty now occupied an old mansion at the corner of Pine and Peel called Purvis Hall, and the classes, given in the dining room, bedrooms, and reception areas, were severely cramped. In 1948, the law library, although an improvement from the late twenties, was still inadequate. Especially after his Harvard experience, Scott felt dissatisfied with conditions in Canadian law faculties. It irked him to think that McGill could pour money into the medical faculty, which enjoyed a prestigious international reputation, while starving the school of law. In spite of these conditions the returning veterans found Scott's teaching first-class. The law faculty at McGill now included three full-time professors and by the end of 1947, there were six on permanent faculty.

Scott lectured easily and spontaneously. Recognizably less conservative than his colleagues, he frequently wore a tweed sports jacket, grey flannels, and a handwoven tie, rather than the conventional navy-blue suit. Yet, when occasion warranted, he would appear in class in the expected attire. Scott did not express himself in eccentricity of dress, but rather through the freshness of his lectures. "Pens down! Brains up!" was one of his maxims – an exhortation that demanded original response rather than rote-learning: the "out-pulling" of knowledge he and Terry MacDermot had so long ago at Lower Canada College defined as the proper function of a teacher.[2] Often stimulated by something he had read in the newspapers, Scott would bring articles into the classroom, put them into a larger historical or political context, and show their relationship to the legal principles under discussion. He lectured in the English fashion, but he had a way of turning what could have been a dull exposition into a Socratic dialogue.

He intended his courses to reflect current practices. For his course on administrative law, he wrote to a former student, Arnold Heeney, clerk of the Privy Council and secretary to the cabinet, explaining that he wanted to teach more than just the analysis of legal actions against administrative officers – the usual component of such courses.

> I want also to give the students some picture of federal departments and their inter-relations. I have seen some charts illustrating the various war committees of the government, and I am wondering whether there exists any chart showing the ordinary government departments and committees. Such a chart would illustrate far better than a mere verbal description just what is involved in the whole problem of conducting the affairs of the modern state like Canada.[3]

Was there such a chart available on the Privy Council and its various committees?

When teaching administrative law, Scott expressed his concern about undue judicial interference with legislative policy. In 1948 he wrote: "Judges must not substitute their notions of social purpose for those of the legislature; indeed, they are there to see that the policy of parliament is carried out, not that it is altered or frustrated."[4] Nonetheless, he believed in the role of the courts in maintaining the rule of the law and in protecting civil liberties. He was convinced that the state should be liable for damage caused by its wrongful acts and he urged the elimination of the immunity of the crown.[5]

Following the example of his teacher H.A. Smith, Scott in his lectures on constitutional law showed his students how the decisions of the Judicial Committee of the British Privy Council had altered the nature of the constitution as drawn up by the Fathers of Confederation. Such changes, he taught, weakened the central government and its power to deal with national problems. He also pointed out that if a democratic government failed to act to define its sphere of power, the vacuum would be filled by the governing power of the large corporations, a thesis later to be developed in depth in J.K. Galbraith's *The New Industrial State* (1967).[6]

Woven through his lectures on constitutional law was an examination of the development of Canadian independence, the striving to make Canada an equal partner in a larger community of nations. Here he also brought in the constitutional relationships among Commonwealth nations and frequently discussed what later came to be known as "the patriation of the Canadian constitution." Scott liked to remark that Canada had "a rendez-vous with the BNA Act." One of his students at this time, Gerald Le Dain, now of the Supreme Court of Canada, recalled that Scott "taught constitutional law as if he wanted his students to be prepared for that rendez-vous, whatever the agenda might be."[7]

Scott's lectures on constitutional law also examined the problem of Canadian unity, with particular attention to the position of French Canada in Confederation with respect to the BNA Act. A French-Canadian student in the early forties, Marc Lapointe, later chairman of the Canadian Labour Relations Board, recalled that the third day he was at McGill University he ran into trouble with Scott's opening constitutional law lecture. Scott said that the Canadian constitution was not the result of an agreement by two founding nations as Lapointe had been taught in his Quebec classical studies but that, in fact, it was Westminster law, English law. He had told the students that if they had any serious questions when he was teaching they might always interrupt. Lapointe immediately jumped to his feet. "Sir, this is awful what you are saying. It is not true, it is most contrary to everything that has been taught to me." Lapointe recalled that Scott listened patiently and then replied, " 'I said that I was willing to be interrupted. What you're raising is so basic, may I ask your permission to wait for an answer after the lecture?' And I sat down simmering."

After the lecture Scott took the young student to his office. "Before I answer your question, Mr. Lapointe, and before you raise it again, may I suggest to you that you take about a week of your time because I have a list of documents and books which I would like to refer you to. In all fairness to you, I would like you to read them before you insist upon my answering your question." Lapointe then spent a "tough but enlightening week" in the library reading the reference books and documents Scott had given him, together with a handwritten paper on the constitution. "That convinced me that I was wrong. The way he handled it impressed me tremendously." Fruitful confrontations such as this one consolidated Scott's reputation with Francophone students.

Scott later encouraged Lapointe to write a thesis on the Quebec labour unions, about which almost nothing had been written. It was quite a difficult topic because the thesis was to show which elements of Quebec labour law had been created from the labour legislation of France and which had been borrowed from American labour legislation. At the end of his first year of study, Lapointe had exhausted all the references Scott had given him, yet the topic had not been covered. He went to Scott's office and said, " 'I have read everything that you have given to me, Frank. I have nothing more to read and I still have a lot of queries'."

" 'Good! Good,' he said, 'because I have news for you. There's nothing else to read and you've got now to find the answers to those queries that you discovered.' He said, 'I can't help you any more. From now on you will be teaching me'." Ultimately, Lapointe produced the first thesis on labour law in Quebec, and with Scott's encouragement, it was written in French. His topic was so specialized that an examining committee could not be found. He was awarded his degree solely on his written work.

When Scott had first advised Lapointe about his graduate thesis and future career, he had pointed out that labour law was a new and most important subject, "especially," as he told the young man, "if you go for the union side. They have practically nobody to advise them. And he was fair with me because he told me, of course, if you go on the management side it's far more lucrative than on the union side. You have to work far harder on the union side to make the same amount of money – and possibly never – as you do on the management side, but, he said, it's more *human*." It was because of Scott, Lapointe acknowledges, that he began a distinguished career in labour law.[8]

As a Quebecer Scott was sympathetic to French Canada's desire for fairer opportunities and more autonomy, and at the personal level he had a stimulating effect on young Francophones who came to McGill to study law. However, his interpretation of the constitution, which insisted that the BNA Act was an English statute, and his belief that the strong federal powers written into the constitution were necessary for the preservation of the country ran into conflict with his position as a Quebecer. Scott resolved this conflict by distinguishing between minority rights and provincial rights. All his experience in Quebec, particularly abuses in the field of civil liberties, led him inescapably to the conclusion that only federal action could ensure minority rights.

In his lectures and public addresses Scott spoke of the necessity of entrenching a Bill of Rights in the Canadian constitution. In a lecture given to the Junior Bar Association of Quebec City circa 1942-43, Scott set out his ideal for the Canadian constitution. A constitution, he pointed out, is not an end in itself, but only a means to an end. "If Canadians can agree upon the great and lasting principles upon which they wish their society to be built, then they can agree upon the broad lines of the constitution needed to achieve those ends." What he emphasized was the need for a national vision of what Canada *ought* to be, a view that extended Scott's earlier concept of the "just society."

After reviewing a number of provincial fears about the increasing federal powers of centralization necessitated by the war, Scott argued that many of these powers are beneficent for Canada. "If we can be happier, healthier and stronger by using all our agencies of government, instead of just our local governments, then let us do so, always maintaining a just equilibrium." Scott foresaw that when the war was over there would be certain fields in which Parliament would be called upon to assume new responsibilities. Far from interfering with provincial rights, these changes would provide economic security so that the provinces and other local governments could function smoothly and efficiently. "We must not abolish the federal system; we must not scrap the BNA Act. We must make it workable under the conditions of our day." The purpose underlying future constitutional law must be the preservation, not only of the social health and welfare of Canadians, "but also of the spiritual and cultural values which our dual civilization presupposes."

He saw three choices facing Canadians in regard to amending the BNA Act. The first was to do nothing; the second was to analyse the problems faced by Canada and divide and allot provincial and federal functions; the third was to recognize that the time had come for Canada, "a nation of dual cultures which has at last attained full political freedom, to adopt a new national constitution." Canadians could draft a new fundamental law after calling a constituent convention representing all parties in the Dominion and the provinces. To secure the new constitution from attack in the courts, it could be approved by all Canadian legislatures as well as by the imperial Parliament. Canadians then would have "achieved that full nationhood that comes from a solemn act approved by a democratic process." This is a difficult step, "yet sooner or later Canadians must face up to the responsibilities of nationhood, and sooner or later, unless we cease to exist as a nation, we shall come to my third alternative." The problem of the constitution, Scott reminded his audience – and later the students in his law classes – is the great question their generation could not escape. "Let us who are members of the legal profession realise that it is our duty to think calmly and coolly about our constitution, and to provide a leadership...."[9]

As a law teacher Scott was highly challenging. Through his lectures and through his speeches and writing, he prepared his students to consider seriously the problems involved in governing a country like Canada. Frequently he offered a sustained critique of the capitalist system and the legal institutions and doctrines that maintained it.[10] Scott's teaching, shaped by his philosophical outlook, was not neutral. Because he did not articulate the fact that he was an active member of the CCF, he liked to say that he never used the classroom as a platform. "I never allowed my political work to interfere with my lectures. I never cancelled a lecture on that account. Our [CCF] meetings were always in Ottawa on weekends and I took great care to give no grounds for saying that I was neglecting my academic [work]." As he also recalled, the students "knew pretty well where I stood, but I didn't ram it down their throats."[11] He did not need to speak out about his socialist affiliations; they were apparent to his students, implicit in his judgement, what he attached importance to, what he found fault with or considered amusing. Indeed, his acknowledged mastery of his subject permitted him to express his social philosophy. Sons of the conservative leaders of the Montreal establishment, many students found Scott's radicalism provocative. At night they would report to their indignant fathers, "Do you know what Professor Scott said today?" One former student speculated that some of the pleasure they derived from Scott, who in his more prophetic mode tore strips off the establishment, was a kind of vicarious expression of revolt against father.[12] Although few of his students took up his socialist views, many report that their sense of the law was enlarged.

Scott taught in the same liberal tradition he had experienced at Oxford, which holds that an education is not just the learning of a specific set of facts of a narrowly defined discipline but rather is based on a broad foundation of learning. His course in public law could have been grasped by upper-division arts students as well as law students, for he drew on his own wider interest in history and politics to make his courses more relevant. But his classes did not lack professional rigour. Students were grounded in fundamentals and the courses were comprehensive. Scott, who specialized in public law, also had a good background in private law. Consequently, his legal views were not narrow. He was not interested in abstractions for their own sake but in the principles, their operations and effects in specific law cases.[13]

For Scott the law had an aesthetic quality. And he himself spoke and wrote with elegance, clarity, and force. His lectures were enlivened by his quiet sense of humour, by his enjoyment of the epigram and aphorism, by irony, and by his strong sense of the ridiculous.[14] When describing the harassment of members of the Jehovah's Witnesses sect by the Premier of Quebec in the *The Canadian Forum*, Scott entitled his discussion "Jehovah versus Duplessis," thus wittily reminding his audience that the issue was not simply a troublesome sect in a provincial context but the greater cause of freedom of religion. In this equation a mere Premier had taken on the God of the Israelites.

In 1946, in addition to his regular law classes, Scott was also meeting privately with a young Francophone who wanted a stronger grounding in constitutional law. Charles Lussier, later director of the Canada Council and clerk of the Senate, then a 1945 graduate in law from the University of Montreal, was unable to go to Harvard because of the rush of returned American veterans. Could he attend Scott's courses in constitutional law?[15]

Scott's primacy in this field was now well recognized by French Quebecers. Moreover, after the 1942 publication of his pamphlet *The Plebiscite Vote in Quebec*, Scott had a reputation as a man sympathetic to Quebec interests. When he had spoken to students at the University of Montreal early in 1943 both Lussier and Trudeau had been in the audience. There he lectured on the Statute of Westminster, tracing the evolution of Canada from Empire to Commonwealth. Lussier had been impressed by Scott's advocacy of "more centralization in order to give Ottawa more flexibility in matters of commerce and finance in dealing with crisis of any kind, and in the field of employment. One of his great ideas was the equalization. As a great socialist, he wanted the greatest possible distribution of wealth." Most important, Scott had recognized the aspirations of French Canada. Lussier recalled: "Since I have known him, Frank Scott has always said that the BNA Act should be construed as making room for our dual culture. As he wrote himself, the Constitution is also important because 'It largely determines the relations of the individual and cultural groups to one another and to the state'."[16]

Lussier, who shared Scott's hopes for Quebecers, found him a great inspiration. The young law graduate was told he would be wasting his time attending lectures. Scott gave Lussier a list of texts and proposed a meeting every two weeks for discussion. In effect, Scott set up a tutorial on the Oxford model. It was the intellectual probity of the man, his openness and his search for truth, that first attracted students. And they continued to return to his office after graduation because he was genuinely concerned about their futures. Lussier remained in touch with Scott and through Lussier, and also Jean Marchand, whom he began to meet through his CCF work with Quebec labour unions, Scott began to move in a circle of young Quebec intellectuals that included Trudeau and Gérard Pelletier. At labour meetings, social gatherings, and through shared interests, Scott and Trudeau began to see more of each other; by the late fifties, as R.I. Cheffins, then doing postgraduate work at McGill, recalled, Trudeau was a frequent visitor to Scott's office.[17]

Over the years Scott taught a number of young men whose future careers were, to some degree, influenced by concepts of law absorbed from Scott. In the twenties and early thirties he taught Carl Goldenberg, later to become a senator; John Humphrey, who became a law professor, a United

Nations official, and finally a colleague at McGill; and David Lewis of the CCF-NDP. In the mid-thirties he taught Abraham Feiner and Albert Marcus, who later were to become his colleagues in the Padlock case. In the forties his students included Emile Colas, a senior partner in a prominent Montreal law firm, Mr. Justice Gerald Le Dain, and Charles Lussier. In the fifties he taught, among many others, Leonard Cohen, who left law for poetry; former Minister of Justice Donald Johnston; Donald Mac-Sween, former director-general of the National Arts Centre; Michael Pitfield, formerly clerk of the Privy Council and now a senator; Timothy Porteous, former head of the Canada Council; and Lionel Tiger, a social anthropologist now at Rutgers.

Above all, Scott impressed his students because he practised the ideals of the law he taught. While he was teaching classes in constitutional law that the citizenship rights of minorities were guaranteed by the BNA Act, he was also writing to newspapers across the country protesting against the constitutional illegality of the deportation of the Japanese Canadians. While he was arguing in administrative law that an administrator must be responsible for his actions, he was taking up the case of a restaurateur, Frank Roncarelli, who had lost his business due to the administrative actions of the Premier of Quebec.

Scott was one of the few individuals in Canada who spoke out publicly against the deportation of Japanese Canadians just after World War II. On January 4, 1946, he drafted an open letter, sent to fifty-five Canadian newspapers, in which he compared the deportations to the expulsion of the Acadians in 1755: "there was at least some military justification for that deportation whereas there is none for this." Scott condemned the hypocrisy of the argument of "disloyalty" levelled against the Japanese by pointing out that German and Italian Canadians were not put into concentration camps. He also exposed the trickery suggested by the way the Japanese Canadians were manipulated into "choosing" repatriation. The deportations, Scott insisted, made a farce of the Citizenship Bill and reflected racist ideology:

> The real problem we have to solve in Canada has nothing directly to do with the Japanese at all: it is the problem of racial intolerance. This problem is only aggravated by the deportations. They mean a victory for intolerance and bigotry. We should be generous to this harmless minority whom we previously admitted to our shores, and apply fully to them the principle that race, religion and colour are no bar to full citizenship in this democracy.

Although objections to the deportation of the Japanese Canadians were not popular, Scott's letter insisted it was a flagrant example of a violation of minority rights. Only eleven of the fifty-five Canadian newspapers to which it was sent published Scott's letter. By their silence, the majority of Canadians tacitly supported the deportation.

To the law students of 1946, the returned veterans, Scott's letter stood as a measure of his principles – and of his willingness to speak out even on controversial issues. Scott, the academic, represented an important element in the legal community, for only the academic, with the time and ability, can probe deeply into issues and provide critical analysis. The judicial branch of the law, in particular, relies on this in-depth interpretation of the law. By inclination and by ability Scott frequently undertook this role.[18]

His habit of examining issues from all sides and, upon discovery of the truth, speaking out in favor of unpopular causes had continued to prove irritating to the McGill administration. In 1942 when Scott was first appointed national chairman of the CCF, Principal Cyril James wrote to the Dean of the Law School, C.S. LeMesurier, warning him it should be made clear to Scott that he could not use any of the office facilities at McGill for political activities. It was even questionable "whether a full professor, expected to devote the major portion of his energies to University work, could be allowed to undertake this supplementary activity."[19]

The argument was that professors should not take an active part in political life. The previous year this issue had caused l'affaire Underhill in Toronto. In practice, this theory of academic impartiality was a convenient smokescreen for attacking political activities which did not find favour with administrations. In fact, several members of the McGill academic community, including Principal Currie, Cyrus MacMillan, head of the English department, and Brooke Claxton, a part-time lecturer, all ran for political office. But all had the good sense to be Conservatives or Liberals. As such they enjoyed the full support of the McGill Board of Governors. Not only were Scott's politics the wrong kind, but he had incurred the serious displeasure of one of the most influential of the governors, J.W. McConnell, who as editor had banned publication of Scott's name in *The Montreal Star*. It was also well known in Montreal in the forties and fifties that McConnell had said Scott would never be Dean of Law as long as he remained on the Board of Governors.

In January, 1947, the matter came to a head when Scott presented the required summary of his preceding year's political activities to Principal James. Scott had arrived at that point in his career where, as an established teacher and scholar, he could expect to be made dean of his faculty – a position he would hold until retirement. But the principal told Scott that the Board of Governors disapproved of his political activities, and that it was unlikely he would be considered for the upcoming vacancy for the deanship. Scott, who could not be faulted for his legal scholarship, was vulnerable in his politics. Shortly after, the McGill Board of Governors passed a resolution stating that no university professor at McGill could hold major office in a political party. In rebuttal Harold Laski wrote from the London School of Economics about the necessity of professors participating in the political process.[20] However, McGill's Board of Governors had gone a little too far. Their resolution was so obviously tailored for F.R. Scott that even hitherto hostile newspapers and journals, such as the *Winnipeg Free Press* and *Saturday Night*, protested in the name of academic freedom. The Scott case was well on its way to becoming a cause célèbre in the academic world. Bowing to this pressure, and embarrassed by the discovery that the resolution would also apply to another McGill faculty member, the Board of Governors quickly withdrew its resolution.

Nevertheless, the Board had its way on the issue of the deanship and Scott was not appointed. He had made a wager with a contemporary, Cecil Wright (better known as "Caesar") of Osgoode Hall who, like Scott, could reasonably expect to be appointed dean of his faculty. They had agreed that the first of the two to be appointed dean would provide the other with a dinner. Then, in February, Scott was officially informed that the Board of Governors had no intention of appointing him to the deanship. C.S. Lemesurier, who had served as dean of the law faculty from 1936 to 1948, was to be replaced by Gerald Fauteux in 1949. A.S. Bruneau was given the position in 1950. Speaking to Charles Lussier of the incident, Scott quipped bitterly on the irony of the situation: McGill, an English institution, much preferred two French lawyers to him![21] In 1950 the Board of Governors called to the deanship W.C.J. Meredith, a Montreal lawyer in private practice. An unhappy correspondence between the two men ensued. Meredith felt that Scott had a better right than he to the job, but if the Board of Governors would not appoint Scott, then his own conscience was clear.

Wright, however, had been appointed Dean of Law at Osgoode Hall in 1947. Scott wrote him, ruefully admitting that he had been passed over, adding, "this letter will serve as legal notice that I intend to hold you to your contract to supply me with a dinner one of these days. Perhaps before I die you can hold me to mine but certainly there is no likelihood of it being enforceable in the near future."[22] Wright, who was depressed by the Board resolution, wrote to Scott. It was clear that the so-called academic freedoms "about which college presidents make Commencement addresses have very little reality in Canadian universities today. The governors certainly dug deep with regard to that resolution in connection with holding executive office in a political party and as for the inference that even if you did drop your executive office it would not make any difference, I give up."[23]

In 1947, when Cyril James first called Scott to task for his political activities, Scott had replied with a stiff note. As his position at McGill for the year was uncertain, "I cannot afford to let that amount of time pass without doing something to help myself over a difficult period, I have come to the conclusion that I must undertake immediately certain work of a remunerative character. I have some requests for articles which I have been too busy to write, and an opportunity has now come of acting as counsel in the Roncarelli case."[24] The Roncarelli case and its companion, the Padlock case, both challenges to autocratic rulings by Premier Maurice Duplessis, were to prove to be two of the most important cases in Canadian civil rights to emerge in the post-war period. Ironically, Scott's failure to achieve promotion at McGill helped drive him into jousts against Duplessis, jousts that finally vindicated his stand as a professor of federal and constitutional law. Persisting in his principles, he would ultimately prove them to be justified.

IN THE LATE SUMMER OF 1941, when motoring home from Harvard, the Scotts had been invited by a friend, Blair Fraser, a journalist and outdoorsman, to stop off and visit at North Hatley in the Eastern Townships of Quebec. This small community clustered around Lake Massawippi had been a favourite summering spot for visitors from Boston, from Harvard University, and from Montreal since the late nineteenth century. Scott had long known of the community – Leacock had immortalized the sleepy Massawippi in his "Maritime Excursions of the Knights of Pythias" – but this was his first real visit. The Scotts liked what they saw: the gently rolling hills, the verdant green of the countryside, and the lake itself – stretching across the horizon as far as the eye could see. What a wonderful lake for canoeing! The Scotts decided to return the following year for summer holidays – there would be young people for Peter, now thirteen, to play with, and there was a pleasant social life available for his parents. For several years they continued to rent a summer cottage at North Hatley. Later into the decade they contracted jointly with the Frasers to buy a summer house. Scott, who preferred hot weather, chose to have the month of July, up to August 1, his birthday. For the Frasers, who were soon to move from Montreal to Ottawa, the cottage proved less accessible and some years later they sold their share to the Scotts.

Summers at North Hatley became an integral part of the cycle of Frank Scott's life. It was a continuation of his childhood summers in the Laurentians and here he was to experience the same vivid appreciation of nature: in the mid-forties he wrote at North Hatley one of his finest poems, "Lakeshore."

> ... And I am a tall frond that waves
> Its head below its rooted feet
> Seeking the light that draws it down
> To forest floors beyond its reach
> Vivid with gloom and eerie dreams.
>
> The water's deepest colonnades
> Contract the blood, and to this home
> That stirs the dark amphibian
> With me the naked swimmers come
> Drawn to their prehistoric womb....
>
> This is our talent, to have grown
> Upright in posture, false-erect,
> A landed gentry, circumspect,
> Tied to a horizontal soil
> The floor and ceiling of the soul;
> Striving, with cold and fishy care
> To make an ocean of the air.
>
> Sometimes, upon a crowded street,
> I feel the sudden rain come down
> And in the old, magnetic sound
> I hear the opening of a gate
> That loosens all the seven seas.
> Watching the whole creation drown
> I muse, alone, on Ararat.  (*C.P.*, pp. 50-51)

The journey down into the water at North Hatley becomes a journey back through evolutionary time to the "prehistoric womb," and, like his earlier plunge at Clovelly, it is also a journey back to the bliss of a more innocent sensual self. Scott always loved water; he felt happiest when rain was falling or when swimming or diving. Too soon, he writes in "Lakeshore," the need for air forces man back up through the water to dry land – the earth that is neither his first home nor his first love. There, as Scott wittily re-marks, he is forced into a new mould, that of "a landed gentry, circumspect."

At North Hatley Scott was free to uncoil; there was leisure for rest and reflection. Here, especially in later years, he found the peace that eluded him in city life. Yet there was a supportive social life when he felt the need for companionship. The Scotts were soon joined by their friends, the Parkins, who found a house just slightly up the hill, by Hugh MacLennan, who bought property nearby, and, in later years, by younger poets and writers such as Louis Dudek, Ralph Gustafson, Ronald Sutherland, and Douglas Jones. Since the mid-thirties, when he had begun teaching at Michigan State, Arthur Smith and his wife Jeannie had returned annually to a summer cottage in nearby Magog. Yet another friend, John Glassco, had a farm in the area at Foster. As time went on, Scott's birthday became the occasion of a poets' party where all the poets and writers gathered.

The decade from the early forties to the early fifties had been a difficult time for Frank Scott. Not only had he experienced a great deal of emotional turmoil but several of the individuals closest to him had died: first Woods-worth and then his mother and father. With the deaths of his two mentors, Woodsworth and the Archdeacon, Scott himself became the father figure. Marian Scott perceived a decided change in her husband. Maturity – and some success – agreed with him. The tall, somewhat lanky man, who had tended in his twenties and thirties to walk with his head a little cast down, now began to assume many of the qualities associated with Archdeacon Scott: the upright, almost military carriage, the avuncular manner, the habit of establishing himself at the centre of an admiring circle, holding forth with witticisms and striking observations. Like Woodsworth, Scott began to be widely known as a man of integrity: a man who could be depended on to speak out against injustice. His own son Peter was now reaching maturity, and Scott found himself a surrogate father for a group of young men, often law students, who were looking to him for direction.

It was a decade of great emotional upheaval, personal as well as political. Certainly he was now forced to rethink his principles regarding the nature of Canada and the democratic socialist state. These principles, expressed in the poem "Laurentian Shield" as well as in the socialist manifesto *Make This YOUR Canada*, reveal a strong nationalism founded on a deep and abiding love of country. The forties taught Scott of the weaknesses of a narrow nationalism. He began to insist on the virtues of an internationalist position, forgetting the significance a strong Canadianism had had in shaping his own character and actions. He was particularly pleased with Canada's developing role at the United Nations and wrote to Escott Reid, then in External Affairs, praising Lester Pearson's role at the United Nations: "we seem to be emerging as the greatest single mediator in the whole picture."[25]

In 1950 Mackenzie King died. Scott wasted little time on the elegiac note; he polished off his old bête noire with the rapier.

> How shall we speak of Canada,
> Mackenzie King dead?
> The Mother's boy in the lonely room
> With his dog, his medium and his ruins?
>
> He blunted us.
>
> We had no shape
> Because he never took sides,
> And no sides
> Because he never allowed them to take shape.
>
> He skilfully avoided what was wrong
> Without saying what was right,
> And never let his on the one hand
> Know what his on the other hand was doing.
>
> The height of his ambition
> Was to pile a Parliamentary Committee on a Royal
>      Commission,
> To have "conscription if necessary
> But not necessarily conscription,"
> To let Parliament decide –
> Later.
>
> Postpone, postpone, abstain.
>
> Only one thread was certain:
> After World War I
> Business as usual,
> After World War II
> Orderly decontrol.
> Always he led us back to where we were before.
>
> He seemed to be in the centre
> Because we had no centre,
> No vision
> To pierce the smoke-screen of his politics.

Truly he will be remembered
Wherever men honour ingenuity,
Ambiguity, inactivity, and political longevity.

Let us raise up a temple
To the cult of mediocrity,
Do nothing by halves
Which can be done by quarters.   (C.P., pp. 78-79)

The death of Mackenzie King symbolized the end of an era. Scott's satiric summary of the Canadian years between 1914 and 1950 is informed by the fury of an idealist, a man who believed in doing "nothing by halves."

# FIFTEEN

# A Grain of Rice

❦

THE FIFTIES was a watershed decade for the Scotts and for the country. Canada, after a new period of internal prosperity, was now increasingly active in foreign affairs; and again, as after World War I, there was a resurgence of nationalist feeling. Now that he was fifty, Scott found himself asking some of the larger questions. He had realized in the forties that an early nationalism had been superseded by internationalism – "the world is my country." Now he began to speak and write of the brotherhood of man. His concepts of religion and socialism, always linked, began to take on a greater international and humanist context. During this decade, Frank achieved full recognition as a lawyer and Marian as an artist. In the fifties he won his most significant legal cases, forged important links with Francophone Quebecers, and published some of his best poetry.

ON JULY 26, 1950, Scott addressed the national convention of the CCF in Vancouver in his final speech as chairman. He was resigning his position and in his speech he paid homage to the Regina Manifesto, acknowledging "the depth of its analysis of capitalism, the vigour of its denunciation of the injustices of Canadian society, and the clarity with which it distinguished democratic socialism from the liberal economic theories of the old-line parties." He believed that it had allowed the CCF to hold "to its own true path." However, he warned the gathering: "The socialist must be aware of world trends, and must realize that he is no more free than anyone else from the danger of becoming old-fashioned."

So began what was to be a very stormy and bitterly debated convention. The CCF National Executive had felt the necessity for some time to make a formal restatement of party principles. There was a strong emotional attachment to the manifesto but many also thought that sections were no longer relevant to the post-war period. The call to eradicate capitalism was damaging since it had so often been misinterpreted by opponents of the CCF. With improved economic conditions many thought that there was room for some private ownership and that isolationism was a pre-League of Nations concept that had, in fact, been abandoned during the war. The Canadian social democratic party was not the only socialist party reconsidering its position; such debates were also being held in the British Labour Party and the social democratic parties of western Europe.

Scott's speech considered some of socialism's fundamental precepts and the changed conditions now facing the CCF. He still believed in the purposes first enunciated at Regina, but "the means of giving effect to them must be adapted to the changing needs and opportunities of society itself." Some of the changed conditions facing the CCF included more employment benefits and other social measures instituted by the Liberal government. But Scott emphasized that socialism is concerned not just with the amount of wealth produced but also with the quality of our social relations.

> It is evident that this thing we may call the spirit of man, this light of faith and conscience and decency on which all civilization depends, is not primarily dependent on the ownership of property, essential though it is to subject all forms of ownership to social controls.... Socialism is first and foremost concerned with the human spirit, with its freedom, its growth, its emancipation, and with its ownership only in so far as some of its forms are obstacles to this freedom just as other forms seem essential to it. Socialism expresses in the fullest degree the great traditions of political democracy.[1]

At the 1950 conference the CCF also put forward its controversial "two nations" policy for French Canada, which accepted Quebec's claim that there existed at Confederation a pact between two national groups. As convention chairman Scott did not publicly differ with this policy, though as a constitutional lawyer he could not have accepted its premises. Eugene Forsey was indignant both with the party and with Scott. Convinced that the CCF had adopted a spurious policy merely to attract Quebec votes, Forsey left the conference and resigned from the party.[2]

Although Scott never withdrew his support from the CCF (and later the NDP), this conference marks the end of his greatest involvement and public role with the party. He did not, however, completely withdraw; later, he served on committees established by the CCF to oversee and eventually facilitate the formation of what became the New Democratic Party. But shortly after his resignation as national chairman, Scott's attention and interest were to be drawn into the wider sphere of internationalism.

IN OCTOBER, 1951, Scott wrote to his old friend Terry MacDermot, now High Commissioner for Canada in South Africa, bringing him up to date on the Scotts. "I continue here, Marian continues painting, Peter continues at Oxford. I turned down a UN job that would have taken me to Burma for a year, but something of this sort is looming again."³ The family was drawing apart, setting out in different directions. Peter was now at Oxford reading for a B.Phil. in politics, Marian's art was blossoming in Montreal, and Frank was about to leave for Burma.

After Peter's graduation from high school he enrolled at McGill. A year later, in the summer of 1946, he drove out to Saskatchewan with some other CCFers for a CCF conference. From there he wrote his cousin Rosemary Kelley, "behind us lie 2200 dusty miles.... The roads here are terrible – the towns are scraggly – the whole province seems poor and I am sure the CCF has a lot of work to do."⁴ He graduated from McGill with a BA in 1949 and spent that summer working in a logging camp at Baie Comeau attempting to organize a Frontier College. There were no books, no magazines, and no newspapers and he had been given a baseball and bat to attract the loggers to the college.⁵ In spite of the problems associated with the job, like his father, he enjoyed the northern wilderness: "the logs keep bobbing endlessly down the flume; the sun goes down; the stars (our stars) wheel slowly around, & finally the sun turns up around 4 in the morning. Here it is so far north that the northern sky glows faintly all night long, & you can also count on a good show of Northern Lights."

Frontier College was followed, in 1950, by a six-month stint at L'Institut d'Etudes Politiques in Paris. For the next two years he studied at University College, Oxford. Unlike his father before him, Peter did not find Oxford difficult although he worked very hard. In October, 1950, Burton Keirstead, a McGill economics professor on leave at Oxford, wrote to the Scotts in Montreal bringing them up to date on Peter and on his own son, who was also studying in England.

> Our children ... poor dears, are really feeling the pressure. They are plunged into homework such as they never imagined even in the worst of nightmares.... They do not get enough play for healthy young animals. But they are learning the lessons of application and sustained concentration, which I fear they would never learn in our schools.⁶

However, like Frank, Peter was becoming interested in poetry and politics. He took Part in the Oxford University Poetry Society, the Oxford *Isis*, and the Oxford Union Debating Society. A young man of independent opinion, he had had a number of serious philosophical disagreements with his tutor and when he did not get his degree he did not have the consolation of knowing about his father's near failure – the third class.

Peter returned to Canada in 1952 and taught for a year at Sedbergh School, a private school in Montebello, Quebec. He then enrolled in a Ph.D. program at McGill and graduated in 1955, spending the next year as a lecturer at McGill. While studying at McGill Peter had visited Cambridge, Massachusetts, where he met Maylie Marshall, the daughter of John Marshall, the associate director of the Rockefeller Foundation and a friend of Frank's.[7] Peter and Maylie were married in June, 1956. That same year he also took the civil service exams in Ottawa that his father had once wanted to take following Oxford. Peter did extremely well in the competition and, in 1957, he was appointed a foreign service officer in External Affairs. He then began a series of postings that took him to the United Nations in New York, to a conference in Geneva, and, in 1959, to the Canadian embassy in Warsaw where he was appointed third secretary.[8]

By the early fifties Marian had consolidated her reputation as an artist. When the family had returned to Canada from Harvard in 1941, Marian brought with her the memory of the murals commissioned under Roosevelt's WPA program. Shortly after their return Hans Selye, then in the Department of Histology at McGill, invited her to paint a mural for the department's conference room. She prepared for the project by doing research in the department itself. Entitled "Endocrinology," the mural took a year and a half to complete and dominated an entire wall of the medical faculty.

Marian Scott was now at a mid-point in her career, working through a transition from pictorial representation to greater abstraction, an interest she was to continue to explore throughout her career. During this period she also continued to teach and exhibit in both group and individual shows. As early as 1939 she had had work exhibited at the New York World's Fair and in 1941 had had an individual show at the Grace Horne Galleries in Boston, Massachussets. During the forties her paintings had been included in group shows in Toronto, Kingston, and Ottawa and in travelling exhibits organized by the National Art Gallery. Twice during the fifties her work was included in the Biennial exhibit in Sao Paulo, Brazil. Over the next three decades she would continue to exhibit almost yearly in Canada and abroad. In the sixties she was to be awarded the Canadian Group of Painters Exhibition Prize (1966), the Centennial Medal (1967), and the Baxter Purchase Award (1969) from the Ontario Society of Painters. In 1972 she became an associate member and in 1975 a full member of the Royal Canadian Academy of the Arts.[9]

In the early fifties, while Marian was busy teaching and painting, Frank was preparing to leave Canada for Burma. John Humphrey, a former student and colleague who had left the McGill law faculty to work at the United Nations, had initially suggested Scott's name as a possible technical adviser with the UN in Burma. Now, in 1952, the invitation was repeated. This time Scott decided to accept. It is possible that he not only wanted to contribute to the public service of the United Nations but also to get away from Montreal for a time. Like many a creative individual, who in his forties feels life passing him by, Scott had experienced a typical mid-life crisis. He had fallen deeply in love with a fellow artist but recognized he could not leave Marian. The "quiet mood of love," the skeins of their lives, were much too intertwined. In the poem "Message" (1950) he wrote of his choice.

> Some wood-paths lead beside a lake
> Lonely with sun and shored by hills
> Where, tenants of one room, we take
> A sky of love, immense, that fills
> Heart to the brim, too brief to break,
>
> And some lead outward from the wood
> Dropping to roads and planted fields
> Where houses stand whose quiet mood
> Of love is seasoned. He would lose
> In choosing, what he did not choose. (*C.P.*, p. 141)

The incident brought considerable pain to both and caused a hiatus in their lives. For an interval – as in his late poem "Dancing" – each moved a little further away from the other.

AS A CCFer Scott was particularly interested in Burma. The old territory of Mandalay had become an independent state outside the Commonwealth in January, 1948, when it formed a parliamentary socialist government under Prime Minister U Nu. And now, having explored the first three ambitions in his Oxford diary: "My line of work must be 1) Canada, 2) the Empire, 3) the English Speaking peoples," he had a chance at the contemporary equivalent of the fourth, "[the] League of Nations."[10] Burma represented the possibility of international service, and in January, 1952, Scott was appointed to go there as a representative of the UN. The trip to Burma strengthened his internationalism, an outgrowth of his socialist belief that the ultimate goal of the good society was to share its benefits with others.

On January 14, 1952, Scott took up his official duties in New York as a technical assistance resident representative to Burma, a function promptly abbreviated in letters home as "the TARR reports." He spent a month in New York and Washington learning the nature of his new duties, which were to assist the government of Burma to co-ordinate various technical services administered by the World Health Organization (WHO), the Food and Agriculture Organization, the International Labour Organization, and UNESCO.[11] On February 20 he left New York. After nearly a week in London he flew to Rangoon after stopovers in Paris, Geneva, Rome, Karachi, and Delhi. He arrived in Rangoon on March 17.[12] He was fascinated by the new and exotic world of the East, by the undulating green landscapes of rice paddy and bamboo, and by the Burmese themselves.

Because Scott had gone to Burma with the assumption that he would stay for twelve months, he prepared himself carefully by readings in Buddhism and the history of Southeast Asia. His brother Elton, a theology professor, had recommended Dr. Slater's *Perdora and Nirvanna*. This encounter with Buddhism widened Scott's concept of religion. He liked to say that he had "never had a road to Damascus experience";[13] that is, he had experienced neither the flash of conversion nor the sudden loss of faith. As a child he had absorbed without question his father's Anglo-Catholicism. During the twenties his readings in Eddington, Bergson, and Einstein had widened his thinking so that science now encompassed religion. However, by the early forties when Scott wrote "Last Rites" he saw both science and religion as equally valid roads to truth. Nonetheless, he still thought of historical Christianity in terms of the fanaticism of the Crusades and the Inquisition. The cross (especially the Jansenist Quebec crucifix) he associated with the images in Foxe's *Book of Martyrs*. Scott's sense of the inherent cruelty of this aspect of Christianity, the fascination with martyrdom and mortification, was now sharpened by contrast with the calm and smiling Buddha of the East. Several poems resulting from the trip to Burma express his recognition of the inherent peace of the Eastern philosophy and in comparison his own Western and personal sense of exclusion from love. Other poems, especially "Finis the Cenci," indict the cruelty of the priestly Italian renaissance. Most importantly, in his poetry of the fifties, Scott expressed his new perception of man's place set against the larger rhythms of nature.

Not only was his concept of religion broadened but his socialism was redefined within an international and humanist context. In politics as in religion, it seemed apparent, the Eastern temperament differed greatly from that of the West. Even the socialism was unique. Of particular interest to Scott was May Day, which was marked by public festivities. The ceremonies in Rangoon were held in the Burmese Athletic Association Grounds and began at seven in the morning with a procession of about 10,000 trade unionists. The event was attended by cabinet ministers and, as Scott noted in his report to the United Nations, decorations of the hammer and sickle were much in evidence. However, as he explained in a report, although Burmese socialism was based on Marxism it was not considered to be of a violent nature; indeed, the Burmese Minister of Defence published a booklet attempting to show that Marxism and Buddhism were not incompatible.[14]

In Burma there seemed to be room for all creeds. When Scott visited a small town outside of Rangoon he was told by U Ba Tu, a leading citizen, " 'I wish the Americans and Russians would have their war and finish it so that we could tell what we should be'." Scott was astonished that the man had no preference between democracy and communism. This, as he recognized, was a fairly common feeling in Burma: "What does it matter? Most people think there is much to be said for and against both sides. It looks like a Big Power fight to them – not their fight. Yet the way of life Burma is trying to establish – tolerant, religious, democratic and socialist – is conceivable only if communism is contained. U Ba Tu would be the first to notice the difference."[15]

Scott was soon involved in meeting government officials and co-ordinating activities with technical personnel. He began to get a sense of what he was later to call "the world's work" when he went to Lashio, a town of some 12,000 people set in hilly country. The town was ramshackle, built primarily of corrugated iron, but the poet in Scott responded to the landscape. "All the vegetation is rich, and flowering trees are all about. The air is full of bird-song and soft and sweet to breathe."[16] Above all, Lashio was cool, only 80°F at noon as compared to Rangoon's daily 100°F plus.

Before he had left Montreal, Scott had received a letter from a professor at Sir George Williams College, Gordon O. Rothney, who joked that he hoped Scott was "about to take up the white man's burden on the road to Mandalay, in a manner, however, more in keeping with your own background than with the traditions of Kipling."[17] Rothney was only partly right. In the twenties Scott had liked Kipling's ballads and he had always enjoyed casting himself as a principal actor within the drama of place. For Scott, one suspects, Burma reverberated with Kipling's "Mandalay" –

especially with its "Burma girl," puffing on her "whackin' white cheroot" and the barracks-room humour of Kipling's description of the young woman "a-wastin' Christian kisses on an 'eathen idol's foot: / ... Wot they called the Great Gawd Budd."[18]

Once in Burma, Scott promptly cast his eye about for the appropriate local colour. At a party given in the home of Sao Hkun Mong, an engineer of noble family, he was delighted to discover that his hostess "sat in the corner and lit a large cheroot." He was served Siamese whiskey, which tasted somewhat like Southern Comfort, and the party nibbled on dehydrated frogs: Scott ate four, which he felt showed "a strong tendency to co-operate."[19] Promptly, the next morning, he purchased a package of cheroots "just to fit myself into the countryside"[20] – and, very probably, Kipling's ballad. This action was to have more serious implications than intended. Scott frequently read himself asleep. Now, with the added impediment of a mosquito net that had to be untucked to turn the light off, he often found himself waking up at four a.m. with the light still on and a book open. One night he discovered his cheroot had "burned a hole through the cotton mattress," fortunately before he had fallen fully asleep.[21]

At first a cautious traveller, taking good care of what he ate and drank, Scott soon threw caution to the winds. He was fascinated by Burmese life and one especially attractive "Burma girl." This was Princess June Rose, daughter of the niece of the last King of Burma. In Burmese her name was Yanada Nat Mai or Goddess of the Nine Jewels, but her mother called her "Babs." She was considered by Scott "the most attractive goddess (age 20) that ever played the game of canasta with F.R.S.,"[22] for so he spent one evening with the girl and her parents. The next morning June Rose was sent to chauffeur Scott around the town of Maymyo. They went first to the local botanical gardens where a UN project was to be initiated and then to the local bazaar. It swarmed with life: "crowded," as Scott reflected, "with dogs, children, nursing mothers and flies." Every now and then sweepers would sweep the narrow walks between the stalls, raising clouds of dust that settled back on the food.

June Rose, known and greeted by all, "kept picking up the oddest fruits and dried edibles of the most dubious appearance and saying, 'Try this'." Scott busied himself by taking a few false bites and dropping things behind him as they walked. Yet he found that "some just had to be eaten." As it was a very hot day, their next port of call was the local swimming pool. Scott eyed the murky water dubiously. But there was nothing to do but get in, especially as he had brought his own bathing suit. "So I slipped in, keeping the eyes and ears above water. June Rose looked even more

like a Goddess than ever. Amoebas be damned." Having slipped, he decided
to plunge, rationalizing all the way.

> I had a solitary lunch in my private dining room, ending up with
> strawberries and thick cream. By this time I was so reckless that I
> didn't care. Maymyo is famous for its strawberries, and this was the
> end of the season – my last chance. You just can't go on observing
> strict rules of health if you are going to travel in this country. At
> least, if you do, you never really know what the country is like. You
> live perpetually on a shelf – as in Rangoon, where the foreigners are
> like foam on the surface of a stream.

Besides, he comforted himself, "An occasional illness – or the risk of it –
is the price of understanding."[23]

Scott was to pay dearly for this ill-conceived foray into international
understanding. Two weeks later, on June 4, he was diagnosed as suffering
from amoebic dysentery. This infection was to undermine severely his
health for the rest of his life. Always relatively frail, he was emaciated after
three weeks of illness. It was clear he could not stay on in Burma. On
June 17 arrangements were completed with the United Nations agreeing
to his return to New York.[24] There he spent the rest of his contract working
with David Owen in the administration of the Technical Assistance Program.[25]

Scott was clearly rationalizing when he wrote: "an occasional illness ...
is the price of understanding."[26] Yet who is to say that he was not right?
It was largely because of his severe illness in Burma that he wrote the
deeply humanist poems of the fifties. These included "Creed," "A Grain
of Rice," and "Water." He had personally experienced the fundamental
needs of the underprivileged East – the need for food and pure water –
so often taken for granted by Westerners.

In "Water" he compares the three kinds of water he had known – the
clear cold water of a northern childhood, the filtered tap water of a Western
world, and the "challenge water" of the East.

> ... the sister water, warm and green,
> Reeking with life and fetid from the swamp
> Whose scum flows slowly under a hum of flies.
> Bring me this rare, this livid water,
> Tribal water, controlling water,
> Charged full of politics and power and race.  (*C.P.*, p. 123)

While still in Rangoon, Scott had been shown a private collection of
moths and butterflies. He arrived just in time to see a moth emerging

from its cocoon and stretching its new wings. This image brought together many of Scott's feelings about Asia and, as he supposed, feelings that went back far before he ever went to the East – to the majestic rhythms of nature he experienced as a young man in the Laurentians.[27] Because Scott sees himself, and indeed man in general, silhouetted against the great movements of nature, his poetry is often structured in terms of man, the microcosm, set against the greater macrocosm of the universe.

It was this experience in Rangoon that later generated the poem "A Grain of Rice." Here the image of the Asian moth is set against the great rhythms of the universe.

> Such majestic rhythms, such tiny disturbances.
> The rain of the monsoon falls, an inescapable treasure,
> Hundreds of millions live
> Only because of the certainty of this season,
>     The turn of the wind.
>
> The frame of our human house rests on the motion
> Of earth and of moon, the rise of continents,
> Invasion of deserts, erosion of hills,
>     The capping of ice.
>
> Today, while Europe tilted, drying the Baltic,
> I read of a battle between brothers in anguish.
>     A flag moved a mile.
>
> And today, from a curled leaf cocoon, in the course of its rhythm,
> I saw the break of a shell, the creation
> Of a great Asian moth, radiant, fragile,
> Incapable of not being born, and trembling
>     To live its brief moment.
>
> Religions build walls round our love, and science
> Is equal of truth and of error. Yet always we find
> Such ordered purpose in cell and in galaxy,
> So great a glory in life-thrust and mind-range,
> Such widening frontiers to draw out our longings,
>     We grow to one world
>     Through enlargement of wonder.   (*C.P.*, p. 126)

The framing evolutionary structure is introduced with the opening line, "Such majestic rhythms, such tiny disturbances." The larger rhythms are the great movements of the universe, "the rise of continents, / Invasion of deserts, erosion of hills, / The capping of ice," the "turn of the wind" that brings the monsoon, and, by implication, the tiny movement that is life, the grain of rice. In one sense, these tiny disturbances are events such as the delicate emergence of a great Asian moth from its cocoon, "radiant, fragile, / Incapable of not being born, and trembling / To live its brief moment." In another sense, the tiny disturbance is man – located midway between cell and galaxy but unnatural, as the Korean War showed, in his cruelty to his fellows: "Today, while Europe tilted, drying the Baltic, / I read of a battle between brothers in anguish. / A flag moved a mile."

The concluding stanza is a summation of the deep structure of Scott's poetry with reflections on religion, love, and science, a belief in the order of the universe as opposed to human order, and a reaching out to the frontiers of life and knowledge. "We grow to one world / Through enlargement of wonder." In effect, Scott is stating his developed poetic creed, an attitude of mind summarized in "Poem for Living": "In all ways, / praise" (*C.P.*, p. 172).

Scott's poems are so often a reaction to a person or event in real life that they provide, as he says, "a mini-biography."[28] His second and best book of poetry, *Events and Signals* (1954), takes its title from an epigraph to an article he had read in the London *Observer*.[29] It expressed his concept of the genesis of his poetry "Between the event and the observer there must pass a signal – a wave, an impulse, or perhaps a ray of light."[30] For Scott certain events in life are charged with intimations of larger meaning that clamour to be expressed by the poet. It is most often an image from nature – like the Asian moth or the great Laurentian Shield – but it can also emanate from human nature. Events like the death of his father, the deaths of Gandhi, of Bryan Priestman (a colleague at McGill who drowned while attempting to rescue a child), and of the vivacious artist, Pegi Nicol. All generate signals that generate poems. Of Pegi Nicol, Scott says:

> Her writing wove through its grammar
> Like a stem through stones,
> As when she wrote on her death-bed
> "There is an excitement in our kind of affairs
> That cannot be compared."
>
> She was a Canadian of these difficult days
> When greatness is in our thoughts
> And our hands are numb.
> Only part of her died.
> Her alive is alive. (*C.P.*, p. 163)

This sacramental view of poetry (the "holy spirit" of "Last Rites," the reference in the Pegi Nicol poem to "her alive is alive") is a transmutation of the old religious spirit or soul into new humanist terms, very likely by way of Bergson's *Creative Evolution*.

Indeed, the fine love poem "Departure" shows that Scott carries both the metaphors of the twenties and his own sense of evolutionary growth and development, an evolution with spiritual overtones, into the poetry of the fifties.

> Always I shall remember you, as my car moved
> Away from the station and left you alone by the gate
> Utterly and forever frozen in time and solitude
> Like a tree on the north shore of Lake Superior.
> It was a moment only, and you were gone,
> And I was gone, and we and it were gone,
> And the two parts of the enormous whole we had known
> Melted and swirled away in their separate streams
> Down the smooth granite slope of our watershed.
>
> We shall find, each, the deep sea in the end,
> A stillness, and a movement only of tides
> That wash a world, whole continents between,
> Flooding the estuaries of alien lands.
> And we shall know, after the flow and ebb,
> Things central, absolute and whole.
> Brought clear of silt, into the open roads,
> Events shall pass like waves, and we shall stay.   (C.P., p. 142)

The young woman, seen as a tree in a Group of Seven painting, is absorbed into the larger natural world of a shared watershed. Death and loss are accepted, for "We shall find, each, the deep sea in the end ...." This is again an evolutionary expression of the older religious concept of eternity.

Scott's characteristic metaphors develop from the exploration of man's relationships to nature and society: they involve time and infinity, world and universe, twentieth-century humanist substitutes for the Christian vocabulary. A typical Scott poem moves from specific image or from the natural or social landscape to a consideration of the significance of the image in the larger pattern of human life. And the human journey, in turn, is seen as a moment in time, a part of the larger cosmic flux in which matter, striving to realize itself, is thrown up briefly in waves – ripples on

Bergson's flowing stream of time. Movement – growth, flux, and reintegration – is the essential aspect of what is a basically evolutionary vision.[31]

The expression of human love in "Departure" and the affirmation of human brotherhood in "A Grain of Rice" transcend the more narrowly national and political concerns of the poetry of the thirties and forties. The most succinct summary of this widened perspective is to be found in "Creed," a poem that had its genesis at Harvard but was not developed as a poem until the fifties.

> The world is my country
> The human race is my race
> The spirit of man is my God
> The future of man is my heaven   (*C.P.*, p. 89)

Scott's moral vision, his politics, and his poetry are so tightly interwoven that "Creed" may be read as a statement of belief, a political manifesto, or an aesthetic credo. In religious terms "the spirit of man" brings together that fusion of Christianity and evolution that developed from his twenties readings. Scott accepts Bergson's view of life as an evolutionary wave, a process of continuous becoming, animated by a vital spirit analogous to the older spirit of God. And in political terms "Creed" reflects the same values that animated his unpublished forties manuscript, "The Democratic Manifesto," and implicitly refutes the values that created so much hardship during the depression.

That Scott chooses to make his ethics explicit is a reminder that he sees both poetry and politics, in their highest forms, as moral activities whose function is the improvement of the human condition and the freeing of the human spirit. This view of poetry incorporates not only the modernist desire to capture human experience through the clearly realized image, but also the more traditional view held by Arnold and even Eliot that one of the functions of poetry is to help us understand our lives, to extract from the fragmentary image its enduring meaning.

In "A Function for Poetry," a talk given in 1946 under the auspices of the Federation of Canadian Artists, he had suggested that the poet can "make us aware of life and our place in it ... by discovering and expressing the significant and important relationships between man and his age." This is not merely a matter of the accumulation of knowledge but "of clarifying the meaning and value of the things we experience."[32] This definition was augmented in 1958 when Scott stated that for him the writing of poetry "opens new roads to truth, gives new insights and understandings about man, society and the gods." He concluded:

If I could define [poetry], it would not be different from my conception of life itself. The making of something new and true. All life
is creation: poetry is creation through language. An exploring of the
frontiers of the world inside and the world outside man. And a kind
of umbilical contemplation from within the poem itself of its own
dynamic and central structure.[33]

What, then, is the relation between his poetic theory and his politics?
Put very simply, it involves the functioning of the creative spirit.

As the flow of events and experiences constantly meets us and passes
behind, we are faced with infinite choices and possibilities. What we
call creative living is the ability to pick out of the total flow those
spacial elements which are significant. The poet, like any artist, selects
these elements, arrests them, expresses them, and steadies us on our
slippery feet.[34]

Scott's remarks on art indicate that he had not forgotten Havelock Ellis's
view in *The Dance of Life* that all human activity can be creative: "I never
felt the slightest contradiction between ... politics and writing poetry,
because the politics I professed and practiced was to me a creative idea
about society.... You can conceive of the state as a work of art."[35] Consequently, in 1963, he declared that "politics is the art of making artists,"
justifying this paradox with the assertion that politics is "the art of planning
and developing the material resources of society for the benefit of all."
The first aim of political action would thus be the individual and his
development so that "the potential which is inherent in each person of an
artistic kind or creative character has the greatest chance of coming out."[36]

# SIXTEEN

# McGill: Law in Society

❦

D URING THE FORTIES AND FIFTIES Scott could often be glimpsed in the Faculty Club at McGill, part of a circle of professors grouped around a large round coffee table in front of the great stone fireplace, hence the name "the faculty circle" or "the round table." There was sufficient room at the table for nearly fifteen men to perch their glasses about its circumference. Unlike other faculty clubs in Canada, McGill at this time served liquor, greatly facilitating a congenial atmosphere, and, like the English "club" it was modelled on, it was a strictly masculine fraternity. No longer as extreme as the Athenaeum Club in London, which required women to enter by a separate entrance, McGill now permitted women faculty members to enter by the front door. Nevertheless, as Joyce Hemlow of the English department remembered, they were expected to hurry upstairs by the front elevator and not dally on the broad curving staircase listening to the gusts of laughter emerging from the faculty circle.[1]

The round table was a daily exchange of conversation among as many as twenty men who came and went irregularly according to their lecture schedules. The catalyst of the group was the biochemist David Thomson, Dean of the Faculty of Graduate Studies. Thomson was tall, thin, and frail, with long tapering fingers; he seemed the essence of sophistication.[2] To Scott, Thomson seemed the typical Scottish intellectual; with the others of the group he enjoyed Thomson's wit, which had "a touch of malice," and his appreciation of the arts. Arthur Lismer, with his long lank hair and his mischievous eyes darting about, was a regular observer at the table. He would often sketch on a drink chit, or a paper napkin – some face would have attracted his attention – and occasionally contribute a bit of dry humour to the conversation.[3]

Other regulars included Pat Baird, director of the Arctic Institute; John Bland, professor of architecture; the ebullient town planner Harold Spence-

Sales, recruited from England; Max Cohen, like Scott a tall commanding figure and a full-time member of the law faculty; George Duthie and Hugh MacLennan of the English department; Kenneth Hare from geography; Nick Walsh from divinity; R.D. MacLennan from philosophy. From economics and political science, then a single department, came Keith Callard; Ben Higgins; Burton Keirstead, formerly from the University of New Brunswick, a short man with a rather dour face that belied his pleasant character; Eric Kierans, later a prominent politician; Keirstead's former student, J.R. Mallory; Fred Watkins. Among the scientists found in the circle were Hank MacIntosh and Ferdie Terroux from physics; Lloyd Stevenson from medicine; Max Dunbar from zoology. Wilder Penfield and Hans Selye, also members of the medical faculty, and Donald Hebb, an animal psychologist, later chancellor at McGill, were not part of the group[+] but occasionally would stop by for a chat. Through the circle Scott was brought into contact with a group of men whose interests were as wide-ranging as his own.

"Scott, with his long nose, his height, his harsh voice and sometimes devastating comments, was a real presence at the table. That is not to say, however, that he dominated. Anybody dominating that lot would have found very quickly he was no longer welcome. It was a table of equals and the kind of talk I had always hoped there would be in universities and certainly did not find at Queen's" – so recalled Arnold Edinborough, then a young assistant professor fresh from Cambridge but immured at Queen's.[5] From the vantage point of Vancouver, Kingston, or even Toronto in 1951, Montreal was a cosmopolitan, civilized city and McGill's Faculty Club reflected this. Edinborough was also conscious when sitting at the round table of the strong spiritual presence of Stephen Leacock, a presence manifested by a delight in the exaggerated tale, or in satire and puns.

Few individuals "talked shop" at the circle: the objective was general conversation enlivened by witty repartee. Good one-liners prevailed. Scott liked to recall Arthur Lismer's bright remark one Friday when faced with the inevitable entrée: "One man's meat is another man's *poisson*."[6] After a dinner supplied by officials of the Imperial Oil Company for a number of the circle regulars, a dinner accompanied by an abundant supply of liquid refreshment and a great deal of self-advertisement, Thomson had remarked urbanely of faculty members: "We all got Imperially oiled."[7]

Despite differences in temperament, or because of them, Scott and Thomson were close friends. They shared a common love of the imagist poetry anthologies, they talked about painting, and together they had read aloud from A.J.M. Smith's new book, *News of the Phoenix and Other Poems* (1943). Some of Thomson's sophistication may also have rubbed off. In the early forties he had taught Scott, hitherto a beer drinker, to enjoy martinis. The ritual of preparation – the chilling of the glass, just the right gin (Beefeaters) not bruised by too much stirring, only a little dry Martini and ice, all offered with great bonhomie – was to become as much a part of the Scott persona as the animated talk about politics and poetry, the hearty slap on the knee, and the uproarious laugh when amused. After Thomson's sudden death in the early sixties, his widow, in recognition of a close friendship, invited Scott to pick out his favourites among Thomson's excellent poetry collection.[8] Several of Thomson's imagist anthologies joined Scott's own well-loved collection.

There was considerable cross-fertilization of ideas at the faculty circle. During the forties and throughout the fifties the Scotts regularly visited with Hugh MacLennan, at first writing *Two Solitudes* (1945) and later, in the fifties, *The Watch that Ends the Night*. It seems likely that MacLennan drew on his friendship with the Scotts for some of the details of his novels; the central scene in *The Watch that Ends the Night*, depicting a meeting of thirties radicals with a thinly disguised Dr. Norman Bethune, is, as MacLennan told a group in Saskatoon, set in the Scotts' living room on Oxenden Avenue.[9]

During one circle gathering Scott was vividly impressed by Wilder Penfield's description of an operation on the brain of a young girl who had suddenly returned to consciousness: in her face the brain surgeon saw proof of the existence of something that had to be called "soul." On another occasion he recalled Hank MacIntosh telling, after the war, of the first testing of the American atomic bomb.[10] Ben Higgins, an economist in Roosevelt's New Deal, spoke fluently on public housing. And it was in this group that Scott began to scribble on a matchbox lines for "A Grain of Rice." He was delighted when Kenneth Hare later explained plate techtonics theory, thus providing a scientific basis for the lines in his poem, "Today, while Europe tilted, drying the Baltic, / I read of a battle between brothers in anguish. / A flag moved a mile" (*C.P.*, p. 126). Generally, the talk around the table was about current events, particularly if Max Cohen was present (he was later international affairs editor of *Saturday Night*), or about cultural matters – the state of poetry, the isolating effect of distances for people in Canada. Nevertheless, as Edinborough perceived, "Nobody, even though the Massey Commission was sitting at the time, really felt that [Canada was] on the edge of a huge cultural explosion, which occurred within the next ten years."[11]

Scott had a stronger sense than most Canadians of the new decade, largely because he was actively engaged in planning change. By the fifties he was an energetic and vocal professional in the three disciplines of law, literature, and politics. And he was beginning to speculate on the possible relations between law and the state and to speak publicly about Canadian culture in terms suggestive of socialist planning.

He was certainly aware of proposals to the Massey Commission, formally known as the Royal Commission on National Development in Arts, Letters and Sciences. Scott had become a member of the Canadian Writers Committee, a national group that had formed to present to the Commission the views of those professional Canadian writers who now disassociated themselves from the Canadian Authors' Association. The brief, to which Scott contributed substantially in the planning stages, was drafted by Joyce Marshall and then augmented by members of the national planning committee.[12] Eventually presented in Toronto in November, 1949, by Claude Bissell, an associate professor of English at the University of Toronto, and Len Peterson, a Toronto writer, the brief emphasized the need for "the further development of a national literature" essential to the continuing progress of Canada and its people. They were critical of the overwhelming American influence on Canadian culture and of the "dumping" of such outside values since Canadians had no voice in shaping these values. "To preserve her national entity [Canada] needs artists as much as she needs diplomats, military men, inventors, technicians, laborers and farmers. She must adapt her economy somehow so that artists can earn a living from their work – from their contribution to the country – the same as the other groups which we have just mentioned." The brief was highly supportive of the role of the Canadian Broadcasting Corporation and critical of commercial radio. Because it was difficult for writers to make a living by their craft, the group recommended "that a body be set up from the Canadian Universities comparable to the Humanities Research Council for the purpose of establishing two types of monetary assistance to Canadian writers: fellowships for work projected, and awards for meritorious work accomplished."[13]

In the Massey Commission report issued in 1951 a large section, "The Artist and the Writer," drew on the brief of the Canadian Writers Committee and endorsed the view that American influence on Canadian letters constituted a threat to cultural survival. In addressing the problems of writers, the Commission felt that the work of Canadian writers lacked national recognition, which isolated them and prevented them from making a full contribution. The Commission believed that "The work with which we have been entrusted is concerned with nothing less than the spiritual foundations of our national life."[14]

From the perspective of 1987 it seems that the primary recommendation of the Massey Commission, establishment of the Canada Council as an intermediary body for channelling, without state control, state assistance to the humanities and social sciences, was also implicit in the Canadian Writers Committee submission. Other recommendations, such as the request for a national library and a national theatre, have also since come into being. The strong nationalism of Scott and other members of the Canadian Writers Committee, a nationalism endorsed by the Massey commissioners, was not shared by some influential members of the larger academic and political community. Individuals like Frank Underhill, a committed North American, writing in *The Canadian Forum*, and J.B. Brebner, the Canadian historian resident at Columbia, reviewing the report in *The Saturday Review of Literature*, condemned what they saw as narrow parochialism.[15] It is tempting to speculate that this adverse reaction to the Canadianism of the Massey report had some influence on the subsequent degree of support given to a national literature. Between publication of the report and establishment of the Canada Council in 1957, the mandate for the Council appears to have altered from the more directly nationalist aim of encouraging the development of a Canadian literature to the more internationalist aim of encouraging the development of all letters in Canada.

AT THE SAME TIME the Massey Commission was bringing forward its report, Scott was helping to found the Association of Law Teachers (1950). In 1948, while on CCF business in Vancouver, Scott had visited Dean George Curtis of the law faculty at the University of British Columbia. The two men sat in Curtis's office and talked shop. After an enjoyable and stimulating hour, as Scott was departing, both said, almost with one voice, "We should do more of this. Why don't we get together? Why not?"[16] They hastily agreed that Scott would write to the faculty of each law school in the East and Curtis to the ones in the West. A meeting was set up at the forthcoming gathering of the Canadian Bar Association to be held in Ottawa that year. The group that met agreed that they should reconvene at the meeting of the Royal Society, to be held at McGill in the spring of 1950. The professors of law from across Canada met in a semicircle in front of the fireplace in the lounge of the McGill law faculty at Duggan House. They agreed the organization would be permanent, that it would be called the Association of Law Teachers (changed later to Canadian Association of Law Teachers), and that Scott would be president. The purpose of the organization was to help "strengthen the sense of professional identity and purpose among law teachers ... [and to afford] an annual opportunity for contact and exchange on matters of mutual interest."[17] It helped to consolidate the teaching of law within the university system and to standardize teaching and materials.

It was also felt that improvements in the training of lawyers would enhance the state of legal research in Canada. In 1954 Scott was appointed chairman of the Committee on Legal Research, set up by the Canadian Bar Association, to inquire into the state of legal research in Canada. Reform in the education and training of lawyers became the major purpose of the committee; its report recommended a new status for law schools and eventually led to the establishment of independent university law schools in Ontario and Manitoba.

From 1951 onward, Scott became active in the Canadian Association of University Teachers and in 1953-54 he was elected president of the McGill Association of University Teachers, a chapter he had helped found. His activity in both the law teachers' organization and the broader field of university teachers was a by-product of the controversy at McGill when they had used his political activities as an excuse not to appoint him Dean of Law. He had come to recognize that university teachers needed an association of their own if they were to have any power to affect university politics.

However, during this period Scott's most important professional contribution to the future of Canada lay in his work on constitutional law. For example, J.R. Mallory recalled that Scott played a significant role in the 1949 amendment to the BNA Act.

> He once told me that Angus McInnis phoned him from Ottawa [to tell him] the amending resolution had just been tabled and that the CCF was disposed to support it. When Frank saw the text he was horrified because it would have enabled a government to bring in legislation at any time extending the life of Parliament beyond the five years provided in the Constitution. At Frank's urging they took the matter up and the government agreed to add at the end of Section 91 (1) the following phrase: "provided, however, that a House of Commons may in time of real or apprehended war, invasion or insurrection be continued by the Parliament of Canada if such continuation is not opposed by the votes of more than one-third of the members of such House."

This now appears as Section 4 (2) of the Constitution Act, 1982.[18]

The next year, on January 10, 1950, the Liberal government under Louis St. Laurent held a dominion-provincial conference to discuss ways to "devis[e] a generally satisfactory method of making amendments in Canada to the provisions of the constitution which concern both federal and provincial authorities."[19] Scott helped in preparing and presenting Saskatchewan's position. The conference ended with an agreement that the governments would meet again in late 1950, at which time each would present its views "respecting the classification of each section of the BNA Act and other constitutional documents."[20] Scott, continuing in his role as an adviser to the Saskatchewan government, worked with Dean Frederick Cronkite of the Saskatchewan law faculty in preparing preliminary work for the Saskatchewan planning board and government. Throughout these conferences the Saskatchewan government was concerned about the adoption of a statement or bill enunciating fundamental rights. Saskatchewan itself, alone in all of Canada, had, in 1947, passed a bill of rights delineating by statute fundamental freedoms and rights.

The issue of a bill of rights in Canada is inextricably tied to the question of federal and provincial jurisdiction. As the BNA Act existed, there was no explicit provision for fundamental rights and freedoms, although Scott had long argued they were implied. The Act guaranteed certain areas of jurisdiction to each level of government, but in those areas where jurisdiction is divided the federal government has ultimate sovereignty. This sovereignty can and has, at times, infringed on fundamental rights and freedoms. It became a question of how best to incorporate, in the BNA Act, a set of statements about rights and freedoms that would limit the sovereignty of Parliament and of the ten provincial legislatures. It would be necessary to entrench these rights and freedoms in such a way that they could not be altered easily, and only if absolutely necessary. The issue was further complicated because the provincial governments could not agree on how the BNA Act could be modified or amended to incorporate such guarantees. Yet the object was to make these rights and freedoms binding on the provinces, where the greatest abuses were taking place.

Acting as legal adviser to the Saskatchewan government provided Scott with an opportunity not only to work on the BNA Act, but also to have some influence through suggestions pertaining to direction. For almost thirty years he had been teaching the BNA Act. In what direction should the Canadian constitution go? Scott's earlier work with the CCF, his views on social policy, and his training in constitutional law, especially his belief in an entrenched bill of rights, were all coming together. In February, 1950, he wrote to T.C. Douglas to say that he and Dean Cronkite had completed a portion of the work on the classification of the BNA Act. In this letter Scott outlined an important point that was to continue to be a contentious issue to successive constitutional conferences attempting to find an amending formula. He told Douglas he felt strongly "that no attempt should be made to remove the Federal power of disallowance of provincial law. This was an integral part of the original concept of Confederation, and it distinguishes the Canadian constitution from almost all other Federal constitutions.... The Debates on Confederation make it clear that the veto power was to be used to see that no local injustice was done without an appeal to higher authority." Scott was convinced that one important function of the federal government was to protect minority rights. He continued:

> If we have a secure Bill of Rights in the constitution to safeguard people in provinces against loss of their liberties perhaps the veto power might be dispensed with, though even then I should be against this; as it is, and considering all the political difficulties the veto is a salutary principle of government. I would not like to see a CCF government sponsor a proposal designed to weaken the authority of the Canadian government.

The link between entrenchment of rights and freedoms and the possible abolition of the disallowance power was not a common perception at this time. Scott was its principal proponent and he advocated it at the 1950 federal-provincial conference attended by Pierre Elliott Trudeau, then working for the Privy Council on a memorandum on federal-provincial relations. Trudeau greatly admired the opinions of Scott ("the thinking man") at this conference and by the sixties and seventies, Trudeau, then Prime Minister of Canada, had adopted the position that disallowance would not be surrendered without entrenchment of a Charter of Rights.

Douglas, although pleased with his legal adviser's efforts, held quite different views from Scott on provincial rights and disallowance. Speaking to Scott of Saskatchewan's position, J.W.W. Graham, Douglas's executive assistant, remarked: "The opinion was expressed that the Constitution set out limits to the jurisdiction of provinces, and that within those limits, the powers should be able to be democratically exercised without a power of disallowance in the federal cabinet." In the event of a dispute it was felt it could be settled by the courts. Saskatchewan was also disturbed that the current power of disallowance did not require a debate in the House of Commons. Such power had often been abused by the federal government. Lastly, the Saskatchewan government argued that the inclusion of a bill of rights in the constitution would protect basic freedoms that a provincial government could not infringe upon.[21]

By the early fifties, Scott had come to feel that a new Canadian constitution was needed. "The present patchwork of statutes," he wrote to Douglas, "is most difficult to understand and to apply. No Canadian citizen could expect to understand it without legal training." He concluded that applying amending procedures to "this legal scrap-pile is rather like (if I may be forgiven the analogy) putting a jet engine in my 1938 Chevrolet."[22]

Scott also expressed his concerns to Eugene Forsey, by then director of research for the Canadian Labour Congress: "I am getting worried at the way the Constitutional Conference is evolving. We are really engaged in rewriting the BNA Act and there is great danger that concessions will be made to provinces that will change some fundamental concepts in the present law. For instance every province demands the abolition of the power of disallowance, and Ottawa seems willing to entertain the idea."[23] In Scott's view the federal government had "bungled" the issue because it had not seriously weighed its implications.

Since the late forties Scott had also been active in civil liberties issues that seemed to require a Canadian bill of rights. He was a member of the Montreal Civil Liberties Association and other affiliated civil liberties organizations. In December, 1946, he had attended a conference that brought together members from the Toronto, Montreal, and Ottawa Civil Liberties Associations and the Civil Rights Union. The conference discussed a number of issues related to human rights and fundamental freedoms, including the plight of the Japanese Canadians, censorship, trade union rights, and a Bill of Rights. At this meeting Scott argued the Canadian constitution contained the beginnings of a Bill of Rights that would limit the sovereignty of Parliament. There were, for example, certain mandatory provisions regarding the use of French and English in Parliament and provisions regarding separate schools. He expressed the opinion that "any Bill of Rights should be enacted as an amendment to the BNA Act rather than as a statute."[24]

The conferences in 1950, however, were not successful in finding a way to repatriate the constitution or in incorporating a Bill of Rights into it. In 1960 the Diefenbaker government, through Justice Minister E. Davie Fulton, decided that a federal Bill of Rights at least would be a first step since provincial agreement on entrenchment was unlikely to occur. This Scott dubbed Diefenbaker's "spurious bill of rights" – spurious because without the backing of entrenchment such rights were easily overruled and at best applied only in regard to federal laws.

IN THE FIFTIES, also, Scott began to crystallize some of his ideas about the role of law in society. After the war there had been a new recognition that the humanist and the social scientist must work together in post-war planning – the whole idea of the welfare state was now a new and exciting concept. Indeed, when Principal Cyril James headed a committee for post-war planning organized by the federal government he invited Harold Spence-Sales, an English architect, to come out to Canada to set up a Committee on Physical Planning that would involve architects, geographers, lawyers, and social scientists. Spence-Sales was ebullient in manner, very quick in his verbal response. A Lismer cartoon shows his head rising from an ostrich's nest, captioned "Eggs-xactly." He captured just that blend of intellectuality and vivaciousness Scott appreciated. The two men sometimes went on expeditions in the North Hatley countryside looking for crenellations and old cannon balls, talking all the while, each capping the other's absurdity with more whimsy, yet in the process developing quite serious ideas about post-war planning.

Spence-Sales organized a series of lectures on planning to be given in the McGill School of Architecture and he invited individuals like David Thomson, Kenneth Hare, Carl Dawson, and Frank Scott as speakers. Publicized by Colonel Wilfrid Bovey, director of the Extension Department, the lecture series drew large numbers of prominent Montrealers. Scott's lecture, "The State as a Work of Art," illustrated the degree to which the nationalist, the artist, and the lawyer were united in his imagination. To some extent the essay is also Scott's apologia, demonstrating the unity of his own widely diverse interests.

In this lecture Scott expressed an idealized view of Canadian federalism – a just society as conceived by a lawyer philosopher-king. "Society is indeed a tangle of institutions, a web of relationships. Over it all and in and around it all stands law and the state, binding the whole together and imposing a degree of unity that no other single factor in the whole possesses by itself." Is there an aesthetics of society? Or are we stretching the meaning of the term "the beautiful" if we apply it to an institution as well as to an art? Scott believed it was not and referred to Jacob Burckhardt's use in his nineteenth-century study of the Italian city-states in *The Civilization of the Renaissance in Italy* (rpt. 1945). There Burckhardt speaks of "the State as the outcome of reflection and calculation, the State as a work of art." Because the Italian states were carefully ordered and designed they were works of art. Scott was captivated by the idea of a "beautiful social order.... Cannot the law arrange the various elements of society, be they individuals or groups, in such a set of relationships that each has his proper place and due rewards according to the style in which the whole is designed." Such a view of society, as Scott recognized, is ultimately as utopian as Plato's *Republic* or Karl Marx's classless society. These are social ideals, not dissimilar to the ideal system of law – "perfect justice to all" – which some lawyers believe in. As the American jurist Roscoe Pound has commented the law is "social engineering" because law "directs the dynamic forces of society into socially desirable channels."

Who would be the maker of Canada's beautiful state and how would this master artist choose the style of his art? Thinking of the dangers of the Russian state, Scott recollected the statue of the buoyant peasant girl and the contrast with the reality of the sculptor's sad and tubercular wife. The harnessing of human idealism was a potent force for social change, but an expression of faith by the artist did not make the society in which he lives beautiful. Was there another kind of technique available? "Can we select the form and shape of our society and move progressively toward it without liquidating all those who stand in the way?" Surely this was what democracy was for? "Politics," he asserted, "is the art of making artists. It is the art of developing in society the laws and institutions which will best bring out the creative spirit which lives in greater or less degree in every one of us. The right politics sets as its aim the maximum development of every individual. Free the artist in us, and the beauty of society will look after itself."[25] From this perspective politics can shape the imagination.

Scott's view of society as being, above all, directed toward cultivation of the individual, and of "the rule of law" as being necessary for the protection of both individual and society, was to have larger repercussions in Canada of the early seventies. His vision of the good society was, above all, the socialist "just society." And his view of the ideal constitution that would create it – a repatriated BNA Act tailored to Canada's needs – was a topic he enjoyed speculating on when meeting with younger lawyers like Trudeau and bright students like Michael Pitfield, Donald MacSween, and Timothy Porteous. All were to help shape Canada's public service and cultural life in the decades ahead.

Pitfield found Scott's lectures to be social commentaries. He was concerned about "the purposes of the law, the ideal of the law. He opened up a view of the constitution as a living, dynamic thing." The most important thing, however, was that he had "a very carefully constructed thesis about the central power which had been revolutionary in its time and which was still regarded as avant garde in many legal circles." To the students, however, "it was so obvious and so well documented that, as I imagine, succeeding generations became the proselytizers to the point where it became the accepted viewpoint in Canadian law."[26] This generation of the fifties, perhaps without realizing it, came at the end of an historical movement, given impetus by the "dirty thirties," which demanded centralized federal power; the pendulum was now about to swing to provincial rights. Scott's students, many of whom took an active part in various public policy issues, have been advocates and even extenders of what might be called the "Scott thesis," dramatically so through the repatriation of the constitution in 1982 with its entrenched Charter of Rights.

# SEVENTEEN

# More Events and Signals

☙

THE TRIP TO BURMA brought Scott back to poetry, but there were other factors. In August, 1950, he attended the Harvard Summer School Poetry Conference organized by his old friend Bill Elliott. The planners had wanted some Canadian representation and Scott suggested himself, A.J.M. Smith, and A.M. Klein.[1] Northrop Frye, then at Harvard, "gate-crashed."[2] The two visiting poets who dominated the conference were Stephen Spender from England and Pierre Emmanuel from France. Spender, Scott recalled, assumed the role of "an illuminating visitor from outer space" and "insisted upon it." The French poet he viewed more charitably as attempting "to do the best he could."[3] Emmanuel, the pseudonym of Noël Matthieu, had made his name as a Resistance poet and essayist. A Christian revolutionary with leftist leanings, he voiced in books like *Tombeau d'Orphée* (1941) and *Qui est cet homme?* (1947) the deep disquiet of his generation. Scott and Emmanuel were to become close friends, and thereafter he frequently stayed with the Scotts in Montreal when meeting with French-speaking poets, novelists, and broadcasters. Scott and Emmanuel, drawn together as poets and by their interest in Quebec poetry, also shared larger philosophical concerns. Emmanuel acknowledged this bond when he wrote to Scott: "You are one of the few persons always present in my thoughts as companions in a common quest for truth."[4]

At the Harvard Conference Scott was relatively well known as a personality, not only because he had spent a year at that university a decade earlier, but also because his poems had won the Guarantors Prize from *Poetry* (Chicago) in 1944. However, E.J. Pratt's *Collected Poems* had appeared in an American edition in 1944, so he was acknowledged as the major Canadian poet. During the conference the American hosts played a record of Pratt reading from *Brébeuf*. "He read very badly," Frye recalls, "and nobody could make much of it. I was embarrassed and I wished they'd either left it out or had something a bit better."⁵ This incident, together with some jostling for primacy among Canadian poets, may have led to Scott's somewhat peevish squib on Pratt's "Towards the Last Spike" (1952):

> Where are the coolies in your poem, Ned?
> Where are the thousands from China who swung their picks with
>     bare hands at forty below?
>
> Between the first and the million other spikes they drove ...
>
> Is all Canada has to say to them written in the Chinese Immigration
>     Act?   (C.P., p. 194)

Scott's indignation is fair enough, but it does ignore the sense of nation-building found in Pratt's poem – an ironic omission in view of his own strong Canadianism. The heart of the matter, perhaps, was that Pratt, a man whom Scott and Smith viewed as an old-fashioned poet, still occupied that place in Canadian poetry the moderns felt was rightfully theirs.

As it happened, the recognition they sought was just around the corner. And Scott was to be a catalyst in bringing about change as well as contributing to the struggle, in the fifties and sixties, to carve out a place for a native Canadian poetry. He had begun to look up old literary friends after his return from Burma, and, inspired by the Harvard Conference, he tried to set up a poetry conference on returning to McGill in 1952. In an outline of the project written to the Rockefeller Foundation, he explained that the great need in Canada was to bring the small community of poets together.⁶ However, the Rockefeller Board of Directors refused the grant on the grounds that the concept was too narrow. Temporarily the idea of a conference fell by the wayside.

A YEAR LATER, however, Scott was cheered to learn that the poet Louis Dudek, just appointed to the English department at McGill, was planning a small poetry conference for the Thanksgiving weekend. This was to be held at Keewaydin, where Doug and Kim Jones, recent graduates of the McGill English department, had a cottage. Scott and Smith, Irving Layton, and some younger poets including Robert Currie and John Harney were invited.⁷ The Joneses' cabins were located on Lake Paudash, north of North Bay, Ontario. Doug Jones, a poet, was then studying English under George Whalley at Queen's.

Scott and Smith came late. When they arrived at Keewaydin they found a large stretch of water separating them from the cabins; the boats were all on the other side. They looked around the boathouse, found an old rowboat, and put it in the water. It leaked like a sieve. Undaunted, they put their baggage (notably, a forty-ounce bottle of Scotch) into the leaky vessel and began to paddle rapidly, attempting to outpace the rising water.

When this apparition appeared on the horizon, Kim Jones was on the dock with her cocker spaniels. At first she thought it was a log. As it drew closer she realized it was a boat, almost down to the gunwales in the water, with two men in it. One was paddling with a board, the other with a broken oar. Finally she realized they were heading toward the dock. She did not recognize the man in the bow, but she had seen pictures of Scott. "As soon as I saw his profile I knew that he *was*...." As they came alongside the dock, Scott grabbed the Scotch and the two men jumped to the dock. The rowboat filled with water and gurgled to the bottom. By this time Kim Jones had been joined by her husband. The couple believed that the man in the bow was a younger American poet: he wore a T-shirt, was very tanned, "and with his sort of drawl, you know, he struck me as some young American friend of Scott." They soon discovered that this was, in fact, *the* A.J.M. Smith.[8]

Smith also recalled this incident when he wrote "Astrea Redux: Kee-waydin Poetry Conference," but from a quite different perspective.

Coming over the water
paddling an old boat
with a broken board
and a bottle in a paper bag

Leaning into the wind
making out an old wharf
in a new land
and a doubtful call

A boy or a female figure
seen in the distance

Nearer, a coughing motor
then a spate of spaniels
leaping and frisking
with Stuart curls
and long sad faces

Coming to land
coming home

to the good people
known anew

My people        lordly ones
the Duke of Dudek        His Grace of Layton
and with me Scott
diaconal, archbishopric
twisted benevolent
with needle eye[9]

Emphasizing the connection between his own return from American exile and the spaniels frisking about the couple on the dock (Charles II was fond of spaniels), Smith casts himself as the exiled monarch returning to England to take up the throne. Surrounding him are his courtiers – Layton, Dudek, and Scott. (Scott, one-eyed, had been contemplating a book of satire entitled *The Eye of the Needle* – thus the allusion in the poem.) Smith's title, referring to Astrea, goddess of justice, is understandable. He had been forced to go to the United States to find college employment during the depression; now justice was finally being done. He was returning to Canada to take his rightful place in the national poetry.

Smith was then reaching the height of his influence. His judiciously edited anthology, *The Book of Canadian Poetry* (1943), had gone through two editions and several reprintings and had established a canon for the study of Canadian poetry. He was respected in the United States and Canada both as a poet and as an anthologist. Indeed, he had always been Scott and Edel's mentor, the major literary figure in *The McGill Fortnightly* group. To Smith they owed their modernism. As Scott liked to quip, "Smith was three years younger than me when I sat at his feet."[10] The younger Smith, to some degree, had patronized both Scott and Edel. "Throw away that crap!" he had said, justifiably, of Scott's early romantic verse, and, not quite so justifiably, "What will the American reviewers think?"[11] His most serious condemnation of Scott's poetry was that it could be easily understood. This was a cardinal sin because for the young Smith the virtue of a poem could be equated with its obscurity. Had not T.S. Eliot said that the modern poet must be obscure, must force language into meaning, to reflect adequately the modern condition?

But the scales were about to shift in a way that none of the group could anticipate. Smith's primacy in the group was challenged a year later when Edel published the first volume of his celebrated biography of Henry James. The following year Scott published *Events and Signals*, which, although not as technically accomplished as the poems of Smith's own *News of the Phoenix* (1943), would ultimately be perceived as more significant in Canadian poetry. And, a year later, in 1955, Layton would successfully wrestle with Smith at the Kingston Poetry Conference for the critical direction of Canadian poetry.

That Kim and Doug Jones had failed initially to recognize Smith and knew Scott only by his newspaper photo is some indication of the lack of personal communication among Canadian poets in the early fifties. They read each other's work, but they did not know each other personally, the country being so wide and poets so widely separated.

That first night at Keewaydin the distances between Montreal, Toronto, and Kingston were bridged in a candlelight poetry reading. Scott and Smith impressed the group greatly "because they read their best things and they read with confidence." As Dudek recalls, "It was so glorious to have our two major poets ..., our great elder poets...."[12] There was a feeling of bonhomie, of being part of a group that respected the craft of poetry. Not surprisingly, there was a desire to repeat the experience. Late at night, recollecting the successful Canadian Artists' Conference held at Queen's University in 1941, Scott proposed a Canadian Writers' Conference, also to be held at Queen's. His 1951 attempt at organizing led him to believe that Rockefeller Foundation money could be obtained.[13] The Kingston Conference, the most important gathering of Canadian writers in the fifties, was a direct outgrowth of the weekend at Keewaydin.

At the height of a heated debate about the feasibility of such a conference, around three a.m., Scott and Smith retired to a small cabin adjoining the main building. Much later, Kim Jones woke up to find Smith standing over her in his underwear. He and Scott were "most urgent and most upset."[14] Kim's cocker spaniel Missy had whelped in their room. Kim and Smith spent the rest of the night acting as midwives to the dog, forever associating spaniels and the Keewaydin Conference in Smith's imagination.

AFTER KEEWAYDIN, Scott began organizing the proposed national poetry conference. Late in November, 1954, he wrote to Robert Weaver at the CBC in Toronto inviting him to lunch at the Victoria College student's lounge early in December to discuss such a conference. Northrop Frye had arranged for a room and Claude Bissell, Joyce Marshall, and some others would be present.[15] In the new year Scott also got in touch with some old friends at Queen's, including J.A. Corry, the vice-principal, and Malcolm Ross in the English department.

Scott had learned from his 1951 application to the Rockefeller Foundation that any conference proposal asking for their support could not deal with poetry alone. "So we invented this idea of the assembly line of literature from the input boys – the poets, the novelists and so forth at the start – [to] the manuscripts which would then go to editors or those little magazines.... Then the thing gets published and goes down the line and goes into libraries and ... booksellers .... We had the representatives of all those interests at the Conference."[16]

During his meetings with Queen's faculty, an organizing committee was established and the general theme "The Writer, his Media and the Public" was adopted. Henry Alexander, head of the English department, agreed to chair the committee; Malcolm Ross, George Whalley, and Kathleen Healey were recruited as members.[17] The aim of the Canadian Writers' Conference was to encourage mutual understanding among author, publisher, critic, and reader. The committee set out questions it wanted considered: "Does the contemporary Canadian scene provide an adequate *milieu* for the Canadian writer? ... How do editors make their choices for the mass-medium audience? Should writers contrive their work with the contemporary 'market' in view? ... Is a writer's integrity threatened by materialist considerations? How do books sell in Canada? Who reads books?"[18] The four-day program was to be centred on evening talks and morning discussions, with the afternoons left free so that writers would be able to meet.

Scott, who had considerable experience with American foundations, agreed to be responsible for conference funding. He and Raleigh Parkin met in Montreal with John Marshall, an associate director for the Rockefeller Foundation. Relations between the three men were especially cordial. Not only had Parkin and Marshall worked together with a number of American foundations for over a decade,[19] but Scott's son, Peter, was now courting Marshall's daughter, Maylie.

After his Guggenheim in 1940, Scott had been instrumental in referring A.J.M. Smith, Bartlett Brebner, Anne Hébert, and a number of others for Guggenheim fellowships.[20] In the late forties, before the Massey Commission and the Canada Council, Scott, with the help of Parkin and Marshall, had also helped to obtain $50,000 from the Rockefeller Foundation for Canadian writers. This fund was administered through a committee and the Canada Foundation. From it a number of established Canadian poets, including Irving Layton and Margaret Avison, received support, as did promising younger writers such as Jay Macpherson, Joyce Marshall, Al Purdy, and Phyllis Webb.[21]

In 1954, the proposed Canadian Writers' Conference did meet the Rockefeller Foundation's requirements and funding was supplied. However, other aspects of organization did not go quite so smoothly. Henry Alexander, the organizing chairman at Queen's, withdrew just before the event. Some of Scott's dismay was averted by a helpful letter from Malcolm Ross, who reminded him that J.A. Corry's presence on the committee had ensured good planning. "I think some people work better when they are ever in the great taskmaster's eye." Ross proposed that Scott take Alexander's place to launch the conference and that Roy Daniells would be a good chairman for the closing session, particularly if Scott ended with a summary and suggestions on future direction that arose from the conference on Canadian writing. "My own feeling," Ross concluded, "is that things are under control, that we are prepared to meet emergencies and that the affair should be a great success."[22]

Others were less convinced. Louis Dudek wrote to urge that Scott not forget promising young poets. Had he asked his son Peter, who had begun to write and publish poetry, Leonard Cohen, Doug Jones, Daryl Hine, Jay Macpherson, and A.W. Purdy?[23] Upon receipt of the official invitation list, Dudek fired off another salvo. The most new and valuable poetry, he argued, had been published in *civ/n* and *Contact*, but among the sixty-five or so invited guests none of this group were included except himself, Layton, and Souster. And they were not new writers. Given this situation, it was unlikely that Souster would now come to the conference. Furthermore, Dudek was not eager to "bring up a car-load of people to Kingston ... since they would all be paying their own way while dozens of much less active people in the cause of literature would be getting official recognition and hospitality."[24] Scott retorted testily. It was no use for Dudek to think that "a conference paid for by Foundation money [was] going to be primarily a stimulus to young avant-gardistes; by definition it [could] not be." He concluded resignedly, "Well, you are not the first person who imagines that I am Lord of this particular creation. I still think a carload of people is a good idea, but I agree that if it would only produce rage and envy it had better not happen."[25]

To add to his troubles, Scott became ill just before the conference began; he half decided not to attend and wrote Anne Wilkinson to say so. She would not hear of it. "You *have* to come to the conference. It's your baby & no one else could possibly manage the rambunctious child – or it might just be flat unless we had your dictatorial self to keep us going." She admonished firmly, "*Come*. In cast and ambulance if necessary."[26]

Despite all setbacks, once the conference was under way there was an overwhelming sense of camaraderie. Poets and novelists who had long read each other's work – who were, in fact, old friends on paper – could now attach names to faces. As Robert Weaver recalls,

> The strongest impression I have of the conference – one of the few conferences I've been to that I still remember with good feelings – was that in those pre-Canada Council days when travel was not something that writers were able to do very much, ... what great pleasure the writers took in meeting face to face, and I remember that people like Ralph Allen of *Maclean's*, John Gray from Macmillan, Jack McClelland and I (who had been able to travel because of our jobs) spent a lot of time introducing writers to other writers and watching the pleasure of these first meetings. A great thing that Frank did.[27]

A.J.M. Smith was there, very witty, speaking in a rather choppy way; Layton, "short, dark and stocky, inclined to push his head forward pugnaciously; he spoke in paragraphs and had a highly sardonic sense of humour."[28] Scott himself, tall and assured, moved from group to group, greeting everyone exuberantly.

The initial sense of meeting was very positive. Roy Daniells, then head of the Department of English at the University of British Columbia, recalled:

> Callaghan I had met once before, in Winnipeg; Child, Reaney, Joyce Marshall, Dudek, Layton, Mrs. Salverson and some of the younger Montreal group I had never before encountered; Sutherland I had seen once and Miriam Waddington I had known only as a student. To see them in action and hear them express what is of current concern to them has been valuable and exciting (in the better sense of that word) beyond all expectation. I can think of no other circumstances in which it could have been achieved.[29]

The list of participants at the Kingston Conference was a *Who's Who* of present and future writing and publishing in Canada. From the media came Ralph Allen, James Bannerman, W.A. Deacon, Kildare Dobbs, James Gray, John Gray, S.P. Kite, Jack McClelland, Hilton Smith, Robert Weaver; prose writers included Morley Callaghan, Philip Child, Hugh Garner, Laura Goodman-Salverson, Ronald Hambleton, Charles Israel, William McConnell, John Marlyn, Joyce Marshall, Malcolm Ross, Mason Wade, and Adele Wiseman. Among the poets were Earle Birney, Elizabeth Brewster, Fred Cogswell, Leonard Cohen, Roy Daniells, Ralph Gustafson, Irving Layton, Dorothy Livesay, Jay Macpherson, Eli Mandel, James Reaney, W.W.E. Ross, A.J.M. Smith, Miriam Waddington, Anne Wilkinson, and

Phyllis Webb.[30] As Mandel reminisced, the Kingston Conference was "one of the very first gatherings of the clan of Canadian poets. I would say that was a key moment because if these writers had previously no sense of themselves as a community, they certainly did at that point."[31]

During the first evening, July 28, there was a public meeting in Convocation Hall on "The Writer" addressed by A.J.M. Smith, Morley Callaghan, and Douglas Grant, then editor of *University of Toronto Quarterly*. The following morning one hundred delegates were divided into three discussion groups. That evening they heard another series of talks on "The Writer's Media" given by John Gray of Macmillan, Ralph Allen of *Maclean's*, and S.P. Kite of Penguin Books. On Saturday morning the discussion groups again converged to talk about the media; that evening the public addresses were about "The Writer and The Public." Speakers were Robert Weaver of the CBC and Hilton Smith of the Toronto Public Library.[32] On the final morning, Sunday, there was discussion of the public reception of writing in Canada. At that time Irving Layton proposed that the conference adopt a number of formal resolutions designed to utilize it as a pressure group.

Wilkinson had rightly predicted the conference would prove to be a "rambunctious child." After the first flush of greeting had subsided, the diverse members of the Canadian literary assembly line found that, although they shared common problems, they did not share the same interests. Some poets turned up their noses at middlebrow writers who wrote for profit; many prose writers felt too much emphasis was being given to poetry and, as a result, the conference was one-sided. And certain poets in the work force made cutting remarks about other poets – academics who had the benefit of a university sinecure. Even Scott blanched at this and observed *sotto voce*, "You call my salary a sinecure?"[33] Poets and prose writers alike damned the media. Predictably, altercations arose as each group justified its position. James Reaney wryly summarized some of the issues in a post-conference note: "The writers, particularly the poets, claimed the mass media people weren't doing enough for them – weren't being daring enough; the mass media people swore they were doing as much as the writers deserved and hinted that the poets might try to make things a bit easier to understand."[34]

One of the problems was that Scott's idea for a poets' conference had not been abandoned but had been extended to cover the general problems of "writing in Canada" in order to meet the requirements of the Rockefeller Foundation. Novelists, dramatists, and media writers were not genuinely integrated into the program, partly, one suspects, because Scott simply did not think that way. One of Doug Jones's most striking images of the convention was the arrival, in staid Kingston, of Layton "in a car full of women. I guess it was probably Leonard [Cohen] and various friends, but it was like the sultan coming with his harem."[35] Recollecting the event, Scott mused that "there arrived from Montreal a group of poets, Dudek and Leonard Cohen who brought up his guitar, and poets began to dominate the thing. They were much more outspoken than the novelists and the few dramatists. And it was Layton who wanted to turn the thing into a sort of pressure group and introduce resolutions to be passed which we never thought we would have."[36]

In retrospect it seems likely that the conference got started on the wrong foot with Smith's opening address on "The Poet." Quoting from Roy Daniells, to insist that the poet had no importance in Canadian society, he said that the excellence of Canadian poetry exists in spite of "immense public indifference, deadly though unspoken." He reminded the audience of A.M. Klein's "Portrait of the Poet as Landscape" (originally "Portrait of the Poet as Nobody"). How did he explain this picture of the poet in exile, as a nobody? Not by the alleged obscurity of poetry, but rather by the fact that the poet is too critical of society. "He is ... the teller of unpleasant truths, the secret conscience of society, the revealer of unconscious guilt."

Poetry, Smith continued, is not a mercantile commodity, but if the poet is willing to simplify his language, conventionalize his image, and "deal with large generalized themes, [or] as often as possible with some heroic episode of Canadian history," there was popularity, even fame, waiting for him with "the middlebrow public catered to by *Maclean's* ..., *Saturday Night*, the Canadian Authors' Association, and the CBC."[37] It is hard to determine whether Smith was seriously affirming higher standards or reverting to that Mencken-induced tone of the twenties and thirties. In any event, his remarks were hardly designed to please the individuals present who represented the magazines, the CAA, and the CBC. Neither could they have pleased E.J. Pratt, who wrote primarily on those "large generalized themes" Smith was so cheerfully indicting. Nor, one suspects, could they have pleased Scott. Once again he was back to the uneasy position he had occupied while trying to edit *New Provinces* in the thirties of trying to hold together two bucking teams of horses, with Smith on one side, and Pratt and the more conservative writers on the other.

A note of querulousness crept into the proceedings. Matters did not improve. Smith went on to justify the poet's obscurity, arguing that the poet is the guardian of a cult that writes primarily for *other* poets.[38] This view of the poet as high priest, writing for a group of initiates, caused considerable dissension. Those who agreed with Smith were forced to defend their positions while those who did not, notably Layton, carried the battle to the barricades. Macpherson later wrote to Scott: "I found myself again and again crammed into a corner with Reaney & Mandel and bitterly defending myth against everything else possible."[39]

The central split of the conference, as far as the poets were concerned, was the split between Smith and Layton on the question of the poet's role in Canada. While Smith argued that poets wrote for other poets, Layton argued that the poet wrote for a wider public, an extension perhaps of his romantic belief, echoing Shelley, that the poet is "the unacknowledged legislator of mankind." Layton, it seemed, simultaneously accepted a pro-letarian and an elitist view of art.[40] On the one hand he proffered the socialist-realist belief that the poet was part of the proletariat; on the other, he gave voice to Nietzsche's idea that the poet is a superior person, one far above the masses, whose mission it is to give direction. Layton no longer believed that poetry was the handmaiden of the revolution, but he was convinced that poetry did not belong in the ivory tower, as Smith seemed to be suggesting.

Smith, on the other hand, was very likely arguing tongue-in-cheek. The "pure poetry" he advocated was a necessary counterview to the persistent forties idea of poetry as a somewhat artless political vehicle. This battle, reflecting contemporary trends in poetry, was really a battle about the direction of Canadian poetry. Should it lean toward Layton's brand of heightened proletarian realism? Or should it go toward Smith's more metaphysical and myth-centred poetry?

This debate marked the point at which Smith's influence as a critic was at its peak; thereafter it began to wane. Other voices would begin to be heard, notably those of Frye, Dudek, and Layton. As Mandel recalled, at this point a shift in sensibility in Canadian poetry began to manifest itself: "to move from whatever the modern period means – Smith, Scott, Klein, Pratt, Finch and Kennedy – to Layton, Dudek, Souster on one hand, and Reaney, Mandel, Macpherson ... on the other."[41] At the Kingston Con-ference, at long last, Scott and Smith were recognized as major figures in the first wave of Canadian modernism. But at the same time the younger poets were now commanding attention.

Despite his best intentions, Scott was not impartial when acting as chairman at the conference. If several people were attempting to be rec-ognized during the discussion periods, Scott invariably gravitated toward the poets and then allowed them to go on at interminable length.[42] Layton, as Dudek recalled, was "the great sounding board. He talked a great deal. And ranted against the journalists."⁴³ Another participant has similar memories: "I remember Irving being very vociferous and ... involved in a conversation in a room full of people sputtering and arguing about whether poetry, art or literature was for people or for a few."⁴⁴ Proletarian poets, Layton said, must oppose capitalism. Society had a duty to support the artist. Private foundations should consider it an honour to support "Great Poets." And the Kingston Conference should be held annually.⁴⁵ In justice to Layton, he had met several times with Scott to help plan the conference. As an avowed leftist, and a founding father of the conference, so to speak, Layton believed he had a duty to give direction to it. It is interesting to speculate what Marshall, sitting quietly in the audience as the representative of the Rockefeller Foundation, thought of these notions.

Edinborough watched Scott attempting to chair the sessions with great interest. "The dominant thing was that he was very tall and he had a droop in one eye and a curious kind of – I can only call it swoop. When he stood up or he made a comment ... then the cutting edge would come out with a great – I think of it as a scimitar. And behind it was this rather sinister face. You felt that, you know, Black Spot was just round the corner ... this guy had one [eye] ... be careful of him." He radiated a sharp intelligence, "particularly [in] his gestures and the way he demolished people. He knew – you knew – that the thrust was coming because the shape of his body and of his head told you it was coming. He telegraphed his wit. He certainly telegraphed his cutting remarks."⁴⁶

But if Scott could be rapier-like, he could also be placatory. At the closing session he attempted to pour oil on troubled waters by reminding the assembled writers that although Smith might complain of isolation and Layton might assert that the poet was essential to society, the actual situation of the writer in Canada had not changed greatly in sixty years. As proof, he read from a letter Archibald Lampman had written to F.G. Scott, his father, in the 1890s. "The gist of it was that Canon Scott might complain of isolation in Quebec, but in the gay teeming national capital of Ottawa there was only one other person Archibald Lampman could talk to about literature."⁴⁷ The moral was clear; one's sense of isolation as a writer is relative. In the largest sense the writer is always isolated.

Scott's role as a mediator and facilitator in Canadian poetry is apparent in the correspondence emanating from the Kingston Conference. No sooner had the delegates dispersed when he received an indignant letter from Layton. "It was wrong to invite the mass media boys to the Conference.... I for one found myself arguing with commercialized apes who no more belonged to any honest gathering of writers than you or I do in a brothel." And he was irritated that Scott had not made a socialist affirmation "that the profit system is hostile to the life of the spirit…. In any case the great writers of our time, and even the minor ones – as surely is not unknown to you – have all been anti-capitalistic, anti-bourgeois, Shaw, Yeats, Pound, Auden, Eliot – but why go on? Christ, don't you read your own poetry?"[48]

Scott replied mildly. He did not think the conference had been "robbed of its fruits" because a list of resolutions had not been supplied to the press. "What we must see to now is the publication of the papers, résumés of discussion, and resolutions in saleable book form. This will have an influence in places where decisions are taken. Of course the resolutions will also go to the appropriate people."[49] Letters were promptly sent to government officials such as Prime Minister Louis St. Laurent; Lester Pearson, Secretary of State for External Affairs; Jack Pickersgill, Minister of Citizenship and Immigration; and Ray Williston, the British Columbia Minister of Education.[50]

Despite the firmness of his reply to Layton, Scott also had a nagging feeling the conference had not quite been successful. That same day, he wrote bitterly to William Arthur Deacon, literary critic of the Toronto *Globe and Mail*, saying that the problems of Canadian writing had not been brought to the public's attention. "Hardly any newspapers bothered to mention it. Though I notified the Star and Gazette in Montreal, they passed it by. The Star of course will never allow my name to be favourably mentioned…."[51] The older man caught the note of anger and, sensibly, raised Scott's perspective:

> In literature we are among the imponderables. The tremendous thing you accomplished for all these people was not in giving them pleasure but providing contacts and inspiration beyond anything you can imagine…. It matters little whether those attending agreed or disagreed, were voluble or silent. For the time [being] they had been enabled to conquer geography and to realize, at least subconsciously, that others, equally earnest, face the same problems, share the same discouragements and frustrations. From that, all gained courage.[52]

Deacon was right. For some participants the immediate image of the conference was, in Jones's words, "a series of contradictions and confrontations and collisions with no sense of direction or harmony coming out of it certainly."[53] But the long-term effect of the 1955 Kingston Conference was to provide direction for Canadian literature as a whole and a new sense of unity for Canadian poets. For most of the younger fifties poets and for many older ones, the Kingston Conference represented a turning point in their work.

More importantly, the recommendations brought forward at Kingston in 1955 laid the foundation for the formal study of Canadian literature. The first three resolutions urged all provinces to give a more prominent place to Canadian literature in school curricula, textbooks, colleges, and universities and to support Canadian libraries. After 1956, a number of Canadian universities, notably the University of British Columbia, included Canadian literature in their curriculum. The fourth resolution stated that "to establish a continuing literary tradition in Canada significant works by Canadians must be kept in print and if necessary republished in inexpensive editions for use both by students and by general readers." The McClelland and Stewart New Canadian Library series, which began with a discussion between McClelland and Ross at Kingston, was a direct response to this. The resolutions further suggested that the Canada Council, then being formed, should subsidize Canadian books in the manner of the Australian Arts Council and help Canadian writers through the provision of literary fellowships and scholarships. The conference also recommended that Governor General's Awards include substantial cash payments and, finally, that the Canadian government increase its purchases of new Canadian writing for distribution in embassies throughout the world.[54]

There was no specific resolution regarding establishment of a journal for the study of Canadian literature, but Scott's report on the conference, published in the *University of Toronto Quarterly* in October, 1955, pointed out that "there does not exist in Canada a literary magazine of the type of *Partisan Review*, *Hudson Review* or the *Sewanee Review*, where a coterie of writers and critics maintain a constant watch for new talent and subject writers generally, both old and new, to an informed criticism. Indeed ... criticism of Canadian literature scarcely exists at all."[55] Several individuals who attended the Kingston Conference shared Scott's view on the importance of Canadian literary periodicals. The decade's most important periodicals and publishing ventures, especially *Canadian Literature* (which emerged from a B.C. conference on writing called by three participants in the Kingston Conference, Daniells, W.C. McConnell, and Dorothy Livesay), *Prism*, and the McGill Poets Series are directly connected with the Kingston gathering.

It is doubtful Scott recognized a direct line between the Kingston Conference and *Canadian Literature* or the New Canadian Library Series. He rarely looked for recognition for himself, always being much more interested in the group. He *was* aware, however, that he had had some influence in acquiring public funds for poetry readings. In June, 1959, he wrote to the secretary of the Canada Council urging favourable consideration of a request from Kenneth McRobbie for a program of poetry readings in Toronto in 1960:

> Poetry readings are well established in many centers in the United States, and have undoubtedly contributed to increasing the audience for poets and the markets for their books. I believe we are at a point in Canada where they would have the same beneficial results if they could be organised. The difficulty, of course, is the usual one of overcoming distance.[56]

Scott's tendency always was to bring new people together in order to get the next exciting project under way. He enjoyed the dynamism of such a life. "Frank has the temerity to sort of push on with things, almost to bulldoze them through, and in so doing to make them happen.... He has a total belief that 'this is valuable' even when most people are full of reservations."[57] This *joie de vivre* made him essential to many of the emerging poets of the forties, fifties, and sixties. He was always willing to talk with them, to have them over to 451 Clarke Avenue for drinks and parties, and to recommend them for fellowships and awards. For younger poets he was, as Doug Jones explained, "a kind of father figure."

> Whenever one went to Frank's place, one felt very much a part of Canadian poetry. Frank had a great capacity to make everybody feel he was great, he was important if you got there at all.... He [had] a tremendous sense of tradition. His own tradition to begin with but the whole tradition of Canadian poetry and of poetry, period. [He felt] the necessity to do things positively and to keep things happening.... He's a man who believe[d] in society and organization and law as a positive thing.[58]

It was primarily the man as poet that Jones saw.

> Every time Frank was with poets he said, "This is where I want to be. Thank God I'm not at this moment a politician or something else." But he may have said that in his law lectures too, because I presume he got as much kick out of his ... brief appearances in court, when he proved he was also a lawyer. He was the only person I ever met who almost convinced me that the law is a good thing. And that it is basic to the whole of Canada, the whole British Empire.... And

Frank saw the law as a piece of poetry in effect, ... as practical poetry....
Most of the time when he was with [mutual friends his attitude said,]
"I feel good and this is the best part of my life."[59]

A circle of poets had been around the Scotts since the twenties. Smith,
Kennedy, and Klein had been augmented in the forties by Anderson, Page,
Layton, Dudek, Souster, and Sutherland, and in the fifties by Ralph Gustafson, Phyllis Webb, Al Purdy, Jones, Cohen, and Daryl Hine. During
the sixties budding poets such as George Bowering, John Newlove, and
Patrick Lane wrote or visited. In all these activities Marian was at hand
greeting the poets warmly, making them feel comfortable, and preparing
gracious dinners for unexpected guests. Her presence added another dimension to the conversation as well. "Poetry is important," Scott's attitude
said. "Painting is important," Marian's attitude said. And those who were
with them felt involved in a common cause.

Throughout the fifties Scott's poetry circle widened considerably. Dudek
was teaching at McGill, Layton at Sir George Williams University, and
Webb at McGill Extension. During the late fifties a number of poets would
gather, usually at Layton's house at Côte St. Luc but sometimes at Scott's,
to talk about poetry. Habitués included Cohen, Aileen Collins, Robert
Currie, Dudek, Yaffa Lerner, Morton Rosengarten, Scott, and Webb. Eli
Mandel, who taught for several years at the College Royale Militaire at
St. Jean near Montreal, was a frequent visitor. Occasional guests were
Dorothy Livesay, Anne Wilkinson, Page, and Smith. The group also en-
tertained Dylan Thomas after he had given a reading at McGill in the early
fifties.

A typical meeting consisted of poets reading from their most recent
work followed by "spontaneous criticism."[60] Cohen recalled that the analysis was blunt and occasionally "vicious," fine training for him as it was
necessary to defend every word of a poem. On one occasion Scott was on
the receiving end. "Frank read a poem that was severely attacked. He wept,
saying, 'I've spread myself too thin. I've wanted to be a poet but I've
spread myself too thin'."[61]

Some time later Scott received a letter from a student at Bishop's University asking if poetry had been the chief concern of his life. He attempted
to weigh his own motives when he responded: "This depends, of course,
on how you estimate 'concern.' It is certainly not the activity which takes
up most of my time; indeed, I've had very little time for it. It is, however,
my deepest concern in the sense that I believe it to be the activity that
most expresses what I feel and think and desire."[62]

Scott's friendships with poets were perhaps the deepest of all – with the exception of old comrades-in-arms like Raleigh Parkin and King Gordon whose friendship, immutable and continuous, was part of the fabric of his life. He was still, however, usually a very private person: people found it very difficult to get through his facade. In the part of his life devoted largely to law and politics there was no role for the private man. But with poets and poetry there was always room for the personal. It is partly that poetry is a subjective expression of feeling; even the satire Scott so often practised was, as he later wrote, "an inverted affirmation of belief."[63] Most importantly, poetry for Scott was restorative. Like the Laurentians, it was a return to the private reaches of self where he found new energy for the next foray outward.

For those who reached for the inner self – Avison, Cohen, Dudek, Jones, Layton, Page, Purdy, Webb – Scott had a great capacity for loving friendship. Dudek later remarked, "I have grown to love the man."[64] Purdy, looking back over his own career, recalled that Scott was "unique among all the people I have known; unique [in] his combination of qualities and abilities; his capacities for friendship.... I have very warm feelings about Scott personally: I owe him, for many reasons. He helped me in all sorts of ways: he tried to get me a job at one time when I was nearly unemployable; he wrote letters on my behalf; he believed in me – he had to act the way he did; and he was a friend."

It was not just the personality of the man that attracted people but the sum of all of his interests, especially, as Purdy remembered, his larger concerns: "there was no one like him in Canada or anywhere else. Just knowing him, being aware that he existed in the world, added to my own strength, was a cause for celebration."[65] This was not a self-conscious nationalism but rather that sense of the land found in his poems, especially narratives like "Lakeshore" and "Laurentian Shield," which were reflected in the work of younger poets like Purdy, Atwood, Newlove, and Lane. Scott was to help shape the new Canadian poetry of the fifties and sixties because he, like E.J. Pratt, showed younger writers how the primary Canadian fact, the northern landscape, could be evoked through metaphors of evolution.

He also had a surprisingly strong influence on younger poets whose work was quite different. Leonard Cohen, for example, entered McGill's Faculty of Law because Scott was there. He reasoned that if Scott had "survived and flourished" there perhaps he, too, could make a contribution to the world that way. He said he liked to hear Scott talk about the law; once he compared it to a coral reef, something that grows and evolves and makes beautiful shapes.[66] Nevertheless, when it became apparent that poetry rather than law was Cohen's forte, Scott encouraged him to write and recommended him for a Canada Council grant.[67]

For Cohen, visits to Clarke Avenue were "warm and wonderful [with] a very open fluid atmosphere; lots of fun; drinking; and talk of politics and poetry." And Marian and Frank began to visit the downtown Montreal clubs where Leonard was beginning to perform with his guitar. Cohen, in turn, was invited to North Hatley to stay with the Scotts at their summer cottage. Once when Cohen arrived in some personal turmoil, he found Scott sitting quietly in his wicker chair on the long verandah. The house, built on the slope of a hill, was surrounded by trees. Scott, sensing the younger man's agitation, motioned to the autumn leaves, saying "Just let it work on you."[68]

Scott's own divided personality found peace at North Hatley, a process reflected in "Autumn Lake."

> the calm of water    becalmed
> flowed into me    covered me
> easing
> what was hurting
> far down
>
> at mid-lake
> a cone of shadow
> from the hill behind
> touched a cone of colour
> mirrored on the water
> from the far shore
>
> and I was drawn
> to that point
> where shadow and reflection
> (two fingers)
> touched
> one and one formed one
> and conflict ended
>
> so calmed
> I glided downward
> melting
> into the wholeness
> into the still
> centre    (C.P., p. 61)

He tried to share with Cohen this feeling of peace. And he helped the younger man to write by encouraging him to stay at his brother Elton's cabin further up the lake, a sparse wooden lean-to Scott had used as a summer retreat in earlier days. There, in 1957, Cohen began to write *The Spice Box of Earth* and in 1958 he stayed longer and worked on *The Favourite Game*. His poem "Summer Haiku: For Frank and Marian Scott" reflects some of the peace he found at North Hatley:

> Silence
> and a deeper silence
> when the crickets
> hesitate[69]

Carved into a rock over many years of successive visits, this haiku was ultimately presented to the Scotts at North Hatley, where it became a doorstop for the summer house.

Scott, always extraordinarily open to new people and new experiences, was introduced, by Cohen, to the new pop poetry of the late fifties and sixties – the Bob Dylan of *Blonde on Blonde* and *Bringing It All Back Home*. This occurred early in 1966 when Scott planned a poetry party. He contrived an invitation, "The EDGE of the PRISM," which brought together the names of many little mags started by the proposed guests.

> The point is
> I firmly believe
> CIV/n is not a one man job
> Hence CONTACT
> Is important
> So please answer
> YES
> As your FIRST STATEMENT
> To 451 Clarke Avenue
> Saturday January 8
> Where the Scotts will provide
> Lunch
> And
> Supper
> Liquid and solid
> Come at Noon
> And be carried out
> After Midnight ...[70]

290 / THE POLITICS OF THE IMAGINATION

Layton, Dudek, Purdy, Gustafson, and a number of others came, including Cohen. As Dudek and Scott recalled, Cohen brought out his guitar and said:

> "What are these poets doing, all writing poetry the way they used to? Do you know who the greatest poet in America is?"
> "Who?"
> "Bob Dylan!"
> "Who's he?"
> "Don't you know? He's already made a million dollars."
> "Then he can't be the greatest poet in the world."
> "Don't you know his records?"
> "Where can you get them?"
> "National Music Store."

Scott dashed out with the names of four records, found they cost $6.95, and bought two. Back at Clarke Avenue he interrupted the general conversation to put on one of the records that Cohen described as "very good music, very good poetry. It's the greatest poetry of the century." Then, in Scott's words, "the music began to blare such as never had been heard in these halls before."

At that point Al Purdy "bounded out of the room as though booted from behind," saying "It's an awful bore. I can't listen to any more of this." He went to the kitchen, probably to get more beer. Cohen's presentation of Dylan as a great poet was "a great fiasco" because, as Dudek reflects, "no one thought him any good." At this point Cohen told the assembled poets that there was an audience out there waiting for him. He would be the new Bob Dylan, a claim no one believed.[71]

Scott's plan for the day had been "drinks, lunch, sit around and rest, resume and then go to see two films from the National Film Board." They saw a Klein film, "A.M. Klein: The Poet as Landscape," followed by "Ladies and Gentlemen, Mr. Cohen," a film Cohen declined to see. After five they came back, rested, had pre-supper drinks and finally dinner. Around ten the conversation began to flag. Scott asked, "Would you like to hear that Bob Dylan record again?" This time everyone got up and danced – "the new rhythms and the beer were having their effect."[72] And Scott added yet another new experience to his list.

ONE SIGN of the increasing cultural maturity emerging in Canada during the late fifties was a new willingness on the part of its writers to satirize things Canadian, to say nothing of the willingness of audiences to laugh with the satirists. Scott, one of the most incisive writers of satirical verse during this period, explained, "I don't quite know why I took to satire so frequently; perhaps because when I was a boy my father used to read Stephen Leacock aloud to us." Of satire itself, Scott observed, "Don't forget that satire, while seeming destructive, is really professing a faith in the opposite of that which is being satirized."[73]

Scott had composed occasional satirical verses most of his writing life, but 1957 saw the production of two works in which this mode predominated, *The Eye of the Needle* and *The Blasted Pine*. The first of these was a collection of Scott's own satirical poems, while *The Blasted Pine*, as its subtitle attests, was *An Anthology of Satire, Invective and Disrespectful Verse Chiefly By Canadian Writers* that Scott and his old friend Arthur Smith put together during the summer of 1957.

The poems in *The Eye of the Needle* were mostly directed against Canadians. The epigraph to the book, "Onward the mighty waters flow, / but where, oh where, is Charbonneau?" alludes to the disappearance of former Archbishop Charbonneau of Montreal, a social reformer well known for his support of the Asbestos strike who suddenly had been removed from power by conservatives within the Roman Catholic Church. Writing to Scott on February 17, 1957, Louis Dudek described the book as "hilarious," but also perceived "the tragic note of your personal drama – namely, the defeat of intelligence in this country of ours." As he added, earnestly, "You are the protagonist for so much good will, civic sense, public wisdom, that the hopeless apathy and stupidity of the world you describe becomes a tragic stage for one's contemplation. 'To Certain Friends' most of all, and the Mackenzie King poem, bring this out."

As a satirist, Scott appreciated the absurdities in subjects that other people thought quite serious, such as the constitution, the role of the Governor General, and the pretensions of a commodity-oriented culture.[74]

> "Culture in Canada is booming"
> Says Toronto *Saturday Night*,
> And *Saturday Night* is always right.
> Quite![75]

He was also able to prick with his satirical needle aspects of Canada that were of supreme importance to him, such as biculturalism, as in "Bonne Entente":

> The advantages of living with two cultures
> Strike one at every turn,

Especially when one finds a notice in an office building:
"This elevator will not run on Ascension Day";
Or reads in the Montreal *Star*:
"Tomorrow being the Feast of the Immaculate Conception,
There will be no collection of garbage in the city"
Or sees on the restaurant menu the bilingual dish:

DEEP APPLE PIE
TARTE AUX POMMES PROFONDES   (*C.P.*, p. 256)

In justifying the social criticism of *The Blasted Pine*, Scott and Smith point out in the introduction that the satirist in times of social change is one "crying in the wilderness, and his critical intelligence and righteous indignation shine like bright lamps in a bleak world." Canadians emigrating to a new country, asserting their individuality against the traditions of their past, are perhaps themselves satirists, revolutionaries rejecting the established order. "The poets and versifiers we have brought together are men who have looked behind the facade of conventional acceptance and ... have refused to play the game." The non-conformist spirit has never been without manifestation in Canada and the "subversive, intelligent reaction to the standardized life will continue to find a voice.... Will anybody listen?"[76] Many did. *The Blasted Pine* received delighted critical reviews and has remained one of Scott's best-selling books.

When Scott and Smith began to collect Canadian satiric verse, many of their friends considered the Canadian climate inhospitable. Why? Scott's McGill friend, David Thomson, wrote a preface for the book in which he remarks that most Canadians are smug about themselves and with what they choose to see. "The political parties are in competition rather than in opposition; the television antenna graces the tar-paper shack;" and, he continued urbanely, "the poor are decently huddled out of sight in the staff-rooms of our schools and colleges; the exactions of the greedy and corrupt are perfected to the point that they suck our blood so painlessly that it is more comfortable to pretend that they do not even touch us."[77]

*The Blasted Pine* is a satiric inventory of Canadian society. Like Scott's miscellany, "An Up-to-Date Anthology of Canadian Poetry," first published in *The Canadian Forum* in 1932, it is organized around an "O Canada" structure, in the sense that there is always a contrast implied between the ideal Canada of the national anthem and recurrent historical realities. The anthology reveals that almost as soon as Canadian poets appeared they began to sound a disruptive note, from Alexander McLachlan's early protest, "We Live in a Rickety House," to Earle Birney's contemporary squib, "Canada: case history." Canada, he says, is "a high-school land, / deadset in adolescence":

> Parents unmarried and living abroad,
> relatives keen to bag the estate,
> schizophrenia not excluded,
> will he learn to grow up before it's too late?[78]

There was even room in the collection for the occasional English visitor, like Samuel Butler, whose early lament against the Canadian commercial spirit – "O God, O Montreal!" – had precipitated Scott's own satire in the twenties.

In the late fifties Scott was also the inspiration for one of the most successful forays into satire that Canadians have achieved. In 1957, two of his law students, Donald MacSween and Timothy Porteous, following Scott's example, wrote a satire on Canadian society for the annual McGill Red and White Revue. They had been invited by the producer, Jim Domville, a rehearsal pianist and skit-writer for former revues, to join him in writing the production. Domville also asked Erik Wang, who with MacSween and Porteous had founded a campus humour magazine, *The Fig Leaf*, to join them. Domville was the composer and MacSween, Porteous, and Wang the writers; eventually Brian Macdonald was lured into the production as choreographer.[79]

MacSween and Porteous had been disgusted by previous McGill skits because they were often based on American content, American humour, and American allusions.[80] It was also clear that the other alternative, the humour of Gilbert and Sullivan or of Flanders and Swann, was quintessentially British, not Canadian. But what was Canadian besides Leacock? During the fifties a Canadian sensibility had begun to emerge partly as a result of such CBC programming as Wednesday night dramatizations of the life of Sir John A. Macdonald or W.O. Mitchell's tales of Crocus, Saskatchewan. Max Ferguson's "Rawhide" poked fun at English Canada and in Quebec Gratien Gélinas's *Tit Coq* (1948) examined Francophone society. Most importantly, for MacSween and Porteous, there at the front of their law classes was F.R. Scott talking about Mackenzie King, who "never let his on the one hand / Know what his on the other hand was doing."

The two young law students talked for almost a year about Canadian themes. There would have to be a Mountie; they wanted something about Parliament; the constitution and the flag debate were important. They adapted a story line around one of the most topical pieces of popular news:

the Grace Kelly-Prince Rainier romance; if Rainier did not marry and have children Monaco would revert to France. The writers invented an Eskimo principality, Mukluko, with a princess who had to marry or her kingdom would revert to Canada. Princess Aurora, seeking a husband in Canada, encounters a reporter, a Mountie, and an anglophobic representative of the newly formed Canada Council but she ends up in the arms of the Governor General, one not given to mere "governor-generalities."[81] The writers cheekily borrowed a title from a reigning London hit, and *My Fur Lady* took Ottawa and then Canada by storm. Ultimately *My Fur Lady* was performed four hundred times in eighty-two centres across Canada.[82] For the first time Canadians throughout the country enjoyed the spectacle of seeing themselves satirized in musical comedy.

It is one thing to satirize Canada, its institutions, and its public figures. It is quite another thing to be the object of such satire oneself. On November 21, 1957, Scott gave a reading at Av Isaac's Greenwich Art Gallery in Toronto. John Robert Colombo, attending the reading, reported for the University of Toronto student paper, *The Varsity*, under the headline "A Lawyer-Poet Talks About Politics." Colombo described Scott as having "steel-gray eyes and ... wearing a steel-gray suit." Under bright lights and surrounded by "great blobs" of impressionistic paintings, "the lanky 59-year-old author of three books of genuine Canadian verse looked like a self-assured New England insurance man." Scott was present for the first of the Contact Press Poetry Readings where he read a number of his own poems as well as his translations of Anne Hébert, Pierre Trottier, and Roland Giguère. Scott's poems, Colombo thought, were readily intelligible, "and a good time was had by all."

At a reception after the reading, "the Montreal poet turned out to be an excellent mixer. He smoked a pipe and drank well. Since he preferred discussing politics to metrics, the soirée broke up into small groups centering around less socially-conscious poets. Drifting from one group to another, one could hear Scott holding his own on the incompetence of the Indian Affairs Department, Burmese nationalism and the 'state of siege' of French-Canadian writers." Scott commented on Jay Macpherson and myth; he had not finished reading Frye's *The Anatomy of Criticism*. "I don't read much about poetry. It is only one of my interests." Scott was joined by the hostess, a translator, and Colombo eavesdropped and reported on their conversation about translation and several Quebec poets. "By 2:00 a.m. everyone decided it was time to go home to bed."

As the noisy group drifted out into the hall of the apartment building the hostess motioned them to be quiet. "Ray Souster's voice carried over the rest: 'Be quiet! Everyone's in bed on Friday nights in Toronto'!" Colombo, stepping into the elevator, recalled Scott's lines on a similar gathering thirty-one years earlier:

> O Canada, O Canada, Oh can
> A day go by without new authors springing
> To plant [paint] the native maple, and to plan
> More ways to set the selfsame welkin ringing?[83]

Three days later Colombo received a letter from Scott, "all muskets blazing threatening to sue me for reporting private conversations."[84] Said Scott, "What kind of journalist you want to be is your own business but my private life is mine. You owe Mrs. Brazeau [the hostess] and myself an apology for so abusing a private invitation."[85] Hastily explaining that he wrote in all innocence, Colombo also pointed out that there were now more open attitudes to journalistic practices. Scott was mollified. He still felt that Colombo "crossed over a line that should be respected. However, I hope you will not let my somewhat sharp expression of feeling create a barrier between us in the future. I was, and I still am interested in your interest in poetry, and there are just too few of us to permit the luxury of alienation. Let's consider the incident closed – and send me the next thing you write."[86] Over the years Scott was to prove amiable, a ready listener to plans for Colombo's latest enterprise. In 1978 he accepted the younger man's dedication of *Colombo's Book of Canada* to himself as "the compleat Canadian."[87]

In 1959 Irving Layton published a new edition of *Laughter in the Mind* and his collected poems, *A Red Carpet for the Sun*. Scott wrote magnanimously, celebrating Layton's achievement. "When seen all together the poems have a total magnitude greater than that of any one.... Most of all it is your poetic rage that is so magnificent, a rage that is not negative but assertive, founded in a felt belief in the greatness of living and ultimately, I think, on a love of man despite the sins for which you so roundly castigate him." By his originality and the directness of his satire Layton had "freed the language" of Canadian poetry. For Scott, who had heard many of the poems as they had been written, the book was also recapitulation of his memories of the fifties.

> I think of all the times we gathered at your house or mine to read
> and talk of poetry. There is a sadness in this looking backward, a

feeling of ending, more for me than for you because I am older. The poems are not ending, but the life that surrounded them and which they distilled is passing. And those who participated in it scatter. Thus we partake of the total process. But you have preserved more of it than any of us.[88]

# EIGHTEEN

# Jehovah's Knight Errant

❧

T HROUGHOUT THE FIFTIES, Scott's thoughts on Canadian constitutional law and the necessity of entrenching a Bill of Rights within the
constitution were reinforced by two protracted legal cases: the Padlock
and Roncarelli cases. Late in 1946, Premier Duplessis had cancelled the
liquor licence of Frank Roncarelli because he had consistently been fur-
nishing bail for members of the Jehovah's Witnesses. Scott, a member of
the Civil Liberties Association, which had sponsored a rally to protest
Duplessis's action, was asked to assist with the case. In addition, he had
taken on *Switzman* v. *Elbling*, a suit for damages that offered an opportunity to test the validity of Quebec's notorious Padlock law. In the Roncarelli case, the larger issue was freedom of religion; in the Padlock case,
as Scott later argued, the primary issue was "thought control" legislation.
He remarked that both cases arose from a climate of opinion in Quebec
where it was considered perfectly all right to condemn a man without a
trial.[1] The legal battle resulting from the two cases lasted from the mid-
forties to the end of the fifties.

EVER SINCE 1937, when Premier Duplessis had introduced the Padlock Act
to plug the loophole left by the repeal in Parliament of Section 98 of the
Criminal Code (permitting the prosecution of Communists), Scott had
been lecturing in his constitutional law classes that the Padlock Act was
*ultra vires*, that is, beyond the authority of the province, since it infringed
on the federal authority for criminal law. During the forties, various civil
rights groups attempted to test its validity, but none were successful. In
1949 the opportunity for a test arose. Two of Scott's former students,
Abraham Feiner and Albert Marcus, were engaged by John Switzman,
who was being sued by his landlady, Mrs. Freda Elbling. Switzman's
apartment had been padlocked for his alleged Communist activities. His

landlady brought suit to recover damages for loss of rent and deterioration of property for one year.

In Quebec Superior Court, March, 1949, Switzman's attorneys took the position that their client admitted the facts but stood on the defence the Padlock Act was unconstitutional. In support of this contention, they argued the province could not pass the Padlock Act because it was beyond its authority: it constituted legislation that dealt with criminal law; it confiscated property without process of law; it was a violation of constitutional rights; the Act prohibited free public discussion; and finally, the words "Communism" and "Bolshevism" were not defined.[2] Mrs. Elbling's lawyer, Louis Orenstein, said in response that he was not there to discuss the constitutionality of the Act. Rather, he based his case on the fact that his client had been deprived of her house. He asked that Switzman be ejected from the house with damages of $2,170.

Mr. Justice Collins of the Quebec Superior Court ruled that the act was *intra vires*. As there had been no substantial proof of damages he did not award any but cancelled Switzman's lease with costs. For direct appeal to the Supreme Court of Canada, awarded damages must exceed $2,000. This choice closed to them, Feiner and Marcus decided, in 1954, to appeal to the Quebec Court of Appeal. The judgement, by a majority of 4 to 1, declared the Padlock Act to be *intra vires*, though a strong dissenting opinion, arguing that the law was unconstitutional, was put forward by Mr. Justice Barclay.

With this judgement, a way to appeal was now open. But before taking any action, the lawyers weighed Supreme Court judgements to ascertain the chances of success or failure. If the whole bench of nine judges sat, there was a possibility their argument might succeed. If only five judges sat, and they were conservative, their chances were poor.[3]

Frank Scott was a recognized authority on constitutional law in Quebec. Although they knew Scott to be strongly anti-Communist, Feiner and Marcus approached him.[4] To complement him they also sought the services of a Francophone lawyer, Jacques Perrault. Scott hesitated about taking the case. The furore over his CCF activities was in full swing at McGill and an editorial in *The Montreal Star* had complained that political activists like F.R. Scott should not be allowed to teach at McGill.[5] He knew he was an annoyance to the university community and this created internal discomfort. Should he go on attacking the people who provided him an opportunity to earn his living in a way he liked? He did not always enjoy his role as a rebel; it conflicted with good relations. "After a while you get sort of bored with always being opposed to authorities."[6]

But he considered the Padlock Act a vicious piece of legislation; surely it was necessary to get rid of it? It was, moreover, a case where it would be possible to argue for human rights by the indirect method – provincial laws that contravene criminal law. "I was sort of made for it. I'd been teaching the law, had the history of the Act at my fingertips." The idea of appearing in court still made him nervous, although by now he had appeared twice to argue the Roncarelli case. The fee was low but he did have his McGill salary. He finally decided, "It would have been impossible not to have taken it." Above all, there was the old impregnation of Father and "Duty": "I couldn't run away from this.... Had I been teaching nonsense for eighteen years?"[7]

The first step was a résumé of legal argument. Scott drafted the factum and Feiner and Marcus contributed cases. The argument went to the Supreme Court in November, 1956. The day appointed for the argument, Feiner rushed to the courtroom at a quarter to ten and came back with glorious news, "Nine little lambs – they're all on! The whole bench is going to sit!"[8]

Chief Justice Kerwin, as Feiner had feared, promptly asked: "Look, Mr. Scott, do we have an Issue before us? After all, this lease was cancelled many years ago, and there has been no award of damages ... you know that we don't hear appeals just on a Matter of Costs. What is the issue before us?"[9] Feiner recalled he had not troubled Frank Scott with that problem because he had retained him for his constitutional expertise. Scott was floundering as Feiner whispered *fortissimo*, "But there is an issue, My Lord."

"There is an issue, My Lord."

"The first of the War Measures Act, My Lord."

"It refers to the War Measures Act, My Lord."

"In 1939 the War Measures Act was proclaimed. By virtue of this act certain proclamations were issued giving tenants vested right in their housing. This order-in-council ...."

"In 1939, by virtue of the War Measures Act ...." Feiner continued to prompt. Scott reinforced. Two issues were raised and at this point the Chief Justice interrupted to remark, "That is sufficient, Mr. Scott. I'm satisfied we have an issue." Abraham Feiner sat back with relief.[10]

The arguments were divided among the lawyers. Feiner claimed the lower court judges had made a fundamental error in their ruling. The judges of the Superior Court and the Court of Appeal had passed a moral judgement on the desirability of the Padlock Act. However, the proper function of the court was to consider "the Pith and Substance" of the legislation. It should inquire if it was in the competence of the province to make such legislation. Scott drew a chuckle from the bench when, presenting his issue, he remarked that Section 3 of the Padlock Act, which defined a house, was sufficiently broad to include and padlock the Canadian Broadcasting Corporation for one of its political broadcasts. He called it "one of the biggest little issues since Confederation."[11] He could not reconcile this interpretation of the Padlock Act with the view of the lower court judges that the law was of a purely local and private nature aimed at combatting what was called a threat to the very marrow of Quebec.

The following day Scott argued that the Padlock Act was "thought control legislation." It invaded the federal government's jurisdiction on criminal law. "If the law ... is held valid ... 'communism, liberalism, socialism – any kind of ism – can be barred from discussion, even in the home'." This law prohibits the use of a "house" so defined to encompass every conceivable type of building to propagate communism. The penalty is a padlock on the door for twelve months. Scott argued that a Communist candidate for federal elections could not even hold meetings to discuss his platform either in his home or in the homes of his supporters without such homes being liable to padlocking. He pointed out there cannot be two types of federal candidates. " 'No province can set up barriers to one type of political candidate for the House of Commons, and give one type of candidate an advantage over another'."

He also contended the Padlock Act drastically altered Quebecers' rights of freedom of speech, of the press, and of assembly. The fundamental purpose of the Padlock Act is "to protect the state against a subversive movement of the most serious kind. 'This, I suggest, is a matter of criminal law'." In effect, this was a provincially enacted amendment to a matter of federal jurisdiction and was therefore unconstitutional.[12] He concluded, on the third day of argument, with an ingenious metaphor suggesting that the Padlock Act was a *lettre de cachet* turned inside out. Such a device, used by the kings of old France, locked a man up, Scott declared; the Padlock Act throws him out of his house. As this was the first time that a challenge of the law had come as high as the Supreme Court, "Your judgements, My Lords, will largely determine two constitutional questions," said Scott.

First whether our basic freedoms of speech, assembly and the press are at the mercy of ten provincial legislatures and exist only at their grace to be removed by a mere majority voice. Secondly whether assuming legislators have such great control over freedom – can they also dare to deprive a man who dares to exercise this right to a trial in an open court of judicial procedure?"[13]

When he said he trembled for what would happen in the next thirty years if the law were upheld, Chief Justice Patrick Kerwin is reported as remarking with a smile, "You and I won't be here then, Professor Scott." "That may well be, My Lord, but I may still turn over in my grave."[14]

Scott appeared before the Supreme Court in November, 1956, but judgement was reserved until March, 1957. He found the intervening months as difficult as the Harvard year of 1940-41, and for the same reasons. Impelled by his ideals, he had pushed himself beyond his capacity too long; his emotional energy was giving out. And events in the province of Quebec were now especially oppressive. Premier Duplessis's influence, Scott felt, was percolating down through the levels of the McGill University administration. Finally, there was no assurance that those ideals for which Scott had battled so long would be upheld by the Supreme Court of Canada.

A renewal of a previously refused invitation from Michigan State University, partly at the instigation of A.J.M. Smith, offered a welcome opportunity to leave these problems behind for two months. Scott's association with Michigan State University had begun in 1955 when he was invited to give an interdisciplinary seminar. But in September, 1955, he had been asked to be Acting Dean at McGill so he had refused the offer but stipulated to Principal James that if it were renewed he would accept. When the offer was again tendered, McGill refused to put up $600 to pay Bora Laskin, Scott's replacement at McGill. Scott was incensed. McGill University had paid $2,300 to assist Dean Meredith in securing a leave of absence. Now that Scott, who had held the fort while Meredith was away, wanted the same privilege, McConnell and the Board of Governors were haggling over a small sum.[15] The matter was ultimately settled in Scott's favour, and in February, 1957, he went to Michigan State disgruntled.

In 1957 Scott was the first in a series of special visiting lecturers. He lived in a guest apartment and gave seminars in the history department on Canadian constitutional law. He also delivered lectures to the English, political science, and French departments, gave at least one poetry reading, and worked with writing classes.

During Scott's tenure at MSU a conference on Canadian-American cultural relations was held. Michigan State's President Hannah was interested in Canada (he had served on the Joint Defence Board with General McNaughton) and both McNaughton and John Diefenbaker later received honorary degrees from MSU.[16] Marshall McLuhan from the University of Toronto and Malcolm Ross, now of Dalhousie University, were also invited. Each was asked to present, with Scott, a short statement to start the discussion. Both Ross and Scott read their statements but McLuhan, popularizing his communications theory, "began talking off the cuff about the [cause of the] development of the Suez crisis which, he claimed, was the introduction of radio into Egypt." As Malcolm Ross recalls, "he then went on to discuss the 'first railroad war' – the American Civil War. The audience seemed bewildered and Arthur Smith began to giggle. Poor Arthur, out of courtesy, stuffed his mouth with a handkerchief and hid behind a large desk."[17] McLuhan's "logic," together with the fact that Smith and Scott were preparing the satiric anthology, *The Blasted Pine*, proved irresistible. Smith soon produced a satiric couplet:

> McLuhan put his telescope to his ear
> What a wonderful smell, he said, we have here!

Ross, who stayed on after the conference, listened to Scott and Smith recall *Fortnightly* days as they took turns reading proposed poems for their anthology aloud. He was amused to hear Scott speak of Lionel Tiger, a promising young undergraduate at McGill. Apparently he had sent Scott some poems for criticism and Scott, quite excited by what he read, decided to phone Tiger at once at home to express his enthusiasm. "I had the devil of a time trying to reach him," Scott told Ross. "Do you know how many Tigers live in Montreal? Pages and pages of them!"[18]

In East Lansing, as in Montreal, Scott soon developed a wide circle of friends and acquaintances, but, as always, when deprived of his roots in Quebec, he began to feel strain. It was at this time he received an offer from Dean Erwin N. Griswold to be a visiting professor at Harvard Law School for 1958-59.[19] While wrestling with the question of acceptance, Scott discussed it by letter with his former pupil, Gerry Le Dain, now a friend and a colleague in the McGill law faculty. Scott felt despondent, his health was not good – the amoebas had been acting up again, and his emotions were again in turmoil over a second important love affair. To make matters worse, he had been passed over again for the deanship. There was also some uncertainty as to whether he could get a further leave of absence from Principal James so soon after the Michigan visit. And finally, he was worried about the future of the McGill Law School.

Le Dain urged him to accept. The invitation was, after all, the highest accolade Scott could receive, "the academic order of the garter." But other considerations, set out in Scott's reply, led him to decline. "But now –

about Harvard. Sure it's the order of the garter. It is also one whole year out of my rapidly disappearing life. It is only justifiable if it speeds me along a road I should be following. I can't afford to run around collecting accolades." The ten weeks at MSU, he told Le Dain, had been a small interruption. He had completed a legal research report, worked on the Padlock case, brought out *The Eye of the Needle*, and was editing *The Blasted Pine*, "a small but distinguished addition to the literary edifice on which I have been a kind of hod-carrier." He had continued researching constitutional law and wondered, "what will I be teaching at Harvard? That is the question. If I could teach straight Canadian constitutional law, with comparative side-lines, it would be first class. But I don't think it will be that." The Harvard appointment, he sensed, would force him "... to deflect into something not my main channel." He would have to acquire new knowledge rather than articulate what he already possessed.

> I do not see myself being able to write at Harvard the book you say I should write on the Canadian Constitution. And in the meantime all the other tendrils on my vine that Canada feeds would starve for lack of soil. Switzman and Roncarelli will still be rolling on – I feel sure of that.[20]

Switzman and Roncarelli were indeed "rolling on." On March 7 the Supreme Court of Canada gave judgement on the Switzman case. The same day Scott received a telegram in Michigan from the president of McGill's Undergraduate Law Society, "Your house has been depadlocked – come home!" There were congratulations all around. "Three cheers and a Lionel Tiger," wrote Malcolm Ross. "And *good for you!*"[21] J.R. Mallory, Scott's political science colleague at McGill, wrote that few lawyers could hope to have "so signal an effect on the law in a single case." He also pointed out that Mr. Justice Abbott had discovered in Scott's plea a telling argument for a Bill of Rights inherent in the constitution.[22]

Scott had left McGill for Michigan State feeling persona non grata; he returned in triumph, acknowledged as a champion of civil rights by newspapers from one end of the country to the other. *The Montreal Star* repeated Scott's arguments in the Supreme Court almost verbatim. It reiterated his remark that if the Padlock Act was held valid, such subjects as communism, liberalism, and socialism would be barred from discussion. It was a significant issue, the very one on which Scott had first written in *The Montreal Star* in January, 1932, when he signed himself "Associate Professor of Federal and Constitutional Law" and aroused the ire of the McGill administration.

While his convictions had not altered, the attitude of others had. Scott's position, inimical to the Quebec of the early thirties, was now acceptable in the more liberal climate of the late fifties. Also, his career as a socialist reformer was vindicated by this decision. Finally, in winning the Padlock case Scott had not only won a victory for civil rights in Canada but he had redeemed himself in the eyes of the Montreal establishment. It was finally recognized that pronouncements on the legality of constitutional statutes were proper activities for a Professor of Federal and Constitutional Law. There was a new demand for Scott's presence at lectures and banquets and he found he enjoyed this novel experience of being praised instead of censured. But there was hardly time to bask in the warmth of public approval. The Supreme Court hearing for the Roncarelli case, now reaching its first stage, was announced for May 16, 1958.

THE RONCARELLI CASE had begun on December 4, 1946, at the carriage trade restaurant of Frank Roncarelli, a prosperous McGill graduate who had inherited the thirty-five-year-old business from his parents. At one p.m., during the height of the lunch-hour rush, several carloads of uniformed policemen descended on the Crescent Street restaurant carrying guns. The restaurant was filled with businessmen enjoying a glass of wine with their meal and with matrons and their children taking a welcome break from Christmas shopping. The police trooped through the dining room, disrupting the guests' meals and removing bottles of wine from the tables. They demanded the restaurant's liquor licence, informing the startled proprietor that it was now cancelled, then confiscated his stock of liquor. On their arrival, embarrassed customers began to trickle out of the restaurant. After a fruitless but chaotic five-hour search for Jehovah's Witnesses literature, the officers left.[23]

Roncarelli phoned the press. Were the police raiding restaurants and cancelling licences everywhere? Several newspapers contacted Premier Duplessis, who offered himself as a champion of law and order – and, indirectly, of Catholic Quebec. " 'A certain Mr. Roncarelli has supplied bail for hundreds of Witnesses of Jehovah. The sympathy which this man has shown for the Witnesses in such an evident, repeated and audacious manner, is a provocation to public order, to the administration of justice and is definitely contrary to the aims of justice'." What Duplessis found particularly objectionable was that Roncarelli had acted as " 'the mass supplier of bails'."[24]

Duplessis no doubt believed that the unpopularity of the Witnesses within Quebec together with the unsavoury patronage overtones of liquor

licences would keep the affair to manageable proportions. He had mis-
calculated. There was an immediate storm of protest. *The Montreal Star*,
*The Gazette*, *The Canadian Register*, and the papers of English-speaking
Catholics united in their objections to this new arbitrary interference with
religious and political freedoms. Magazines soon picked up the issue.
*Saturday Night* ran a parody of Byron called "The Destruction of Roncarelli":

> Duplessis came down like a wolf on the fold,
> And his edicts were gleaming in purple and gold;
> And the sheen of his padlocks was hid by the pall
> Of the laws that hang heavy o'er French Montreal.[25]

The newly founded Montreal Civil Liberties Association, of which Scott
was a prominent member, called a public meeting on December 12. A
large rally was held in the Monument National, usually a centre of French
nationalist activity, and the platform party included a number of prominent
French and English Montrealers. All spoke against the government action.

Persecution of Jehovah's Witnesses had actually begun with the federal
government. In the atmosphere of tension that had gripped Canada fol-
lowing the outbreak of World War II, Ernest Lapointe, the Minister of
Justice and Mackenzie King's lieutenant from Quebec, had introduced in
1940 an order-in-council declaring the Jehovah's Witnesses illegal. Two
MPs, John Diefenbaker from Saskatchewan and Angus MacInnis from
British Columbia, had futilely protested. The ban was not lifted until
October 14, 1943.[26] But with or without federal sanction the Jehovah's
Witnesses, who had launched a vigorous proselytizing campaign early in
1933 in Quebec City, were virtually outlawed in that province.

The name of the organization was taken from the forty-third chapter
in Isaiah: "Ye are my witnesses, saith the Lord." Each member considered
himself a minister of the gospel and opposed organized religion on the
grounds that it interposed between man and his God. Since 1933, when
German Catholics had co-operated with Hitler in the suppression of German Witnesses, they had become particularly opposed to the Catholic
Church, which they described as the "whore of Babylon." Following a
Jehovah's Witness convention in Quebec City in the fall of 1933, forty
carloads of adherents had begun distributing *Watch Tower* booklets. This
had caused a furore, especially as forty-seven Catholic bishops and archbishops from across Canada had gathered in Quebec City for an episcopal
meeting. Their blitz, viewed as an invasion of heretics, had caused Quebec
City Council to pass By-law 184, which made it illegal to distribute printed
material without police permission.[27]

Nevertheless, over the next decade adherents continued to stand on Quebec street corners distributing the pamphlet *Awake!* The Montreal municipal authorities were soon arresting members: at first, under municipal laws for peddling without a licence, then under the provincial Padlock Act, and ultimately under charges of sedition, justified by a book written by Dr. Damien Jasmin, a priest. Prosecution of the Witnesses in Quebec became so extreme that the journalist Leslie Roberts said of this period, "To many outside Quebec, that province had become the home of religious persecution reminiscent of the days of the Inquisition."[28]

Then Frank Roncarelli stepped in. Because arrests were often made on a Friday, any Witnesses unable to pay bail spent the weekend in jail. Roncarelli was an adherent of the faith and a relatively prosperous man and, knowing it is a right under the democratic process, he began to provide bail. By the time Duplessis cancelled his liquor licence in 1946, Roncarelli had posted bail in 383 cases. He was able to do so by arrangement with city lawyers because he owned "substantially valid immoveable property. His bail bonds were readily accepted, and this simplified the procedure of releasing arrested parties."[29]

The confrontation between Quebecers and the Witnesses accelerated during the fall of 1945. The Witnesses would converge on sleepy Quebec villages surrounding Montreal, knocking on every door, urging repentance, and distributing pamphlets critical of the Catholic Church. Residents, offended by their zeal, soon rallied to oppose them. In Chateauguay on September 9, 1945, a mob of 1,000 Quebec Catholics appeared with a truck loaded with tomatoes, potatoes, and stones. Witnesses, including Frank Roncarelli, were beaten and pelted in a similar incident a week later. At the same time in Lachine, a mob was laying siege to the shop and home of Joseph Letellier, a member of the sect, forcing its occupants to barricade themselves within the shop against a hail of stones.[30]

In November, 1946, the Witnesses published a pamphlet, *Quebec's Burning Hate For God and Christ and Freedom Is the Shame of all Canada*, attacking both Quebec and the Catholic clergy. To Premier Duplessis, who was also acting as Attorney-General, this was too much. He issued two warnings. When they were not heeded he concluded that some mastermind directed the activities of the Jehovah's Witnesses. The search for "le grand distributeur" of the pamphlets was on.[31] Then, after consulting with the head of the Liquor Commission, Edouard Archambault, it seemed to Duplessis that both culprit and remedy were close at hand when he learned that a certain Frank Roncarelli had advanced bail for the Jehovah's Witnesses in over three hundred cases, and Roncarelli also held a liquor licence. Duplessis instructed Archambault to cancel the licence and so informed the press.

Unexpectedly, Roncarelli fought back. He asked A.L. Stein, a Montreal lawyer, to represent him. Stein had acted as counsel for Jehovah's Witnesses in the past; on one occasion he had secured an exemption from the Conscription Act for a Witness who claimed to be a minister of the gospel. At that time, Stein had decided to go to the Kingdom Hall where the applicant minister presided. He found the service to be "serious, religious, and in good faith." This had helped him to decide "that Frank Roncarelli had always acted in good faith and therefore was entitled to full protection under our law at the time."[32]

Roncarelli had also asked Stein to approach Scott, well known as a civil libertarian. Scott was in a dilemma. He understood perfectly well the theoretical principles involved. But (as the initiation of the Roncarelli case preceded the Padlock case) he had never actually pleaded a case in court. He was not familiar with court procedures. He was not even sure that his dues to the Quebec Bar Association were up to date. Was he still entitled to be a practising member? But his sense of injustice was strongly aroused. "At the present moment," he wrote in the January, 1947, *Canadian Forum*, "with a pretence of legal process, and in Mr. Roncarelli's case without even a pretence, a small religious sect is being persecuted and indeed martyred in many parts of Quebec." Premier Duplessis's action had demonstrated a contempt for a concept dear to Scott's heart – "the rule of law." Roncarelli's liquor licence had been removed not because he had conducted his restaurant improperly while using it but because his religious beliefs collided with Quebec Catholicism.

In later years Scott was to say that he had taken the case partly because he was relatively secure at McGill. The university was financially independent and therefore not subject to the Premier's vengeance.[33] But personal reasons may have loomed large at the time. A new dean was soon to be appointed in the law faculty and Scott knew he would not get either the promotion or a deserved raise. On February 14, 1947, he had written to Principal James explaining that it would be necessary to take on the Roncarelli case for financial reasons. In addition to the justice of Roncarelli's cause, there may have been some sense of hitting back at an unjust establishment. Duplessis was hand-in-glove with church and business in Quebec; indeed, one of his strongest allies in the Anglophone establishment was Scott's nemesis, J.W. McConnell, owner of *The Montreal Star*.

To downplay the emotional and racial aspects of the case and to emphasize its legal importance, Scott and Stein brought in a prominent member of the Montreal legal establishment, Lionel Forsyth, KC, from one of the largest legal firms in Montreal, popularly known as "The Factory." Forsyth assisted Scott and Stein in their first attempt to sue the now former chairman of the Quebec Liquor Commission, Edouard Archambault. Under the Liquor Law of Quebec, Archambault could be sued only with the permission of the Quebec Chief Justice, a position now occupied by Archambault himself.[34] The three lawyers prepared a petition, filed on January 31, 1947, that set out the grounds of complaint and requested the authority to sue. On February 5 Judge Archambault dismissed the petition against himself. The trio understood from this judgement that if they had made their case more clearly, they might be given permission to sue.[35] Accordingly, they made a second submission to Judge Archambault on April 16. It was rejected two weeks later.

Meanwhile, they had concluded that not only the manager but also the Liquor Commission as a legal body could be sued. They wrote to Attorney-General Duplessis requesting permission to sue. The man who had committed the fault, if there was one, was also in a position to judge his own case. Duplessis did not reply. After some time had elapsed, the newspapers reported that the Premier had no intention of allowing the petition. Scott and Stein were now blocked. There seemed no remedy available since the two avenues for appeal provided in the Quebec Liquor Act had been denied to Roncarelli. Was there any other way?

As they discussed the matter, there emerged the concept of a personal action against Duplessis, based on the ancient English Common Law right of every citizen to sue any government official, no matter how highly placed, if he had done him a personal wrong for which there was no justification. Scott's studies at Oxford were standing him in good stead. A well-known statement of Dicey's was in his mind that "with us every person from the Prime Minister down, is liable to answer for his wrongs in the ordinary Courts of Law." This principle applied to Premier Duplessis, providing he had done wrong in ordering the cancellation of the licence. To be sure, in Quebec the measurement of the wrong depended on the Civil Law, but this did not impede the application of English constitutional law principles. It seemed there was a legal case.

Scott and Stein faced the primary issue. Either they sued Duplessis personally or Roncarelli would be quietly defeated. This raised a further legal problem. Under Quebec law no public officer can be sued unless action is taken within six months after the event and unless notice of one month is given. They had lost precious time making fruitless petitions. And Duplessis had delayed. It was now too late to institute action against the Premier with a month's notice. Also, there were the psychological difficulties of instituting a personal action for damages "on behalf of a member of a most unpopular sect, against a Prime Minister, who from all appearances had the complete support of the vast majority of the population of Quebec and had done nothing wrong in defending them against subversive elements."

Scott never forgot the day when he and Stein sat in the latter's office and looked at each other considering a decision. It was not too difficult for Scott to say that he was prepared to go ahead with the attempted vindication of Roncarelli in its new form, but the decision for Stein was much harder. "He did have clients who did not want him to be a persona non grata with the government." If he took the case against Duplessis he ran the same danger as that of his client, who less than three months after Duplessis's action had been forced to close his restaurant for lack of business. Nevertheless, after the two men had considered the whole situation Stein said, "I am prepared to go along if you will come with me." The two men then made preparations for the final phase of the legal proceedings.

As Forsyth was unable to continue with the case, they attempted to find another counsel of top rank, preferably French-speaking. The two men approached a number of distinguished representatives of the bar. All refused: some sympathetically, some abruptly. None, it seemed, felt free to undertake so risky an operation as suing Duplessis.

Earlier in the forties Scott had begun to write a satiric poem, "To Certain Friends," which he now filed with the papers dealing with the Roncarelli case:

> I see my friends now standing about me, bemused,
> Eyeing me dubiously as I pursue my course,
> Clutching their little less that is worlds away.

> Full of good will, they greet me with offers of help,
> Now and then with the five-dollar bill of evasion,
> Sincere in their insincerity; believing in their unbelief.

Such individuals, he concludes, fear above all "... the positive formation of opinion, / The essential choice that acts as a mental compass, / The clear perception of the road to the receding horizon...."

> Till one day, after the world has tired of waiting,
> While they are busy arguing about the obvious,
> A half-witted demagogue will walk away with
>     their children.    (*C.P.*, p. 77)

A sense of just cause, as well as a degree of self-righteousness, informs Scott's satire, for he is exploring motives – his own as well as those of others. The search for a legal colleague had been greatly discouraging, for Scott did not like the sense of being cut off from his friends in the Quebec bar. And his feelings were mixed about carrying the burden alone.

Meanwhile, the two men prepared the plaintiff's declaration. The action was instituted in June, 1947, but the case was not scheduled for hearing until May, 1950. Mr. Justice McKinnon was the presiding judge. On May 10, the day of the trial, Scott went down to the Ritz-Carlton Hotel at eight a.m. to spruce up for his appearance in court. There, in the barber shop chair nearest to him, was Premier Duplessis – also having his hair trimmed. Scott sat waiting for him to leave the chair, which he himself then occupied. As he sat down he felt that the seat was still "Duplessis-warm." Scott's quick mind flashed to intimations of a "hot seat." He said to the barber, "Est-ce que c'est le Premier Ministre?" The barber replied, "Oui, il est dans les Cours cette semaine."

When Scott reached the courthouse, he discovered Duplessis had taken the extraordinary step of barring the trial to the public. The courthouse was filled with provincial police, "with pistols in their belts, marching up and down as though some sort of siege were taking place." Further, Scott was informed that Duplessis had ordered someone to check on Scott's standing at the bar; he hoped perhaps Scott might have forgotten to pay his fees. A few visitors were admitted, including Marian, who sketched the room, but the general public was prevented by the police from entering.

The small attic room, overflowing with some thirty people, was dominated by a huge crucifix. In 1947, crucifixes were installed in all Quebec courtrooms by Premier Duplessis, a symbolic reminder, perhaps, that the customary division between church and state did not apply. As Scott looked around he recognized Dr. Damien Jasmin, the priest who had written *Les Témoins de Jehovah* in which he had sought to prove that the evil religious ideas and practices of the Witnesses were seditious and comparable to the Albigensian heresy of the thirteenth century. Scott knew about the Albigenses and how they had been ruthlessly slaughtered and burned by John of Gaunt. He still remembered two long introductory chapters in Foxe's *Book of Martyrs* on their martyrdom. As he looked at this man he wondered whether he would be a witness against the defendant. Scott's vivid imagination "could almost smell human flesh burning."

It was the power of the medieval church over the human body – a power to burn, rack, or crucify – that Scott feared and dreaded. It was an image of totalitarian control now symbolized by Jasmin's presence and by the agonized figure of Christ on the wall. For Scott, as for the presiding judge at an earlier trial, the persecution of the Witnesses was a lesser form of the medieval inquisition. Such images were fresh in Scott's mind. He had recently helped Glen How, counsel for another Jehovah's Witness case, the Boucher case, to refute Jasmin's charges of heresy by providing the background of the Albigenses and the details of John Wycliffe's trial. Wycliffe, condemned in his time for heresy by the pope and the clergy, was vindicated by posterity. There was a clear historic parallel with the actions of the Jehovah's Witnesses.

Scott felt an initial strangeness as he entered the courtroom. He had never worn a bib and gown and owned neither. He had borrowed a gown from Charles Lussier and bought a waistcoat and bib. He later remarked that he was "almost more worried about getting my robes in order than I was about the legal argument which I knew I was going to present." The argument continued for three days, and it seemed to him that "in the first day I delivered the entire course I give to the First Year students, on the second day I gave the second course and on the third day I gave the Third Year Administrative Law course, which was then being presented at the Law Faculty."[36] Arguing from Dicey that even a premier was accountable for his actions if he acts outside the limitations of his office, Scott pointed out that the Quebec Liquor Commission had been constituted as an independent body and Duplessis, in commanding Archambault – if he indeed had commanded him – had committed a "fault" and was therefore responsible for subsequent damages to his victim, Roncarelli.

On the first day of the trial, Roncarelli took the stand, stating that he was an adherent of the Jehovah's Witnesses. He had given bails that had been approved by the court, but he denied he was a ringleader of a group or a distributor of literature. M. Emery Beaulieu, Duplessis's counsel and Dean of Law at the University of Montreal, asked Roncarelli if there was any truth in a document prepared by a Quebec liquor inspector, identified only as "Y-3." It was alleged that during the ration years Roncarelli had Jehovah's Witnesses buy liquor for him and that his restaurant was frequented by "fast women." Roncarelli replied with dignity, " 'There were no fast women and no slow women frequenting my restaurant.... They were ladies'."[37]

When the Premier took the stand he was in good form, answering questions at length and undertaking a little electioneering on the side – so much so, the presiding judge, Mr. Justice McKinnon, on several occasions told him to be brief. Duplessis contended that the Jehovah's Witnesses were an obnoxious sect and that it was his duty as Prime Minister to cancel Roncarelli's licence on behalf of the Quebecers who had given him such an excellent mandate in the recent election. " 'In my opinion a man like Roncarelli was not worthy of holding a privilege from the province'."[38]

Stein was careful and tenacious in his cross-examination. He repeatedly asked the Premier whether he had been correctly quoted by newspapers when he stated in Quebec City he personally, as Attorney-General, gave the order cancelling Roncarelli's liquor licence. Duplessis wiggled on the stand. He attempted to argue that he approved the cancellation after receiving telephone calls from the general manager of the Quebec Liquor Commission indicating his intent to do so. But finally, in response to Stein's insistent cross-examination, he flashed, "When a superior officer gives an order, an inferior officer obeys." It was hubris, Scott later thought, "pure hubris" that led to his downfall.[39]

At that moment Scott felt the case had been won. Stein had forced Duplessis to admit that he was indeed the *causa causans* of the action, the person who is responsible. And it was so taken later as a fact by the trial judge. Stein also made another important point when he demonstrated that Duplessis had made no effort to allow Roncarelli to come before him and explain his position. " 'That's ridiculous,' Duplessis replied. 'The premier of the Province of Quebec, with a population ...' "[40] Scott also argued that Roncarelli's permit had been cancelled "for now and for good" – thus illustrating a degree of personal vengeance in his action.

The judgement of the Quebec Superior Court was given in 1951. Roncarelli had sought damages of $118,741 for loss of his business and possible profits. Mr. Justice McKinnon agreed with Roncarelli's claim that the liquor permit for his licence was cancelled without just cause through the intervention of Duplessis. However, he awarded damages of only $8,123.53 on the ground that he could not allow for profits lost because of the loss of a liquor licence because " 'no licence holder has any inherent right to such a licence'."[41]

Roncarelli was now approaching bankruptcy. His restaurant had failed and his bank had cut off credit. He instructed his lawyers to appeal for a higher settlement. Duplessis, in turn, launched a cross-appeal. Both sides began to prepare their briefs for the Court of Queen's Bench, the Quebec Court of Appeal. Due to a backlog of cases the Roncarelli case was not heard until June 2, 1956. Although both sides presented their original arguments, the Appeal Court reached quite different conclusions, accepting Duplessis's appeal and holding that the Premier was not liable for damages. The Chief Justice held that there had been no order given by Duplessis, an interpretation put forward by all but one of the judges. In so doing the Court of Appeal set aside what had been accepted as "fact" by Judge McKinnon of the Superior Court: that is, that Duplessis had ordered the head of the Quebec Liquor Commission to cancel Roncarelli's licence.[42]

What now? Stein, Scott, and Roncarelli were beginning to feel like Don Quixotes tilting at windmills. Roncarelli was now a poor man. Since Duplessis had "shot off his mouth," as Roncarelli told reporters, no one would employ him. He was now attempting to find some construction work to feed himself and his family.[43] And since the two lawyers had lost their case in the Court of Appeal, the Jehovah's Witnesses' Watch Tower Association had decided to withdraw its financial support. Should the Witnesses association wish to appeal it would retain other lawyers. Roncarelli, however, would have none of this. Stein and Scott had stood by him in the past and he was not going to leave them now. The next step in the process, however, would be an expensive appeal to the Supreme Court. Roncarelli said he could find $500; Scott had no money; Stein agreed to bear the costs and keep them to a minimum.

When the case came before the Supreme Court of Canada in May, 1958, the issue was now a question of the interpretation of the law based on the earlier rulings. With some trepidation, Scott and Stein came before the nine justices of the Supreme Court. Stein submitted there was no proof that Roncarelli had violated the province's liquor laws during the time he ran the family restaurant, that the defendant had failed to prove Roncarelli was a leader of the Jehovah's Witnesses, that it had not been proved that any of the pamphlets distributed were of a seditious nature, that Roncarelli had not given bail for gain, and, moreover, he had ceased to give bail before publication of *Quebec's Burning Hate*.[44]

As Scott came forward to begin the case, Chief Justice Kerwin said, "Get closer, Mr. Scott." The hierarchy of the Supreme Court reserves the place closest to the judges for Queen's Counsel; ordinary lawyers sit behind the brass bar in the front row, below the salt. Scott, a man who might have expected to have been made a QC by his province, had not been recognized by the Union nationale under Duplessis. The Chief Justice, in inviting him forward, was, in effect, conferring this honour. In Scott's words – "He QC-fied me."[45] The Montreal law professor was fluent in his discussion of the issues of constitutional law raised by the case; essentially, he argued that any act by a public officer for which there was no specific provision in law was *ultra vires*.

For Scott, the most significant moment in the hearing came when Emery Beaulieu, counsel for Duplessis, was asked by one of the justices of the

Supreme Court, "Tell me, what was the real reason why this licence was cancelled?", and he answered with perfect frankness,

> It was to cut Roncarelli's credit, meaning to reduce his financial position so he couldn't give any more bail! When I heard that admission from Duplessis's counsel I said to myself, we've won the case. No court in a democratic country can contemplate a public official deliberately destroying a man's credit so he can't give bail. Giving bail is a human right. A tremendous human right. Each bail bond must be approved by the court; it was approved by the court every single time that Roncarelli gave bail. Then where was Roncarelli at fault?

This, as Scott concluded, "really was just too much."[46] Certainly the popular press thought so. The next morning a headline in *The Globe and Mail* quoted Beaulieu's admission.

One afternoon, as Scott went out after the day's adjournment, he saw Frank Roncarelli sitting in the back of the courtroom reading from the Old Testament in Greek. "Don't worry, Frank," he said. "We've got Jehovah on our side." "I hope we have the Supreme Court, too," Scott replied.[47] In fact they did, although the judgement was not pronounced until a year later, on January 27, 1959. Scott and Stein were not in Ottawa for the decision, but they did have a representative at hand to hear it. Stein phoned Scott at the McGill law faculty. "We've won, Frank," he said, "by a decision of 6 to 3."[48]

Within a few minutes of Stein's phone call to Scott, the news was all over the law faculty. There were no further lectures that day. A general assembly of students was called with Professor Max Cohen presiding. Scott sat at the front and a few points of the case were discussed. Students brought two bottles of Mumm's champagne. This gave Scott a chance to answer, whenever asked a question to which he ought not to reply – as the case was still before the courts in the sense that Duplessis had the option of appeal to the Judicial Committee of the Privy Council – "Mum's the word." General rejoicing that day was followed by a party that night at Clarke Avenue with a gathering of personal friends, including Thérèse Casgrain, Pierre Trudeau, Eric Kierans, and others.[49]

One day later Scott's students delivered their verdict in *The McGill Daily*. The name of McGill, the editor remarked, was associated with the names of its leading faculty members: Osler, Rutherford, and Penfield. There was now one other member of the faculty who deserved to be ranked with the greats in McGill's history – Professor F.R. Scott of the Faculty of

Law. Scott's activities in the Roncarelli case would be remembered as among the most significant in Canadian history. Yet it was not because of such headlines that McGill students owed him their respect, but rather as a teacher and adviser to law students at McGill since 1928 and as a poet and an editor of literary magazines. The editorial concluded with a citation by which Scott had been awarded an honorary Doctor of Laws at Dalhousie University, where he had delivered the convocation address at a celebration marking the seventieth anniversary of the law faculty there. The man once seen by Montrealers as analogous to the hapless young man of Leacock's satire – a Don Quixote who had jumped on his horse to ride madly in all directions – was now seen by his colleagues in quite another light:

> At this university we think of him particularly as a distinguished teacher and writer on Canadian constitutional law, a man instrumental in the founding of the Association of Canadian Law Teachers, the Chairman of the Canadian Bar Association's Committees on Legal Research and the recent champion before the courts of human rights. Like the knight of another age, truly he is *sans peur et sans reproche*. In him is exemplified that best product of the professional, the scholarly humanist who is also a man of action.[50]

At the McGill students annual law dance this metaphor was emblazoned across a large red banner depicting a champion on a white horse: "KNIGHT F.R. SCOTT VANQUISHES NIGHT DUPLESSIS."

The Supreme Court of Canada had awarded Roncarelli $33,123.53 in personal damages plus interest dating from the Superior Court ruling in May, 1951, plus costs, estimated at between $20,000 and $30,000. The majority opinion, written by Mr. Justice Rand, stated that Duplessis had exceeded his authority: "In public regulation of this sort [the Liquor Law] there is no such thing as absolute and untrammelled 'discretion,' that is, that action can be taken on any ground or for any reason that can be suggested to the mind of the administrator."[51] Two of the dissenting judges, Taschereau and Fauteux, disagreed on the technicality that one month's notice before instituting the suit had not been given. Mr. Justice Cartwright, who also dissented, took the view that the cancellation of Roncarelli's liquor licence by the Quebec Liquor Commission, even if invalid, would not give rise to liability in damages.

Many newspapers in Canada commented on the judgement. *The Montreal Star*, which printed the entire text of the decision, emphasized, in an editorial on January 28, 1959, its "profound importance in relation to public order and the rule of law." Although all the justices had noted Duplessis believed himself acting "in the best interests of the people of his province," their decision said "good intention is not enough if it conflicts with the rule of law." The *Star* concluded: "Thus the judgement becomes one of relating to the liberty of the subject and his right of recourse when he is damaged. It puts a curb on the exercise of arbitrary authority and establishes the supremacy of the rule of law in this country." Readers of the *Lethbridge Herald* (February 4, 1959) were reminded that although the court upheld the principle of civil liberties, the fact that two judges dissented on the basis of a technicality "indicates how uncertain a bastion existing law is and how great is the need for that constant vigilance which is the price of freedom."

A number of editorials saw the decision within the context of other civil rights decisions made in Canada during the fifties. Robert Duffy, in *The Globe Magazine* (February 21, 1959), argued that the Witnesses in a "backhanded" way had provided a service to Quebec by strengthening the fundamental liberties and rights with regard to unorthodox minorities. The Roncarelli case, and other cases in which the Witnesses had been successful in the lower courts in Quebec, had established a body of law that enhanced civil liberties in the province. As a result there was now a more tolerant social climate in Quebec, which was "just as much necessary to Quebec's evolution as is its industrial economy."

Among Duplessis supporters the decision was not necessarily seen as a defeat. The *Red River Valley Echo* in Manitoba quoted the Union nationale paper, *Montreal Matin*, which praised Duplessis for "the courage he showed before the insults of the Witnesses of Jehovah." The *Echo* also noted that even anti-Duplessis forces had tempered their praise of the decision by continuing to denounce the "evil menace" of the Jehovah's Witnesses.[52]

What Scott had introduced to Canadian constitutional law in the fifties was a concept based less on technicalities than on the history of British government and parliamentary democracy. From his Oxford background, Scott had acquired the larger social and historical perspectives espoused by English scholars, and because of this he taught constitutional law from a different perspective than others. Most constitutional law courses in Canadian universities dealt primarily with Sections 91 and 92 of the BNA Act, the division of federal and provincial responsibilities. Scott was the only constitutional law teacher to teach it in two separate courses over two years. He started his first-year course with the theory of the British constitution – the narrow escape from an absolute monarchy and the evolution of the English practice in Parliament and responsible government. This background allowed him to advance his arguments to the Supreme Court of Canada as to the real effect and nature of a piece of legislation like the Padlock Act. Similarly, because of his background in both English Common Law and the Quebec Civil Code, he was able to show that neither system of law permits even the highest public official to exceed the authority of his office. Finally, he brought to his teaching and practice of law a large humanistic concern, moral in nature, which may derive, in part, from the whole Anglican tradition of a government being a government where people have responsibilities as much as rights, where there are duties that must be performed. In this last respect he was very much his father's son.

# NINETEEN

# Letters from the Mackenzie River

If an idea is to be found great enough to evoke a common loyalty amongst all races in Canada and to overcome their differences sufficiently to make stable political union possible, it can only be found in the idea of Canada, the nation. The building of an orderly and just society within this vast territory, the elimination of poverty and insecurity through a wise utilization of natural resources, the development of arts and sciences, of political liberty and spiritual freedom – all of this while maintaining a fair balance between the claims of racial and religious minorities – that is a task ... that can hardly be achieved, however, except at the expense of the old imperialist foreign policy.

F.R. SCOTT
"A Policy of Neutrality for Canada," 1939

IN THE SUMMER OF 1956 Scott wrote to Maurice Lamontagne, then economic adviser to the Privy Council in St. Laurent's government, asking him for help arranging passage to the Canadian North.[1] Scott was preparing to go to Michigan State University as a visiting professor and his duties would include lecturing about Canada and Canadian-American relations. As he had never visited the North, he felt it necessary to get some first-hand experience. Lamontagne put Scott in touch with officials of Eldorado Mining and Refining Limited, who agreed to transport him down the Mackenzie to Norman Wells during the last trip of the season before freeze-up, about mid-August.[2] Scott was delighted with these arrangements and expressed his pleasure to several friends. Shortly thereafter he received a phone call from one of them, a Montreal lawyer associated with the CCF. "Frank," he said, "would you mind if I came too?" Scott was not pleased. He did not like other people "horning in" on his plans, even a younger colleague as bright and congenial as Pierre Trudeau.[3]

Scott had known Trudeau since the early forties. In 1943 Trudeau, then an embryo socialist, and Charles Lussier had heard Scott speak on the Canadian constitution to a group of students, many of whom opposed Quebec's participation in the war, at the University of Montreal.[4] After 1946 when Lussier began his special tutorials on constitutional law with Scott, the older man began to encounter the two of them at CCF meetings and more informal gatherings. Trudeau recalled that in 1942-43 he was reading Scott's "little mag" *Preview*, the LSR book *Social Planning for Canada* (where he would have encountered the Regina Manifesto), and the CCF submission to the Rowell-Sirois Commission, "Canada – One or Nine."[5] Trudeau was also aware of Scott's 1942 essay "Why Quebec Voted No," which had been translated into French and widely circulated throughout the province. Scott's belief in neutrality and his concept of one Canada, a "just society," had been articulated in "A Policy of Neutrality for Canada," published in *Foreign Affairs* in 1939. By the time Scott spoke to the University of Montreal students he was asserting the necessity of patriating the BNA Act. He did not advocate a complete remaking of the constitution; he believed that with certain modifications it could be made to work for the benefit of French and English Canada equally.

By the mid-forties Trudeau was attending CCF meetings and by September, 1950, when he had participated in the Dominion-Provincial Constitutional Conference in Quebec as a secretary to Gordon Robertson, who was preparing a fifty-page memo on federal-provincial relationships, Trudeau had absorbed many of Scott's views on Canada and the constitution as an adjunct to a socialist philosophy. Trudeau had also acquired a healthy respect for Frank Scott as contrasted to Duplessis. Recollecting the Quebec conference, he remembered the striking difference between "the thinking man [Scott] and these politicians."[6]

For Trudeau and others it was the violent strike at Asbestos that had provided the glass through which they could focus on Quebec society. This strike, generally recognized as a turning point in the social history of Quebec, consolidated the labour movement and brought together those activists opposed to Duplessis. Included in this group were Jean Marchand of the Canadian Catholic Confederation of Labour, Gérard Pelletier, a reporter for *Le Devoir*, and a bearded Trudeau, just back from travels in the Middle East, dubbed "St. Joseph" by the strikers because of his beard and his oratory.[7] The fiery young activist dismayed the more sober Marchand when he spoke to an excitable group about throwing medicine to a sick cow: the strikers were not slow to take the hint; that evening they hurled bricks through the windows of company buildings.[8]

In 1950 the radical quarterly *Cité libre* had been founded to provide a forum for the expression of contemporary thought and writing. Trudeau indicated the magazine's direction in the first issue: like *Esprit*, the French Catholic magazine, it would speak for a socialist, Christian, and French society within the North American context. The political legacy of the past must be scrutinized, not to repudiate Confederation, but to understand and rectify the failure of French Canada (by which he meant Quebec) to use the powers provided to it by the BNA Act.[9] Trudeau, who had begun within a nationalist stream – he had been caught up by that chanting group of students who in the mid-thirties had demonstrated against the Spanish Loyalists – was, by the mid-fifties, strongly opposed to those clerical and nationalist groups he believed had kept Quebec a feudal state.[10] By the early sixties he was to become vehemently anti-separatist. In an article in *Cité libre* in March, 1961, he attacks separatism, explaining the aim of the magazine had been "to unshackle the superstructures, desanctify civil society, democratize politics, break into economic life, relearn French, get unessentials out of the university, open the borders to culture and minds to progress."[11] It was in the struggle for a more democratic society in Quebec, in particular in the fight against Duplessis, that Scott and Trudeau found common ground.

Scott's jousts against Duplessis in the fifties were followed closely by Trudeau and his group. Jacques Hébert recalled the extent to which Scott's courage was respected by Francophone intellectuals. "For them Frank Scott was certainly one of the great men of the time ... because he was a great mind, ... [because] he was a passionate man for justice, for human rights. He was sensitive even before it was fashionable about the Third World." Scott, as an English Canadian, was "a pure WASP, naturally, but at the same time he was really a Quebecer and you could feel that. He was from Quebec, he had his roots here ... and he was always with us – us, the intellectuals – whenever there was something important to do related to human life, democracy and all that. He was always there so he was one of us."

What had impressed the *Cité libre* group was that this "man of quality who was older" than most of them would go out of his way to be present at significant meetings. "I remember there was this huge gathering each fall of L'Institut canadien des affairs publiques ... Frank was always there, naturally. So because of that we felt that he was really one of us and that he understood the French Canadian. He went out of his way to do so.

He was one of the few Anglophones of that period, especially a Quebec Anglophone, that spoke French."[12] At the first meeting of L'Institut in 1954 on "Le Peuple Souverain" Scott and Eugene Forsey were asked to speak, as were Thérèse Casgrain, Jean Marchand, Gérard Pelletier, André Laurendeau, and Pierre Trudeau.[13] Throughout the fifties and early sixties Scott continued to attend L'Institut.

In 1956, when Trudeau telephoned Scott about the Mackenzie trip, he, Scott, and Laval sociologist Jean-Charles Falardeau had just finished several years of collaboration on *La Grève de l'amiante* (1956), a penetrating study of the events leading up to and following the strike at Asbestos. In many ways the book was an attempt to analyse Quebec society through the prism of 1949. Scott was the catalyst who brought the book into being. He had initiated a new study group, Recherches sociales, to focus on social problems that affected French and English in Canada. The group, founded in 1951, received an initial grant of $2,500 from the estate of Scott's late friend Alan Plaunt. His widow, Bobbie Dyde, who had remarried and moved west, promised that $2,000 would follow annually.[14] In establishing this fund, Bobbie Dyde was paying tribute to Plaunt's dream of a united Canada: just before his death Plaunt had talked to Scott about providing funds for the "promotion of social studies relating to French-English relation[s] and to the impact of contemporary social ideas upon them."[15] Scott became secretary-treasurer, recruited Jacques Perrault as chairman, and invited Falardeau, Eugene Forsey, and, later, McGill sociologist Aileen Ross to join the executive of Recherches sociales.[16]

Several projects were planned by the group but the primary emphasis was placed on a series of studies examining the significance of the confrontation at Asbestos. Gérard Pelletier, who had reported on the strike for *Le Devoir*, provided an outline for the book and undertook the preliminary organization; his work was supplemented by Jean Gérin-Lajoie, union representative for the United Steelworkers of America.

In April, 1954, Bobbie Dyde wrote to Scott: "On the whole I feel that the experiment [Recherches sociales] has not been a success in spite of all your efforts."[17] She appeared discouraged with the slowness of the Asbestos project (most of the people working on the book had full-time jobs) and by the lack of tangible evidence of improved English-French relations. Scott asked Trudeau, who as a radical could not find employment in Quebec universities in the fifties, to edit the book. Trudeau agreed. On May 21, 1954, Scott received a note from Falardeau saying, "Pierre Trudeau is ... beginning to edit the available chapters. Indeed, he tells me he cut short his stay in Bali by one week in order to return to Asbestos. Greater love hath no man."[18] Shortly after, armed with the manuscript, a number of reference texts, and a bristling array of statistics, Trudeau left Montreal for Paris. There, in voluntary exile, he proceeded to write the introduction between July and December of 1955.

In late September he wrote Scott from Paris explaining he wanted to "crash" the forthcoming socialist conference at Margate [England] where he hoped to meet members of the Labour Party. Would Scott write him a letter of introduction to "any big-wig in the Labour Party?" Scott wrote to Philip Noel-Baker, a Labour MP who had been Secretary of State for Commonwealth Relations in the Attlee government.[19] Two months later Trudeau reported he had not had to trouble Noel-Baker personally as just waving Scott's letter was enough. He added, "Margate was full of lessons for me. But the party seems to be in a very bad shape. The Left in every country (including Canada) seems to be going through an 'agonizing reappraisal.' Something for us to discuss, when we get this book out of the way."[20] The Margate Conference may well have disillusioned Trudeau about the efficacy of socialism in an international context.

The book, in the meantime, required a great deal of work. A series of letters sped in a triangle from Paris to Montreal and Quebec City and back again. Scott soon found himself in the role of mediator, or "gentleman" as Trudeau quipped.[21] Forsey, who was verifying data in the manuscript, objected to Trudeau's statistics, which he considered out of date. Falardeau objected to the polemics of Trudeau's chapter; in his view, this was not the objective scientific appraisal of the Quebec situation that the committee had planned.[22] And Trudeau objected to the tardiness of publication plans. After the manuscript had been turned down by two French publishing houses, Le Seuil and Editions ouvrières, Trudeau wrote: "In view of the improbability of any French Editor of great repute taking our book, there is really no great point of having it printed in France, if we can help some struggling young Canadian publisher instead."[23] Near the end of the year he returned to Montreal to arrange personally publication of the book with Editions Cité libre. The book went to the publishers in March and came out in May. It was to help mould a climate of opinion that led directly to the Quiet Revolution.

SHORTLY AFTER PUBLICATION OF *La Grève de l'amiante* Trudeau telephoned Scott about the Mackenzie River trip. Although Scott was at first unsure he wanted to share his expedition (as he remarked later, "There is something in me that likes to keep my copyright"),[24] the trip was a success.

Trudeau was an agreeable travelling companion. And Scott's spirits always lifted when he got out into the wilderness.

The journey began in Edmonton about August 9 when a government plane flew the two men to Fort Smith. Lifted into what Scott in his poem "Flying to Fort Smith" called "long lanes of space," they peered "through panes of glass":

> The plain of lakes below
>     Is bound with bands of green
> Fringed by darker green
>     Pocked with drops of ponds.
>
> Everywhere
>     A huge nowhere,
> Underlined by a shy railway.   (*C.P.*, p. 223)

Following the "snaking brown streams" with the eye, they began to enjoy themselves; this was a world both knew well. To be sure, this trip was not quite what Scott had experienced paddling up the Murray River with his brothers – portaging, camping out, living on fish and salt pork. Nor was it the outdoor life that Trudeau had described in a 1944 essay, "Exhaustion and Fulfilment: The Ascetic in the Canoe," where he speaks of the paddler entrusting himself to nature "stripped of [all] worldly goods" but "canoe and paddle, blanket and knife, salt pork and flour, fishing rod and rifle." Yet, in the largest sense, this journey down the Mackenzie River was the journey into nature – and into human nature – that Trudeau had advocated in his essay, that larger psychological journey in which physical adventure leads to new insights into self and others.

> It involves a starting rather than a parting. Although it assumes the breaking of ties, its purpose is not to destroy the past, but to lay a foundation for the future....
>
> What is essential at the beginning is the resolve to reach the saturation point. Ideally, the trip should end only when the members are making no further progress within themselves. They should not be fooled, though, by a period of boredom, weariness or disgust; that is not the end, but the last obstacle before it. Let saturation be serene![25]

At Fort Smith, as Scott had been warned, they were obliged to put in time waiting nearby at the company camp at Bell Rock for the tug from the Northern Transportation Company, which was to carry them down the river. During six days of enforced idleness they explored the surrounding countryside, climbing down to the Slave River "To the rock polished by ice / And the roar of the great rapids" (*C.P.*, p. 227). They now stood on the edge of the Great Canadian Shield: to the east lay Precambrian rock all the way to Labrador; to the north, south, and west the great central plain stretched from the Arctic Ocean to the Gulf of Mexico. Scott was now deep in that northern space his father had spoken of when he said, "There's nothing between you and the North Pole, Frank."[26]

As Scott and Trudeau looked out at the tremendous surge of water that poured down, draining the whole of the Peace River and Lake Athabasca, seventeen miles of rapids with great waves surging toward the shore, Trudeau announced, "I'm going in." "Here, don't be silly," Scott replied. "You can't go into that." "Oh, I'm going in," he said.[27] Scott had his camera at hand, and just as Trudeau began to walk out, he snapped a photograph.

> Pierre, suddenly challenged,
> Stripped and walked into the rapids,
> Firming his feet against rock,
> Standing white, in white water,
> Leaning south up the current
> To stem the downward rush,
> A man testing his strength
> Against the strength of his country.   (*C.P.*, p. 227)

Scott was fascinated by the way Trudeau entered the foaming water, getting one foothold firm, searching for another and leaning upstream as the waves kept threatening to topple him.[28]

Scott also recognized a familiar attitude in Trudeau's response to the land. The reference to "strength" in this poem, "Fort Smith," echoes A.J.M. Smith's "The Lonely Land," his twenties portrait of the Canadian landscape that spoke of "... the beauty / of strength / broken by strength / and still strong." Behind Scott's poem lies the romantic nationalism of the twenties, especially the conception of a strong, rugged, and lonely North in which a man must be equally strong to prove his own worth.[29] It is this brand of Canadian nationalism, an "idea of Canada" grounded in the land itself, that the two men shared. Trudeau, for example, concludes "Exhaustion and Fulfilment" by asserting that a sense of nationality and of historical continuity is derived from the land: "I know a man whose school could never teach him patriotism, but who acquired that virtue when he felt in his bones the vastness of his land, and the greatness of those who founded it."[30]

When the tugboat from the Northern Transportation Company finally arrived at Fort Smith, Scott and Trudeau were given a cabin with two bunks for their journey downstream. It took about seven and a half days to go down the river. Mile after mile they travelled, the river sometimes widening a little as streams came in from the side.

> This river belongs
>   wholly to itself
>     obeying its own laws
>
> Its wide brown eye
>   softens what it reflects
>     from sky and shore
>
> The top water      calm
>   moves purposefully
>     to a cold sea
>
> Underneath      its stone bed
>   shows sunken rock
>     in swirl and surface wave ...   (*C.P.*, p. 238)

There was little to see on the low banks, but occasionally mountains could be viewed in the distance. After the initial excitement of the land and the North it began to be a somewhat dull trip: mile after mile of sameness.

It was now late August. The days were beginning to get cool; by mid-September all navigation would cease. Scott, who enjoyed warmth, closeted in the cabin and busied himself by keeping a record of the trip. He began to jot lines for what would become a poetic sequence describing the journey, "Letters from the Mackenzie River." Trudeau also began to write. He found a sun-warmed niche on the deck, stripped to the waist, wrapped a towel around his head, and leaning back on the deck and surrounded by a pile of books, he began to draft an article for a symposium on biculturalism organized by Mason Wade for the following month.[31] The article, "Some Obstacles to Democracy in Quebec," was ultimately published in *The Canadian Journal of Economics and Political Science* in August, 1958, and later republished in *Canadian Dualism: Studies of French-English Relations* (1960), a series of articles collected by Falardeau and edited by Wade for the Social Science Research Council of Canada, to which Scott also contributed.

In writing of democracy Trudeau was raising one of Scott's favourite subjects. Not only had the latter codified his feelings on democracy in his

"Democratic Manifesto," but the insights gleaned when writing this essay permeated much of his later thought and conversation. Significantly, a week after their return from the Mackenzie River Trudeau produced his own *Manifeste démocratique* calling for a union of all opposition parties to make a common front, Le Rassemblement, against the powerful Union nationale. It was precisely the lack of democracy in Quebec that had spurred Scott's first efforts for reform in 1931 and informed his battles against Duplessis in the late forties and most of the fifties in the Padlock and Roncarelli cases.

Trudeau had wanted to accompany Scott on his trip down the Mackenzie River, not just because of the adventure but because, as he said, "[Frank] was a great hero of mine.... I never studied under him.... But he was the man who was taking sides in a courageous way in important causes ... whether it be Jehovah's Witnesses, [or] in his writings." In the early forties at the University of Montreal little constitutional law was taught. "It's been [from] my contacts with Frank in his person and his actions that I absorbed much of my constitutional thinking." Scott taught the younger man informally, by association, "almost as much by his poems, by his being and by his actions as by his writings.... in an intellectual argument he always did me the honour of a fair hearing. So going on the Mackenzie with him wasn't just another adventure, of which I had many and which I like ... it was a chance also to be exposed to Frank Scott for days and weeks."[32] Trudeau may have wanted to try out some of his ideas on democracy with the undoubted expert and, perhaps, do a little proselytizing of his own. He approached the subject of democracy from a perspective diametrically opposed to that of the older man, putting to Scott the thesis that "Historically, French Canadians have not really believed in democracy for themselves; and English Canadians have not really wanted it for others."

What Trudeau wanted was a critical reappraisal of democracy in Canada. He began, as did Scott in his 1940s jottings on Canadian democracy, with the Constitutional Act of 1791. This act, Trudeau remarked, ushered in representative government at a time when the *canadiens* were not psychologically or politically prepared for it. Accustomed as they were to an autocratic monarch, an authoritarian church, and a quasi-feudal seigneurial system, they valued representative government less for its intrinsic value than as a means to racial and religious survival. French Canadians learned to use what Trudeau calls "the arsenal of democratic 'fire arms'" to their own advantage. There were two possibilities open to them: sabotage of Parliament from within by obstruction or outward acceptance of Parliament without acceptance of its inner principles. Consequently, what Trudeau typified as "an unusual approach" to civil liberties is typical of French Canada: he cited as examples the French-language press's support for Duplessis's authoritarianism in the two cases Scott was then fighting, the Roncarelli case and the Padlock case. But such examples were legion. Were Trudeau to cite all the material proving that Quebecers fundamentally do not believe in democracy he would "exhaust time and encroach upon eternity."

Trudeau was probably aware such comments might alienate both French and English Canadians: even Scott, perhaps, to whom he talked at length about the article he was writing. But he remained unrepentant, noting "that such exercises are necessary if Canadians are to know how to provide the whole of Canada with a common and enduring democratic faith."[33] The reference to "a democratic faith" must have struck a resonant chord in Scott. It was a phrase used by leftist writers and one he had made his own. But the paradox central to Trudeau's thesis was less congenial. Later, reminiscing about the trip and Trudeau's article, Scott remarked, "[Trudeau believed] that democracy was something we were being taught by the English but [he] didn't think the English practised it. So why should [Quebecers] take it?" Furthermore, and Scott found this extraordinary, Trudeau thought the English should have taught it to the French Canadians. But how? For a short time Scott considered refuting Trudeau's article; he was surprised to discover that some political observers considered it an excellent analysis.[34]

Scott's reaction to Trudeau's article is not hard to understand, although years earlier, in 1936, he too had made the same argument, strenuously advocating "liberty" and asserting that Quebec Catholics opposed democracy.

> The democratic state – in the sense of a state which is neutral toward religious beliefs, political theories and economic doctrines, and which merely demands that constitutional methods must be followed in their propagation – is a state which has never been accepted, save as a political necessity, by Catholic dogma, and Cardinal Villeneuve has recently denounced it in no uncertain terms in Quebec. The Church is simply striving to make Quebec's political life conform as far as possible to the Catholic concept, in which truth is Catholicism, error is anything non-Catholic, and liberty is liberty to speak and live that truth.[35]

The problem, perhaps, was that he had never quite taken to heart the implications of this fact. Had he been somewhat naive in his formulations regarding democracy? The full implications of Trudeau's article – if accepted – made it all too clear why socialism had not taken root in Quebec. A socialist society, as Scott understood it, could not function without the foundation of a democratic state. If democracy was repugnant to Quebecers, had he been beating his head against a stone wall during all these years of attempting to establish the CCF in the province? In addition, any nagging recognition that the English, despite professions of democracy, might not have been particularly democratic in their dealings with the conquered French would have been a bitter pill to swallow. Finally, Scott may have recognized he himself was far more of an elitist than a democrat. In his personal relations the principles of interaction that prevailed were often more hierarchical than democratic.

Scott believed passionately in democracy and in egalitarian principles, but co-existence of a democratic philosophy and an aristocratic manner in Scott's person (so reminiscent of his father, who once asserted that he was "an aristocrat by birth but a socialist by conviction") was apparent. And the incongruity of the combination did not fail to attract comment. Once in 1940, at Harvard, when Scott had made a cutting remark about "the tradesman's entrance," a quick-witted Harvard professor had riposted, "If this is one of your Canadian socialists I certainly wouldn't like to meet a conservative."[36]

It was these aspects of Scott's character that Trudeau, whose character also contained elements of the elitist and the democrat, may have found congenial. Moreover, on Trudeau's Scottish side there were affinities with the older man's emotional reserve. But the younger Trudeau, who moved relatively easily within each solitude of English and French society, was then an exception in Quebec. To many Quebecers, Scott's elitism and his typically "WASPish" qualities were an anathema.

The gulf between English and French in Quebec, both before and after the Quiet Revolution, was perhaps, as Jean-Charles Falardeau speculated, the difference between two quite different ways of looking at the world. Falardeau acknowledged Scott worked hard to understand French Quebec: "He would ask me questions, questions, questions.... Of all the English-speaking colleagues whom I have known ... Frank Scott is the one who has gone the farthest in trying to understand." But Scott's family background and his intellectual training had produced a habit of mind that made it very difficult for him. As Falardeau recalled:

He has always, to my knowledge, been extremely courteous of what were the essential ingredients of the French-Canadian culture, not only its language, its history, but I refer to what you might call in general the totality, the attitudes, the political orientation, the traditional ideologies of the French-speaking population, and [there] I must say he was quite lost. He just could not grasp why, for example, a person like Duplessis would have remained Premier of the province of Quebec for fifteen years as he did, because Frank had an irrepressible faith in democracy, human rights. He was a lawyer, and he had been reared, of course, in the British variety of democracy, which is historically the most important brand of democracy. So he had politically a credo or a faith which prevented him from being able to understand the people [who] had different ideologies or views.

In effect, as Falardeau suggested, to some degree Scott was "congenitally unable to go very far into understanding the mentality of his French-speaking compatriots ... [although] he remained all the time curious about it."[37]

As Scott and Trudeau continued their journey down the Mackenzie River, they began to make further discoveries about each other. At one point, looking over the vast number of English place names – Fort Smith, Fort Fitzgerald, Norman Wells, Fort Simpson – Trudeau had said angrily, "I can't see a single indication that there were any French here." "Pierre, of course there were never any French," Scott replied. "There may [have been] the odd person wandering through but this was never part of the occupied part of Canada under the French regime. Never at all."[38] Trudeau had not recognized the chronology of exploration in the North. In fact the Mackenzie Valley had been first explored by Alexander Mackenzie in 1789, and although he may have had some French in his crew, all the place names were inevitably English. And Scott, aware of the historical reason for this fact, failed to recognize the emotional importance of the omission of French to Trudeau, the Quebecer. On this occasion, and again later, when the two addressed a group of students from Sarah Lawrence University and Trudeau began to speak in an impassioned manner about the injustices suffered by Quebecers ("almost like René Lévesque"), Scott finally began to perceive that at the heart of Trudeau's character was a strong Quebec patriotism.[39] It was this Trudeau who had written in the introduction to *The Asbestos Strike* of "a people which had been defeated, occupied, decapitated, pushed out of commerce, driven from the cities, reduced little by little to a minority, and diminished in influence in a country which it had none the less discovered, explored, and colonized."

In a sense, both Scott and Trudeau were sending back "Letters from the Mackenzie River." But where the form of Scott's letters was poetic, the content, although mainly descriptive and narrative, was full of politics:

> Curving in toward shore
> We read on a kind of gallows
> In this utterly public land
> The words PRIVATE PROPERTY.
> Behind is its counterpart:
> TRESPASSERS WILL BE PROSECUTED
> BY ORDER, IMPERIAL OIL.
> Trespassers! In this North!
> Man is the absent fact
> Man is the aim and need
> Man is the source of wealth
> But Property keeps him out.
> And the Indians wonder, who first
> Lived off this very soil
> And now are outcast and dying
> As their substance is drained away.   (*C.P.*, p. 234)

At the Mission School, at Fort Providence, Scott found a grey fort-like school where "Priests from France, nuns from Quebec, / Taught Slavies (who still speak Indian) / Grades I to VIII, in broken English."

> We walked through the crowded classrooms.
> No map of Canada or the Territories,
> No library or workshop,
> Everywhere religious scenes,
> Christ and Saints, Stations of the Cross,
> Beads hanging from nails, crucifixes ...   (*C.P.*, p. 231)

In a series of images Scott finds that upstairs in this Indian residential school "Seventy little cots / Touching end to end / In a room 30' x 40' / Housed the resident boys / In this firetrap mental gaol" (*C.P.*, p. 231). Scott's sense of the needs of the native people and his perceptions of the river itself later led Mr. Justice Thomas Berger to quote from this poem in his report on the northern pipeline: *Northern Frontier, Northern Homeland: The Report of the Mackenzie Valley Pipeline Inquiry* (1977).

For Scott, the Mackenzie itself became the true symbol of Canada:

> A river so Canadian
> it turns its back

on America

The Arctic shore
  receives the vast flow
    a maze of ponds and dikes

In a land so bleak and bare
  a single plume of smoke
    is a scroll of history.   (*C.P.*, p. 239)

This view of Canada, the bare northern land, was to influence strongly Canadian poetry of the fifties and sixties. A year after Scott's journey, Ralph Gustafson followed his footsteps and produced a book of poetry, *Rocky Mountain Poems* (1960). Five years later Al Purdy wrote *North of Summer: Poems From Baffin Island*, which included paintings of the Arctic by A.Y. Jackson. The book was dedicated to Frank Scott.

On the trip down the Mackenzie both Scott and Trudeau saw Canada as a land of rivers, a rugged land of canoe and portage. And both understood that, to remain independent, Canada must maintain a defensive ideology like the river, belonging "wholly to itself, / obeying its own laws." But whereas Scott's nationalism related primarily to the larger English Canada, Trudeau's nationalism was rooted in French Quebec. Scott the poet (as opposed to Scott the Anglophile historian), like Trudeau the patriot, understood perfectly well that French and English had shared in its exploration. This perception is revealed in the phrase "a single plume of smoke / is a scroll of history." In this poem, as in "Laurentian Shield," Scott speaks of his old theme – man writing on his landscape. The "plume of smoke" invokes the first writing, Indian smoke signals. "Plume" also suggests the quill pen and is French for pen and thus is a bilingual pun. Nor should we miss the chivalric overtones of this noun: the "plume" or feathers of identity in the helmet of the adventurous knight.[40] In one noun the poet has captured the multi-racial past of Canadian history. He has also reminded us of the evanescence of this history – like a plume of smoke it is quickly blown away.

Both Scott and Trudeau were attracted to this northern land but each saw it through the "plume" – the historical pen – of his own racial ideology. Each wanted to leave an imprint on this land by leaving his name in the history books. In this context, Scott was a kind of wilderness guide who provided the constitutional expertise, the example of personal courage, and the friendship the younger man needed and which, perhaps, he could not find elsewhere in Quebec. Of equal importance, Scott embodied a strong sense of moral direction. In the Quebec of the forties and fifties only the journalist André Laurendeau had similar moral stature. Years later, at a 1981 symposium on Scott, Trudeau stated, "Frank taught me everything I know."[41]

They had returned to Montreal by September 5. Scott promptly wrote to the secretary of Eldorado Mining and Refining Limited, R.C. Powell, to report his safe arrival. The trip from Fort Smith to Norman Wells "was taken in good weather and most comfortable accommodation in a spare cabin." Scott and Trudeau had flown from Norman Wells to Aklavik. At Inuvik they had encountered Gordon Robertson, the Commissioner of the Northwest Territories, who invited them to sit in on the first session of the Territories' council to meet north of the Arctic Circle. Scott also told Powell that the northern journey "has enlarged my understanding of the problems and opportunities of development in this country."[42] What he reserved for his poem was his objection to exploitation of the North by this company and Imperial Oil and his indignant observation that the council meeting, the Arctic's "birth of democracy," was attended only by southerners – a commissioner and nine whites with himself, Trudeau, a priest, and members of the RCMP in ceremonial braid looking on "Were all the public around, / No Indian or Eskimo face" (C.P., p. 236). But Scott, as one of the participants remarked, "was mischievous": the whites included four representatives from Northwest Territories constituencies, elected in most cases by native majorities; and the site, then described as "E-3," was merely a construction camp in the wilderness; there was no resident native community to come to the meeting.[43]

Shortly after his return, Scott asked some friends to Clarke Avenue to view his slides, among them Northrop Frye, then visiting in Montreal. Frye discovered "that a trip down the Mackenzie could be a fascinating experience if one gets someone with a sharp eye and a well-focused camera to take the trip instead." He added, "the other guests I met suggested that living in Montreal would have a lot of compensations."[44] Scott's memory is that one of the guests leapt from his chair when a picture of an athletic nude snapped from behind appeared on the screen. Trudeau had retrieved the slide from the projector. Scott was bemused at this unexpected display of modesty. "It must have touched something in him that was built in the way I was built," he reflected. "I must say the difference between the two cultures as I knew mine and saw his was not very different."[45] Trudeau's memory is that a decade later, after he had decided to enter public life, Scott returned the slide to him together with a letter wishing him well.

There were indeed parallels between Scott's Anglo-Catholicism and Trudeau's Jesuit training. This basic affinity, reflected in a common socialism, had brought them together. To some degree, Scott seems to have played the same role in relation to Trudeau as Woodsworth did for Scott. But where Scott had attempted to bring to realization many of the undertakings and ideals that Woodsworth had advocated – such as patriation of the constitution and the struggle for a Canadian socialism – in the fairly straightforward manner of master to protégé, Trudeau's relation to Scott was far more dialectical. He was first attracted to a democratic and Christian socialism, indeed, those were the principles that animated *Cité libre*. But by exploring the ramifications of some of Scott's theories – as, for example, in the essay on democracy – Trudeau reached his own, sometimes opposite conclusions. This characteristic of his own mental processes he recognized in the foreword to *Federalism and the French Canadians*, where he remarks, "The only constant factor to be found in my thinking over the years has been opposition to accepted opinions."[46] This oversimplification obscures the fact that the process of Trudeau's intellectual development was one of gradual – and dialectical – evolution through which he clarified his goals for French Quebec within a Canadian federal system.

To assess the influence of one man on another is always difficult, but Frank Scott did play an important part in providing some basic concepts for Trudeau. Scott's pioneering articles clearly provided direction to Trudeau. Trudeau began as a democratic socialist, much in the Scott mould, who gravitated to socialist philosophy because of his repugnance for the "injustice" of society. In looking for remedies, as Trudeau recalled, "I found them first of all in the study of socialist thought." He had, however, certain reservations about the transference of socialist thought from one country to another. "I became aware later that the systems that these people had elaborated, whether it be called socialism or something else, were designed for a certain country or a certain period, and that we would be wrong to try to apply them to another country and another period."[47] This view, however, delivered to *The Toronto Star* in 1968, reflects an older Trudeau. One suspects that the Trudeau of the early fifties believed much more passionately that socialism was a practical solution to Quebec's problems.

IT WAS SUBSTANTIALLY Scott's analysis of Quebec society – buttressed with even more statistics, a more intimate knowledge of Quebec's institutions, and a greater sense of moral outrage – that characterized "The Province of Quebec at the Time of the Strike," Trudeau's introductory chapter to *La Grève de l'amiante*. Conscious that "History knows no abrupt turns; the forces at work in the present have arisen in the past," Trudeau searched out the essential principles governing Quebec's religious, political, and social past in order to understand her present society. Like Scott, he identified a greatly accelerated industrialization as the contemporary problem and saw both the Roman Catholic Church and national institutions as factors militating against progress.[48]

Church and universities – obliged to live by ideals and yet respond to realities – were unable to bridge the gap between their out-of-date economic ideas and the realities of industrialization. Political parties abandoned theory for opportunism. In the end, French Canadians owed their survival not to any of the institutions that had set out to defend their way of life but to the empiricism and "materialism" of the new institutions they had made their own – the trade unions.[49] The Asbestos strike, Trudeau argued, signalled the end of an era – the era of the submission of the French-Canadian working class to ideologies and institutions no longer valid. In the "Epilogue" Trudeau revealed his concern for the future and his aim in writing: "A whole generation hesitates on the brink of commitment. We hope that this work has offered it some basic principles to assist it in making its decision."[50]

One of the most striking aspects of this essay is the degree to which Trudeau was grieved by the fact that the Catholic Church hierarchy opposed socialism – the logical mode for Quebec's needed economic reforms.

> In the area of politics, we condemned ourselves to an equally discouraging impotence, because our political ideas were imbued with authoritarianism.... This attitude, combined with the pope's condemnation of atheistic socialism, gave us an excuse to reject the new Canadian social-democratic party, the Co-operative Commonwealth Federation (CCF), though it was concerned neither with atheism nor philosophy, but offered us concrete political means for putting an end to the economic colonialism which our nationalism found so offensive.[51]

Again and again he returns to the unfairness of this attack on the CCF by the church. One suspects that in writing this chapter Trudeau tacitly recognized the impossibility of ever establishing the CCF in Quebec. In his essay, "Some Obstacles to Democracy in Quebec," drafted on the Mackenzie trip, he offered faint praise to the Liberal Party, which after all had demonstrated amazing "astuteness," "foresight," and "courage" in making overtures to Quebec in the latter half of the nineteenth century.[52] His own path, perhaps, was beginning to emerge.

In 1956 Quebec was indeed at the crossroads. A number of individuals – Scott, Trudeau, Gérard Pelletier, René Lévesque – stood united in their opposition to Duplessisism. In Le Rassemblement Trudeau had attempted a union of all opposition parties to oppose Duplessis. At initial planning sessions for the movement Jacques Perrault, analysing the political situation in Canada and Quebec, showed "need for a new movement of a socialist kind, attached to popular groups in Quebec. He explained CCF position and asked whether it wasn't the answer."[53] It seems apparent that socialism was not acceptable to the majority as an answer, even though Trudeau was himself inclined in that direction. Le Rassemblement was to fail, as also did the later Union démocratique, because of the lack of a power base in Quebec.

Trudeau had been active in CCF circles for over a decade. He had campaigned for Thérèse Casgrain and a number of other CCF candidates, and as a regular participant in CCF meetings he was considered by Casgrain the logical inheritor of the leadership of the Quebec CCF. Jean Marchand acknowledged that Trudeau was strongly tempted in that direction. "I was to a certain extent responsible for Pierre refraining from coming out for the CCF, for convincing him that we had some immediate problems to solve – like to get rid of Duplessis. And if we tried to build a new party in Quebec, particularly a party which is composed almost entirely of Anglophones – well, we'd spend our lives building a party." Trudeau had spoken to Marchand about formally joining the CCF, but when Premier T.C. Douglas came to speak to the Quebec group, as Marchand recalled, "we were impressed, but we knew very well that those people will never be in a position to communicate with Quebecers."[54]

In 1959, however, political alliances in Quebec suddenly changed with the unexpected death of Maurice Duplessis. Writing to Dean Erwin Griswold of the Harvard Law School in October, Scott expressed his hope that matters would now improve. He added a paragraph on Duplessis. "It is said that on hearing the news of the death Cardinal Léger remarked 'History will judge of his actions; God will judge his soul. It only remains for us to pray for him.' Rather neat?"[55] Such epigrammatic conclusions, neat as they were, did not dispose of the problems represented by Duplessis. Certainly his death precipitated a shifting in political alliances; those formerly united by their opposition to Duplessis now began to move tentatively in other directions. In the early sixties, as Marchand recalled, "it was a problem of conscience for us. Normally we should support the CCF, but again, the Separatist Movement was threatening. We had a poor representation in Ottawa.... If we spend all our life building the CCF, well that means we would not have time to prevent what is coming."⁵⁶ Subsequently Trudeau, Pelletier, and Marchand went into the federal Liberal Party, primarily to counterbalance the new nationalism of the provincial Liberals.

In late January, 1968, when the federal Liberals were urging Trudeau to become leader of the party, Scott wrote urging that Trudeau accept:

28 January 1968

Dear Pierre,

I am not, as you know, a Liberal in the party sense of that word. I am convinced that had the CCF and the NDP had more electoral success many of the difficulties we find ourselves facing in Canada could have been avoided. Certainly Quebec's legitimate claims for a more equal partnership across Canada would have received earlier recognition. But despite my position, I am deeply concerned that the Liberal Party choose the best leader possible at this time. This must be a man who stands for a new concept of Canada, and one who is not suspect because of long association with the old-style Liberal politicians. Above all he must understand the constitutional realities, and be able to distinguish between mere change for change's sake and genuine functional growth. You are obviously this man. I really feel that, however much you may be dismayed at the prospect, you are called to undertake this responsibility. There is too much human happiness at stake, too great an opportunity for making a unique contribution to the building of a bi-cultural nation state, for you not to accept the challenge. I do hope you agree with me.

Just summon up the courage that led you to wade out into the fierce rapids of the Slave River!

Yours sincerely,
[Frank]

In subsequent years, Trudeau, who remained in touch with Scott, seems to have carried forward certain concepts associated with the older man. Not only did he share Scott's belief in the democratic ideal but he held the same view of the law as "social engineering," a view he developed not at the University of Montreal but later, in the forties and fifties, after his friendship with Scott had begun. Trudeau was later to say that law can be instrumental in social change, a *creative* thing. " 'My delight with the law developed a couple of years after I'd begun ... to realize that here was an instrument of social control, and it was an extraordinary creation of society. I wasn't interested in the lawmakers as much as I was interested in the whole process'."[57] The two now held a common belief about "one Canada" and Quebec's place in a federal state, about the necessity of repatriating the constitution, and, above all, about the need to entrench a Bill of Rights in the constitution. They also shared an internationalist view of the world; Trudeau called himself a "citizen of the world," a phrase that reflects not only the spirit of 1944-45 but also, perhaps, Scott's formulation. Both held at the back of their minds a conception of the lawmaker-politician as philosopher-king with the power of bringing into being the ideal state, "the state as a work of art." Many of these early views Trudeau carried into his fifteen years in power as Prime Minister of Canada. Indirectly, in the next two decades, Scott may have helped shape the future of Canada, especially as it related to Quebec and the constitution.

# TWENTY

# "A Citizen of the World"

I am an iamb
    because the bones of my social fish
were so precise
    I was meant to be embedded
    in the soft mud of my ancestors
or to be drawn on stone
    giving out words dreams ideas
    regular as ribs
crisp in the perfection of pattern
    dated
    a trilobite in limestone

But the earthquake came
    the sea-bottom cracked
    the floor rose to an island
no time for quiet death
    the tranquillity of fossilization
these were mountain days
    a new language in birds
diaspora of dactyls
    iambs split to the core
    now my ancient frame
cries for the deeps of Zanzibar
    and is answered only by
    I AM

        "COELACANTH"

FRANK SCOTT was sixty-one on August 1, 1960, and so began his most turbulent decade. Superficially, these years were the apogee of his career. He won another significant legal victory, this time for the freedom of the press, with the *Lady Chatterley* case. And he was finally "respectable" in terms that his father and elder brother would have recognized: in 1961 he was appointed Dean of Law at McGill University and in 1963 invited to become a member of the Royal Commission on Bilingualism and Biculturalism, in recognition of his work with civil liberties in Quebec. He also published two excellent books of poetry: *St-Denys Garneau & Anne Hébert: Translations / Traductions* (1962) and *Signature* (1964), the latter a collection of his recent work.

Yet the decade that might have been the fruition of his life's work brought more disillusionment than contentment. A Canada Council Senior Research Fellowship in 1960 allowed him to make a trip around the world that also became a kind of interior journey, an emotional and intellectual stock-taking of his past and present life. On this journey Scott began to perceive the subjectivity of ideas and institutions he had formerly considered absolute. As he wrote in the poem "Japanese Sand Garden" (1963), "... the eternally relative / absorbs / the ephemeral absolute" (*C.P.*, p. 127). The absolutes of his earlier Galahad phase – his faith in himself as an agent to effect change, his belief that socialism would bring in the new millennium – were rapidly dissolving into more relative and disillusioned pronouncements. The process was painful.

Everything was coming at once: a recognition of increasing age, retirement in the offing, the student revolt of the sixties, the trauma of Quebec separatism. Although at first attracted by the freedom of the hippie movement, he was increasingly alienated as he found that the new radicals did not share the same positive ideals for social change as had his contemporaries in the thirties. And, most distressing, all his desires for peaceful change in Quebec, for an accommodation with English Canada through constitutional reforms directed toward the preservation of minority rights within a strong Canadian federalism, seemed to be going up in smoke – in the bombs of the terrorist Front de Libération du Québec. With the assassination of Pierre Laporte and the invocation of the War Measures Act, Scott reached a nadir in his emotional life and in his hopes for Canada.

He felt a sense of enormous change – of a world cracking apart. As he wrote in a poem of the early sixties, "the earthquake came / the sea-bottom cracked" (*C.P.*, p. 183). In this new revolution Scott saw himself half-humorously as a living fossil, one like that ancient fish, the coelacanth, then recently discovered off the coast of Zanzibar. This Scott, who wanted to retain the old social pattern, again used metaphors of evolution and the language of poetry to describe his state of being. As a coelacanth, he preferred to remain "embedded / in the soft mud of my ancestors," where he can give out "words dreams ideas / regular as ribs" (*C.P.*, p. 183). But the revolution of the sixties, like the earlier upheavals of the twenties and thirties, had intervened. The difference was that Scott was no longer a vigorous young radical; the effort required to meet the new order – both social and poetic – was now incomparably greater. Scott, "the iamb," as he punned, is divided, "split to the core," by new revolutions requiring new action. His aging frame called out for some peace, "for quiet death / the tranquillity of fossilization" (*C.P.*, p. 183), as he half-jested. Yet he answered "I AM" – the traditional assertion of the Old Testament Jehovah, the old resonant call to duty. His first public "duty" was the fight against censorship in Quebec.

> I went to bat for the Lady Chatte
>     Dressed in my bib and gown.
> The judges three glared down at me
>     The priests patrolled the town.
>
> My right hand shook as I reached for that book
>     And rose to play my part.
> For out on the street were the marching feet
>     Of the League of the Sacred Heart.   (*C.P.*, p. 264)

WHEN SCOTT ROSE in the Court of Queen's Bench, Appeal Side, on April 7, 1961, to submit that the Quebec Superior Court had erred in pronouncing D.H. Lawrence's *Lady Chatterley's Lover* obscene his eyes fell on a large crucifix at the front of the courtroom. To his left was the British coat of arms with its motto *Honi soit qui mal y pense*. This motto, Scott later mused, encompassed the whole problem of determining questions of obscenity: what is judged obscene by one man or one culture may well be judged as not obscene by another.[1]

To some extent these two emblems – the cross and the plaque – were also symbolic of the social conflict involved in reaction to *Lady Chatterley's Lover* in Quebec, a conflict between a Jansenist Catholicism with its belief in the primacy of the spirit over the body, and the more open British tradition that tended to shy away from what John Milton, that great seventeenth-century defender of free speech, called "a cloistered virtue." However, definitions of obscenity are invariably related to community standards and the social climate in Quebec in 1959 was overwhelmingly conservative. "You have to remember," Manuel Shacter, counsel for the defence, recalled in the eighties, "this was before any of the so-called revolutions in Quebec."[2] Reading material was still censored by the Board of Cinema Censors; there was, in fact, an "Index" of prohibited literature. Not surprisingly, in the eventual appeal to the Supreme Court of Canada, Scott and Shacter were to invoke in the defence of D.H. Lawrence's novel Milton's paean to the freedom of the press, the *Areopagitica*.

Much has been written of the *Lady Chatterley* cases in the United States and Great Britain, but it has not been recognized that the Canadian trial preceded, and indeed may have given direction to, the more celebrated English trial. Moreover, the Canadian trial proved a much more difficult case to win, largely because of Canada's – and Quebec's – highly conservative social mores. Unlike the American trial, won on appeal, and the English trial, which was successful in the court of first instance, the Old Bailey, the Canadian trial went all the way to the Supreme Court of Canada. The ultimate acquittal of *Lady Chatterley's Lover* affirmed, like the novel itself, a social as well as a sexual revolution.

The English trial rested on a new definition of obscenity. Prior to 1959 obscenity had been defined in England, as in Canada, with reference to the old Hicklin Rule: that is, would the effect of a work be "to deprave and corrupt" those innocents into whose hands it might fall? This was Mr. Podsnap's principle of Victorian morality – "Would it bring a blush into the cheek of a young person?" – and by such principles many classics of literature could be, and indeed were, condemned. In 1933 in the United States Judge John M. Woolsey of the District Court for Southern New York reversed this trend by lifting the ban on *Ulysses*. Instead of the *jeune fille* as the chief consideration, Woolsey proposed "what the French would call l'homme sensuel moyen," the normal adult reader, "a person with average sex instincts." He also ruled that a book must be judged as a whole rather than as a sampling of "salacious titbits."[3]

Not until 1959 did English and Canadian law move toward the liberality of American legislation. In 1959 both countries brought in new definitions of obscenity. The British Parliament had enlarged the old Hicklin definition to read that an article "shall be deemed to be obscene [if] ... the effect of any one of its items is, if taken as a whole, such as tend to deprave and corrupt persons who are likely, having regard to all relevant circumstances, to read, see or hear the matter concerned or embodied in it."[4] An item must be corrupting or depraving as a whole and not merely show a tendency. Moreover, the English legislation permitted the argument that a work could be justified as literature and was thus for the public good.

In Canada on July 18, 1959, Parliament passed Bill C.150 (8) amending the provisions of the Criminal Code in regard to obscene publications. Under this Act, an individual commits an offence when he has in his possession, for the purpose of distribution, any obscene matter, or when he knowingly exposes such to public view. Under this legislation either the work or the individual or both may be charged. But an individual cannot be convicted of an offence if it is established that the public good was served by the act that is alleged to constitute the offence. Subsection 8 states that "For the purposes of this Act, any publication a dominant characteristic of which is the undue exploitation of sex, or of sex and any one or more of the following subjects, namely, crime, horror, cruelty and violence, shall be deemed to be obscene."[5]

On November 5, 1959, the Montreal newsstands of Larry Brodie, Joseph R. Dansky, and George Rubin were raided by the police, who seized copies of a new unexpurgated edition of *Lady Chatterley's Lover*. A paperback edition, the book was priced at fifty cents per copy. The publishers, the New American Library, were aiming at the Canadian mass market as they were reputed to have printed 40,000 copies of the book in Winnipeg. When the book was charged as obscene and the news dealers were found in possession of obscene material, the publishers engaged Manuel Shacter, a Montreal lawyer and a former student of Frank Scott, to undertake the defence.

Shacter prepared the case for trial to be held on April 12, 1960, at the Quebec Superior Court. As only the book itself was on trial, the prosecution provided as its sole evidence a copy of *Lady Chatterley's Lover*. The book submitted by the prosecution was heavily underlined in thick blue ink to indicate those passages alleged obscene.[6] Not only did the emphasis of the Criminal Code on the "dominant characteristic" of a work discourage the reading of the book as a whole but, in effect, the court was exposed to a slanted text.

Unlike the British law the new Canadian legislation, directed toward ridding newsstands of pornography, provided no protection for works of literature. Despite this, counsel for the defence began by calling experts to show the book was a work of art. Up to this point only the court had been considered competent to judge what was obscene; this approach was now met by the argument that experts were testifying to the literary quality of the work rather than to its obscenity. However, an important rider to this argument was the fact that a work of art, by definition, could not be obscene. Defence counsel also argued that juveniles should not set the standard for obscenity. And a new argument was advanced: the guideline of prevailing community standards.

Expert witnesses included the Canadian novelists Morley Callaghan and Hugh MacLennan, and Harry T. Moore, an American scholar and a recognized specialist on D.H. Lawrence. All testified Lawrence was a major twentieth-century novelist, the work was not pornographic, and the passages involving sexual intercourse were not meant to degrade and corrupt but were integral moral concerns of the novelist. Professor Moore considered the dominant characteristic of the book a condemnation of the sterile industrialization of England, a condition symbolized in the novel by Lord Chatterley's impotence.[7]

Moore reminded the court that Lawrence himself had resisted efforts by his publishers to censor the novel. Mr. J. St. Laurent, the counsel for the prosecution, cross-examined: "Would you give me a definition of 'Expurgated'?" Moore replied, "That merely means, – well, – castrated, – castrating a book, – that's all."[8] The presiding judge, Judge T.A. Fontaine, leaned over and asked his clerk in a stage whisper, "What does he mean by that?" The clerk told him. The judge reddened perceptibly and appeared upset.[9]

Judge Fontaine heard the literary witnesses on April 12, and then the prosecution asked for and received an adjournment until May 5 in order to obtain literary witnesses to testify on the pornographic quality of the work. On May 5, still unable to produce witnesses, a further postponement was requested until June 1. On this date, still unable to proceed, the prosecution submitted that no literary evidence be accepted. To this the judge agreed.

Judgement of the first Canadian trial of *Lady Chatterley's Lover*, known as *Brodie, Dansky and Rubin* v. *The Queen*, was given on June 10, 1960. Judge Fontaine ruled that the morality squad had been legally justified in seizing copies of the novel, *Lady Chatterley's Lover*, as it was an obscene book.

Shacter had expected this verdict. The obscenity legislation was new, this was the first time it had been tested before the courts, and the Quebec court was notoriously conservative. He had only taken the case with the understanding the publishers would, if necessary, support it all the way to the Supreme Court. He now asked Scott, whom he had consulted earlier, for help in arguing the appeal. The two lawyers spent that summer in preparing the factum for the Court of Appeal. Shacter recalled, "I would draft several pages, go up to the law faculty, and we would review it for a couple of hours. He would reduce my drafts to short, concise, hard-hitting sentences, which I think was a marvellous lesson for me and indicative of just how good he was both as a lawyer and as a writer."[10]

Meanwhile, in October, 1960, charges of obscenity were brought against *Lady Chatterley's Lover* in England. Curiously, the attorney for the defence was Gerald Gardiner, an old friend of Scott's from his rowing days at Oxford; both, as Scott was later to quip, became "Lady Chatterley's lawyers." Gardiner wrote to the Canadian defence counsel requesting a transcript of the trial for use in preparing his own case. He followed the procedure established by Schacter and Scott in the first Canadian trial of calling literary witnesses; he also argued that juveniles should not be the standard for obscenity but rather that community opinion should be the yardstick.

The defence counsel for the English trial, *Regina* v. *Penguin*, had assembled a cast of witnesses including such literary notables as Rebecca West, Helen Gardner, and E.M. Forster. All testified that *Lady Chatterley's Lover* was a great work of literature. Helen Gardner briskly observed that as the sex act itself was not immoral, neither were four-letter words describing it; Forster submitted that Lawrence was a Puritan, one of that long list of English moralists that began with Bunyan. The prosecution was able to call only one witness, Katherine Anne Porter, to speak against the novel. The jury brought in a verdict of acquittal on November 3, 1960. Kenneth Tynan, commenting wryly on the case in *The Observer*, remarked, "Now that the case is over, and Lady Chatterley's adventures are speeding two-hundred-thousand-fold to every outpost of literacy in the country, it seems suddenly unthinkable that the jury could have brought in any other verdict. But it was desperately thinkable right up to three o'clock on Thursday afternoon, as anyone knows who sat through the six days of the trial, and sweated out the dragging hours of the jury's retirement."[11]

Even in the relatively liberal English social climate of the early sixties, the *Lady Chatterley* case had been difficult to win; it was incomparably more difficult in Catholic Quebec, where the sexual and the immoral were so often equated. The Canadian case went to appeal in April, 1961. Scott's first task was to argue, with reference to the new legislation on obscenity, that the treatment of sexuality in *Lady Chatterley's Lover* could not be described as pornographic because the preoccupation with sex in the novel was not "undue." As a result of appearing before the Quebec court he began to versify the issues:

> The word "obscene" was supposed to mean
>   "Undue exploitation of sex."
> This wording's fine for your needs and mine
>   But it's far too free for Quebec's.

I tried my best, with unusual zest,
  To drive my argument through.
But I soon got stuck on what rhymes with "muck"
  And that dubious word "undue."   (*C.P.*, p. 264)

It is possible that the combination of a four-letter word and the portrayal of adultery may have led the Quebec court to extend its judgement of the immorality of the actions of the characters to a judgement on the morality of the book itself. Scott contended that the new Bill of Rights, passed by Prime Minister Diefenbaker's government, allowed freedom of the press.

So I raised their sights to the Bill of Rights
  And cried: "Let freedom ring!"
Showed straight from the text that freedom of sex
  Was as clear as anything.   (*C.P.*, p. 264)

The new Bill of Rights, as Scott knew, was a weak piece of legislation that did not apply in general terms; it applied only to some – but not all – federal legislation.

Scott further argued the attempt to censor *Lady Chatterley's Lover* was the ultimate folly of trying to censor one's own human sexual response.

Then I plunged into love, the spell that it wove,
  And its attributes big and bold
Till the legal elect all stood erect
  As my rapturous tale was told.

The judges' sighs and rolling of eyes
  Gave hope that my case was won,
Yet Mellors and Connie still looked pretty funny
  Dancing about in the sun.   (*C.P.*, p. 264)

However, that section of the novel describing Lady Chatterley and her lover braiding wild flowers into her pubic hair was, not surprisingly, considered "excessive" by the Quebec Court of Queen's Bench. And there was consternation over the wide availability of the book as a paperback.

What hurt me was not that they did it a lot
  And even ran out in the rain,
'Twas those curious poses with harebells and roses
  And that dangling daisy-chain.

Then too the sales made in the paperback trade
  Served to aggravate judicial spleen,

> For it seems a high price will make any book nice
> While its mass distribution's obscene.   (*C.P.*, p. 265)

During the appeal and shortly after, when Scott began to satirize his own interpretation of the Lady Chatterley case, he sent a copy to Shacter. But because the case was still in progress he did not attempt to publish it. A year later when a tabloid, *The Justice Weekly*, reported on March 31, 1962, the progress of Lady Chatterley in the Supreme Court of Canada it also published, on the facing page, a titillating account of a young man called Alan who had undergone a sex change. The title read THE FURTHER ADVENTURES OF ALAN, NOW CALLED "ALICE" IN WONDERLAND. One suspects that Scott seized on the connection with delight: he titled his own verse "A Lass in Wonderland," punning on Alice and Alas! The American literary critic Harry Levin, writing on pornography and the Lady Chatterley case some four years later, savoured the same element of absurdity and made the same connection when he remarked that even the name of the English trial *Regina* v. *Penguin*, suggesting as it did "a chapter from *Alice in Wonderland*, aptly announced the procession of church dignitaries, lady dons, schoolmasters, librarians, editors, critics, and publicists who took the witness stand."[12]

On April 7, 1961, Justices Paul Casey, Fernand Choquette, and J. Larouche dismissed the appeal to the Quebec Court of Queen's Bench, holding that *Lady Chatterley's Lover* represented "an undue exploitation of sex." Mr. Justice Casey feared the book would not be sought out for its literary merits or its sociological significance: "the majority of its readers will ... be found among the young and among the impressionable, those very persons with whose moral stability Parliament is primarily concerned." He added, "ours is a Christian civilization," and remarked "we must not allow an articulate minority to impose its will and its standards on the majority." It had not been customary to call literary witnesses in the past and he made short shrift of them now: "If the issues involved matters of science or skill, or if the ability to form an opinion presupposed special learning or experience, the evidence of experts would be admissible. But our problem is not of that type."[13]

When the case finally came before the Supreme Court of Canada on March 15, 1962, the court was asked for the first time to rule on the meaning of the new definition of obscenity embodied in Section 150 (8) of the Criminal Code. Scott argued there was no more undue exploitation of sex in *Lady Chatterley's Lover* than in the nude figures painted by Michelangelo in the Vatican's Sistine Chapel. Montreal lawyer Claude Wagner, prose-

cuting the case for Quebec, "countered that the book was not only obscene
– 'it develops no moral teaching whatsoever'" – but was characterized by
"promiscuity and adultery." Debate centred on the following issues: "[Did]
the new definition completely exclude application of its predecessor, ...
the Hicklin Rule? What do the key words ... 'dominant,' 'undue,' and
'exploitation' really mean? Is expert testimony as to the literary value of
the book ... admissible in evidence? What protection, if any, is afforded
by the Canadian Bill of Rights to serious writers? ... Is the defence of
public good – i.e., literary or artistic merit – available to a book [charged
as being obscene?]"[14]

Scott and Shacter, building on Harry Moore's testimony, submitted
that the dominant characteristics of *Lady Chatterley's Lover* were the evils
of industrialization in England, an emphasis on intuition as opposed to
intellectualization, and the power and beauty of physical love between
man and woman.[15] "[These] parts of the book which deal with sex," Scott
argued, "deal with the developing love of the characters in the book. The
dominant characteristic is the human relationship. The existence of sex
does not make it dominant."[16]

On March 16, 1962, a judgement of five to four in favour of *Lady
Chatterley's Lover* was given. The majority judgement, written by Mr.
Justice Judson, pointed out the test under the new legislation "was whether
the dominant characteristic of the novel was the undue exploitation of
sex." The majority were convinced the book was "a serious work of fiction"
and the sexual scenes were not written for pornographic intent. Mr. Justice
Judson, accepting Scott's argument, pronounced the novel a means of
expressing Lawrence's views on modern society and its effect on relations
between a man and a woman. The dissenting judgement, by Mr. Justice
Fauteux, was that the exploitation of sex was "a dominant characteristic
of the publication [and] has been carried to a shocking and disgusting
point." Not surprisingly, perhaps, the decision was made along denominational lines, with four Anglicans and one non-denominational supporting it and three Roman Catholics and one Anglican opposing.[17] This
split was to lead a Quebec newspaper to inquire rhetorically, "Y a-t-il deux
Cours suprêmes du Canada?"[18]

Clearly, Scott did not accept the idea of literary censorship in a democracy. Some years later, writing to an individual who had asked him
to define pornography, Scott replied, "I cannot give you any definition of
pornography that would be satisfactory to me, or probably to anyone else.
I do not think it is a definable concept. I would consequently let people
publish whatever they wanted to publish, whether in pictures or in print.

It's all part of our universe, and I don't think we should hide a fraction of it. In any case we shan't succeed in doing so, no matter how much we try."[19] However, Scott's preoccupation with individual freedom in society was shortly to be tempered by an extended consideration of responsibility in an international context.

IN MARCH, 1960, Scott was awarded a Canada Council Senior Research Fellowship to continue his studies of constitutional law with reference to comparative constitutional law. He decided, as this was a travel fellowship, the best way to get first-hand information on comparative law would be to take an around-the-world trip to the major centres of constitutional law and to those nations, such as Japan and Ethiopia, currently developing new constitutions.

Throughout the summer of 1960 Scott prepared for the trip by writing letters to friends and acquaintances in embassies in the Middle East and Europe. He decided to circumnavigate the globe, travelling westward from Vancouver. En route he would pass through San Francisco and Honolulu and from there go on to the Far East: Tokyo, Singapore, Djakarta, Rangoon, New Delhi, Cairo, and Addis Ababa. Back in Cairo again he would be joined by Marian and jointly they would visit the Valley of the Nile and the cradle of Greek civilization at Athens. From there they planned to travel to Europe – to Geneva, Paris, and Strasbourg. The journey would end in England.

Scott set out as a solitary pilgrim. "What am I doing on this trip?" he recognized as the big question.[20] Although he travelled alone, his journey was punctuated by meetings with old friends and acquaintances: Chester Ronning in India, George Cadbury in Cairo, the King Gordons in Tokyo, Allan Gotlieb in Geneva, Scott's son Peter and family in Vienna, Charles Lussier and Pierre Emmanuel in Paris. With a far-flung network of friends and students, supplemented with numerous letters of introduction, he was handed on from friend to official as he passed from city to city. Every now and then he put aside time for thinking and writing – trying to make sense of what he was seeing and feeling. Because Marian did not join him until near the end of the trip, his travel journal, like the Oxford diaries, became a confidante.

On the first leg of the trip he sought out old friends in Vancouver – Dean George Curtis of the law faculty at UBC and poetry friends Earle Birney, Phyllis Webb, and Bill and Alice McConnell. The journey began on a self-conscious note, partly because McConnell asked Scott to put together a collection of his translations of Quebec poets for Klanak Press.

Scott felt uneasy about accepting. "Between me and poetry – indeed, between me and many things – has come a fear: I distrust my own ability," he wrote in his diary.[21] Now sixty, he was highly conscious of the passage of time.

And the journey he had now started was one he associated more and more with a shrinking life journey. He was also very conscious of failing capacities. Recently, when lecturing at Carleton, he had made a serious error about Section 86. And when visiting the UBC law faculty, he found himself forgetting names.[22] Memory, the capacity to marshall accurate precedents, is a primary requirement of a legal scholar. Scott liked to quote the remark made by an Anglican bishop in a London play: "Two things can save us: the grace of God, and, if that fails, accuracy."[23] He recalled his embarrassment for a senior judge in the Padlock case who had made a spectacle of himself by confusing persons and statutes.[24] Now it seemed he was doing the same thing. For Scott the memory lapses brought with them nagging doubts about his own competence, doubts that his overly strict super-ego translated into "consuming monsters who eat up my will to work."[25]

With these pessimistic thoughts he left Vancouver for San Francisco. There he sought out old Montreal friends: Betty Layton, Irving Layton's first wife, and Avi and Naomi Boxer. They all talked about old times, especially about the friends and poetry of the forties and fifties. The Boxers also provided an introduction to the thriving beatnik colony in San Francisco. Scott found this new phenomenon of "beatnikery" fascinating. In his diary he recorded impressions of the "pad," reached by a secret door: the floor covered with rush mats on which visitors walked silently in stocking feet; a bar in one corner holding paper cups and a large gallon jar of red wine; in front of the bar a small area of hardwood floor to dance on; and along the brick wall of the room mattresses with cushions, "admirably suited," Scott speculated, "for conversation or copulation."[26]

He watched the beatniks sitting or lying about in groups: "occasionally one would leave to join another conversation, or pick a partner for a dance. Some of the dancing was expertly expressionist, the couple facing one another but not touching, speaking and sharing through spontaneous movement." From a young college student named Paul, formerly in Cuba with the United States Army during the Castro revolution, he learned there were three types in the room: those who come for the kicks; those who would always drift along on the fringes of society; and a middle group like himself who would try to keep alive the values of dissidence as they grew older and began working. Paul told Scott that he had broken from his family completely; his protest was against the conformity of American life. " 'If you show yourself to be the least bit different from the others you're called a Red,' he said. 'They'll blacklist you and keep you from jobs. They expect you to go steady, think like the rest, marry young and aim to raise a family in the suburbs. That's not good enough for me and these others'."

Talking with Paul reminded Scott of the reforming zeal of the 1930s. On the plane trip between San Francisco and Honolulu he began to compare the young man with himself at his age. "I never broke with my family, only with W.B.S. [his brother William]. He was, in a way, a father, since it was he who told me what to do when I came back from Oxford.... But Father and Mother were always the same no matter what causes I was espousing. They never understood what I was after, but that made no difference." He realized he had never known complete freedom from family ties. In this sense Scott's revolt was less complete than Paul's.

> And at first it was directed against old forms of belief in religion and art rather than in politics. Poetry was my emancipator.... It was a revelation, a discovery. Scales fell from my eyes and, falling, brought down other trappings. I began to see shams everywhere; my greatest concern was not to be fooled by appearances. The mock religion inside the Fraternity made religion outside more of a mockery. I read Eddington, Jeans, and other books on science. (H.G. Wells had given me this bent: so had Father's love of astronomy). Slowly and without shock or pain I shifted from one set of working concepts to another which seemed to me truer, fresher and more exciting. I could never go back.

Scott's jotted reminiscences, which began in Vancouver and San Francisco, were kept up on the long trip to Japan. Each mile of the journey continued the internal voyage into the self – one of his first attempts to make sense of his past life and to find a continuing basis for the future.

The immediate purpose of the trip, however, was to gain further information about comparative constitutional law. In Japan he interviewed Dr. Kenzo Takanayagi, chairman of the commission for the investigation of the constitution of Japan. Japan, Scott concluded, had accepted certain basic concepts such as the welfare state and the rule of law in its new proposed constitutional reforms, but the divisions between conservatives and socialists rendered the future of parliamentary government insecure.[27] At Rikyo University he met Professor Miyazawa, Dean of the Law School. The latter did not expect much from the new constitution because the socialist opposition held sufficient seats to prevent the two-thirds majority needed for Diet approval. Another Japanese specialist, Professor Oishi, former Dean of Kyoto University Law School, dismissed the present Japanese constitution as " 'good for those who want Japan subservient to China and Russia'."²⁸

As Scott passed through the Far and Middle East he visited with former students and colleagues. In Singapore, he met with members of the law faculty at the University of Malaya to discuss their new constitution.²⁹ In Ethiopia he was delighted with a reunion of nineteen former students now involved in an attempt to implement a new constitution. Were they implicated in the last coup? he asked. " 'Not this time'," they replied.³⁰ The highlight of this visit was the former students' affectionate reminiscences of the McGill Law School. He was touched to find in one home a picture of the class of 1957 over a McGill crest. "I would never have believed, from my feeling about the Faculty at that time," he recorded, "that we could have made that much impression on them."³¹

Only when he reached Paris was he able to spend an extended period in the library of a law school. There he did some general reading and began to prepare, for the Canadian Labour Congress, an opinion on Bill 42, the labour legislation passed by the British Columbia Social Credit government regarding union contributions to political parties. At Strasbourg, at the International Court of Human Rights, he again installed himself in the library and began to work, reflecting that it was "Very satisfactory to be back at this academic treat."³² Between April 25 and 29 he watched the Consultative Assembly of the Council of Europe discussing a proposed new "Protocol on Human Rights affecting minorities." Later, at Cambridge in May, Scott spoke on the nationalization of the Canadian constitution – "Bringing home the Grundnorm" – using the German "grund" to emphasize that the BNA Act was Canada's foundation stone. To the English audience he described the processes that had been going on in Canada at the conference of attorneys-general and predicted that Canada "would not emerge without a rigid amending procedure, probably based on the unanimity rule."³³

The most fruitful contacts of Scott's journey, however, involved a combination of politics and law. When lecturing in Indonesia he was delighted to discover he was more highly regarded for his socialism than for his expertise in constitutional law. "The millstone around my neck has become a halo around my head," he gleefully confided to his journal.³⁴ Indeed, because Scott was a socialist Chester Ronning, Canada's High Commissioner to India, was able to arrange an appointment for him with Jawaharlal

Nehru, Prime Minister of India, on February 24. For a day or so before the visit, Scott prepared a list of questions to ask; immediately after the interview he pencilled in some of Nehru's responses.

When he entered the large office Scott found the Indian leader seated at a large desk "dressed in [a] long brown coat with one rose-bud on it, and no cap to cover his bald head." After introducing himself Scott asked, " 'Are you making a planned advance towards socialism'?" Nehru's answer must have been a source of ironic amusement to his listener: the primary problem experienced by Indian socialists was that " 'you cannot carry out your plans for the public sector unless you keep control of the private sector. Of course, the private interests have all sorts of ways and means of getting around the controls – always evading or twisting. And they own the press'."[35] The evasions of capitalism and questions of freedom of the press were old stories to Scott. However, in the latter area the Indian socialist party enjoyed a great advantage. Very fortunately, as Nehru said, the masses were protected from the press by their illiteracy.

When Scott asked if he had any message for the New Party of Canada (the precursor to the New Democratic Party), the Indian leader replied, " 'I believe some form of socialism is coming everywhere. It is the course of history'." And was there anything special Canada might do for India? Nehru remarked: " 'We have always got on well with Canada. Better than with any other part of the Commonwealth.... Perhaps it was a question of personalities – Mackenzie (he forgot the King), St. Laurent, Pearson'." Wishing luck to Scott's New Party, Nehru went back, as Scott reflected, "to his task of trying to move 400,000,000 people, mostly illiterate, mostly hungry, mostly sick, all shot through with notions of caste and status, from their present backwardness toward the industrialized democratic socialist society."

Despite Nehru's evident approval of Canadian statesmen, this view was not shared generally. Through his many contacts in Canadian embassies and legations in the Middle East and Europe, Scott was told again and again that Canada's prestige abroad was dropping below its previously high standard. He also heard a particularly revealing anecdote from Chester Ronning. During Prime Minister Diefenbaker's visit to India, Ronning had had a long talk with him about China, reminding him that Pearson and Prime Minister St. Laurent had gone to Washington in 1956 because they believed the time had come for Canada to recognize Peking. As they believed Secretary of State Dulles would be too rigid and emotional to accept this idea, they had talked directly to President Eisenhower. To their astonishment, he was much more emotional than Dulles could have been. He told them if Canada recognized China it would turn the tide in the

General Assembly: China would then be admitted to the United Nations. Should this happen the United States would not only pull out of the United Nations but also "throw the UN out of the US lock, stock and barrel." Pearson and St. Laurent promptly dropped the subject. Diefenbaker, hearing this story, asked Ronning, " 'Are you sure of this'?" Ronning was. Then Diefenbaker remarked, " 'I wanted to be sure, because that is exactly what Eisenhower told Sidney Smith and I when we broached the same question with him in 1958'." To Scott this story disclosed Canada's true satellite position. He felt Canada should have recognized China anyway; "the mistake lay in asking permission."³⁶ It is likely Scott would have later told this story to Pierre Trudeau who, in his term as Prime Minister, did not ask permission before recognizing China.

While in Vienna Scott had a bird's eye view of embassy life and Canada's place in the world while visiting his son Peter, a member of the Canadian delegation at the International Conference on Diplomatic Privileges in Vienna. After a particularly distressing diplomatic dinner (saved only by a National Film Board film on the Eskimo hunting life) Scott reflected, "what a life to lead, and at this level what does it achieve? I hope Peter does not stay with it."³⁷ Later, in Geneva, visiting with Peter and his wife Maylie, Scott talked with the young couple about various possibilities for a change of job. Shortly after, to Scott's great relief, the young man was to take an appointment in the English department at the University of California at Berkeley. There he continued to write poetry, becoming a stalwart of the peace movement and, in the late sixties and early seventies, after the assassination of President Kennedy, an acknowledged expert on the topic.

During his journey around the world Scott also encountered a number of poets. Besides Birney and Webb in Vancouver, he also saw Pierre Emmanuel and Daryl Hine in Paris, Patrick Anderson in England, and, most importantly, Edmund Blunden in Hong Kong. Blunden was "so bright and alive" that Scott instantly felt a rapport with him. "His voice," Scott recalled, "was the only true voice I heard on the journey." When the older poet asked him to stay for lunch, Scott, conscious that he had previously refused a "duty" invitation, declined. He regretted it bitterly: "How bound I am by stupid conventions!"³⁸ In London, chatting with Patrick Anderson at the George Pub, he met Bern Singer, who had slighted A.J.M. Smith's *The Oxford Book of Canadian Verse* in *The Times Literary Supplement*. Singer drank so much beer that he fell asleep in his chair, leaving Scott to snap of this "little nonentity who knows nothing of Canada, its people or its literature. Of such is the Times thunder made."³⁹

Scott now had a storehouse of memories for poems. He had been impressed by the vast serene compound of the Japanese garden at the Ryoan-ji Temple. Founded in 1450, the temple extends toward the western foot of Mount Kinugasi and commands a view of Mount Otokogama River to the north. The quintessence of Zen, the sand garden is the focal point of the temple and consists of fifteen precisely positioned stones. Scott marvelled over its "exactly rightness." This he translated into a poem with the proportions of the rocks (5-2-3-3-2) reflected in the lines of the poem.

Japanese Sand Garden

raked
in long lines      by bamboo prongs
the white sand
is endless      a distance
is waves
circling small rocks
islands
placed here three      here two
and faraway
three      two      and two
in rock clefts
moss
makes river deltas

In this world of the Japanese temple garden all horizons vanish as "the most / is made from the least / and the eternally relative / absorbs / the ephemeral absolute."[40] Here, as later, when participating in a delicate Japanese tea ceremony, Scott recognized once again that so many of his so-called Western absolutes were in fact relative.

At Angkor Thom, Scott was delighted by the Bayon and what he perceived in the structure as "a sustaining single architectural concept underneath: the parts make a massive whole." The following day, climbing a nearby hill in a cooling late-afternoon breeze, he discovered the view from the top: "All around stretched the flat land that had once housed a million or more inhabitants whose work and skill had erected these vast monuments. Now Angkor Vat stood up magnificent below us, and far to the west the sun gleamed on the Great Lake where Chams defeated the Khmers in 1177-80. Sounds of pastoral life below floated up, seeming to increase the calm around." On his descent, at the foot of the mountain, he saw a bonze, a Buddhist monk, sitting beside a stone basin depicting

Buddha's footprint.⁴¹ From this date Scott became fascinated by replicas of the Buddha, especially the portrayal of the great calm stone face. As he had noticed on his trip to Burma, there is a striking contrast between Eastern religious representations and the Western depiction of the crucified Christ.

In Cairo on March 3, Marian Scott joined her husband for visits to the Karnak and Luxor temples. At Karnak, when thinking about a tour of the Valley of the Kings, Scott wrote, "The achievement of grandeur through the union of religion and temporal kingly power – it is in Japan, in Angkor, in India, in Mexico – [it is] in all 'civilisations' no matter what form of government. It was the primitive expression of 'social welfare,' something lifting the individual above his own limited environment." Yet, Scott objected, there was no sense of individual benefit, "no concept of inner resources in human beings needing and capable of development." Karnak, he recognized, was a slave state "for other-worldly glory." Was religion, he wondered, a "spiritual fertilizer making the soil produce more?" No doubt it was because it represented a "poetic system" that many people accepted it: "for all but the slaves!" he reminded himself.⁴²

His reaction to Greece was quite different. In Athens on March 18 he reflected on the temples he had seen, struck by the paradox of "failure and success, ruin and permanence" and again "the deadly combinations of priest and king."⁴³ From this context Scott's poem, "Cloth of Gold," emerged.

> The king I saw who walked a cloth of gold,
> Who sat upon the throne a child of God,
> He was my king when he was most a myth.
>
> Then every man paid homage at his feet.
> Some fought his battles and shed ransom blood,
> Some slew their rights to magnify his claims.
>
> It was our centuries that cut him down.
> Bold kings would totter with the lapse of time.
> We pushed them over with our rebel shout.
>
> Yet of this metal are new kingdoms struck.
> The unknown kings that filter through the laws
> Make baron plans to multiply their fiefs....
>
> While far across the ploughlands of the East
> The single master who is history's dream
> Holds up his hand to daze the patient throngs.

It seems the shadow of a king is here
That strides before us to the rising sun,
Some shadow of a king that will not fade.

The tumbled limbs of monarchy are green.
A hundred heads survive our mightiest stroke.
These broken dreams, these fragile interludes.... (*C.P.*, p. 175)

Yet the tyranny of priest and king, Scott recognized, was only part of the story,

> ... no more true than the other part which sings, even shouts aloud, of man's greatness when a system of beliefs releases his individual and social energies for a vast collective achievement. And always within the embracing architecture the individual artist emerges who creates his own single works of art through sheer joy in his own vision, not caring much where his work is used. The man who can snap his fingers at theology and laws other than those he sets for himself.

It does not matter, he concluded, what kind of gods prevailed at the time: decline comes from a settling into moulds, from human conformity.[44] Priests, he recognized, had always asked the really important questions, the "why" of man's existence.[45]

At Athens, Frank and Marian Scott felt themselves most strongly in touch with the democratizing ideals of Western culture. Visiting the Temple of Dionysus, they listened to a young guide explain the early Greek drama and the mode of Greek theatres. "Memories and imagined scenes flooded over us; I turned to look at M. and there were tears in her eyes. The frieze at the back of the hemispherical stage contained a goddess of democracy. How far we are from Karnak!" For Scott this was a return to one of the central concerns of his emotional and spiritual life: here democracy had started. At the Acropolis, they viewed "Ruins, but outpouring of man's spirit and pride, the tragedy and partial survival being fused into a new whole. A live tomb: A death and resurrection."[46]

In England both Scotts revived their emotional roots; Frank reflected on the joys of his Oxford years while Marian visited her mother, Mrs. Dale, and her sister Anna, who had married David Keir, now Sir David, Master of Balliol College, Oxford. At Cambridge early in May, the day after he had spoken on the Canadian constitution, the couple "took the morning roaming about quietly, absorbing the sunlight and the sweet orderliness of everything."[47] Viewing King's College Chapel, he judged it "Truly a poem in stone, not matched by the great monuments of the East." At Trinity the couple was given a guidebook to the college, and at the end Scott found a list of "some Trinity men" ranked in order: "Royal Family / Poets / Prime Ministers / Other Public Men / Men of Science and Mathematicians / Classical Scholars / Philosophers / Historians / Judges and Lawyers / Ecclesiastics and Divines [please note! he inserted] / Other Writers. (Where, oh where, are the Great Executives, Bankers, Brewers, Mining Magnates and Wizards of Finance? Can this be a University?)," he exulted.

The major discoveries of the journey, however, were more serious. They related to one of the shaping concepts of his own life – a sense of the evolution of the human spirit. While in the Middle and Far East he had been reading Julian Huxley's *Knowledge, Mortality and Destiny*. Scott liked the book; it confirmed his own belief in man's capacity to shape his future:

> His overall view of evolution, with the place it now gives to conscious cultural evolution on the part of man, thus making politics and law two essential and ontological activities – this exactly fits my feelings and long held beliefs. Moreover it fits in with this tour of the world, for nothing less than a world view is meaningful, and by this travel I see the factors which must be brought in to the total concept, at least in their geographical distribution and to some degree in their cultural levels.[48]

Scott's early readings in evolution, his sense of an evolving spirit of man, and his forties internationalism – all were now coming together into the larger concept of "a citizen of the world." The statement, "the world is my country," found in his 1952 poem, "Creed," had now widened into a more specific comment: citizenship in a world community carries with it larger legal and moral overtones.

While Scott had been travelling, absorbing and reflecting on a larger world spirit, events in Montreal had changed drastically. In Europe, he received news that Cyril James had suffered a coronary attack. The old order was changing. In Paris, he received a letter from his good friend David Thomson, Dean of the Faculty of Graduate Studies and Research, informing him the Board of Governors wished him to become McGill's new Dean of Law replacing the late Dean Meredith. Scott's feelings were mixed. If Meredith had not died, he reflected, "I would never have been put into the post everyone seems to think I am so well fitted for." He scribbled a few terse lines on the subject:

> I am not McGill's choice: I am
> something she could not escape.
> She has had greatness thrust upon her.[49]

Scott, likening himself to Shakespeare's Malvolio, displayed a curious satiric mixture of humility and pride.

At Paris, also, he received news that he had been appointed Queen's Counsel by the newly formed Quebec government of Premier Lesage. Again the appointment troubled him. "Everything changes at once! These particular initials I have never wanted; they make me out to be more of a lawyer than I am or even asked to be. Goes back to my sinking of the heart when Willum told me I was to go to McGill and study law back in 1924. Any pretence of being a poet must surely be cast aside if one calls himself a QC! But again, like the Deanship, if it comes and your life is as it is, why not? It's sad, though."[50]

At Oxford yet another link with the past was severed when a cable informed him of the death of his brother Elton. The death itself was not unexpected – Elton, who had been severely gassed during World War I, had recently undergone a difficult operation. It just seemed strange the news should arrive at Oxford, where they had shared digs in 1920-21 and where they had been closest. Elton had influenced Frank greatly, "both in my early childhood, when he taught Arthur and me how to do all the things boys must do and later at Oxford." In later years, as Scott reflected, they lost touch "as he went more churchman and I more layman. Yet it was I in my youth that Father had picked out for the Church, whereas Elton's skill at making and inventing things seemed to mark him out as an engineer. I always thought this was his real bent, whereas – God knows – I have enjoyed preaching!"[51] News of Elton's death brought a crisis of conscience: should he spend his last few days in England or cut short his visit to get back to Canada for the funeral? Scott decided to complete the journey. He salved his conscience by phoning Willum to explain there were still further contacts to be made at the London School of Economics that would be of help to the law faculty at McGill. Four days later, on May 21, the Scotts returned to Canada. "Now what?" Scott wrote. "I don't see at all clearly. One step enough for me."[52]

# TWENTY-ONE

# Committing Deanery

I N THE SPRING OF 1961 Scott took up office as Dean of Law at McGill
to a barrage of congratulations from overseas and from one end of
Canada to the other.[1] He began his duties in a happy glow, modified only
slightly by an inner voice that said he ought not to be doing it. He had
merely three years left to retirement. What good could he possibly do in
that time? Yet the appointment seemed somehow "inevitable." Later in
the decade he explained to Roy St. George Stubbs, an old CCFer and later
a judge, that when the deanship was finally offered he had decided to
accept it "simply to clear the matter away and remove the stain on McGill
which a new Board of Governors was anxious to erase."[2] Scott was being
somewhat disingenuous. The deanship was a vindication of his own position, tangible evidence he had deserved it all along – a point made by
many of his colleagues when they wrote to congratulate him. Eugene
Forsey, for example, considered the appointment "poetic justice rare indeed."[3]

However, he did believe there had been a social revolution at McGill
just as great as that described by Robert Graves in dismissing the war and
the old order of England in *Goodbye to All That* (1929). Scott had a rare
first edition of the book, bought when it came out. Now, in the early
sixties, he wrote his own version, "Goodbye to All That," a piece of
pregnant doggerel dismissing the old order of McGill governors, trustees,
wardens, and overseers.

> Your kind founded us, they built us, we are grateful. That era is past.
> Now we are waving you good-bye.   (*C.P.*, p. 212)

J.W. McConnell was no longer chairman of the Board of Governors; Cyril
James was no longer principal; professors were now taking an active part
in university administration. And F.R. Scott – at long last – was Dean of

359

Law. The old era had been vanquished and the urge to crow a little was irresistible.

> The poor scholars are awake at last. They have seen the new vision.
> They feel in their probing hands the form of the future.
> They know that the evolution of man
> Is shaped by the knowledge they accumulate, test and impart....
>
> You cannot afford to admit the first principle of a university –
> That all truth is relative
> And only the obligation to search for it is absolute.   (C.P., p. 212)

He had some right to brag: the principle to which Scott held – that the function of the university was the search for truth and not its suppression – was valid. But the administration of knowledge was another matter. What if he didn't like being Dean? When he assumed the position he specified he would serve for two years with the third year to be negotiable.

To celebrate Scott's appointment a party was organized by Gerald Le Dain for the McGill law graduates on November 30, 1961. A host of friends and distinguished members of the legal community attended, including Scott's brother William, now Chief Justice of Quebec. In a speech at the dinner Scott put forth his strong belief in the "rule of law," referring to a speech by Abraham Lincoln – "He who bids the law rule, may be deemed to bid God and Reason alone rule, but he who bids man rule adds an element of the beast; for desire is a wild beast, & passion perverts the minds of rulers, even when they are the best of men. The law is reason unaffected by desire." In its widest sense, Scott argued, law is "the state itself, the system of government." Reviewing the distinguished graduates of McGill Law School, beginning with Sir Wilfrid Laurier, Scott outlined the task of a law faculty in training lawyers, in research, in writing, and in community leadership. After an appeal for first-rate men to consider the teaching of law, he then moved to one of his favourite topics – the library at McGill. It had always been his dream to build up the law library; now, as Dean, he urged those members of the bar assembled to support a new building project.[4]

The dinner was a highly emotional gathering. Scott's brother William wrote on December 1, 1961: "*Scripta manent.* I just want to say that it was indeed moving to be present last evening when you received such a warm, spontaneous and well-deserved tribute from the graduates of the McGill Law Faculty."[5] The two brothers were reunited at the dinner when the Chief Justice made a gallant reference to the speech of "my brother Scott," a speech he admitted he could not match, thus implicitly acknowledging the younger man had achieved pre-eminence – both in law and in the family. It was a great turnabout in their relationship. Shortly after, Frank was startled by a telephone call with a gruff inquiry, "Frank, have you seen to your plot?" William Scott, who was planning to be buried with his wife Esther in the Aird family plot in Mount Royal Cemetery, wondered if Frank intended to take his place with the Scotts?[6] Just as if a thirty-three year hiatus had not intervened, William was taking up his old role as responsible elder brother.

Scott's appointment did indeed signal the end of an era. The humorous aspects of the change were recognized by the undergraduates of the McGill Law Society in the spring of 1962 when they wrote a burlesque of Scott's career. Just as the Captain of Gilbert and Sullivan's H.M.S. *Pinafore* had become "Ruler of the Queen's Navy" without "ever having been to sea," so Frank Scott had become McGill's Dean of Law "by thumbing his nose at society."

> I hated capital so heartily
> That they made me the Dean of the Law Faculty....
> So students take a tip from me,
> If renowned Professor you want to be
> If you want to rise to your profession's fore,
> If you want to be a Queen's Counsellor.
>
> (Chorus: If you want to be a Queen's Counsellor).
>
> Just thumb your nose at society
> And you may all be Deans of the Law Faculty.
>
> (Chorus: Just thumb your nose at society,
>          And you may all be Deans of the Law Faculty).[7]

Scott was optimistic as he settled in the Dean's office, the huge living room on the second floor of what had once been the old J.K.L. Ross mansion, now renamed Chancellor Day Hall. There was space for the large Oxford oar over the mantelpiece, for the photographs of Woodsworth and Coldwell on the wall, and for his piles of law books, his CCF pamphlets, and his file cabinets. Scott's formal duties began on June 1 but he was in his office hard at work before then. The sense of political change in Quebec – the Liberals under Premier Jean Lesage in June, 1960, had defeated the Union nationale on a comprehensive reform program – was reflected in Scott's hopes for the law faculty. He began to write to colleagues in the legal profession about plans for innovative programs in legal education in Quebec: "With the new wind blowing in the province, perhaps we could make some progress toward a more liberal program of studies, and one less dominated by Bar regulations."[8]

Scott began his deanship as a popular teacher, probably one of the most popular at McGill; he was excellent when dealing with individuals with whom he felt a rapport. Unfortunately, administration did not bring forth the same response. It confined his creative spirit. In the fifties he had written about the grind of office life in "I Am Employed":

> by my idea of myself. I conceive
> work in an office, so I arrive,
> Hang my coat on a peg, ring for a girl.
> She too is but a thought of herself, though she comes in the flesh,
> and poses a little as she hands me the mail.
> I have a plan of the days activities –
> A to meet, B to write, C to avoid. I obey....
>
> How hard to strike against this management,
> picket one's habits, unionize dreams,
> down tools and march into the thoroughfares
> holding the banner high: UNFAIR TO MYSELF.   (C.P., p. 82)

Scott still disliked office routine and now it tended to make him even more autocratic than usual: he laid down firm rules regarding various situations so that he would not have to be bothered with details. When circumstances inevitably required that his rules be modified, he tended to judge his colleagues and assign blame. He began to run a very tight ship. Professors, who had been accustomed to a certain loosening of the administrative reins during Dean Meredith's illness in the late fifties, now found themselves under sharp control. Not surprisingly, they reacted angrily. One recalled Scott as a Roman Emperor issuing edicts: " 'Caesar' Wright multiplied by three" – that is, an administrator in the old style who would brook no nonsense.[9]

Scott, who had become Dean some two decades later than might have been expected, brought to the office a now outmoded authoritarianism. The students became aware that the "rule of law" was now associated with the Dean's office in quite a new way. One wag described a visit to Scott's huge office as "like going down a corridor that is one yard wide and a mile long."[10] Scott's least attractive quality as an administrator was that he did not inspire ease. He had a habit of drawing himself up to his full six-foot-three and staring icily down at hapless petitioners. There was little patience for those he considered inept. And he had always lacked a facility to pour soothing amounts of oil into the academic machinery. Indeed, he found the normal process of deanery, the placating of opposite sides in a dispute, abhorrent.

Demanding much of others, he demanded more of himself, and the deanship began to take its toll almost at once. Scott took on far more work than he should have and in May, 1962, he became ill and was briefly hospitalized. At that time recurring attacks of tachycardia, which were to dominate the late sixties and seventies, were diagnosed. Scott felt sufficiently ill to cancel a planned trip to England with good friends Jim and Jean Milner of Toronto. He wrote the couple in July admitting he was in "a terrible stew." Looking over his commitments for the summer, he could not imagine taking eighteen days off "without throwing [everything] out of kilter. The very thought of it starts me worrying, and once I start worrying I get into a dreadful state in which almost anything might happen." As Scott explained, he was indeed over-committed:

> I am editor of the Royal Society's volume on "Jargon" this year; I must write a preface and see it through the U. of T. Press. I have to write a chapter for the CAUT book on the Government of Universities. I have a report to make to the Committee which is revising the Japanese constitution. I am seeing my volume of translations through the press. I am supposed to write a report of the Quebec Royal Commission on Education regarding the control of the legal profession over the Law Faculty. I have just completed my annual report on the Law Faculty for the Principal, and have two other committee reports to get ready. Then on top of all this I am senior counsel in a crucially important trade union case.

All of this, he concluded, was his punishment for not obeying the great commandment, " 'Thou shalt not commit Deanery'."[11]

Occasionally, whenever he could escape from the office, Scott would drive up Peel Street to Pine Avenue, turning west, and then up Côte des Neiges Road, up past the ribbed layers of sedimentary rock to the park of Mount Royal, halfway up the mountain, overlooking the city. There, leaning against a parapet of grey square-cut stone, he found wider horizons. Below and to the left in early summer were lilac trees and fragrant honeysuckle; beyond was a small grassy plot with an old lamp post in the middle. Over the green plumes of trees the eye travelled over still more trees, past the city of Montreal to the blue of the St. Lawrence River and the mountains beyond. There Scott felt the exhilarating freedom of moving out into space.

> Every day I go up this hill
> Onto the lonely plateau
> And take off quietly into space.
>
> The traffic and all the trivial sounds
> Fade far away. I mount
> Swiftly, for time is short, flight beckons
> Out where the world becomes worlds, suns pass, galaxies
> Shrink and explode, time bends, and motion,
> A sweep of laws,
> Rolls up all my strength and all
> Into one marvel.
>
> Yet it is always the same. A loved voice, a touch,
> A phone ringing, and the thrust dies.
> Another journey ends where it began
> Shipwrecked on ground we tread a little while.   (C.P., p. 134)

Scott was feeling not only the pressure of events, but also a sense of narrowing time. Jerked back to the office routine – the "shipwreck" of human contact (even loved contact) and office telephones – he was both saddened and testy. Added to the normal duties of Dean were the tasks required of him as chairman of the building committee for a new law building – fund-raising, meetings with committees, and supervising the technical details of the construction. He began to irk some individuals when he adamantly held to the position that it would be better to preserve the stately old mansion in which the law school was housed and add a modern library building to it. Others considered it more sensible to demolish the whole edifice and build a modern school of law.

In addition to his regular duties, Scott had taken on another case involving civil rights, a challenge to the repressive labour legislation, Section 5 of the Labour Relations Amendment Act, enacted in British Columbia by Premier W.A.C. Bennett. This legislation prevented union members from contributing funds to all political parties but was directed at the NDP, which enjoyed union support. While considering this case in Paris for several days during his around-the-world trip, Scott had observed, "This kind of real wedding between con.[stitutional] law, human rights and Canada's future does immensely please me."[12] His involvement with the case had begun in May, 1961, when Thomas Berger, a Vancouver lawyer, wrote to Scott saying he had been retained by the Oil, Chemical and Atomic Workers International Union, Local 16-601, to sue Imperial Oil and test the validity of the legislation. Berger asked Scott to submit his opinion on the constitutional questions of the case,[13] and Scott acted as an adviser on the constitutional issues as it was argued up through the B.C. Supreme Court and the B.C. Court of Appeal.

In March, 1962, when it was obvious it would go all the way to the Supreme Court of Canada, Scott wrote to Berger, "I just don't believe I can win four cases in a row in the Supreme Court. It is contrary to nature."[14] Berger rejected this idea. Both he and his clients agreed only Scott should act as senior counsel. Berger continued humorously, "Anyway I have lost four cases in a row in the Supreme Court and, whether or not this is contrary to nature, I think the law of averages would to some extent operate against the Oil Workers case becoming the fifth loss in a row."[15] Scott stayed on the case but later in April he again wrote to Berger, warning him that as his health had been poor, he must take things easier.[16]

As the year progressed others were drawn in to argue against Section 5: the Canadian Labour Congress, the Ontario Federation of Labour, the Quebec Federation of Labour, and the government of Saskatchewan.[17] The appeal was heard by seven judges on February 11-13, 1963. On October 1 the judgement was handed down and the appeal was dismissed.[18] It seemed the "law of nature" had prevailed.

Although Scott had begun his tenure as Dean of Law with the hope it might be possible to institute new programs, he soon found himself bogged down with administrative details. As time passed, he realized there was little he could do in the short duration of his term and began, instead, to oppose change and innovation. These expectations were opposite to those held by younger members of the full-time faculty. At the outset they had admired Scott and they looked to him for leadership. Now they were badly disappointed. Suggestions for change (such as adding to the course offerings, ordering new books, and allowing law students more options) found Scott unreceptive.[19] Increasingly he fell back on "the bar regulations" as a bastion against innovation. He, who had always disputed these regulations in the past, now became intransigent: "Like a lion at the foot of Gibraltar guarding the Mediterranean against all suggestions of change," as one former colleague recalled.[20]

Not surprisingly, as in his father's tenure in the parish of Drummondville, there soon arose a palace revolt. Several members of the McGill law faculty went to the new principal of McGill, Rocke Robertson, requesting that Scott not be renewed as Dean for the third year. Cooler heads within and without the department prevailed: here was a man who had been treated unjustly by McGill for many years, and these, after all, were minor issues. The matter blew over and the appointment was renewed for a final year. But Scott, who knew of the difficulties, was both hurt and angry. He nursed a grudge against his old colleague Maxwell Cohen, who had been Acting Dean in 1959-60 and was the dissident's candidate as the proper replacement for Scott.

The relationship between the two men, relatively close in the early fifties after Cohen had joined the law faculty in 1946, became strained. Both were fully qualified for the Dean's office and both deserved it. The problem was that the natural succession to the office had been delayed; as a result Scott's tenure came at a time when Cohen could justifiably expect to be made Dean. Then, too, there were differences in personality and in their respective approaches to the teaching of law. Scott, an Oxford product, tended to be personally reserved and succinct in his judgements. Cohen, a product of the American legal system with its emphasis on the case-book method, very probably questioned the relaxed English style of lec-turing, which did not seem to encourage rigorous analysis. In fact, both methods brought excellent results when employed by first-class minds. Ultimately, the differences between the two men were accentuated when the controversy of cutting short Scott's tenure arose and when Cohen, who did eventually succeed Scott as Dean, became actively involved in a visionary new program for reorganizing McGill Law School. This was a four-year program in which students obtain, at the undergraduate level, degrees in both Civil (B.C.L.) and Common (LL.B.) Law. There were advantages to students in having a knowledge of Canada's two law systems. Few lawyers who practise in Quebec deal exclusively with Quebec private law, and a knowledge of another legal system deepens the understanding of one's own legal system. In addition, the program allowed greater mo-bility in Canada for its graduates.[21]

Scott opposed the program, which was again a great disappointment to younger faculty. Angry and disappointed, they did not understand his objections. But he had another agenda. Like several other "civilians," or Civil Law specialists within the Faculty of Law at McGill, he had worked hard to build up the teaching of Civil Law. It now seemed that an am-bitious Common Law program would draw off diminishing funds, and he was bitterly disappointed that some of the foundation money Cohen had acquired for another program did not go directly to the library. A colleague, Donovan Waters, recalled meeting Scott on several occasions in the stacks of the law library; again and again Scott would point to various sets of journals, remarking "this set stopped in the thirties, this set here, this set there."[22] By the mid-sixties he felt increasingly alienated from the law faculty. And it was clear the new teaching program would go ahead, with or without his support.

In 1965 Scott's term as Dean of Law at McGill came to a close. Undoubtedly he was left with the unhappy feeling that he had not been a good Dean. His failure to implement change in the faculty is highly ironic, especially in light of his first intentions and his earlier struggles with former deans and administrators. Despite all his professed beliefs in democracy, Scott remained something of the autocratic Victorian. In part, his character preferred command to consensus: when a statement can be uttered as a request or as a command, Scott, drawing on his past experience of deans and principals, preferred to command.

The difference between the young reformer and the same man in power is too striking to be passed over. In part he had come to the deanship too late and was facing some of the greatest challenges in his life at a period when he was no longer physically able to deal with them. He had driven himself hard during the preceding two decades. His general health was giving way: his memory was not always reliable and the amoebas badly sapped his energy. More importantly, many of his old ideals had rapidly vanished over the horizon; in particular, his belief in the CCF, and later the NDP, as a vehicle for social progress for Canadians could not be supported by the success of the party. Even the few converts the CCF seemed to have made in Quebec, like Trudeau, had moved toward the Liberals. His hopes for Quebec were rapidly dissipating as the Quiet Revolution changed into open revolt.

To what extent did the hippie revolution of the sixties contribute to his disillusionment? He felt he could no longer look to the young for continuity as he had in the forties and fifties. Indeed, he seemed to have felt largely alienated from the young people of the early sixties who derided the old values of "work" and "responsibility" and, later in the decade, from the radicals whose demands for equal representation on academic committees denied the conception of the university as a hierarchy of knowledge.

Or was it that Scott, like many creative individuals, proved not to be a good administrator? He, who could never suffer fools gladly, lacked the patience and tact for equitable administration. As well, he may have been torn between the head and the heart, between the profession of law and what he really wanted to do, which was to write. Then, too, any power, when tied to the realities of office, tends to moderate the idealist? It seems reasonable to conclude that Scott, who came to the Dean's office with hopes for change, also came with a special background in the law faculty based on his own past experience. As a result, his tenure was influenced as much by past considerations – which included the establishing of his own authority and the strengthening of the law library – as by future plans for the faculty. In any event, the long-awaited deanship proved the opposite of his hopes. His prestige among some of his immediate colleagues diminished rather than increased and he seems to have felt a nagging sense of personal failure. It became difficult to keep depression at bay, and the three- and four-martini lunch began to extend the lunch hour into a buoyant post-prandial period followed by a querulous afternoon.

Scott, a man who had lived for his work, was facing not only retirement from the Dean's office but the greater trauma of retirement from McGill. The practice of law was important to him, not only as a chosen vocation, but also, very likely, because it represented psychological control. In a sense, his repeated insistence on the "rule of law" throughout his life was directly proportionate to the depths of his own emotional responses. Only an individual who feared deeply the dangers of emotional *bouleversement* in himself and others could advocate, as strongly as Scott did, the necessity of the rule of law in society. A man of deep feeling, he had integrated his own personality through law. Law was, in effect, the new scripture – the ultimate guide to action.

Now he must leave all this behind. Admittedly there was work still in progress with his appointment to the newly established Royal Commission on Bilingualism and Biculturalism, and he had been invited by Michael Oliver, a member of the Department of Economics and Political Science who had been the moving spirit behind the founding of the French Canada Studies department at McGill, to take part in their program for the coming year. But there was no longer room for him in the law faculty. It was not until several years later that he was provided with a small room, "a broom closet," he snorted, where he might keep a few of his books and continue his professional life.

As he prepared to move out of his office at Chancellor Day Hall, he was swept by a wave of nostalgia for the room – and the life – he must now leave.

Rude and rough men are invading my sanctuary.
They are carting away all my books and papers.
My pictures are stacked in an ugly pile in the corner.

There is murder in my cathedral.

The precious files, filled with yesterday's writing,
The letters from friends long dead, the irreplaceable evidence
Of battles now over, or worse, still in full combat –
    Where are they going? How shall I find them again?

Miserable vandals, stuffing me into your cartons,
This is a functioning office, all things are in order,
Or in that better disorder born of long usage.
    I alone can command it.

I alone know the secret thoughts in these cabinets,
And how the letters relate to the pamphlets in boxes.
I alone know the significance of underlinings
    On the pages read closely.

You scatter these sources abroad, and who then shall use them?
Oh, I am told, they will have a small place in some basement.
Gladly some alien shelves in a distant library
    Will give them safe shelter.

But will there be pictures of J.S. Woodsworth and Coldwell
Above the Supreme Court Reports? The Universal Declaration
Of Human Rights, will it be found hanging
    Near the left-wing manifestos?

And where are the corners to hold all the intimate objects
Gathered over the rich, the incredible years?
The sprig of cedar, the segment of Boulder Dam cable,
The heads of Buddha and Dante, the concretions, the arrowheads,
    Where, where will they be?

Or the clock that was taken from my 1923 air-cooled Franklin?
The cardboard Padlock, a gift from awakened students?
The Oxford oar, the Whitefield Quebec, the Lorcini?
    These cry out my history.

These are all cells to my brain, a part of my total.
Each filament thought feeds them into the process
By which we pursue the absolute truth that eludes us.
    They shared my decisions.

Now they are going, and I stand again on new frontiers.

> Forgive this moment of weakness, this backward perspective.
> Old baggage, I wish you goodbye and good housing.
> I strip for more climbing.   (*C.P.*, pp. 218-19)

Scott is only half joking when he refers to his office as a "sanctuary" and remarks "There is murder in my cathedral." He does see himself as a kind of Saint Thomas à Becket, betrayed and set upon by assassins. The office becomes a central metaphor: it is the history of his past life – the air-cooled Franklin, the pictures of Woodsworth and Coldwell, the cardboard padlock – as well as the means by which thoughts are fed to the brain, thus sustaining his present intellectual life. Without the office the body dies. There is gallantry in his last salute: "Old baggage, I wish you goodbye and good housing. / I strip for more climbing." Scott, the mountaineer, was beginning his final ascent up Mount Royal.

# TWENTY-TWO

# The Tomb of the Kings

❦

EARLY IN DECEMBER, 1966, Scott wrote to Micheline Sainte-Marie, a young poet who had helped with his translations of Quebec poetry. The letter spoke honestly of his fears.

> Great changes loom ahead, with a menacing undertone of something ominous – is it the little forefinger of death? – yet we are too busy to think much about them. Take my case, for instance: what I shall do next year I do not know and can scarcely imagine. Where shall I put myself and all my books and papers that fill a large room at McGill about to be taken from me? I have invitations to be a visiting professor, but that would only last a year and I don't think I could take the removal from accustomed paths. Any intelligent person in my position would be making careful plans; since all my life interesting things have always happened to me without my planning them I just go along like a dog following his master. When the master vanishes, what does the dog do?[1]

Scott had always considered himself a passive agent; he liked to leave matters to providence. Modernizing his father's concept of a guardian angel, he joked about "little hands" – the benevolent workings of the universe that regularly produced from nowhere a parking space, an outlet for his poetry, a biographer.

After speaking of death in his letter, Scott mentioned he had just seen Anne Hébert. The Quebec writer was in Montreal to supervise production of a play. "Now she is back in Paris working on a novel. A life dedicated to writing because, I think, of early tragedy."[2] The connection between death, Hébert, and early tragedy was firmly linked in Scott's mind. When he first met Hébert in the early fifties, she had told Scott of her childhood fear of English Canadians. Sometimes, when passing a certain bridge, she had been admonished by the nuns who taught her, "Look, this is the road to Ottawa." The image was dark and menacing. Scott was so struck by the anecdote that he promptly wrote it down and put the scribbled note in a file he labelled "régime en peur."[3]

He had a similar reaction when he first met, in 1942, the poet Hector de Saint-Denys Garneau, Hébert's cousin. In Garneau's *Journal* Scott had recognized an "anguished" sensibility, one shaped by a monolithic Roman Catholic society. He had a strong sense of what this meant; his early readings of Foxe's *Book of Martyrs* made him especially sensitive to the tormented religious mind.

In the mid-fifties, as a result of his friendship with Pierre Emmanuel (who had written the introduction to Anne Hébert's *Le Tombeau des rois* in 1954), Scott began to meet regularly with small groups of French- and English-language poets invited to his home. Scott by this time had established an easy familiarity with Francophone poets and poetry and despite the language problems – there were unilinguals in both languages – lively communication took place. In 1955, when A.J.M. Smith had been invited to prepare a new anthology, *The Oxford Book of Canadian Verse*, he had written to Scott for advice. He suggested Smith should start with "my young friends around the *Cité Libre* magazine" and offered numerous ideas on who should be included and emphasized.[4]

Scott had also met Quebec poets on a more formal basis. He had been invited to the first of the annual Rencontres des Poètes Canadiens held in September, 1957, and organized by Jean-Guy Pilon. This first meeting was at the Maison Montmorency, just below Quebec City, where the Scott family had often picnicked so many years before. Among a number of special sessions was one on "Poetry and Language." Quebec poets Jacques Brault, Gilles Constantineau, Roland Giguère, Gilles Hénault, Gaston Miron, Yves Préfontaine, and Gilles Vigneault attended.[5] Scott, who had been translating Quebec poetry since the early fifties, was the only Anglophone present. This prompted Jean Bruchési, then Undersecretary of State and Deputy Registrar for Quebec (which had helped finance the conference), to greet Scott "with the cheery – and somewhat revealing – salutation, 'Quoi, vois êtes le seul paien ici'?"[6] In terms of the old Quebec Catholicism, Scott, a "Protestant," was indeed the only pagan or outsider at the conference. Yet, in ways Bruchési could not recognize, Scott had many affinities with the Catholic poets present.

The second Rencontre des Poètes Canadiens was held the following year at Morin Heights, near Montreal. This time a number of Anglophones attended, among them Doug Jones, Jay Macpherson, and Scott Symons, later to write *Place d'Armes*. Scott was invited to speak. Macpherson has dim recollections of being "at the back of a crowded, smokey, low-ceilinged room & seeing Frank and someone else holding forth up front – [Jean-Guy] Pilon possibly? ... Much envied Scott's amphibiousness I do remember."[7] At this gathering Scott spoke about his own poetic impulse.

> Why do I write poetry? Because I feel something inside me urging me to write. A voice which keeps saying "You should write, you should write, you should write." I have not paid much attention to that voice; actually I have spent more time in my life playing the piano than I have writing poems. The necessity of earning a living, and interest in other things, have taken me away from poetry. Yet the voice persists....
>
> Because of this inner voice, writing poetry has always been for me a kind of discharge of accumulated energy. As the poem is coming to the surface and before it is written I feel uncomfortable and heavy with responsibility, like an angry cloud; in writing, this new and curious thing grows before your eyes, takes on shape and character, draws off the current of the imagination, brings release and calm. More than that, it opens new roads to truth, gives new insights and understandings about man, society and the gods. Sometimes it brings ecstasy – "cet élan pour éclater dans l'Au Dèla." Who would not want to write poetry?

"Translation," he told the assembled poets, "is at least a valuable poetic exercise, at best a creative act." However desirable it might be that all Canadians should be able to read French and English, translation between the English and French literature in Canada was certainly essential. "Though I have lived in Quebec all my life and may perhaps claim to know something of the spirit and meaning of French Canada, no experience has been so rewarding for me in this respect as my endeavours to render into English certain poems of contemporary Quebec poets. Besides," he added, "it has brought me the inestimable advantage of meeting the poets themselves."[8]

It was the meeting between Scott and the Francophone poets that most struck Doug Jones. In the middle of the plenary session there was extended discussion of the problems of the Quebec poet as a minority. Jones was conscious of a sense of isolation, of frustration and alienation among the French-speaking writers. "Depression ... was so thick there you could cut it with a knife.... The sense that people had been castrated was almost literally evident in the air, in the way people were talking ..." Scott stood up and, speaking in French, made some comments prefaced by the observation that he spoke for the minority among the minorities. "... It was very nicely phrased, with this tall man in the middle of this whole group ...

who were proclaiming their minority. Here was a member of the majority coming in to say he was a minority, [part of the] English minority." Yet he also saw Scott as a mediator "creating an ambience in which people could say whatever it was they had to say that they thought was important to say and maybe wouldn't say to a half-a-dozen other people ... given that ambience [they] would speak."

Jones also retained two other images from the conference. After taking a walk with Scott and four or five others after midnight, almost blind, down a road in the Laurentians he was conscious of "Frank's sense of the Laurentians out there." Later, after listening to and observing Anne Hébert, he had a sudden insight of her as a surgeon for whom "words are arrayed like surgical instruments ... probing" the psyche.[9]

Jones's association of Scott with the wilderness and his perception of Hébert dissecting the psyche represent in a generalized way two opposing tendencies in modern poetry in Canada. English-Canadian poets are most often concerned with external space while many French-Canadian poets are primarily fascinated by inner space. Thus, when actively translating poetry from French, as Scott did throughout the fifties, he was also exploring this inner psychological space. In the past he had concerned himself with the externals of Quebec law and society; now he looked inwardly to the Quebec psyche, to a character structure he somewhat shared.

Providence or "little hands" had brought Saint-Denys Garneau and Anne Hébert into Scott's orbit, and providence (now in the form of greater contact with Francophone poets) encouraged him to continue. Gael Turnbull, who occasionally came to the Montreal poetry group and collaborated on translations with a teacher from Iroquois Falls, Jean Beaupré, published *Eight Poems* (1955), a translation of Roland Giguère's work. Turnbull had hoped to include Hébert, but she withheld permission since Scott,[10] who had earlier translated "La Fille maigre" and "En guise de fête" for *Northern Review* in 1952, had started a translation of "Le Tombeau des rois," a poem that was to fascinate him for over thirty years.

He sent his first fifties translation of the poem to Hébert. She wrote back suggesting certain aspects of his rendering did not agree with her conception of the poem. For example, the first two lines of the original had read:

> J'ai mon coeur au poing
> Comme un faucon aveugle.

The first Scott translation was:

> I hold my heart in my clenched hand
> Like a blind falcon.

The dialogue between the two poets continued:

ANNE HEBERT — *in my clenched hand*: l'oiseau est ici comme écrasé dans la main, au lieu d'être porté sur le poing comme le faucon à la chasse.

FRANK SCOTT — You bring out a point my version had obscured, namely the fact that the bird is free to leave the hand of its own volition. It is "on" rather than "in" the fingers. Yet in line 3 the phrase *pris à mes doigts* suggests also that it is perhaps fastened to the hand, caught as it were by its talons. I have suggested this by using *held on*.

Nouvelle version: I BEAR MY HEART ON MY FIST.[11]

This translation together with the correspondence appeared in 1960 in *Ecrits du Canada Français*, together with an explanatory note by Jeanne Lapointe.

After the poem appeared in *Ecrits*, Scott recorded he had "met Anne Hébert (it was the evening Frère Untel appeared on television) and had the rare pleasure of going over with her personally the supposedly final draft. We agreed on 10 more changes."[12] These changes were incorporated into the poem and this version was published, again with the correspondence with Hébert, in *The Tamarack Review* in 1962. Scott's rather stiff, literal translation of the opening line now becomes more fluently colloquial:

> I have my heart on my fist
> Like a blind falcon.[13]

Eventually the whole correspondence between the two Quebec poets appeared as a book, *Dialogue sur la traduction: à propos du 'Tombeau des rois'* (1970), with an introduction by Jeanne Lapointe and a preface by Northrop Frye. There Frye comments, "Scott went directly to the real meaning, the imagistic and metaphorical meaning of what he was translating: this caused Mlle Hébert to think long and deeply about the real meaning of her poem." He also notes Scott's tendency toward exact rendition: "every one of Mr. Scott's improvements is a step toward a more literal rendering."[14]

Describing the process of translation, Scott later remarked that "to translate means to take words and phrases out of the space they occupy in the original composition, and to replace them with other words and phrases that have never quite the same shape or size or sound or meaning. Try as one will, the round hole is never wholly filled by the square peg of another language."[15] The greater the poem, the more it resists translation, yet the more likely it is to be worth reading – even in translation. Scott persisted in his attempts to find precise equivalents for the French text; in 1978 for a second edition of the book he had further "corrections" to make. Later, just before his final illness in 1984, he was still making changes. This desire for accuracy reflected, in part, his legal training, but Scott may have felt also that in penetrating to the precise meaning of the poem he was penetrating to the heart of the society it symbolized. In this sense the poem recapitulated his own political experience in Quebec. Beyond this it appears to have resonated with symbols that particularly evoked aspects of his own psychic and poetic life.

By chance, providence speeded Scott's work on Anne Hébert's poem. On January 2, 1961, W.C. McConnell of Klanak Press in Vancouver re-minded him: "We would very much like to bring out a good translation of representative poems by some of the younger French-Canadian poets, who apart from the remarks of Pilon and a few others, are practically unknown here"; nor, he suspected, was the West "any different from Toronto or English-speaking Montreal in this respect." Scott was his first choice as editor and translator, but if he could not take on the task himself, perhaps he could recommend someone?[16]

The initial request had come when Scott was starting his around-the-world trip. He was at first reluctant, doubting his own capacity; ultimately, however, he assented and a lively correspondence between the two men ensued. It was finally decided the volume would contain only the poems of Saint-Denys Garneau and Anne Hébert, it would be a bilingual edition, and the design and typography would be the finest possible. To ensure this result, McConnell engaged the artist Takao Tanabe to design the book and Morriss Printing Company of Victoria, well known for its fine pro-ductions, to print it.[17]

*Saint-Denys Garneau & Anne Hébert: Translations/Traductions* appeared in 1962 with a preface by Gilles Marcotte and a translator's note by Scott, which explained he had translated the anthologized poems because he thought them "representative of the best work of the two French-Canadian poets I most admire." His principal aim in translating was "to alter the poem as little as possible, and to let it speak for itself in the other tongue. This means a preference for literalness rather than for alternate renderings: for one poem in two languages, instead of two similar poems."[18]

George Whalley, reviewing the book on the CBC program *Critically Speaking*, was highly enthusiastic about the quality of the translation. "So

readable are Scott's English versions, so devoid of the inexact inflations
to which the translator easily falls prey, so evidently turned word for word
from the original that the reader is tempted to take this beautifully designed
and printed book for a do-it-yourself translating kit and make confident
suggestions for improvement. The translucency," Whalley concluded, "is
deceptive."[19] John Glassco had a similar reaction. "You make the work of
rendering these difficult poems seem so deceptively simple – and yet I feel
as if I had never before read them with such a full understanding of their
*essential* meaning. What is their very *own*." The book, he added, "is really
as much a revelation of your own genius as it is of Garneau's & Anne
Hébert's, and I hope everyone realizes it. For me, it is truly a landmark.
The absolute fidelity to the poetry itself, the suppression of any self-ness,
has made me quite ashamed of my own efforts in the same line."[20]

There was a certain logic in publishing Garneau and Hébert in a single
book; not only were they first cousins but there was an affinity in their
work, in the theme of the artist as exile in a static and repressive Canadian
society and as a rebel against religious upbringing. This concept, as A.J.M.
Smith's talk at the Kingston Conference had shown, was one shared by
English-Canadian poets. It was more strongly accentuated in Quebec,
because of the extent of ecclesiastical control of Quebec society and because
exile was a recurrent theme of the French surrealists, symbolists, and
existentialists, who had strongly influenced the Quebec literary world.

But it was Hébert's "Le Tombeau des rois" that most intrigued Scott.
The power the poem exerted on his own imagination may have resided
in an affinity between the perceptions of two poets who had been raised
in Quebec in a fundamentally Catholic tradition, a "régime en peur" as
he had labelled the file containing Hébert's anecdote of her childhood. In
his early Anglo-Catholicism, as in Hébert's Jansenism, an overwhelming
sense of original sin, a belief in confession and the ritual of the mass, and,
above all, a sense of the primacy of the spirit over the body had engendered
in Scott both a repressed sexuality and a determination to revolt against
such constraints. "Le Tombeau des rois," which sought to erase the divisions between body and spirit and to throw off the old repressive Catholicism, was thus magnetic to Scott. What's more, the poem may have
evoked symbols resonant of his own childhood tragedy, Harry's death, a
tragedy long repressed by his conscious mind.

In Hébert's poem (here in Scott's translation) the protagonist descends
into the underworld of the tomb where she is described in images suggestive of the crucified, the sacrifice of the mass, and the risen Christ.

I carry my heart on my fist
Like a blind falcon.

The taciturn bird gripping my fingers
A swollen lamp of wine and blood
I go down
Toward the tombs of the kings
Astonished
Scarcely born.

What Ariadne-thread leads me
Along the muted labyrinths?
The echo of my steps fades away as they fall.

(In what dream
Was this child tied by her ankle
Like a fascinated slave?)

The maker of the dream
Pulls on the cord
And my naked footsteps come
One by one
Like the first drops of rain
At the bottom of a well.

Already the odour stirs in swollen storms
Seeps under the edges of the doors
Of chambers secret and round
Where the folding beds are laid out.

The motionless desire of the sculptured dead lures me.
I behold with astonishment
Encrusted upon black bones
The blue stones gleaming.

A few tragedies patiently wrought
Lying on the breast of sleeping kings
As if they were jewels
Are offered me
Without tears or regrets.

In single rank arrayed:
The smoke of incense, the cake of dried rice,
And my trembling flesh:
A ceremonial and submissive offering.

A gold mask on my absent face
Violet flowers for eyes,
The shadow of love paints me in small sharp strokes,
And this bird I have breathes
And complains strangely.

A long tremor
Like a wind sweeping from tree to tree,
Shakes the seven tall ebony Pharaohs
In their stately and ornate cases.

It is only the profundity of death which persists,
Simulating the ultimate torment
Seeking its appeasement
And its eternity
In a faint tinkle of bracelets
Vain rings, alien games
Around the sacrificed flesh.

Greedy for the fraternal source of evil in me
They lay me down and drink me;
Seven times I know the tight grip of the bones
And the dry hand that seeks my heart to break it.

Livid and satiated with the horrible dream
My limbs freed
And the dead thrust away from me, assassinated,
What glimmer of dawn strays in here?
What then makes this bird quiver
And turn toward morning
Its blinded eyes?   (*C.P.*, pp. 332-34)

"Greedy for the fraternal source of evil in me / They lay me down and drink me": the protagonist, the body, becomes the spirit or offering. As her blood is drunk by the dead kings, described in images suggesting a perverse mingling of the spiritual and the sexual, the poem becomes a black mass. Like the traditional mass, the black mass offers spiritual recovery, the "glimmer of dawn," even though the bird, the spirit, is blinded. In this poem the closed chamber, the sense of spiritual and sexual repression, echoing Sartre's theme of "No Exit," is given a uniquely Quebec context, symbolizing a static and imprisoning society that crucifies the artist (as indeed it crucified Garneau) and from which he or she *can* emerge, but maimed.

For Scott, as for Hébert in this poem, the subject of death was always obsessive. So many of his poems are elegies – "For R.A.S. 1925-1943," "On the Death of Gandhi," "On Watching Margaret Dying," "Epitaph," "For Bryan Priestman," "For Pegi Nicol," "Bedside," and "Last Rites." Even "W.L.M.K.," his best-known satiric verse, is an epitaph. Scott sometimes writes of death in terms of literary myth ("Finis the Cenci") or fertility myth ("The Spring Virgin Cries at Her Cult"), but more often he reworks the traditional Christian cycle of death and resurrection. In "March Field," written in the thirties, he identifies Christ's body (and, by implication, his own body also) with the land:

> There is a warm wind, stealing
> From blunt brown hills, loosening
> Sod and cold loam
> Round rigid root and stem.
>
> But no seed stirs
> In this bare prison
> Under the hollow sky.
>
> The stone is not yet rolled away
> Nor the body risen.   (C.P., p. 45)

Here the earth carries sexual as well as religious overtones; Scott is offering a modern version of the Easter myth shaped by his reading of Sir James Frazer's *The Golden Bough*. In later poems, such as "Calvary" and "Resurrection," the figure of the crucified Christ fascinates him. The continued lesson of mankind, especially for would-be saviours (as, perhaps, for would-be social reformers), is the utter impossibility of their task, "The vision beyond reach / Becomes the grave of each" (C.P., p. 190). Despite this, however, it is this divine spirit, or impulse, in man that Scott celebrates.

> And that of him which rose
> Is our own power to choose
> Forever, from defeat,
> Kingdoms more splendid yet.   (C.P., p. 190)

Not only did "Le Tombeau des rois" express the same metaphysical concerns that had so often preoccupied Scott – death and the relation of the spirit to the body – but Hébert saw Quebec society as he did. Indeed, "Le Tombeau des rois" has been described as "national allegory" by some critics of Quebec literature because it so perfectly symbolizes an individual fascinated and trapped by the dead past. In the poem the young serving girl, compelled or fascinated, descends into the tomb of the past where she is raped by the seven dead pharaohs. The turning point of the poem comes implicitly, rather than explicitly, in the recognition that it is the past, the dead, or ancestral giants who pull the strings, reduce one's life to a merely instrumental one. Doug Jones remarked of the poem that the girl has, as it were, paid her dues, served the dead kings. She has also recognized this and begins to heed her own impulses and desires, if not clearly and articulately (since the "eye" of introspection is "crevé") then at least by registering light as opposed to dark, a feeling for life as opposed to death. She thus can turn away from the past to start living her own life.[21]

Moreover, the symbols of the poem (especially the reference to the dead hand of the past, which reaches out to grasp the living) may have resonated with Scott because they evoked his own childhood tragedy – the death of his brother Harry at the Somme in 1916. It is possible Scott responded to the symbols of Hébert's poem without fully understanding why. Like his father's report of the search for Harry's body and his symbolic descent into the grave to perform the Anglo-Catholic service for the dead, or Scott's own poem "Recovery" (about digging for Mrs. Miller's body during World War II), "Le Tombeau des rois" depicts a descent into the tomb. Moreover, the descent ultimately seeks to reorient the living in terms of spiritual resurrection. For Canon Scott and the older generation, the ritual magic of the old faith sustained life. For Scott and Hébert, new metaphors that reshaped the old religion into a new creed were vital. Thus, in his own poem "Resurrection," Scott celebrated the divinity of man:

> Play Easter to this grave
> No Christ can ever leave.
> It is one man has fallen,
> It is ourselves have risen.   (*C.P.*, p. 190)

In support of this reading of Hébert's "Le Tombeau des rois," it is worth noting that in Scott's first translation, which Hébert objected to, as the critic Kathy Mezei points out, he completely ignored the feminine gender in "Cette enfant fut-elle liée par la cheville." He translated it:

> (In what dream
> Was this child tied by the ankle
> Like a fascinated slave?)[22]

Did Scott so identify with the protagonist of the Hébert poem that the clearly feminine persona is given the possibility of being a young boy? In

382 / THE POLITICS OF THE IMAGINATION

any event, on Hébert's request the child became female with a new trans-lation referring to "her ankle."

In retrospect, one might hazard a guess this complex of images was central to Scott's psychological makeup. In November, 1975, when he was facing a serious operation after a severe heart attack, brought on by the strain of attempting to fight Quebec's newly enacted language bills, he spoke of that legacy of duty, "the dead hand of the past," as he called it, which forced him to strive far beyond his capacity. As he said, using a central image from "Le Tombeau des rois," "something has me by the ankle and won't let go."[23]

In his letter to Micheline Sainte-Marie, Scott links death, Anne Hébert, and early tragedy when he mentions the "little forefinger of death." In this beckoning image is Scott's consciousness of his own mortality. More-over, the collocation of "death" and a little "finger" evokes F.G. Scott's description of his search for Harry's grave and his recognition of the body when he unearthed his hand wearing the Scott family ring on his "little finger." The legacy of duty and responsibility, the "dead hand of the past" symbolized by the ring, was assumed by Frank, then sixteen. He had written to Canon Scott saying he knew he must spend the rest of his life doing something worthwhile to make up for Harry's death.[24] Not sur-prisingly, Scott repressed this memory when the letters describing the incident disappeared into the family files, but the theme of death was to pervade his poetry.

After publication of *St-Denys Garneau & Anne Hébert*, and indicative of his growing involvement with both French and English poetry in Que-bec, Scott worked with John Glassco and Louis Dudek, in 1963, to organize the Foster Poetry Conference. Although it was meant to be a conference to bring together English and French poets in Quebec, the conference, held in West Bolton in the Eastern Townships, consisted only of English participants. Because of emerging separatist violence the Quebec govern-ment, which had agreed to fund the conference, had held up financing until all participants could be scrutinized. Consequently, no French poets were able to attend.[25]

It was not until 1977 that Scott again became actively involved in French poetry in Quebec. That year, he published an anthology of translations, *Poems of French Canada*, with Blackfish, a small press in British Columbia. It included an introduction in which Scott discussed his career as a trans-lator of Quebec poetry. The period from 1945 to 1965, he remarked, was one of profound change in Quebec in which the old and monolithic social and religious order gave way to a new industrialized society and mass communications. The French-Canadian poets, who exposed a tradition that had become repressive and dogmatic, appealed to Scott's own basic convictions. In translating their work he was celebrating the fact that they, too, were sweeping away the darkness of the Duplessis era to bring in the Quiet Revolution. And it was, above all, a revolution.[26] As Scott's translation of Roland Giguère's "Polar Season" puts it: "Silently, we sought a new horizon on which to find a foothold for a new life, to start all over again, to re-invent everything beginning with ourselves."[27] With this revolution Scott could intellectually agree, for it was "largely internal and not yet aggressively nationalistic or politically indépendantiste."[28]

With these poems, also, Scott the poet recognized an emotional affinity. And, up to the time of his final illness, he continued his translation:

> I have my heart in my hand
> Like a blind falcon ...

# TWENTY-THREE

# The Royal Commission on Bilingualism and Biculturalism

❦

I had the feeling ... Canadians were capable of analyzing their problems with sympathy and genuine desire to find a solution. I also believe that while sympathy for Quebec is evident amongst most people who are given a chance to think about its position, there is a profound underlying feeling, not often outwardly expressed, that the country called Canada is very much worth maintaining as an independent single state, with its bilingual and bicultural character and its various other ethnic groups not obliged to absorb their whole personality in a larger community.

(B and B Journal, 23-25 March 1964)

O NE OF THE FIRST casualties of the revolution is the revolutionary[1] – so runs a wise and witty French maxim. By 1963-64, Frank Scott was beginning to realize the truth of this aphorism. He was no longer close to the Quebec intelligentsia. The new Liberal Premier, Jean Lesage, was bringing about the Quiet Revolution with the help of young Francophone progressives like René Lévesque and Pierre Laporte. Anglophones were no longer needed, especially when the cry "maîtres chez nous" yielded to the more strident voices of younger radicals calling for "Québec libre." Forces of moderation were still present, but they were now working behind the scenes, some at Ottawa. Maurice Lamontagne, now special adviser to newly elected Prime Minister Lester Pearson, was influential in persuading him to implement a special inquiry to help dispel Quebec unrest. In the spring of 1963, Scott was asked to become a member of the Royal Commission on Bilingualism and Biculturalism.

The idea of a fact-finding commission had originated with an editorial by the journalist André Laurendeau in *Le Devoir*. In it, he challenged English Canada to stop offering piecemeal solutions to the problems of

Quebec and to institute a Royal Commission on Bilingualism. "At stake is the French language, the language spoken by nearly a third of the population of Canada. At stake is the participation of nearly a third of Canadian people in the life and administration of the central government."[2] The proposed commission would have three objectives: to find out what Canadians from coast to coast thought of bilingualism; to ascertain how countries like Belgium and Switzerland had dealt with the same problem; and to examine the role played by two languages in the federal civil service.

When called to an informal discussion with Maurice Lamontagne at the home of Jean Marchand, Laurendeau enlarged on what he thought should be the terms of reference for the Commission, and a new concept, biculturalism, was added. The mandate for the Commission eventually read:

> [the Commission is] to inquire into and report upon the existing state of bilingualism and biculturalism in Canada and to recommend what steps should be taken to develop the Canadian Confederation on the basis of an equal partnership between the two founding races, taking into account the contribution made by other ethnic groups to the cultural enrichment of Canada and the measures that should be taken to safeguard that contribution.[3]

A. Davidson Dunton, president of Carleton University, was appointed English co-chairman of the Commission with Laurendeau, but it was, in fact, Laurendeau's Commission. The other members were selected because of regional, linguistic, and party affiliations with an eye to a balance reflecting the composition of Canada. There were four French, four English, and two "Others." When Scott arrived at the first meeting in Ottawa on September 4-5, 1963, he was pleased to find that he knew three of the French members well enough to call them by their first names. He had worked with Laurendeau in French-English study groups off and on since the forties; he had offered legal help to Marchand at the time of the Asbestos strike and, occasionally, since then.[4] He was on friendly terms with Jean-Louis Gagnon, a newspaperman and *bon vivant* originally from Quebec City. The only unknown entity among the French was Father Cormier, a priest from Moncton, New Brunswick. Of him Scott had heard "good reports."[5]

Of the English commissioners, Scott knew Davidson Dunton as editor of the *Montreal Herald* and later through the CBC. He reserved judgement on Gertrude Laing, a French teacher from Calgary, and Royce Frith, a lawyer with a broadcasting background. Laing, Scott noted with approval, was attractive and Frith "tall [with] rather aquiline features."[6] As the meeting proceeded, Scott saw that Frith was informed and articulate, and that Laing, who spoke excellent French, gave a western dimension to their discussions. J.B. Rudnyckyj, a Ukrainian from the University of Manitoba, and Paul Wyczynski, a Pole teaching French-Canadian literature at the University of Ottawa, were new Canadians representing the ethnic minorities. Rudnyckyj recalled an amusing exchange with Scott over their newness. "Frank asked us jokingly what would have happened to us if we, after [a] few years of stay in 'another country,' would have tried to change its constitution? 'Where would you land?' – asked Frank, thinking of Siberia. I recall my reply very exactly: 'This is why we came to Canada, Frank'."[7]

Nevertheless, there was some truth to Donald Creighton's indignant observation that no one had been appointed to the Commission to represent English Canada.[8] Certainly all the English-speaking commissioners spoke for Canada, yet the dynamics of the group was such that their roles were directed toward differing constituencies. Dunton, the English co-chairman, was responsible for the internal co-ordination of the Commission and externally for public relations – the difficult task of explaining the Commission's aims to English Canada. Frith, one of the younger members, was junior as a representative of English Canada.[9] He had been chosen, Pearson told Scott on the phone, because he spoke reasonable French. This was a great advantage, Pearson added, since trying to find a member of the family compact in Toronto who could speak French was utterly impossible. Scott recognized the implications of this remark at once: if Frith "was not a member of the family compact in Toronto ... [he] probably could not speak for that great solid lump or heart of English Canada which is as much a basic fact of our national life as the Catholic core of Quebec is."[10] And Laing, chosen to represent the West, proved to be an ardent Francophile. At one point, when she endorsed sweeping suggestions from a Commission member for constitutional change desired by Quebec, Frith leaned over to whisper in Scott's ear, "Boy, are we in trouble!"[11] Scott copied the remark in the journal he kept for the Commission meetings. In fact, as three of the five Francophone members of the Commission later recalled, the split in the Commission was not what one would expect. Laing, Frith, and sometimes Dunton could be expected to be sympathetic to the Quebec cause; for many English-Canadian small "l" liberals of the sixties, there was a strong sense that the French of Quebec had been badly treated and that only sweeping reforms could remedy past injustice. Scott agreed with the first premise, but his adherence to the second was qualified by his concern for the English minority in Quebec.

Not surprisingly, several of the French-speaking members of the Commission were more sympathetic to the federalist vision of Canada that Scott advocated. He, in turn, wrote affectionately of Marchand, whom he found "a wonderful companion," and of Father Cormier and Jean-Louis Gagnon. Marchand and Gagnon, now established Liberals, were known federalists. And Father Cormier spoke for the Acadian French of New Brunswick as well as the French of Manitoba. A humorous element underlining Scott's belief that the English minority in Quebec were not adequately represented on the Commission surfaced when he complained testily that whereas the French were represented by briefs from such institutions as the St. Jean Baptiste Society and the Knights of Columbus, there was no institution to represent English Canada. "I'll trade you the St. Jean Baptiste Society for the Royal Bank of Canada any day," riposted Gagnon.[12]

Laurendeau was faced with the difficult task of holding the Commission together. As a man who had begun his life as a strong nationalist, he sympathized with the nationalist cause; but as a cosmopolitan, a product of a European education, he also perceived that Quebec must find its place within a larger world. He was not a Liberal; indeed, he distrusted that party. However, a belief in the federal system had been consolidated during a mid-fifties trip across Canada when he made many friends, both Francophone and Anglophone, especially in western Canada. From then on, his concern for Quebec autonomy, which included the possibility of constitutional reform, was balanced by his concern for the French who lived outside Quebec.

Laurendeau, the Commission's intellectual leader, was committed to a tightrope equipoise between separatism and federalism. Initially he had been reluctant to co-chair the Commission, but now that he had committed himself to the task he was determined to see it through. Tall and frail, he was also gentle in manner. Several members of the Commission saw him as an artist – the Proustian artist in his manifest ill health and his desire to be both descriptive and precise. It was partly the way he looked and the way he held his cigarette: "his hands ... the way he smoked, he had a way of looking at the world, I suppose, through a smoke screen ... or shielding behind it.... You felt that he was a very soft man, tender man, and that the kind of fight he had been leading since the early forties ... was not the real Laurendeau."[13]

During the war, Laurendeau had been leader of La Ligue pour la défense du Canada and had campaigned vigorously against conscription. In 1942 he helped found the Bloc populaire canadien and was briefly a member of the Quebec legislature. It was at McGill he had met Scott. During the fifties, Gérard Filion and Laurendeau, as editors of *Le Devoir*, had led the fight against the increasingly corrupt Duplessis administration; they had also defended Quebec autonomy against growing encroachment by Ottawa. Laurendeau thus was both experienced and battle-scarred. Behind the gentleness perceived by colleagues on the Commission lay an integrity of purpose combined with extreme vulnerability. He was determined to produce a report both English and French Canada could support.

Laurendeau's aim of equal partnership for Quebec necessitated agreement between the diverse views of French and English as represented on the Commission. When Jean Marchand resigned and Paul Lacoste – formerly a co-secretary to the Commission – was recommended as his replacement, Laurendeau told the other commissioners that if Lacoste, whose views were identifiably nationalist, were appointed as a commissioner, it would relieve him of the necessity of presenting this view himself.[14] Lacoste eventually came to believe that when he spoke of Quebec's political and constitutional aspirations, he was also speaking for Laurendeau.[15] On the other hand, when it was first proposed that Lacoste replace Marchand, Scott was alarmed. Lacoste, he felt, "had a thorn in his soul." He seemed to be advocating what amounted to an associate status for Quebec; nor was he willing to recognize the amount of time that would be required to bring English Canada around. Scott was mollified only by Laurendeau's explanation that the more extreme Quebec position needed to be represented. Reconciliation often involved finding an acceptable compromise between individuals like Scott and Lacoste who were literally embodiments of the polar opposites in the Canadian confederacy. Lacoste later recalled that Laurendeau's most frequently repeated aim was to find a resolution in which "the minimum that one side would accept would not exceed the maximum that the other would be willing to grant."[16]

There was a further difficulty because, as well as emphasizing the relationship between the two founding nations, French and English, the mandate also sought an accommodation with other ethnic groups. But what should this be? How could one stress the two major language groups without antagonizing other minorities who felt that an unfair "racial aristocracy" was being established in a country they had always understood to be English?

Despite his English-Quebec credentials, Scott was perhaps the essential English Canadian in the subsequent debates. He *did* speak for that solid core of English Canada that could not conceive of Confederation as other than an historical union between separate colonies in British North America, a union that made certain provisions for the continuance of French language and religion. His willingness to concede only up to a certain point – language rights for Quebec, yes, but language rights for the minority English in Quebec also – augmented by his socialist belief in the necessity of a strong central government (for only such, he believed, could deal with the complexities of the modern world and the dangers to national sovereignty of the multinational corporations) made him a formidable opponent to Quebec's demands for increasing autonomy. Thus he opposed attempts by some commissioners to move toward political and constitutional recommendations. Doing so, he insisted, was not part of their mandate.

His conception of Canada as a federal state in which French, as the language of one of the two founding nations, should receive equal consideration (though not at the expense of federalism itself) was not to find favour among all members of the Commission. And, as so often happens, this position affected the dynamics of the group. When one strong member of a group becomes identified with a specific position, other members, even when they agree with him, feel it unnecessary to add their weight to the argument. Consequently, Scott frequently felt alone when arguing the case for Canada.

Initially, he had had high hopes for the Commission. The individual commissioners enjoyed one another's company, the witty exchanges, the heady sense of being part of another cultural world. And several had caught a glimpse of a vision of Canada. After the first public meetings of the Commission, held in Ottawa on November 7-8, 1963, Scott had lunch with Jean-Louis Gagnon and Father Cormier. The trio discovered that they had been greatly moved during the morning sessions "at the feeling that there was a great potentiality in the country, and by the possibility that our work might come to some fruitful results. We had seen emerging glimpses of something that might be called Canada."[17]

Representatives from seventy-six organizations, including two provincial governments, ethnic groups, the media, the civil service, universities, business, labour unions, political parties, and the arts, attended those first public meetings, commented on the meaning of the terms of reference, and suggested how the Commission should proceed. Scott knew at least two former Montrealers among the group, Burton Keirstead, formerly a political science professor at McGill and now at the University of Toronto, who spoke emotionally of Canada, this country "we all love,"[18] and Pierre Trudeau, then in Prime Minister Pearson's office. Michael Oliver, soon to be appointed director of research for the Commission, was also present.

He recalled the gist of Trudeau's advice to the Commission: "You must take a narrow view of what you are doing. Do not get into the constitutional questions. Do not get into the federal-provincial relations questions. Deal with language. Deal with cultural relations. That is what your mandate is, should be."[19]

Scott, Gagnon, and Cormier also recognized that the Commission needed a more definite plan of action to focus the audience's response during the coming months. Gagnon and Royce Frith, both experienced with the media, were to prove helpful in developing this audience response. Their procedures were dictated by the shape of Canada itself; to reach as many people as possible, it was decided to hold regional meetings throughout the country. From March 18 to June 16, 1964, twenty-three regional meetings were held across Canada, from St. John's, Newfoundland, to Victoria, British Columbia. The Commission met a staggering total of approximately 11,800 people. The format of such meetings was ambitious and innovative: prior to the appointed day, a Commission staff member travelled to the designated region to draw in as many individuals and members of community groups as possible. These meetings, at which the commissioners did not speak but only listened, were structured around discussion groups asked to address the following questions: "Can English-speaking and French-speaking Canadians live together, and do they want to? Under what new conditions? And are they prepared to accept those conditions?" At the end of morning, afternoon, and evening discussions, representatives from each group would report on the group discussions to the commissioners and the meeting as a whole. Most frequent responses from English-Canadian audiences were: "Why do you want to make us speak French here in x? What do you want us to do? Around here we all get along well together. There are no problems here. What does Quebec want?"[20]

For the commissioners the unavoidable travel across the country was emotionally and physically exhausting. Laurendeau, like Scott, kept a journal. On May 2, 1964, he wrote:

Within a short period of time we enter into contact with a considerable number of people. We hear things said that sometimes touch and move us – often rubbing us the wrong way. And the next day the same thing starts over again somewhere else. It is exactly as though we were being subjected to a machinegunning. It is easy to see why the weak cave in right away and the strongest go through periods of being wrought up. It is rough treatment for everybody, but at the same time useful, I think.

Co-existence, he recognized, was going to be more difficult than he had imagined. He had not expected the degree of negativism to be found in English Canada, negativism toward the Commission and toward French Canada itself: "the density and the depth of ignorance and prejudice truly cannot be fathomed." The big question remained, "do these two peoples, anglophone and francophone, wish to and can they live together?"[21]

This question also surfaced during private, informal and internal meetings of the Commission. Frequently, at the end of evening sessions, Laurendeau would go to Scott's hotel room to talk over the day's events. The two men respected each other. Like Laurendeau, Scott had been reluctant to join the Commission. He had been persuaded, against his first inclinations, that his voice was needed. He recognized from the start the Commission was really French Canada's opportunity to put forward what Quebec wanted in the areas of language and culture. Thus it was the French, and Laurendeau especially, who must state their case. In response, Scott was obliged to take up the reactive role of stating whether or not he thought such proposals would be acceptable to English Canada.

As Michael Oliver recalled, Laurendeau's aim was to produce a new agreement between English and French. Thus, he "relied on Frank to a quite considerable extent" for his constitutional expertise and for his understanding of both French and English Canada.[22] Laurendeau, or Oliver, as research director, "would often schedule a morning or afternoon for Frank to talk [to his fellow commissioners] about some aspect of the material, or he might intervene impromptu. He would stand at the front, give a two- or three-hour talk and exchange of questions and answers totally without notes and apparently without any preparation, giving facts, events, dates, perspectives, dimensions on our problems in historical, constitutional and yes, even poetic context."[23]

Commissioners like Royce Frith found such performances "absolutely marvellous" because through Scott one saw glimpses of a larger Canada.

[He] brought you up to a perspective of the country that you couldn't see from your own day-to-day [life]. We all get flashes of it but ... it seemed like a permanent thing with him. He had a vision. It was that he seemed always aware of this bigger dimension of Canada –

This vision "was little bits of talking about Riel and something about his father going out into the forest and getting natural woods and burning them as incense in the church, and some of his more poetic allusions to the Laurentians – it was kaleidoscopic." Frith continued, "and of course what you saw when you started to put these fragments together [there] was a country that made you very proud."[24]

As a constitutional specialist, Scott had one of the keenest general minds on the Commission; as a trained jurist and an accomplished debater, he frequently perceived the weak links in an argument. Oliver recalled it was necessary "to test everything against Frank. You had to test it for its intellectual quality, for whether it really did stand up as an argument ... he was *the* constitutional authority."[25] Finally, and perhaps this was most important in terms of his role on the Commission, Scott, as one colleague commented, was the only English commissioner who had the sort of "track record" that allowed him to be critical of Quebec's more extreme demands without fear of being accused that he was unsympathetic to French Canada.[26]

Even while serving on the B and B Commission Scott had continued to try to interpret Quebec for English Canada when in 1964 he and Michael Oliver published *Quebec States Her Case: Speeches and Articles from Quebec in the Years of Unrest*. The collection had been planned before either editor was involved with the B and B Commission. Despite their subsequent involvement, both felt justified in completing the collection because of continuing interest in Quebec's Quiet Revolution and the almost complete lack of information regarding it.[27] This book provided a wide spectrum of contemporary Quebec opinion, ranging from the economic and political demands for increasing Quebec autonomy made by Jean Lesage, Daniel Johnson, and René Lévesque, to Jean-Jacques Bertrand's proposal for "Estates-General of the French Canadian nation" that would determine the objectives to be pursued for a new constitution. Also included were Marcel Chaput's separatist manifesto; a justification of terrorism by André Major, the editor of *Parti Pris*; and the manifesto of the FLQ, with its ringing slogans: "Only a full-fledged revolution can build up the necessary power to achieve the vital changes that will be needed in an independent Quebec.... QUEBEC PATRIOTS, TO ARMS! THE HOUR OF NATIONAL REV-OLUTION HAS STRUCK! INDEPENDENCE OR DEATH!"[28]

The rebuttal of separatism in *Quebec States Her Case* is provided in several articles by André Laurendeau and one by Léon Dion. It is given more emphatically by Trudeau in an article originally entitled "La nouvelle trahison des clercs," in which he argues that the new separatism is a "self-deluding passion of a large segment of our thinking population."[29] *Quebec States Her Case*, as a cross-section of contemporary opinion, is a clear indication of the political factors that brought into being – and subsequently undermined – the work of the Royal Commission on Bilingualism and Biculturalism.

Scott knew well the varying demands being made by Quebecers and he was, to a large degree, sympathetic to French Canada's aspirations for a new deal. But he was not afraid to voice his objections to what he saw as excessive demands. Laurendeau, in turn, shared Scott's belief about extremes. And because he wanted to produce a report acceptable to both English and French moderates, he looked to Scott as uniquely qualified to assess the situation. "You'd be an idiot if you pushed anything past one of the most sensitive English Canadians you'd ever want to meet, one who had a real understanding of much of what French Canada was all about." Scott was "the door through which everything had to go."[30] For Scott this role was to prove exhausting.

One of the most traumatic aspects of the first round of regional meetings was the realization that, while English Canada refused to recognize that Quebec was demanding new terms for Confederation, feelings of separatism in that province were rapidly accelerating. Meetings in Sherbrooke and Quebec City were stormy. The extremists dominated at Sherbrooke on March 17-18, 1964 – young students and professors who spoke at length to what Scott felt was "orchestrated applause." One young *séparatiste* said he was not interested in the French-speaking minorities in the other provinces – they were lost anyway; the English-speaking minority in Quebec was the only one that mattered and the sooner they moved west the better. Scott replied, "J'y suis, j'y reste." This comment, he reported in his journal, drew laughter as well as some sympathy for his position.[31] Scott had dealt gracefully with the confrontation but more and more he began to feel emotionally shaken. He had been born in Quebec City; he had lived in Quebec all his life; this was his soil, too. Were his rights and those of other English Quebecers of no account?

In Quebec City on June 16, 1964, there was general shock when public discussion groups were taken over by separatists. Prior to the evening sessions, Rudnyckyj had stumbled upon a private meeting of separatist groups who were "getting their orders from their leaders." At the plenary sessions they spoke vehemently on the Americanization of Canada and the necessity to build an independent Quebec state from which the English would be removed. There was only one voice of moderation. When the separatists began to insult the commissioners, particularly the French-speaking ones, Marchand, still a commissioner at this time, became so angry he broke the silence imposed by the meeting format. He reminded the audience of what unions had done for the French-Canadian population. Would this be forgotten? Scott wrote that the attempt to stifle democratic procedures by verbal violence reminded him of the antics of Jacques Ferron's Rhinoceros Party.[32]

These and other indications of the strength of Quebec separatism forced the unsettled commissioners to wonder whether Canada now faced a crisis in its national life. Laurendeau did not believe the majority of Quebecers held separatist views but rather that their voices had been paralysed. Lacoste disagreed. It was no longer just a question of moderate as opposed to separatist views because moderate opinion, in his view, "had now reached a point where it put the development of a powerful Quebec state first in its thinking and relations with the rest of Canada and with Ottawa in second place."

Time was running out. Rudnyckyj, drawing on his European experience, said he had seen two identical situations in European nations that had ended in disaster. Metaphorically speaking, the time in Canada was 11:45 and there were just fifteen minutes left. Scott was at first reluctant to endorse the idea of a "crisis." Ultimately, however, he agreed there was a crisis and assented to the Commission's preliminary report because they had reached "a time when decisions must be taken and developments must occur leading either to [Canada's] break-up, or to a new set of conditions for its future existence."[33] Before going to the country with this alarming message, the Commission members decided to consult with Prime Minister Pearson, who agreed that it was a "good thing for Canadians to realize what deep feelings existed" and quipped, "I did not learn this from Mackenzie King."[34]

On February 1, 1965, the Commission issued *A Preliminary Report*, which came right to the point in the preamble: "*Canada, without being fully conscious of the fact, is passing through the greatest crisis in its history.*" The source of this crisis was identified with Quebec. "The state of affairs established in 1867, and never since seriously challenged, is now for the first time being rejected by the French Canadians of Quebec." The commissioners, in enunciating this problem, considered themselves to be "*demonstrating a supreme confidence in Canada,*"[35] for they were saying to the country they had faith in it and in its future.

With the crisis acknowledged, the problem was how to establish priorities. Some commissioners, including Lacoste, argued that if the country was facing a crisis, the first issue on the agenda ought to be a consideration of the political dimension of the problem, which would recognize Quebec's constitutional relations with Ottawa.[36] Laurendeau also believed the Commission could make suggestions for constitutional change if necessary; indeed, he stated he would not have taken up his position with the Commission were this eventuality not provided for.[37]

Others, like Scott, disagreed; he argued the mandate did not include proposals for constitutional change. Then, too, he did not feel the commissioners were capable of dealing with the issue because they lacked sufficient constitutional knowledge. Laurendeau and Dunton resolved this conflict with what Lacoste described as a "gentlemen's agreement."[38] Since it was apparent there was no unanimity among the members, why not get on with issues like language in the civil service, in education, and in the workplace? The political and constitutional ramifications of bilingualism and biculturalism were to be postponed to a later date. Meanwhile, some accommodation would be maintained. Describing the Commission to Prime Minister Pearson on June 29, 1964, Dunton remarked: "We have always interpreted our mandate in the following terms: we are not primarily a constitutional commission, but if our subject takes us into this field we will go into it as far as necessary."[39] Regardless of what individual commissioners thought about this issue, the Commission had to consider questions of the constitution because any discussion of the vital issue of language involved Section 133 of the BNA Act, which set out the respective powers given to the French and English languages.

Relations on the Commission became strained over the question of whether or not Quebec's needs could be met by the Canadian Confederation and constitution as they then existed. Scott opened a discussion on "A Strong Central Government" by making an economic argument. He identified two types of governments: public and private. The public government is the one organized by the society, the private by the large industries and corporations. The private government, he pointed out, can have as much influence over our lives as can the public, and it is one role of the public government to try to find a balance. In Canadian federalism, government is divided, according to the BNA Act, between various levels and institutions. However, some institutions, evolved after 1867, were not found in the constitution and could give more flexibility than had hitherto been thought. For example, federal-provincial conferences were not required by law, and provinces had been presented with such choices as opting-out devices and with such joint programs as tax-sharing arrangements. "Indeed at times it seems that the constitution is the last thing to be looked at in current Canadian discussions."[40]

Of those whose views were opposite to Scott's, the most articulate commissioner was Lacoste, also a constitutional lawyer. During internal meetings held between April 26-30, 1965 (when he was still co-secretary), he suggested constitutional changes in Quebec. Scott noted indignantly that what the younger man called "Minor Changes" involved:

the abolition of a power of disallowance, nomination of Lieutenant Governor by the provinces, nomination of all judges in Quebec by the province, the taking over of penitentiaries, divorce, and possibly the criminal law. Then, of course, bankruptcy, the treaty power, Eskimos and Indians in Quebec, plus control of TV were to be provincial in all those provinces that wished to enlarge their jurisdictions. Beyond this, the residue of powers was to go to the provinces and in any case of conflict between provincial and federal laws the former would prevail. There must be a new constitutional Supreme Court, and drastic reform of the Senate. He felt these trivial changes, however, could not go to the roots of the problem of federalism, which he felt still had to be thought out. Should we change from Federalism to Con-federalism? Should we have an associate state solution? These matters he left for further contemplation. I can see merry times ahead if this type of constitutional change is considered by the French speaking members to be quite within the bounds of possibility.[41]

Lacoste's proposals, however, were not too different from those put forward by Jean-Jacques Bertrand in *Quebec States Her Case*, or for that matter, from the policy directive to the Parti Socialiste du Québec written by Michel Chartrand, Jacques-Yvan Morin, and André L'Heureux.

At the forty-fifth meeting of the Commission, on July 5-6, 1966, Scott read an opening paper on "The Place of the Federal Government." Before long he felt very sleepy and had a hard time just sitting upright as the talks wandered on. He was jolted out of this post-luncheon snooze by Lacoste, who had been working on a document entitled "Schéma Préliminaire: Problème," which argued for a major transfer of jurisdiction from the federal government at Ottawa to the Quebec provincial government to ensure equal partnership in Canada. Scott snapped that if Lacoste were going to suggest a list of subjects that Quebec wanted to take over then "we" (presumably English-Canadian federalists) should provide another list of subjects that the federal government must have to fulfil its functions. Scott later wrote in his journal, "The atmosphere in the room became charged with a certain amount of emotion as the confrontation developed. I found myself being thrust into the position of sole defender of Federal rights and duties. As it became impossible to resolve the conflict the meeting adjourned."[42]

Scott was well aware of the grievances of Quebecers, but his solution was based on British political traditions, especially those relating to civil liberties. H. Blair Neatby speculated this meant "he was fundamentally opposed to 'minority rights' whenever they discriminated against 'individual rights'." This attitude was to condition his later objection to "territoriality" in the determination of rights. One result of this stand was, as Neatby explained, that

> Scott found himself more and more isolated in the Commission, where cultural duality seemed to most commissioners to depend upon the existence of two cultural groups or even "two nations." French Canadian nationalism, filtered through the federal system, led to demands for greater Quebec autonomy; Scott's defence of individual rights more and more frequently took the form of opposing these demands in order to defend the rights of the Anglo-Québécois.[43]

In the summer of 1965, confrontation between Quebec and Ottawa had become more intense. Scott, who had learned from Michael Pitfield that Prime Minister Pearson had not appointed a special minister in his cabinet to deal with Quebec, made an appointment with the Prime Minister for the evening of August 16, 1965, to discuss this and other matters. He found Pearson comfortable in "lounge coat and slippers." After drinks had been served, the two men chatted agreeably. Scott asked Pearson directly whether or not he expected the B and B Commission to recommend constitutional change. Pearson said he did not. Scott then outlined some of the problems involved. The commissioners, he said,

> ... could hardly avoid dealing with even major constitutional problems because they were being widely discussed in the country at large and particularly in Quebec. If the B and B Commission said nothing about such gravely important matters which could justifiably be considered to come within its terms of reference in the development of the concept of "equal partnership" it could be considered to have failed in its duty to the Canadian people.

It would be possible, Scott thought, to appoint a subcommittee of the Commission to deal with constitutional problems, but he was concerned about the lack of constitutional expertise within the Commission. It would be preferable if Pearson were to appoint another committee to deal with this aspect of the problem and leave the Commission "to make our recommendations on bilingual and bicultural matters." His suggestion regarding expert advice inside the cabinet on constitutional developments was considered helpful by Pearson. Would Michael Pitfield make a good secretary for a group of experts? Scott thought he would.[44] This committee was the nucleus for what later became Senator Carl H. Goldenberg's

Committee on the Constitution, which reported directly in 1967 to Minister of Justice Pierre Trudeau.

In October, 1967, the first B and B report was issued. In the preface Laurendeau explained the reports for the Commission would be issued serially and indicated the general areas to be covered. These included the official languages, the work world, education, the federal capital, and the contribution of other ethnic groups in Canada. He also indicated there would be a last book summarizing the general findings of the Commission. In one sentence Laurendeau offered hope to those members of the Commission who wished a political and constitutional approach to the problem. "Finally," he said, "in the general conclusions we shall offer a synthesis of our views and shall approach important constitutional questions concerning the relations and the future of the two societies."

The Commission's terms of reference were interpreted in the general introduction. "In our view the reference to the two 'founding races' or 'peoples who founded Confederation' is an allusion to the undisputed role played by Canadians of French and British origin in 1867, and long before Confederation." Bilingualism, it was emphasized, did not mean a country where all the inhabitants have to speak two languages but "rather it is a country where the principal public and private institutions must provide services in two languages to citizens, the vast majority of whom may very well be unilingual." Similarly, "biculturalism" was not meant to be a mixture of two cultures but rather the existence of two dominant cultures in Canada embodied in distinct societies.

Among the recommendations were that English and French be declared official languages of the Parliament of Canada, of the federal courts, of federal government and administration; that New Brunswick and Ontario, and any other province whose official language minority reaches 10 per cent or greater, recognize French and English as official languages; that other provinces and municipal governments accept French and English as the language of debate in the legislature and offer services in French; that bilingual districts be defined; that the federal capital area be equally bilingual. In education it was recommended children be educated in the language of choice of the parents, and further, that a paragraph known as 93A be added to the BNA Act, which would allow for schools to be English, French, or bilingual. Also suggested was a new version of Section 133 of the BNA Act to establish English and French as the official languages of Canada and guarantee the above recommendations. Most important, the Commission recommended the adoption of an "Official Languages Act" to apply to the provinces designated as bilingual.[45]

The regional meetings had left individual Commission members distressed: the Francophones by the extremes of English-Canadian negativism and the Anglophones by Quebec separatism. They recognized the crisis was a kind of unavoidable tragedy in Canadian national life. They did not, however, readily extract from this metaphor the recognition that each of the commissioners, representative of a certain segment of Canadian society, was also an actor with a predetermined destiny in this drama. By birth, by training, and by temperament, Scott was slotted into an awkward role, one in which he was obliged to be a constitutional specialist, English Quebecer, and Canadian – sometimes each in turn but often all at once. As long as André Laurendeau remained stage manager of this drama, it was possible for him and each commissioner to play his or her part with some hope of a successful performance.

Tragedy was compounded, however, when Laurendeau died. In November, 1967, he had recognized the coming year would be difficult. Within ten days three events happened simultaneously: the first book of the B and B Commission was submitted to the public; Quebec independently set up an Estates-General to recommend constitutional change; and finally, an interprovincial conference was scheduled in Toronto to discuss constitutional matters. It was, Laurendeau mused, pure chance that all three had occurred at the same time, though it appeared as if it had been consciously planned. This he found disturbing:

> The years ahead don't look too promising. I am going to find myself allied with people I do not regard highly (money, the old parties, the masses – and let it be hoped that these will not be drawn into the separatist maelstrom); and I will have most of my friends ranged against me – that is, those with whom friendship is natural and spontaneous for me. The best examples are René Lévesque and the young. Only one thing is more repugnant to me than being booed by the young and that is to flatter them like a demagogue. Here is a new situation in which I shall be condemned to solitude. Life won't be exactly a bed of roses.[46]

In the spring of 1968 Laurendeau suffered an aneurysm at the B and B offices in Ottawa while meeting with a research group. By June he was dead. Just thirty-six hours before his fatal attack Laurendeau had called Scott and Lacoste to his home in Outremont, to get their agreement on a paragraph he had already rewritten fourteen times. As Lacoste later remarked, this "showed how far things had gone."[47] Laurendeau, by eliciting the arguments on both sides and by patiently rewriting and refining, slowly worked toward consensus. The contested paragraph, it appears, dealt with minority English rights in Quebec.

For many individuals, the tragedy of the Commission was the death of Laurendeau before consideration of Book VI, the final report that would have considered the question of Quebec and the constitution. Only his sensitivity and intellect, many felt, could have mediated between the extremes of Quebec separatism and English-Canadian centralism. The question remains, however, whether or not the primary issue that has bedevilled Canada since Confederation, and indeed since 1759 – the relations between French and English – could be effectively settled by one royal commission, however ambitious and well-meaning.

Undoubtedly with Laurendeau's death there was more pressure placed on the remaining Commission members. By 1969, however, many had good reason to be pleased with their accomplishments. Recommendations for change contained in the first volume had already been implemented by the Official Languages Act passed in October, 1969, by Trudeau's government. The Goldenberg Committee was now dealing with proposals for repatriation of the constitution and possible constitutional change. Many English Canadians accepted the concept of a crisis in Confederation and were even willing to accept the recommendations for bilingualism advanced by the Commission.

What had caused the change? In part, it was the renewed assertion of nationality occasioned by the hundredth anniversary of Confederation – an assertion embodied in Expo '67 – and in the recognition of a dynamic French community. Curiously, President De Gaulle's "Vive le Québec libre" helped. As one of the B and B jokes collected by Scott points out, it is all very well for a visitor to come to a man's home and say to his wife "Vive l'amour." But it is another matter entirely if this same visitor says, "Vive l'amour libre."[48] De Gaulle's call to arms, welcomed by the younger generation, was considered highly inappropriate by many older Quebecers; it also generated a nationalist backlash in English Canada. There was, by 1969, a stronger sense of one Canada. However, by early 1971, any sense of accomplishment that might have been enjoyed by Commission members was shattered by new events in Quebec – the abduction of James Cross and Pierre Laporte in October, 1970, and the revelation, days later, of Laporte's murder. And, as before, the fragile sense of Canadian unity was dissipated by the invocation of the War Measures Act in October, 1970.

These events hung heavily over the Commission on February 27, 1971, when it met to discuss the final book. Jean-Louis Gagnon had replaced Laurendeau as co-chairman and André Raynauld, an economist, had taken

Gagnon's place as a commissioner. The group was divided about whether or not it would be advisable to deal with the constitutional aspects of the question. A preliminary attempt to put together a consensus was rejected as unsatisfactory. Lacoste, however, reminded the Commission " 'the whole question of political equal partnership' " was still with the Commission; the crisis noted in the first volume had not ended. "People are suspecting that we opened up a great question and then ran away from it. We must say – or he himself would have to say – that our work was very important, but there was much more to be done to provide the necessary psychological breakthrough." During the coffee break there was amusement among the commissioners to discover that Lacoste was drinking from a mug with the Union Jack on it. Finally, however, the majority decided against putting out a volume dealing with the political aspect of the problem because, as Raynauld remarked, he was not sure the Commission could have agreed on a final constitutional volume. "To which Frith answered, we can't only not agree, but we can't agree to say we can't agree." The Commission, as Scott now recognized, "in its composition and in its divergent views, was very like Canada itself."[49]

After the Commission had submitted its final volume, Paul Lacoste appeared on Quebec television to assert that Laurendeau's vision had not been fulfilled. Claude Ryan, editorializing in *Le Devoir*, agreed with him. Scott, not surprisingly, again differed. "The majority of the Commission had enough sense to know that they were not appointed to write such a volume and were incapable of doing it well."[50] Later, writing an introduction to Philip Stratford's *André Laurendeau: Witness for Quebec* (1973), Ryan added, "When the B and B Commission decided to terminate its work without following up on the [constitutional] proposals that Laurendeau had promised, many people spoke sadly of 'the betrayal of Laurendeau's dream'. History will confirm the validity of this harsh verdict."[51]

It is doubtful whether history will endorse this verdict. The Commission had accomplished a great deal. For the first time there had been a national soul-searching to determine what ought to be the relations between the two founding nations, and important conclusions were drawn on the nature of Canada, on education, and on minority and ethnic rights.

If a betrayal of Laurendeau's vision had taken place, it was primarily in relation to establishing true biculturalism in Canada, and that "betrayal" resulted from events outside the control of the Commission. History had caught up with the B and B Commission. Indeed, it had passed it by. The intellectual approach to the problem represented by the Commission, still viable in the early sixties, made little sense after Trudeau took power and none at all after René Lévesque was elected Premier of Quebec. Trudeau, by legislating the Official Languages Act in 1969 and by directly confronting separatism with the War Measures Act in 1970, had changed the issue into a personal one. Quebec's place in Canada was now a matter to be settled by Québécois among themselves. In this sense the significance of the Royal Commission on Bilingualism and Biculturalism – and with it the visions of both Scott and Laurendeau – was diminished.

Scott, although irritated by Lacoste's censorious remarks, was relatively well pleased. The Commission had accomplished more than any previous royal commission. Its primary recommendations had been promptly legislated. His own position in Quebec, however, had changed considerably. Michel Brunet, the Québécois historian, had once said the Anglo-Québécois would have to learn to be a minority. Scott fought valiantly against this, but in the end he became a defender of this minority, "a tragic figure whose noble commitment to civil liberties had become a commitment to a marginal cause, pushed to one side by French Canadian nationalism."[52] In the new Quebec, the young radical who had protested injustice in Montreal during the thirties and forties, the hero of the Roncarelli and Padlock cases and the anti-Duplessis reformer of the fifties, was largely forgotten. For many Québécois, F.R. Scott was persona non grata, an advocate of an Ottawa-based centralism who denied Francophone Quebecers their legitimate constitutional rights. The revolution had claimed its revolutionary.

# A Viable Federalism

I N AUGUST, 1971, Scott was at North Hatley smarting over the Quebec situation. "How do we," he wrote to King Gordon, "establish the fact ... that the cultural needs as well as the economic needs of [the province] are far better served by a viable federalism than either by separation or even such a special status for Quebec as will make the rest of the system unfit to survive in a modern world.... Quebec has already more than enough jurisdiction to save and develop its own culture." What he feared was the kind of economic splintering that would make it impossible for the rest of the country to survive. The real battle, he told Gordon, was not economic but psychological: a battle for the hearts of Quebecers. And it was Canada that was at stake.

> If Ottawa would show some signs of caring for the real values, and would say YES to some progressive ideas instead of only NO to bad ones more people might be convinced federalism was useful, even to Quebec. I do not believe Quebec will ever vote in majority for separation unless things get much worse, and even then people may be frightened into greater co-operation. But I am sure the Liberal party under the present kind of Trudeauism won't save us. And if we cannot save all then we must save what we can of the rest of the country. No one seems to be thinking about that, or at least not out loud.
> I tried for forty years to make things better
> And all I know is
> This lake is beautiful.[1]

The letter to King Gordon was the sigh of an old warrior who saw his life's work slipping away. He had always sought to explain Quebec to the rest of Canada and to justify Canadian federalism to the Québécois. But Canadian unity was now threatened as French and English polarized into two antagonistic camps within Quebec. It was clear to him, and to many others in the English community, that a series of language bills enacted by the Quebec government was intended to create a unilingual French Quebec, and this had greatly antagonized the English minority in Quebec. What was worse, the application of the War Measures Act in the preceding October, an action that 85 per cent of Quebecers had appeared to accept at the time, was now viewed by many Québécois as a unilateral display of power by Ottawa. No common ground seemed possible.

When he supported the War Measures Act, Scott found himself increasingly ostracized, not only by leftists but by liberals of all political persuasions. The events of the previous year in Quebec profoundly darkened the last years of his life. Unable to rest on his laurels, he felt the ideals to which he had devoted his life – above all, the ideal of one Canada – were in danger of being swept away in a wave of separatist violence. The only escape from such increasingly pessimistic thoughts was communing with nature itself – the beauty of Lake Massawippi as it shimmered just beyond the North Hatley verandah where he so often sat.

It is now almost impossible to recreate the Quebec of the late sixties and early seventies. It involved: an atmosphere of emotional strain generated by the growing separatist movement, the McGill français movement, a series of strikes in Montreal, and, as occurred in other cities, an increased political activism by students. Despite the proposals for linguistic equality advocated by the B and B Commission, despite the Official Languages Act in 1969, which stated that "the English and French languages are the official languages of Canada for all purposes of the Parliament and Government of Canada, and possess and enjoy equality of status,"[2] and despite an increasing desire on the part of English Canada to accommodate many of Quebec's needs, separatist violence had accelerated in that province throughout the sixties.

Day after day new targets, mainly in Montreal, were bombed by the Front de Libération du Québec: the National Revenue Building, the RCMP building in Westmount, the Black Watch armoury, Dominion Textiles factories in both Montreal and Drummondville, the Paul Sauvé Arena, Eaton's, the home of the president of Murray Hill limousine service, the Bank of Nova Scotia building, two bombs (one exploded) near the Montreal City Hall, the Queen's Printer bookstore in Montreal, the Montreal Stock Exchange, the Château Frontenac in Quebec City, Loyola College, an explosion behind Jean Drapeau's house, the Army Recruiting Centre.[3] In seven years, between 1963 and 1970, there had been six deaths. Quebecers, and especially Montrealers, became fearful of stepping outside.

This sense of a breakdown in public order was heightened in the early seventies when accelerating strikes paralysed the Quebec economy. Writing to an English law colleague in April, 1972, Scott expressed his dismay:

We have just had a startling example of law enforcement in Quebec. All the unions engaged in the public service called a general strike, which included even hospitals, schools and old-people's homes. Dreadful situations developed, and the government has just passed a back-to-work law which union leaders at first ordered their members to disobey. Many did and are being tried, but then the strike collapsed and for the moment we are wondering whether new forms of civil disobedience will develop. It was 200,000 people against a rather shaky government.[4]

Scott was especially distressed by the continuing use of force by the FLQ. The bombings had begun in 1963. One night in May, he and Gerald Le Dain had been having an animated discussion after dinner at Scott's home when there was a loud bang. The two men were too absorbed in their argument to investigate. The next morning they discovered that the FLQ had blown up a mailbox just a few blocks down the street from the Scotts' house.[5] Shortly after this, Scott was walking with his former student Donald MacSween (who had just been appointed director-general of the National Arts Centre) not far from where the mailbox had exploded. The two men passed another mailbox. Noting the box, MacSween remarked, "We [had] better be careful." "Fine, no problem," Scott replied. "Revolutions never go uphill."[6] There was truth in Scott's jest: popular revolutions require not only general support, but also the momentum of an easily travelled path. By the early seventies in Quebec it was easier, and far more natural, for the intellectual to follow the FLQ rather than a moderate path.

The violence of the late sixties culminated in the October Crisis of 1970, an event Scott followed closely not only because the events in Quebec impinged on Canadian unity but also because he was in direct communication with the major participants in both Quebec City and Ottawa. The crisis began on October 5 when James Cross, British trade commissioner in Montreal, was kidnapped by an FLQ cell that demanded, among other things, the release of political prisoners and payment of $500,000 in gold. On October 10, Quebec Labour and Immigration Minister Pierre Laporte was kidnapped from his home in Montreal by a second FLQ group. On October 12, the army took over security duties in Ottawa, which included guarding politicians. As a result of this, two nights later, there was a rally of 3,000 people, mostly students, at the Paul Sauvé Arena in Montreal. Michel Chartrand, Pierre Vallières, Charles Gagnon, and Robert Lemieux spoke. CBC films of the event show a large, sometimes hysterical crowd screaming "FLQ, FLQ." Some speakers appealed for cool-headedness, but Vallières and Chartrand said that the presence of the army in Quebec was a "provocation."[7]

The emotional component of this rally determined Scott's attitude. To him it was the same threat of mob violence he had experienced earlier in his life – in the Quebec conscription riots, in the mob that threatened the representatives from the Spanish Loyalist government. To him, as indeed to most Quebecers at the time, the call for Quebec separatism put forward at the rally was highly menacing. To others, Marian Scott among them, this threat was overrated. She seriously doubted violence would ensue. This difference of opinion was to prove a bone of contention between the Scotts. He grumbled half-humorously of his wife to a neighbour at North Hatley, "She is an FLQ cell all by herself."[8]

For Scott the primary issue was that revolutionary separatism in Quebec threatened the rule of law in a democratic society. Writing in *The Montreal Gazette* on October 24, he denounced "a determined and well organized revolutionary movement applying new techniques of terror aimed at the polarization of our society and the fracturing of those elements which enable Canadian federalism to exist at the moment and give assurance that it can exist in the future. It is a global attack upon all institutions in our present system."

Scott's belief in the rule of law was shared by Prime Minister Trudeau, to whom he had so often expounded the necessity of the rule of law in a democracy. Gordon Robertson, then clerk of the Privy Council, later remarked in a CBC retrospective that a fundamental part of Trudeau's political philosophy had been that "the rights of individuals, which are paramount in the state, depend on the rule of law and therefore he saw this as the attack on that rule of law which is fundamental for individual rights and therefore an attack on the whole purpose for which the state exists."

Members of the federal cabinet had negotiated with the Quebec government in an attempt to restore order. Jean Marchand, Minister of Regional Economic Expansion, had been delegated by the cabinet to meet with Mayor Drapeau and municipal authorities in Montreal and with Premier Bourassa in Quebec City. Marchand recalls that Drapeau's lawyer and the chief of police in Montreal painted a frightening picture. They said that they knew the FLQ had some remote-controlled trucks full of dynamite that could be parked under Place Ville Marie in downtown Montreal or, for that matter, any other building in Montreal. The police were exhausted. They had just been on strike and there were students threatening to strike at the University of Montreal. According to Marchand, the police felt they were "no longer in control. Anything [could] happen. And Bourassa ... told me exactly the same. We [could] not control the situation."

He also recalled that although many individuals were suspected of terrorism, they could not be arrested because there was no evidence. "The judge [would] just release them right away and so our problem [was] to be in a position to make an arrest without a warrant.... And outside that we [needed] some help in order to ... guard the public utilities that [could] be blown up at any time ... in Montreal – water, electricity, and so forth." Unfortunately, there was little precise information from the RCMP, beyond showing Marchand and Gérard Pelletier a list of about 150 suspects. As Marchand reminisced, there were ten or fifteen people they knew, some great talkers "but so frightened of guns that [they would] never hurt anyone!"⁹ Other individuals they did not know: there the danger lay.

At the request of Premier Bourassa, a day after the rally in the Paul Sauvé Arena the army moved into Montreal and Quebec City. The Quebec government then offered to recommend parole for five prisoners in exchange for Cross and Laporte. Prime Minister Trudeau, when asked by a reporter about the extent he would go to quash the FLQ, replied,

> There's a lot of bleeding hearts around [that] just don't like to see people with ... guns. All I can say is go on and bleed. But it's more important to keep law and order in this society than to be worried about weak-kneed people....
>
> The reporter interjected, "At any cost? How far would you extend that?" Trudeau replied, "Well, just watch me."¹⁰

Trudeau's remark was unfortunate, yet to many individuals watching this televised interchange across Canada, the gleam in Trudeau's eyes as he uttered these last words was most striking. With this intrusion of personality, the crisis had narrowed from a question of national policy to a clash between Québécois of opposing political persuasions. It was now Trudeau and the federal Liberals versus the Quebec separatists. At four a.m. on October 16, the War Measures Act was proclaimed.

Trudeau's reaction, combined with his personal statements, antagonized Quebec separatists, many of whom believed the War Measures Act was simply a tactic implemented by federal Liberals to vitiate the separatist movement in Quebec. Jacques Ferron, the popular Quebec fabulist, flayed Trudeau mercilessly in an essay called "The Dragon, the Maiden and the Child," in which he suggested that Trudeau, when speaking to the nation on the Quebec crisis, was, in reality, playing a highly Jesuitical role. Ferron genuinely believed the imposition of the War Measures Act was little more than a cruel political game designed to crush Quebec independence.[11]

One day after the imposition of the War Measures Act, the body of Pierre Laporte was found in the trunk of an abandoned car; he had been strangled by the chain from his own scapular medal. As Marchand recalled, the situation then deteriorated rapidly:

> Laporte was killed. There it became a real crisis. I remember at the House it was terrible. All the MPs were there running, answering the phones and everybody asking us [when to leave] because they really thought, wrongly, but they thought that [it would be so]. So ... we [reasoned] if we don't send the army and *something* happens, of course we'll be held responsible. You know? We'd be held. And they'd say, well, we asked you, we told you and so on and so forth. So ... we sent people [the army] and the condition was that [for] those people outside – I don't talk about the RCMP – that just is a normal job.... [it] has as a mandate to protect public utilities. This was the mandate of the army – you know? Not to search people or to arrest people or anything [like that] but just to replace policemen so that the others do their own job.[12]

In a Gallup poll conducted the day the invocation of the War Measures Act became common knowledge but the death of Laporte was not known, the following question was asked: "Do you feel the governments in Ottawa and Quebec are being too hard and tough on the FLQ kidnappers so far, or not enough?" In Canada as a whole 4 per cent said too tough, 37 per cent said not tough enough, 51 per cent said about right, and 8 per cent were undecided. In Quebec alone 5 per cent said too tough, 32 per cent said not tough enough, 54 per cent said about right, and 9 per cent were undecided.[13]

Scott shared the majority opinion. In correspondence about the War Measures Act in 1946 with the historian and civil libertarian, A.R.M. Lower, Scott had said he did not like "these extraordinary powers which can be picked off the shelf and applied in emergencies without Parliamentary approval." But he had also expressed caution, perhaps looking to a time when a CCF government might find such a tool useful. "On the other hand the possible necessity of defending ourselves against organized sabotage is one that cannot lightly be dismissed."[14] Scott's fear of an organized sabotage of democracy possibly reflected the socialist view then that the capitalist class and the civil service would be unwilling to co-operate with a democratically elected left-wing government. Now, in the seventies, he believed such a moment had arrived, that the whole parliamentary system of democracy was threatened by the FLQ.

> I have lived seventy-one years in Quebec, and have been under the application of the War Measures Act four times. While its procla-mation was drastic, there was no other means at hand and it has already been replaced by a much less dangerous piece of legislation, itself due to expire soon unless the terrorists in Quebec foment more civil disorders. While there was no likelihood of any "insurrection" here, there was an imminent collapse of civil government. Unfortu-nately, we live in a fragile civilization which can be brought to the brink of disaster by a few ruthless and determined men.[15]

In Quebec itself, despite widespread dismay over Laporte's death, there was an unexpected surge of popular support for the FLQ following a broadcast of the FLQ manifesto and dissemination of the names of FLQ members. A Quebec sociologist speculated this support was an acknowl-edgement that many of the FLQ's claims for the reorganization of society were just. Also, many Québécois saw that the so-called terrorists were ordinary Quebecers, young people such as one would meet in one's neigh-bourhood. The most persuasive factor, however, was the recognition that implementation of the War Measures Act was unfair.

In Parliament, Robert Stanfield of the Conservatives and David Lewis and others in the NDP opposed use of the War Measures Act. Of their stand Scott remarked: "They did and I understand why they did, but they hadn't been living in Quebec under seven years of bombing and they hadn't been living in Quebec in a volatile atmosphere, they hadn't seen seven thousand or six thousand students approving the FLQ manifesto." The Attorney-General of Quebec, a former student of Scott's, had taken refuge on the top floor of the Queen Elizabeth Hotel guarded by police. It was the threat to the rule of law in a democracy to which he objected. "Now they [the executive] may have got frightened but whatever it was they were the legitimate government of Quebec and I was going to defend their right to govern against any terrorist ...."[16]

Outside Quebec, the common view among liberals of all persuasions was that the federal government had overreacted. Subsequent evidence, they later argued, proved there was no danger of insurrection or civil collapse. However, those individuals involved in making the decision, Prime Minister Trudeau, Jean Marchand, and Gérard Pelletier, clearly felt that a judgement had to be made. And one might argue that even if the danger was only one in twenty for Canada's security, then the government did have a responsibility to act. Certainly Scott believed this.

At the time the issue was badly clouded by the fact that it was to the political advantage of the federal Liberals to take a tough stand on separatism. And Trudeau's authoritarian attitude leant credibility to those who believed his actions were partisan. However, in fairness to the Prime Minister, it is clear from his mid-fifties essay on democracy that he had believed Quebecers misunderstood the concept and had historically subverted it for nationalist purposes. This belief was undoubtedly confirmed by the actions of the FLQ, which proclaimed the democratic rights of Québécois while subverting such rights through violence. And rumours of a projected coup (even if only rumours) that was to be followed by the installation of a new cabinet made up of prominent figures from outside the National Assembly also kept the issue murky. All these factors were further complicated by the existence of a relatively weak Liberal government in Quebec City. Premier Bourassa and Justice Minister Jérôme Choquette, together with Mayor Drapeau of Montreal, insisted they could not maintain order and requested federal troops be brought into Quebec. Finally, while it seemed clear that most Québécois were disgusted with accelerating violence and wanted the federal government to take firm action, there remained a residue of suspicion because the War Measures Act emanated from Ottawa, the traditional enemy of Quebec.

Once the crisis was over Québécois began to have second thoughts, which were supported by liberals and leftists outside the province who had not been subjected to the FLQ terrorism of the preceding years, but who objected to the general curtailment of civil liberties. What tipped the balance in public opinion was the manner in which the War Measures Act was implemented. The Quebec police had been released from their normal duties by the army and the RCMP was overzealous. Although the original list of suspects had only 150 names,[17] over 400 people were rounded up on suspicion of being members of the FLQ. As the Act went into force early on that Friday morning, people were pulled from their beds without warning and taken to jail, where they were not allowed legal counsel. Many innocent people were imprisoned in what soon became a general purge. Even the home of Gérard Pelletier, a Liberal cabinet minister (hardly a separatist supporter), was raided.[18] A young English-Quebecer thought "very much to the point" the publication of an Aislin cartoon showing

Jean Marchand with a Montreal phone book under his arm, announcing: "We now have a list of suspects."[19] As it was possible under the Act to hold an individual seven weeks without trial, Quebec jails rapidly filled. Scott, convinced the first regulations were far too strict, nonetheless believed the situation demanded severe action. He recalled, "In a crisis like that you have to act quickly, and innocent people [are] thrown into jail, if you don't throw them all into jail at once the ones that are thrown into jail notify all the others of their friends who immediately escape."[20]

Despite such justifications he was feeling a great deal of internal strain. On the one hand he had always believed in the civil rights of minorities, but counterbalancing this belief was the fact he had always fought for minorities *within* the legal system. The October Crisis brought these beliefs into conflict. Scott considered his support of the War Measures Act consistent with his earlier stand on individual freedom and civil liberties, since he felt individual liberties can only be protected by the rule of law. If the law is wrong, the citizen is responsible for attempting change by democratic means. He later said, "the War Measures Act gave my civil liberties back to me taken away by the FLQ. It was a response to government by terror. The FLQ held Quebec's democratically elected government to ransom and dictated to it an evil policy. It had to be stopped quickly."[21]

After the crisis he found himself in a most uncomfortable position. As he later wryly observed, "I seem to have a facility of getting a persona grata swinging both ways."[22] Formerly admiring Québécois friends now saw him as a traitor to Quebec, and many English liberals were convinced he had renounced his position as a civil libertarian. Scott was quite accustomed to advocating minority causes but, like that invincible knight-errant of his younger years whose strength was as "the strength of ten," he had always believed that his cause was just. This moral justification, in turn, redoubled his energy. The problem with the October Crisis was there were so many grey areas.

He was dismayed to discover that his wife and some of his younger friends and colleagues disagreed with him vehemently. The Scotts knew both Robert Lemieux, a former student at McGill and the FLQ lawyer, and Michel Chartrand personally. Chartrand, especially, was a gentle man, a former CCFer and an active trade unionist. To Marian, it seemed most unlikely that real violence would ensue. Talking to Marcel Rioux, a Quebec sociologist and a neighbour at North Hatley, she found they held similar views. Both considered it unfair the War Measures Act should make the FLQ, hitherto a legal political party, retroactively illegal.[23] This legal issue, one that Scott had considered so important in the early thirties at the time of the imprisonment of the Toronto Communists, he now tended to dismiss. He believed there was a larger issue at stake – the primacy of the rule of law in democracy.

In this matter Marian and Frank were at loggerheads. One of the cornerstones of his philosophy was the belief in the rule of law, whereas Marian had always respected the rights of the revolutionary. As a child listening to her governess, the descendant of Charlotte Corday, Marian had come to sympathize with those driven to use force in overthrowing tyranny during the French Revolution. During the twenties this understanding had been reinforced by her readings of Jean Cocteau, who had written that every true artist is a revolutionary. In the thirties, she had admired the idealism of Norman Bethune. In the sixties, both she and their son Peter felt impelled to speak out against the war in Vietnam. Marian attended demonstrations and signed a letter of protest to President Nixon. Now once again in the seventies, she signed a petition published in *Le Devoir* asking that political prisoners be exchanged for the release of James Cross and Pierre Laporte, as requested by the FLQ. In essence the clash between Marian and Frank on this issue was a clash between a belief in the individual's right to self-determination versus the belief this right must be qualified if it threatens law and order in society.

On October 17, the night after the War Measures Act had been enacted, the Scotts had accepted an invitation for dinner at the home of Doug Jones in North Hatley in honour of two poets, Irving Layton and Paul Chamberland, who were being awarded honorary degrees by Bishop's University. However, the Scotts missed the dinner. They had to remain in Montreal, where their phone was continuously ringing as people of all political persuasions asked Scott's advice. The next day, a Saturday, they drove to North Hatley where they were visited by a number of younger friends, including Jones, the translator Sheila Fischman, Ron Graham, and Kathy Mezei, then taking Canadian Studies at Carleton. It was a tense visit because relations between Scott and Graham had temporarily cooled. The young man, a former McGill student who later became a political journalist, had become a friend. Just a month earlier he had written to Scott flatly disagreeing with his views on Quebec nationalism. It was a courageous letter because Graham admired Scott, but he did not mince words: Scott, with his insistence on the rule of law, was ignoring the emotional force behind Quebec. This was true both in reference to his attitude on the impending language bills as well as in his response to Quebec politics in general.

What emerged from Graham's letter was the difference between the generations. Whereas Scott's experience had been with Premier Duplessis, Graham had grown up with the liberalism of the Quiet Revolution, with Lesage, Bertrand, and Bourassa. He did not believe the Quebec government would enact unjust linguistic laws unless provoked. In his view, Scott should recognize the English "must be sensitive to what is involved in a society in the process of rebuilding its sense of confidence, of losing its fear, of establishing its self-respect." Quebec was a society in upheaval; "intense individual suffering that the discontinuity and alienation create is often relieved by unifying goals of collective actions.... People, caught up in the suffering caused by social and historical forces, can act together in this way because it fulfills a *human need*."

Graham made an important distinction between law and practical politics. Scott's perception was that "linguistic freedom is a legal responsibility remaining with the legal authorities.... But my political training and interest suggests that the *political* action of restricting the freedom of a minority is often the result of that minority allowing itself to appear as an outside, alien and threatening force at a critical period of history. Therefore I see the *political* responsibility as resting with the minority *now*." Recently Scott had given speeches in Windsor and Winnipeg condemning Quebec's failure to protect its English minority; this, Graham felt, exacerbated the situation.

What's more, he felt that Scott, who emphasized the "regime of fear" experienced by the English in Quebec, too lightly dismissed Québécois fear. What "regime of fear," Graham asked, caused him to be insulted by French-Canadian friends who, in attempting to discover lost confidence, speak only French, or to inflate minor incidents into threats of "creeping unilingualism," or to see the composition of the Gendron Commission as so unjust that he denied them assistance (Scott had taken exception to the fact the Commission, set up to examine Quebec's language laws, included as its only Anglophone representative an immigrant to Canada)? What, Graham asked, caused him to dismiss Québécois fears and indignities as irrational? Indeed, what "regime of fear" made Scott "fight this cause for this minority at this time, when the rights and power of English Quebeckers are so strong? You can list injustices to minorities anywhere, *everywhere*, but surely those experienced by Anglophones in Quebec are now relatively petty, compared to most."

Graham was convinced Scott had lost his "spirit of challenge, of confidence and of broad understanding. You often, in discussing this issue, seem defensive, petty and unsympathetic." To be sure, he had exaggerated Scott's position somewhat,

> but that's because you exaggerate it too, in conversation, and I especially wanted to emphasize here how rigid and uncomparative you seem to have become. Less and less do you seem to be looking deeply into the other side of a question, particularly where it involves emotional and irrational social forces which can cause great human misery and which should not be dismissed as lightly as your rational approach suggests.[24]

In the immediacy of the October Crisis, Scott was experiencing considerable personal strain. He had direct connections with all participants in the larger political drama. Trudeau and Chartrand were long-time friends. He knew Laporte, who had once asked him to act as legal counsel. Robert Bourassa, Robert Lemieux, Michael Pitfield, and Jérôme Choquette were all former students. Drawing on his own beliefs and his information about the crisis, he had arrived at a decision to support the invoking of the War Measures Act. But surrounding him at North Hatley were a number of individuals (Marian, younger friends like Jones, Graham, and Larry Shouldice, a bilingual professor at Sherbrooke, and Quebec sociologist Marcel Rioux) who held quite different views. He was caught in an emotional cross-fire that was both generational and philosophical. The tension between Scott and Graham was apparent to others during the visit. Writing to her mother about the weekend, Kathy Mezei expressed her belief that Scott had information not available to the others and this made his position even more difficult.[25] In retrospect, it seems likely this information related to the rumours regarding a possible coup: any threat of this nature would harden Scott's attitude.

During the course of the visit, Scott apologized to Jones, explaining he had missed the previous evening's dinner party because he had been receiving telephone calls from Trudeau through Pitfield, at that time an assistant secretary to the cabinet, and from FLQ spokesmen Chartrand and Lemieux. Ironically, both sides were looking to Scott, the constitutional specialist and civil libertarian, for direction. As Timothy Porteous perceptively remarked,

> it's a personal tragedy because there were only two things that mattered to Frank in his lifetime – one was human rights and the other was Canada ... and here at the end of his long life ... the two are in

conflict.... If 5,000,000 people wish to create a state of their own that's probably something that they might well be allowed to do but if it destroys "my dear Canada" it's a tragedy, a classic Greek tragedy to have these two central trends inside a human being ultimately in conflict.[26]

It is not difficult to speculate on why Scott was reluctant to face the emotional aspects of Quebec separatism emphasized in Graham's letter, for in this issue both his philosophy and his psychology coalesced. Scott focused on the legal aspects of the October Crisis partly because it was the only way he could deal with the issue. A relatively rigid personality whose strong will controlled volatile emotions, Scott was a man who had unified his personality through law – "reason over passion." For him any choice between invoking the higher authority of the War Measures Act and not invoking it became, both philosophically and emotionally, a choice between democracy and anarchy. Thus his support of the Act was inevitable.

Inevitable also was the rejection of this position by many of the younger generation at North Hatley, such as Larry Shouldice, who felt that regardless of questions as to the primacy of law, the federal and provincial agencies were abusing their powers.

As a relatively young academic at the time, I found myself *very* disillusioned .... In what seemed to me to be a typically Anglo-Quebec establishment reaction, Frank was apparently prepared to support the federal government's doing essentially the same things as he had fought against the Quebec government for doing two decades or so earlier – namely, ignoring or abusing people's civil rights. Certainly I enjoyed Frank's company, but since I inevitably argued with him about Quebec matters, which he seemed to find intolerable in a young whippersnapper like me, I ended up believing that age or breeding or proximity to power had turned him into not so subtle a reactionary.[27]

Graham, Jones, Mezei, and Shouldice were products of the fifties and sixties, a generation sympathetic to Québécois aspirations for political and cultural independence. In the fall of 1969, Jones had started the bilingual journal *Ellipse*, which translated French poets into English and English poets into French. (Paul Chamberland and Frank Scott were featured in the first issue.) Members of this younger generation, who met frequently with Francophone poets and artists, were impressed by the cultural manifestations of the independence movement: by its articulateness and by the quality of people associated with it. There was no parallel in English

Canada. To them, as to their Québécois friends, it seemed inconceivable an intellectual could be jailed for his beliefs.

In addition, they tended to see social revolution as a necessary liberation from oppression. Scott and others of his generation had held similar views on social revolution in the early thirties, but these opinions had been drastically revised in the mid-thirties by the horrors of Stalinism and the Spanish Civil War. Talk of "human values" now seemed beside the point to Scott. In a democracy, any popular uprising that threatened insurrection or social change by non-democratic means was to be greatly feared and instantly stopped. The eventual human cost would be too great. At this point the polarization between the two groups was so extreme there was no common ground.

The larger question was later raised by Walter Tarnopolsky, an authority on constitutional law and civil liberties: to what extent should the state limit human rights and fundamental freedoms during an emergency? "Are there some rights and freedoms which are so fundamental that even consideration of the security of the state cannot be permitted to nullify them?"[28]

Near the end of the seventies, looking back on the decade, Scott summarized his views on the issue:

> The first regulations to confirm the War Measures Act were unnecessarily severe and innocent people were undoubtedly arrested. This was an injustice which I protested against with the Civil Liberties Union in Montreal. New regulations were subsequently adopted which were more in accord with democratic rights as well as effective national security. But there was no way to stop the secret conspiracy except by mass arrest followed by a sorting out of the guilty from the innocent. The fact that so few charges were laid in the courts against those who were arrested does not prove that guilty people were not found; it is quite consistent with the wise decision of the government to minimize the number of prosecutions in order not to clutter up the courts and prolong the agitation.[29]

He later pointed out that the proof of the Act was in its application,[30] that is, the War Measures Act did effectively quash terrorism in Quebec.

Because he felt the initial regulations were far too drastic, Scott met with thirteen other members of the Montreal Civil Liberties Union on October 25, 1970, to establish a "committee to aid persons arrested under the Emergency Powers legislation."[31] At that time the Union executive consisted of Thérèse Casgrain as honorary chairman, Jacques Hébert as president, and Frank Scott as vice-president. Hébert later pinpointed the difference in emotional climate between Quebec and Ontario when he observed the Quebec Civil Liberties Union could not take a position like that adopted by the Canadian Civil Liberties Association in Toronto, which condemned the use of the Act, because Québécois members were so conscious of living in "a climate of fear." In the Montreal group, there was complete unanimity about the need to restore order, but the middle-of-the-road position they took annoyed both the moderates and the extremists. Premier Bourassa gave a committee of three permission to enter the prisons to interview prisoners. Hébert did the bulk of the visiting, but Scott assisted and was an active liaison in setting up legal counsel for the prisoners.[32]

Later in the year, in December, 1970, at the time of the launching of Gérard Pelletier's *The October Crisis* at Editions du Jour, two independently motivated groups of extremists picketed Hébert's publishing office, ostensibly because the Civil Liberties Union was not doing its job with him as president. Scott was enraged at this display of hypocrisy; clearly, their intent was to prevent the launching of Pelletier's book. This book, as Hébert has said, presented "a rather serene view of the whole situation [which] was not really well accepted, even before reading it, by ... hard-core separatists, the gang of Reggie Chartrand." This group of "more-or-less bouncers," known as Les Chevaliers de l'indépendance, together with a second group directed by Dr. Serge Mongeau, a Marxist whose mandate was the defence of political prisoners, occupied the building. They constructed large signs reading "Hébert is Traitor" and stood by the door with two-by-fours. No one could get in or out. Hébert, who did not want to precipitate further violence by calling the police too quickly, slept there for a day or two.

The evening before the scheduled launching, Scott heard of the occupation. Hébert remembered Scott bursting into his office. He was no longer young, he walked with the aid of a cane, yet he was so furiously angry about the attack on the Civil Liberties Union that he pushed his way through the men blocking the door of the press:

> He came in, right in, and there was this Reggie Chartrand and the other bouncers that were there with big sticks and he was pushing them around. They allowed it because he was Frank Scott. You know? They couldn't hit him on the head. So he came into the office and he was shouting "Get out of my way. Who said that I won't get into this place?" ... He was raging mad with his cane, tearing apart the signs in front of bouncers with big sticks and he didn't care.... God, he is a man of courage. He just came to comfort me and to make

sure that I was okay. That I didn't need anything. And to say that he was solidaire with me and that I could count on him.[33]

Scott's ties to Editions du Jour dated from the late sixties and early seventies when he had continued to meet Québécois informally at book launchings. As Hébert recalls, there was "a launching every week, every Wednesday – sometimes two or three in good weeks and a certain number of people would come there, *knowing* that they would be all mixed up. There would be some Francophones, some Anglophones, some federalists like Mme Casgrain or Gérard Pelletier or others like that and some extreme separatists like Jacques Ferron and Gaston Miron." As Hébert remarked, "If you have a place where you can put together Gaston Miron, Mme Casgrain, Frank Scott, and then Jacques Ferron, well, you have achieved something." These parties were "the last place in those years where federalists and separatists would meet and have a drink together on the occasion of publishing a book."[34]

But the War Measures Act changed the nature of Scott's relations with Québécois, especially with Jacques Ferron, with whom Scott had had a casual acquaintance since the 1950s when Ferron had been briefly interested in the CCF. (Ferron was a CCF candidate in the 1958 federal election but broke with the party in 1960, disillusioned by its lack of support for French nationalism.) Also in the fifties, Ferron had been one of the French writers attending meetings in Scott's living room on Clarke Avenue. But by 1970 he had become a prominent separatist, and he had acted as an intermediary between the police and the kidnappers Paul Rose and François Simard during the October Crisis. A doctor by profession, Ferron was also a gifted writer whose short stories, novels, and essays were often allegories of Quebec society. His own position in that society was unique: he was frequently described as the conscience of Quebec. The significance of Scott's position in Quebec society is revealed by the fact that throughout Ferron's writing, from the early sixties to his death in 1985, Scott most often functioned as the significant "other," a kind of alter ego in a continuing dialogue on the role of the English in Quebec, and of Quebec in English society. In fact, it is not going to far to say that, after 1963, Scott dominated Ferron's creative imagination: it would have been impossible for Ferron to write about the relationship of Quebec to Canada without dealing with Scott as a symbol of the English in Quebec.

Ferron's use of Scott as a symbolic figure in his fiction was initially inspired by a story Scott himself had told about a marmalade jar his father had persuaded workmen to place under the Wolfe Monument in Quebec City during the restoration of Wolfe's statue at the turn of the century.

In this jar Canon Scott had placed one of his poems and a penny for each of his six children. In 1963, separatists blew up the Wolfe Monument. Shortly after this, Scott's brother Arthur phoned from Quebec City to let Frank know that the jar was still intact. Scott told this story to a number of young students with separatist leanings during meetings of the B and B Commission and they were amused by the anecdote.

However, Ferron's response was more complicated. For him the story of the marmalade jar became symbolic of the relationship between the French and English in Quebec. In 1964 he published an essay entitled "All Is Not Lost," in which he retells the story of the Wolfe Monument with the wry comment that "all these important objects miraculously saved (no doubt through the intervention of Saint George) authorise us to believe that all is not lost for the English memory and that, having no other place for it, we shall smile with amusement and keep a tiny niche in the *Québécois* heart."[35]

Ferron's tone is not easy to define. Certainly, he portrays the English as exploiters, but, as his translator Betty Bednarski remarked of the incident, "the satirical little portrait of Scott that grows out of it is, to my mind, quite affectionate.... Indeed, Ferron is attempting in all he writes to assign a *place* to English Canadians in Quebec, a place that will no longer be threatening to the French majority."[36]

In a series of novels published after 1965, Ferron employed the marmalade jar (transformed by this time into a jar of quince jam) and introduced Frank Scott as a major figure in his narratives. In *La Nuit* (1965) Scott is caricatured as Frank Archibald Campbell, a portmanteau name encompassing poets of Canon Scott's generation (Archibald Lampman, Wilfred Campbell and Duncan Campbell Scott). An archetypal WASP, tall, forbidding, and beak-nosed, this "Frank" undertakes a pub crawl that is also a harrowing of hell, perhaps by way of Joyce's *Ulysses*. The "Scot," as he is known, drinks prodigiously and makes love to his girlfriend from Monday to Saturday. He refuses to do so on Sunday, saying even God rested on the Sabbath. As Scott recalled bemusedly, Ferron "seemed to be praising me all the time for retaining a hold on my religion and yet performing so magnificently."[37] *La Nuit* was followed by *La Charrette* (1968), *Le Ciel de Québec* (1969), and *Les Confitures de coing* (1972) (a reworking of *La Nuit* together with Ferron's views on Quebec autonomy), and an appendix, "Le congédiement de Frank Archibald Campbell."

In Ray Ellenwood's translation of *La Charrette*, Campbell, or "Night's Blarneyman-Bailiff," has come to "Hell's Gates," a cabaret / dance hall in old Montreal. There, as was Canon Scott's practice, he begins to recite his verse. The novel refers both to the Wolfe Monument and to Scott's own role in Quebec. Ferron's character, Frank, is a rake described as "a Messiah for straw men."

> Come down from an English
> Pedestal, his own brand of Sinai,
> Bearing tablets of stone,
> No doubt another bloody bailiff
> Serving subpoenas....
>
> I protested, I begged for mercy,
> I told them my name was
> Frank Archibald Campbell,
> Nationality Québécois,
> Just like them.[38]

Ferron's lines parody Scott, the habitué of nightclubs, and his role as a lawgiver, his function as a messiah in the fight against Duplessis (one of the initial hurdles in the Roncarelli case was the struggle to find a bailiff with the courage to subpoena the feared Duplessis), and his claim to be a Quebecer. To Ferron, Scott's desire to associate himself with the Québécois is laughable, a mere affectation by one of the privileged English.

By the summer of 1969, Scott was becoming irritated by Ferron's caricatures. Simultaneously, Ferron wrote to Scott in his characteristic tongue-in-cheek manner observing that since Scott was a public man, "your opinion must certainly concur with mine which is as follows: that between a public man and a public woman there ought not to be a difference." In as much as the phrase "une femme publique" also carries the implied meaning of prostitute, Ferron has neatly suggested that Scott the public figure is also a prostitute of a sort. As such, he can hardly complain if Ferron had made a convenience of him.

> The first time [Ferron goes on] it was in the night [*La Nuit*] – you were more or less poisoned with quince jelly. If my memory is good Naïm Kattan found this a deplorable happening. With more insight Gérard Bessette saw in it a parental conflict constructed along Oedipal schéma.... the Son in order to defend his rights to the future, must kill the Father. It appears that this happens in all families: in a very minor little ceremony, very banal in fact.[39]

Ferron's message is clear. Scott, a representative of the overpowering parental English presence, must be assassinated by the Québécois (and indeed eaten, as Saturn was eaten by his sons) if they are to achieve manhood. Ferron, through metaphor and allegory, is also conducting this "banal little ceremony," as he terms it, in writing about Scott.

By the time *Le Ciel de Québec* was scheduled for the fall of 1969, Ferron had misgivings about his treatment of Scott. Hurtubise Press had returned his manuscript to him on the advice of a lawyer who considered it libelous. Curious about Scott's opinion, Ferron asked Jacques Hébert to invite Scott to a launching. "This would be a good opportunity, as they say in your language of the forest, to let me know it," he wrote.[40] At the reception Scott appears to have agreed to publication: the book, after all, was described as "a little joke" and everyone knew that Ferron was a great practical joker.

Ferron's mixed feelings about Scott – his admiration balanced against his anger – are apparent in a letter he wrote to Ray Ellenwood, the translator of Ferron's novels. "Campbell has lost his language ... I think he'd really like to be a true *québécois*, but that's not easy.... In *La Charrette* he doesn't succeed and remains a kind of disinherited witness, but at the end of *Le Ciel de Québec* he does succeed. Of course after that, the October Crisis came along and spoiled everything."[41]

Subsequently, at a meeting of L'Institut canadien des affaires publiques in the early seventies, Ferron attacked Scott personally. The unfairness of this gesture angered Pierre Trudeau:

> One of the things that made me most angry [about] nationalism in Quebec of the people of my generation [was when they] began to get up and heap scorn on Frank Scott. I remember at L'Institut des affaires publiques, one of the rare meetings I didn't attend but I heard about it from friends, that Jacques Ferron had attacked Frank and said, "Oh well, you know, he's really small potatoes. He's always been the Anglo. He's on the side of the exploiters." You know, the vilest stuff. Separatist thinking from a man as distinguished as Ferron just made me boil with rage because they really didn't know the greatness of this guy and his contribution to all of us.[42]

After October, 1970, there was no common ground between the staunch federalist and the staunch separatist. In 1971 Ferron wrote a fable for a medical journal about the patriots of 1837, emphasizing Jean-Olivier Chenier, a figure he considered more representative of Quebec than the commonly eulogized Papineau. In concluding he remarked, "according to the English custom, they had torn away the heart of the still warm body of Jean-Olivier Chenier. What a great pity it wasn't preserved: Frank Anarcharcis Scot would have been able to flourish it above Quebec, bilingual district."[43] Scott wrote to Dr. R.E.L. Watson, who had sent him a copy of the essay, that he knew and admired Ferron's writing, "but there is an unfairness in this particular piece that I am surprised he would commit to print. He virtually accuses me of wanting to tear the heart out of Quebec! But why would he make it? His judgement seems increasingly warped by his bitterness."[44]

When Ferron was asked, just before his death in 1985, why he had caricatured Scott so relentlessly, he replied: "He was the most outstanding English Canadian, English Quebecer, during the period. He was a brave man but the best part of Frank was Marian."[45] Not surprisingly, he most admired Marian's revolutionary impulse. Commenting on the political love-hate relationship that Ferron felt for Scott, translator Ray Ellenwood noted "It is an amiable quirk of Ferron's work that this recovery of identity often takes place in opposition to various manifestations of Frank Scott, the devil's Queen's Counsel, a worthy enemy, symbol of all that is admirable and deplorable in what Ferron calls the Quebec Rhodesians."[46] Scott is an alter ego, another self. Betty Bednarski has observed, "To come to terms with [the English 'other'], to deal with him, is absolutely essential if the Québécois narrator is to recover his soul – his own and, by implication, Québec's."[47]

In 1981, when the proceedings of a Scott symposium held in Vancouver were going to press, Scott insisted it was the Wolfe-Montcalm Monument in Quebec City under which the jar had been placed and requested this correction be made in an essay by Michael Oliver included in the book. Later, however, a letter was found in Scott's papers from a man whose father had been involved in the turn-of-the-century reconstruction of the Wolfe Monument. It was indeed under this unquestionable symbol of English domination that Canon Scott had buried his jam jar, a kind of time capsule, which the separatists had blown up in 1963. Scott's mental substitution indicated he was adjusting the facts of his life to accord with his vision of history. By metamorphosing the Wolfe Monument into the Wolfe-Montcalm Monument, he also metamorphosed an English imperialist past into the joint heritage of Wolfe and Montcalm, the Canada that he hoped to bring into being. In a sense, Ferron was doing something similar to this in his novels, using Scott and others as symbols within the myth he constructed to make sense of his world. For Ferron, the separatist, it was necessary to assimilate the English in order to ensure the future of Quebec. For Trudeau, the federalist, on the other hand, this aspect of Scott's influence was benign, since Quebec's future could only be perceived from the perspective of one Canada.

Though Frank Scott and Pierre Trudeau agreed (in opposition to Ferron) that Quebec's future could only be perceived from the perspective of one Canada, other events were emerging in the constitutional field which they were to differ about strongly. From Scott's point of view, the greatest threat to Canadian unity was now a series of language bills enacted by the Quebec provincial government. In the late sixties T.P.M. Howard, general counsel for the Protestant School Board of Greater Montreal, had invited Scott to be part of a committee to study constitutional aspects of proposed language bills. Successive Quebec governments had passed a series of language bills designed to establish a unilingual Francophone society. Bill 85, dealing with the language of instruction in schools, had died in the legislature in 1967-68, but in 1968 there had been confrontations with the St. Léonard School Commission concerning the bill. Then, in 1969, Bill 63 was passed, in which the public schools lost the right to choose the language of instruction. This legislation was followed by Bills 27 and 28, which completely reorganized Quebec's education system. Members of the Protestant School Board of Greater Montreal felt increasingly threatened and recognized the argument for English as a language of instruction in Protestant schools in Quebec would have to be based on the BNA Act.

Accordingly, Howard selected a committee consisting of Frank Scott, Jean Martineau, and Peter Laing, with Peter Graham acting as secretary. Howard chaired the committee. For three days a week for three years from 1967 to 1969 the committee assembled at the Windsor Hotel, where they had a special room supplied with reference books. There they worked all day. In 1969 they produced the massive Howard Report, which provided a legal basis for the argument that the language of instruction in Protestant schools in Quebec is guaranteed by Section 93 of the BNA Act. Howard later said that it should have been called the Scott Report because Scott's constitutional expertise provided much of the argument.[48] However, there was little official response to their efforts from either Quebec City or Ottawa.

On February 26, 1971, Scott wrote directly to Prime Minister Trudeau:

I am writing to express my deep concern, indeed consternation, at the proposal to remove the entrenched rights of the English minority in Quebec to the use of their language.

Such a change would violate one of the fundamental principles underlying the Confederation agreement, would destroy the historic rights of the largest minority group in the country, and would mean the rejection of the principles laid down by the B & B Commission which you have hitherto so courageously followed.

May I take the liberty of reminding you of the negotiations that took place at Confederation on the use of language. Bilingualism had been practiced in Quebec from the day of the cession, and in the old Province of Canada from 1841, though not till 1848 were the two versions of the statutes given equal status. But not until Confederation was the discretionary power of the Legislature changed into an entrenched duty in the manner provided by Section 133. And it was at the express request of certain French-speaking members that the duty to publish the statutes and proceedings bilingually was imposed on parliament and the Quebec Legislature.

He also reminded Trudeau that "we have told this story in Chapter III of Volume I of the B and B Report."

No sooner had the committee finished a second report in 1973 than Premier Robert Bourassa's government produced Bill 22, the Official Languages Act, which made French the official language of the province, requiring that it be the language of normal usage in government and business. However, the educational requirements excited the greatest controversy. Bill 22 stated that French was to be the language of instruction in public schools, and this particularly affected immigrants because children whose parents did not have English as a mother tongue would be required to go to French schools.[49]

Scott recalled that in July, 1974, he was one of a group of seven McGill professors who issued a public statement "criticizing not the purpose but some of the harsh provisions" of Bill 22:

We saw in it a direct attack upon the concept of equality between the two principal cultures in the province, as well as upon rights and freedoms long established and in part entrenched in the BNA Act. We objected to the excessive use of Regulations, free from debate in the Assembly, to implement the Bill; to the immunity from judicial review granted to officials enforcing the law; to the evident disregard of the constitutional protection for the denominational schools, whether Protestant or Catholic; and to the form of "statutory patronage," the withholding of all government contracts and aid, from businesses not certified as being "francisé" to the satisfaction of an entirely French governing body. I personally found it inconceivable that a supposedly democratic government should claim the right to limit the growth of the English minority in Quebec by denying access to its schools to any Protestants it chose to exclude by provincial law. The idea of equal partnership and fair treatment of new Canadians, which the B & B Commission sought to achieve, was utterly repudiated. It would obviously have the effect of driving out the anglophones, particularly the younger ones, and thus would achieve a form of "genocide by erosion." The purpose of making French the working language of Quebec could better have been achieved by following the consultation methods urged by the B & B commissioners instead of by this Draconian legislation.[50]

The Protestant School Board brought its case before Chief Justice Deschênes of the Quebec Superior Court, and in 1976 received a 105-page judgement that was felt by many to be "more a social judgement than a legal judgement."[51] In essence Deschênes argued that Section 93 did not give rights to the Protestant School Board with respect to its choice of language of instruction, nor did it otherwise protect language. The committee then prepared to go to the Court of Appeal, but the appeal was rejected. René Lévesque had just been elected Premier; Bill 22 had been repealed and a successor, Bill 101, had now been enacted. The court ruled that since Bill 22 no longer existed, it could not hear the case.

Scott and Trudeau had always enjoyed an amiable correspondence on constitutional matters. But now Scott was writing letters in which he strongly disagreed with Trudeau's attitude to Bill 22. He bitterly resented the fact that the federal cabinet would not exercise the power of disallowance. In his view, this was precisely why this power had been built into the BNA Act, to protect the country from unjust provincial legislation. After receiving a particularly unsatisfactory letter from Trudeau, Scott began an indignant reply:

> If your statement is correct, that Bill 22 is "generally within the legislative authority" of Quebec, then we English speaking Protestants have been living in a fool's paradise for 200 years. We have imagined our right to English-language denominational schools, on which the Quebec system was based by pre-Confederation law, was entrenched. No other province had more than a guarantee for denominational schools. Now the federal government through you says that all that is guaranteed is the existence, the financing and the religious teaching in the schools....
>
> In view of the lengthy study made of the question by Messrs. Martineau, Laing, Howard and Scott in Montreal, how could you possibly state so blandly that past decisions of the courts indicate the

absence of a language guarantee in Section 93? Who is there in the Dept. of Justice with superior knowledge of the law? Who ever studied the pre-Confederation law in Quebec from this point of view before we did? Our opinion is not necessarily correct, but it surely makes it clear that the right to have English text-books and English teachers was provided by law for Protestant denominational schools in 1867.

The difficulty with Scott's position was that in comparable cases involving French-language education rights in the Anglophone provinces, the courts had said that the separate school guarantee for Catholics did not include the right to trial in French.

Scott was particularly irritated at Trudeau's suggestion that they would have to wait to see how the bill was applied in specific situations before the federal cabinet decided whether intervention were necessary. This was a specious argument because, as he pointed out, "disallowance must be exercised within one year from receipt of the official text of the law." He ended his letter with a personal plea to Trudeau to intervene in the Quebec language situation to secure justice.

> Every now and then certain elements in Quebec have to be checked, Pierre, and this is one such occasion. We would still have the Padlock Act if the Supreme Court had not saved the day for Quebec liberals. Same with arbitrary executive action but for Roncarelli. Same with terrorism but for your action against the FLQ. The forces growing stronger in Quebec which threaten Confederation will not be stopped, but made more hungry, by appeasement. You must assert a higher moral set of values. You and your ministers must openly defend the cultural rights of the anglophone Quebecers as well as French minorities elsewhere, not suggest they don't matter any more than what goes on in B.C. or Newfoundland. The moral shoe is now on the other foot. I know the situation is difficult, but so was your going into the rapids in the Slave River. You give money to the Indians to fight their case: the Protestant School Boards are just as deserving: they fear Bourassa will cut their grants if they use them to defend their rights.

After completing this draft on August 27, 1975, Scott reconsidered. He did not like making personal pleas. And his letter asked for consideration on the basis of past friendship. He may also have retained some hope that the Prime Minister would still intervene. Trudeau did not, probably because he and his advisers considered it too dangerous to do so in such a volatile political situation and risk losing the federal Liberal constituency in Quebec. Little more than a year after finishing the letter Scott wrote in the upper left-hand corner: "*Not Sent*. Regret it now. F.R.S. 24-10-76."

By late 1976, Premier Lévesque's government had been installed and was preparing Bill 101, which in essence made Quebec a unilingual Francophone society for all purposes within the control of the provincial government. This bill, passed in 1977, stipulated that the quality and influence of the French language were to be assured in all provincial government business, in the law, and in normal everyday usage of work. Thus French became the language of instruction, commerce, and business. A unilingual Francophone society that denied rights Quebec Anglophones considered had been accorded to them, whether by history or by law, had now been legislated into existence.

Eugene Forsey speculated in the mid-seventies that passing the language bills in Quebec changed Scott's favourable view of the "Two Nations Policy," approved by the CCF at its founding convention:

Judging by some of the things he said to me at the time of Bill 22 I think he probably has had second thoughts. I know on one occasion during our discussion on Bill 22 he said to me: "You know for years I've spoken French whenever I've had the opportunity. Now I'm damned if I'll speak French." Frank has found himself, tragically I think for him, towards the end of his life. I hope he'll live many years yet, but he's now getting up into his seventies. He's several years older than I. He's found himself tragically after a lifetime of fighting for the rights of French Canadians very much a member of the English-speaking minority in Quebec, willy-nilly.[52]

For some English Quebecers the matter was a tempest in a teapot. It was not all that difficult to learn French and co-exist. Why had Scott become so agitated over Bills 22 and 101 to become the typical Westmount Englishman, an apparent reactionary? Robert Stocks, a young Montreal lawyer who worked with Forsey in trying to nudge the Trudeau government on the language issue, understood:

Scott felt truly that the English language rights were enshrined in sections 93 and 133 of the BNA Act as they were not enshrined in the

Quebec constitution and that this guarantee or constitutional right was violated by the successive language bills. It was important because English was a large minority in the province of Quebec. One of the largest minorities in Canada. This was a serious violation of civil liberties and civil rights and Frank had been fighting for this all his life.[53]

# TWENTY-FIVE

# "Take Care – of Canada"

❧

FOR SCOTT, the seventies were a particularly painful decade. He was disillusioned about politics in Quebec and anguished over the larger problem of Canadian unity. Now, in the twilight of his life, he began to reflect on his own life and its connections with Canada's past. As so often had been the case in the past, his deeper feelings found relief in satiric verse. Now an old man and fretting that Quebec might no longer be a part of Canada when he died, Scott liked to declaim, parodying Rupert Brooke:

> If I should die, think only this of me:
>     That there's some corner of a foreign field
> That is for ever Canada. There shall be
>     In that rich earth a richer dust concealed ...[1]

There was bitter humour in this metaphor. Quebec, under the Parti Québécois, seemed determined to eradicate both the English in the province and the idea of Canada. It was not just the increasing attack on English minority rights posed by Quebec's successive language bills that made Quebec an effectively unilingual Francophone society. Nor was it merely pressures from the province for new constitutional arrangements with Canada. It was the very real fear Quebec would become foreign soil. The White Paper on Sovereignty-Association tabled in the Quebec National Assembly in 1979 proposed the province become a politically sovereign state with citizenship, passports, membership in NATO, NORAD, the United Nations, and, possibly, the British Commonwealth. It defined sovereignty-association as "the power to make decisions autonomously, without being subject in law to any superior or exterior power."[2] In effect, if Quebecers voted in the 1980 sovereignty-association referendum to negotiate with Canada the terms of this White Paper, it was quite conceivable the Quebec that Scott loved so well could indeed become "foreign soil." His rational self did not believe the average Quebecer would vote to leave Canada: there was too much at stake on the economic side. But his emotional self, rooted in Quebec, had an apocalyptic side. When it was a choice of two options he invariably feared the worst.

Scott had followed the hard-fought referendum campaign closely. The federal Liberals, including Prime Minister Trudeau and Justice Minister Jean Chrétien, had countered with an effective plan that ridiculed sovereignty-association and concentrated on the economic dangers to Quebecers should they separate from the rest of Canada. Scott had the distinct pleasure of watching Trudeau, his one-time protégé, fight for a united Canada. And he received immediate reports of activities on the Quebec scene from his close friend Thérèse Casgrain, who took an active part on the federal side, campaigning for a "no" vote. Nearly 86 per cent of the eligible voters turned out on May 20, 1980, and the result was approximately a 60-40 split in favour of the "no."³ For Scott the immediate danger of Quebec's physical separation from Canada was alleviated. But it had been a close battle and a worrying period. He was emotionally exhausted and the matter of the language bills was still not settled. For Quebecers, the result of the referendum was that Premier Lévesque went to a new round of constitutional negotiations a few months later with far less power than Quebec had possessed before the confrontation.

Scott had remained very much a part of the continuing debate on the constitution. His *Essays on the Constitution: Aspects of Canadian Law and Politics*, one of the major texts depicting the historical context of the constitutional issue, had, in fact, won the 1978 Governor General's Award for non-fiction. As this volume shows, Scott's belief that Canada needed to reassess or replace the BNA Act and that any revision must have an entrenched Bill of Rights can be traced to his essays of the thirties and forties. It was not an uncommon idea at that time. The intriguing question is the extent to which Scott, through his friendship with Trudeau and other key individuals involved in constitutional reform, and indirectly through the publication of articles included in his *Essays on the Constitution*, specifically influenced debates in the seventies. He himself never made this claim; indeed, it is doubtful if he considered it at length. Nonetheless, the historical evidence is persuasive.

Throughout the thirties Scott had been one of the strongest advocates of Canada's need for greater autonomy in foreign affairs. And for him, as for many Quebecers, the possibility of World War II had made this matter all the more acute. In "A Policy of Neutrality for Canada" (1939) he had argued for "the idea of Canada, the nation. The building of an orderly and just society within this vast territory ...."[4] As the ring of this phrase the "just society" indicates, it was also a concept adopted by Trudeau, who shared Scott's belief that to bring such a society into being it was first necessary to patriate the constitution. Only then could Canada properly direct its domestic and foreign affairs.

Scott believed that the BNA Act set out the proper division of powers between federal and provincial governments and was a flexible document, adaptable to changing events. However, like most commentators in the thirties, he believed the intent of the Fathers of Confederation had been frustrated by successive interpretations of the BNA Act by the Privy Council, especially by Lords Watson and Haldane. In his view, a constitution designed to guarantee a strong federal government had been whittled down, through misinterpretation, to the benefit of the provinces. When the Privy Council struck down Bennett's "New Deal" Scott felt Canada had been shorn of the power it required to remedy the exigencies of the depression. It was at that time he had insisted that this Privy Council decision had been made by "none but foreign judges ignorant of the Canadian environment and none too well versed in Canadian constitutional law ...."[5] Scott subsequently made it his central theme that Canadians must bring home the constitution, to fulfil their "rendez-vous with the BNA Act."[6]

In the twenties his own mentor, J.S. Woodsworth, had been an early advocate of both patriation of the BNA Act and entrenchment of a Bill of Rights. As early as 1933 the Regina Manifesto, a document Scott helped refine, urged protection of minority rights, as did *Social Planning for Canada* a few years later. Writing in 1948, he argued that a Bill of Rights should be entrenched because a mere statute could easily be repealed by the government of the day. "The addition of a new section to the BNA Act containing a list of further rights, entitled Bill of Rights, should therefore be looked upon as something which would carry forward and enlarge upon rules already formulated in our constitution."[7]

After his return from his world tour in 1948, Pierre Trudeau had become economic adviser to the Privy Council. As assistant to Gordon Robertson, then a member of the cabinet secretariat in the Privy Council Office, he worked on a fifty-page memo on federal-provincial relationships for two dominion-provincial conferences on patriating the constitution and the entrenchment of human rights.[8] There his earlier tutelage by Scott was undoubtedly reinforced. Scott had always believed the purpose of a constitution in a democratic state is to define and protect the rights of the individual. Similarly, throughout the fifties and early sixties, Trudeau strongly advocated democracy because it best protected the rights of the individual. Scott believed, and Trudeau concurred, the best way to ensure democracy is through a Bill of Rights. During the fifties, the Roncarelli and Padlock cases had demonstrated once again to Scott (and perhaps to Trudeau, who invariably was in the courtroom when Scott pleaded) that only the federal government and the constitution of Canada could protect the rights of minorities.[9]

For both Scott and Trudeau, Prime Minister John Diefenbaker's 1960 Bill of Rights was inadequate. In four talks prepared for CBC radio in 1959, *The Canadian Constitution and Human Rights*, Scott pointed out the purpose of Diefenbaker's proposed bill was "not the enactment of a strict legal rule which the courts can enforce but a statement of principles."[10] Such declarations made public the vague yearnings for liberty inherent in all human beings, but they fell far short of what he would call a true Bill of Rights, one laying down rules binding on courts or legislatures. As one of three choices open to Canadians, Scott proposed an amendment to the BNA Act that would cover the whole of Canada and place certain freedoms beyond the control of any legislature. Diefenbaker assumed, however, and probably correctly, that this was a utopian proposal impossible to attain at that time.

Scott also kept a keen eye on proposed revisions to the constitution as they affected Quebec. In fact, he helped initiate what might be termed the second cycle of federal-provincial constitutional negotiations in the sixties. Concerned that the Royal Commission on Bilingualism and Biculturalism was getting beyond its commissioners' expertise, Scott had made his suggestion to Prime Minister Lester Pearson that he establish a special committee to take cognizance of the constitutional needs of Quebecers.[11] As a possible member of the proposed constitutional committee he had recommended Michael Pitfield. This committee, working in the Privy Council Office, had included not only his former student Pitfield but also senior officials like Gordon Robertson and R.B. Bryce, and for a time Trudeau until, in 1965, he joined the Liberal Party and was elected to Parliament.[12]

In January, 1966, Trudeau was appointed parliamentary secretary to Prime Minister Pearson and in April, 1967, Minister of Justice. In this capacity he took charge of Pearson's constitutional committee. Initially Trudeau, like Scott, was not enthusiastic about wholesale constitutional reform. However, he did want to see a Charter of Rights entrenched in the constitution, primarily, one suspects, to protect French-language rights.

As earlier noted, in 1967 Prime Minister Pearson had agreed with the provinces to carry out a constitutional review. It began in February, 1968, with Trudeau an active participant as Minister of Justice and, after April, 1968, with him as Prime Minister. The talks continued until 1971.

After application of the War Measures Act and the 1971 failure to reach an agreement in Victoria (the Victoria Charter), Scott became increasingly pessimistic about constitutional reform. Several years later, writing to Allan Blakeney, he itemized his thoughts on the Constitution:

1. Patriation must be stopped immediately. How can you make sensible plans for amendments and amending procedures when you don't know what kind of country you are foreseeing? You must accept the possibility that Quebec will at some time vote for independence.

2. The next question is, assuming the rest of us want to save what we can (look at the map – it's a big piece) what parts of the present constitution must we save? It is the constitution we shall have to work with. So don't allow any further pieces to be chipped off in the hope of holding Quebec in. Trudeau was absolutely right in saying that it is a grave illusion to think that those who seek the break-up of Canada will suddenly cease to pursue their objective simply because the provincial governments have increased their powers in some areas. Feeding bits of power to those who want more just makes them more hungry.

3. No more vetos over future amendments at this stage. All this talk is premature. As long as the constitution stays in England, we control its changes through the federal Parliament. We may have to act fast to avoid other break-aways.

4. Stall for time. Appoint more committees. Ask for statistics. Quebec is out to prove she pays more to Ottawa than she gets. Apply psychological warfare; she has been getting more than her share in many ways. (Canada Council has just bought 106,000 books to give away – 370 French titles and 320 English!). Remind Quebec that the boundaries of 1912 would have to be re-established, since James Bay area was given to a province, not a foreign country. If a common currency and customs union is what is meant by "sovereignty," then start a long study of its implications, which would imply a common tariff and free movement of workers across provincial boundaries. And demand the entrenchment of a real Bill of Rights, not just French language rights – not forgetting the million anglophones in Quebec, Canada's fourth largest English-speaking province.[13]

By mid-August of 1978 a parliamentary constitutional committee working in Ottawa was considering a draft document, Bill C-60, which the government had presented for purposes of debate. Scott was asked by Prime Minister Trudeau to revise and condense the Bill of Rights to be included in the new Constitutional Act. Scott agreed to do so, but almost instantly regretted the decision.

In his small study at North Hatley, writing laboriously by hand, he sent a letter to Pitfield explaining his withdrawal.

Dear Mike.

I owe you some explanation of my sudden change of mind over the revising and condensing of the Bill of Rights statement. As you did not call me back I would like to indicate briefly what my reasons were.

The first was the fear of re-awakening my erratic heartbeat, which I have now under good control. Once I had accepted your invitation to try my hand at revising so important a document as the B/R [Bill of Rights] must be I began to start worrying. Did I have to accept the basic principles already agreed on? Suppose, as is highly probable, I found them inadequate or even offensive (like the present phrase about "the Supremacy of God"?). Would I become involved in a series of committee meetings this autumn, thus destroying any hope of completing the new book of essays [to be edited by Michiel Horn] and the Collected Poems now well underway?

A deeper reason for withdrawing my collaboration was a profound sense of hopelessness in our constitutional future. I am afraid I have not recovered from the blow to all my beliefs dealt by Bill C-60. If the previous constitution was unworkable, the one that seems to be emerging will be doubly so. The rot that started as far back as the constitutional conferences of 1950-1960, (when the word *Canada* did not appear on the Conference Table) which I attended, has not been checked; on the contrary Pierre himself, despite some brave words about the need for a strong government at Ottawa, has aided and abetted the disintegration. I dubbed him a "separatist by abandonment" as he let fall the unity of CBC, the monitoring of medicare payments, the opportunity of preventing the vast flood of unconstitutional PQ legislation under Bills 22 and 101, etc. What I asked myself was, how does a Bill of Rights fit into the new constitution? Will there be a preamble to the revised BNA Act different from the preamble to the B/R? I don't want to try to improve the wording of a part of the document in ignorance of the shape and power-distribution in the whole structure.

To some degree the letter reflects the legal theorist and the idealist confronted with the pragmatics of practical politics. One could always argue that Scott's "one Canada" had been held together since before he was born by such political compromises. Indeed, the confederation of British North America was itself such a compromise.

Nonetheless, the result of these internal questionings was Scott's realization that he had agreed too hastily. He then began to experience bouts of tachycardia that left him weak and breathless, unable to think or work. These attacks, in turn, forced him to recognize that he could never go back into legal harness. However, after the election in 1980 it was some comfort to him that Pitfield was once again clerk of the Privy Council. He concluded his letter of refusal to Pitfield on a lighter note. "It is cheering to know that you are back in your old office. And Trudeau may save something from the wreckage if he can summon up the courage to use some of the powers he still has. Otherwise I fear we are doomed, and I must complete two private jobs that no one else can perform for me." He ended his letter, "Take care – of Canada."[14]

One of these private jobs was, as he had said, collecting his poems; the other was gathering his additional legal and social essays. Scott now began to withdraw more and more from the public world of constitutional debate into the more private world of his own writings. On August 16 he wrote his biographer a testy letter expressing his annoyance, mostly with himself (he had been frustrated in attempts to find two of his books) but also with the larger proposals for constitutional reform that fell so short of his earlier ideals. "Still haven't found [my Thomas] à Kempis, or my Democratic Manifesto, but frankly I have been pestered by visitors and well-wishers, not to mention Ottawa pundits who want me to make their constitutional proposals less stupid. I feel that if a thing is not worth doing at all it is not worth doing well; some reforms are needed, but not these ones."[15]

After federal-provincial meetings in 1978 and 1979 and the post-referendum conference of 1980 had failed, and after diverse judgements rendered by the Manitoba, Quebec, and Newfoundland courts of appeal, Prime Minister Trudeau was forced to request the Supreme Court of Canada to rule on the legality of Parliament's direct request to the British Parliament for patriation with the support of only two provinces, Ontario and New Brunswick. The Supreme Court rendered a complex judgement in September, 1981, to the effect that although the Trudeau government had legal authority to proceed with patriation of the constitution, constitutional convention required a substantial measure of provincial consent. Faced with this ruling, the federal government had no option but to attempt to secure agreement with the provinces. At the conference of November, 1981, a "brutal compromise," which excluded Quebec, was secured among the provinces. René Lévesque, Premier of Quebec, left the conference infuriated, and the emotional climate between French and English in Quebec deteriorated further. However, the agreement of nine provinces had been achieved. A constitutional solution had at last been found.

Scott watched the patriation ceremony of April 17, 1982, on television in King Gordon's living room in Ottawa. The two couples popped a bottle of champagne and proposed a toast. Marian, granddaughter as she was of that staunch Presbyterian, Dr. Barclay, sang along with the hymn, her face shining.[16] The Canadian constitution, which first Woodsworth and then Scott had always said should come home, was finally back in Canada. And it was complete with the new Canadian Charter of Rights the two men had advocated and Trudeau had finally brought into being.

Predictably, however, Scott was not pleased. The Charter of Rights, with its "notwithstanding" clause, permitted provinces and Parliament to opt out: "to set aside fundamental freedoms, legal rights and equality rights by passing legislation which expressly declares it will operate 'notwithstanding' the provisions of the Charter."[17] This clause, in Scott's view, gutted the protection offered to minorities. Moreover, he did not approve of the imperial style with which Trudeau had stage-managed the patriation ceremony. Scott was annoyed that there was so little reference to the English in the actual ceremony. Like the younger Trudeau when travelling down the Mackenzie River, Scott was indignant at the omission of his own racial past, and for the same reason – only now there seemed to be no *English* names. In a letter to his niece, Rosemary Walters, he complained: "Trudeau browned me off the patriation ceremony by his overloading it with French speeches & French names; imagine not an English-Canadian name on the official document recording the event. But Trudeau himself is there, signing as though he were making the gesture.... He is stirring up anti-Quebec feeling everywhere by such tactics: Ontario is now more bilingual than Quebec, despite [Section] 133 of the BNA Act."[18]

Two years earlier, following the Quebec referendum in May, 1980, Scott had reminisced on his life's work on the constitution.

Almost I reached the point that Donald Creighton had reached when he said "I spent my entire life writing the history of a country that no longer exists." He said, "I've wasted my life." This made it impossible for me to take part in any active way in the debate because if the federalist forces won, which they did, they have already committed themselves to a further aggravation of our difficulties by a further decentralization and a further break-up of the old notion of Confederation. Even Pierre Trudeau himself contributed to this disappearance of the old concept of Canada by his willingness to make concession after concession to the demands of the Quebec nationalists.... This turned me towards a greater interest in literature and poetry, and I have plenty of work I could do there and I didn't see what I could do that would be helpful on the political and constitutional side. Hence I have kept a very low profile in this whole debate.

Maybe I was intended [to be] on the poetical side from the start more completely. This is an old story, but we had made great progress in building the country and it showed the power of the original concept of federal responsibility on matters of common interest to the whole country. World War II required that the federal government be the mainspring of initiative in developing new war industries.... We put the unemployed back to work and the effort left us with a feeling of what is capable [of being done] under the old constitution when there was this co-operative spirit about.[19]

It was one of the last sustained laments of the old warrior.

WHENEVER LIFE on the political side became more than he could bear, Scott turned back to his old love – poetry. Long before, in the forties, he had written a poem, "Archive," which was an assessment of his own past life.

> Table this document: to wit, one page
> Found in the odd detritus of this age.
> A simple chapter, in the English tongue,
> Of normal length and paragraphed. Begun
> In gentle language, probing for the heart,
> But soon involuntarily made a part
> Of social change and crisis; men at war
> Defending systems rotten at the core.... (*C.P.*, p. 83)

By the early seventies, the impulse toward self-definition returned more strongly than before. It was partly a sense of narrowing time, the urge to make one's mark on history. "Save me from oblivion," he remarked to Elspeth Chisholm, a freelance journalist for the CBC who interviewed him early in the seventies.[20]

He was beginning to recognize what a remarkable life he had led. All kinds of people wanted to write profiles, do films, and consult his files; all recognized his continuing involvement with "Canada's century." Michiel Horn, a history student at York University, later a professor, was researching his early papers for a history of the LSR. A decade earlier Walter Young had done the same for his history of the CCF. The Ontario Institute for Studies in Education made a film on Scott the poet. Mavor Moore was dramatizing the Roncarelli case for the CBC. Publishing houses such as Knopf in New York and friends and editors such as William Toye of Oxford and Douglas Gibson of Macmillan urged Scott to write his autobiography.

Scott remained hesitant. Another old friend, John K. Fairbank, director of the East Asian Research Center of Harvard University, put forward the strongest case when he wrote Scott in 1971, "Life is an assertion of values, but they may be better perceived in retrospect." What were Scott's efforts really about? "Autobiography," Fairbank reminded Scott, "is a double life: you now, observing you then. This makes it fun, often funny. The mis-efforts and blind alleys are instructive. The continuing themes emerge. It is a great challenge to create a piece of literature, given this wealth of subject matter." Fairbank added a firm note. "Your scope has been so wide and multi-channelled, you are challenged to get yourself into a single perspective ...."

> This task is a remaining duty. One can't interact with history and then be a hit-and-run artist, go away and leave it. You have to pull it together, even if it's a schizoid history of a triple life. An accounting is due. You have still to be heard from. If you told the world off earlier, you must now have the last word. Toss a tack in the path of the juggernaut.[21]

Fairbank's remarks were shrewd. The remaining task was to bring his careers in law, poetry, and politics into a coherent whole that would illuminate the man. For this, the Canadian content was essential. Even behind the verbal thrusts of his latest book, *Trouvailles: Poems from Prose* (1967), was Scott's abiding concern for social justice in Canada. *Trouvailles*, as the name suggests, consists of "found poems," that is, poems not conceived directly in the imagination of the poet but found, pre-existing, in adjacent lines of prose.

Scott saw the truth of Fairbank's remarks; moreover, his vision of auto-biography was congenial, but, he told his friend, there were other problems to be faced.

> My greatest enemy now is a distrust of my capacity to sustain the story well. I have always been harsh with myself. Guilt, the dirty rat, gnaws away. Maybe I am my own juggernaut. Maybe I'll have to put that tack in front of myself! I'm tempted to relax and play tick-tack-toe. There are always green leaves on trees, or, as today, dark branches overlined in white snow. Such things are all about us, if we look.[22]

Scott, with his profound self-awareness, was moving to the heart of the problem – guilt induced by an overly severe super-ego. His memory for dates and events was failing and, a perfectionist, he could not bear to write anything not first rate. The temptation was to throw it all up and do other things. This appealed to the poet in him. Just outside his study on Remembrance Day in 1971, as he replied to Fairbank, the dark branches on Clarke Avenue were overlaid with white snow: it was the beauty of the Canadian winter he had first glimpsed back in the rectory garden in Quebec City at the start of the century. Memoir writing would mean subordinating the poet to the scholar and, he wrote, "I am only partly a scholar, as I seem to be only partly everything else."[23]

But he did want to talk out some of his story in a context allowing for accuracy. Scott liked working in tandem; his long years with the CCF had given him a facility for group work. In the late fifties and sixties he had particularly enjoyed working on his translations of Quebec poetry with Micheline Ste-Marie and Jeanne Lapointe. Now he began to talk informally with a number of students who were writing master's and doctoral theses on his work. There were longer interviews with Horn and other individuals on the significance of the LSR and the CCF. He encouraged Victor Hoar (later Howard) from Michigan State University, who was writing on the depression. He asked his younger brother Arthur to bring Foxe's *Book of Martyrs* from Quebec City. At North Hatley the two men began to record what they could remember of early days in the rectory. Scott was especially pleased when Elspeth Chisholm began several biographical interviews. In the meantime, he made additional efforts to record his life as a poet. When Fred Cogswell decided against writing a book on Scott's poetry for the Copp Clark series on Canadian criticism, he approached Doug Jones, who admired his work. Would Jones do a book on the poetry? Jones was provided with several armloads of documents but at the end of a year he brought them all back. As Scott wrote in reply to a query from Stephen Williams, an editor at Clarke Irwin, on March 13, 1977: "Two poets have already been asked to take on the assignment; one refused, the other lasted a year and then withdrew. Both could face the poetry side, but were fearful of my law and politics. I don't blame them."

Scott was in a quandary. He wanted to write his memoirs, and indeed he had had several offers of assistance from fine political historians. But he had been unwilling to commit himself, perhaps because memoir writing implied a recognition of mortality. "The question of my autobiography," he assured Williams, "has often arisen.... Then I remember that Bertrand Russell did not begin his until he was around ninety. As I have decided to live till the year 2000 so as to intrude on three centuries, there still seems to be time ahead." The question of a biography or someone to help with his memoirs was another matter. But who? Undoubtedly he was casting around for some suitable individual when, on Remembrance Day of 1974, the author interviewed him for a projected history of English-Canadian poetry.

Although he had first thought of memoirs, this concept soon changed to biography. This was a genre in which Scott took great technical interest: he liked to refer to his life as an "onion," the layers of which the biographer would have to peel back, presumably not without some discomfort. During the next few years he remained bemused by the "process" of biography to which he (a "patient lump of clay") and his life were being subjected. On July 1, 1979, he wrote to Leon Edel, thanking him for a copy of *Bloomsbury: A House of Lions* (1979), and speculated on how he would come through the biographical mill. The note ended with a whiff of mortality: "Hatley life moves gently along. AJM hopes to be in his cottage by July 11th. Alas, we see each other waiting our turn." Scott was right. His birthday party on August 1, 1979, proved to be the last that he and his close friends, Arthur Smith and John Glassco, would share together.

A decade earlier, Smith and Scott had visited a small graveyard in the Eastern Townships and recorded their visit in photographs. Smith stood by a tombstone marked "SCOTT" and Scott posed by another marked "SMITH." Together they wrote a parody for future generations about the identity of "the great Canadian poet" of the years 1920-1970. "Some say his name was Smith, others thought Scott ... the founder of a Communist Youth movement known as the CFC .... His love poetry ... was both passionate and witty ... Some of his nature poetry was inspired by the beautiful lakes and mountains of the Eastern Townships...." A tomb equidistant from Magog and North Hatley was thought to be the poet's resting place.[24] Their lives and their poetry, as both understood, had been intertwined ever since the twenties, when they had first encountered modernism together. Now they were growing old and both acknowledged and quipped about the inevitability of approaching death.

Scott's eightieth birthday party was held in North Hatley on a misty grey day that turned sunny toward noon. The white cottage, colonial in style with a wide front verandah, stands on the side of a wooded hill with Lake Massawippi shining below. Throughout the morning there was a bustle of preparation: the picking up of groceries, the setting out of food and the filling of the house with wild flowers: Queen Anne's lace, loosestrife, ironweed, and the mustard-coloured tansy, "Frank's birthday plant," because it always seemed to come out in time for his birthday.

On the wide verandah facing the lake there were several rockers and other chairs made of white wicker: homey, faded, pleasant. Hanging from pillars supporting the roof were several bird-feeders made by Scott from sticks and scraps of wood. He particularly liked to watch the feeding birds. One of the best photographs of the poet as an old man, one revealing a gentleness hidden in his younger self, was taken on just such an occasion by another friend, the New York photographer Lois Lord.

As the guests arrived, they joined others sitting on the verandah drinking coffee: Eloise Street, a long-time summer visitor to North Hatley, and A.J.M. Smith, who arrived on the arm of Buffy Glassco, Parisian in a cravat. Smith had become nearly blind during the preceding year and was unable to recognize other guests until he moved quite close to them. A little later a contingent of other literary friends arrived: Louis Dudek and his wife, Aileen Collins; Doug and Monique Jones; Ron and Jean Sutherland.

When everyone had arrived, Smith suddenly felt very tired. Off the verandah was a large window opening on to the living room. There, next to the window, he lay quietly but could still participate in the conversation. And while lunch was served a circle gathered around him. After lunch, Dudek and Sutherland, with bagpipes and mandolin, marched in in processional. "We must strike a solemn note as befits the occasion," said Scott. "I'm singing my swan song," said Smith. And everyone laughed. None wanted to face the fact Smith was dying and that Scott had little time left. In fact, Arthur Smith died the following year, and Buffy Glassco the year after that. Scott was to outlive these two important friends, though not by very long.

Early in the following year in Vancouver the F.R. Scott Conference was held on February 20-22, 1981. It was organized by faculty associated with the Centre for Canadian Studies at Simon Fraser University to honour Scott and to assess his life and work. In the sense that the conference was a retrospective, it was a continuation of the "summing up" or recovery of the past that had preoccupied him throughout the seventies. Scott was dubious about attending: "Should I attend my own symposium? I really don't want to. There seems something wrong about it. Is Morley Callaghan going to Ottawa U for his? Smith sat through his one at MSU: I can see his face slightly worried, looking at me as I gave the final paper. Because he was there, nobody said a nasty word."[25] Scott did not approve of conferences for living people. During the 1976 Smith Symposium at Michigan State University in East Lansing he had snorted his disapproval: "Smith is erecting his own mausoleum."[26] Eventually, however, at a dinner given by Senator Carl Goldenberg and attended by his younger colleague in the Oil Workers' case, then Mr. Justice Thomas Berger, he was prevailed upon to attend. His sense of humour rose to the occasion; the chance to view his own "pre-mortem," he decided, was irresistible.[27]

Once in Vancouver he was surprised to discover the whole process was enjoyable. He justified his presence with a few lines of doggerel. "Gather your honours while you may, / Your fame is soon forgotten, / And that bright silk you wear today / Tomorrow will be cotton."[28] Later, writing to Hugh Keenleyside, he confessed: "when I first heard of it I [said] I would not go, not being totally dead, but in the end I am glad to say I changed my mind and thoroughly enjoyed it all. So many old friends, so many nostalgic memories. The gut feeling all the time was Canada, not me: I provided an excuse for looking over the scene."[29]

And so it was. In many ways the Scott symposium was an index to Canadian history and culture of the past sixty years. Certainly there seemed to be no other individual in Canada for whom the Prime Minister of the country, the Chief Justice of the Supreme Court, the first mandarin of the Ottawa civil service, the director-general of the National Arts Centre, and the associate director of the Canada Council would gather to take part in a pre-conference entertainment. But all did so for Frank Scott because he had had such a direct influence on their lives. The skit, written by Timothy Porteous and Donald MacSween, was, like their earlier joint effort, *My Fur Lady*, highly topical. One Wilbur Throckmorton, Cherubim Second Class, fired from the Celestial Civil Service for his role in creating Scott, an irritant in the celestial machinery, has appealed to the Celestial Supreme Court. His advocates, the Archclerk Michael (Pitfield) and St. Peter (Trudeau), advise Jehovah, J., the presiding judge, "to hold his nose" and grant the appeal. This comment parodied Prime Minister Trudeau's remark to the British Parliament, whose Kershaw Committee was then suggesting the Canadian federal government was exceeding its power in unilaterally requesting patriation of the BNA Act without the provinces' consent. In the skit, Jehovah (Chief Justice Bora Laskin) reinstates Throckmorton, observing the issue turns on the question of "whether or not Scott has been good for Canada."[30]

The skit was amusing but the implicitly nationalist comment was serious. Many of Scott's contemporaries shared his nationalist vision of Canada as a self-governing nation north of the 49th parallel; a lesser number shared his socialist vision of a humane society where all Canadians might be equal. But few had his range of concern, the force of personality, and the gift of language to convey this vision to all those he encountered. Some of his achievements in poetry, law, and politics were well known but others emerged during the proceedings, notably Walter Tarnopolsky's judgement on the significance of Scott the legal essayist in establishing minority rights and civil liberties in Canada. Still other aspects of his contributions to Canadian culture, especially his significance as an *éminence grise* in the patriation of the Canadian constitution, were not made known to the audience – indeed, they were perhaps not recognized by Scott himself or by Trudeau. The last image of Frank and Marian Scott at the conference is that of two shadows – one tall and gangly, bending over to meet the other, petite, looking up; they were holding hands and swinging them, like happy children, as they walked down the long winding corridor at Vancouver airport.

A few months later, in Winnipeg in early June, Scott received the Governor General's Award for his *Collected Poems*. He had been busy collecting and arranging the poems ever since the mid-seventies when a severe attack of tachycardia had reminded him that there was one task remaining which only he could complete. Working from a preliminary bibliography (prepared by British Columbia bibliographer Marilyn Flitton), he received a small grant from the Canada Council to track down the poems. These he xeroxed and put in a three-ring binder. This unwieldy manuscript went into a shopping bag he carried around for seven years between Montreal and North Hatley and once, in the early stages, to Vancouver. Scott agonized over the selection and arrangement of his poems, consulting with a number of his friends, including Smith, Dudek, and Glassco, among others. Should the satires be included with the serious poems? And what about the early juvenile verse? To be sure it would give the reader a better sense of his development, but who wants to put lesser verses first?

He had become convinced that the proper order for the poems was chronological for, as he liked to remark, they constituted a "mini-biog-raphy," covering his life from the early twenties when he was first courting Marian ("Below Quebec") up to "The Indians Speak at Expo '67." But given this premise, what should be the internal order? Within a series of thematic categories he arranged his poems roughly by date of composition and then made use of a technique he had learned from Smith. He had always admired Smith's method of organizing a book of poems. This was simply to fan the pages of typed poems, like a pack of playing cards, and arrange them by "feel," or similarities in theme and tone. The first section, "Indications," is a selection of juvenile verse; "Laurentian" covers most of the Laurentian poems up through the forties, while later sections cover the depression, the war, and the fifties.

Ultimately he decided to divide the satires, with the lesser ones coming near the end. Also included are a series of found poems and a collection of his translations, including the last published translation of "Le Tombeau des Rois." The book ends with his translation of Pierre Trottier's suggestive "Time Corrected."

> So I retraced my steps
> I retreated to my birth
> And rolled back to their beginnings
> My family and all my ancestors ...
>
> And then
> Nothing remained for me
> But to give up the first sigh
> In order to blow out the light
> And everything returned to darkness   (C.P., p. 357)

Scott has always been known as an incisive satirist and as a poet of the Laurentians. Yet, when all the poems were gathered, it was the reflective and strongly humanist Scott, especially the love poet, who proved dom-inant. The section "Insights," which covers the poems of his middle years and contains "Message," "Departure," "Excursion," "Dancing," "Vision," and "Last Rites," is among the most powerful in the book, followed only by the section "Journeys" with the moving humanist poems "A Grain of Rice" and "Japanese Sand Garden." In these poems a perception of nature combines movingly with the poet's own larger meditation.

With time the satirist poet has become somewhat eclipsed; admirable, but not quite to the extent as when engaged in the thick of battle, nearly forty years ago. Some of the targets of this satire no longer exist. To be sure, the wit and energy of his ripostes at subjects like "W.L.M.K." and "The Bartail Cock" (a self-portrait) are savoured. Ironically, however, one of the strongest impressions from the satiric poems is Scott's moral indignation – his rage for social order. Scott, who had once indignantly complained that his predecessors in Canadian poetry, "Roberts, Carman, Lampman, Scott," were valued for "their faith in philanthropics, and their earnest thought," must also be appreciated, if only partially, for his social – and thus philanthropic – concerns.

How are we to rank Scott in Canadian poetry? He takes his place with Pratt and Birney as one of the three primary modernists, perhaps a little behind both. He takes primacy before Smith, a better craftsman, and before Klein, whose moral indignation was nearly as great as his own. But Scott's poetic canvas is greater than either of these poets and neither has had quite his influence on younger poets. Like Pratt (and sometimes in combination with the older poet), Scott showed a new generation new ways of handling a Canadian evolutionary landscape in their poems. The flippant, astringent tone of Scott's "Teleological" permeated Birney's "Canada: case history" just as his "Trans Canada" helped shape Birney's "North Star west." Al Purdy, whose *North of Summer* is dedicated to Scott, learned about the northern poem from him and there are joint echoes of both Pratt and Scott in the early verse of Margaret Atwood. A fine craftsman, Scott greatly enlarged the subject matter of Canadian poetry and introduced a freer and more open conversational line. His best work is a rare combination of intelligence and deep feeling; curiously, however, this feeling is generated through a surface reticence that creates a tension between expressed and unexpressed emotions. In the finer poems these qualities unite, giving the poems resonance.

It seems probable that Scott and Smith perceived that their relative positions in Canadian poetry had changed by the mid-sixties. Once, when the two men were driving down to the Eastern Townships after a joint recording session with the CBC, Smith remarked, "Frank, people seem to like your poems better than mine. They're about things they recognize." "Yes, Art," replied Scott, "but your poems are *sub specie aeternatis.*" It was a graceful rejoinder. Scott's poetry had deeper resonance for Canadians – and for an emerging tradition – but in the larger poetic world of universals several of Smith's poems might well be ranked above Scott's.

The Governor General's Award ceremony was held late in the afternoon in the main ballroom of the Fort Garry Hotel. That afternoon Scott was visibly frail. At one point, as he walked up the steps to receive his award, his foot hesitated, not quite meeting the stairs. For a moment he swayed, nearly toppling, and those sitting in the front rows held their breath. On stage he received the award from the novelist Adele Wiseman, whose welcoming speech bestowing the award acknowledged Canada's "Mr. Poetry."

That night the winners and friends, together with Canada Council officials, went to a restaurant in St. Boniface, where Scott and Marian were the centre of attention. Scott was amused to hear from publisher Douglas Gibson of a frosty response provoked from a lady member of a local writers' association who had been in attendance at the afternoon cocktail party. "[She] felt (with some justice) that F.R.S. had been satirising her and her peers when he wrote 'The Canadian Authors Meet' ...." When one of the guests had remarked, " 'Isn't it wonderful that Frank Scott was able to come for the Award?' this worthy answered 'No!' and pursed her lips in a manner that discouraged further discussion."[31] The story delighted Scott; once more his poetic past was intersecting with the present. The occasion of the Governor General's Award for poetry, the prize Scott coveted more than any other, was to be one of his last public appearances.

# TWENTY-SIX

# The Closing Years

I N HIS LAST YEARS Scott's health seriously disintegrated and he was forced to withdraw more and more from his accustomed activities. Since the late 1960s, his erratic heartbeat had periodically forced him to reduce his activities. But now the sustained effects of using a pacemaker for nearly a decade were beginning to show. With the insertion of this pacemaker in 1974, his tachycardia had been stabilized, but by 1980 his whole body was clearly in a state of attrition. Scott had always been somewhat conscious of his own mortality. Even before he was thirty, he had written about growing old.

> Growing old is withdrawing
>     From the fire
> In the little clearing
>     Of desire.
>
> It is moving to the cooler
>     Air on the fringe
> Where the trees are nearer
>     And voices strange.
>
> We need not shudder
>     Or be afraid
> Till we cross the border
>     Of that dark wood.
>
> Till in the dark glow
>     Suddenly
> We find the shadow
>     Become the tree.    (*C.P.*, p. 33)

Growing physical weakness and the illness and death of contemporaries deepened this sense of his own mortality. At the end of the seventies even Bora Laskin, a much younger man, was in hospital in the intensive care ward. Scott wrote on November 7, 1979, to Laskin's wife Peggy, expressing his deep concern. "He has done so much to make Canada a viable and free nation through his writings and judgments that at this crucial moment of our history his eventual return to the bench is supremely important. I feel deeply that this nation cannot be healthy while he is unwell." Now in the eighties Laskin was seriously ill again.

The old generation was passing away: Frank Underhill in 1971; Raleigh Parkin and Jeannie Smith in 1977; John Bird in 1978; Patrick Anderson in 1979; Arthur Smith in 1980; and David Lewis and Thérèse Casgrain in 1981. At the Scott conference in Vancouver, Lewis had mentioned Scott had spoken at the funeral service for his father, who died of leukemia in Montreal in 1950. He quite likely knew, even then, that he was also dying and that within a few short months Scott would perform the same service at his own funeral. Scott was already the last survivor in his family of seven. Mary had died in the fifties and Elton and William in the sixties. With the death of his younger brother Arthur in 1979 (whom he had expected would outlive him), Scott was feeling very much an exposed tree – bare to the blasts of winter. Writing to Eugene Forsey, he joked: "I am quite well, but a silly nerve in a back tooth has just died. Funeral soon. It can't have heard that I hope to live to the year 2000! If this sort of thing goes on, maybe I'll change my mind."[1]

All sorts of little ailments were bothersome: the nerve in his tooth, a sty in his eye, a growth on a finger. But far worse than any of these problems was a terrible arthritis that at first cramped his fingers and then the larger limbs. It became increasingly difficult to move, finally impossible. He began finger exercises and signed up for physiotherapy treatments. But it was difficult to travel to the clinic. Subject to toppling – his long frame would suddenly crash to the ground – he began to take the precaution of propping himself up with a cane. He was also having considerable difficulty with his eyes and it was now necessary to use a large magnifying glass for general reading. But what he most regretted about his failing sight was that he could no longer sit at Mrs. Dale's piano and play his favourite hymns; religious music had always been a solace.

Even worse for a man of Scott's keen intellect was the awareness his attention span had become severely limited. After a good dinner, especially one accompanied by wine and perhaps preceded by martinis, he began to nod. Eventually, on "doctor's orders," he was forced to give up his beloved martinis in favour of a tomato drink he dubbed a "Virgin Mary." By the early eighties, he sometimes dozed even before dinner was over. Once, telephoning long distance on March 28, 1983 (he could no longer manage letters without a secretary), he catalogued his long list of ailments, ruefully summarizing, "I am in a stage of convalescence from an illness that all the doctors agree can never be cured."

In 1980 he had a severe attack of bronchitis and pneumonia that required hospitalization. He was not sufficiently well in May to go to A.J.M. Smith's memorial service in East Lansing, Michigan, but he retained vivid and distressed memories of Smith's earlier funeral. There had been no religious service and the urn containing Smith's ashes had simply been placed in the ground. "It was just a little hole in the ground that sucked him in,"[2] he recalled with horror.

During these lonely and saddening years, the one positive force was Scott's renewed closeness with Marian, who was a great comfort to him during his days of despair and pain. Despite the inevitable ups and downs of two highly creative personalities, the Scotts' marriage had been a sustaining one. As one of their friends recalled, "It was something very different what they have achieved – something creative in the art of living."[3] As parents and grandparents, proud of their son Peter, his wife Maylie, and their grandchildren, they had had a rich life together. In "Question," from *The Dance is One*, Scott wrote a love poem recollecting his and Marian's courtship those many years ago on the slopes of Mount Royal.

> Suppose I took your hand
> or just the tips of
> your fingers
> and led you again
> up a mountain side
> where first we walked
> and pointed to the island
>
> far away
>
> would an old yesterday
> shine clear of now
> would the whole of time
> come to a silent stop
> as it did
> as we did
> among the ferns on our first shining day
> when we held

as only lovers hold
all anti-time within our clasping palms?[4]

In the spring of 1983, Scott became seriously ill and was hospitalized for several months. At that time he was visited by Donald MacSween, who was moved as he came toward the hospital to find Marian sitting on a little hill, her chin on her knees, watching the children play. She had been keeping vigil and had just left the ward for a few minutes. When he went up to Scott's room he found him propped in a chair with pillows stuffed between the arms to keep him from falling. He was wearing a kimono and sitting straight as a rod, gripping the sides. MacSween asked him if he had seen Gerry Le Dain recently and Scott replied, "Oh yes, Gerry Le Dain. He goes back a long way in my life. In fact, I go back a long way in my life."

The joke was all the more powerful because it came from a man who was in great pain. As MacSween remarked, "to have the mind under that kind of control despite physical ailments is very moving." At Marian's request, he talked about specific subjects and Scott responded with a combination of his usual quizzical, wry comments and a new stillness. In the silences between conversation a strange atmosphere was generated by this gaunt, somewhat spectral, silhouetted figure. MacSween sensed Scott's double feeling about time – there was not much time left for him, but on the other hand time would go on forever.

While MacSween was still there Scott began to do his exercises, which involved bending forward in his chair and "kissing his knees," as he put it. "So he'd bend down *very* slowly and obviously in great pain, lower this great torso down and kiss his left knee and congratulate himself on having that achievement behind him and then straighten up and come down and kiss the right knee and all with absolute dignity. Not a drop of self-pity. And all the while, in effect, spoofing himself as he was doing all this."[5]

This was an exceptionally difficult time for the Scotts. Marian, who spent most of her days and nights at the hospital, became severely exhausted. Scott then returned home, where Marian continued to nurse him. One morning, utterly weary, she burned her arm severely on the stove and was in turn confined to hospital. Without Marian to tend him Scott became worse and his mind began to wander. She returned home, rested to some degree, and took up her household chores with her right arm in a sling. Scott then began to rally.

By the late summer of 1983, a visitor would find Scott sitting upright in a wheelchair in front of the open window looking out on the old tree on Clarke Avenue. In profile he was appallingly thin, his face emaciated.

He talked on a poetic rather than on a rational level. He discussed the CCF and medicare, but confused the thirties with the eighties. He spoke of the attitude the French were taking to medicare. In order to have harmony within the party, the CCF was going to have to go along with the French attitude to medicare. Scott felt "very distressed." He urged his biographer to "consider the state of Quebec."[6] His words still came out with great force. Their order was more or less what they would be in a normal sentence, but they were not always conceptually correct. There was also a real awareness of a division of aims: a recognition he was going to have to change his philosophical position, and of how this change would be regarded. Scott, after a lifetime of holding adamantly to a strongly centralist strategy, was now in his last illness willing to take a somewhat more flexible attitude on Quebec.

That fall the proceedings of the Scott conference, *On F.R. Scott: Essays on His Contributions to Law, Literature and Politics*, were published. Copies were sent to the Scotts, and in December Marian wrote to say she was reading excerpts from the book to Frank: "So many memories that can be stirred."[7] At this point, too, a slight bump on Scott's forehead was diagnosed as a tumour. A year earlier he had catalogued it as one of the increasing annoyances of age, a slight stinging sensation whenever he pressed the middle of his forehead. The tumour had begun to grow at that point where pieces of lead remained from the explosion, so many years ago, when he had been testing gunpowder. He was at first bemused to have such a tangible link between his present physical frame and that long-ago incident. The tumour, however, was not benign; pressing on the brain, it began to affect his coherence.

In late December, Scott suffered a mild stroke that left him much weaker but seemingly more at peace. There were still good times in the day. He enjoyed music intensely. "He has times of being very lucid and *very* witty – and at other times makes sense on a poetic level."[8] In April, 1984, however, Scott was hospitalized again. By mid-May he had an operation in which part of the tumour was removed. Marian was very relieved when he recovered sufficiently to come home. By now he required nursing around the clock, and the young French-Canadian paramedic who had been assisting in his care was replaced by a day and a night nurse.

During the last year he was very hesitant about seeing people. He hated to have his weakness exposed, and he was aware his mind was wandering. By mid-December his mind failed. When Marian read aloud to him he could no longer understand: "My mind is like a perforated piece of asbestos," he told her.[9] As his tumour enlarged Scott became progressively weaker. The pressure in his head and the effects of the drugs caused confusion and anxiety. By the turn of the year it was clear he was dying.

On the morning of January 31, 1985, Scott was very weak. His lungs were filling and he had had a particularly bad night. Marian sent away the morning nurse, saying she would like to stay with her husband and make him comfortable. His breathing was raspy. Sitting beside him, Marian held his hand and stroked his forehead and said, "I'm here." Scott died quietly in her presence. "His breathing became less and less and there wasn't even a tremor between his life and death."[10]

WHILE PREPARING *The Dance is One* in 1973, Scott had written his final thoughts on the activity that had been the central passion of his life. This statement was filed among his papers.

> Every poem is a partner with the poet in the dance of creation. Are they two? Are they one? Does he make it, does it make him? Or do the two make the one?
>
> The rhythms change, the fashions come and go, from metrical stanza and rhyme, from free verse and imagism, from surrealism, concrete verse and anti-poems, from this and that new intensity, the forms emerge, but always it is the dance of life, of the vision standing on the commonplace, of man and womb and woman, of yin and yang, of beginnings and endings without end.[11]

*On the afternoon of July 6, 1985, Frank Scott's ashes were interred in the family plot on Mount Royal. During the morning, there had been thunderstorms, but by mid-afternoon the day was calm and sunny. Scott's nephew, the Reverend Brian Kelley, had driven up from Boston. He conducted a short and moving ceremony, referring to King Gordon's tribute to Scott at the memorial service in McGill's Redpath Hall, and the hymn that had been sung, "Guide Me, O Thou Great Jehovah." He prayed and read the Service for the Dead. The plain box was then placed in the Scott grave. Only the immediate family was present – Marian, Peter Scott and his wife Maylie, and Scott's nieces and nephew, Brian, Rosemary, and Frances, the children of Mary Scott Kelley.[12] A modest stone was placed in direct line with the magnificent old oak. On it is written:*

*F.R. Scott*
*1899 – 1985*
*Marian Dale Scott*
*1906 –*
*The Dance Is One*

# Afterword

A S HE APPROACHED the seventh decade of his life, F.R. Scott was urged by many friends and by several publishers to embark on an auto-biography or, failing this, at least on a collection of memoirs. But he had doubts about his ability to write autobiographically. "My greatest enemy," he said, "is a distrust of my capacity to sustain the story well." Realistic considerations also intruded, for he was always "too infernally busy with immediate things." As the prospect of writing a first-hand account of the three-ring circus that had been his life (in law, politics, and poetry) became less and less likely, he began to look for a biographer. He was aware the widely separated facets of his career complicated the task. He feared the law historian or the political scientist might not view his poetry with the primacy he gave it, and he realized that the literary critic might not ap-preciate law and politics. But in Scott's own mind, he was first of all a poet. Ultimately he selected a literary critic as his biographer in the belief that such a person would inevitably recognize that his poetry, his political life, and his work in law were the unified expression of one personality.

As a literary historian, I became a candidate for this task on November 11, 1974, when interviewing Scott in connection with a projected history of English-Canadian poetry. Shortly after nine o'clock on a cold, grey Remembrance Day, I went to his office in the law faculty on the McGill campus. There I found Scott slumped over his desk, suffering a severe attack of tachycardia. I issued orders: he was to lie quietly on the floor; a doctor was phoned. Shortly after this a taxi took us both to the Scott home. Unaccustomed to being treated in such an unceremonious manner, Scott was surprised and grateful. And, while waiting for a late afternoon doctor's appointment, he insisted we get on with the interview. Despite his discomfort, he spoke animatedly about his poetry and about Canadian poetry in general. Gradually the talk moved to a discussion of his childhood

– his memories of the garden in his boyhood home, of the northern lights above Quebec City, of the sense of infinity he had experienced as a young child. Later that evening he telephoned to say he was to be hospitalized for the insertion of a pacemaker. "If I get hit by a truck," he asked, "will you collect my poems?" I agreed to put together a chronological list of his poems as a first step. Eventually the *Collected Poems of F.R. Scott* was published by McClelland and Stewart in 1981.

Several months passed, and when the transcript of our interview had been typed out, I sent him a copy, pointing out that he had been talking more about his life than about poetry. Wasn't it about time that he did some work on his memoirs? He was not enthusiastic about autobiography but invited me to "come back and talk, soon." A year later, in 1976, he formally requested I undertake the writing of his biography. Thus began the first stage of this work, our joint endeavours to outline the main events of his long and eventful life, a task shared by his wife Marian and by his younger brother Arthur. Scott enjoyed reconstructing the past. During frequent interviews at Montreal and at North Hatley from 1976 onwards, he would stride up and down his living room or front porch, chewing pipe and words together, gesturing, laughing, becoming indignant, tumbling out opinions of people and issues long since dead – "or worse," as he wrote in one of his poems, "still in full combat."

The advantage of autobiography, as opposed to biography, which involves the interpretation of a life by another, is that it allows the subject complete autonomy. This Scott well knew. Years earlier, in 1926, when contemplating a number of missed entries in his diary, lacunae that very likely related to his sexual awakening, he wrote gleefully:

> But what have I been doing since February 13th last? Ha Ha! Ho Ho! (and a little ha ha!) That is just what I don't need to answer now. There are twenty-five good days of my youth gone, and, thank heavens, no mention need be made of them. What relief for me, what confusion for my biographer!
> Wait – I may be forced, for safety, to write an auto-b.!

Even at twenty-six Scott anticipated that his life would be worth recording; but whatever version this record took, he intended to retain some control.

In the mid-seventies when this biography began he was still thinking in terms of autobiography-cum-memoir. He offered to participate in taped interviews and allowed me free access to his papers. Informally we visited old friends like Raleigh Parkin and Percy Corbett and others were notified they would be contacted. The process of giving interviews was a stimulating one and Scott liked the sense that his vision of events was getting down on paper. As late as 1978 Scott had quipped to Michiel Horn, "I am ghost-writing my own memoirs," but by July, 1979, he recognized the difference between memoir and biography.

What brought about this change was his acknowledgement of the difference between a subject's and a biographer's vision of a life. The journey into the past also proved to be a journey into the unremembered self. A younger and more callow Frank Scott emerged, a young colonial fired by military zeal. His older brother, William, whom he had always blamed for forcing him into law when he would much rather have been a poet, was found not responsible after all. The pages of Scott's diaries revealed that he, rather than his brother, had weighed the pros and cons and made the final decision. Memory, a living thing, had played tricks: it had adjusted the past to correspond with his contemporary vision of himself.

Initially Scott found it difficult to accept this new version of his life, especially when it conflicted with his view of his father, whose authority, he insisted, he had never rejected. Yet, the Frank Scott who had admired and internalized the positive aspects of Canon Scott, particularly his moral courage, could not recognize his father's negative qualities, notably his egotism, without acknowledging that he shared some of these qualities. Such an insight, implying disloyalty, could not be faced. Through much of his life Scott seems to have coped with this potential division in his feelings by banishing Canon Scott (of whom he saw very little in the thirties) and by dividing the psychological aspects of the father into the "good" and the "bad" father and applying these qualities to others. The good aspects he associated with J.S. Woodsworth and the bad he assigned to his brother William. Arbitrary father substitute that he was, William Scott gave his brother ample reason for this attribution. Scott maintained this stance until the mid-seventies; then, when reading Lionel Trilling's *Sincerity and Authenticity*, he suddenly realized his insistence on individual freedom and his revolt against dominating power in society was, like Shelley's, related to rejection of a father's domination.

Scott was a rich and demanding subject for biography, both as a highly complex personality and because his life touched upon so much of Canada's social history. As we moved into his past, he was sometimes repelled and sometimes moved to tears by the young man revealed in his long-unread Oxford diaries ("a bit of a young prig," he thought) and by the occasionally sharp-tempered respondent to his earnest but untried Boswell. "Why was I so angry over that?" he pencilled on a typed interview in which he had adamantly rejected a suggestion that J.S. Woodsworth had become a father in spirit. "I laughed and I cried," he said on another occasion. He was always a challenge to work with because of his intellectual honesty and because of his scorn for the second-rate. And, as the nine years of working on his biography slipped by, although we differed on matters of fact, and indeed sometimes came to sharp words, he did not attempt to exert control over the interpretation that would be placed upon past events.

Indeed, as the facts of the past emerged – as opposed to the myths of his recollected past – he began to see that there were aspects of his life he had not fully perceived. It is a commonplace of autobiographical writing that most individuals remake their vision of their past with each passing decade. Scott was no exception to this general rule. He knew himself to be motivated by a pressing inheritance of "duty" but he did not ascribe it to any specific incident other than his early religious training. He believed that he had always been opposed to war.

The task of his biographer was thus to find concrete evidence – diaries, letters, and other contemporary accounts – from the first three decades of the century that would help determine, as far as was possible, the accuracy of views expressed in taped interviews. And, as was the case, when some of these beliefs proved to be without foundation, the distortions of memory had to be reinterpreted in the light of discovered fact. In effect, the search was for the essentials of personality beneath the public persona. Furthermore, as Scott was both a significant public figure and one of the few English Canadians to have had a genuine impact on Quebec society, there was the additional task of relating a highly charismatic personality to some of the many individuals he had influenced.

Scott himself was not aware of his real position as English alter ego to the Quebec allegorist, Jacques Ferron; nor did he recognize (as Pierre Trudeau himself did not) the profound influence his vision of Quebec and his constitutional thinking had on the former Prime Minister. Indeed, the whole question of showing Scott's relation to Quebec was problematic because largely undocumented. Because the Quebec chapters required candid discussion with prominent Québécois they are broadly based on oral as well as written reports. As co-editor of *Quebec States Her Case*, Scott undoubtedly read Michael Oliver's introduction where the latter remarked on Trudeau's "novel" idea of entrenching a Bill of Rights in the constitution. But Scott had not reminded Oliver that he had been advocating this idea to Trudeau and others ever since the forties. It is unlikely he thought of it, for, as he so frequently said, "there is no copyright on ideas." Yet the parallel between Scott's forties constitutional writings on Quebec and those of Trudeau in the fifties and sixties seems apparent.

However, the validity of this connection was not fully documented until September, 1984, when I read aloud a paragraph on the "just society" from Scott's 1939 essay on "A Policy of Neutrality for Canada" to Pierre Trudeau: momentarily, neither of us could decide whether he or Scott had been the author.

Scott himself ultimately came to the wry recognition that biography is not simply the mere recording of memoirs but rather the events of a life as selected, reconstructed, and interpreted by another. In July of 1979, he wrote to Leon Edel, "I think I already see what you mean by your theory of biography: concentration on the nature of the personality being portrayed as shown in the events of his life, rather than a series of events happening to a character who takes second place ... I can't help wondering how I shall come out in the process of sifting the essence from the events."

For the biographer the sifting process involved separating the young colonial of the twenties – tentative, strongly religious, determined to be "of some use in this world" – from the urbane, articulate, and not infrequently dogmatic public man of the seventies. It meant attempting to pull from Scott's memory incidents that had been blurred over the years and sharpening their outlines through the transcription of diaries and letters, the interviewing of friends and family, the sorting through hundreds of letters, at first in Scott's small office at McGill University and then at the Public Archives of Canada. It meant separating the poet from the lawyer and the political activist and emphasizing each one of these three vocations in the decade where it was most dominant. Because the thirties were primarily concerned with the depression and the CCF, I have had to give short shrift to some of the literary aspects of the life during this decade, particularly the story of *New Provinces*. However, I have passed all the relevant letters on to D.G. Pitt, who is writing a literary life of one of the other *New Provinces* poets, E.J. Pratt. Above all, the process of developing this biography involved the attempt to see Scott's world with the poet's eye, whether at the site of the old rectory in Quebec City, at Cap à l'Aigle, the Oxford quadrangle, the lookout at Mount Royal, or the shimmering Lake Massawippi at North Hatley. This journey finally led to Mount Royal Cemetery and the cross.

In many of these attempts to perceive Scott's life as an evolving process the common denominator turned out to be Canada – and often the land itself. This is hardly surprising. Historically, as acknowledged in the national anthem, the Canadian poetic and political imagination has had a circular relation to what is seen as the physical realities of the landscape itself: "the true North strong and free." Ever since Confederation, and especially in the formative twenties when F.R. Scott came to maturity, that old question, "Can we have a Canadian art and literature?" has been another way of asking, "Can we have a Canadian nation?" Scott's multi-faceted career in law, literature, and politics is in itself a unified response to the nationalist concerns of the twenties: the desire for a Canadian literature, a Canadian legal and political order (especially a new constitution to remedy problems not addressed by the Statute of Westminster), and a uniquely Canadian social order.

One of the pleasures of writing this biography of F.R. Scott has been the discovery of how the creative imagination of one constitutional lawyer, political activist, and poet has both reflected and helped to shape the cultural and political climate in which we now live. Despite the exceptional nature of Scott's achievements (and he is, as F.H. Underhill once said of J.S. Woodsworth, an "untypical Canadian"), F.R. Scott's life in broad outline contains much of what we recognize as central to the Canadian experience.

SANDRA DJWA
Simon Fraser University
April, 1987

# Acknowledgements

❧

Many individuals have helped bring this book into being. Above all I am grateful to Ann Herstein, M.J. Coldwell's first and volunteer secretary, who transcribed early interviews with F.R. Scott and continued, over the years, her enthusiasm and support. Next is Frances Hord, who generously gave of her time and patience deciphering the Scott diaries, transcribing over 300 taped interviews, and typing successive drafts of the manuscript. Beyond this I owe most to Leon Edel for his unfailing generosity of spirit.

The research for this book could not have been undertaken without the bibliographic expertise of Marilyn Flitton, who helped gather background material, established reference files, and assisted on research trips to Montreal, Toronto, and the National Archives. I am also grateful to Ruth Yates, who indexed the Scott diaries and helped with research and typing of the first three chapters of the manuscript. Perry Millar took over from Marilyn Flitton in 1983 as research associate and worked with me on successive drafts of the manuscript; she remained a pillar of strength throughout, especially when seeing the manuscript through the press. A number of graduate students, including Rob Campbell, Elizabeth Gowland, Jim Janz, Carol Lane, Carey Vivian, and Lynne Whenham, assisted over the years; to all, my thanks.

The time and support required to write this book were provided by a Senior Killam Fellowship and by a research grant from the Social Services and Humanities Council of Canada. During one particularly lean year the project was funded by the President's Fund at Simon Fraser University, the Boag Foundation, the Foundation for Legal Research, and the Law Foundation of British Columbia. Without this assistance the book could not have been written. I am especially grateful to Dr. R.C. Brown, Dean of Arts, Simon Fraser University. Barbara Barnett typed the manuscript up to the thirties and Anita Mahoney promptly and cheerfully brought it to completion. My family, Peter and Phillip Djwa and Bill McConnell especially, have been a support throughout.

Catherine Carver, Alan Dawe, Michiel Horn, J.R. Mallory, Ruth McConnell, William Robbins, and Peter Scott read and helpfully commented on the manuscript in whole or in part. The following individuals contributed their expertise to specific sections: Betty Bednarski, Alan Cairns, Norman Chalmers, George Curtis, Glwadys Downes, Louis Dudek, Davidson Dunton, Leon Edel, Ray Ellenwood, Barbara Godard, Ron Graham, Doug Jones, W.C. McConnell, Kenneth McNaught, H. Blair Neatby, Frank Newby, Ivon Owen, Gordon Robertson, Malcolm Ross, Justice Barry Strayer, and William Toye. I am indebted to each of them for the information they provided. Any errors or omissions are my own. A special thanks to the Special Collections Division at the University of British Columbia Library, especially Anne Yandel, Laurenda Daniells, and Joan Selby. I am grateful to the staff at the National Archives in Ottawa, particularly R.S. Gordon, Anne Goddard, and David Walden. Finally, I would also like to thank the many friends and acquaintances of F.R. Scott who generously set aside time for interviews. Their names are listed in the notes.

This book has been published with the help of a grant from the Canadian Federation for the Humanities, using funds provided by the Social Sciences and Humanities Research Council of Canada.

# Notes

THE BIOGRAPHY draws upon a number of sources, including unpublished diaries, taped interviews, and unpublished papers. The late F.R. Scott and Marian Scott were unfailingly helpful in providing overviews of successive decades through taped interviews and generous access to unpublished diaries and papers. Many of Scott's relatives, friends, and colleagues willingly shared memories that stretched back, in some cases, over sixty years. I am particularly grateful to Peter and Maylie Scott, to the late Arthur Scott and his wife Janet, to Grace Scott, widow of Elton Scott, to A.J.M. Smith and his wife Jeannie, both deceased, to the late Raleigh Parkin and his wife, Louise, and to the late David Lewis.

The F.R. Scott Papers are located in the Public Archives of Canada and include political and legal papers, miscellaneous journals, manuscripts of published and unpublished poems, and several pages of "Notes Towards an Autobiography." References to these papers are identified as FRSP. Quotations from Scott's diaries (1912-1928) are cited by date and entitled "Diary." The Frederick George Scott Papers, abbreviated as FGSP, are located at the McCord Museum, Montreal, and include the papers of Dr. William Edward Scott. Other relevant papers include:

| | |
|---|---|
| John Glassco Papers | PAC |
| Frank Underhill Papers | PAC |
| J.S. Woodsworth Papers | PAC |
| H.R.C. Avison Papers | PAC |
| Brooke Claxton Papers | PAC |
| M.J. Coldwell Papers | PAC |
| J.W. Dafoe Papers | PAC |
| E.A. Forsey Papers | PAC |
| Grace MacInnis Papers | PAC |

| | |
|---|---|
| Mackenzie King Papers | PAC |
| Angus MacInnis Papers | Special Collections, University of British Columbia Library |
| Alan M. Plaunt Papers | Special Collections, University of British Columbia Library |
| McGill University Records | McGill Archives |
| G.M.A. Grube Papers | Queen's University |
| Harry M. Cassidy Papers | Victoria University |
| E.A. Forsey Papers | (Fellowship for a Christian Social Order) Victoria University |
| Leon Edel Papers | In the possession of the owner, Hawaii |
| John Robert Colombo Papers | Special Collections, McMaster University |

All references to Scott's poems are to *The Collected Poems of F.R. Scott* (Toronto: McClelland and Stewart, 1981) unless otherwise identified.

In the preparation of this biography I have drawn on discussions or interviews with the following individuals:

The Honourable Douglas Abbott, 25 August 1983, Ottawa
Patrick Anderson, 8 June 1974, Ottawa
Geoffrey Andrew, 23 February 1981, Vancouver
Murray Ballantyne, 26 October 1978, Montreal
Inglis Bell, 22 April 1985, Vancouver
Thomas Berger, 19 January 1981, Vancouver
Jacques Bieler, 25 April 1979, Montreal
Florence Bird, 27 April 1979, Ottawa
Earle Birney, 31 August 1983, Toronto
Roma Blackburn, 8 June 1977, Eastern Townships
Alan C. Cairns, 25 July 1985, Vancouver
Senator Thérèse Casgrain, June, 1978, May, 1980, Montreal
R. Cheffins, 3 October 1983, 31 December 1983, Victoria
Leonard Cohen, 9 January 1983, 11 January 1984, New York
Maxwell Cohen, 24 August 1983, Ottawa
Emile Colas, 18 February 1985, Montreal
Ramsay Cook, 23 August 1983, Toronto
Percy Corbett, 8 June 1977, Eastern Townships
Paul Crépeau, 19 September 1984, Montreal
George Curtis, 3 August 1982, Vancouver
Guy Desaulniers, 27 August 1983, Montreal
Louis Dudek, 1 October 1975, 24 May 1979, 26 April 1979, Montreal

Davidson Dunton, 18 February 1985, Montreal
Abraham Edel, 6 September 1979, London
Leon Edel, 21 February 1981, 25 October 1982, Vancouver
Arnold Edinborough, 6 November 1984, Toronto
Jean-Charles Falardeau, 22 November 1979, Quebec City
Abraham Feiner, 2 December 1980, Montreal
Mary Filer, 13 December 1983, Vancouver
Senator Eugene Forsey, 1 October 1977, 13 May 1983, Ottawa
Senator Royce Frith, 25 September 1984, Ottawa
Northrop Frye, 23 August 1983, Toronto
E. Davie Fulton, 15 December 1983, Vancouver
Jean-Louis Gagnon, 24 September 1984, Montreal
Senator Carl Goldenberg, 19 September 1984, Montreal
J. King Gordon, 30 September 1977, 5 February 1982, Ottawa
Hamish Gow, 30 December 1983, Victoria
Ronald Graham, 18 February 1985, Montreal
J.L. Granatstein, 15 May 1983, Toronto
Ralph Gustafson, 4 May 1975, Ottawa
Jacques Hébert, 17 September 1984, Montreal
Joyce Hemlow, 2 December 1980, Montreal
Ralph Hodgson, 21 September 1984, Ottawa
Michiel Horn, August, 1982, 20 February 1983, 15-18 February 1985, Vancouver
Glen How, 31 August 1983, Toronto
T.P.M. Howard, 18 February 1985, Montreal
John Humphrey, 27 August 1983, Montreal
W.A. Irwin, 2 October 1983, Victoria
Doug and Monique Jones, September, 1975, 28 August 1983, North Hatley
Lady Anna Keir, 13 September 1979, Oxford
Leo Kennedy, 24 April 1979, Montreal
Paul Lacoste, 19 February 1985, Montreal
Marc Lapointe, 26 September 1984, Ottawa
John Lawrence, 26 September 1984, Ottawa
Irving Layton, 10 September 1975, Toronto
The Honourable Gerald Le Dain, 24 October 1981, 22-23 August 1983, 5
    October 1984, Ottawa
Douglas LePan, 7 May 1983, Toronto
David Lewis, 3 August 1976, 18 February 1981, Vancouver
Dorothy Livesay, 15 December 1974, 2 August 1975, Vancouver
Senator Charles Lussier, 23 August 1983, Ottawa
R. St John Macdonald, 21 May 1981, Halifax

Grace MacInnis, 8 July 1981, Vancouver
Hugh MacLennan, 2-4 December 1980, Montreal
Donald MacSween, 24 August 1983, Camp Five Lakes
J.R. Mallory, 28 August 1983, Montreal
Eli Mandel, 5 January 1975, Toronto
Senator Jean Marchand, 23 August 1983, 25 September 1984, Ottawa
Ronald McCall, 25 April 1979, Montreal
W.C. McConnell, 8 December 1974, 30 June 1984, Vancouver
Kathy Mezei, May, 1985, Vancouver
Mavor Moore, 31 August 1983, Toronto
Anne Moreau, 28 August 1983, Montreal
Mary Naylor, June, 1982, Cap à l'Aigle
John Newlove, 9 September 1975, 1982, Toronto
Michael Oliver, 28 August 1983, Eastern Townships
Michael and Kim Ondaatje, 24 September 1975, Toronto
P.K. Page, 20 July 1975, 3 October 1983, Victoria
Raleigh and Louise Parkin, 7 June 1977, 22 April 1979, North Hatley
Léon Patenaude, 17 September 1984, Montreal
The Honourable Gérard Pelletier, 28 September 1984, Ottawa
The Honourable Jack Pickersgill, 5 February 1982, Ottawa
Senator Michael Pitfield, 28 August 1983, Ottawa
Timothy Porteous, 24 August 1983, Camp Five Lakes
Margaret Prang, 20 May 1976, Vancouver
Al Purdy, 4 January 1975, Ameliasburg
Gordon Robertson, 26 September 1984, Ottawa
Aileen Ross, 25 April 1979, Montreal
Malcolm Ross, 25 May 1981, Halifax
Bruce Ruddick, December, 1983, New York
Micheline Ste-Marie, 5 June 1985, Montreal
Douglas Sanders, November, 1981, British Columbia
Arthur and Janet Scott, 25-26 May 1976, 15 September 1976, 20-23 November
    1979, Quebec City and North Hatley
F.R. Scott, 15 July 1974, 11 November 1974, 6-11 January 1975, 1 October
    1975, May-June, 1976, 13-15 September 1976, 27 January 1977, 6-8 June
    1977, 27 November-1 December 1977, 19-22 May 1978, 18-25 July 1978,
    26-27 October 1978, 1-2 February 1979, November, 1979, 24 May 1980,
    June, 1980, 8 October 1980, 3-4 December 1980, 23 February 1981, 29
    October 1981, February, 1982, October, 1982, 26-31 January 1983, 23
    February 1983, August, 1983, Montreal, Vancouver, and North Hatley
Grace Scott, 29 October 1978, Toronto

Marian Scott, 15 September 1976, 22 May 1978, 29 October 1981, 27 August
   1983, 4 June 1985, Montreal
Peter Scott, 11-13 April 1982, San Francisco
Stephen Scott, 19 September 1984, Montreal
Manuel Shacter, 19 February 1985, Montreal
Neufville Shaw, 8 January 1975, Montreal
Terence Sheard, 29 October 1978, Toronto
A.J.M. Smith, 8 November 1974, 28 May 1975, November/December, 1975,
   Vancouver, Edmonton, and East Lansing, Michigan
Fred Soward, 11 December 1978, Vancouver
Harold Spence-Sales, 13 December 1983, Vancouver
Graham Spry, 30 September 1977, Ottawa
A.L. Stein, 29 August 1983, Montreal
Robert Stocks, 18 February 1985, Montreal
The Honourable Barry Strayer, 10 April 1985, Vancouver
Margaret Surrey, 24 April 1979, Montreal
William Taylor, 28 September 1984, Ottawa
George Tompkins, 11 June 1984, Vancouver
William Toye, 1 January 1980, Toronto
Phillipe Vaillancourt, 19 September 1984, Montreal
Rosemary Walters (now Cartwright), 9 June 1985, London
Donovan and Marilla Waters, 31 December 1983, Victoria
Sir Edgar Williams, 13 September 1979, Rhodes House, Oxford
Paul Wyczynski, August, 1984, Ottawa

I also had access to transcripts of interviews with F.R. Scott by the following individuals:

Elspeth Chisholm, 28 May 1963, n.d. (ca. 1975)
Doug Francis, 15 June 1978
King Gordon, 12 June 1977
Arthur Scott, 7 May 1966
Vincent Tovell, n.d. (ca. 1971)
William Toye, 18 September 1976, 9 April 1977

## ONE: THE SCOTTS

1. F.G.S., Diary, 1 August 1899, FGSP.
2. F.R.S. to F.G.S., letter, 8 December 1916, FGSP.
3. Marian Scott to author, interview, 4 June 1985.

4. All genealogical information from Scott family tree and papers in possession of Peter Scott.

5. One of a series of reminiscences written by readers of the *Montreal Daily Witness*, "The Witness Jubilee Symposium" (n.d.), published in the paper on Saturdays in 1895-96 to commemorate the paper's 50th anniversary. McGill University Archives.

6. Minutes of McGill medical faculty meetings, 28 May 1883, McGill Archives.

7. Elizabeth Scott, Diary, Dominion Day, 1883, FGSP.

8. Elizabeth Scott to F.G.S., letter, 11 March 1883, FGSP.

9. Canon Sydenham Lindsay, *Old Boys Association of Lower Canada College News Letter*, 4 (Fall, 1959), p. 2.

10. F.G.S., "A Mood," *Poems* (London: Constable & Company Ltd., 1910), p. 146.

11. F.G.S., reminiscence of his visit to Cardinal Newman written on his return to Canada, n.d., FGSP.

12. FGSP.

13. Bishop of Montreal to F.G.S., letter, 18 December 1883, FGSP.

14. "Answers," manuscript of F.G.S. examination in Divinity, FGSP.

15. Amy Brooks to F.G.S., letter, dated: St. Michael's and All Angels, FGSP.

16. Amy Brooks to F.G.S., letter, dated: New Year's Eve 1885, FGSP.

17. *Ibid.*, dated: St. Michael's and All Angels, FGSP.

18. Cited in Matilda Preddy to F.G.S., letter, 6 September 1886, FGSP.

19. *Ibid.*

20. F.G.S., "The Soul's Quest," *The Soul's Quest and Other Poems* (London: Kegan Paul, Trench & Co., 1888), p. 10.

21. Bishop Williams to Church Wardens, 18 April 1887, FGSP.

22. Bishop Dunn to F.G.S., 22 March 1893, FGSP.

23. F.G.S. to Mr. Würteh, 24 February 1891, FGSP.

24. Amy Scott to F.G.S., 29 March 1886, FGSP.

25. *Ibid.*, 18 August 1886, FGSP.

26. A stag's head is listed with the College of Arms as part of the crest of the Scotts, but F.G. Scott had no real right to use it. Moreover, he may have appropriated the concept from the stationery of the Anglo-Catholic community at Coggeshall.

27. F.R.S. in discussion with author, November, 1979.

28. F.G.S., *Elton Hazelwood: A Memoir, by his Friend Henry Vane* (New York: Thomas Whittaker, 1892), p. 18.

29. F.G.S., *The Unnamed Lake and Other Poems* (Toronto: William Briggs, 1897), p. 8.

30. F.G.S. to Rev. Lennox Williams, letter in possession of F.R.S.
31. Sermon preached in St. Matthew's Church, Quebec City, 27 January 1901, FGSP.
32. André Siegfried, *The Race Question in Canada*, ed. and intro. Frank Underhill (Toronto: McClelland and Stewart, 1966), pp. 86-87.
33. Melvin O. Hammond, Diaries, Toronto, 21 April 1909, Ontario Archives.
34. Anecdote related by F.R.S. and other Scott family members.
35. Henri Bourassa to F.G.S., 3 December 1903, FGSP.
36. F.R.S. to author, interview, 26 October 1978.
37. Micheline Ste-Marie to author, interview, 5 June 1985.
38. F.R.S. to author, interview, November, 1979.

### TWO: A QUEBEC CHILDHOOD

1. F.R.S. and Arthur Scott in conversation, 7 May 1966.
2. F.R.S. to author, interview, 13 September 1976.
3. Arthur Scott to author in conversation, November, 1979.
4. Family photograph.
5. F.R.S. to author, interview, 28 November 1977.
6. *Ibid.*, 14-15 September 1976.
7. *Ibid.*, 14 September 1976.
8. F.R.S. and Arthur Scott to author, interview, 14-15 September 1976.
9. *Ibid.*
10. F.R.S. to author, interview, 13 September 1976.
11. F.R.S. to author, interview, October, 1980; F.G.S., "Duty," *In Sun and Shade: A Book of Verse* (Quebec: Dussault & Proulx, 1926), p. 37.
12. F.R.S. to author, interview, November, 1979.
13. F.G.S., "The Key of Life," *Collected Poems* (Vancouver: Clarke & Stuart, 1934), p. 153.
14. F.R.S. to author, interview, 11 November 1974.
15. *Ibid.*, 13 September 1976.
16. *Ibid.*, 11 November 1974.
17. *Ibid.*, November, 1979.
18. F.R.S. and Arthur Scott in conversation, 7 May 1966.
19. *Ibid.*, to author, interview, 13 September 1976.
20. Arthur Scott to author in conversation, November, 1979.
21. F.R.S. to Vincent Tovell, interview, 1971.
22. Scott recalls the incident as one in which he represented the French and a childhood friend, Jack Price, represented the British. In a letter to Scott on November 26, 1969, John H. Price wrote, recollecting a stage performance, and asking him if he remembered when, "You were the Marquis of Levis and I was the Earl of Quebec."

23. F.R.S. to author, interview, 14 September 1976.
24. *Ibid.*, 13 September 1976.
25. F.R.S. and Arthur Scott to author, interview, 13 September 1976; F.R.S. to author, interview, 27 May 1980.
26. F.R.S. to author, interview, November, 1979.
27. *Ibid.*, May, 1976. See also Stephen Leacock, *Nonsense Novels* (London/ New York: John Lane, The Bodley Head Ltd.; John Lane Company, 1911), p. 45.

### THREE: KNIGHTHOOD

1. F.G.S., *The Great War as I Saw It*, 2nd ed. (Vancouver: Clarke & Stuart, 1934), p. 15.
2. F.G.S., "Blood Guilt," *In the Battle Silences: Poems Written at the Front* (Toronto/London: The Musson Book Company Limited, Constable and Company Limited, 1917), p. 31.
3. F.R.S. and Arthur Scott to author, interview, 13-14 September 1976.
4. Diary, 1914.
5. F.G.S., *The Great War*, pp. 34-37.
6. F.R.S. to author, interview, 13-14 September 1976; November, 1979.
7. Amy Scott to F.G.S., letter, 26 June 1916, FGSP.
8. F.G.S. to Amy Scott, letter, 5 July 1916, FGSP.
9. Newspaper report, no date, FRSP.
10. F.R.S. and Arthur Scott to author, interview, 13 September 1976.
11. F.R.S. family photograph album.
12. Mary Naylor to author, interview, June, 1982.
13. F.R.S. to author, interview, 28 November 1977.
14. Photograph in family album.
15. "Knighthood," *In the Battle Silences*, p. 23.
16. F.G.S. to Amy Scott, letter, 15 October 1916, FGSP.
17. F.G.S., telegram, 30 October 1916, FGSP.
18. F.R.S. to author, interview, 28 November 1977.
19. F.G.S. to Elton Scott, letter, 31 October 1916, FGSP.
20. F.G.S. to Amy Scott, letter, 17 November 1916, FGSP.
21. F.R.S. to F.G.S., letter, 8 December 1916, FGSP.
22. This thesis regarding the significance of the chivalric overtones of Canadian war poetry was developed in 1973 and explicated in an application to the SSHRC to undertake work on a biography of F.R. Scott in 1979. Subsequently, this concept has been generally accepted because of Mark Girouard's *The Return to Camelot: Chivalry and the English Gentleman* (New Haven: Yale University Press, 1981).

23. Diary, 24 March 1918.
24. Diary, 30 March 1918.
25. F.R.S. and Arthur Scott to author, interview, 14-15 September 1976.
26. *The Great War*, pp. 319-20.
27. F.R.S. to author, interview, 27 November 1977.
28. *Ibid.*, 13-14 September 1976.
29. F.R.S. to author in conversation, November, 1977; George B. Shaw, "Socialism: Principles and Outlook" (London: The Fabian Society, 1930; rpt. from Encyclopedia Britannica), FRSP.
30. F.R.S., "The Brotherhood of Man," FRSP.
31. F.R.S. to author, interview, 20 July 1978.
32. Diary, 11 September 1919.
33. F.R.S. and Arthur Scott to author, interview, 14-15 September 1976.
34. Diary, 19 October 1919.
35. *The Great War*, p. 317.
36. Diary, 31 December 1919.
37. *Ibid.*
38. F.R.S. to author, interview, 27 May 1980.
39. *Ibid.*
40. Diary, 11 June 1920.

### FOUR: OXFORD: "MY GREAT ADVENTURE"

1. Diary, 5 October 1920.
2. Stephen Leacock, *My Discovery of England* (London: John Lane, The Bodley Head Ltd., 1922), p. 81.
3. Diary, 2 February 1921.
4. *The Mirrors of Downing Street: Some Political Reflections*, by A Gentleman with a Duster (New York/London: G.P. Putnam's Sons; The Knickerbocker Press, 1921), pp. 46-47.
5. Diary, 7 August 1921.
6. F.R.S. to author in conversation, July, 1979.
7. Diary, 12 August 1921.
8. *Ibid.*, 5 August, 2 August 1921.
9. *Ibid.*, 20 April 1923.
10. *Ibid.*, 27 May 1921.
11. *Ibid.*, 11 April 1923. He first saw the painting at the National Gallery on April 11, 1923.
12. F.R.S. to author in conversation, June, 1980.
13. Diary, 28 April 1923.
14. John Darlington to author, 20 October 1981.

15. *Ibid.*
16. Diary, 16 September 1921.
17. *Ibid.*, 2 January 1923.
18. *Ibid.*, 3 April 1923.
19. *Ibid.*, 2 September 1923.
20. F.R.S. to author, interview, 14-15 September 1976.
21. Diary, 26 January 1921.
22. *Ibid.*, 6 February 1921.
23. Cited by F.R. Scott in a tape on "Christianity and Industrial Problems" made for S. Djwa, September, 1977. A transcript of this tape was published in *Canadian Poetry*, No. 4 (1979) under the title of "F.R. Scott: Discussing Oxford Study Groups on Christianity and Industrial Problems," pp. 83-93.
24. R.H. Tawney, *The Acquisitive Society* (New York: Harcourt, Brace and Company, 1920).
25. Thomas à Kempis, *The Imitation of Christ* (London/New York: J.M. Dent & Sons Ltd.; E.P. Dutton & Co. Inc., 1910, 1960).
26. Diary, 29 December 1921.
27. *Ibid.*, 4 July 1921.
28. Rupert Brooke, *The Collected Poems of Rupert Brooke With a Memoir* (London: Sidgwick & Jackson Ltd., 1918), p. 9.
29. *Ibid.*, 19 July 1922.
30. H.G. Wells, *The Undying Fire* (New York: Macmillan Company, 1919).
31. All preceding citations from Diary, 20 July 1922.
32. F.R.S. to author, interview, 27 November 1977.
33. Diary, 23 August 1921.
34. *Ibid.*, 5 April 1922.
35. *Ibid.*, 17 July 1922.
36. F.R.S. to author in conversation, July, 1980.
37. Diary, 17 July 1922.
38. *Ibid.*, 20 August 1922.
39. Later published in *The McGill Fortnightly Review* (January, 1926), p. 43.
40. Diary, 11 December 1922.
41. Cited in Christopher Hollis, *Oxford in the Twenties: Recollections of Five Friends* (London: Heineman, 1976), p. 14.
42. F.R.S. to F.G. Scott, letter, 6 November 1922, FGSP.
43. F.R.S. to author, interview, 14-15 September 1976.
44. Diary, 26 July 1921.
45. *Ibid.*, 19 August 1923.

46. F.R.S. to author, interview, July, 1978.

47. Diary, 16 July 1921.

48. *Ibid.*, 2 July 1922.

49. Terence Sheard to author, interview, Toronto, 29 October 1978.

50. Hollis, *Oxford in the Twenties*, p. 15.

51. Diary, 7 November 1922.

52. F.R.S. to author, interview, 18 July 1978.

53. F.R.S. to Amy Scott, letter, 20 November 1921.

54. Diary, 5 May 1922.

55. *Ibid.*, 2 March 1923.

56. *Ibid.*, 4 July 1923.

57. *Ibid.*, 5 January 1922.

58. *Ibid.*, 3 January 1924.

59. F.R.S. to author in conversation, July, 1980.

60. Diary, 11 April 1921.

61. *Ibid.*, 14 August 1921.

62. Unpublished poem, FRSP.

63. Diary, 15 August 1923.

64. *Ibid.*, 7 December 1921.

65. *Ibid.*, 23 June, 25 June 1923.

66. *Ibid.*, 23 February 1923.

67. F.R.S. to author, interviews, 26-27 October 1978; October, 1981.

68. Diary, 18 May 1923.

69. F.R.S. to F.G.S., letter, 15 October 1922, FGSP.

70. F.R.S. to Amy Scott, letter, 24 March 1923, FGSP.

71. F.R.S. to F.G.S., letter, 24 April 1923, FGSP.

72. Diary, 9 July 1923.

73. F.R.S., Notes made after conversation with Jacques Parizeau, FRSP.

74. Diary, 30 August 1923.

75. *Ibid.*, 31 October 1923.

76. *Ibid.*, 2 November 1923.

77. *Ibid.*, 3 November 1923.

FIVE: A NEW SOIL

1. Diary, 10 November 1923.

2. *Ibid.*, 12 November 1923.

3. F.R.S., typewritten speech, untitled, but with the following notation at top: "This is not about poetry in general so much as about poetry and Frank Scott – this is all I can be sure of," dated 1958, FRSP.

4. Diary, 23 December 1923.

5. *Ibid.*, 26 January 1925.
6. *Ibid.*, 2 November 1924.
7. *Ibid.*, 21 May 1924.
8. *Ibid.*, 26 October 1924.
9. *Ibid.*, 1 February 1925.
10. *Ibid.*, 30 April 1923.
11. *Ibid.*, 20 February 1925.
12. *Ibid.*, 6 July 1924.
13. *Ibid.*, 1 December 1923.
14. *Ibid.*, 3 June 1924.
15. *Ibid.*, 10 May 1924.
16. Carleton Stanley, "Spiritual Conditions in Canada," *Hibbert Journal* (June, 1923). Besides decrying materialism in Canada, Stanley wrote (p. 276), "To say that life is unstable, spasmodic and haphazard is at the same time to say that we have no Canadian art and no Canadian literature."
17. Diary, 1 November 1924.
18. *Ibid.*, 3 May 1924.
19. *Ibid.*, 21 August 1924.
20. *Ibid.*, 12 October 1922.
21. *Ibid.*, 15 November 1923.
22. *Ibid.*, 3 February 1924.
23. F.R.S. to author in conversation, September, 1976.
24. Diary, 3 February 1924.
25. *Ibid.*, 21 November 1923.
26. *Ibid.*, 26 June 1924.
27. F.R.S. to author, interview, 20 July 1978.
28. Diary, 5 July 1924.
29. *Ibid.*, 13 July 1924.
30. *Ibid.*, 15 July 1924.
31. F.R. Scott, "My First Memories of the Law Faculty," *The McGill You Knew: An Anthology of Memories 1920-1960*, ed. E.A. Collard (Don Mills: Longman Canada Limited, 1975), p. 189.
32. Stephen Leacock, *Montreal: Seaport & City* (Garden City, N.Y.: Doubleday, 1942), p. 290.
33. Scott, "My First Memories," p. 190.
34. Diary, 20 November 1924.
35. F.R.S. to author, interview, 27 January 1977.
36. Diary, 9 March 1925.
37. *Ibid.*, 18 November 1924.

38. *Ibid.*, 11 March 1925.
39. *Ibid.*, 11 October 1924.
40. *The Canadian Forum*, I, 1 (October, 1920), p. 1.
41. Diary, 10 November 1924.
42. *Ibid.*, 13 May 1924.
43. *Ibid.*, 26 March 1925.
44. *Ibid.*, 18 March 1925.
45. *Ibid.*, 22 March 1925.
46. *Ibid.*, 30 April, 12 May, 29 June, 12-14, 24 August, 25 November 1925, 22 July 1926.
47. Ronald McCall to author, interview, 25 April 1979.
48. F.R.S. and Marian Scott to author, interview, 2 December 1980, October, 1981.
49. Marian Scott to author, interview, November, 1979.
50. Author's notes from a conversation with Marian Scott, June, 1977.
51. F.R.S. in conversation with author.
52. Marian Scott to author, interview, 29 October 1981, 27 August 1983.
53. *Ibid.*
54. Dora Russell, *The Tamarisk Tree* (London: Elek/Pemberton, 1975), p. 156.
55. Marian Scott to author, interview, 29 October 1981.
56. Diary, 21 March 1925.
57. Diary, Marian Scott, 10 January 1926, read to author 4 June 1985.

SIX: THE ORTHODOX WAS WRONG

1. Diary, 20 October 1925.
2. *Ibid.*, 25 October 1925.
3. *The Canadian Forum*, I, 1 (October, 1920), .p. 1.
4. *The McGill Fortnightly Review*, I, 1 (21 November 1925), pp. 1, 2.
5. *Ibid.*, p. 2.
6. "Nordic" (F.R.S.), "Talks on the Mountain," *ibid.*, p. 7.
7. Diary, 11 December 1925.
8. Harold Files to author, letter, 1 January 1976.
9. *MFR*, I, 9/10 (22 March 1926), p. 80.
10. *MFR*, II, 4 (15 December 1926), p. 1.
11. F.R.S., "Student Government at McGill," *MFR*, II, 7 (10 March 1927), pp. 50-51.
12. A.J.M. Smith, "Contemporary Poetry," *MFR*, II, 4 (15 December 1926), p. 32.
13. *MFR*, II, 9/10 (27 April 1927), p. 66.

14. Diary, 22 March 1925.

15. Leon Edel, *"The McGill Fortnightly Review:* A Casual Reminiscence," *The McGill News* (Autumn, 1939), p. 22.

16. *MFR*, II, 9/10 (27 April 1927), p. 66.

17. Diary, 29 November 1925.

18. A.J.M. Smith, "Symbolism in Poetry," *MFR*, I, 2 (5 December 1925), pp. 11-12, 16.

19. "R.S." (F.R.S.), "The Royal Canadian Academy," *ibid.*, p. 14.

20. Diary, 24 December 1924.

21. Sandra Djwa, " 'A New Soil and a Sharp Sun': The Landscape of a Modern Canadian Poetry," *Modernist Studies: Literature and Culture 1920-1940*, 2, 2 (1977), pp. 11, 12, 15.

22. F.R.S., "Frost in Autumn," *The Collected Poems of F.R. Scott* (Toronto: McClelland and Stewart, 1981), p. 39. Unless otherwise noted all further citations of Scott's poems are from this edition and will be designated by *C.P.* and the page number.

23. F.R.S., "XXX," *MFR*, II, 2 (17 November 1926), p. 14; revised version in *Collected Poems*, p. 29.

24. D.H. Lawrence, "Fidelity," *Pansies: Poems by D.H. Lawrence* (London: Martin Secker, 1929), p. 69.

25. F.R.S. to author, interview, July, 1978.

26. Diary, 11 June 1924.

27. *MFR*, II, 6 (18 February 1927), p. 41.

28. F.R.S. to author, interview, 3 December 1980.

29. A.J.M. Smith to author, interview, East Lansing, Michigan, 8 November 1974.

30. F.R. Scott to Leon Edel, letter, 22 March 1976.

31. *MFR*, I, 8 (6 March 1926), p. 61.

32. Leon Edel to author, interview, 25 October 1982.

33. A.J.M. Smith to author, interview, Vancouver, November/December, 1975.

34. Wilfrid Bovey to Major General J.H. MacBrien, letter, 17 December 1932, McGill Archives.

35. Diary, 2 May 1925.

36. Henry Festing Jones and A.T. Bartholomew, eds., *The Note-Books of Samuel Butler* (New York: AMS Press, n.d.), p. 392.

37. F.R.S. to author, interview, 8 June 1977.

38. Diary, 2 May 1926.

39. Diary, 1 July 1927.

40. F.R.S. to author, interview, October, 1981.

41. F.R.S., "H.G. Wells" (February, 1925), unpublished paper, p. 18. All further citations from this paper will be noted in the text and designated HGW with page number.

SEVEN: A SEARCH FOR FORM

1. Diary, 12 August 1927.
2. Diary, 29 June 1925.
3. F.R.S. to author, interview, July, 1978.
4. Diary, 22 September 1924.
5. A.J.M. Smith to F.R. Scott, letter, 1 December 1927.
6. Diary, 5 July 1927.
7. *Ibid.*, 22 July 1927.
8. F.R.S. to author, interview, October, 1981.
9. Diary, 29 August 1925.
10. *Ibid.*, 2-4 September 1925; Arthur Scott to author, interview, November, 1979.
11. Diary, 5 September 1925.
12. *Ibid.*, 31 August 1925.
13. F.R.S., "The Poet in Quebec Today," *The McGill Movement: A.J.M. Smith, F.R. Scott and Leo Kennedy*, ed. Peter Stevens (Toronto: Ryerson, 1969), p. 51.
14. Djwa, " 'A New Soil and a Sharp Sun,' " pp. 3-16.
15. Diary, 18 August 1928.
16. Interview with Marian Scott, 29 October 1981.
17. *The Poetry of Ernest Dowson*, ed. Desmond Flower (Rutherford: Fairleigh Dickinson University Press, 1934, 1970), p. 52.
18. Marian Scott to author, interview, 29 October 1981.
19. Diary, 17 October 1927.
20. "Sonnet (Written on a May Morning)," *MFR*, II, 2 (17 November 1926), p. 11.
21. Marian Scott to author, interview, 2 December 1980.
22. D.H. Lawrence, *Look! We Have Come Through!* (New York: B.W. Heubsch, 1919), p. 1.
23. Marian Scott to author, interview, 29 October 1981.
24. Havelock Ellis, *The Dance of Life* (Boston: Houghton Mifflin Co., 1923), p. 259.
25. F.R.S. to author, interview, October, 1981.
26. *Ibid.*, interview, 2 December 1980.
27. Dora Russell, *The Right to be Happy* (Garden City, N.Y.: Garden City Publishing Co., 1927), pp. 153-55.

28. F.R.S. and Marian Scott to author, interview, October, 1981.
29. Diary, 23 May 1927.
30. Marian Scott to author, interview, 29 October 1981.
31. F.R.S. to author in conversation, October, 1980.
32. Marian Scott to author, interview, 29 October 1981.
33. F.R.S. to W.B. Scott, letter, 8 January 1928.
34. Diary, 12 March 1928.
35. F.R.S., "Little Body of Baby," *The Auto-Anthology of F.R. Scott* (Montreal, 1939), p. 54, unpublished manuscript, FRSP.
36. "Metamorphosis," *ibid.*, p. 51.
37. Diary, 29 December 1924.
38. "The Labour Party in Canada," *MFR*, II, 5 (1 February 1927), p. 35.
39. Kenneth McNaught, *A Prophet in Politics: A Biography of J.S. Woodsworth* (Toronto: University of Toronto Press, 1959), pp. 244-45.
40. F.R.S. to author, interview, 27 January 1977.
41. F.R.S. and Marian Scott to author, interview, 7 June 1977.
42. F.R.S., "What Prof. Frank Scott Thinks About Grace MacInnis's Book," *CCF News* (February, 1954).
43. E.A. Pulker, "The Social Concern of Canon Scott," *Journal of the Canadian Church Historical Society*, XXII (October, 1980), p. 1.
44. *Ibid.*, p. 4.
45. Olive Ziegler, *Woodsworth: Social Pioneer* (Toronto: Ontario Publishing Co., 1934), p. 128.
46. *Ibid.*, pp. 124-25.
47. F.R.S. to author in conversation.
48. A.S. Eddington, *The Nature of the Physical World* (Cambridge: Cambridge University Press, 1929), p. 276.
49. Henri Bergson, *Creative Evolution*, trans. Arthur Mitchell (New York: Random House, 1911, 1944), p. xi.
50. Handwritten notes inserted into *The New Machiavelli* in Scott's collection.
51. Diary, 11 November 1926.
52. F.R.S. to author, interview, 30 November 1977.
53. Author's notes from conversation with F.R.S., July, 1978.
54. Literary article written between 1929 and 1931. Published in *Canadian Poetry* and dated 1927. However, on the basis of internal references to *All Quiet on the Western Front* (first published in 1929) it is apparent that the article could not have been written until after March, 1929, the dating of Scott's copy of the book.
55. J.S. Woodsworth, *Following the Gleam: A Modern Pilgrim's Progress – To Date* (n.p., 1926), p. 6.

56. *Ibid.*, p. 18.
57. "New Poems for Old: I – The Decline of Poesy," *The Canadian Forum*, XI (May, 1931), p. 297.
58. "New Poems for Old: II – The Revival of Poetry," *ibid.* (June, 1931), p. 338.

EIGHT: POLITICS – THE ONLY ROAD TO HEAVEN NOW

1. FRSP.
2. F.R.S. to author, interview, 27 January 1983.
3. Cited in John W. Dafoe, *Canada: An American Nation* (New York: Columbia University, 1935), p. 22.
4. F.R.S., "The Value of Imperial Sovereignty," *The Canadian Forum*, X (August, 1930), pp. 398-99.
5. H. Blair Neatby, *The Politics of Chaos: Canada in the Thirties* (Toronto: Macmillan, 1972), p. 5.
6. F.R.S. to author in conversation, July, 1980.
7. *Ibid.*, interview, 13 September 1976.
8. J.S. Woodsworth to F.R.S., letter, 28 October 1932, FRSP.
9. "J.E. Keith" (F.R.S.), "The Fascist Province," *The Canadian Forum*, XIV (April, 1934), pp. 251-52.
10. F.R.S. to author in conversation.
11. Terence Sheard to author, interview, 29 October 1978.
12. F.R.S., "The Trial of the Toronto Communists," *Essays on the Constitution: Aspects of Canadian Law and Politics* (Toronto: University of Toronto Press, 1977), p. 59. "Happier far are those who inherit revolutions than those who attempt to make them."
13. J. King Gordon, "The Politics of Poetry," in *On F.R. Scott: Essays on His Contributions to Law, Literature, and Politics*, eds. Sandra Djwa and R. St. J. Macdonald (Montreal: McGill-Queen's University Press, 1983), pp. 21, 27.
14. Florence Bird to author, interview, 27 April 1979.
15. *Ibid.*
16. Gordon, "The Politics of Poetry," p. 21.
17. F.R.S. to author, interview, 30 November 1977.
18. *Ibid.*, October, 1981.
19. *Ibid.*, 11 November 1974.
20. *Ibid.*, 27 January 1983.
21. David Lewis to author in conversation, 18 February 1981.
22. From handwritten notes on socialism made by F.R.S. He notes this quote is taken from [G.D.H.] Cole, "The Intelligent Man's Guide" [to Socialism], n.d., ca. 1930-1935, p. 1.

23. Gordon, "The Politics of Poetry," p. 21.

24. Speech to Young People's Socialist League, 1931, pp. 1-4, FRSP.

25. David Lewis to F.R.S., letter, 24 October 1932, FRSP.

26. David Lewis to author, interview, 18 February 1981.

27. David Lewis, "F.R. Scott's Contribution to the CCF," *On F.R. Scott*, p. 83.

28. Michiel Horn, *The League for Social Reconstruction: Intellectual Origins of the Democratic Left in Canada 1930-1942* (Toronto: University of Toronto Press, 1980), p. 18.

29. Eugene Forsey, "Montreal Is A Quiet City," *The Canadian Forum*, XI (June, 1931), pp. 327-29.

30. F.H. Underhill, "O Canada," *The Canadian Forum*, X (April, 1930), p. 235.

31. *The Montreal Star*, 18 October 1933.

32. Principal Arthur Currie to Arthur Purvis, letter, 24 October 1933; Premier Taschereau to Arthur Currie, letter, 20 October 1933, McGill Archives.

33. F.R.S., "The Trial of the Toronto Communists," *Essays on the Constitution*, pp. 50, 59. An editorial in the Toronto *Globe* in August, 1932, commended Scott's style, noting that "little in it could be objected to by those who are determined to suppress in Toronto the habit and practice of thinking. Yet in it there is a sort of bland astonishment that the verdict and sentences could have been what they were in a country where everybody can read and write."

34. B.K. Sandwell to F.R.S., letter, 15 October 1932, FRSP.

35. McGill Inter-departmental Correspondence from Principal Currie, 26 October 1933, p. 2, McGill Archives.

36. Wilfrid Bovey to Major General J.H. MacBrien, letter, 17 December 1932, McGill Archives.

37. F.R.S. and Marian Scott to author in conversation, February, 1982.

38. Sandra Shaul, "Marian Scott: The Balance of Structure and Expression in Abstract Art," *The Modern Image: Cubism and the Realist Tradition* (Edmonton: Edmonton Art Gallery, 1981), pp. 31-35. Catalogue to exhibit of same name.

39. Marian Scott to author in conversation, 4 June 1980.

40. F.R.S., "The Efficiency of Socialism," *Queen's Quarterly*, 42 (Summer, 1935), pp. 215-25.

41. Marian Scott to author, interview, 29 October 1981.

42. "Christian Ethics at a Discount," *Saturday Night*, 8 April 1933, p. 1.

43. Gordon, "The Politics of Poetry," p. 27.

NINE: MISSIONARIES OF A POLITICAL CHARACTER

1. David Lewis, *The Good Fight: Political Memoirs 1909-1958* (Toronto: Macmillan, 1981), p. 84.
2. Cited in Kenneth McNaught, *A Prophet in Politics: A Biography of J.S. Woodsworth* (Toronto: University of Toronto Press, 1959), p. 253.
3. Described in Grace MacInnis, *J.S. Woodsworth: A Man to Remember* (Toronto: Macmillan, 1953), p. 179.
4. F.R.S. to F.H. Underhill, 7 March 1932, FRSP.
5. *Handbook of The League for Social Reconstruction* (February, 1933), pp. 1, 2, 10.
6. Michiel Horn, *The League for Social Reconstruction: Intellectual Origins of the Democratic Left in Canada 1930-1942* (Toronto: University of Toronto Press, 1980), pp. 27-28.
7. F.R.S. to author, interview, 8 October 1980.
8. King Gordon to author in conversation, 30 September 1977.
9. FRSP.
10. Horn, *The League for Social Reconstruction*, p. 55.
11. F.R.S. to author, interview, 20 July 1978.
12. Horn, *The League for Social Reconstruction*, p. 31.
13. F.R.S. to G.W. Allen, letter, 25 August 1932, FRSP.
14. McNaught, *Prophet in Politics*, p. 259.
15. F.R.S. to M.J. McPhail, letter, 15 June 1932, FRSP.
16. J. King Gordon, "The L.S.R. – Thirty Years After," speech to The Humanities Association, University of Alberta, Calgary, 2 December 1963, p. 17, FRSP. See also McNaught, *Prophet in Politics*, pp. 258-65.
17. MacInnis, *J.S. Woodsworth*, pp. 267-68.
18. Gordon, "The L.S.R. – Thirty Years After," p. 17.
19. F.R.S. to F.H. Underhill, letter, 7 September 1932, FRSP.
20. *Ibid.*, 20 October 1932, FRSP. Scott gives a different version in his 1961 recollections when he writes the following: "At Calgary only a short, eight point program had been adopted: F.H.U. saw the opportunity of providing something more complete. So he prepared the first draft of the Regina Manifesto and circulated it to us for comment. Graham Spry showed a revised version to Woodsworth, who was so taken with it that he arranged to have it put before the National Executive of the CCF which was to meet in Regina two days before the National Convention. He also arranged for representatives of the LSR to be

there when it was being discussed. Thus it was that Eugene, King Gordon and I were able to sit in on the National Executive meeting of a new party we had not formally joined." Travel Diary, 13 January 1961, FRSP.

21. F.H. Underhill to F.R.S., letter, 1 December 1932, FRSP.

22. Michiel Horn, "The L.S.R., the C.C.F., and the Regina Manifesto," speech to Conference Commemorating the 50th Anniversary of the Regina Manifesto, Regina, 24 June 1983.

23. T.C. Douglas, banquet address to Conference Commemorating the 50th Anniversary of the Regina Manifesto, 25 June 1983. Author's notes.

24. Laurence Grolund, *The Cooperative Commonwealth*, ed. Stow Persons (1884; rpt. Cambridge, Mass.: Harvard University Press, 1965).

25. F.R.S. to King Gordon, letter, 11 August 1937, cited in "The Politics of Poetry," p. 26.

26. Reproduced on agenda for Conference Commemorating the 50th Anniversary of the Regina Manifesto.

27. F.R.S., Travel Diary, 13 January 1961, FRSP.

28. Horn, *The League for Social Reconstruction*, pp. 44-45.

29. Travel Diary, 13 January 1961, FRSP.

30. "Co-operative Commonwealth Federation Programme," adopted at First National Convention held at Regina, Sask., July, 1933, reprinted in McNaught, *Prophet in Politics*, p. 321.

31. *Ibid.*, p. 330.

32. Walter Young, *The Anatomy of a Party: The National CCF 1932-1961* (Toronto: University of Toronto Press, 1969), p. 44, note 16.

33. George Curtis to author, interview, 3 August 1982.

34. *The Leader Post* [Regina], 21 July 1933.

35. *Le Canada*, 21 August 1933.

36. Horn, *The League for Social Reconstruction*, pp. 44, 46.

37. Ivan Avakumovic, *Socialism in Canada: A Study of the CCF-NDP in Federal and Provincial Politics* (Toronto: McClelland and Stewart, 1978), p. 59.

38. *Toronto Daily Star*, 10 November 1932.

39. *The Ottawa Journal*, 10 November 1932.

40. *Ibid.*, 15 November 1932.

41. F.R.S. to author, interview, 8 October 1980.

42. F.R.S. to Editor, *The Ottawa Journal*, 18 November 1932, FRSP.

43. Horn, *The League for Social Reconstruction*, p. 34.

44. *Ibid.*, p. 40.
45. *Ibid.*, pp. 67-69.
46. F.R.S. *et al.*, *Social Planning for Canada* (Toronto, 1935; rpt. Toronto: University of Toronto Press, 1975), pp. vii, viii.
47. Horn, *The League for Social Reconstruction*, p. 69. Full title of the book is: *A Criticism of the Book Written by Eugene Forsey, J. King Gordon, Leonard Marsh, J.F. Parkinson, F.R. Scott, Graham Spry and Frank H. Underhill and Published by the League for Social Reconstruction Under the Title "Social Planning for Canada."*
48. F.R.S. in conversation with author.
49. Horn, *The League for Social Reconstruction*, p. 69.
50. *Ibid.*
51. John Strachey, *The Coming Struggle for Power* (London: Gollancz, 1933).
52. Horn, *The League for Social Reconstruction*, p. 135.
53. *Ibid.*, p. 14.
54. F.R.S. to author, interview, 26 October 1978.
55. F.R.S. and H.M. Cassidy, *Labour Conditions in the Men's Clothing Industry* (Toronto: Thomas Nelson & Sons, 1935), p. vi.
56. "People Who Do Things," *Saturday Night* (12 October 1935), p. 20.
57. J.H.R. Wilbur, "Stevens Upstages Bennett," *The Bennett New Deal: Fraud or Portent?*, ed. J.H.R. Wilbur (Toronto: Copp Clark, 1968), pp. 118-20.
58. F.R.S., "Why Stop With Radio?," *ibid.*, pp. 58-59.
59. F.R.S. to author in conversation.
60. H. Blair Neatby, *The Politics of Chaos: Canada in the Thirties* (Toronto: Macmillan, 1972), p. 66.
61. "A Pox on all your Houses," *The Bennett New Deal*, p. 186. From an editorial in *The Canadian Forum*, XV (1935).
62. "Goodbye Dominion Status," *ibid.*, pp. 208-11.
63. F.R.S. to author in conversation.
64. F.R.S., "The Consequences of the Privy Council Decisions," *The Canadian Bar Review*, 15 (June, 1937), pp. 485, 494.
65. See Alan C. Cairns, "The Judicial Committee and Its Critics," *Canadian Journal of Political Science*, IV, 3 (September, 1971), p. 323. Cairns argues the Privy Council had a decentralizing effect better suited to Canada's diversity and that it placated Quebec, thereby having a positive influence on federalism. See also Mr. Justice Gerald Le Dain, "Sir Lyman Duff and the Constitution," *Osgoode Hall Law Journal*, 12, 2 (October,

1974), pp. 261-338. Le Dain provides a tempered explanation of both the legal antecedents for the Privy Council decisions and the climate of opinion surrounding them.

66. F.R.S., "The Need for a Canadian Penal Association," speech to the Canadian Penal Congress, Montreal, 14 June 1935, pp. 1-5, FRSP.

67. J.A. Edmison, "Perspective in Corrections," *Canadian Journal of Corrections*, 12 (October, 1970), pp. 534-48.

68. F.R.S. to author, interview, February, 1982.

69. D.V. Smiley, "The Rowell-Sirois Report, Provincial Autonomy, and Post-War Canadian Federalism," *The Canadian Journal of Economics and Political Science*, XXVIII, 1 (February, 1962), p. 54.

70. F.R.S., "The Royal Commission on Dominion-Provincial Relations," *University of Toronto Quarterly*, 7 (January, 1938), p. 150.

71. *Canada – One or Nine? The Purpose of Confederation*, brief submitted by the League for Social Reconstruction to the Royal Commission on Dominion-Provincial Relations, n.d., FRSP.

72. Maxwell Cohen, "Couchiching," *The Canadian Forum*, xx (October, 1940), p. 202.

73. "Impressions of a Tour in the U.S.S.R.," *The Canadian Forum*, xv (December, 1935), p. 382.

74. Diary, Russia/Sweden trip, 20 July 1935, FRSP.

75. "Impressions," p. 384.

76. Diary, Russia/Sweden trip, 16 July 1935, FRSP.

77. *Ibid.*, 29 July 1935.

78. *Ibid.*, 18 July 1935.

79. F.R.S. to author, interview, 7 June 1977.

80. *Ibid.*

81. *Ibid.*

TEN: CANADA

1. F.R.S. to author in conversation, October, 1978. Leacock actually joined the Department of Economics and Political Science at McGill in 1903.

2. Diary, 8 November 1921.

3. F.R.S. to author, interview, September-October, 1976.

4. *Ibid.*

5. Notes on proposed book on Canadian Politics and Reform, FRSP.

6. Horn, *The League for Social Reconstruction*, pp. 21-22.

7. F.R.S. to Lester Pearson, letter, 21 July 1931, FRSP.

8. Lester Pearson to F.R.S., letter, 22 July 1931, FRSP.

9. F.R.S., "The Permanent Bases of Canadian Foreign Policy," *Foreign Affairs*, 10 (July, 1932), p. 631.

10. Minutes of the Royal Institute of International Affairs, 1932, v.2 (September), pp. 696, 699.

11. F.R.S. to author, interview, 8 October 1980.

12. Brooke Claxton, unpublished "Memoir," Claxton Papers, pp. 371, 393, PAC.

13. F.R.S. to author, interview, 6 June 1977.

14. F.R.S. to King Gordon, letter, 11 August 1937, cited in "The Politics of Poetry," p. 27.

15. F.R.S. to author, interview, June, 1977.

16. *Ibid.*

17. F.R.S., "Russia, Japan and the Pacific," radio broadcast, ca. 1936, FRSP.

18. F.R.S., *Canada Today: A Study of Her National Interests and National Policy*, 2nd rev. ed. (Toronto: Oxford University Press, 1939), p. ix.

19. F.R.S. to author, interview, 8 June 1977.

20. Fred Soward to author, interview, Vancouver, 11 December 1978.

21. *Ibid.*

22. *The Montreal Daily Star*, 23 November 1938.

23. *Ibid.*, 25 November 1938.

24. J.L. Granatstein, "The 'Man of Secrets' in Canada, 1934," *Dalhousie Review*, LI, 4 (Winter, 1971-1972), p. 510.

25. A Quebecer (E.K. Brown), "French Canadian Nationalism," *Forum*, eds. J.L. Granatstein and Peter Stevens (Toronto: University of Toronto Press, 1972), p. 143.

26. "J.E. Keith" (F.R.S.), "The Fascist Province," *The Canadian Forum*, XIV (April, 1934), pp. 251-52.

27. "S" (F.R.S.), "Embryo Fascism in Quebec," *Foreign Affairs*, 16 (April, 1938), pp. 455-56.

28. *Ibid.*, p. 464.

29. Montreal *Herald*, 23 October 1936.

30. F.R.S. to author, interview, 8 October 1980.

31. *The Gazette* [Montreal], 24 October 1936.

32. *Ibid.*

33. F.R.S. to author, interview, 8 October 1980.

34. *The Gazette* [Montreal], 24 October 1936.

35. *The Montreal Star*, 24 October 1936.

36. *Ibid.*

37. *Ibid.*, 26 October 1936.

38. *La Presse*, 26 October 1936. "Les grandes théories de la liberté, de

l'égalité et de la fraternité ne valent rien. Ce qui compte ce sont les trois vertus théologales: la foi qui illumine l'intelligence, la charité qui en richit les coeurs, et l'esperance qui réconforte."

39. Humphrey Carpenter, *W.H. Auden* (London: Unwin Paperbacks, 1981), p. 214.

40. W.H. Auden, "Impressions of Valencia," *The New Statesman and Nation*, XIII (30 January 1937), p. 159.

41. Carpenter, *Auden*, p. 218.

42. *The Gazette* [Montreal], 26 October 1936.

43. J.R. Mallory to author, interview, 28 August 1983.

44. H.R. Trevor Roper, "Acts of the Apostles," review of *After Long Silence* by Michael Straight, *New York Review of Books*, 31 March 1983, p. 3.

45. F.R.S., "Where Do We Go From Here?" *Winnipeg Tribune*, 5 December 1938, p. 11.

46. *The Gazette* [Montreal], 10 August 1934.

47. F.R.S. cited in *The Gazette* [Montreal], 28 October 1936.

48. J.L. Granatstein, *Canada's War: The Politics of the Mackenzie King Government, 1939-1945* (Toronto: Oxford University Press, 1975), p. 20.

49. "Our Position When Britain Enters War," *McGill Daily*, 3 March 1937.

50. F.R.S. to J.S. Woodsworth, letter, 3 February 1937, J.S. Woodsworth Papers, PAC.

51. R.A. Mackay from a chapter for a projected book sponsored by the CIIA, *Canada's Status in Peace and in War*, sent to F.R.S. for comment, pp. 1, 2, FRSP.

52. MacInnis, *J.S. Woodsworth*, p. 237.

53. *The Montreal Star*, 23 February 1937.

54. Claxton "Memoir," p. 414.

55. R.C. Brown and Margaret Prang, eds., *Confederation to 1949* (Toronto: Prentice-Hall, 1966), III, p. 309.

56. F.R.S., *The Winnipeg Tribune*, 5 December 1938, pp. 11-12.

57. F.R.S., "A Policy of Neutrality for Canada," *Foreign Affairs*, 17, 2 (January, 1939), pp. 1, 7.

58. *Ibid.*, pp. 8-9. Italics mine.

59. Unpublished statement, "Toward a Canadian Foreign Policy," p. 1, FRSP.

60. Michael Oliver, "F.R. Scott as Quebecer," in *On F.R. Scott*, p. 168.

61. "Toward a Canadian Foreign Policy."

62. Arthur R.M. Lower, *My First Seventy-Five Years* (Toronto: Macmillan, 1967), pp. 232-33.

63. F.R.S. to author, interview, June, 1976.

64. F.R.S., notes taken at National Council meetings, Ottawa, 6 September 1939, FRSP.
65. F.R.S. to author, interview, 28 November 1977.
66. David Lewis to author, interview, Vancouver, 18 February 1981.
67. David Lewis, *The Good Fight: Political Memoirs 1909-1958* (Toronto: Macmillan, 1981), pp. 173-74.
68. McNaught, *Prophet in Politics*, p. 306.
69. F.R.S. to author, interview, 28 November 1977.
70. Granatstein, *Canada's War*, p. 26.
71. F.R.S. to Rt. Hon. Mackenzie King, letter, 5 January 1940, FRSP.
72. Mackenzie King to J. Pickersgill, memo, 12 January 1940, Mackenzie King Papers, PAC.
73. O.D. Skelton to Mackenzie King, memo, January, 1940, Mackenzie King Papers, PAC.

ELEVEN: WHO HEARS A SHOT?

1. F.R.S. to author, interview, 8 October 1980.
2. *Ibid*.
3. Jack Pickersgill to author, interview, 5 February 1982.
4. F.R.S. to author, interview, 8 October 1980.
5. F.R.S. to Stuart LeMesurier, letter, 6 October 1940, FRSP.
6. F.R.S. to author, interview, February, 1982.
7. F.R.S., "Personal Stuff Mostly Ideas Such as Come Casually," 20 September 1940, unpublished notes, FRSP.
8. I am indebted to Douglas LePan for drawing my attention to this parallel.
9. Constantine FitzGibbon, *The Blitz* (London: Macdonald, 1957, 1970), p. 78.
10. F.R.S., Diary of Commonwealth Labour Conference, 15 September 1944, FRSP.
11. Douglas LePan to author, interview, Toronto, 7 May 1983.
12. F.R.S. to author, interview, 8 October 1980.
13. *Ibid*.
14. *Ibid*.
15. Rainer Maria Rilke, *Duino Elegies*, trans. & intro. J.B. Leishman and Stephen Spender (New York: W.W. Norton, 1939), p. 21.
16. F.R.S. to author, interview, 11 November 1974.
17. *Ibid.*, 8 October 1980.
18. John Strachey, *The New Statesman and Nation*, xx (9 November 1940), p. 466.
19. F.R.S. to author, interview, 8 January 1975. In fact, Barker wrote one

of the greatest elegies of the Second World War, "Sonnet to My Mother."

20. "The Democratic Manifesto," p. 16.

21. *Ibid.*, pp. 58, 59, 60.

22. *Ibid.*, p. 56.

23. *Ibid.*, p. 36.

24. Thomas Paine, *Rights of Man*, in *The Oxford Dictionary of Quotations*, 2nd ed. (London: Oxford University Press, 1966), p. 373. I am indebted to Ramsay Cook for drawing my attention to this parallel.

25. F.R.S., "Personal Stuff," 24 November 1941, FRSP.

26. John Bird, "A Political Poet," *Ottawa Evening Citizen*, F.R.S. Scrapbooks, FRSP.

27. Bartlett Brebner to F.R.S., letter, 19 October 1942, FRSP.

28. Granatstein, *Canada's War*, p. 234.

29. Walter D. Young, *The Anatomy of a Party: The National CCF 1932-61* (Toronto: University of Toronto Press, 1969), p. 231.

30. Granatstein, *Canada's War*, p. 227.

31. F.R.S. to M.J. Coldwell, letter, 7 May 1942, FRSP.

32. F.R. Scott, "What Did No Mean?" *The Canadian Forum*, XXII (June, 1942), p. 72.

33. *Ibid.*, p. 73.

34. Gérard Pelletier to F.R.S., letter, 5 juin 1942, FRSP.

35. Louis Morisset to F.R.S., letter, 6 June 1942, FRSP.

36. F.R.S. in conversation with author.

37. Louis Dudek to F.R.S., letter, 25 July 1942, FRSP.

38. J.M. Macdonnell to F.R.S., letter, 6 July 1942, FRSP.

39. Eugene Forsey, letter to *The Canadian Forum*, XXII (August, 1942), p. 141.

40. Editorial, *Saturday Night*, 8 August 1942, p. 3.

41. *Ibid.*, 26 September 1942, p. 1.

42. *Ibid.*, 10 October 1942, p. 3.

43. B.K. Sandwell, *ibid.*, 21 November 1942, p. 20.

44. A.R.M. Lower to F.R.S., letter, September, 1947, FRSP.

45. Harold Innis to F.R.S., letter, 21 August 1942, FRSP.

46. Brooke Claxton to F.R.S., letter, 19 July 1942, FRSP.

47. F.R.S. to author, interview, July, 1978.

48. Elton Scott to F.R.S., letter, 22 August 1942, FRSP.

49. *The Gazette* [Montreal], 11 November 1942.

50. *The Gazette* [Montreal], 14 November 1942.

51. Thérèse F. Casgrain, *A Woman in a Man's World*, trans. Joyce Marshall (Toronto: McClelland and Stewart, 1972), p. III.

52. F.R.S. in conversation with author.

53. Jacques Bieler to author, interview, 25 April 1979.

54. F.G. Scott, in *Colombo's Canadian Quotations*, ed. John Robert Colombo (Edmonton: Hurtig Publishers, 1974), p. 527.

55. *The Gazette* [Montreal], 26 August 1943.

56. F.R.S. to author, interview, 7 June 1977.

57. *Ibid.*, September, 1976.

58. *Ibid.*

59. Brooke Claxton, unpublished "Memoir," Claxton Papers, pp. 433-34.

60. Murray Ballantyne to author, interview, Montreal, 26 October 1978.

61. Grace Scott to author, interview, Toronto, 29 October 1978.

62. F.R.S. to author, interview, 10 January 1975.

63. F.R.S., "Personal Stuff," 1944, FRSP.

64. *The Standard* [Montreal], 22 January 1944.

65. Order of Service, FRSP.

66. *Quebec Chronicle-Telegram*, 22 January 1944.

## TWELVE: PREVIEW

1. F.R.S. to Leon Edel, letter, 4 February 1944, FRSP.

2. "Statement," *Preview* [No. 1] (March, 1942), n.p.

3. Patrick Anderson to author, interview, 8 June 1974.

4. Margaret Surrey to author, interview, 24 April 1979.

5. F.R.S. to author, interview, February, 1982.

6. P.K. Page to author, interview, 20 July 1975.

7. *Ibid.*

8. *Preview*, No. 11 (February, 1943), n.p.

9. John Sutherland. [Story contained in inventory put out by Golden Dog Press.]

10. Louis Dudek to author, interview, 1 October 1975.

11. *Ibid.*, 24 May 1979.

12. John Sutherland, "Introduction," *Other Canadians: An Anthology of the New Poetry in Canada 1940-1946*, ed. John Sutherland (Montreal: First Statement Press, n.d.), pp. 5-20.

13. Louis Dudek to author, interview, 1 October 1975.

14. P.K. Page to author, interview, 20 July 1975.

15. Patrick Anderson, "Poem on Canada," *Return to Canada* (Toronto: McClelland and Stewart, 1977).

16. F.R.S., "Four of the Former *Preview* Editors: A Discussion," *Canadian Poetry*, No. 4 (Spring/Summer, 1979), p. 109.

17. F.R.S. to author in conversation, 27 January 1983.

18. *Poetry* (Chicago), LXV, II (November, 1944), p. III.

19. Earle Birney to author, interview, 31 August 1983.

THIRTEEN: MAKE THIS YOUR CANADA

1. F.R.S., "The C.C.F. Program Today," typewritten manuscript of speech, October, 1942, FRSP.
2. David Lewis, "F.R. Scott's Contribution to the CCF," *On F.R. Scott*, p. 83.
3. Roger Lemelin to author, letter, 20 June 1984.
4. George Tompkins to author, interview, 11 June 1984.
5. Thérèse Casgrain to author, interview, May, 1980.
6. David Lewis and Frank Scott, *Make This YOUR Canada: A Review of C.C.F. History and Policy* (Toronto: Central Canada Publishing Company, 1943), p. 122.
7. *Ibid.*, p. 56.
8. *Ibid.*, pp. 147-48.
9. *Ibid.*, p. 187.
10. Lewis, *The Good Fight*, p. 252.
11. F.R.S. to author in conversation, January, 1983.
12. Lewis, *The Good Fight*, p. 230.
13. F.R.S. to author in conversation, January, 1983.
14. Totalitarian Govt. in Sask. – After June, 1944. F.R.S. Scrapbooks, FRSP.
15. See *The Leader-Post* [Regina], 30 December 1944.
16. F.R.S. to author, interview, 27 January 1983.
17. *Ibid.*
18. Brian Moore to author, letter, n.d. [ca. August, 1983].
19. F.R.S. to author, interview, 27 January 1983.
20. Cited in Lewis, *The Good Fight*, p. 238.
21. *Ibid.*, p. 240.
22. F.R.S., Diary of the Commonwealth Labour Conference, 18 September 1944, FRSP.
23. *Ibid.*, 12, 15, 30 September 1944.
24. *Ibid.*, 9 September 1944.
25. *Ibid.*, 21 September 1944.
26. George Tompkins to author, interview, 11 June 1984.
27. *Saskatchewan Commonwealth*, 19 July 1944.
28. Granatstein, *Canada's War*, pp. 392-410.
29. Stephen Spender, "The Making of a Poem," *Partisan Review*, XIII, 3 (Summer, 1946), pp. 300-01.

30. Arthur Lismer, "Techniques in the Education of Children in Art," typewritten transcript of 1933, CBC Radio talk, FRSP.
31. F.R.S., *I.F. Stone's Weekly*, 17 May 1943.
32. George Cadbury, "Saskatchewan 1944-1951," unpublished speech to Conference Commemorating the 50th Anniversary of the Regina Manifesto, Regina, 24 June 1983, p. 7.
33. Young, *The Anatomy of a Party*, p. 119.
34. Lewis, *The Good Fight*, p. 456.
35. *Ibid.*

### FOURTEEN: THE LAW TEACHER

1. Gerald Le Dain to author, interview, 24 October 1981.
2. F.R.S. to author in conversation.
3. F.R.S. to Arnold Heeney, 22 January 1946, FRSP.
4. Gerald Le Dain, "F.R. Scott and Legal Education," *On F.R. Scott*, p. 104.
5. *Ibid.*
6. *Ibid.*
7. *Ibid.*, pp. 104, 106.
8. All preceding material from Marc Lapointe to author, interview, 26 September 1984.
9. All preceding citations from F.R.S., typewritten lecture, "Some Thoughts on the Constitutional Question," given to the Junior Bar Association, n.d. [ca. 1943], pp. 3, 10, 12, 13, 14, FRSP.
10. Le Dain, "Legal Education," pp. 103-04.
11. F.R.S. to author, interview, 8 October 1980.
12. Le Dain to author, interview, 24 October 1981.
13. Le Dain, "Legal Education," p. 107.
14. *Ibid.*, p. 108.
15. Charles Lussier to author, interview, 23 August 1983.
16. Lussier to author, letter, 13 February 1984.
17. Ron Cheffins to author, interview, 31 December 1983.
18. Le Dain, "Legal Education," pp. 111-12.
19. Cyril James to C.S. LeMesurier, letter, 14 August 1942, FRSP.
20. Harold Laski to F.R.S., letter, 27 January 1948.
21. Charles Lussier to author, interview, 23 August 1983.
22. F.R.S. to C.A. Wright, letter, 14 April 1948, FRSP.
23. C.A. Wright to F.R.S., letter, 23 October 1947 [*sic*], FRSP. From contents of this letter it is apparent it is incorrectly dated.

24. F.R.S. to Cyril James, letter, 14 February 1947, FRSP.
25. F.R.S. to Escott Reid, letter, 13 November 1947, FRSP.

FIFTEEN: A GRAIN OF RICE

1. F.R.S., speech to CCF Convention, 26 July 1950, FRSP. All preceding quotations are from this speech.
2. Eugene Forsey to author, interview, 1 October 1977.
3. F.R.S. to T.W.L. MacDermot, letter, 16 October 1951, FRSP.
4. Peter Scott to Rosemary Kelley (Cartwright), letter, 4 August 1946; Rosemary Cartwright to author, interview, 9 June 1985.
5. Peter Scott to Rosemary Kelley (Cartwright), letter, 11 July 1947.
6. Burton Keirstead to F.R.S., letter, 12 October 1950, FRSP.
7. "Peter Scott – Maylie Marshall Wedding," itinerary, FRSP; Rosemary Walters to author, interview, 9 June 1985.
8. Peter Dale Scott, Curriculum Vitae, FRSP.
9. Marian Scott, Curriculum Vitae.
10. Diary, 8 November 1921.
11. Secretary General to His Excellency Justice U Aye Maung, letter, 14 March 1952, FRSP.
12. F.R.S. to Mr. Mandereau, letter, 31 March 1952, FRSP.
13. F.R.S. to author, interview, 27 May 1980.
14. F.R.S., "Monthly Report No. 3 Covering the Period 1 May-30 June [1952]," p. 1, FRSP.
15. F.R.S., Burma Diary, 13 May 1952, FRSP.
16. Ibid., 7 May 1952.
17. Gordon O. Rothney to F.R.S., 20 December 1951, FRSP.
18. Rudyard Kipling, Rudyard Kipling's Verse 1885-1932 (Toronto: Copp Clark, 1933), p. 411.
19. Diary, 8 May 1952.
20. Ibid., 9 May 1952.
21. Ibid., 11 May 1952.
22. Ibid., 12 May 1952.
23. All preceding incidents described in Diary, 13 May 1952.
24. Owen, Keenleyside to Rangoon, Burma, telegram, 27 June 1952, FRSP.
25. F.R.S. to T.W.L. MacDermot, letter, 21 May 1953, FRSP.
26. Diary, 13 May 1952.
27. F.R.S. to Elspeth Chisholm, interview, 27-28 August 1962.
28. F.R.S. in conversation with author.
29. F.R.S. to Elspeth Chisholm, interview, 27-28 August 1962.

30. Epigraph, *Events and Signals* (Toronto: The Ryerson Press, 1954), frontispiece.

31. Sandra Djwa, "F.R. Scott," *Canadian Poetry*, No. 4 (Spring/Summer, 1979), pp. 1-16.

32. F.R.S., typewritten speech, "A Function for Poetry," n.d. [1946], FRSP.

33. F.R.S., typewritten speech, untitled, but with the following notation at top: "This is not about poetry in general so much as about poetry and Frank Scott – this is all I can be sure of," dated 1958, FRSP.

34. F.R.S. to Elspeth Chisholm, interview, n.d. [ca. 1975].

35. *Ibid.*

36. S. Djwa, unpublished paper on F.R.S.

SIXTEEN: MCGILL: LAW IN SOCIETY

1. Joyce Hemlow to author, interview, 2 December 1980.

2. Harold Spence-Sales to author, interview, 13 December 1983.

3. J.R. Mallory to author, interview, 28 August 1983.

4. Donald Hebb to author, letter, 24 August 1983.

5. Arnold Edinborough to author, letter, 7 September 1983.

6. See epigram to "Bonne Entente," *Collected Poems*, p. 256.

7. F.R.S., typewritten account of "The Day We All Got Imperially Oiled," 1950, FRSP.

8. F.R.S. in conversation with author.

9. Elizabeth Brewster to author, conversation, Summer, 1984.

10. F.R.S. to author, interview, January, 1983.

11. Arnold Edinborough to author, letter, 7 September 1983.

12. Joyce Marshall to author, letter, 19 March 1984.

13. Brief to the Royal Commission on National Development in the Arts, Letters and Sciences from The Canadian Writers' Committee, pp. 1, 2, 3, 6.

14. *Report of the Royal Commission on National Development in the Arts, Letters and Sciences 1949-1951* (Ottawa: King's Printer, 1951), pp. 18, 227, 271.

15. Frank Underhill, "Notes on the Massey Report," *The Canadian Forum*, XXXI (August, 1951), pp. 100-02; J.B. Brebner, "In Search of a Canadian Accent," *The Saturday Review of Literature*, 1 September 1951, pp. 6-8, 31.

16. George Curtis to author, interview, 3 August 1982.

17. Le Dain, "F.R. Scott and Legal Education," p. 112.

18. J.R. Mallory to author, November, 1985.

19. Louis St. Laurent to T.C. Douglas, letter, 7 December 1949, FRSP.
20. Memo from J.W. Corman, Attorney General of Saskatchewan, to The [Saskatchewan] Planning Board, 16 January 1950, p. 1, FRSP.
21. J.W.W. Graham to F.R.S., letter, 6 March 1950, FRSP.
22. F.R.S. to T.C. Douglas, letter, 20 February 1950, FRSP.
23. F.R.S. to Eugene Forsey, letter, 17 October 1950, FRSP.
24. Minutes of Civil Rights Conference, Ottawa, 28-29 December 1946, pp. 1, 3, 7, FRSP.
25. All preceding citations from F.R.S., "The State as a Work of Art," FRSP.
26. Michael Pitfield to author, interview, 28 August 1983.

SEVENTEEN: MORE EVENTS AND SIGNALS

 1. F.R.S. to author, interview, 3 July 1978.
 2. Northrop Frye to author in conversation.
 3. F.R.S. to author, interview, 14-15 September 1976.
 4. Pierre Emmanuel to F.R.S., letter, 28 August 1955, FRSP.
 5. Northrop Frye to author in conversation.
 6. "Proposal for a McGill Poetry Session in 1951," FRSP.
 7. Kim Ondaatje to author, interview, 24 September 1975.
 8. *Ibid.*
 9. A.J.M. Smith, "Astraea Redux," *A.J.M. Smith: Collected Poems* (Toronto: Oxford University Press, 1962), pp. 62-63.
10. F.R.S. in conversation with author.
11. F.R.S. to author, interview, 29 July 1978.
12. Louis Dudek to author, interview, 26 April 1979.
13. Doug Jones to author, interview, 28 August 1983.
14. Kim Ondaatje to author, interview, 24 September 1975.
15. F.R.S. to Robert Weaver, letter, 25 November 1954, FRSP.
16. F.R.S. to author, interview, 8 January 1975.
17. Program, "Canadian Writers' Conference," 28-31 July 1955, FRSP.
18. *Ibid.*
19. F.R.S. to author, interview, 8 January 1975.
20. F.R.S., Recommendations for Margaret Avison, Hugh MacLennan, draft recommendation P.K. Page, n.d., FRSP.
21. F.R.S. to author, interview, 8 January 1975.
22. Malcolm Ross to F.R.S., letter, 28 June 1955, FRSP.
23. Louis Dudek to F.R.S., letter, 9 July 1955, FRSP.
24. *Ibid.*, 15 July 1955, FRSP.
25. F.R.S. to Louis Dudek, letter, 18 July 1955, FRSP.

26. Anne Wilkinson to F.R.S., letter, Monday (n.d.), FRSP.
27. Robert Weaver to author, letter, 27 December 1983.
28. W.C. McConnell to author in conversation.
29. Roy Daniells to F.R.S., letter, 8 August 1955, FRSP.
30. "List of Delegates," *Writing in Canada*, ed. George Whalley, intro. F.R. Scott (Toronto: Macmillan, 1956), pp. 144-46.
31. Eli Mandel to author, interview, 5 January 1975.
32. *Writing in Canada*, pp. v-vi.
33. W.C. McConnell to author in conversation.
34. James Reaney, "Another View of the Writers' Conference," *The Canadian Forum*, xxxv (October, 1955), p. 158.
35. Doug Jones to author, interview, 28 August 1983.
36. F.R.S. to author, interview, 8 January 1975.
37. A.J.M. Smith, "Poet," *Writing in Canada*, pp. 13, 16, 19.
38. *Ibid.*, p. 20.
39. Jay Macpherson to F.R.S., letter, 1 August 1955, FRSP.
40. Eli Mandel to author, interview, 5 January 1975.
41. *Ibid.*
42. W.C. McConnell to author, interview, 23 April 1985.
43. Louis Dudek to author, interview, 24 May 1979.
44. Doug Jones to author, interview, 28 August 1983.
45. W.C. McConnell to author, interview, 23 April 1985.
46. Arnold Edinborough to author, interview, 6 November 1984.
47. Reaney, "Another View," p. 158.
48. Irving Layton to F.R.S., letter, 2 August 1955, FRSP.
49. F.R.S. to Irving Layton, letter, 11 August 1955, FRSP.
50. F.R.S. to Rt. Hon. L. St. Laurent, Hon. L.B. Pearson, Hon. J.W. Pickersgill, letters, 26 October 1955; F.R.S. to Hon. Ray Williston, letter, 2 December 1955, FRSP.
51. F.R.S. to W.A. Deacon, letter, 11 August 1955, FRSP.
52. W.A. Deacon to F.R.S., letter, 13 August 1955, FRSP.
53. Doug Jones to author, interview, 28 August 1983.
54. F.R.S., "The Canadian Writers' Conference," *University of Toronto Quarterly*, No. 25 (October, 1955), pp. 101-02.
55. *Ibid.*, p. 98.
56. F.R.S. to Secretary, Canada Council, letter, 17 June 1959, FRSP.
57. Doug Jones to author, interview, 28 August 1983.
58. *Ibid.*, September, 1975.
59. *Ibid.*, 28 August 1983.
60. Irving Layton to author, letter, 24 April 1985.

61. Leonard Cohen to author, conversation, 9 January 1983.
62. F.R.S. to Helen Digby, letter, 8 March 1962, FRSP.
63. F.R.S. to Judith MacKnight, letter, 18 April 1969, FRSP.
64. Louis Dudek, address at Memorial Service for F.R. Scott, McGill University, 18 February 1985.
65. Al Purdy to author, letter, 24 April 1985.
66. Leonard Cohen to author, interview, 9 January 1983.
67. F.R.S. to author, interview, 8 January 1975.
68. Leonard Cohen to author, interview, 9 January 1983.
69. Doug Jones to author, interview, 9 August 1983. See also Leonard Cohen, "Summer Haiku," *Selected Poems 1956-1968* (Toronto: McClelland and Stewart, 1964), p. 70.
70. F.R.S., "The EDGE of the PRISM," FRSP.
71. All preceding citations are from Louis Dudek to author, interview, 26 April 1979.
72. *Ibid.*
73. F.R.S. to Judith MacKnight, letter, 18 April 1969, FRSP.
74. Donald MacSween and Timothy Porteous to author, interview, 24 August 1983.
75. F.R.S., "Canadian Culture," *The Eye of the Needle* (Montreal: Contact Press, 1957), p. 43.
76. F.R.S. and A.J.M. Smith, "Introduction," *The Blasted Pine: An Anthology of Satire, Invective and Disrespectful Verse*, eds. F.R. Scott and A.J.M. Smith (Toronto: Macmillan, 1957, 1965), pp. xvii, xix.
77. David L. Thomson, "Preface," *ibid.*, p. vii.
78. Earle Birney, "Canada: case history," *ibid.*, p. 3.
79. "The Triumph of *My Fur Lady*," *The McGill You Knew: An Anthology of Memoirs 1920-1960*, ed. Edgar Andrew Collard (Toronto: Longman Canada, 1975), pp. 123-24.
80. Donald MacSween and Timothy Porteous to author, interview, 24 August 1983.
81. *Ibid.*
82. "The Triumph of *My Fur Lady*," pp. 127-29.
83. All preceding citations from John Robert Colombo, "A Lawyer-Poet Talks About Politics," and "Social Criticism in Poetry," *The Varsity*, Monday 24 November 1958, FRSP.
84. John Robert Colombo to author, letter, 27 March 1985.
85. F.R.S. to John Robert Colombo, letter, 27 November 1958, FRSP.
86. *Ibid.*, 5 December 1958, FRSP.
87. John Robert Colombo to author, letter, 27 March 1985.

88. All preceding citations from F.R.S. to Irving Layton, letter, 28 July 1959, FRSP.

EIGHTEEN: JEHOVAH'S KNIGHT ERRANT

1. Ken Lefolii, "The Poet Who Outfought Duplessis," *Maclean's* (11 April 1959), p. 72.
2. Bruce Taylor, "Padlock Law Unconstitutional, Switzman's Lawyers Tell Court," *Montreal Herald*, 3 March 1949.
3. Abraham Feiner to author, interview, 2 December 1980.
4. *Ibid.*
5. Lefolii, "The Poet Who Outfought Duplessis," p. 74.
6. F.R.S. to author, interview, December, 1980.
7. *Ibid.*
8. Abraham Feiner to author, interview, 2 December 1980.
9. *Ibid.*
10. *Ibid.*
11. "Padlock Case Defense Scores Moral Judgement in Quebec," *The Montreal Star*, 8 November 1956.
12. "Attack Quebec Law As Thought Control," *ibid.*, 9 November 1956.
13. *Ibid.*, 10 November 1956.
14. F.R.S. to author in conversation.
15. F.R.S. to Dean W.C.J. Meredith, letter, 28 December 1956, FRSP.
16. R.B. Nye to author, letter, 22 January 1984.
17. Malcolm Ross to author, letter, 17 January 1984.
18. *Ibid.*
19. F.R.S. to Dean Erwin Griswold, letter, 25 February 1957, FRSP.
20. F.R.S. to Gerald Le Dain, letter, 10 February 1957. Quoted by Le Dain in Le Dain to author, letter, 28 July 1983.
21. Malcolm Ross to F.R.S., letter, 8 March 1957.
22. J.R. Mallory to F.R.S., letter, 15 March 1957, FRSP.
23. F.R.S. to author, interview, 3 December 1980.
24. F.R.S., "Duplessis Versus Jehovah," *The Canadian Forum*, XXVI (January, 1947), p. 222.
25. Ronald Hambleton, "The Destruction of Roncarelli," *Saturday Night* (8 February 1947), p. 29.
26. *Awake!*, "Jehovah's Witnesses Banned," 8 June 1973, p. 23.
27. M. James Penton, *Jehovah's Witnesses in Canada: Champions of Freedom of Speech and Worship* (Toronto: Macmillan, 1976), pp. 111-15.
28. *Awake!*, "Happy Changes in Quebec," 8 March 1975, p. 16.
29. A.L. Stein to author, memorandum, 23 August 1983.

30. Penton, *Jehovah's Witnesses*, pp. 183-84.
31. F.R.S. to Elspeth Chisholm, interview, n.d. [ca. July, 1975], FRSP.
32. A.L. Stein to author, letter, 4 August 1983.
33. F.R.S. to author, interview, 3 December 1980.
34. *Roncarelli* v. *Duplessis*, Dominion Law Reports, 1952, p. 689.
35. A.L. Stein to author, interview, 29 August 1983.
36. All preceding citations from F.R.S., "Pure List for Roncarelli Case," unpublished history of case, pp. 5, 7, 9, 11, 12, 13, FRSP.
37. *The Herald*, 11 May 1950.
38. *Ibid.*
39. F.R.S. to author, interview, 3 December 1980.
40. *The Herald*, 11 May 1950.
41. *The Montreal Star*, May, 1951.
42. *Rapports Judiciaires*, Duplessis v. Roncarelli, 1954, pp. 447-49.
43. *The Montreal Star*, 27 July 1973.
44. *The Montreal Star*, 16 May 1958.
45. F.R.S. to author, interview, 3 December 1980.
46. F.R.S. to Elspeth Chisholm, interview, n.d. [ca. July, 1975], FRSP.
47. F.R.S. to author in conversation.
48. *Ibid.*
49. Names signed on the flyleaf of André Malraux's *The Walls of Silence*.
50. *The McGill Daily*, 28 January 1959.
51. *The Montreal Star*, 28 January 1959.
52. *The Red River Valley Echo*, 11 February 1959.

NINETEEN: LETTERS FROM THE MACKENZIE RIVER

1. F.R.S. to Maurice Lamontagne, letter, 12 March 1956, FRSP.
2. R.C. Powell to F.R.S., letter, 4 July 1956, FRSP.
3. F.R.S. to author, interview, 3 December 1980.
4. Charles Lussier to author, letter, 13 February 1984.
5. Pierre Trudeau to author in conversation, 27 September 1984.
6. *Ibid.*
7. F.R.S., "Foreword," *The Asbestos Strike*, ed. Pierre Trudeau, trans. James Boake (Toronto: James Lewis and Samuel, 1974), pp. ix-x.
8. Jean Marchand to author, interview, 25 September 1984.
9. Edward M. Corbett, *Quebec Confronts Canada* (Baltimore: The Johns Hopkins Press, 1967), p. 50.
10. Michael Oliver to author, interview, 28 August 1983.
11. Cited in Corbett, *Quebec Confronts Canada*, p. 51.
12. Jacques Hébert to author, interview, 17 September 1984.

13. "Programme," L'Institut des Affaires Publiques, 29 septembre-2 octobre 1954, FRSP.
14. F.R.S. to Walter Herbert, letter, 18 January 1951, FRSP.
15. *Ibid.*
16. F.R.S. to Herbert, letter, 2 December 1953, FRSP.
17. Bobbie Dyde to F.R.S., letter, 12 April 1954, FRSP.
18. F.R.S. to Jean-Charles Falardeau, letter, 21 May 1954, FRSP.
19. Pierre Trudeau to F.R.S., letter, 28 September 1955, and F.R.S. to Philip Noel-Baker, letter, 6 October 1955, FRSP.
20. Pierre Trudeau to F.R.S., letter, 8 November 1955, FRSP.
21. *Ibid.*, 28 September 1955, FRSP.
22. Jean-Charles Falardeau to F.R.S., letter, 7 September 1955, and Eugene Forsey to F.R.S., letter, 29 August 1955, FRSP.
23. Trudeau to F.R.S., letter, 28 September 1955, FRSP.
24. F.R.S. to author, interview, 3 December 1980.
25. Pierre Trudeau, "Exhaustion and Fulfilment: The Ascetic in a Canoe," in *Wilderness Canada*, ed. Borden Spears (Toronto: Clarke, Irwin, 1970), p. 3.
26. F.R.S. to Vincent Tovell, interview, 1971.
27. F.R.S. to author, interview, 3 December 1980.
28. *Ibid.*
29. Sandra Djwa, " 'A New Soil and a Sharp Sun,' " pp. 3-17.
30. Trudeau, "Exhaustion and Fulfilment," p. 5.
31. F.R.S. to author, interview, 3 December 1980.
32. Pierre Trudeau to author in conversation, 27 September 1984.
33. All previous citations from Pierre Elliott Trudeau, "Some Obstacles to Democracy in Quebec," in *Federalism and the French Canadians* (Toronto: Macmillan, 1968), pp. 103, 104, 106, 107, 114, 123.
34. F.R.S. to author, interview, 3 December 1980.
35. "S" [F.R.S.], "Embryo Fascism in Quebec," pp. 464-65.
36. F.R.S. to author, interview, 26 October 1978.
37. Falardeau to author, interview, December, 1979.
38. F.R.S. to author, interview, 3 December 1980.
39. *Ibid.*
40. I am indebted to Ruth McConnell, Professor Emeritus, UBC, for her perceptive comments on this poem.
41. Alan Twigg, "The Achievements of F.R. Who?" *The Province* [Vancouver], 1 March 1981.
42. F.R.S. to R.C. Powell, letter, 5 September 1956, FRSP.
43. Gordon Robertson to author, interview, 26 September 1984.

44. Northrop Frye to Marian Scott, letter, 13 November 1956, FRSP.
45. F.R.S. to author, interview, 3 December 1980.
46. Trudeau, "Foreword," *Federalism*, p. xix.
47. George Radwanski, *Trudeau* (Toronto: Signet/Gage, 1978), p. 55.
48. Trudeau, *Asbestos Strike*, p. 1.
49. C.B. Macpherson, review, *La Grève de l'amiante* (source unknown), p. 269, F.R.S. Scrapbooks, FRSP.
50. Trudeau, "Epilogue," *Asbestos Strike*, p. 349.
51. Trudeau, *Asbestos Strike*, pp. 15-16.
52. *Ibid.*, *Federalism*, "Some Obstacles to Democracy," pp. 118-19.
53. F.R.S., handwritten notes of Perrault's speech written on "Aide Memoire," FRSP.
54. Jean Marchand to author, interview, 25 September 1984.
55. F.R.S. to Dean E.N. Griswold, letter, 6 October 1959, FRSP.
56. Jean Marchand to author, interview, 25 September 1984.
57. Radwanski, *Trudeau*, p. 53.

TWENTY: "A CITIZEN OF THE WORLD"

1. F.R.S. to author, interview, 3 December 1980.
2. Manuel Shacter to author, interview, 19 February 1985.
3. All preceding citations from Harry Levin, "The Unbanning of the Books," *Refractions: Essays in Comparative Literature* (New York: Oxford University Press, 1966), p. 297. Also, concerning Podsnap: "The question [with Mr. Podsnap] about everything was, would it bring a blush into the cheek of the young person?" Charles Dickens, *Our Mutual Friend* (London: Oxford University Press, 1864-1865, 1963), p. 129.
4. Great Britain, Obscene Publications Act (1959).
5. Canadian Criminal Code, Obscene Matter, Sec. 150 (8) (1959).
6. Manuel Schacter to author, interview, 19 February 1985.
7. See Harry T. Moore, "*Lady Chatterley's Lover* as Romance," *A D.H. Lawrence Miscellany*, ed. Harry T. Moore (Carbondale: Southern Illinois University Press, 1959), p. 263. Also F.R.S. to author, interview, 3 December 1980.
8. Transcript of evidence of *Brodie, Rubin and Dansky* v. *Her Majesty the Queen*, 12 April 1960, p. 133.
9. Shacter to author, interview, 19 February 1985.
10. *Ibid.*
11. Preceding description of English trial from Kenneth Tynan, "Lady Chatterley's Trial," *The Observer Weekend Review* [London], 6 No-

vember 1960, p. 21. See also Levin, "The Unbanning of Books," p. 298.

12. Levin, "The Unbanning of Books," p. 298.

13. Casey, J., *Rapports Judiciares* [1961], B.R., le 7 avril 1961, pp. 614-18.

14. Morris Fish, " 'Lady Chatterley' Ban Not Needed, High Court Told," *The Montreal Star*, 16 November 1961.

15. Draft of appellant's factum, "Larry Brodie v. Her Majesty the Queen," filed in Supreme Court of Canada (in appeal), p. 30, FRSP.

16. Fish, " 'Lady Chatterley' Ban Not Needed."

17. Bruce MacDonald, "Lady Chatterley's Lover Cleared, May Now Be Brought in Canada," *The Globe and Mail*, 16 March 1962, p. 8.

18. Pierre Chaloult, "Y a-t-il deux Cours suprêmes du Canada?," *le nouveau journal* [Montréal], 16 mars 1962.

19. F.R.S. to H. Craig Campbell, letter, 23 March 1967, FRSP.

20. F.R.S., Travel Diary, 12 January 1961, FRSP.

21. Diary, 11 January 1961.

22. *Ibid.*

23. F.R.S., London Conference Diary 1944, 13 September 1944, FRSP.

24. F.R.S. to author in conversation.

25. Diary, 11 January 1961.

26. *Ibid.*, 13 January 1961. All further recollections of this evening are from diary entry on this date.

27. *Ibid.*, 24 January 1961.

28. *Ibid.*, 25, 30 January 1961.

29. *Ibid.*, 14 February 1961.

30. *Ibid.*, 27 February 1961.

31. *Ibid.*, 2 March 1961.

32. *Ibid.*, 20 April 1961.

33. *Ibid.*, 11 May 1961.

34. *Ibid.*, 15 February 1961.

35. *Ibid.*, 24 February 1961. All further citations from interview with Nehru are from diary entry on this date.

36. *Ibid.*, 20 February 1961.

37. *Ibid.*, 27 March 1961.

38. *Ibid.*, 4 February 1961.

39. *Ibid.*, 16 May 1961.

40. F.R.S., "Japanese Sand Garden," *Signature*, p. 10. See also revised version, *Collected Poems*, p. 127.

41. Diary, 6 and 7 February 1961.

42. *Ibid.*, 7 March 1961.

43. *Ibid.*, 18 March 1961.
44. Diary, 18 March 1961.
45. F.R.S. to author, interview, October, 1981.
46. Diary, 17 March 1961.
47. *Ibid.*, 12 May 1961. All further citations on time at Cambridge are from diary entry on this date.
48. *Ibid.*, 10-12 February 1961.
49. *Ibid.*, 24 April 1961.
50. *Ibid.*, 1 May 1961.
51. *Ibid.*, 16 May 1961.
52. *Ibid.*, 21 May 1961.

## TWENTY-ONE: COMMITTING DEANERY

1. Letters to F.R.S. from April, 1961, to January, 1962, in FRSP.
2. F.R.S. to Roy St. George Stubbs, letter, 26 November 1969, FRSP.
3. Eugene Forsey to F.R.S., letter, 21 May 1961, FRSP.
4. F.R.S., notes for speech to McGill law graduates, 30 November 1961, FRSP.
5. William Scott to F.R.S., letter, 1 December 1961, FRSP.
6. F.R.S. to author, interview, 18-25 July 1978.
7. Song sheet from McGill Law Society party, Spring, 1962, FRSP.
8. F.R.S. to L'hon. Gérald Fauteux, letter, 12 June 1961, FRSP. Fauteux was Dean of Law, University of Ottawa.
9. Ron Cheffins to author, interview, 31 December 1983.
10. *Ibid.*
11. F.R.S. to J.B. Milner, letter, 20 July 1962, FRSP.
12. F.R.S. Travel Diary, 14-16 April 1961, FRSP.
13. Thomas Berger to F.R.S., 4 May 1961, FRSP.
14. F.R.S. to Berger, letter, 26 March 1962, FRSP.
15. Berger to F.R.S., letter, 28 March 1962, FRSP.
16. F.R.S. to Berger, letters, 12 and 30 April 1962, FRSP.
17. Berger to M. deFeyter, Oil, Chemical & Atomic Workers, letter, 5 November 1962, FRSP.
18. Berger to J.L. LeBourdais, OCAWIU, letter, 1 October 1963, FRSP.
19. Ron Cheffins to author, interview, 31 December 1983.
20. Donovan Waters to author, interview, 31 December 1983.
21. J.E.C. Brierley, "Developments in Legal Education at McGill, 1970-1980," *The Dalhousie Law Journal*, 7, 2 (April, 1983), pp. 364-74.
22. Donovan Waters to author, interview, 31 December 1983.

TWENTY-TWO: THE TOMB OF THE KINGS

1. F.R.S. to Micheline Ste-Marie, letter, 4 December 1966, FRSP.
2. *Ibid.*
3. F.R.S. to author in conversation.
4. F.R.S. to A.J.M. Smith, letter, 20 March 1955, FRSP.
5. "Horaire," Première Rencontre des Poètes Canadiens, 27-29 September 1957, FRSP.
6. F.R.S., "Preface," *Poems of French Canada*, trans. F.R. Scott (Whiterock, B.C.: Blackfish Press, 1977), p. v.
7. Jay Macpherson to author, letter, 26 April 1985.
8. F.R.S., typewritten speech untitled but with following notation at top: "This is not about poetry in general so much as about poetry and Frank Scott – this is all I can be sure of," dated 1958, FRSP.
9. All preceding citations from D.G. Jones to author, interview, August, 1983. Jones's impressions later found poetic expression. See D.G. Jones, "Sketches for a Portrait of F.R.S.," *The Sun Is Axeman* (Toronto: University of Toronto Press, 1961), p. 5, and "A Portrait of Anne Hébert," *A Throw of Particles* (Toronto: General Publishing, 1983), p. 25.
10. Gael Turnbull to author, letter, 6 April 1985.
11. F.R.S. and Anne Hébert, "Dialogue," *Ecrits du Canada Français*, VII (1960), pp. 202, 203, 215.
12. F.R.S., handwritten "Final Note by Frank Scott," 1962, FRSP. Frère Untel was the pseudonym of Jean-Paul Desbiens, later an editor at *La Presse*. As Frère Untel he was an early critic of Duplessis.
13. F.R.S. and Anne Hébert, "The Art of Translation," *The Tamarack Review*, No. 24 (Summer, 1962), p. 88.
14. Northrop Frye, "Foreword," *Dialogue sur la traduction: à propos du 'Tombeau des Rois'* (Montréal: Editions HMH Limitée, 1970), p. 13.
15. F.R.S., "Translator's Note," *St-Denys Garneau & Anne Hébert: Translations/Traductions*, trans. F.R. Scott (Vancouver: Klanak Press, 1962), p. 9.
16. W.C. McConnell to F.R.S., letter, 2 January 1961, FRSP.
17. W.C. McConnell to F.R.S., letter, n.d. [1961], FRSP.
18. F.R.S., *St-Denys Garneau & Anne Hébert*, p. 9.
19. George Whalley, "Critically Speaking," transcript of review given on CBC, 16 December [ca. 1962], FRSP.
20. John Glassco to F.R.S., 21 September 1962, FRSP.
21. D.G. Jones to author in conversation, 11 June 1985.

22. Anne Hébert et Frank Scott, *Dialogue sur la Traduction*, pp. 37, 65; see also Kathy Mezei, "A Bridge of Sorts: The Translation of Quebec Literature into English," *The Yearbook of English Studies*, 15 (1985), p. 209.
23. This incident occurred during a conversation with F.R.S. and the author, 11 November 1975.
24. F.R.S. to F.G.S., letter, 8 December 1916, FRSP.
25. John Glassco to F.R.S., letter, 25 June 1963, FRSP.
26. D.G. Jones, "F.R. Scott as Translator," *On F.R. Scott: Essays on His Contributions to Law, Literature and Politics*, eds. Sandra Djwa and R. St. J. Macdonald (Montreal: McGill-Queen's University Press, 1983), p. 161.
27. Roland Giguère, "Polar Season," *Poems of French Canada*, p. 44.
28. Jones, "F.R. Scott as Translator," p. 161.

TWENTY-THREE: BILINGUALISM AND BICULTURALISM

1. "There was reason to fear that the Revolution, like Saturn, might devour in turn each one of her children." Pierre Vergniaud, *Histoire des Girondins*, quoted in *The Oxford Dictionary of Quotations*, 2nd ed. (London: Oxford University Press, 1953), p. 552.
2. André Laurendeau, "A Proposal for an Inquiry Into Bilingualism," *André Laurendeau: Witness for Quebec*, ed. and trans. Philip Stratford (Toronto: Macmillan, 1973), p. 189.
3. Davidson Dunton, André Laurendeau, *et al.*, "Terms of Reference," *A Preliminary Report of the Royal Commission on Bilingualism and Biculturalism* (Ottawa: Queen's Printer, 1965), p. 151.
4. Jean Marchand to author, interview, 25 September 1984.
5. F.R.S., B and B Journal, 4-5 September 1963, p. 1, FRSP.
6. *Ibid.*, p. 4.
7. J.B. Rudnyckyj to author, letter, 15 March 1985.
8. Ramsay Cook to author, interview, 23 August 1983.
9. Royce Frith to author, interview, 25 September 1984.
10. Journal, 4-5 September 1963, p. 1.
11. *Ibid.*, 5-6 June 1966, p. 324.
12. *Ibid.*, pp. 165-66.
13. Ralph Hodgson to author, interview, 21 September 1984.
14. Journal, 13-14 September 1965, p. 245.
15. Paul Lacoste to author, interview, 19 February 1985.
16. *Ibid.*
17. Journal, 7 November 1963, p. 33.

18. *Ibid.*, p. 34.
19. Michael Oliver to author, interview, 28 August 1983.
20. *Preliminary Report*, pp. 27, 155-59.
21. Laurendeau diary excerpts, 2 May 1964, "Upon returning from Vancouver," *The Vancouver Sun*, 11 August 1978, p. A6.
22. Michael Oliver to author, interview, 28 August 1983.
23. Royce Frith to author, letter, 11 July 1984.
24. *Ibid.*, interview, 25 September 1984.
25. Michael Oliver to author, interview, 28 August 1983.
26. Ralph Hodgson to author, interview, 21 September 1984.
27. "Preface," *Quebec States Her Case: Speeches and Articles From Quebec in the Years of Unrest*, eds. Frank Scott and Michael Oliver (Toronto: Macmillan, 1964), n.p.
28. "The FLQ Manifesto," trans. Claude Savoie, *ibid.*, p. 87.
29. Pierre Elliott Trudeau, "The Conflict of Nationalisms in Canada," *ibid.*, p. 61.
30. Michael Oliver to author, interview, 28 August 1983.
31. Journal, 17-18 March 1964, p. 75.
32. Following description of Quebec City meeting from *ibid.*, 15-19 June 1964, pp. 123-25.
33. *Preliminary Report*, p. 133.
34. Journal, p. 135.
35. *Preliminary Report*, p. 13.
36. Paul Lacoste to author, interview, 19 February 1985.
37. Journal, p. 116.
38. Paul Lacoste to author, interview, 19 February 1985.
39. Laurendeau diary excerpts, 29 June 1964, "Memorandum of a meeting with the Prime Minister, Lester B. Pearson," *The Vancouver Sun*, 11 August 1978, p. A6.
40. F.R.S., "A Strong Central Government," handwritten draft for B and B discussion, April, 1965, FRSP.
41. Journal, 26-30 April 1965, p. 210.
42. *Ibid.*, 5-6 July 1966, p. 322.
43. H. Blair Neatby to author, 13 December 1985, in response to a preliminary version of this chapter.
44. Journal, 16-17 August 1965, pp. 238-39.
45. All preceding citations from Davidson Dunton, André Laurendeau, *et al.*, *The Report of the Royal Commission on Bilingualism and Biculturalism, Volume I* (Ottawa: Queen's Printer, 1967), pp. xviii, xxii, xxviii, 147-49.

46. Laurendeau diary excerpts, 26 November 1967, "A few days after delivery of Book I of the Report to the Prime Minister," *The Vancouver Sun*, 11 August 1978, p. A6.

47. Paul Lacoste to author, interview, 19 February 1985.

48. F.R.S., "B. & B. Stories," *The Tamarack Review*, Nos. 83-84 (Winter, 1982), p. 31.

49. Journal, 27 February 1971, pp. 557-58.

50. *Ibid.*, pp. 559-60.

51. Claude Ryan, "Introduction: André Laurendeau," in *Witness for Quebec*, n.p.

52. H. Blair Neatby to author, interview, 13 December 1985.

## TWENTY-FOUR: A VIABLE FEDERALISM

1. F.R.S. to King Gordon, letter, 9 August 1971, FRSP.

2. From Section 2 of the Official Languages Act, quoted in J.T. Thorson, *Wanted: A Single Canada* (Toronto: McClelland and Stewart, 1973), p. 87.

3. Gérard Pelletier, *The October Crisis*, trans. Joyce Marshall (Toronto: McClelland and Stewart, 1971), pp. 197-205.

4. F.R.S. to R.M. Jackson, letter, 24 April 1972, FRSP.

5. F.R.S., *F.R. Scott: Rhyme and Reason*, dir. Donald Winkler, National Film Board, 1982.

6. Donald MacSween [and Timothy Porteous] to author, interview, 24 August 1983.

7. "The Santo Domingo of Pierre Elliott Trudeau," *The Last Post*, I, 5, p. 11.

8. Marcel Rioux to author, letter, n.d. [September, 1985].

9. Jean Marchand to author, interview, 25 September 1984.

10. Cited in "More Than Words: The Official Languages Act," National Film Board, 1980.

11. Ray Ellenwood to author, letter, 7 August 1985.

12. Jean Marchand to author, interview, 25 September 1984.

13. Gallup Poll, Canadian Press Index, 19 October 1970.

14. F.R.S. to A.R.M. Lower, letter, 3 April 1946, FRSP.

15. F.R.S. to Donald Cameron, letter, 25 January 1971, FRSP.

16. F.R.S., *Rhyme and Reason*.

17. Jean Marchand to author, interview, 25 September 1984.

18. Pelletier, *October Crisis*, p. 142.

19. Larry Shouldice to author, letter, 30 July 1985.

20. F.R.S., *Rhyme and Reason*.

21. F.R.S. to author in conversation.
22. F.R.S., *Rhyme and Reason*.
23. Marian Scott to author, interview, 4 June 1985.
24. Ron Graham to F.R.S., letter, 16 September 1970, FRSP.
25. Kathy Mezei in conversation with author, May, 1985.
26. Timothy Porteous [and Donald MacSween] to author, interview, 24 August 1983.
27. Larry Shouldice to author, letter, 30 July 1985.
28. Walter Tarnopolsky, "Emergency Powers and Civil Liberties," *Canadian Public Administration* (1972), p. 196.
29. F.R.S. to author in conversation, 1978.
30. *Ibid*.
31. *Rapport préliminaire du Comité d'aide aux personnes arrêtées en vertu des lois d'urgence de la Ligue des Droits de l'homme*, p. 1, FRSP.
32. Jacques Hébert to author, interview, 17 September 1984.
33. *Ibid*.
34. *Ibid*.
35. Jacques Ferron, "All Is Not Lost," *The Cart*, trans. Ray Ellenwood (Toronto: Exile Editions, 1980), p. 143.
36. Betty Bednarski to author, letter, 9 August 1985.
37. F.R.S. to author, interview, January, 1983.
38. *The Cart*, pp. 58-59.
39. Jacques Ferron to F.R.S., letter [ca. summer, 1969], FRSP.
40. *Ibid*.
41. *The Cart*, p. 143.
42. Pierre Trudeau to author in conversation, 27 September 1984.
43. Jacques Ferron, "Le coeur de Jean-Olivier Chénier," *L'Information médicale et paramédicale* (16 November 1971), p. 14. "La frousse rend féroce et il est fort probable que, selon l'usage anglais, on ait arraché le coeur du cadavre encore chaud de Jean-Olivier Chénier. Dommage qu'on ne l'ait pas conservé: Frank Anacharcis Scott pourrait le brandir au-dessus du Québec, district bilingue."
44. F.R.S. to R.E.L. Watson, letter, 25 November 1971, FRSP.
45. Jacques Ferron to author in conversation, 17 September 1984.
46. Ray Ellenwood, "Translator's Note," in Jacques Ferron, *Quince Jam*, trans. Ray Ellenwood (Toronto: Coach House (1972), 1977), p. 11.
47. Betty Bednarski, unpublished article.
48. T.P.M. Howard to author, interview, 18 February 1985.
49. John Saywell, *The Rise of the Parti Québécois 1967-76* (Toronto: University of Toronto Press, 1977), p. 106.

50. F.R.S. to author, "Opposition to Bill 22," 19 December 1977.
51. Robert Stocks to author, interview, 18 February 1985.
52. Eugene Forsey to author, interview, 1 October 1977.
53. Robert Stocks to author, interview, 18 February 1985.

TWENTY-FIVE: "TAKE CARE — OF CANADA"

1. F.R.S. to author in conversation, ca. 1979.
2. Graham Fraser, *René Lévesque & the Parti Québécois in Power* (Toronto: Macmillan, 1984), p. 197.
3. *Ibid.*, p. 234.
4. F.R.S., "A Policy of Neutrality for Canada," *Foreign Affairs*, 17, 2 (January, 1939), p. 8.
5. F.R.S., "The Privy Council and Mr. Bennett's 'New Deal' Legislation," *Essays on the Constitution* (Toronto: University of Toronto Press, 1977), p. 99.
6. Gerald Le Dain, "F.R. Scott and Legal Education," in *On F.R. Scott*, p. 106.
7. F.R.S., "Dominion Jurisdiction over Human Rights," *Essays on the Constitution*, p. 214.
8. Gordon Robertson to author, interview, 26 September 1984.
9. Pierre Trudeau to author in conversation, 27 September 1984.
10. F.R.S., "A Bill of Rights for All Canadians," *The Canadian Constitution and Human Rights* (Toronto: Canadian Broadcasting Corporation, 1959), p. 44, FRSP.
11. B and B Journal, 16-17 August 1965, pp. 238-40, FRSP.
12. Barry Strayer to author, interview, 10 April 1985.
13. F.R.S. to Allan Blakeney, letter, 30 November 1976, FRSP.
14. F.R.S. to Michael Pitfield, letter, 6 August 1980, FRSP.
15. F.R.S. to author, letter, 16 August 1978.
16. F.R.S., *Rhyme and Reason*.
17. Keith Banting and Richard Simeon, eds., *And No One Cheered: Federalism, Democracy and the Constitution Act* (Toronto: Methuen, 1983), p. 9.
18. F.R.S. to Rosemary Walters (Cartwright), letter, 30 October 1982.
19. F.R.S. to author and Elizabeth Gowland, May, 1980.
20. F.R.S. to Elspeth Chisholm, letter, 18 March 1973, FRSP.
21. John Fairbank to F.R.S., letter, 27 October 1971, FRSP.
22. F.R.S. to John Fairbank, letter, 11 November 1971, FRSP.
23. *Ibid*.
24. A.J.M. Smith dictated to Jean Milner, Keewaydin, 24 July 1960, FRSP.

25. F.R.S. to author, letter, 29 January 1980.

26. F.R.S. to author in conversation, May, 1976.

27. Thomas Berger to author in conversation.

28. F.R.S., conversations at Scott Symposium, 21-22 February 1981.

29. F.R.S. to Hugh Keenleyside, letter, 5 March 1981, FRSP.

30. Sandra Djwa, "Introduction," *On F.R. Scott: Essays on His Contributions to Law, Literature and Politics*. The following summaries are from this book.

31. Douglas Gibson to author, letter, 9 September 1985.

TWENTY-SIX: THE CLOSING YEARS

1. F.R.S. to Eugene Forsey, letter, 21 August 1979, FRSP.

2. F.R.S. to author in conversation.

3. Gerald Le Dain to author in conversation, 1983.

4. F.R.S., "Question," *The Dance Is One* (Toronto: McClelland and Stewart, 1973), p. 26.

5. Donald MacSween [and Timothy Porteous] to author, interview, 24 August 1983.

6. F.R.S. to author in conversation, August, 1983.

7. Marian Scott to author, letter, 8 December 1983.

8. *Ibid.*, 15 February 1984.

9. *Ibid.*, 14 December 1984.

10. *Ibid.*, interview, 4 June 1985.

11. FRSP.

12. Rosemary Cartwright to author, letter, 5 July 1985.

# Index